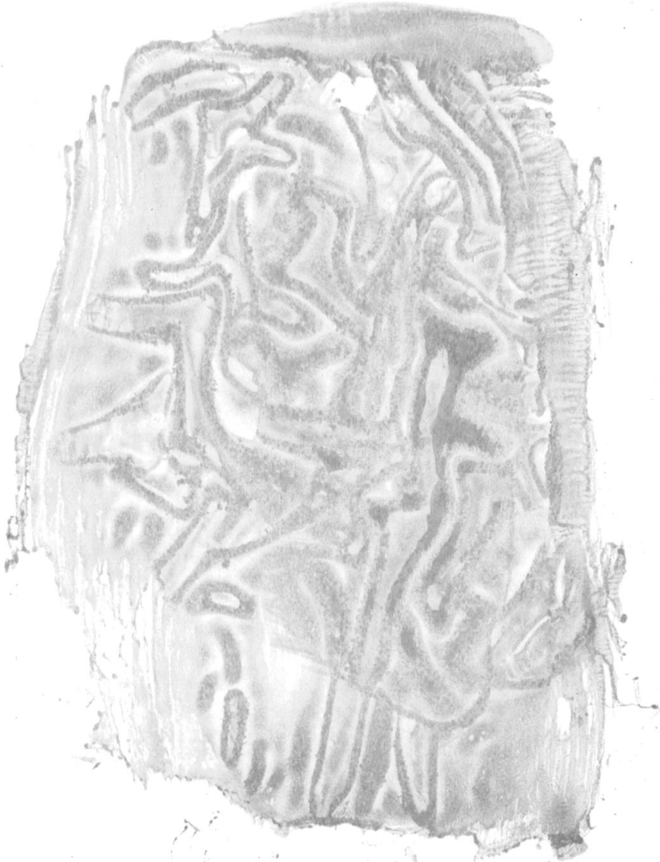

Problems in
THE HISTORY OF COLONIAL AFRICA
1860–1960

Problems in

THE HISTORY

OF
COLONIAL AFRICA
1860–1960

Edited by
Robert O. Collins
Department of History
University of California
Santa Barbara

Prentice-Hall, Inc., Englewood Cliffs, New Jersey

Problems in
THE HISTORY OF COLONIAL AFRICA 1860–1960

Edited by
Robert O. Collins

P-13-716605-2
C-13-716613-3

Library of Congress Catalog Card No. 70-113845

Printed in the United States of America.

Current printing (last digit):
10 9 8 7 6 5 4 3 2 1

PRENTICE-HALL INTERNATIONAL, INC., *London*
PRENTICE-HALL OF AUSTRALIA PTY. LTD., *Sydney*
PRENTICE-HALL OF CANADA, LTD., *Toronto*
PRENTICE-HALL OF INDIA PRIVATE LTD., *New Delhi*
PRENTICE-HALL OF JAPAN, INC., *Tokyo*

Contents

Preface

In 1968 I published a collection of readings entitled *Problems in African History*. My purpose in compiling these readings was to provide, in a single, compact volume, excerpts from interpretive articles, essays, and books dealing with Africa which are not readily available to the general student. I grouped these materials around seven "Problems" constructed to present controversial and conflicting interpretations as well as to provide themes for discussion and further inquiry. Although not suitable for every teaching situation, *Problems in African History* has been well received by both students and instructors from a large number of colleges and universities. Some teachers have complained, however, that the volume does not contain any "Problems" dealing with colonial Africa. This omission was not accidental; I deliberately excluded themes associated with Africa under colonial rule. First, students are generally less familiar with precolonial African history and consequently need materials for this fascinating period more than they require readings for the age of European imperialism in Africa. Second, I did not believe that either the precolonial or the colonial period of African history could be adequately presented if both had to be compressed into one volume. I thus limited the compilation of materials to the precolonial period, and although this concentration made the volume more substantial, it did not satisfy the critics. The solution, however, was obvious to my friends and to my publisher, and acting on their suggestion I have produced the following reader as a companion to *Problems in African History*.

Conforming to the pattern established in *Problems in African History*, I have constructed seven "Problems" dealing with the partition, occupation, and administration of Africa by the European Powers. As before, the appellation "Problems" refers not only to those topics which at present invoke controversy and conflicting interpretations, but also to those subjects which lend themselves to discussion and inquiry. I have made no attempt to present a narrative for Africa in the colonial period; that is the task of the instructor.

In choosing the selections for each problem, I have sought to include the most authoritative statements, interpretations, and analyses by well-known and distinguished scholars. Future contributions will add to our understanding of each area, but they will undoubtedly elaborate on, refine, or revise the basic positions which these scholars have already assumed. One may quarrel with the choice of problems and with the choice of authorities used to elucidate them. In defense I can only plead my own experience and knowledge and the favorable reactions of my students to my experiments in the presentation of the history of colonial Africa.

I want to express my appreciation to Martin Legassick, Michael Coray, Ralph Herring, and the students of my graduate seminar for their criticism and suggestions. I am particularly grateful to Michael Coray and Ralph Herring who have so ably assisted me in compiling the enclosed materials without whose help, interest, and ideas the project would remain unfinished.

My thanks also goes to the many authors and publishers who granted me permission to reprint passages from their works, and especially to John Wiley and Sons, Inc., for permission to reprint passages from my *Introduction to The Partition of Africa.*

All but the most necessary footnotes have been eliminated from the selections that follow.

Robert O. Collins
Santa Barbara, California

Acknowledgments

The editor is grateful to the publishers and individuals who have granted permission to reprint passages from the works of the following authors:

Ntieyong U. Akpan, *Epitaph to Indirect Rule* (London: Cassell & Co., Ltd., 1956), pp. 26–30.

Georges Balandier, "Messianism and Nationalism in Black Africa," from Pierre L. Van den Berghe (ed.), *Africa, Social Problems of Change and Conflict* (San Francisco: Chandler Publishing Company, 1965), pp. 443–48, 457–58. First published in *Cahiers Internationaux de Sociologie* by the Presses Universitaires de France, Paris (1953).

Raymond F. Betts, *Assimilation and Association in French Colonial Theory, 1890–1914* (New York: Columbia University Press, 1961), pp. 106–28 and 165–76.

James S. Coleman, "Nationalism in Tropical Africa," from *American Political Science Review,* XLVIII, 2 (1954), 404–14. Reprinted by permission of the author and the publisher, The American Political Science Association.

———, *Nigeria: Background to Nationalism* (Berkeley: University of California Press, 1963), 145–66, 170–72, 175. Reprinted by permission of The Regents of the University of California.

W. R. Crocker, *Nigeria: A Critique of British Colonial Administration* (London: George Allen & Unwin, Ltd., 1936), pp. 213–22.

Michael Crowder, "Indirect Rule—French and British Style," from *Africa,* XXIV, 3 (1964), 197–205. *Africa* is published for the International African Institute by Oxford University Press, London.

———, *West Africa Under Colonial Rule* (Evanston: Northwestern University Press, 1968), pp. 273–75, 345–53.

A. B. Davidson, "African Resistance and Rebellion Against the Imposition of Colonial Rule," from T. O. Ranger (ed.), *Emerging Themes in African History* (Nairobi: East African Publishing House, 1968), pp. 177–88.

Hubert Deschamps, "Et Maintenant, Lord Lugard?", from *Africa,* XXXIII, 4 (October, 1963), 293–305. *Africa* is published for the International African Institute by Oxford University Press, London.

D. K. Fieldhouse, *The Colonial Empires: A Comparative Survey from the 18th Century* (New York: Delacorte Press, 1966), pp. 380–87, 391–92. Copyright

© 1965 by Fischer Bucherei KG, Frankfurt am Main. Copyright © 1966 by Dell Publishing Co., Inc. and George Weidenfeld & Nicholson Ltd., London. Used by permission of the publishers, Delacorte Press and George Weidenfeld & Nicholson Ltd.

Lewis Gann and Peter Duignan, *The Burden of Empire, An Appraisal of Western Colonialism South of the Sahara* (New York: Frederick A. Praeger, Inc., 1967, and London: Pall Mall Press Ltd.), pp. 227–51.

———, *White Settlers in Tropical Africa* (London: Penguin Books, Ltd., 1962), pp. 110–21.

John Hargreaves, "West African States and the European Conquest," from L. Gann and P. Duignan (eds.), *The History and Politics of Colonialism,* Vol. I (Cambridge: Cambridge University Press, 1969), 199–200, 205–16.

Elspeth Huxley and Margery Perham, *Race and Politics in Kenya* (London: Faber and Faber Ltd., 1956), pp. 27–39, 42–49, 228–43.

Martin Kilson, *Political Change in a West African State: A Study of the Modernization Process in Sierra Leone* (Cambridge: Harvard University Press, 1966), pp. 252–56, 259–64. Copyright 1966 by the President and Fellows of Harvard College.

Martin D. Lewis, "One Hundred Million Frenchmen: The 'Assimilation' Theory in French Colonial Policy," from *Comparative Studies in Society and History,* IV (1962), 129–49 and 149–52. Reprinted by permission of the publisher, The Cambridge University Press, London.

J. M. Lonsdale, "Some Origins of Nationalism in East Africa," from the *Journal of African History,* IX, 1 (1968), 120–29, 135–38, 140–46. Reprinted by permission of the author and the publisher, Cambridge University Press.

D. A. Low and R. C. Pratt, *Buganda and British Overrule: 1900–1955* (Kampala, Uganda: Copyright 1969 by Makerere Institute of Social Research, Makerere University College), pp. 163–76. First published by Oxford University Press, London, 1960.

Lord F. Lugard, *The Dual Mandate in Tropical Africa* (London: Frank Cass & Co. Ltd., 1965, by arrangement with William Blackwood and Sons Ltd.), pp. 94–97, 102–5, 193–218.

C. W. Newbury and A. S. Kanya-Forstner, "French Policy and the Origins of the Scramble for Africa," from the *Journal of African History,* Vol. X, No. 2 (1969), 270–75. Reprinted by permission of the authors and the publisher, Cambridge University Press.

Roland Oliver and J. D. Fage, *A Short History of Africa* (Harmondsworth: Penguin Books Ltd., 1964), pp. 202–3.

Dame Margery Perham, "A Re-Statement of Indirect Rule," from *Africa,* VII (1934), 321–23, 328–34. *Africa* is published for the International African Institute by the Oxford University Press, London.

T. O. Ranger, "African Reaction to the Imposition of Colonial Rule in East and Central Africa," from L. Gann and P. Duignan (eds.), *The History and Politics of Colonialism in Africa,* Vol. I (Cambridge: Cambridge University Press, 1969), 293–317, 319–21.

———, "Connexions between 'Primary Resistance' and Modern Mass Nationalism in East and Central Africa," from *Journal of African History,* IX, 3 (1968), 440, 443–48, 452–53; and IX, 4 (1968), 631–39, 641. Reprinted by permission of the author and the publisher, Cambridge University Press.

Ronald Robinson, John Gallagher, with Alice Denny, *Africa and the Victorians: The Official Mind of Imperialism* (London: Macmillan and Company, Ltd., 1961, The Macmillan Company of Canada Ltd., and St. Martin's Press, Inc.), pp. 163, 166, 168–74, 177–80, 274, 281–89, 376–78.

Ronald Robinson and John Gallagher, "The Partition of Africa," from F. H. Hinsley (ed.), *New Cambridge Modern History,* Vol. XI (London: Cambridge University Press, 1962), 639–40.

G. N. Sanderson, *England, Europe and the Upper Nile, 1882–1899* (Edinburgh: Edinburgh University Press, 1965), pp. 386–92.

Ndabaningi Sithole, *African Nationalism,* 2nd Ed. (London: Oxford University Press, 1968), pp. 131–37.

Jean Stengers, "L'Imperialisme Colonial de la Fin du XIXe Siècle: Mythe ou Réalité," from *Journal of African History,* III, 3 (1962), 471–91.

A. J. P. Taylor, *Germany's First Bid for Colonies* (London: Macmillan and Company, Ltd., 1938, and Hamden, Conn.: Archon Books, 1967), pp. 1–7.

Henry A. Turner, Jr., "Bismarck's Imperial Venture: Anti-British in Origin," in Louis, Gifford and Smith (eds.), *Britain and Germany in Africa* (New Haven: Yale University Press, 1967), pp. 49–53.

Jack Woddis, *Africa: The Roots of Revolt* (New York: The Citadel Press, 1962), pp. 1–2, 4–5, 7–13, 16–20, 31–34, 36–43, 46–47.

Leonard Woolf, *Empire and Commerce in Africa* (New York: Howard Fertig, Inc., 1968, and London: George Allen and Unwin, Ltd.), pp. 316, 328–31, 333–38, 343–58. First published by George Allen and Unwin, Ltd., 1920. Reprinted by permission of the author and publishers.

AFRICA: 1914
ADMINISTRATION:
Independent
British
French
Spanish
Portuguese
Belgian
German
Italian
0 500 1000 1500
miles
NORTH ATLANTIC OCEAN
SOUTH ATLANTIC OCEAN
INDIAN OCEAN
Mediterranean Sea
Red Sea
London
Brussels
Berlin
Paris
Madrid
Lisbon
Rome
SPANISH MOROCCO
Algiers
Fez
MOROCCO
IFNI (Sp.)
CANARY IS. (Sp.)
ALGERIA
TUNISIA
Tripoli
CYRENAICA
LIBYA (It.)
Cairo
EGYPT
Nile
RIO DE ORO (Sp.)
MAURITANIA
FRENCH WEST AFRICA
Senegal R.
Niger R.
SENEGAL
Dakar
GAMBIA (Br.)
PORTUGUESE GUINEA
SIERRA LEONE (Br.)
LIBERIA
IVORY COAST
GOLD COAST
TOGO
NIGERIA
Lagos
L. Chad
FR. EQUATORIAL AFRICA
ANGLO-EGYPTIAN SUDAN
ERITREA (It.)
FRENCH SOMALILAND
BRITISH SOMALILAND
Addis Ababa
ABYSSINIA
ITALIAN SOMALILAND
Mogadiscio
KAMERUN
Fernando Póo (Sp.)
Principe
São Thomé (P.)
RIO MUNI (Sp.)
GABON
CONGO
Congo R.
BELGIAN CONGO
Brazzaville
Léopoldville
CABINDA (P.)
UGANDA
BRITISH EAST AFRICA
Nairobi
L. Victoria
GERMAN EAST AFRICA
ZANZIBAR (Br.)
EQUATOR
St. Paul de Loanda
ANGOLA
Lubango
NORTHERN RHODESIA
Zambezi R.
SOUTHERN RHODESIA
NYASALAND
MOZAMBIQUE
MADAGASCAR
GERMAN SOUTHWEST AFRICA
Walvis Bay (Br.)
Windhoek
BECHUANA-LAND
Lourenço Marques
SWAZILAND
Vaal R.
Orange R.
UNION OF SOUTH AFRICA
BASUTOLAND
Capetown
20°
40°
60°
0°

Problems in

THE HISTORY OF COLONIAL AFRICA

1860–1960

problem I

The Partition of Africa

During the first four centuries of contact with Africa, the European Powers had been content to restrict their holdings to a handful of scattered trading stations along the coast, the control of which passed from one state to another as each state's strength in Europe waxed or waned. Finally, in the nineteenth century European explorers penetrated into the interior and opened the enormous hinterland of Africa; yet no European government rushed to follow in their footsteps. Missionaries began to work out from the coastal enclaves, but they never regarded themselves as agents of their imperial governments. Merchants expanded their trade, but they realized that they would not necessarily gain by the intervention, occupation, and rule of any single European Power. To be sure, the presence of missionaries, merchants, explorers, and soldiers served to clear the way for the expansion of Europe in Africa, but nothing in history is inevitable until it occurs. Yet within less than twenty years, the continent was conquered and divided amidst rising national feeling at home and increasing belligerency abroad. Why? The explanations are nearly as unsatisfactory as they are numerous. The interpretations are as controversial as they are doctrinaire. The misconceptions are as enduring as they are erroneous. To scholar and student alike, the search for understanding this dynamic period, which resulted in European colonial rule in Africa and dramatically altered the future of a vast continent, is the Problem of the Partition of Africa.

There were hesitant beginnings to the Partition of Africa in the 1870's. The discovery of diamonds in South Africa in 1869 provided the incentive and capital for a large influx of Europeans that ultimately spilled across the Limpopo into Central Africa. The opening of the Suez Canal in the same year not only made the East African coast more accessible but also became the great pivot in British imperial strategy, eventually shifting British interest from Constantinople to Cairo with repercussions as far south as the great lakes of equatorial Africa and as far west as Wadai and

Lake Chad. In 1881, the French extended their control over Tunis, but in Tunis the French were reluctant empire builders. The repercussions to their occupation might reverberate in North Africa but not south of the Sahara. The Partition of Africa required greater stimuli than the discovery of diamonds in South Africa or political intrigue on the Mediterranean littoral. The partitioners did not have long to wait. Between 1882 and 1885 the British occupied Egypt, precipitating additional conquests that carried them as far as East Africa; Savorgnan de Brazza claimed the north bank of the Congo for France, while Leopold II, King of Belgium, began to carve out a personal fief in the vast hinterland of the Congo Basin. And not to be outdone, Otto von Bismarck decided that Imperial Germany needed colonies. Who then began the scramble for Africa—the British in Egypt, King Leopold in the Congo, the French in West Africa, or an acquisitive Bismarck? The interpretations are as numerous as the candidates.

Ronald Robinson and John Gallagher have argued that the scramble for Africa was begun, not by the intrigues of King Leopold or the heroics of Brazza, but rather by the British occupation of Egypt in 1882. Hitherto the governments of Britain and France had agreed not to permit the quarrels of their traders and officials along the coasts of Africa to become reasons for acquiring additional African territory. The British occupation of Egypt destroyed this Anglo-French collaboration. Henceforth, France consciously sought to acquire colonies elsewhere in Africa as compensation for Cairo and a means to apply diplomatic and commercial pressure on London. On the Niger and the Congo French officials and explorers were active, and British attempts to enlist the Portuguese and King Leopold in order to check the French soon proved abortive. Moreover, Britain's occupation of Egypt provided Bismarck with the opportunity to exacerbate Anglo-French differences while carving out an African empire for Germany. From every European capital the Egyptian affair had seemed to precipitate the scramble for Africa.

Jean Stengers cannot agree. He has argued that the Partition of Africa was inaugurated neither by King Leopold nor Egypt but rather by French ratification of Savorgnan de Brazza's treaty with Makoko followed by the declaration of protectorates in West Africa. Chauvinism made possible French acceptance of the Makoko Treaty; economic motives resulted in the acquisition of French protectorates in West Africa. French claims to political control on the north bank of the Congo forced Leopold to assert his sovereignty on the south bank. French activity on the West African coast stirred the British to preserve their economic interests on the Niger from fear of French annexations. Driven on by the inexorable demands of public opinion, the interior markets were ready for European commercial competition which would have begun the scramble for Africa even if Egypt had never existed.

C. W. Newbury and A. S. Kanya-Forstner have agreed with Jean

Stengers that the French, indeed, were responsible for precipitating the scramble for West Africa, but the ratification of the Brazza Treaty was not the turning point in French expansion nor was the British occupation of Egypt any significant influence on French acquisitions in West Africa. From the beginning Admiral Jean Jauréguiberry, the Minister who was responsible for colonial affairs, sought a forward course in West Africa, not only to protect French coastal traders but to create a vast French empire in the interior of West Africa. The genesis of French imperialism in West Africa, Newbury and Kanya-Forstner argued, was not Brazza and his treaty with Makoko in 1882 but earlier in 1879–80. At that time public opinion was an important, if sporadic, factor but it did not initiate the scramble. Commercial interests were pervasive but not decisive. As with the late Victorians on the Nile, the motives for French expansion were to be found within the "official mind" of French imperialism. Both Freycinet and Jauréguiberry were prepared to commit the power of France to intervention in Africa for the purpose of future economic profits at the expense of present political control. Much of their policy was based on myth, but it was this myth which precipitated the Partition of West Africa.

Whether it was Egypt, King Leopold, or the French who began the scramble for Africa, it was Bismarck who sought to take advantage of it. A. J. P. Taylor, one of Britain's most controversial and influential historians, has argued that Bismarck had no real interest in German acquisitions in Africa but expected that German colonial adventures would draw France and Germany together over imperial quarrels with Great Britain. Bismarck's map of Africa lay in Europe.

Henry A. Turner has disagreed. He remains unconvinced that Bismarck's change of policy can be attributed to considerations of European diplomacy. Turner has argued that, in fact, Bismarck simply changed his mind in 1884 and decided that Germany must expand overseas. He was motivated not so much by foreign policy as by the uncertain future of Germany in a world of predatory states. Observing these developments Bismarck simply decided that colonies were necessary more as an attempt to insure the future of Germany than as a product of any complex diplomatic maneuver.

Not only did Bismarck seize territory on both sides of the continent, but in October 1884 he joined with France to invite twelve other states to a conference in Berlin to discuss the partitioning of Africa. The conference opened in November 1884 and in 1885 passed the Berlin Act incorporating vague and pious pronouncements regarding the slave trade, free trade, and the ground rules for the occupation. In practice, they were to prove largely ineffectual, but when the Berlin Conference ended in February 1885, the scramble for Africa should have been in full swing. Paradoxically, it was not. Once having agreed on the rules for the partition, each of the contestants seemed reluctant to scramble for African territory, and it was not until the Prime Minister of Great Britain, Lord Salisbury, decided that the British occupation of Egypt would have to become more permanent that the second round in the scramble began. Once the British determined to remain in Egypt, they were committed to its defense. Ronald Robinson and John Gallagher have carefully delineated the consequences of Salisbury's decision. Egypt is a desert that is made to bloom only by the waters that pour out of equatorial Africa and from the highlands of Ethiopia. No African people possessed the technological skills to interfere with the northward flow of the Nile waters. The European Powers did. Thus, to protect Suez, that lifeline of empire, the British had to remain at Cairo. When they decided to take up permanent residence in Egypt, they had to defend the Nile waters, wherever they might be—Khartoum, Lake Tana, Fashoda, Uganda.

Lord Salisbury first checked the Italian threat to the Nile waters by warning them to stay away from the Nile Valley. Deeply embroiled with Menelik in Ethiopia, the Italians readily agreed. Having gotten rid of the Italians, Salisbury next had to face the more powerful Germans. The conclusion of the Anglo-German (Heligoland) Agreement of 1890 resolved that problem diplomatically. And then there were the French. From 1893 until 1898 the French, fitfully at first but eventually with Gallic fervor, sought to reach the Nile at Fashoda. In July 1898 a French expedition under Captain J. P. Marchand succeeded. Throughout the nineties, successive British ministers had attempted to seal off the Nile Valley from the French by diplomacy. They all had failed, and Lord Salisbury, who had returned to power in 1895, determined that the only way to preserve the Nile Valley for Britain was to conquer it. In 1898 General H. H. Kitchener and his Anglo-Egyptian Army advanced into the heart of the Sudan, defeated the forces of the Mahdist State outside Omdurman, and raced south to meet Captain Marchand at Fashoda.

Fashoda was the greatest Anglo-French confrontation in nearly a century, and the most serious crisis in Africa between European rivals. G. N. Sanderson has demonstrated that, for France, Fashoda was the result of separate, irreconcilable, and, therefore, conflicting policies of French imperialism. Despite formidable opposition within the government to this foolhardy mission, the French sent Marchand to Fashoda in their desperate pursuit of prestige. Prestige, not economic considerations, dominated the march to Fashoda. The result only proved the folly of a policy motivated by glory and formulated in a crucible of conflicting objectives.

For Britain the great confrontation of French and British imperialism at Fashoda was the climax of half a generation of colonial rivalry. Although acknowledging that the Fashoda crisis aroused public opinion in Britain for the first time to near hysteria, Ronald Robinson and John

Gallagher have regarded Fashoda as the logical conclusion of the strategic outcome of the Egyptian policy assiduously practiced for over a decade by the men who controlled affairs in Britain.

The conclusion of the Fashoda crisis virtually ended the Partition of Africa. Only a handful of states on the periphery of the continent remained free of European control and by the outbreak of World War I only two countries, Liberia and Ethiopia, maintained their independence. Two others, Morocco and Libya, had slipped under French and Italian administration respectively, but neither the Franco-German dispute over Morocco nor the Italian-Turkish struggle for Libya possessed the drama or the danger of the Fashoda crisis and were, in fact, the peripheral and rather sandy remains of the scramble for the more tropical regions further south.

Many scholars have sought to provide a comprehensive interpretation for the Partition of Africa. Some have argued that British participation in the scramble was the result of strategic considerations arising from the British occupation of Egypt. To be sure, financial, humanitarian, and commercial interests were always present but of less influence on the official minds who made policy than the strategic requirements of the British empire. Although this interpretation has provided a more defensible explanation for the British presence at Cairo, Khartoum, and Kampala than appeals to economic inevitability, the extension of this thesis becomes less convincing when attempting to explain the partition in West and southern Africa, where personal ambitions, national prestige, and economic factors outweigh strategic consideration. Others have emphasized the complexities of the scramble for Africa which defy a general, comprehensive interpretation. European imperialism in Africa must be written only in a "polycentric fashion," for "no unitary theory will ever untangle for us the richness and variety of the historical skein."[1]

[1] Lewis Gann and Peter Duignan, "Reflections on Imperialism and the Scramble for Africa," in *The History and Politics of Colonialism in Africa,* Lewis Gann and Peter Duignan (eds.), vol. I, p. 128.

Robinson and Gallagher: Egypt and the Partition of Africa

Without the occupation of Egypt, there is no reason to suppose that any international scrambles for Africa, either west or east, would have begun when they did. There seem to have been no fresh social or economic impulses for imperial expansion which would explain why the partition of tropical Africa should have begun in the early 1880's. Gladstone's second administration was totally devoid of imperial ambitions in west Africa. Granville was unimpressed by the dingy annals of the west coast. Kimberley, at the Colonial Office, was eager to give sleeping dogs every chance of lying. The pessimistic Derby, who succeeded him in 1882, was temperamentally opposed to any suggestion, however modest, for expansion on the west coast. Finally there was Gladstone, himself, who knew little and cared little about the problem. In so far as these men possessed any coherent view of the situation in tropical Africa, it was the view sometimes of Cobden, sometimes of Palmerston and the mid-Victorian imperialism of free trade. As in Gladstone's first ministry, they still concurred in looking on tropical Africa as a third-rate adjunct of the British economy, which might be worth the exertion of coastal influence, but did not justify the effort of administration inland. There were none of them likely to plant the flag in the middle of the African bush in a fit of absence of mind.

For decades all the European governments concerned with the coast of Africa both east and west had tacitly agreed not to allow the petty quarrels of their traders and officials to become occasions for empire. The ministries in London and Paris wanted nothing more than to continue their gentleman's agreement, although each faintly suspected the other of wanting to break it. . . .

It was the British invasion of Egypt which shattered this system, because it shattered the general Anglo-French collaboration. When France came out in open opposition to the new *régime* in Egypt toward the end of 1882, she began to cast around for ways of putting pressure on London. There was plenty of scope for a policy of pin-pricks in west Africa, and these now began in earnest. Two French firms were on the lower Niger, trading not only at the coast, but pushing into the interior. The alarming feature of this activity was that the French consular agent in the river was now hard at work making treaties as far upstream as the kingdom of Nupe and along the Benue. In Paris they had

From Ronald Robinson and John Gallagher, with Alice Denny, *Africa and the Victorians: The Official Mind of Imperialism* (London, 1961), pp. 163, 166, 168–74, 177–80.

no illusions about their chances on the lower Niger, for the British position seemed too strong. But the Minister of Marine and Colonies had high hopes of the Benue. . . .

At the same time, another British sphere looked like slipping away. Trade in the Delta of the Congo was dominated by British firms; in the interior Lieutenant Cameron had made a set of treaties in the Seventies which gave the United Kingdom an option on the inner basin of the river. Then Her Majesty's Government had rejected it. Now French and Belgian private enterprises were ready to take the Congo seriously. There was a vast river behind the mouths of the Congo, as Stanley had shown; and it had become possible to break into the hinterland, as Brazza had found. King Leopold II of the Belgians, who had floated an International Association to explore central Africa at the end of the Seventies, launched Stanley on another mission to open communications between the navigable Congo and Stanley Pool in the interior. At the same time Brazza too went back, acting in the name of the French section of the International Association. Here was a scramble, but only at the personal level of two explorers racing each other to the interior, each with the skimpiest of credentials. Stanley was little more than the personal agent of a petty monarch, for the International Association was a piece of mummery, and the Belgian Parliament would have nothing to do with its King's speculations. The status of Brazza was no less peculiar. He too was nominally the agent of the International Association. Although his expedition was given a tiny grant by the French government, the chief inspiration of his mission came from his own pleadings. Paris had little desire to be involved in his adventures. Brazza however had heard that Leopold intended to seize all the interior basin of the Congo, and this would cut off the French colony of Gabon from its hinterland and cast it into bankruptcy. To avoid the ruin of their colony, the French government in 1879 authorised Brazza to make a treaty at Stanley Pool. Just as the Foreign Office in the Eighteen-fifties had worked to open the Niger hinterland, so the French government in the Eighteen-seventies worked to open the Congo basin. They were far from wanting to extend their political control into the interior; their aim was simply to block the political extensions of others. Brazza's treaty was meant to "reserve our rights, without engaging the future."

Between 1880 and 1883 Stanley and Brazza played out their game in the Congo. This raised awkward questions for the British government. Leopold was a puny rival, and his Association could be pushed into the wings if the need arose. But after Brazza had made his treaty at Stanley Pool, the Foreign Office had to rely on the French disinclination to move in central Africa. In April 1882 the British ambassador in Paris asked the Quai d'Orsay whether the Congo mission had an official character. The discussion that followed showed that in the opinion of the Ministry of Marine and Colonies Brazza had no right to have made a treaty at all. But on the Congo, as on the Niger, all this was to change. After the Egyptian affair had reached its climax, Paris did not feel the old need to pay deference to British susceptibilities; on 10 October the Foreign Minister overrode the protests of the Marine, and announced that he intended to ask the Chamber to approve the treaty. Ratification followed on 30 November. On 15 December the Foreign Office countered by recognising Portugal's claims to the Congo and its hinterlands—claims which Britain had steadily rejected for the past forty years. In return Britain was to enjoy most favoured nation treatment in the trade of the Congo, a maximum tariff rate, and the setting up of an Anglo-Portuguese commission to supervise the traffic on the river. The treaty took fifteen months to complete, because the Portuguese went on hoping to get better terms from France than from the United Kingdom; but its purpose was always painfully clear. When it had at last been signed, the French ambassador in London caustically defined it as:

"... A security taken by Britain to prevent either France or an international syndicate directed by France from setting foot in the Congo Delta. . . . The British Government . . . would rather parcel it out with Portugal, whom it can influence at will, than leave France with an open door."

That was true enough. During 1883 and 1884 the Gladstone Cabinet hoped to use the Portuguese as a sort of holding company which would decently veil the pre-eminence of British interests. Lisbon would do the governing, London would do the trade. In fact, British optimism went further than that. It was rumoured in the Foreign Office that King Leopold's own organisation might become ". . . as I hear is not unlikely, an English company." Both these sanguine hopes are very revealing. As a direct result of the Egyptian occupation, British interests in the Congo were now threatened by Leopold and the French. If their sphere were to be saved, then ministers could no longer rely on the old gentleman's agreement; from now on, official acts of policy would be needed. This they understood. Yet they refused to meet the new situation by any territorial extension of their own. Instead, they fell back on a variant of their technique of informal empire. Others could administer on paper, while they enjoyed the trade. With the King of Portugal as their caretaker on the coast and the King of the Belgians as their manager in the hinterland, all might still be saved, thanks to these regal subordinates. . . .

In fact, British plans went astray both in the Niger and in the Congo. Ministers had had their doubts already over the Anglo-Portuguese Treaty. They were to end by thoroughly repenting of it. Although the treaty had been designed to guarantee the interests of British traders, they were loud in opposition to it, because of the nominal Portuguese control and the actual Portuguese tariff. Their protests were joined by the ancestral voices of the Anti-Slavery Society and the Baptist Union. Behind all this agitation there may have lain, as Granville suspected, the fine hand of King Leopold. The complaints of these pressure groups however were not enough to stop the treaty. That it failed was another of the consequences of the Egyptian crisis. After the occupation of Cairo, it seemed to French observers that Britain was driving for African empire. French diplomacy attacked the Anglo-Portuguese arrangement, both as a way of keeping the Congo open, and of putting pressure on the British in Egypt. The treaty was signed on 26 February, 1884, and during March the Quai d'Orsay was actively inciting opposition in Belgium, Holland and the United States, the Powers with trading interests in the Congo. But in his search for supporters Ferry hooked a bigger fish than these. On 31 March he tried to get the Germans to join the resistance. This overture was to begin the partition of west Africa.

Bismarck too had his grievances against British policy. To his rooted dislike of Gladstone as a man fit only to chop down trees and make up speeches, he could now add a splenetic indignation at Granville's dawdling. In February 1883 he had enquired whether Britain would be ready to protect the German settlement at Angra Pequena; in December he repeated the enquiry. But for a further six and a half months the only reply he could get from London was a series of vague observations about British claims in that region. In part the muddle was caused by the objections of the Cape, in part by the British feeling that the colonial politicians had to be listened to, if south Africa was one day to be united around that province. But it was an important muddle. The occupation of Egypt gave Bismarck the chance to deepen the rift between Britain and France and to enter the African game. In March and April of 1884 the Germans took steps to assert their own protectorate over Angra Pequena, but the ambiguity of their statements and the imperceptiveness of Gladstone's ministers (one of whom as late as June did not know where Angra Pequena was) left the British as naively ignorant as ever about where their attitude was taking them. It was beginning to take them a long way. On 5 May Bismarck hinted at this in two messages to London, in which German colonial claims and the question of the Congo were ominously linked. By another in this chain of muddles the messages were not delivered. Thereafter Bismarck swung the weight of Germany behind the Congo revisionists and then against the whole British position in west Africa. On 7 June he let the Foreign Office know that Germany refused to recognise the Anglo-Portuguese Treaty and wanted a conference to settle the Congo question. Granville was too discouraged to press on with ratification, and that was the end of the Treaty. But the retreat did not stop there. On 4 August the Germans suggested to the French that they should co-operate over west African questions generally at the impending conference, and at the end of the month the French persuaded their new collaborators to join in an onslaught against the least expendable of the British spheres—the Niger. . . .

It seems then that any attempt to analyse British policy in terms of some one decisive factor breaks down before the facts. There is nothing for it but to approach the problem from another direction. Instead of postulating a single, necessary and sufficient cause of these events, it is well to be less pretentious and to define them as the result of an interplay between non-recurrent factors in the early Eighteen-eighties. Government policy in west Africa seems to have evolved as a by-product of three major crises, one in Egypt, another in Europe, a third in the domestic politics of Great Britain, and a minor crisis on the west coast itself.

The Egyptian affair had started off the "scramble." It had ended the standstill arrangement in Africa. It had run British policy into a noose held by Bismarck. When Germany's policy swung towards France, the two of them squeezed hard on the British position in west Africa. That position was already susceptible to change, as the bases of tribal societies and economies were eroded by the gradual commercial penetration of the interior. So long as other things stayed equal, Gladstone's Cabinet thought it could cope with the results of this erosion by making only small adjustments in its traditional policy. But things did not stay equal, and the Egyptian aftermath shifted the European balance, blowing these calculations sky-high. . . .

It would seem that the claiming of the Niger in 1884 was motivated neither by increased enthusiasm for enlarging the empire nor by more pressing economic need to exploit the region. The incentive to advance here was no stronger than of old. It sprang from a passing concatenation of minor trade rivalries in west Africa with major changes of front by the Powers in Europe and the Mediterranean, mainly provoked by British blunders and difficulties in Egypt. The Liberals claimed the Lower Niger merely to prevent an existing field of British trade from disappearing behind French tariff walls; and they limited their new commitment to this negative purpose. They had not decided to found an ambitious west African empire. All they had done in the face of French hostility was to make a technical change in the international status of the Lower Niger. Henceforward the Powers recognised this country as a British sphere, but government still had no serious intention of administering, developing or extending it.

Stengers: King Leopold, Savorgnan de Brazza, and the Beginning of the Scramble for Africa

Was it Leopold II who began [the scramble for Africa]? One could so imagine when reading the first treaty signed by the agents of the expedition which he sent into Africa. In this treaty—which was published in 1884 by the American Senate to whom the King had sent it—the political idea was apparently the most important: the Vivi chiefs of the lower Congo ceded their rights of sovereignty over a part of their territory of the *Comité d'Etudes* [du Haut Congo], the organ which served as a screen for the King. This was June 13, 1880. If the text was

From Jean Stengers, "L'Impérialisme Colonial de la fin du XIXe Siècle; Mythe ou Réalité," *Journal of African History,* Vol. III, No. 3 (1962), 471–91. Translated by Nell Elizabeth Painter and Robert O. Collins.

authentic, the political initiative would be striking. Unfortunately, it is not. Leopold II had sent the American Senate a falsified version. The real Vivi treaty of June 12, 1880, has been found, and it does not provide for any abandonment of sovereignty.

At its beginnings, Leopold II's enterprise in Africa had no political nature. This does not mean that the King, from time to time, did not envision or contemplate political projects, but they never progressed beyond the stage of ephemeral plans. The central idea, the program, in every sense of the word, of Leopold II was elsewhere. It consisted in the organization of the commercial exploitation of Central Africa. To establish trading stations, to get started a big commercial enterprise, this was Leopold's first objective.

It was not until 1882 that he was forced to change direction, to impress a new orientation upon his enterprise. It was necessary to face a danger, that is, Brazza. Was he not going to plant the French flag in the regions of the Congo where Leopold II wanted to penetrate, even as far as the stations where the *Comité d'Etudes* [du Haut Congo] was already established? In order to stop Brazza, to prevent his annexations, the only method was to plant another flag before his and one which would also be the emblem of a political power. Henceforth, Leopold II sought for a way to acquire sovereignty: now began the march toward the formation of the Congo State.

But all this, which began in 1882, was only a counterweight to Brazza's policies, to the intentions reputed to be Brazza's. In our search for first initiatives, should we not turn directly toward France?

It is in France, in fact, that we think the two real initiatives of the "scramble" began. The first was the conclusion of the Brazza-Makoko treaty and, even more, its ratification in 1882. The second was the protectorate policy inaugurated in West Africa in January 1883. The first episode is well known, although France's reasons for installing herself in the Congo have never been sufficiently analyzed. The second, we believe, has never been brought into focus.

In 1882 Brazza returned to France. He brought what he himself called, and what everybody would soon be calling, his "treaty" with Makoko. It was, in fact, two documents in bizarre legal form—and which were certainly not the work of a specialist in international law—dated September-October 1880. The explorer declared in the first that he had obtained from King Makoko, reigning sovereign north of Stanley Pool, the "cession of his territory to France." Makoko had put his "mark" on this declaration. In the second, he declared that he had occupied, in the name of France, part of this territory situated on the edge of Stanley Pool itself (that is to say, what became Brazzaville). This "treaty," to use Brazza's expression, installed France in a small territory whose strategic and commercial importance was great, being situated on the doorstep of the navigable Congo, but which was isolated by hundreds of kilometers from both the coast and the existing French possessions. . . .

The government, as we have seen, would propose approval of the Brazza-Makoko treaty to Parliament. This would be accepted unanimously in November 1882, by the

Chamber. "The Chamber," commented the *Temps,* "high spirited and warm hearted, has put aside all dissension: it was truly French. . . ."

In this enthusiasm, it is easy to distinguish the dominant major part played by national pride. It could be felt alive everywhere. A competition was opened in Africa between two rivals: Brazza and Stanley. France supported her champion and wanted his triumph. Stanley, who had returned to Europe in 1882, attacked Brazza and declared that the treaty with Makoko was worthless. One more reason for French public opinion to form a solid block around the man who wore its colors.

While making the cause of Brazza in the Congo triumphant and achieving this victory for France, it was possible to get even with England. It is here that we rediscover the question of Egypt—but from a point of view, it must be emphasized, that Robinson and Gallagher [*Africa and the Victorians,* London, 1961] have not noticed. After the hurt, the humiliation that the occupation of Egypt caused it, French public opinion instinctively looked for a way to compensate for the British success. It needed a French success. The Congo offered itself at this point. For us it is, wrote a Parisian newspaper, "the best and the surest revenge" to the "frustrations" that we have just suffered. Brazza, of course, did not fail to play on these sentiments. "A speaker who preceded me," he declared during a ceremony at the Sorbonne, "said that the English have left us behind everywhere. There is, however, one place where we have put our mark before them; that is the Congo [prolonged applause, notes the report]. The French flag flies over this land and the Parliament has only to say the word for it to be ours forever. . . ."

In the Congo the French policy had been more chauvinistic than calculating, dictated far more by patriotic exaltation than by considerations of economic matters. In West Africa—where the second French initiative took place in January 1883—the game was completely different. It was, without interference by public opinion and without public outcry, a game calculated to promote the interests of national commerce.

Commercial interests and territorial occupation had been linked on the West Coast more than once during the nineteenth century. These were always limited occupations, responding above all to local or regional preoccupations. The last of these local maneuvers carried out "to support national commerce" had been the reestablishment in 1882 of the French protectorate over Porto-Novo.[1]

In January 1883 the designs apparently were enlarged. Texts came from the Ministry of the Marine and Colonies in Paris which, when brought together, defined a new policy, and which one would be tempted this time to call grand policy. . . .

A protectorate on the coast from the Gold Coast to Dahomey, political treaties on the Benue, agreements with the chiefs in the eastern delta of the Niger, eventually protectorates at Bonny, Old Calabar, or in that region, treaties to the south of the Cameroon estuary: one recognizes that there is here, in the trea-

[1] The declaration reestablishing a French protectorate at Porto-Novo was signed in Paris in 1882, but not carried out in Africa until April 1883. *Ed.*

ties of January 1883, a far-reaching political program. . . .

The plans were grand, but the means actually employed were mediocre, and all in all, the policy defined in January 1883 produced only very minor results.

To the west of Dahomey action was reduced to really very little. It was put off essentially for fear of diplomatic complications. Farther to the east, in the Niger and the Cameroons, those who tried to execute the new policy with slender means hardly succeeded at all. . . .

Thus, between the program conceived on paper in January 1883 and its realization in West Africa, there was a world of difference. The little that the French did was sufficient however—just as the approval of the Brazza-Makoko treaty had been sufficient in Central Africa—to set off the "scramble." In fact, there is no doubt, once the English documents are taken in hand, that it was the French initiatives which, taken together and, in a way, regarded as one by the Foreign Office and the Colonial Office, were at the origin of the decision taken by the British government to act.

Already the Brazza-Makoko treaty had begun to cause worries for West Africa, as well as for the Congo, for a "coup" like that which Brazza had succeeded in pulling off might well be repeated elsewhere, and, for example, on the Niger. "The tactics of M. de Brazza may be imitated on the Niger, and that great highway into the interior of Africa be converted into a French river," wrote a British trader to the Foreign Office, where his words were listened to. Then came the news of the reestablishment of the French protectorate at Porto-Novo, which reinforced the alarm. Then came the announcement that a French warship was at Bonny and that the officers of the ship were trying to obtain a treaty from the native chiefs. Under these conditions, it became "a question of the first importance to consider . . . how British interests are to be protected." From June 1883, Percy Anderson, in the Foreign Office, makes the point. He brought together the different elements of the French activity and particularly emphasized the last.

"The Captain of the *Voltigeur* is trying to induce the natives of the mouths of the Niger to accept his treaties. If he succeeds in this, the final step will have been taken, and British trade will have no chance of existence except at the mercy of French officials."

The conclusion, from that point onwards:

"Action seems to be forced on us. . . . Only one course seems possible; that is, to take on ourselves the protectorate of the native states at the mouth of the Oil Rivers, and on the adjoining coast. . . . Protectorates are unwelcome burdens, but in this case it is . . . a question between British protectorates, which would be unwelcome, and French protectorates, which would be fatal."

Later news from the west coast—the treaty concluded with Passall, the activities of Mattei—did nothing but further reinforce the reasoning so well defined by Percy Anderson. This reasoning resolved the British government to act. In a second region of Africa, the "scramble" began. . . .

In analyzing the events of 1882–1883, we see the new face of imperialism emerge, which it acquired from that moment and which it kept to the end of the parcelling of the lands that were still free in the world. Three characteristics particularly emerge: the development of colonial chauvinism; the new type of occupations designed to safeguard economic interests as their end; finally, the role of public opinion. National pride, national *amour-propre,* and chauvinism entered into colonial affairs with a force which they had never before had. In this case, Brazza appeared as a great instigator. His propaganda in 1882 used, without a doubt, numerous economic arguments; it indicated to France the direction of rich and fertile lands. But Brazza would never have been acclaimed if, in a moral sense, he had not waved the national flag. It was when he invoked the tricolor which he had planted in the heart of Africa that he had his audience in his hand, that he carried off the country. Even the economists who agreed with his views did so more as patriots than as economists. Leopold II, a great admirer of Paul Leroy-Beaulieu, sadly reported that "chauvinism seemed to have possessed" the eminent author of *Colonisation chez les peuples modernes* [The Colonialism of Modern Peoples]. . . . [2]

Here we see the new aspect of colonial policy; it satisfied a need for grandeur which, in more than one case, passed well above considerations of material interest. Yves Guyet in 1885, shocked by the mental habits of the traditional economist used to serene calculations in all matters, wrote of the psychological evolution of his colleagues, and particularly of their attitude *vis-à-vis* the British colonial empire:

> "We are jealous of that vast domain, and we want to have one like it to oppose theirs at any price. We no longer count, we listen only to passion. We want annexations, of which we see only their size, without worrying about their quality."

In virtue of the opinion it has of itself a great country must spread overseas. And thus it proves to itself and shows to others its national vigor. "One believes," said the German chancellor in 1890, "that if we only had colonies, and bought an atlas and colored Africa blue, we would then be a great people." Not to act, not to expand, is to give to oneself the label of incapacity, the prelude of political decadence. Jules Ferry proclaimed in 1885:

> "It is necessary that our country put itself in a position to do what the others are doing, and because colonial expansion is the most important means at this time used by all the European powers, it is necessary that we play our part. Otherwise what happened to other nations which played a great role three centuries ago and which now find themselves, no matter how great they once were, fallen to the level of third or fourth class powers, will happen to us."

The rank: it was their rank in the world—an absolutely new phenomenon whose appearance is vainly sought before this time—which the European countries would defend by means of overseas partitions.

This was especially so in the partitioning of Africa. There, more than in Asia or Oceania, the process is definite and well defined: it was a

2 Pierre Paul Leroy-Beaulieu, French economist and writer. *Ed.*

continent that could be taken apart piece by piece. The success of each one was visibly measured on the map. "In this partitioning," declared the *Comité de l'Afrique française* [Committee on French Africa], "France has the right to the largest part." And in trying to realize this program, the majority of those who supported the work of the *Comité*—secondary school students, for example, or officers, which were found in such great numbers among the subscribers—evidently thought above all of the grandeur of their homeland.

On the race which was begun, economic preoccupations of course were present, but they very often changed their character in comparison with those of the past. During the period which Jules Ferry very correctly called that of "modest annexations and of little actions, of bourgeois and parsimonious conquests," a well-planned annexation was sought more than once, in order to gain economic advantages or to improve the condition of national commerce. Those were the classic and traditional objectives. French commercial houses on the west coast pushed for annexations; they wanted to procure a privileged position there. The British consul in the Gulf of Benin, Hewett, recommended the protectorate policy. In his eyes the best way to stimulate national commerce would be to establish direct commercial relations with the hinterland. Calculations of this kind had a positive character. But after 1882–1883 the fear of annexations by others would be substituted for positive calculations. Conquest would be made in the name of protection to defend an area considered endangered by the interventions of another power because it was necessary to make good one's own commercial interests there. The "tariffs" of others: that was what became, on the economic plain, the major obsession which seized all minds. . . .

Finally the third new element: the role of public opinion. In the autumn of 1882, in the affair of Brazza and the Congo, observers were unanimous in agreeing that such an unleashing of the press and public opinion had never before been touched off by a colonial question. Thus began in colonial matters a series of movements of public opinion at the end of the nineteenth and the beginning of the twentieth century. It is necessary to speak in the plural of movements and not of a movement, for it was never a question of one emotion, such as we know in politics, that literally take over and dominate imaginations in a lasting manner. It was by sporadic spurts that colonial enthusiasm would flare up in one country after another separated by periods of indifference which so upset the champions of the colonial cause. . . .

To conclude, let us come back again to Egypt. Without the occupation of Egypt, would things have happened as they did in Africa south of the Sahara? If the Egyptian question had not inspired a desire and a need for revenge, would French opinion have embraced Brazza's cause as it did? When it is a question of movements of collective emotion, the "what would have happened if," we must recognize, is nearly always a futile question. There are always too many imponderables in emotions which escape analysis.

But the "scramble" also had a basis in economic reasons. And here there is no doubt possible: Egypt or no Egypt, economic factors would have in any case begun the movement sooner or later.

The fundamental element that must be kept in mind is the following: from the moment when the economic penetration of the dark continent was begun, the temptation to reserve certain advantages for oneself in the regions penetrated was strong, even irresistible. The march toward the interior became almost of necessity synonomous, in many cases, with the acquisition of economic privileges. . . .

Remarkably, despite his forward entrance on the scene, Leopold II did not set off the process. From 1882, in fact, by a political about face whose genius must be acknowledged, he abandoned his designs on a privileged exploitation to make himself, to the contrary, the champion of free trade in Central Africa. In this way he played the card which would lead to triumph. When some of the exclusive treaties that Stanley and his collaborators had signed at the beginning were brought to light, they evidently made the King uncomfortable, but he was able to overcome the bad effect they produced by burying them under torrents of solemn promises to respect free trade. And so the bomb was dismantled.

Whether by Leopold II in the first phase, whether by Goldie, whether by the French eyeing the Benue, Africa in the 1880's, or rather, the interior markets of Africa, were opened for commercial competition, which would have engendered the "scramble" in any case. And this would have been so had Egypt never existed.

Newbury and Kanya-Forstner: French Policy and the Scramble for Africa

What was the significance of these French moves [up the Senegal, in the Niger Delta, and on the Congo]? What were their motives and the reasons for their timing? One cannot answer these questions by concentrating exclusively upon the immediate origins of the scramble for territory which they provoked. The ratification of the de Brazza treaty, for example, was not a crucial turning-point in French expansion as some have pictured it. De Brazza had no official powers to negotiate, and the government was reluctant to accept the results of his unauthorized diplomacy. Jauréguiberry regarded the explorer as a foreign upstart in the pay of a private organization closely linked with King Leopold of the Belgians, and he tacitly opposed the submission of the treaty to Parliament. Even after its

From C. W. Newbury and A. S. Kanya-Forstner, "French Policy and the Origins of the Scramble for West Africa," *Journal of African History,* Vol. X, No. 2, 1969, 270–75.

ratification, both he and the Quai d'Orsay warned their agents: "The question of the Congo is not the only important one. The need to concentrate our efforts at other points, the necessity to bind together our colonial empire, and the complications which it can lead to will point out the prudent limits beyond which you cannot go in a country where thus far our interests are relatively weak."

As is well known, the pressure of public opinion forced the government to act. But the success of the Congo lobby's propaganda campaign and the popular enthusiasm which it aroused did not reveal "the new face of imperialism." De Brazza's supporters had done just as well with their agitation over the trans-Sahara railway three years before, and the reasons for their success were the same in both instances. Parliament ratified the de Brazza treaty because it gave France a new route into the vast and wealthy lands of the West African interior. Rouvier's report to the Chamber had a strangely familiar ring:

> This vast commercial enterprise, of which one can hardly catch a glimpse of the future and of which one does not know today the measure of its extent, will certainly develop to the profit of those who first penetrate these regions barely opening them to world commerce. More a neighbor of Africa than most other nations, more directly interested in the future of this continent by her possessions of Algeria, Senegal, Gabon, and by the numerous commercial outlets which she possesses on the west coast [of Africa], France will seriously fail to recognize her interests, most certainly, if she allows others to precede her in the movement which is sweeping the civilized world toward these still mysterious regions of yesterday.

Not even the phrasing had been changed since 1879.

The repercussions of the occupation of Egypt also had little significance for French expansion in West Africa. Certainly, the British occupation had a profound effect upon the general course of Anglo-French relations, and it may have facilitated the adoption of more overtly anti-British policies, just as public reaction to the occupation may have contributed to the success of de Brazza's publicity campaign. But Jauréguiberry's protectorate policy was designed to defend French interests in West Africa, not to drive the British out of Egypt. And Anglo-French hostility was no new phenomenon; fears of British expansion had plagued Jauréguiberry ever since he first came to office in 1879. Even the suddenness of the Minister's actions in January 1883 can be explained without reference to Egypt. There is strong circumstantial evidence that he and his advisers were forced by domestic considerations to activate their plans while they still had the opportunity. At the time, France was in the grip of a serious ministerial crisis over the proposed expulsion of the princes from the armed forces. Jauréguiberry was violently opposed to the measure, and when the Government asked for discretionary powers to deal with individual cases on 19 January, he must have known that his days in the cabinet were numbered. On that same day, his proposals for the occupation of Porto-Novo and the extension of a French protectorate along the Slave Coast were sent to the Quai d'Orsay. His orders to the South Atlantic Naval Division, issued without consulting the Foreign Ministry, were actually signed two days after his resignation and the day before he was finally replaced.

Those who emphasize the commercial factor in French expansion have a much stronger case. The protection of coastal trade had been a prominent theme since the 1870s, and, after the failure to reach a comprehensive settlement, the pressures to assume territorial commitments in its defence became powerful indeed. But coastal trade was not the policy-makers' sole concern. Jauréguiberry himself was much more interested in the future commercial prospects of the interior. The extension of French influence along the Niger-Benue complex was the most important element in his protectorate programme. The Benue treaties were intended to give France "the route to Lake Chad and the rich borderlands of Adamawa and Bornu." The treaties with Bonny and Calabar were intended to give French trade, "established on the Niger up to Egga, and also on the Benue where he dreamed to carry all our efforts now," an independent outlet to the sea. The gunboats operating from Bamako were intended to give France control over the Niger as far as Bussa. Jauréguiberry's protectorates were not simply an attempt to safeguard the coastal trading interest; they were also part of a two-pronged assault aimed at the creation of a vast territorial empire in the West African interior. Admittedly, this was a long-term and a rather vague objective; the minister himself never described the occupation of Bamako and his plans for the Lower Niger as two related elements in a fully developed policy of imperial expansion. But the simultaneous advance on both fronts was clearly more than pure coincidence. Soleillet had talked of such an empire in 1876, and the Colonial Department had noted his views. Rouvier's speeches had echoed the same theme after 1879. Twenty years before them, Faidherbe had drafted detailed plans for the empire's creation, and his were the blueprints which the Ministry of Marine was using.

Certainly, there had been a revolution in French African policy; but one cannot grasp its significance by studying the diplomacy of imperialism, because this revolution preceded the diplomatic phase of the partition. The French entry into the politics of the Lower Niger and the Congo was not the start but the continuation of a new policy. By then the fascination of Sudanese wealth, the fear if not the reality of foreign rivalry, and the triumph of protectionist sentiment had already whetted appetites for African territory and rendered the old techniques of informal expansion obsolete. The crucial change in French policy was the transition from informal to formal empire; it took place not in 1882–3 but in 1879–80.

What brought this change about? Local crises in Africa cannot provide the complete answer. The breakdown of the traditional pattern of trade along the coast may have forced the French to intervene politically; but even here their objectives were not limited to the protection of existing trade from British competition. And in the western Sudan no growth of African opposition forced them to adopt the techniques of military conquest. Tokolor resistance did not provoke the capture of Murgula or the occupation of Bamako; the fall of Murgula and the loss of Bamako did not even provoke Tokolor resistance. The conquest of the western Sudan was not an involuntary response to the pressure of local African circumstance but a determined European bid for territory.

Developments in French political life can provide only a partial explanation. The stabilization of the republic after the elections of 1877 and 1879 and the resignation of MacMahon, the return of France to the diplomatic stage at the Congress of Berlin, and the new spirit of self-confidence which these developments engendered should all be kept in mind. But they merely provided the back-drop to the process of policy-making. The nationalist and expansionist sentiments of French public opinion are more directly relevant. The popularity of the trans-Sahara railway was one of its most significant characteristics; the popularity of de Brazza was his most powerful weapon. Parliament was sympathetic to all the government's West African schemes. 25,000,000 frs were spent on the Senegal railway before the Chambers finally called a halt, and even the government's sternest critics did not dare to criticize its political objectives or to question the value of its projected African empire. But the impact of public opinion was sporadic and selective, and opinion itself was unstable; the agitation in favour of the trans-Sahara railway and de Brazza was more than matched by the furore over the Tunisian campaign. Nor can sudden bursts of nationalist fervour account for the origins of the policies pursued after 1879. Public opinion may on the whole have supported African expansion; it did not initiate the process.

Pressure from private commercial interests also played its part. Bordeaux merchants, the most influential group in Senegal, had long coveted the trade of the western Sudan. In 1851 and 1854 they campaigned for the appointment of Faidherbe and petitioned the government to open up the river *escales*. In 1879 the firm of Maurel et Prom supported the railway scheme; in 1880 it set up shop at Médine; by 1883 it had two steamers plying between Saint-Louis and Kayes. Along the Southern Rivers Verminck and his associates tirelessly demanded official protection and support, as did the C.F.A.E. in the Niger Delta. Governments did not remain deaf to their appeals. But ministers like Jauréguiberry were anything but traders' cats-paws. They made a clear distinction between the national and the private interest, and it was the former, not the latter, which they tried to serve. Nor were the traders empire-builders to a man. They were divided on important issues such as fiscal control and administrative responsibility. Their operations were limited to the coast and the river *escales;* even the Bordeaux merchants on the Upper Senegal were more interested in the profits to be had from supplying the expeditionary forces and transporting material for the railway than in gum or gold. And those who saw their trade threatened by the increased competition which the railway would bring, actively opposed and obstructed the government's plans. In France, moreover, the most influential commercial pressure groups, the Bordeaux and Marseille chambers of commerce, lagged far behind the government in their appreciation of Africa's future commercial importance.

Indeed, it was the local Senegalese administration which often stated the commercial arguments most forcefully. Brière de l'Isle was the most insistent in his demands for the revival of mercantilist principles in French African trade, and the most effective in undermining the government's commitment to peace. Once the military advance began, the military themselves became the focus of local initiative. The agents of expansion exerted the pressures which most affected the policy-makers. But French expansion in Africa was more than a case of 'a little local imperialism.' Senegal alone could not secure the massive capital outlay on which the Niger plan depended. And the decision to introduce the military factor was taken in Paris; Jauréguiberry was the man who sent Desbordes to the Sudan.

Ultimately, the motives for French expansion are to be found within the policy-making framework itself, within the 'official mind' of French imperialism. What transformed French policy after 1879 was a change in official thinking on the vital questions of cost and military effort. Freycinet and Jauréguiberry were the ones who broke with the tradition of limited government intervention in African affairs. Alarmed by the imagined threat of foreign competition, they made the state the principal agent of African expansion. Convinced of Africa's legendary wealth, they invested public funds in its future profitability. Discarding the old notions of informal empire, they made political control the basis for economic development, and they set out to win their empire by military means. This last was the crucial decision, and for it the Ministry of Marine rather than the Ministry of Foreign Affairs was the department primarily responsible. Within the Ministry a group of dedicated and energetic officials—Legros, Dislère and the head of the Upper Senegal Bureau, Lieutenant-Colonel Bourdiaux—provided a strong supporting cast; but, on the evidence available, Jauréguiberry himself seems to have acted the leading part.

French expansion in West Africa had its peculiarities. Its economic objectives were all-important, but these did not derive from any profound changes within the structure of the French economy or even from any serious assessment of Africa's economic potential. The policy-makers of the 1880s, like their predecessors of the 1820s and 1830s, fell victim to the myth of Sudanese wealth. Their calculations were no more solidly based than they had been half a century before. Jauréguiberry's estimate of a Sudanese market of 80,000,000 people was hardly the product of careful study, and Jauréguiberry was by no means unique. More intelligent men like Freycinet and more sophisticated economists like Rouvier talked blandly of markets three times the size. When policies are based on myths, they can be as fanciful as the objectives they seek to attain. But this does not make them any the less significant. The age of imperialism was not an Age of Reason, and French policies were nothing if not the product of their age.

Any interpretation of the partition must take this imperialist phenomenon into account. The policies of Freycinet and Jauréguiberry contained the very essence of late-nineteenth-century imperialism; they were the Gallic 'doctrine of tropical African estates' enunciated fifteen years before Chamberlain came to office. And this difference in timing was vital. By 1895 the scramble for West Africa was virtually over; in 1880 it had yet to begin. Chamberlain's doctrine may have 'inspired the beginnings of . . . modern administration' in Britain's African territories; its French counterpart inspired the actual process of expansion. The beginnings of British imperialism in West Africa may have been a consequence of the partition; the beginnings of French imperialism were its cause.

Taylor: Germany's First Bid for African Colonies

Thirty years of European concussions came to an end at the Congress of Berlin. In the ensuing period the European powers shrank from European conflicts, and the problems which continued to divide them were, as the French said of Alsace-Lorraine, *"reserved for the future."* European rivalries were temporarily diverted to the less dangerous field of *extra-European expansion,* and in the years between 1881 and 1912 the European powers extended their influence or their empires over Africa and large parts of Asia.

This imperialist expansion was of two kinds. The more important was the struggle for the heritage of decaying states, themselves very often the relics of earlier epochs of imperialism. The struggle over the succession to the Turkish Empire had gone on since the end of the seventeenth century; but what distinguished the "Age of Imperialism" was that more of these decadent states came into the market and that the process of absorption was rendered more and more difficult by the interference of some other European (and in one case of an Asiatic) power. Thus France was able to establish her control over Tunis, Annam, and Madagascar without serious difficulty; but she extended her influence over Morocco only after coming twice to the brink of war with Germany. Great Britain annexed the Boer republics (relic of an earlier Dutch empire) after a period of conflict with Germany; and she asserted her predominance in Egypt after a period of conflict with France. It was owing to the rivalry of England and Russia that Persia and Afghanistan preserved their independence—though Persia nearly lost it to Russia in the last years before 1914; and, thanks to the jealousy of all the powers, China preserved her independence, except for the loss of a few ports in what proved to be an abortive partition in 1898. It is not necessary to speculate at length on the reasons for

From A. J. P. Taylor, *Germany's First Bid for Colonies* (London, 1938), pp. 1–7.

these imperialist activities: the objects of conflict were going concerns; their economic and political importance was known; and in many cases they adjoined possessions or strategic routes of European powers (Morocco on the frontier of Algiers, Egypt and Persia on the route to India, the Boer republics on the frontier of Cape Colony, and so on). The rival powers were still primarily influenced by European considerations; and though the extra-European questions provoked crises, it was the old problem of the Balkans which produced the War of 1914, with the even older problem of the Franco-German frontier as a contributory cause.

The predominance of European considerations is even greater in relation to the second form of European expansion in these thirty years —the occupation of hitherto ownerless territories, or rather of territories with no ruler substantial enough to be treated as an independent power. Under this head come most of Africa and the islands of the Pacific. The enormous areas of tropical Africa appear impressive on the map; but of most of them the plain truth is that they had remained so long ownerless because they were not worth owning. The principal exception was the basin of the Congo, which, curiously enough, slipped through the hands of the two traditional colonial powers, England and France, and was secured by a royal speculator, Leopold II. of Belgium, masquerading as a philanthropic society. Portugal, with a shadowy traditional claim to all Africa, managed to retain one colony on the west coast, and one on the east. France, who created a great North African empire within a few years, had intelligible political reasons for doing so: the republican government wished to demonstrate by colonial expansion that France was still a great power despite the humiliations of 1870; part of the expansion was undertaken to protect the frontiers of the existing colony of Algiers; and much of the rest aimed at opening for France an overland route to the Sudan, where —it was commonly believed—it would be possible to divert the upper Nile and so make the English position in Egypt untenable. France regarded Egypt as part of the heritage of Napoleon, and, in endeavouring to oust the English, was seeking to recover what had once been hers.

England had two interests in Africa, which she meant to preserve —a settlement of British colonists in South Africa, and a predominant influence in Egypt, which was both valuable in itself and a vital point on the route to India. The new English acquisitions were made in order to protect what England already possessed by cutting off the Nile from foreign interference, and the Boer republics, and neighbours of Cape Colony, from foreign help. It is true that these new possessions sometimes proved to have a value of their own, such as the diamond mines of Kimberley and the cotton plantations of the Sudan; but it was not for this that they had been undertaken.

In these years of "the scramble for Africa" there was suddenly added to the old colonial rivals, France and England, a power which had hitherto confined itself strictly to the European continent. The German colonial empire, or rather the formulation of its theoretical claims, was virtually the work of a single year: the Cameroons were established in July 1884, German South-West Africa in August, New Guinea in December 1884, and German East Africa was begun in May 1885 (though its frontiers were not settled until 1890); Samoa was added in 1899; otherwise—apart from some minor adjustments of the Cameroons frontier at the expense of France after the second Moroccan crisis (1911)—the German colonial empire was complete. The success of Germany, as previously of Prussia, had been due to freedom from all concern in non-German questions: Prussia had been able to secure the support of Russia because of her indifference to the Near East, and of Italy, because of her indifference to the maintenance of the treaty settlement of Europe. It is therefore surprising that Germany should have deliberately pushed her way into the hornets' nest of colonial conflicts. The explanation of this German outburst of colonial activity has usually been found in the rising enthusiasm for colonies, and it is true that there was in Germany a certain amount of colonial agitation. Imperial Germany was a "made" state, an artificial reproduction of French nationalism tinged with echoes from the Holy Roman Empire; the new Germany had no political tradition, and had therefore to ape the political traditions of others. Many Germans demanded a colonial empire simply because other great powers had colonial empires, and their demand was reinforced by the current belief that the possession of colonies was in itself a profitable thing. Many writers, not only German, at this time failed to grasp the truth about the British empire—that it had come into being as the result of British commercial enterprise and industrial success; and they asserted the reverse, that the prosperity and wealth of Great Britain were due to the existence of her empire. The German campaign for colonies rested on the simple dogma—give Germany colonies and the Germans will then be as prosperous as the English.

It is difficult to believe that this primitive outlook was shared by the German government, particularly in the days of Bismarck. It has often been suggested that Bismarck was driven into a policy of colonial expansion against his will. Lord Sanderson, who was a member of the British Foreign Office in 1884, put forward this explanation in a defence of Bismarck written some twenty years later: "Prince Bismarck was personally opposed to German colonisation. . . . He therefore encouraged us to make fresh annexations on the West Coast of Africa, to which we had been previously indisposed: hoping that the clamour for such annexations by Germany would subside. Suddenly he found that the movement was too strong for him, and that his only expedient, in order to avoid a crushing Parliamentary defeat, was to make friends with the party which urged the acquisition of Colonies. He went to Lord Ampthill [the British Ambassador], explained his dilemma, said he should have to take up the Colonial policy vigorously, and begged that we should give him our support."

To imagine that Bismarck was influenced by public opinion, or that he was swayed by fear of "a crushing parliamentary defeat" is to transfer to Germany the conceptions of constitutional government as practised in England or France. The Imperial German government did not depend upon a parliamentary majority, and the German press was only slightly freer than the press in Russia. There are, of course, plenty of instances—the history of the Schleswig-Holstein affair is full of them—when Bismarck gave the signal for a popular campaign to compel him to do what he wanted to do, but there seems to be no other case in which Bismarck is supposed to have bowed to the force of public opinion. Nor is it conceivable that Bismarck was suddenly converted, after years of scepticism, to a belief in the value of colonies. He was contemptuous enough of those who were ready to disturb the quiet of Europe for the sake of the "sheep-stealers" of the Balkans. But even Bismarck could not have found words of condemnation strong enough for a policy which provoked a quarrel with Great Britain for the sake of the "light soil" of South-West Africa or of the head-hunters of New Guinea.

. . . Bismarck's colonial policy . . . alone seems meaningless and irrational; but when to the relations of England and Germany are added those of Germany and France, and those of France and England, Bismarck's policy in 1884 and 1885 becomes as purposeful as at any other time in his career. Such an examination shows that Bismarck quarrelled with England in order to draw closer to France; and that the method of quarrel was the deliberately provocative claim to owner-less lands, in which the German government had hitherto shown no interest. These lands had a certain negative value to Great Britain, in that they adjoined existing British colonies or lay near British strategic routes; but their value was not such as to provoke the English government into a war. Moreover, they were of no concern to any other power, and claims to them would not cause any international complications, such as would have been occasioned by German demands in China or Persia. The German colonies were the accidental by-product of an abortive Franco-German Entente.

It may be asked whether the later colonial disputes and discussions between England and Germany were similarly related to the European situation. It would be rash to attempt to discover in German policy after 1890 any such persistent and successful planning as in the days of Bismarck, particularly when to the gross incompetence of his successors were added the planless impulses of William II. Moreover, with the passing of time the German colonies did acquire a spurious ideological value; they became a white elephant, a sacred relic of Bismarck's era. He could contemplate passing on their useless burden to England, and even in 1890 the German government could surrender vast theoretical claims in East Africa in exchange for the really valuable island of Heligoland. Ten years later the value of colonies was taken as an axiom by the Germans, and from the failure of their colonial ventures they drew the moral not that colonies were a mistaken luxury, but that they ought to have more, and better, colonies. In the first decade of the twentieth century the Germans demanded "a place in the sun"; by this they meant someone else's place in the sun, their own having proved too hot.

Turner: Bismarck Changes His Mind

It is not difficult, however, to point out circumstantial evidence that casts considerable doubt on the validity of Taylor's reasoning. For example, just prior to Bismarck's move into the colonial world his utterances to his most trusted confidants contain strong indications that he was very skeptical about the prospects for reconciling France and Germany genuinely and permanently. The attempt to placate the French was, contrary to the impression conveyed by Taylor, nothing new, having been a basic component of Bismarck's policy at least since 1878. But even while pursuing this goal, Bismarck did not cease to doubt the possibility of quickly overcoming French resentment at Germany's possession of Alsace-Lorraine. It therefore seems questionable whether the Chancellor would have been willing to saddle his new German Reich with the sort of uncertain obligations and dangers that overseas possessions entailed, solely in order to pursue a goal he suspected was unattainable in the foreseeable future.

As Taylor himself admits, if Bismarck had really been looking for a quarrel with Britain in order to test the possibility of a Franco-German entente, there was a simpler and less risky alternative to the seizure of overseas possessions: he could instead have sided with France against Britain in the dispute over Egypt. Taylor dismisses this alternative in characteristically apodictic fashion. It would not, he states, have served Bismarck's purpose, "which was to convince the French that he had a grievance of his own and therefore actually needed French help. A grievance had to be created, and Bismarck turned to the colonial topics, which he had hitherto despised." However, if Bismarck had actually been seeking a rapprochement with Paris he would certainly, as a master diplomat, have sought it initially at the lowest price. Before resorting to such extravagant means as an imperialist policy he surely would have at least tried playing the Egyptian card.

More important than these objections to Taylor's theses is the fact that, like all the other interpretations that attribute Bismarck's change of policy to ulterior motives, it fails to accord with the documentary record of the Chancellor's words and actions. Some of this documentary evidence is new, having come to light only after Taylor's book was written. But much was available in print even in 1938, in German monographs and in documents published by the Reich in the 1880s. As will be shown below, these sources

From Henry A. Turner, Jr., "Bismarck's Imperial Venture: Anti-British in Origin?", in *Britain and Germany in Africa,* Roger Louis, Prosser Gifford, and Alison Smith, eds. (New Haven, 1967), pp. 49–53.

indicate clearly that Bismarck was not primarily motivated by any of the ulterior motives imputed to him. They reveal instead that he simply changed his mind and decided there must be German overseas possessions. This is not to say that Bismarck suddenly became an ardent imperialist. From all indications he was a very reluctant convert and retained a high degree of skepticism even while presiding over the founding of Germany's overseas empire. This was obviously because he was moved to reverse his policy not by the confident expectation of gaining concrete advantages but rather by a mounting concern about the possible adverse consequences of continued abstention. He acted, that is, only in order to avert what he feared might be the damaging effects of not doing so.

Bismarck's apprehensions stemmed initially from his growing concern lest the failure to stake out a German claim in the colonial world might have grave economic consequences. This was by no means an immediate possibility. Although Germany's commerce with Africa and Asia had been increasing rapidly since the mid-1870s, it remained only a miniscule fraction of the country's total foreign trade. But the non-European world was still the great unknown factor: there was always the chance that the extravagant predictions of the colonial zealots would eventually be borne out. As long as the principle of free trade prevailed in the colonial world, this possibility caused Bismarck no apprehension, for there was no reason to assume that Germany would lack access to Africa and Asia if those continents should prove to be of great economic importance. What brought Bismarck to reconsider his policy were the multiplying signs in the early 1880s that the era of free trade, which he himself had dealt such a heavy blow in Europe by the adoption of the protectionist German tariff of 1879, was also drawing to a close in the colonial world. Quite clearly, his attitude began to change under a barrage of reports to the effect that the colonial powers were beginning to favor their own nationals by means of differential tariffs and other discriminatory policies.

The Chancellor's doubts about the wisdom of continued opposition to German overseas possessions were further heightened by the developments that foreshadowed the partition of Africa, beginning with the well-publicized de Brazza-Stanley race to claim territory along the Congo in the early 1880s. As long as large parts of the non-European world were free of colonial rule, German commerce could get access to the markets and resources of Africa and Asia regardless of the discriminatory policies of the imperialist powers. But if those powers were to carve up all of the non-European world, German overseas merchants would be at their mercy. And without territorial possessions of her own overseas, Germany would be unable to obtain for her subjects the sort of economic privileges the colonial powers could gain for theirs through reciprocity agreements. The indications are that Bismarck had these eventualities in mind and that they contributed to his decision to break with his old policy.

Bismarck was also not immune to the *Torschlusspanik* that was to play such an important role in the partition of the non-European world—

the fear that the gate was rapidly closing and that the last chance was at hand. A major factor in his turn to imperialism was the thought that if he failed to authorize the hoisting of the German flag, the flag of another European power would quickly go up. In Germany's case at least, it is impossible to account for the new imperialism of the late nineteenth century without taking into account the dynamics of the highly competitive European state system.

Finally, it should be said that there was undoubtedly a domestic political dimension to Bismarck's reversal of policy. He was, after all, primarily a man of politics who instinctively sought out the political significance of almost everything that came into his purview. Still, it would be a mistake to conclude, as have some, that he limited his assessment of the political ramifications of such a major policy decision to tactical, short-range considerations such as the impact on a single election campaign. He was without question aware in 1884 that the popular colonial issue would be a useful cudgel against the anti-imperialist Radical Party in the campaign for the autumn Reichstag elections. However, the line of argument that would attribute the origins of his imperialist venture to his concern about those elections founders on the fact that he continued to enlarge Germany's overseas commitments even after the Radicals had been dealt a resounding setback at the polls. It is far more likely that long-range considerations played a greater role in Bismarck's assessment of the domestic aspects of overseas questions than did the campaign of 1884. This was, it must be remembered, the mature Bismarck, who was seeking to stabilize the political system he had imposed on the German people and to convince them his government really served their interests. Moreover, the early 1880s was a period when, under the impact of a severe economic depression, Bismarck had committed his government to the task of restoring and furthering the material welfare of Germany. The possible effect that continued abstention from the colonial arena might have on the attitude toward the government of such an important component of society as the business community, particularly if Africa and Asia became as important economically as the imperialists had predicted, must therefore have given the Chancellor pause. There are also indications that he was very much concerned about the effects on his own place in German history. In remarks that have an unguarded, sincere ring, he later explained that in considering whether to take the plunge into colonial affairs he had to ask himself "whether after twenty, after thirty years, people will charge that fainthearted Chancellor back then with not having the courage to ensure for us a share of what later became such valuable property."

It was this complex of economic and political considerations that brought Bismarck to reconsider his position. Formerly, he had opposed overseas possessions for Germany on the grounds that they would be a two-fold liability, externally because the country lacked a fleet adequate to defend them, and internally because the costs of administering them would "widen the parliamentary parade ground" by increasing the government's financial dependence on the Reichstag. In searching for solutions to the new developments described above, however, he began to relax his rigid attitude, gradually moving away from his old position. When he finally became convinced he had found an administrative formula that circumvented at least his domestic objections, he acted to commit Germany to the imperialist scramble.

Robinson and Gallagher: Britain's Nilotic Imperative

If the strategic reasons for staying in Cairo were strong, the internal Egyptian reasons against withdrawal were overwhelming. By 1889 Baring had convinced the Prime Minister that there could be no stability or security in Cairo without occupation. As the British Agent saw it, the internal crisis which had come to a head in 1882, was still unsolved. Revolution still simmered beneath the surface tranquillity of the occupation. The chances of setting up a reliable Egyptian *régime* and so returning to a supremacy wielded from outside, were smaller than ever. . . .

By June 1889, Salisbury had come round entirely to Baring's point of view. The British Agent had stated his case in these words:

> ". . . the real reason why the evacuation policy is well nigh impossible of execution . . . is based on the utter incapacity of the ruling classes in this country. . . . [They] are almost exclusively foreigners. . . . Now, all this class are detested by the people, and they are more disliked now than they ever were before . . . if he [Riaz Pasha] were left to himself he would go far to produce a revolution in six months. . . . Really, the more I look at it, the more does the evacuation policy appear to me to be impossible under any conditions."

From Ronald Robinson and John Gallagher with Alice Denny, *Africa and the Victorians: The Official Mind of Imperialism* (London, 1961), pp. 274, 281–89.

Baring warned the Prime Minister that even if the French agreed to give the British a right of re-entry, a withdrawal now would lead to anarchy and disaster for British influence. Moreover he could see another and even worse danger in evacuation. Reopening the entire Egyptian question would shatter any chance of reconciliation between Britain and France and might well lead to war. . . .

Having reached this conclusion by the middle of 1889, Salisbury soon drew others, more momentous still for the future of Africa. Within the next six months he decided at Baring's prompting that if they were to hold Egypt, they could not afford to let any other European Power obtain a hold over any part of the Nile Valley. In so doing, he took what was perhaps the critical decision of the Partition. Henceforward almost everything in Africa north of the

Zambesi River was to hinge upon it.

The idea that the security of Egypt depended upon the defence of the Upper Nile was as old as the pyramids; and the government had been reminded of it often enough. Sir Samuel Baker, the well-known explorer and once the Khedive's governor in the Sudan, wrote about it in 1884 and 1888. He pointed at the danger that a hostile Power could readily dam the Upper Nile, starve Egypt of water, and so destroy the country. This had been one of the objections of the forward party to abandoning the Sudan, and for the same reason Riaz Pasha had pressed upon Baring the need to win it back.

> ". . . The Nile is the life of Egypt. . . . The Nile means the Soudan. . . . If [any European Power] . . . took possession of the banks of the Nile it would be all over with Egypt. . . . The Government of His Highness the Khedive will never willingly consent, not without compulsion, to such an attack on its existence."

But the British Agent was not at this time persuaded. He had strongly advised Salisbury against reconquering the Sudan for the time being; and the Prime Minister had agreed. . . .

So far they had had good reason to be complacent about the Upper Nile and its headwaters in Uganda and Ethiopia. As long as no other Power was in sight of seizing these regions, they could have little bearing on Egyptian security. The Dervishes who held the Sudan could not cut off the flow of the river on which the life and stability of Egypt depended, for they were no engineers. No European Power had yet reached the point of sending menacing expeditions towards the Upper Nile, and it was still possible that Britain would leave Egypt soon.

But things were very different by 1889. The British were certainly intending to stay. Cairo was becoming more and more the pivot of their Mediterranean strategy. A foreign Power astride the Upper Nile would be in a position either to levy blackmail or to lever them out of Egypt. It was the Italians, advancing from the Red Sea towards the eastern Sudan, who presented the first threat of this kind.

In May 1889, the Italian minister, Crispi, made the Treaty of Uccialli with Ethiopia—an agreement designed to give Rome great influence in the country of the Blue Nile. He also laid claim to Kassala which commanded the Atbara tributary of the Nile. With this town as a base the Italians might edge their way towards Khartoum at the confluence of the White and the Blue Nile. Crispi's vaulting African ambition and the challenge at Kassala goaded Salisbury to make up his mind about the Nile Valley as a whole.

How long he had meditated it before putting on paper the policy of closing the Valley of the Nile, who can say? But by August 1889, the Prime Minister was anxious enough about Kassala to ask Baring what he thought about it. The reply must have been emphatically against letting foreign Powers into the Nile Valley, because on 15 November, "[the Prime Minister] concurred fully as to the inviolability of the valley of the Nile even in its affluents. . . ." The doctrine was already fully formed.

The reasons for adopting this policy are plainly disclosed in Baring's correspondence with Salisbury. If the Italians took Kassala, he wrote,

"... They would soon strike the valley of the Nile ... at Khartoum ... the establishment of a civilised Power in the Nile Valley would be a calamity to Egypt."

When Baker and others had put forward similar views in 1888, Baring went on, he had thought them "unnecessarily alarmist":

"The savage tribes who now rule in the Sudan do not possess the resources or the engineering skill to do any real harm to Egypt."

But the Italian threat had now converted Baring,

"... The case would be very different were a civilised European Power established in the Nile Valley. ... They could so reduce the water-supply as to ruin the country. ... Whatever Power holds the Upper Nile Valley must, by the mere force of its geographical situation, dominate Egypt."

There was already enough discontent inside the country without inviting Foreign Powers to manufacture subversion by drought. But Baring the administrator still guided Baring the strategist. He did not want Salisbury to stop the Italian advance at the expense of a premature reconquest of the Sudan, for this would disorganise the Egyptian finances which the British Agent had been at such pains to set in order. He urged the Prime Minister to keep 'a strictly defensive policy' for the time being; and to keep the Italians out of the Nile Valley by diplomacy.

Just as the Prime Minister in June had concurred in Baring's counsel to stay in Egypt, so after November he took up Baring's policy of defending the occupation of the Upper Nile.

"In respect to Kassala," Salisbury wrote in March 1890, "it gives the Power occupying it command over one of the main affluents of the Nile, and therefore a power of diverting a portion of the supply which is vital to Egypt." And he agreed to "... such measures as may be necessary for the purpose of protecting your Nile Valley against the dominion of any outside Power."

It was, he declared, "... essential to the safety of Egypt" that this should be done. The policy was comprehensive. At first it applied specifically to the Italians and Kassala. But Salisbury and Baring had plainly adopted it from November 1889 as a general principle; and the principle held good for all Powers and for all parts of the Nile Valley, indeed as far south as the headwaters of the river in the Uganda country.

Thus the safety of the Nile had now become a supreme consideration, and the policy was quickly put into effect. On 7 March, 1890, Salisbury warned the Italians off the Nile, and later Baring was sent to Rome to try and set safe limits to their advance. The new strategy also forced Salisbury and Baring to reconsider the defensive policy of the past six years in the Sudan. Baring gave three reasons for doing so; in the first place, Egypt's finances had now turned the corner; secondly, "the dervish movement has been going rapidly downhill"; and thirdly, diplomacy could not be relied upon for ever to ward off other Powers. In the end, occupation alone could make certain of the Upper Nile. The Prime Minister agreed that sooner or later the Sudan would have to be reconquered. But like Baring, he preferred to wait—so long as diplomacy would suffice to keep foreign rivals away. Salisbury as usual was against giving the imperialists at the Horse Guards a free hand. More important, he took it for granted that an "imperialist" advance would jar upon the prejudices of the electorate at Home.

> "They were so deeply impressed with the disasters of six years ago," Salisbury explained, "and the apparently inexorable necessity which had driven them into situations where those disasters were inevitable, that they shrink instinctively from any proposal to advance into the Egyptian desert. I do not say that this is a sufficient argument to prevent such an advance, if there is a clear balance of undoubted advantage in its favour; but in the absence of any such evidence, it must be accepted as a strong presumption. As far as I can see matters, I should say that until you have money enough to justify you in advancing to Berber, you had better remain quiet."

For the time being, diplomacy must remain the chief defence of the security of Egypt in the Nile Basin. If he was not yet ready to re-occupy the region, he made it plain that he would oppose its occupation by any other Power. Having already warned off the Italians, he quickly gave the French and the German ambassadors a similar message. The new strategy was now operating.

For all the worldly wisdom which prompted this strategy, it flowed less from hard-headed reckoning than from a change of heart. Behind it lay a sea-change in the Victorian spirit and the official mind. A new age was struggling to be born. To the old men who sat at the head of affairs—as old men usually do—it seemed that imperialism was entering on its greatest epoch. But European expansion was already at odds with the new forces of colonial nationalism which it had goaded into life. The dynasts were beginning to lose their way in history. The shadows were falling over the times and themes they knew best. The end of the European age was in sight. Beset with problems for which their historiography offered no solutions, the old men in the chancelleries came more and more to combat their manifestations rather than to grapple with their causes. . . .

In the event ministers began to fear that Providence and the laws of progress were no longer working on their side. Shocked by nationalist intransigence and Oriental fanaticisms, jostled by new rivals in Africa and new enemies in the Mediterranean, they were losing their nerve. Self-confidence had carried the English to the ends of the earth. Drop by drop it was dribbling out of them.

For the Victorians at mid-century the excellence of moral suasion and free partnership had seemed self-evident. But now this belief was being shrunk by fears of subversion and disloyalty. Too often the old aspirations to liberate and improve the world had been ungratefully accepted or surlily refused. Orientals and Africans had been shown the way. They had not followed it. Boers and Irishmen had been given equal rights with Englishmen. They had misused them. Step by step, the easy British optimism modulated into an injured resentment and a harsher outlook. Since the Irish bit the hand that fed them, they should undergo twenty years of resolute government. Since the Indians could not be assimilated, the Ilbert Bill and the Indian Councils Bill were Radical treachery to the *Raj*. Since the King of Burma was a bad risk, he should be deposed. Having failed to find willing partners by policy, the Victorians condemned them to be involuntary subjects.

Hence they were driven into abandoning creative policy and replacing it by cold administration and control. Prestige became all important to them. So too did insurance. Policy grew more and more committed to the warding off of hypothetical dangers by the advancing of frontiers. When Salisbury put his Nile strategy into practice, the defensive psychology which kept watch over northern India had been transplanted into Africa. The frontiers of fear were on the move.

And so the Prime Minister at the end of the Eighteen-eighties had decided upon an enlarged Egyptian policy. Not that there was any popular demand for it. It had emerged from the subjective calculations of national interest made by the small group which still decided such matters. To them supremacy in Egypt was becoming crucial, as the balance in Europe and the Mediterranean shifted. In Salisbury's mind, the pivot of the British position in the Mediterranean, and therefore in the world, was moving from Constantinople and the Straits to Cairo and the Canal, from south-eastern Europe and Asia Minor to the Nile Valley and north-east Africa. The Nile Valley strategy was something of an anomaly among the traditional concepts of the national interest handed down from Pitt, Canning, and Palmerston to Salisbury. He became the first Victorian statesman to discover a vital interest in the middle of tropical Africa, but if he was the first, he was not the last, to do so. The decisions of the winter of 1889 to 1890 set the priorities of British policy for the remainder of the Partition, and the Nile Valley headed the list. Salisbury stamped his new design upon tropical Africa, but it was a new design for an old purpose. Hitherto Britain had given way to her rivals in both east and west Africa, in order to protect Egypt. Henceforward, she could yield only on the west, for the Nile Valley and its approaches from the east coast were now considered vital to Egypt. The Mediterranean and Indian interest, like a driving wheel in some vast machine, was now engaging the lesser wheels of the eastern-central Africa and connecting them one by one to its own workings. At the turn of Salisbury's strategy, these once remote and petty interests in the Sudan, Uganda and the northern hinterlands of Zanzibar were changing into safeguards of Britain's world power.

Sanderson: French Policy on the Upper Nile

Except for a moment in June 1894, the Germans always kept their action, or inaction, on the Upper Nile subordinate to their general foreign policy. In France, and the other extreme, policy towards the Upper Nile often followed a completely autonomous course which was sometimes in direct opposition to the broader trends of French diplomacy. Indeed, by 1897 the Foreign and Colonial Ministries were pursuing two separate and irreconcilable policies. Something not dissimilar occurred in London during 1897-1898, when Salisbury and Chamberlain differed radically on policy towards France in West Africa. But not even "pushing Joe" ever dared to imitate the off-hand arrogance with which the Pavillon de Flore sometimes ignored the directives—indeed, almost the very existence—of the Minister for Foreign Affairs.[1]

Between 1889 and 1892 Eugène Etienne [Under-Secretary for the Colonies] had striven to introduce some order into the chaos of French activity and stagnation on the mainland of Africa. His scale of priorities, on which the upper Ubangi and the Upper Nile ranked very low, was maintained by his successor Jamais. But Jamais quite failed to control either the soldiers in West Africa, or the forces which Etienne himself had released. When Delcassé took over in January 1893, the under-secretary's control over expansionist activity was little more than a legal fiction. Mizon was levying private war in Adamawa, a region which London and Berlin regarded as their private bone of contention. In West Africa the *commandant supérieur* Archinard passed on Delcassé's instructions to his subordinate Combes—but with explicit orders not to obey them. On the upper Ubangi the younger men were going as far as they dared in opposition to the "politique de moindre effort" for so long enforced by Paris and by de Brazza. Even Liotard, normally the most loyal of subordinates, had caught the prevailing infection when he advanced on Bangasso in March 1893. In this situation Haussmann, the *Directeur Politique* at the *Colonies,* tended to regard his function as that of a brake on local excess of zeal. In 1893 he was not looking for new adventures, above all not on the Upper Nile, but rather to liquidate old ones, especially the potentially very dangerous Adamawa affair.

To these hazards Delcassé seems to have been quite indifferent. He did indeed recall Mizon, but evidently with the greatest reluctance. He did

From G. N. Sanderson, *England, Europe and the Upper Nile, 1882–1899* (Edinburgh, 1965), pp. 386–92.

[1] Pavillon de Flore was the location of the French Colonial Ministry and "pushing Joe" was Joseph Chamberlain, British Colonial Secretary. *Ed.*

not get to grips with the *officiers soundanais* until in December 1893 heavy pressure from press and parliament forced him to appoint a civilian Governor-General, Albert Grodet, with the directive that "the period of conquest and territorial expansion must be considered as definitely over." Meanwhile, influenced by Victor Prompt's dangerous hydrological speculations and perhaps by the sudden enthusiasm of d'Arenberg and Harry Alis, Delcassé launched a drive for the Nile. Leopold had promoted this idea through his agent Harry Alis, hoping to enforce a diplomatic settlement on the upper Ubangi as an indispensable preliminary to the French expedition; but to Leopold's dismay Delcassé proposed to challenge the Congolese by armed force as well as to "re-open the Egyptian question" by a threat to the Nile waters of Fashoda. Meanwhile, Delcassé kept even his own *Direction* as far as possible in the dark. Develle, the Foreign Minister, was no wiser, though he was on record as approving at any rate a mission "towards" the Bahr al-Ghazal. However, Delcassé invoked the assistance of the President of the Republic himself to overcome Monteil's reluctance to undertake the mission; and Sadi Carnot, usually regarded as a model of constitutional rectitude, associated himself completely with a mere *sous-ministre*'s private and unauthorised project to challenge the British occupation of Egypt.

The Monteil Mission of 1893 was not so much a policy as a conspiracy in the margin of policy. It was neatly frustrated when Leopold II, a conspirator beside whom Delcassé was a beginner, inspired the probably unwitting Monteil to insist on a previous agreement with the Congo State as a *sine qua non* of his departure for Africa. Delcassé could not dismiss out of hand the colonialist hero of the hour and a man who still enjoyed the powerful support of Etienne. The Mission therefore languished from August 1893, when Monteil delivered the ultimatum embodying his "conditions," until it was given its quietus by Casimir-Périer early in 1894. Casimir-Périer's suppression of the mission was certainly prompted by his desire to assert his own ministerial authority against Presidential encroachment; he was moreover prepared, from whatever motives, to go to almost any length to please King Leopold. At the beginning of 1894 there were however good objective reasons for putting a sharp curb on adventures in Africa. The British had protested again Mizon's proceedings in language which, if used in any but an African dispute, might have heralded an early ultimatum. In December 1893 there had been an accidental but bloody clash between British and French troops in the hinterland of Sierra Leone. In January 1894 a French column, sent to relieve a junior officer who had advanced to Timbuktu in direct contravention of orders, was ambushed and annihilated. *Le Matin* thundered: "Les Romains, qui furent le modèle des conquérants dans l'antiquité, châtiaient sans pitié l'héroïsme indiscipliné."

The early months of 1894 were the high-water mark of "héroïsme indiscipliné." Thereafter the *Colonies* (since April 1894 a full Ministry) seems to have exerted a more effective control over its agents overseas. The details of this process are unknown. Boulanger, despised for his lack of expert knowledge, initiated an internal re-organisation of his Ministry; and this may have had some effect. The appointment of Grodet certainly went far to spike the guns of the *officiers soudanais,* in spite of—or perhaps because of—Grodet's quarrelsome, unscrupulous and generally unpleasing personality. Haussmann's rather ineffective *immobilisme* began to be eclipsed by the influence of younger men, more in sympathy with the forward policy and perhaps for that very reason better able to control it. After his return to the Pavillon de Flore in June 1894, Delcassé no longer seems to have held his *Direction* at arm's length; he evidently worked closely with it in opposition to the proposed Phipps-Hanotaux settlement.

In the second half of 1894 the Colonial Ministry launched a series of successful missions—Decoeur, Toutée, Ballot—through the Dahomey gap towards the middle Niger. These successes, and the *esprit de suite* of the whole operation, showed a professional touch which had been lacking in the planning of the Monteil Mission; and they extorted the rueful admiration of a fellow-professional, Sir Percy Anderson: "It is impossible not to be struck by the admirable way in which the numerous French expeditions are conducted by capable officers." In sharp contrast to these successes, the Liotard Mission to the Upper Nile, authorised by the French Cabinet in November 1894, made no progress worthy of the name. But compared with the West African expeditions, the "Liotard Mission" was little more than a *façon de parler*. There was no independent mission under an experienced military explorer. Instead, the drive to the Nile was entrusted to a rather pedestrian administrator already over-burdened by routine tasks for which his resources were barely adequate. Delcassé's apparent satisfaction with this rather half-hearted arrangement invites speculation; it is at least possible that his policy towards the Upper Nile was no longer so headstrong as in 1893.

Delcassé's successor Chautemps was a clear-headed administrator, who took the first and decisive step towards remedying the 'situation anarchique' of conflicting and overlapping jurisdictions in French West Africa. The setbacks to Delcassé's forward policy in the Ivory Coast and elsewhere had raised an outcry in the Chambers; Chautemps insured against a similar danger on the Upper Nile by simply neglecting to reinforce Liotard. This quiet reversal of Cabinet policy may not have been to the taste of his *Direction;* but no one else objected—least of all Hanotaux, who had in November 1894 openly opposed the Liotard Mission. In September 1895, Marchand, presumably with support from the permanent officials, submitted his proposals to Chautemps. Administratively, the essence of Marchand's scheme was that the Upper Nile mission should be given an organisation and status similar to those of the successful West Africa expeditions. This was a technically sound proposal which Chautemps was prepared to consider; but he was not prepared to act until the political implications of Marchand's plan had been explicitly approved by the Quai d'Orsay. In September 1895 the relations of France with Russia, and of Russia with Germany, were moving Hanotaux actively to seek a rapprochement with England, rather than to initiate action which could, as he well knew, lead only to a violent quarrel. But he seems to have lacked the nerve to kill the project outright. Instead, he hedged and procrastinated. Meanwhile, so long as Chautemps was in office, the *Colonies* took no further action, and the Marchand Mission remained a paper project.

The mission was finally launched, after the fall of Chautemps and Hanotaux, by those who had doubtless supported it from the first—the permanent officials, notably Ernest Roume. Approval was obtained from Guieysse, the new and professionally inexperienced Colonial Minister, when he had been only a week in office. Berthelot, the new Foreign Minister, was if anything even less qualified for his position than Guieysse. Roume found an ally at the Quai d'Orsay, presumably Benoît, the high colonialist *Directeur des protectorats.* Pleading overwhelming urgency—a plea totally belied by their later action—these men rushed Berthelot into approving a project of which the full political implications had never been explained to him. This concealment was almost certainly deliberate; and the mission to the Upper Nile, in 1895 as in 1893, was promoted by methods which can only be described as conspiratorial. But this time the conspiracy was not merely in the margin of policy; it was a conspiracy directly opposed to Berthelot's policy of amicable settlement with England, if possible even in Egypt.

In 1896 the able and aggressive Gustave Binger became *Directeur des affaires d'Afrique* at the Colonial Ministry. Given a tough-minded Minister who would underwrite their policies, the *bureaux* of the Pavillon de Flore could now disregard the directives of a mere nonpolitical Foreign Minister like Hanotaux. The *Colonies* found their tough-minded Minister in André Lebon; and Hanotaux' efforts to assert his control over this formidable combination were pathetically futile. He apparently watered down Marchand's instructions by omitting all mention of the White Nile and of Fashoda, in the attempt to convert the mission from "a pistol-shot on the Nile" to a means of comparatively gentle pressure in the Bahr al-Ghazal. He certainly opposed the Colonial Ministry's foolhardy and irresponsible policy—supported, however, by his own *Direction*—of enlisting the military support of the Negus Menelik. But after he had been over-ruled in full Cabinet on Ethiopian policy in March 1897 he seems to have admitted defeat; and he took no traceable action when early in 1897 the Pavillon de Flore issued instructions quite incompatible not only with Hanotaux' own watered-down version but with the original objects of the Mission as approved by the Quai d'Orsay. While the *Colonies* did its best to set the Nile on fire, Hanotaux pursued an expectant and unprovocative policy in this sphere, presumably hoping that "Marchand n'arriverait pas"—at least, not on the Nile itself.

The Marchand Mission was the last and most spectacular manifestation of the "imperialism of prestige" which came to dominate French colonial expansion in the eighteen-nineties. In this movement, economic motives played very little part; in the Marchand Mission itself, none at all. Marchand's own motives were those common to the *officiers soudanais* who conquered a sub-continent while Ministers protested and businessmen placed their investments elsewhere: a hunger for action and adventure, ennobled by the concept of 'la plus grande France', and in Marchand's particular case (which was certainly not unique) spiced by a hearty detestation for 'greedy and hypocritical' England. Until 1893 the "imperialism of prestige" had been restrained rather than encouraged, at least in its more extravagant forms, by the Office tradition at the *Colonies;* Haussmann was utterly opposed to its extension to the Nile valley. Moreover Etienne, from motives which can at least in part be justly described as economic, saw French expansion in Africa largely as the creation of a "Greater Algeria." To this vision the Upper Nile was quite irrelevant. But from 1894 the control of policy fell increasingly into the hands of permanent officials who were, in Monson's words, "extremely combative" towards England. To these men, always ready to assert the prestige of France by "inventing and intensifying" difficulties with England, the Nile project was very relevant indeed; for its fundamental object was to restore French prestige in the theatre where national pride had received its most grievous wound since 1871.

Precisely because the British occupation of Egypt was so widely felt as an intolerable affront to national self-respect, the Nile project enjoyed support far outside the ranks of convinced colonialists once its connection with Egypt had been clearly established. In June 1894, at the close of the debate in which Etienne established this connection, the Chamber voted unanimously in favour of what at least appeared to be a policy of active reprisal against the Anglo-Congolese Agreement. In December 1896, when a Deputy queried the inflated upper Ubangi budget which, as almost everyone knew, concealed the credits of the Marchand Mission, even the Socialist Jean Jaurès demanded "une vote nationale"; and obtained one, by an enormous majority. It is hardly relevant to discuss the influence of the Parliamentary Colonial Group in this connection. The Chamber needed no convincing; all that the Colonialists had to do was to make the keynote speeches and to provide any necessary detailed information. In 1882 the French Chamber had shrunk from the largely imaginary hazards of joint intervention in Egypt. In 1885 it had destroyed Jules Ferry because he had become involved in petty hostilities, for the moment unsuccessful, with China. But in 1894 and 1896 the Chamber gave its overwhelming approval to a policy carrying risks beside which those of 1882 and 1885 were negligible. Behind this policy there was little rational calculation. It rested rather on a quite irrational conviction that a successful expedition to the Upper Nile *must* somehow lead to a favourable solution of the Egyptian question; and on the further assumption, less irrational but almost wilfully erroneous, that economic interests would always keep England from making the Nile a *casus belli.* These views were not confined to an ill-informed public and parliament. Astonishingly, they were shared by French diplomatists and by the professional experts not merely in the Colonial Ministry, but in the Foreign Ministry. Even had Hanotaux' position been stronger than it was, it is doubtful whether, after his return to office in 1896, he could have halted the Marchand Mission against the combined pressure of the permanent officials and of public opinion.

Beneath the surface of events, however, the "imperialism of prestige" was losing ground to the economic imperialism of the *Union Coloniale Française*. The businessmen who formed this organisation relaxed their hostility to further expansion to the extent of regarding Morocco as an indispensable acquisition; but they never had the slightest sympathy for an imperialism of prestige in the Nile valley. They well knew that in Egypt Cromer safeguarded their investments better than any conceivable alternative régime was likely to do; better, indeed, than they were safeguarded by the *fonctionnaires* in some French possessions. As for the Sudan, profits here were obviously a chimaera. In the shock and disillusion which followed Fashoda, the interests embodied in the *Union Coloniale* were able to use the influence which they had been quietly accumulating during the previous five years. If the Marchand Mission was the last grandiose fling of the old imperialism of prestige, its dénouement in 1898–1899 was the first victory for an imperial policy based on more material calculations. It was at a meeting sponsored by the *Union Coloniale* that Eugène Etienne read the obituary of the imperialism of prestige; Marchand had known what he was about when he so bitterly denounced "les coloniaux d'exploitation rationnelle."

French policy towards the Upper Nile was certainly the outcome of a conflict of interests; indeed of a multiple conflict which even included personal interests, not always of a reputable kind. But once the Upper Nile had been publicly linked to Egypt in 1894, French intervention was sustained by a wider enthusiasm which rose to a climax in 1897 and 1898, only to collapse thereafter with a surprising rapidity. In England, too, similar conflicts played their part in the determination of policy; but here too there was a wider enthusiasm for intervention and ultimately for acquisition. Until the end of 1894 this wider enthusiasm scarcely existed so far as the Sudan was concerned; but in 1898 and 1899 it reached a peak from which it did not decline until it had undergone the chastening experience of the South African War. By 1898 it had endowed with strongly acquisitive overtones a Sudan policy which had in the later eighteen-eighties been gradually and rather reluctantly initiated as a purely defensive strategy to protect the Nile waters and so to safeguard the British position in Egypt.

Robinson and Gallagher: The Meaning of Fashoda

At first sight there is a certain absurdity about the struggle for Fashoda. The massive advance of Kitchener's army took two and a half years, and it ended by browbeating a few men marooned by the side of the Nile. There was a strange disproportion between ends and means, as there was in building two railways from points two thousand miles apart to run into the deserts of the Upper Nile. A still deeper absurdity seems to lie in the French speculation about damming the river and in the labours of the British to stop them. Even Marchand himself came to see that the scheme was hare-brained, for it turned out that there was no stone within miles of Fashoda. To this extent, the great rivalry for the Upper Nile was based on a myth. The greatest absurdity of all might seem to be that for two months two great Powers stood at the brink of war for the ownership of the *sudd* and desert of the Upper Nile.

It is true that after 1895 there was an irrational fringe to the British attitude towards the Nile. It is no less true that this attitude commanded the assent of British opinion during the dramatic climax of the struggle. Nearly all the English newspapers stood firm behind the government during the crisis, and their tone was considerably more strident than that of the French press. The abstract analysis of editorials is not worth much as an evaluation of public opinion, but there is no doubt that there was plenty of warlike spirit in the country. Even the British and Foreign Arbitration Association let it be known that while they remained devoted to their doctrine they did not think that it should be applied to Fashoda.

The aggressive mood of 1898 has often been regarded as an example of the hysterical passion for aggrandisement which is supposed to have swept through Britain at the end of the century. This 'new imperialism' is said to have been produced by the spread of literacy, the coming of the mass vote and the rise of the yellow press. This may be so, or it may not. At the end of the century there may have been a new imperial spirit rising in some sections of English society. Perhaps the new voters and the new readers may have applauded a policy of swagger and bluster towards the foreigner. The newly fashionable theories of Social Darwinism may have introduced a racial arrogance towards lesser breeds without the law. More people by this time may have come to believe that Africa could be made into another India.

From Ronald Robinson and John Gallagher with Alice Denny, *Africa and the Victorians: The Official Mind of Imperialism* (London, 1961), pp. 376–78.

All this may have been true; but it is not to say that new public pressures drove the government down the road to Fashoda, or that popular demand in September 1898 compelled government to do what it would otherwise not have done. During the Fashoda crisis the leaders of both parties came out openly in favour of the Nile Valley strategy. In a speech on 12 October, Rosebery warned the French not to make a mistake ". . . which can only lead to a disastrous conflagration"; the next day Asquith spoke in the same sense; on 28 October Harcourt spoke of the need for national unity; while Campbell-Bannerman said on 24 November that ". . . we ranged ourselves as one man in determining to resist the aggression." This chorus of patriotic union was joined by the Liberal and Radical press. Among the politicians only Morley, among the newspapers only the *Manchester Guardian* stood out against this general line of approval and support for the British government. At the time of Fashoda opinion in the country was being exhorted by two political parties both saying the same thing and both casting it in stereotypes of the national honour and the civilising mission. It may well be true, as Chamberlain asserted, that British policy was strengthened by ". . . the spectacle of a united nation," but it does not follow that the policy was determined by that spectacle. To assert that it was, is to study the situation of 1898 from the standpoint of other centuries and, it may be, from the standpoint of other countries.

The Fashoda crisis was not the outcome of a ferocious popular will then, although it evoked signs of one. It was the logical conclusion of a strategy followed by the Foreign Office for a decade. Of the calculations and interests involved in this, the public knew very little. The leaders of both parties understood the strategy, and most of them approved of it; but time after time they refrained from any public explanation of the vital issues it involved, lest this should hinder British diplomacy abroad and provoke the intervention of the ignorant at home. Foreign policy was a matter of an *élite,* and they conducted it according to their own view of national interest and world policy. The British electorate found that their country now enjoyed a condominium over the Sudan, whether they liked it or not. However it may have appeared to the man in the street, to the initiated few Fashoda was simply the climax to an old policy of imperial defence.

In the eyes of the real makers of policy, there was obviously a scramble in Africa; but it was hardly for Africa or for empire for empire's sake. Throughout the partition their over-riding concern was to claim those regions of the continent which seemed vital for security in the Mediterranean and therefore in the world.

problem II

Collaboration or Resistance to European Rule in Africa

Having partitioned Africa, the European powers set out to occupy the continent. In fact Chapter VI of the General Act of the Conference of Berlin of 1884/1885, which was designed in part to regulate the scramble for Africa, stipulated the conditions by which the powers would mutually recognize what constituted an effective occupation in Africa. Although such conditions were seldom put to the test, no European state could ever claim to rule where it could not claim sovereignty. Once the technical criteria of occupation had been settled, however, the European powers were free to occupy Africa, exerting control with an ease more apparent than real. Equipped with superior weaponry and resources, a relatively small number of Europeans, usually assisted by African troops or allies, were able to impose their control over large African populations. The conspicuous facility by which the Europeans asserted their authority seemed to indicate a moral, as well as a technical, superiority, at least in the minds of the imperialists, while often obscuring the reality of African resistance. Although even the imperialists have today ceased to confuse superior morality with superior technology, the dominant role of the latter in the European occupation of Africa remains irrefutable but has eclipsed the nature of the African response. Not only have the alternatives available to Africans facing the European invaders appeared clear and distinct, but the results, favorable for the collaborators and detrimental for the resistors, seemed so obvious as to require no further inquiry. This sharp distinction between collaborators and resistors has now been challenged. The clarity with which scholars once viewed the African response has now become blurred by the growing awareness both of the complexities of human motivation and of the rational calculations made by the Africans after assessing their interests and the probable consequences to themselves and their society of collaboration or resistance. This confusion has created the historical problem of African collaboration with or resistance to the imposition of European control.

Until recently historians of Africa have not specifically examined African resistance. Traditionally, scholars have focused their attention on the means by which vastly outnumbered Whites imposed their rule over large indigenous Black populations and upon those Africans whose collaboration not only insured their own survival, but enabled them to adapt successfully to the imperatives of European colonial rule. Thus, historians came to regard the resistors as romantic reactionaries, or even "proto-nationalists," determined to sacrifice themselves needlessly on the altar of lost causes in a futile attempt to preserve an authority that the European presence had reduced to an anachronism. Conversely, those Africans who accommodated themselves to the European incomers have been regarded by many historians as sensible realists attuned to the changing situation in Africa, as progressive and sophisticated collaborators whose cooperation secured and frequently enhanced their own authority and the well-being of their people.

Thus, James S. Coleman in his pioneering study of nationalism in Nigeria regarded both initial resistance and later revolts against British administration not only as "proto-nationalist" in character, but also as impulsive retorts against the disruption accompanying the advent of alien control. Moreover, primary resistance ended with pacification and generally played little role in later nationalist appeals. Although subsequent, sporadic revolts against British rule were regarded as equally reactionary, their causes were employed to further the nationalist movement (see Problem VII). Like James Coleman, Ronald Robinson and John Gallagher accept the negative character of African primary resistance, as well as its "proto-nationalist" nature. They regard the resistors as romantic reactionaries and contrast their fruitless savagery to the prudence of the collaborators who gained by accommodation what the protestors lost. Roland Oliver and John D. Fage concur, arguing that the farsighted and well-informed leaders perceived the futility of resistance. These African statesmen reaped the rewards of cooperation, while the less prescient and less well-advised leaders jeopardized their authority and often the integrity of their society by resistance.

These conclusions have, in the past, seemed so apparent, so patently obvious to historians of Africa that they appeared self-evident, requiring little elaboration or explanation no matter how fundamental to the course of European colonial rule in Africa. Recently, however, historians of Africa have reexamined the period of pacification by challenging the accepted interpretations with new hypotheses. To them the division of African reactions to the imposition of colonial rule into negative resistance on the one hand and prudent collaboration on the other appeared increasingly artificial and inadequate. Rather than a simple dichotomy, the revisionists argue, African responses, including resistance as well as accommodation, can be explained as rational calculations of self-interest and not simply irrational, instinctive reactions. Indeed, African resistance can be regarded in positive terms. Thus, the very manner of resistance, as well as the results, conditioned the character of future European administration and profoundly influenced, usually to the advantage of the Africans, their relationship with the colonial rulers. Moreover, the African response was not simply a reaction to European initiatives. It was in fact a complex pattern produced by the interplay of European and African interests that were far more subtle than the arbitrary division into progressive collaborators and reactionary resistors.

Surveying African resistance throughout the continent, the Soviet Africanist, A. B. Davidson, emphasizes that resistance took different forms in different parts of Africa at different times. Africans were not merely "objects" in the scramble, but interested subjects whose means, organization, and aims have been largely ignored by historians oriented to European imperialism in Africa. Moreover, African resistance was not simply "accidental" but calculated wars of liberation, or in Soviet terminology, "national wars or national rebellions of oppressed peoples." Although to regard African response as wars of national liberation goes far beyond the "proto-nationalism" which James Coleman and Robinson and Gallagher perceived in African resistance, this theme presages the connection between African primary resistance and modern mass nationalism argued by T. O. Ranger in Problem VII.

The role of African resistance specifically in the history of West Africa is delineated by J. D. Hargreaves who argues that the African leaders who chose resistance were neither less far-sighted nor less progressive than those who collaborated. "In fact they were often the same men." Some, like Samory, discovered that collaboration brought intolerable restrictions. Others, particularly the Fulani, found that a willingness to accommodate themselves to European overrule was an essential ingredient in preserving their privileges and perquisites as a ruling minority. Even the resistance of the Ashantehene, which ultimately led to British subjection of the Ashanti, did not lead to the end of the Ashanti nation. In fact, it regenerated Ashanti nationalism which proved such a formidable opponent to the national liberation movement of Kwame Nkrumah. In Dahomey the success of a collaborator like Tofa, with the failure of a resistor like Behanzin, cannot be sharply distinguished since the former achieved immediate but ephemeral success, while the latter met defeat but acquired lasting fame.

In East and Central Africa, T. O. Ranger has argued that the Africans were active participants, not just objects, in the "pacification," and that their actions directly conditioned the Europe occupation and administration. Moreover, historians have generally underrated the strength of the indigenous societies of East and Central Africa which in fact resisted European encroachment more successfully than hitherto believed. The result of their resistance did not mean the unconditional subjection of the African but a "balance of power" in which many African societies held their own against the Europeans while a few were so formidable the Europeans chose not to fight them. The Africans were thus often able to exploit the needs, weakness, and ignorance of the incomers to their own advantage. In this process there were not exclusively collaborators or resistors, but both. Indeed, during the colonial period the historian frequently has difficulty determining who are the resistors and who are the collaborators.

Although the revisionists have reexamined the rather simplistic assumptions of the past with subtlety and sophistication, their most important contribution to understanding the African response to the imposition of European rule is in dissolving the sharp differences hitherto drawn between collaboration and resistance. Nevertheless, the danger still remains of reducing historical interpretation to the peculiarities of each confrontation between African and European and replacing fallacious clarity with the chaos of precision.

Coleman: Resistance as a Negative Response to European Initiatives in Nigeria

Throughout the four centuries preceding the imposition of formal British control, African chiefs in the Niger Delta area effectively prevented intrusions of the white man. In his recently published study, Dr. K. Onwuka Dike has emphasized that such opposition, and not disease, was the primary force tending to exclude the white man from the hinterland. The opposition compelled European traders to recognize the sovereignty of African states, and remained effective so long "as Africans had the equipment, the means, and the numbers to maintain their independence." But there were two developments that weakened or overcame this barrier to penetration. One was the decline in the power of the semimilitary coastal kingdoms which resulted from revolutionary economic changes, as well as from other internal developments. The other was the decision of the British government in 1885 to support a more determined and systematic penetration of the interior which was to culminate, fifteen years later, in the establishment of a formal protectorate supported and controlled by British power.

Once Britain had made this decision, the occupation and pacification

From James S. Coleman, *Nigeria: Background to Nationalism* (Berkeley and Los Angeles: University of California Press, 1963), pp. 170–72, 175.

of Nigeria were carried out with comparatively little difficulty and with relatively little expense in arms, money, and men. In general, the acquisition was accomplished by force, or by the threat of force. The British obtained the cession of Lagos by duress, after launching an armed attack during which most of the town was destroyed by fire. In the Western Region, the Ijebu and the Bini were both the victims of military conquest, the latter after putting up substantial resistance. In the Delta area, the Royal Niger Company met sporadic opposition to the establishment of its authority from the riverian tribes, whose bitter resentment over the white intrusion was well demonstrated in the Akassa Massacre. In the Eastern Region, between 1900 and 1920, several expeditionary forces (Aro, Northern Hinterland, Niger–Cross River, North Ibibio) were necessary to establish British control, and as late as 1918 constant patrolling was still the order of the day. In the north, the Nupe and the Ilorin, with armies of 30,000 and 8,000, respectively, resisted the forces of the Royal Niger Company. After the company's charter was revoked, and during the transition to formal British rule, the Nupe and the Kontagora revolted against British authority. The Yola, Kano, Sokoto, and Hadeija emirates were all conquered in 1903 by Lugard's forces, after offering initial resistance. The vast areas of the Middle Belt were not completely pacified until the end of World War I. Even after pacification, however, there were frequent revolts in this area, which Sir Alan Burns has suggested were prompted "less by a zeal for independence than by a desire to continue the habits of murder, robbery, and cannibalism, which had become the second nature of these primitive people."

To what extent was their conquest by superior forces, after they had offered maximum resistance, a factor in sparking a nationalist reaction among Nigerian peoples? It is suggestive that the Ijebu, the Bini, the Nupe, and several of the Ibo groups, who resisted the British most strenuously, have had a disproportionately heavy representation in the nationalist movement; yet there are other factors that could serve as an explanation. Part of the prejudice of many nationalists against indirect rule stemmed from the replacement of chiefs who resisted the alien intrusion by chiefs who were "good boys" and who willingly signed protectorate treaties. Certainly the protracted agitation of educated elements in Lagos was partly stimulated by their resentment over the duress employed by the British in acquiring the colony, and over the lowered status of the House of Docemo.

There seems to have been nothing in the conquest of Nigeria to compare to the famous Ashanti wars of Ghana. Moreover, the thoroughgoing application of indirect rule in Nigeria helped to alleviate the initial sting of subjugation. At most it can be said that the ease of British conquest and rule was a factor in creating an exaggerated belief in white superiority and black inferiority among the first generation after occupation, and that the reaction of educated Nigerians to white lordship and black depreciation ultimately had nationalistic implications. Being made acutely aware of one's own weakness by superior force can be a powerful stimulus to subsequent self-assertion and retaliation. Nationalists could later appeal to resentment based upon the indignities and injustices, the shame and wounded pride of subjugation, and could use it as a focus for mobilizing resistance to foreign rule.

Except for descriptive purposes no sharp line can be drawn between the initial resistance to the establishment of British authority and later protest or revolt against specific administrative actions which Africans deemed offensive. In both instances, the response was an impulsive negative retort to an alien disruptive force. Yet there is clearly a difference of degree in native consciousness of alien control between compelling a chief under military threat to rule his people with the guidance of a British administrative officer, and directing the same chief to impose unaccustomed taxes upon his people. Moreover, there is an important time differential: the bewilderment and resentment over and the resistance to initial intrusion ended with pacification, whereas the sporadic revolts against specific administrative actions occurred after final submission and temporary accommodation to superior force. Nationalist leaders could capitalize on the latter by channeling grievances into the nationalist movement; the former, except as a rankling memory to be kept alive, had less utility.

Precipitated and fed by specific grievances, postpacification revolts were territorially uncoördinated, and haphazard in their occurrence. Subject to local leadership which before 1938 normally had no affiliation with or direction from strategists outside, they were usually short-lived, collapsing at the show of force, the release of emotional tension, or the removal of the grievances. . . .

During the interval between the initial shock of alien control and 1950, minor nativistic religious movements arose throughout southern Nigeria. They reflected accumulated tensions within the social fabric of the community—tensions created by the shock of rapid culture change and urgently demanding release or dissipation.

In the Moslem areas of northern Nigeria, a related type of protest occurred during the decade immediately following initial pacification. Several minor uprisings, which were led by local Mahdis, did not present any serious challenge to the political order (Fulani or British). But in order to crush an outbreak of Mahdism at Satiru in Sokoto Province in 1905, the British had to rush troops from Lagos and from the Tiv country where pacification was still in progress. Since World War I there have been no known incidents of this nature, which is attributable at least in part to the British policy of not offending Moslem sensibilities. These early outbreaks, together with the fact that the Fulani jihad was part of the famous Wahabi movement, were evidence of the ever-present potentiality of religious revolt.

Robinson and Gallagher: Romantic Reactionaries versus Sophisticated Collaborators

Despite the astounding games of partition it played with the maps of Asia and Africa at the end of the nineteenth century, the so-called new imperialism was merely a second-order effect of the earlier work of European expansion. Colonising the Americas and the other white dominions had been a durable achievement, constructed out of the manpower, the capital and the culture of the lands on the Atlantic seaboard. By this time their growth in self-sufficiency was throwing them outside the orbit of European control, whatever relics of that overlordship might still exist on paper, or might still be fleetingly reasserted by force of arms. Yet far from this being a period of decay for Europe, its energies were now developing their maximum thrust. The potential of the old colonies of settlement had matured so far that they were generating local expansions of their own. The Canadians and Brazilians had organized their backlands. The Americans and Australians had spilled out into the Pacific. The South Africans had driven north of the Zambezi. Whatever the flag, whatever the guise, the expansive energies of Europe were still making permanent gains for western civilisation and its derivatives.

From Ronald Robinson and John Gallagher, "The Partition of Africa," in F. H. Hinsley (ed.), *The New Cambridge Modern History* (Cambridge: Cambridge University Press, 1962), Vol. XI, Chap. 22, 639–40.

None of this was true of the gaudy empires spatch-cocked together in Asia and Africa. The advances of this new imperialism were mainly designed to plaster over the cracks in the old empires. They were linked only obliquely to the expansive impulses of Europe. They were not the objects of serious national attention. They have fallen to pieces only three-quarters of a century after being thrown together. It would be a gullible historiography which could see such gimcrack creations as necessary functions of the balance of power or as the highest stage of capitalism.

Nevertheless, the new imperialism has been a factor of the first importance for Asia and Africa. One of the side-effects of European expansion had been to wear down or to crack open the casings of societies governed hitherto by traditional modes. Towards the end of the nineteenth century this had produced a social mobility which the westerners now feared to sanction and did not dare to exploit by the old method of backing the most dynamic of the emergent groups. Frontiers were pushed deeper and deeper into these two continents, but the confident calculus of early nineteenth-century expansion was over and done with.

It is true that the West had now advanced so far afield that there was less scope for creative interventions of the old kind. The Russians had as little chance of fruitful collaboration with the Muslim emirs of Khiva and Bokhara as the French and British were to have with the theocrats of the Sudan. When the time of troubles came to the peoples of China or Tongking or Fiji, their first response was to rally around the dynasty, just as in Africa the Moroccans and Ethiopians were to group under the *charisma* of the ruler. Movements of this sort were proto-nationalist in their results, but they were romantic, reactionary struggles against the facts, the passionate protests of societies which were shocked by the new age of change and would not be comforted. But there were more positive responses to the western question. The defter nationalisms of Egypt and the Levant, the 'Scholars of New Learning' in Kuang-Hsü, China, the sections which merged into the continental coalition of the Indian Congress, the separatist churches of Africa—in their different ways, they all planned to re-form their personalities and regain their powers by operating in the idiom of the westerners.

The responses might vary, but all these movements belonged to a common trend. However widely the potentials might range between savage resistance and sophisticated collaboration, each and every one of them contained growth points. In cuffing them out of the postures of tradition and into the exchange economy and the bureaucratic state, western strength hustled them into transformation. One by one, they were exposed to rapid social change, and with it came conflicts between rulers and subjects, the rise of new élites, the transforming of values. All that the West could hear in this was distress signals. But just as its ethnocentric bias has obscured the analysis of imperialism, so its Darwinism has stressed the signs of decrepitude and crack-up in these societies at the cost of masking their growth points.

In dealing with these proto-nationalist awakenings, Europe was lured into its so-called age of imperialism; from them, the modern struggles against foreign rule were later to emerge. But the idiom has hidden the essence. Imperialism has been the engine of social change, but colonial nationalism has been its auxiliary. Between them, they have contrived a world revolution. Nationalism has been the continuation of imperialism by other means.

Oliver and Fage: The Futility of Resistance: The Success of Collaboration

For the African peoples the most important factor at this stage of colonial history, however, was probably not the issue of European settlement or its absence, not the relatively concrete issues of land and labour, certainly not the difference between the policy of one colonial power and another, but the far more intangible psychological issue of whether any given society or group was left feeling that it had turned the colonial occupation to its own advantage, or alternatively that it had been humiliated. To a large extent this was a result of the accidents of occupation in each particular territory. Every occupying power inevitably made both friends and enemies. Every occupying power, before it could train a local army or police force, needed native allies and was prepared to accord substantial privileges to those who would play this part.

According to the value judgements of modern Africa, such peoples were traitors and quislings; but these categories hardly fit the circumstances of eighty years ago. Then, the primary choice lay not with individuals but with their political leaders. If these were far-sighted and well-informed, and more particularly if they had had access to foreign advisers such as missionaries or traders, they might well understand that nothing was to be gained by resistance, and much by negotiation. If they were less far-sighted, less fortunate, or less well-advised, they would see their traditional enemies siding with the invader and would themselves assume an attitude of resistance, which could all too easily end in military defeat, the deposition of chiefs, the loss of land to the native allies of the occupying power; possibly even to the political fragmentation of the society or state. In trying to see the early effects of the colonial occupation upon the African peoples, it is essential to realize that the rivalries and tensions between African communities did not end with the colonial occupation. They continued, with the colonial administrations both using them and being used by them. As with the slave trade in earlier times, there were gainers as well as losers, and both were to be found within the confines of every colonial territory.

From Roland Oliver and J. D. Fage, *A Short History of Africa* (Harmondsworth: Penguin Books Ltd., 1964), pp. 202–3.

Davidson: African Resistance and Rebellion Against the Imposition of Colonial Rule

This topic is important for many reasons. First of all because the African peoples have the right to demand that the most forgotten and sometimes deliberately counterfeited pages of their history be re-established. The resistance of each African people to the establishment of colonial rule is a very important aspect of their life over decades and for many of them over centuries. It is impossible to understand the African past without the re-establishment of the truth about this resistance. This is the main reason why it must be re-established. Without making a study of what was the answer of one or another people to the establishment of colonial rule it is difficult to understand not only the past of that people but its present as well; it is difficult to comprehend the character of the liberation movement in the recent revolutionary years. Many things in this struggle and even in its demands were defined (and in countries that are still colonies are defined up until today) by long-standing traditions of resistance.

An attentive study of the history of popular resistance in Africa will inevitably prove that this struggle acted as one of the most important stimuli to historical development for the African peoples. This struggle has never ended because whenever oppression exists, resistance to this oppression exists as well; this resistance can change its character and forms but it never ceases.

In fact the character and effectiveness of the resistance which one or another people offered to a considerable extent defines the place this people has occupied in colonial Empires: that is whether it became a protectorate or a colony or whether it was able to preserve its independence like Ethiopia. In other words, in the course of the struggle against the imposition of colonial rule each people founded positions from which in our days it waged a struggle for complete liberation.

This resistance left its mark on the most important internal processes of the development of African peoples. As a rule in the course of the resistance tendencies to change developed more quickly; for instance in some countries feudalism started gaining in strength much more rapidly than before.

In the course of resistance to colonialism, tribes which up to that time had lived more or less in isolation gradually began to comprehend the identity of their interests. Nationalities and large ethnic units formed

A. B. Davidson, "African Resistance and Rebellion Against the Imposition of Colonial Rule," in T. O. Ranger (ed.), *Emerging Themes in African History* (Nairobi: East African Publishing House, 1968), Chap. 16, pp. 177–88.

more rapidly; the features of national self-consciousness were crystallising. Tribal unions were being created; the rudiments of State organisations came into being. The active forces that led the struggle made use of the religions which existed at that time, for example Islam in Northern Africa. All these and many other processes were inseparably linked with the struggle against the imposition of colonial rule and therefore it is impossible to understand them without careful study of the resistance of every people. Proceeding from the cardinal importance of the history of resistance, I think it would be expedient to discuss at this Congress how the question itself is to be defined; to lay down its chronological limits and identify the practical tasks which arise.

What are the stages of this struggle?

This question is inseparably linked with the more general division into periods of the history of Africa as a whole since the beginning of colonial penetration. For the whole continent (but of course not for each country taken separately) it should be possible to accept the following division into periods. The first stage is up to the 1870s when colonial rule was exercised only over 10 per cent of African territory. Then the period from the 1870s till about 1900 when this rule affected over 90 per cent of the territory. Next, the period from the beginning of the 20th century up to the first world war, when the system of colonial rule and imperialist exploitation already had been brought to most parts of Africa. Then the epoch between the two world wars when the crisis of the colonial system and imperialism started. And lastly the period after the second world war, when this system was broken down and dozens of young states appeared in place of colonies.

At these different stages of African history the African struggle took different forms. Up to 1870 it often took the form of uprisings of slaves against slavers. It was the struggle of coastal, very often separate, tribes and peoples. Fortresses and strongholds were being built on the coasts, local peoples were being put into a dependent and subordinate position and did not want to accept it. The resistance of the Hottentots against the establishment of Dutch rule in the Cape of Good Hope started in the fifties of the 17th century. In other areas whole peoples refused to work for their conquerors. That was why colonial powers had to import to Africa, Indians, Malayans and representatives of other non-African peoples. Considerable armed conflicts began to arise by the end of this period, but only in those regions where colonisation had penetrated very deeply (as in Northern Africa, in Ashanti and the south of the continent).

The period between 1870–1900 is usually thought of in Africa as a struggle between European powers competing against each other. But in reality at that time the struggle between imperialist countries was *much less bloody* than skirmishes between colonialists on one side and Africans on the other side. It was the time when tribal and feudal African societies showed the most decisive resistance to colonialisation; when Ethiopians defeated the Italian army near Adowa; when the Sudanese crushed the British Army near Khartoum; when Zulus gained the victory over English forces.[1] At the same time it was in that period that new forces were arising, and together with them new forms of struggle. This applies to those areas where colonialism had dominated at that time for more than one decade and traditional foundations—tribal and feudal—had been strongly shaken.

This process went furthest in Southern Africa. Hundreds of thousands of Africans were working there on European farms, in towns and miners' settlements. During this period it was possible to see in Southern Africa forms of struggle that appeared in other parts of Africa considerably later. There was for instance the protest against colonisation that arose amidst African Christians leading to sectarian movements—the so-called 'native churches.' Associations of electors (African voters) in Cape Colony favoured the emergence of the rudiments of national and political consciousness. The same part was played by the African Press that was already being published in Cape Colony at that time. In the 1880s also the first, very timid attempts were made to set up organised working-class movements. At that time the first attempts to organise a strike of African workers were made; the first very weak political organisation came into being.

From the end of the 19th century till the first world war the last great struggle against colonisation within the tribal system took place in Africa—the rebellion of the Herero and the Hottentots, the 'Maji-Maji' rising and others. But sometimes these rebellions differed from previous ones—this means that the traditions of a tribal society were falling to the ground. Thus in the course of the 'Zulu' rebellion in 1906 a great part was played by a native (Ethiopian) church, and the leader of the whole rebellion was a chief of one of the comparatively small tribes.

At that time also in many African countries there arose, still in embryonic forms, new forces—workers, an intelligentsia. In connection with them the first political organisations appeared. The African National Congress (South Africa) created in 1912 appears to have been the first political organisation on the scale of a whole country. But the leadership of the liberation movement was still in the hands of tribal chiefs and elders.

In the period between the two wars colonial exploitation became stronger but at the same time a gradual accumulation of the forces of the liberation movement was going on. This was favoured by the influence of revolutionary events in Russia and some other European countries. In many countries the leadership of the liberation movement passed into the hands of the intelligentsia and bourgeois elements. This can be easily observed in the activities of the political organisations which were often created after the pattern of the African National Congress (South Africa) and even took the same nature. Often, for instance, in Nyasaland or Rhodesia, political organisations were created on the base of welfare associations or other

[1] The author is probably referring to the Mahdist defeat of a British led Egyptian army at Shaykan in 1883 and the destruction of a British force by the Zulu army of Cetshwayo at Isandhlwana in 1879. ed.

urban associations. At that time the last significant movements of religious sects took place for example in the Congo and some other countries. In many parts of the continent riots of peasants took place.

The workers' movement became stronger. The mining areas of the Transvaal during the first war years were disturbed by big strikes. In 1935 and 1940 tens of thousands of 'Copper belt' miners went on strike. *The actions of the workers were not only class but anticolonial in character.* In South and North Africa communist parties appeared and came out with a comprehensive programme for the struggle against colonisation. The Pan-African movement which manifested itself at four Pan-African congresses between the two wars witnesses the arising of connections between forces of resistance of different African countries.

The last period—the post second-world war years, saw not merely a resistance to the imposition of colonial rule, but a preparation and implementation of national liberation revolution aimed at the complete destruction of colonial régimes.

It goes without saying of course that this outlined scheme of division into periods is not final or complete. The history of an immense continent in its diversity cannot be put into the limits of any strict scheme. Resistance took different forms in different parts of Africa and at different stages of its history. Differences in the nature and methods of colonial policy of the *parent states* had an influence on the forms of resistance. Of course it is impossible to cover in one report all these stages of the history of liberation movements. That is why I consider it possible to limit my historiographical report and pay most attention to the period of 'The Scramble for Africa.' Apparently the organisers of the conference meant this too since they suggested the question 'resistance to the imposition of colonial rule' as the topic of my report.

We can say that for the time being the studying of the question of the struggle of African people is still in embryo. As a matter of fact, historians have not really raised yet the problems of African resistance to colonialism. It is to be supposed that many rebellions are not yet known; that historians have not 'discovered' them yet. Often we do not have concrete information about those rebellions that are considered an established fact. It is not discovered yet what were the motive forces of rebellions, how they were organised, why rebels undertook one or another action, what was the intercommunication between different events, linked with a rebellion. About other forms of resistance we know even less than about armed rebellions.

How does historiographical literature consider the question of the African peoples' resistance during the period of 'The Scramble for Africa?' If we try to summarise the traditional, European historiographical view about the problem, first of all we shall find a frank defence of colonialism. According to one of these versions the African people apprehended the coming of colonialists as good fortune; as deliverance from fratricidal internecine wars, from the tyranny of neighbouring tribes, from epidemics, and periodic starvations. This school wrote about the peoples who did not resist as 'peace loving.' Other peoples who from the very beginning treated colonialism with such an evident enmity that it was impossible to hide this fact in literature were called 'bloodthirsty' and readers were told that they merely imbibed with their mothers' milk a hatred of all 'strangers.' As is known European powers often explained their invasion as necessary to save 'peace-loving' people from their 'bloodthirsty' neighbours. Later on both peoples—the one that was 'saved' and the one that was 'bloodthirsty' might rise together or at the same time against European newcomers. Thus in the early 1890s Rhodes saved the Shona from the Ndebele, but in 1896 there broke out the almost simultaneous rebellion of both these peoples.

But facts of this kind did not modify the traditional scheme of interpretation which remained unchanged. According to another version which is not less widespread African chiefs without a moment's hesitation signed one-sided agreements and sold their lands and all the riches of their tribes for rum and beads. No doubt this sometimes happened. But there were many other cases. We know a great number of examples when chiefs and rulers of independent states entered upon diplomatic single combat with arch-colonial politicians who were not squeamish about the means they used. Skilfully and wisely they carried on negotiations and upheld the independence of their peoples at any rate for a certain period of time. Examples of this are Menelik II, Moshesh, Mutesa, Lobengula. The supporters of the beads and rum version, perhaps, idealise the colonialists in subtler ways—they openly admit the policy of lies and deceit, but they depict Africans as such primitive and irrational *semi human beings* that the reader is prompted to accept the justice of the imposition of colonial rule.

In openly procolonial literature the struggle of Africans has been ignored. 'The Scramble for Africa' was considered to be a struggle between imperialist powers only, and in these events Africans were given the part of an object, but not a subject. It was only the largest rebellions of Africans that were mentioned; the tendency existed to write only about so-called 'colonial wars' but authors did not understand or did not want to understand the nature of these wars. German, Portuguese, Italian and other historians did not call the wars their countries waged in African countries 'predatory wars.' On the other hand they ignored the fact that for Africans these wars were wars of independence.

While analysing 'colonial wars' they described as a rule the actions of European forces only. They described in detail what one or another column was doing, how and in what direction it moved. But the African remained a mass without a distinctive personality. Africans were mentioned only as an object of European troop actions. Authors as a rule wrote very little about the internal organisation of African rebellions. Their readers cannot picture the rebels; what kind of people they were or what they were fighting for—what they felt—all these questions were unanswered. Europeans killed during these wars and rebellions were proclaimed national heroes. After Cecil Rhodes' war against the Matabele (1893), 36 Englishmen killed while trying to capture Lobengula were proclaimed national heroes and were built monuments. A heroic tragedy about their fate has been performed in British theatres. But the Matabele, who were really heroically defending the independence of their people, who were fighting with spears against maxim guns were only counted to the nearest thousand corpses. Again articles have appeared devoted to the question of whether General Gordon's fatal wound was a breast or a back wound. But the date and circumstances of Lobengula's death seem to be unknown up to now.

Authors who tried to explain African rebellions looked for their reasons to accidental or superficial circumstances. According to them rebellions were caused not by the interests of the whole tribe or people but by the yearnings of some part of this tribe. Often they took as this part the youngsters; the young warriors who desired 'to wet their spears in blood' and to capture cattle for a marriage settlement. Very often misunderstandings were announced as the reason for a rebellion. Protectors of colonial rule refused to consider rebellion a regular phenomenon. They rejected the only correct explanation which regards rebellions as just wars for liberation, which is why they were supported by the overwhelming majority of Africans.

Colonial novels played a most painful part in the spreading of colonial theories. The formation of the traditional colonial literature was closely linked with racial theories. Colonial literature was born out of scornful treatment of the African peoples and in its turn favoured the taking root of racial prejudices. Literature of this kind caused damage to the study of the African peoples' struggle because it spread wrong ideas. Documents and materials were not collected. Official European historiography didn't regard peoples' uprisings a subject that was worthy of serious studies.

It is necessary to note to the credit of Europeans that in the period when Africa was almost totally under colonial rule, there were some people in Europe and America that defended uprising colonial people. Among them there were famous writers, for instance, M. Twain, political figures, like N. Chernishevsky, publicists, like Moral [E. D. Morel], scientists, like Hobson. But their voices were not heard in official procolonial circles.

In that period the founders of Marxism took a clear position in their treatment of the African people's struggle. Engels wrote with admiration about the military skills and the art of war of Zulus in connection with the Anglo-Zulu war of 1879. Lenin wrote that the history of the 20th century, the century of unbridled colonialism, is full of colonial wars. But these colonial wars 'were very often national wars or national rebellions of oppressed peoples.'

Unfortunately the traditional colonialist literature has adherents up until today, although their number is less than before. And up to today its influence can be found in many historical papers, text-books and in mass media propaganda. The pseudo-modern ideas that have appeared during the last years are closely linked with this traditional colonialist opinion, but they are more hypocritical and harmful. The historian advocates of apartheid doctrine are a very good example. In theory, supporters of this doctrine accept that the traditions of each people have to be treated respectfully, and that every nation has the right of independent development and the right to struggle against foreign domination. But in practice, according to the racial essence of this doctrine, official historians of the South African Republic and their adherents in other countries are taking away the rights of the African people to resist and are impudently falsifying real history.

Some historians and publicists calling themselves liberals have taken a position which may be called neocolonialism in historiography. They agree that some aspects of colonialism are bad, but they subtly justify it by different arguments. For example, one of them admits, 'Yes, of course, colonisers who killed rebelling Africans did evil, but often the rebels were the more war-like tribes, who oppressed and enslaved other tribes.' And the conclusion was that Europeans were very cruel, but these African tribes deserved such a fate.

Another point of view holds that in the past parent states certainly quarrelled with their colonies, but that at present the two sides have re-established very good relationships. What reason to make mention of the past? It is profitable for communists only. It isn't necessary to study the past. The idea that by analysing the past it is possible to cause damage in the present is disseminated not only in history of Africa and of colonialism, but it is propagated by the reactionary forces in connection with different problems. For example, the Neo-Nazis are declaring that study of the Nazi history may cause damage and embitter contemporary mankind. The truth is quite the opposite; knowledge of history helps us to understand modern problems.

In many modern books an opinion is expressed that the reason for African rebellions was not colonial rule by itself, but cruel forms of it. Such a judgement objectively justifies colonialism as a phenomenon. On the other hand a reader gets the impression that the cruelties of colonialism are divorced from us by the whole epoch and that they are facts of historical interest only. While the real contemporary situation in some South African countries demonstrates quite the opposite. All abovementioned approaches to the problem, of course, do not help us much to comprehend it properly. Although it is necessary to note that sometimes we can find very interesting material in the most procolonialist papers.

When we come to discuss the positive results achieved in the study of the African peoples' struggle it has to be noted that there are very few papers written about this problem and most of them are not scientific, but popular or pesudo-scientific in character. However we are able to see some regularities.

The history of rebellions is mainly presented in the form of biographies of famous African leaders of the past. Much has been done recently to bring to life Cetewayo, Samory, Mzilikazi, Lobengula and the Ethiopian emperors. This is a very gratifying fact because earlier we had accounts only about those people against whom Africans rebelled. (For instance, there are so many works about Cecil Rhodes that several bibliographies have been already printed.)

Moreover, the material of such

biographies is destroying the schematic image of an African leader, created in the colonialist literature —the image of an irrational semi-human being ready to sell everything from 'rum and beads.' This old image favoured the rooting of racial prejudices in the minds of Europeans. But it is not only scientists and publicists who are trying to re-create the images of the great persons who struggled against colonialism. It is this side of the African past that attracts the attention of African poets and writers. Many novels and poems are devoted to the great rulers and chiefs of Africa. The production of these biographical works is very important because while writing them historians are obliged to turn to African sources for historical information. Around these biographies materials dealing with national liberation movements are accumulated. And yet the biographical *genre* is fraught with great danger. In concentrating on the personality it is possible to miss the laws of social development. It must not be forgotten that in African countries as all over the world the motive force of history was the people. It was the people that rose in rebellion against colonialism. And any ruler or a chief was able to bring out his people in rebellion only if the idea of the struggle was congenial to the people, and if this idea had matured in their consciousness. That is why the restoration of the picture of the liberation struggle cannot be limited to the biographical form. It is a pity that a comprehensive analysis of the resistance and peoples' uprisings has not yet become the subject of intensive study. In some cases this is because to give such an analysis is much more difficult than to write a biographical novel. But this is only a partial explanation. Fundamental researches into the most important rebellions as, for example, the book by Shepperson and Price about the Chilembwe uprising in Malawi in 1915 have only just begun to appear. But in general works, attempts to re-interpret the problem of resistance are undertaken not infrequently.

Marxist historians, considering it their task to study first of all the history of a people and their struggle for a better future, pay much attention to African resistance. This can be seen in books and articles by J. Woddis, J. Suret-Canal, M. Diop, and other marxists from Africa, Europe, Asia and America.

In the Soviet Union the study of the struggle of the African people began long ago. In 1950 appeared *The Revolt of the Mahdists in the Sudan* by S. Smirnov and very soon his new book, developing this subject further, will be published. In the Soviet Union works have also been published about the peoples' struggle in South Africa, West Sudan, Somali. In 1964 was published a collective monograph, the *Contemporary history of Africa,* and next year will be published *The history of Africa from the 19th century to the beginning of the 20th century*. In both books Soviet historians write about the resistance against colonialism all over the continent. In 1962–1963 was published a two-volume reference book, *Africa*. Besides a great number of articles dealing with resistance against colonialism there is a map being compiled of the most important up-risings. For a long time the Soviet historians worked in unfavourable conditions.

Till the gaining of independence by African states they could not come to Africa. And even now South Africa is closed to them.

The study of the history of the African peoples' resistance is only beginning and faces many difficulties.

The most important task at the present time is the accumulation of sources for such study. There is no doubt that for the historian each stage of struggle requires its own methods of research. For each period different sources of material must be used.

Obviously folk-lore is of the greatest importance. It may be we can collect participants' and eye-witness accounts. It is necessary to begin collecting these materials as soon as possible. In the near future it may be too late; many valuable things will be lost. Maybe it is expedient to give careful consideration to the problem of combining the efforts of different scientific centres and scientists for the collection of such materials and for the organisation of field work.

The history of the African peoples' struggle is up to now so little investigated that it is difficult even to enumerate the most important tasks in this field of knowledge. One of the most urgent tasks is the working out of the problem of period division of African resistance and rebellion. A discussion on the problem would be an important task for this conference. The conclusion of such discussion might be useful towards the realisation of the ten-volume history of Africa proposed by UNESCO and the Encyclopaedia Africana.

African historians' tasks are great and complicated. Their successful solution will be found only through the united and persistent efforts of historians all over the world. And certainly the leading role in African historical study belongs to African historians themselves. The very land where they were born, the very air they breathe from their childhood helps them to understand the history of the struggle for independence, the struggle of their fathers, grandfathers, great grandfathers.

The prominent researcher into the Zulu past, Bryant who died in 1953, expressed the hope that after a century the African historians would appear and would be able to use his books. Bryant did not imagine forthcoming events in Africa. Now, not after a century but after 10–15 years, prominent African historians have appeared and their appearance is a pledge of success for African historical study.

For the fruitful study of the history of African resistance and rebellion the efforts of progressive historians from all over the world are necessary. The history of Africa developed and is developing now in accordance with general laws of the history of other countries and continents. The African struggle against colonialism is inseparably linked with the struggle of the European peoples against capitalism and it is possible to understand the history of African resistance only in interdependence with the history of all mankind.

Hargreaves: African Reaction to the Imposition of Colonial Rule in West Africa

A common though superficial view of the partition of Africa is that Europeans, having decided to impose their power, proceeded to do so, enabled by the superior technology represented by Belloc's famous Maxim gun.[1] J. S. Keltie, author of the earliest and still the most detailed general account, believed that "we have seen the bulk of the one barbarous continent parcelled out among the most civilized powers of Europe." In such a perspective, European occupation inaugurated such a radically new phase in African history that the methods and motivations of the conquerors seemed a vastly more important subject for study than the reactions of the conquered.

From the new frontier of African historical studies, the view is rather different. We can trace how, in the centuries before the partition, African states, entering into more or less stable relations, grew or diminished in power as a result of commerce, statecraft, war, and internal changes.

From John D. Hargreaves, "West African States and the European Conquest," in L. H. Gann and P. Duignan (eds.), *The History and Politics of Colonialism in Africa* (Cambridge: Cambridge University Press, 1969), Vol. I, Chap. 6, 199–200, 205–16.

1 Whatever happens we have got
The Maxim gun and they have not.

The nineteenth century provided in Africa many examples of what philosophic historians might earlier have called "great revolutions . . . and the rise and fall of states." One may see what has been described as a sort of African partition of Africa, a radical reshaping of political structures and boundaries, taking place throughout the century. It is most evident in the Muslim countries of the Western Sudan, with the great Fulani *jihad* in Sokoto, the consolidation of Bornu, the rise and defeat of Macina, the foundation of the Tukulor state of El Hadj 'Omar and later of the military empires of Samory (Samori) and Rabeh. But in coastal areas, too, many peoples were adapting their attitudes and institutions in response to the challenges presented by foreign traders, missionaries and governors. Wolof states took to peanut-growing and to Islam; the Fon state in Dahomey reorganized its economy and extended its power; the "city-states" of the Oil Rivers perfected their mechanisms for controlling trade.

Not all such states were completely wiped from the map by European imperialism. Although some, like the Muslim empires that faced the French military in Haut-Sénégal-Niger, were deliberately broken up by the conquerors, the cultural identity, institutional structure and ruling personnel of others survived not only under colonial rule but after its termination. The Tolon Na, traditional Dagomba chief, represented Nkrumah's radical republic of Ghana in Lagos; the ancient dynasty of Mossi played active if somewhat conservative roles in Voltaic politics during the 1940s and 1950s; rulers of small Mende and Temne chiefdoms provided much of the basis for the rule of the Sierra Leone People's Party. Most striking of all was the power wielded within the Nigerian federation by representatives of the ruling houses of the Fulani empire. It is therefore relevant to many present problems to inquire how such survivals became possible, what forces or conditions determined whether African states could retain their identity, what characteristics were needed for survival through the violent mutations induced by the European partition.

Historians of colonial policy might propose a simple hypothesis: that the decisive factor was the policy and attitudes of the occupying powers, whose material superiority was such that they could reshape the continent in accordance with their national interests and ideologies. British governors and consuls, their activities watched on the one hand by ministries drilled in the need to economize by administrative improvisation, and on the other by merchants anxious not to damage potential customers too badly, were unable to press so severely upon the African states that confronted them as ambitious French *militaires,* shrugging off civilian control as they sought Napoleonic conquests. One mode of expansion pointed towards the pragmatic philosophy of Indirect Rule, the other towards an integrationist ideal attainable only after French control had imposed rigorous processes of levelling and indoctrination. . . . [See Problems III and IV.]

Comparisons between French and British policies need to be taken no further in this discussion. Neither side embarked on the occupation of its African empire with a fixed and monolithic policy, pointing towards a single inevitable fate for the African polities in its path. If the aims and aspirations of those Europeans who led the advance sometimes implied a need for military conquest, more often they were such as could be satisfied by some form of treaty, providing access to commercial markets, denying land to rival imperialisms, laying foundations for political control. Of course, . . . there were treaties and treaties. Some were taken seriously by both signatories, some by neither; some were far-reaching in their terms, others almost meaningless. After the onset of the scramble, and the enunciation by the Berlin Conference of the principle of 'effective occupation', African signatories were usually required to make more far-reaching surrenders of their rights of independent action than in the days of 'informal empire'. Yet, since they were more liable to diplomatic challenge, these later treaties needed to be better authenticated. When the European signatory needed collaborators in policies which he was still too weak to carry out directly, there might still be genuine reciprocity of obligation. Even when imperial control had become secure, it was still necessary to find *interlocuteurs valables* within the colony; ex-employees of the postal department, however shrewd, did not make ideal 'chiefs'.

Given this range of possible attitudes on the part of the European invaders, a number of options might be open to African rulers. Among the short-term advantages obtainable from treaties or from collaboration with Europeans were not merely access to fire-arms and consumer goods, but opportunities to enlist powerful allies in external or internal disputes. Why then did so many African states reject such opportunities, choosing to resist the Europeans in battle? In West Africa, as in East and Central Africa, it cannot be said that those who opted for resistance were less far-sighted or forward-looking than the "collaborators". In fact they were often the same men. Wobogo, for example, first received Binger cordially; became much more suspicious of the French after his accession; but only fought them after the Voulet mission had made their hostility unmistakably clear. Lat-Dior, *damel* of Cayor, a Senegalese kingdom with much longer experience of the French, was a "modernizer" in his acceptance of commercial groundnut production, and adjustment to its social consequences. After resisting Faidherbe's attempts to replace him by a more compliant ruler, he co-operated with succeeding governors on the more generous terms they offered, but finally reached the sticking-point when the French began to build a railway through his country. Convinced (rightly) that this "steamship on dry land" would erode his sovereignty, he chose to die resisting in 1886. . . .

Examples could be multiplied indefinitely. Nearly all West African states made some attempt to find a basis on which they could coexist with Europeans. Virtually all seem to have had some interests which they would defend by resistance or revolt—some conception of what can only be described as a rudimentary "national cause", anterior to, and distinct from, the national loyalties demanded by modern independent states. An analysis of the "national cause" of any specific people would need to embrace some values deeply rooted in their own culture and not very readily comprehensible to outsiders, together with some that can be universally understood—claims to territories, freedom to settle matters of internal concern without foreign interference. On this basis they would face the problem of relations with foreigners. Whether it was judged necessary to defend the national cause in battle, and at what stage, depended on variables on both sides of the Afro-European relationship—on African statecraft as well as on European intentions.

In countries where African political structures had already been deeply affected by the growth of export trade, Afro-European relationships were conditioned by economic change. In the Niger delta, among the Yoruba, in coastal areas near Sierra Leone or on the Ivory Coast, political authority was diffused, and many African rulers were moved by considerations of commercial advantage or profit. Studies of "conjecture" may be needed to explain not only the pressures behind the European advance, but certain African reactions. Trading chiefs and heads of houses, as well as European merchants, sought to maintain the rate of profit in times of falling produce prices. The present discussion approaches the study of African resistance chiefly through rather simple cases, where centralized monarchies possessing the physical means of resistance, defended national causes that can be described in fairly simple terms. To extend such an analysis to West Africa as a whole will, however, involve detailed studies of the relations between trade and politics, such as the one A. G. Hopkins is undertaking for the Lagos hinterland.

One of the classical cases of military resistance seems to be that of Samory who between 1891 and 1898 fought the French with remarkable tenacity and military skill. Yet the record of his relations with France and Britain in the preceding decade shows many examples of his readiness to negotiate bases for genuine co-operation with either or both, provided that such bases safeguarded certain fundamentals of his independence. His early contacts with the French, beginning with the armed conflict at Keniera in February 1882, were indeed characterized by mutual mistrust and antagonism. But the French had to act circumspectly while building up their military force in the Niger valley, and it was only in early 1885 that Commander A. V. A. Combes's invasion of Bouré (whose gold was so important to Samory's economy) revealed prematurely the full extent of their hostility.

Samory's response was to develop his contacts with the British in Sierra Leone, first established in 1879-80. After occupying Falaba in 1884 he sent emissaries to Freetown to invite the Governor 'to ask the Queen to take the whole of his country under her protection'. The purpose of the offer was clearly to obtain British support in warding off the French, and Governor Rowe was doubtless correct in interpreting it as a diplomatic flourish not intended to alienate sovereignty. More intent on protecting Sierra Leone's sphere of commercial and political influence among Temnes and Limbas than in seeking influence on the Niger, he did not even report the offer to London until a year later. His reply to Samory was amicable but cool, simply welcoming his promise to respect Temne country—"the Queen's garden"—and agreeing to develop friendly relations and trade.

Yet this was not without importance for Samory. Commercial contacts alone gave him a vital interest in collaboration with Freetown. Until 1892, when the Sierra Leone government enforced the licensing of arms sales according to the Brussels convention of 1890, this route provided Samory with his supply of modern breech-loading rifles, which he was increasingly aware might be needed for use against the French.

Even now, Samory had not accepted armed conflict with France as inevitable. He was not leading a jihad against all Christians, nor a pan-African revolt against imperialism. He was concerned, practically, with governing and extending the empire he had conquered, with controlling its resources of gold, agricultural produce and men (including, of course, its slaves) and with enforcing the observance of Islam. It was perhaps less evident in the 1880s than later that these conditions were incompatible with the purposes of the French forces on the Niger. French relations with the Tukulor empire of Ségou remained somewhat ambivalent until 1890; and the

French military, desperately anxious to forestall supposed British ambitions and chafing under restraint from Paris, were reduced to signing treaties with Samory also.

In March 1886, when Colonel L. L. Frey was obliged to divert his forces against Mamadou Lamina, Samory was able to make a French mission under Captain Tournier modify the terms which they had intended to impose upon him. He secured French recognition not only of his territories on the right bank of the Niger, but of his rights over the contested districts of Bouré and Kangaba. This left him more independence of action than the French were prepared to tolerate; and the following year, J. S. Gallieni (of all the French commanders the one most susceptible to the idea of protectorate relationships with Muslim rulers) sent Captain E. Péroz to negotiate new terms. Samory, although reluctant to damage his prestige by surrendering territory, wished to avoid further battles against French military power at a time when he was about to attack his arch-enemy Tiéba, chief of Sikasso. After discussion he therefore agreed, by a treaty of 23 March 1887, to abandon the gold of Bouré to the French and to accept a boundary line on the Tinkisso river. According to the French, he agreed also to place his state and any future acquisitions under their protection.

As is often the case with such treaties of protection, it is difficult to tell how far Samory was aware of having entered into some new relationship with France under the protectorate clause. Certainly he interpreted it quite differently from the French (whose immediate concern was not to define their permanent status in his territories, but to acquire a legal title against the British). There is some evidence that Samory believed that the French had undertaken to assist him to further his own designs, in particular against Tiéba; counting on the alliance, he asked Binger for troops and artillery to help in his siege of Sikasso. But he certainly did not regard himself as having made an irreversible surrender of sovereignty. When the French refused to assist him, began to encroach on his territory, and tried to prevent his trading with Freetown, Samory "began to doubt whether, after all, the white man's word could be thoroughly relied upon" and tried, somewhat naïvely perhaps, to reverse his policy.

There still seemed to be possibilities of balancing British against French. In May 1888 Samory, while still besieging Sikasso, was visited by Major A. M. Festing, an official from Sierra Leone. This devout, garrulous, and pompous man had exaggerated faith in his personal powers of persuasion and influence. He had an unrealistic vision of Samory, with Festing as adviser, making peace with his enemies, consolidating his dominions into a genuinely united kingdom, and admitting the railway which the house of F. and A. Swanzy hoped to build from Freetown. Samory was interested, accepted the principle of a railway, and promised to sign a treaty when he returned to Bissandougou; but he refused to risk provoking a French attack before defeating Sikasso. In February 1889, indeed, he signed a new treaty with the French, accepting the Niger as the frontier everywhere, and agreeing to direct trade towards French ports; but soon afterwards he returned this treaty (though not that of 1887) to the French. He told another British travelling commissioner that he now considered himself free of obligations and ready to place his people and country under British protection; and on 24 May 1890 he signed a treaty promising not to alienate territory or undertake obligations to third powers except through the British government. It was, however, too late. London had already decided that the French protectorate treaties must be recognized, that war with France for West Africa was excluded, and had agreed with France on a partition of influence through the middle of Samory's empire. G. H. Garrett's treaty was not ratified, and Samory's partisans in Freetown tried in vain to persuade the government to work with him.

Samory's diplomacy was thus doomed to failure by the constant hostility of most French soldiers. Although some civilians wanted to avoid, or at least defer, a conflict, the ambitious and thrusting Colonel L. Archinard was hostile to any policy of tolerating Muslim empires. In April 1891 he again slipped the long rein of civilian control and attacked Kankan, intending to cut Samory's supply route to Sierra Leone. Thus the final period of armed resistance began. Until all of Yves Person's work has been published, assessment of Samory's personality and achievements can only be tentative. His dealings with the French were so marked by mutual mistrust and cultural incompatibility that a sober judgment is difficult; but it seems that Samory's attempts at coexistence were at least as seriously intended as those of the Frenchmen with whom he was dealing. For both sides, collaboration involved accepting restrictions of their rights, interests and prestige, which came to seem intolerable.

Samory's case thus hardly supports the view of Professors Oliver and Fage that "nothing was to be gained by resistance and much by negotiation"; nothing that he held important could have been permanently gained by either method. (J. Suret-Canale suggests that something might have been achieved had Samory, Amadou, and Tiéba been "capable of rising above their quarrels in time to present a common front to the invader". Although such a coalition might have postponed the French conquest, however, it is doubtful whether it could have averted it.)

On the other hand, resistance—if combined at other times with willingness to accommodate and skill in doing so—could further the cause of national survival. In Northern Nigeria, most evidently, the military resistance of the Emirs did much to determine the basis of the very special relationship which their successors enjoyed with the British administration. Even here, however, D. J. M. Muffett has argued that the conflict of 1903 was due less to intransigent resistance by Sultan Attahiru than to Lugard's determination that, before the British could utilize the Fulani as a "ruling caste", the military basis of British suzerainty should be asserted by conquest. Muffett cites reports by Burton and Temple to show that before the expedition to Kano and Sokoto Lugard was receiving "a mounting tale of evidence of the Sultan's readiness to be amenable and of the ripeness of the time for a diplomatic approach"; and he questions the translation and the dating of the famous assertion by Attahiru's predecessor that "Between you and us there are no dealings except as between Mussulmans and unbelievers—War, as God Almighty has enjoined on us". Lugard may indeed have hoped that the conquest of Kano would make that of Sokoto unnecessary. But as Attahiru saw British soldiers invading his provinces from the south, as he was joined by the stream of Tijaniyya fugitives from the French in the west, it must have seemed increasingly clear that "the doings of the Europeans" threatened the independence of Muslim Africa. It was left for his successors to discover how much could be preserved by collaboration with the British conquerors.

Ashanti, faced with ambivalent British attitudes touched on above, may have missed opportunities of profiting by a more flexible diplomacy. Even hostile officials like W. Brandford Griffith presented a less formidable menace to African autonomy than did Combes or Archinard. Anglo-Ashanti relations have been described as "a mutual and protracted misunderstanding between peoples with fundamentally different conceptual frameworks". The freedom which British imperialists claimed to be bringing to the peoples of Ashanti were not the freedoms demanded by the resisters of 1900—freedom "to buy and sell slaves as in the old time", freedom "from demands for carriers . . .", "from the obligations of building houses and supplying thatch", and from the unwelcome attentions of "huxters and strangers".

Yet contradictions of this sort, which existed along the whole front of Afro-European relations, did not inevitably have to be resolved by head-on conflict. Might not Prempeh have preserved more of Ashanti political and cultural autonomy by accepting, for example, Griffith's unauthorized Protectorate of 1891? He would have preserved the unity of the confederacy, its right to levy customary revenue, and some, at least, of the "habits and customs of the country"; and although the Ashantehene would in many respects, no doubt, have become increasingly dependent on the British Resident who was to be appointed, an adaptable Ashantehene would doubtless have made the Residency equally dependent upon his own collaboration. In retrospect Prempeh's decision that "Ashanti must remain independent as of old" seems to have led logically on to his own deposition in 1896, to Governor Hodgson's ill-advised claim in 1900 to assume the authority of the Golden Stool, and so to the final military conflict and the subjection of Ashanti to direct British administration.

Yet this was by no means the end of the Ashanti nation. In 1900 some of the outlying peoples of the Confederacy, who had not always been noted for their loyal support of ruling Ashantehenes, rallied to defend Ashanti against British aggression. Prempeh in exile became a more powerful focus of unity than he had been in Kumasi; British administrators in Ashanti, cherishing their separate status under the Governor of the Gold Coast, came better to appreciate the strength and complexity of Ashanti national feeling. The advice of R. S. Rattray, appointed as government anthropologist in the 1920s, furthered this reassessment. Ashanti began to seem a natural theatre for experiments in Indirect Rule. In 1924 Prempeh returned to the country; in 1926 he was recognized as Omanhene of Kumasi. The confederacy was restored under his nephew in 1935, and in 1943 crown lands in Kumasi were restored to the Ashantehene. One may reasonably ask whether, but for the resistance of the 1890s, Nkrumah's Convention People's Party would, over fifty years later, have faced such strenuous opposition from the National Liberation Movement. ". . . a Kumasi-centred Ashanti movement, which appealed for support in the name of the Ashantehene, the Golden Stool, Ashanti interests, Ashanti history and Ashanti rights." References to military exploits against the British enabled the Ashanti to counter the anti-imperialist centralism of the Convention People's Party with claims to have been anti-imperialist from the first hour. In the long run, something was after all gained by resistance for the Ashanti "national cause", if not for that of a future unitary Ghanaian nation.

This conclusion is reinforced by a comparison of the experience of the Fon and the Gun during the French occupation of Dahomey. The Fon state of Abomey throughout the nineteenth century exhibited attitudes of proud resistance towards all European attempts to encroach upon its sovereign rights or to compel changes in a way of life which Europeans found particularly abhorrent. This does not imply that it was "hostile to modernization". King Gezo, although unable to fully meet British demands that he should cease exporting slaves and conducting the sacrificial "customs", did much to encourage and participate in the production and sale of palm-oil as soon as Europeans showed interest in buying it. But although trade and diplomatic intercourse were welcome, the Dahomeans were uncomfortably aware that Europeans who entered African states to trade sometimes ended by ruling. Thus in 1876, Gelele preferred to undergo a British naval blockade rather than admit European interference in a commercial dispute which lay within his own jurisdiction. Yet he was anxious to avoid a military conflict, for "he who makes the powder wins the battle". When the French sent troops to Cotonou under a treaty of cession of 1878 (made in Gelele's name but probably without his consent), he confined himself to obstruction and protests.

Rulers of the Gun kingdom of Porto-Novo were more ready to cooperate with Europeans, both politically and commercially. In part, this attitude reflected fear of Abomey, whose armies for much of the nineteenth century constituted an intermittent threat to this smaller Aja state; in part it was caused by the desire of one of the ruling lineages to secure external support for its dynastic and territorial claims. In 1862 King Soji made an unsuccessful attempt to preserve these interests through a French protectorate. After 1874 his son, King Tofa, revived this policy. Tofa was a shrewd politican who worked with European traders to increase his wealth and power; "his succession", say the traditional historians of Porto Novo, "marked the transition into modern times". At first the French could do little to protect his territories against either Abomey or British Lagos, and Tofa showed bitter disappointment with the protectorate. But when Behanzin, who succeeded Gelele at the end of 1889, took more active steps to enforce his territorial claims, the French government was drawn somewhat hesitantly into military operations against him, largely through the intrigues of their ally Tofa.

How did Tofa, the "collaborator", fare by comparison with Behanzin, "the shark that troubled the bar"? Although Behanzin defended Dahomean rights more vigorously than Gelele had latterly done, he, like his predecessors, at first tried to avoid fighting France. In March 1891, after the initial clashes, Behanzin received French emissaries with apparently sincere expressions of friendship and desire for peace, and agreed not to make war on Porto-Novo, since the French were there. But he refused formally to renounce his title to Cotonou, or his liberty to send armies to other parts of his dominions; and he rejected as infringing his internal sovereignty French demands for the release of some of his own subjects whom he had detained during the fighting. In 1892, after receiving new arms supplies from German merchants, he proudly reaffirmed his right to coerce all the towns which he considered as his, excepting Porto-Novo, even at risk of a war with France.

> 'I am the king of the Negroes,' (he wrote to the French representative), 'and white men have no concern with what I do . . . Please remain calm, carry on your trade at Porto-Novo, and on that basis we shall remain at peace as before. If you want war I am ready. . . .'

By this time the French had come to the conclusion, somewhat apprehensively and reluctantly, that war would be necessary to defend the position which their subjects had established in Dahomey. Accordingly, in 1892 the Senegalese Colonel A. A. Dodds carried out that march on Abomey which tough Dahomean diplomacy had thus far helped to postpone. But even now France hesitated to destroy the structure of the Dahomean state. During 1893 Behanzin continued to resist with much popular support; and the French, finding difficulty in identifying other *interlocuteurs valables,* contemplated accepting his offers to negotiate. In January 1894 they recognized his brother as ruler of an area corresponding roughly to the seventeenth century rump of Abomey, and as a temporary expedient practiced a form of indirect rule until 1900. Even afterwards the dynasty continued to enjoy widespread prestige, which the French acknowledged in 1928 by arranging the ceremonial return from exile of Behanzin's ashes. (One wonders how far they had considered the implications of the analogy with the return of Napoleon's ashes to France in 1840.) Nor was this prestige confined to traditionalist circles. A clandestine newspaper published by two nationalist schoolteachers in 1915 took the name *Le Recadaire* (ceremonial messenger) *de Behanzin.*

By comparison, Tofa's policy of collaboration won certain advantages in the short run. He remained ruler of Porto-Novo under the French protectorate until his death in 1908, but with dwindling privileges and functions. He seems to have become bitterly conscious of accusations that he had sold his country to the French. With his funeral, say the traditional historians, the monarchy of Porto-Novo came to an end. His heirs, for whom he had sought French support, were mere French clients, their influence among the Gun eclipsed by others. On 28 November 1965 the author of this essay visited Tofa's successor in Porto-Novo. Elsewhere in the town revolutionary manifestations were taking place on behalf of the Gun President of the Dahomean Republic, who had been declared deposed by a Fon prime minister. Even though this constitutional conflict clearly reflected old antagonisms of Fon and Gun, however, the royal palace had become an irrelevant backwater. President S. M. Apithy, representative of the Gun "national cause", had begun his eventful political career as a young intellectual associated with the Catholic mission. But Justin Ahomadegbe leader of the Fon, spoke not merely as a trade unionist, but as a member of the house of Behanzin.

Until more research has been done on the policies and aims of individual African states, a survey of this kind must be superficial and tentative. It is hardly profound to conclude that the most important element making for the survival of African polities under colonial rule was simply a strong sense of ethnic or political identity—the attachment of their subjects to what has been called the "national cause". This sense of identity tended to be strengthened when the rulers who represented it could point to some record of resistance to imperialism. This does not mean blind or reactionary opposition. Those leaders who achieved most for the national cause, whether immediately or in the longer run, combined military action with more or less discriminating attempts to find some basis for coexistence or collaboration. Indeed, their success in keeping old national causes alive has sometimes presented problems to modern leaders who seek to represent a broader form of nationalism.

Ranger: African Reaction to the Imposition of Colonial Rule in East and Central Africa

The myth of the early colonial period in Africa dies hard. Scholars have challenged the old assumptions concerning the white man's overwhelming moral force and the Africans' acquiescence to the invaders' rule. But opposing assumptions concerning the overpowering military superiority of the Europeans and the despairing inability on the part of Africans to determine their own fate have all too often taken the place of

From T. O. Ranger, "African Reaction to the Imposition of Colonial Rule in East and Central Africa," in L. H. Gann and P. Duignan (eds.), *The History and Politics of Colonialism in Africa* (Cambridge: Cambridge University Press, 1969), Vol. I, Chap. 9, 293–317, 319–21.

these long-standing conceptions. 'The "balance of power" had moved right over into the European side of the scales', writes Basil Davidson.

> The armies and expeditions of Europe could now do pretty well whatever they liked in Africa, and go more or less wherever they pleased. Backed by their wealth and increasing mastery of science, the European kings and soldiers carried all before them. In doing so they found it easy—and convenient—to treat Africans either as savages or as helpless children.

Africans were not completely helpless, however, during the early colonial period in East and Central Africa. They could not avoid the imposition of colonial rule, but they were not simply objects or victims of processes set in motion outside Africa and sustained only by white initiative. Even in this period Africans helped to make their own history. Many scholars have shown how Africans necessarily participated in the early colonial administrative systems. Others have demonstrated how black men shared in the economic development of the new colonial territories. Here I wish to stress that the 'balance of power' in East and Central Africa also allowed of African political initiative during the 'pacification'.

Britain and Germany of course possessed very great technical, manpower and capital resources. But they employed only a minute proportion of these for the colonization of East and Central Africa. In the first instance, responsibility for their paper spheres of influence was handed over by the two governments to chartered company administrations. The power of European capital was called in to transform Africa, but European capital did not respond. Every company administration was grossly underfinanced. . . . Only the British South Africa Company, drawing upon Rhodes' private fortune and the expanding economy of South Africa, was able to mobilize more capital and employ larger numbers of men. The 700 police and pioneers who entered Mashonaland in 1890 represented an exercise of European power quite without parallel anywhere else in East and Central Africa. But the B. S. A. Company, for all its resources, was unable to establish a strong administration in Northern Rhodesia. . . . Even in Southern Rhodesia the Chartered Company's resources proved inadequate to the task in hand. . . .

These Company administrations have been severely criticized by historians. Freeman-Grenville has told us that 'not one' of the employees of the German East Africa Company 'appeared suitable for the task in hand'. I have myself declared that Company rule in Southern Rhodesia 'was inevitably producing a society whose atmosphere was profoundly different from any conceivable crown colony, and different for the worse'. But when the Company administrations were replaced in Uganda, Kenya, German East Africa, and Nyasaland with official colonial administrations, the new regimes were initially not much more efficient or powerful than the old.

In Kenya, so an ex-government official tells us, the new official regime inherited 'little more than an embryonic administration in the coastal belt, a few poorly garrisoned stations on the Uganda road, and an appreciation of the difficulties which had to be overcome'. The arrival of the Imperial Government with all its potential resources of men and money made little immediate difference to the administration. No 'deliberate planned and directed operation of conquest' was set on foot; 'none of the Commissioners was given the forces necessary to implement such a plan had one been sanctioned. As conquest was ruled out . . . and staff and forces were insufficient to establish law and order throughout the country, the handful of administrative officers had to concentrate their efforts in maintaining and improving their position in the established posts.' 'Here we are', recorded R. Meinhertzhagen in his Kikuyu diary for 1902,

> three white men in the heart of Africa, with 20 Nigger soldiers and 50 Nigger police, 68 miles from doctors or reinforcements, administering and policing a district inhabited by half a million well armed savages who have only quite recently come into touch with the white man . . . the position is most humourous to my mind.

In German East Africa the new regime was similarly short of men and money. The first Governor, Baron Von Soden, attempted wherever possible to avoid further commitments in the interior. 'The establishment of military stations', he wrote, 'is impossible without increased burden to the budget.' Harry Johnston in Nyasaland was weaker still. 'No other administration in what became British tropical Africa', writes Dr. Stokes, 'started out with such slender financial and military backing. . . . Johnston lacked the power to subdue [and] was also lacking in the means to persuade.'

If the power of European governments in East and Central Africa has been overestimated, the strength of some East and Central African societies has often been underrated. Many scholars have argued that the nineteenth-century history of the area was a 'progress to disaster' which left African societies on the eve of colonization greatly weakened and divided. Perhaps the century saw a decline in terms of agricultural production, of population growth or of life expectancy. But in terms of military strength and of the ability of the stronger East and Central African societies to defend themselves, the European colonizers probably faced a more formidable task than they would have done a century earlier. The stresses of the nineteenth century had provoked reactions. Some societies at least had developed both stronger military institutions and more centralized political machinery. There were the intrusive Ngoni military systems whose decay has been greatly overestimated. There were other societies that responded to Ngoni pressure or to Ngoni example—the Bemba, the Hehe, the Sangu. There were the Swahili-Arab trading empires and enclaves and the Nyamwezi and other interior state systems which had risen to emulate them. The pastoral peoples of Kenya, especially the Nandi, had also been moving towards more effective and centralized action. Kingdoms, long established on different bases, like Buganda and Barotseland, responded successfully to the challenge of the nineteenth century and built up military and raiding systems. Some of these had increasing access to fire-arms; many had widespread trading or diplomatic connexions which assisted them to take the white man's measure.

There were also, of course, many small-scale societies unable either to comprehend what was involved in colonization or to offer initial resistance. In armed clashes the superiority of modern weapons generally made up for lack of numbers. In any case it was always possible to supplement small numbers of whites with African 'friendlies'. Where the colonial power did suffer initial reverses it was provoked into committing more men and more money. The resistance of African societies was bound to be broken in the end. Nevertheless the confrontation of relatively weak colonial administrations with relatively strong African military systems did produce a practical 'balance of power' very different from that described by Davidson. There were, in fact, some African societies or peoples whom the early colonial administrators could not easily afford to fight.

We may give a few out of many examples. Harry Johnston, for instance, for all his belief that the white man was destined to take over and develop the land of East and Central Africa, had to entrench the land rights of the Ganda aristocracy in 1900. He justified this policy with the explanation that he was dealing with 'something like a million fairly intelligent, slightly civilised negroes of war-like tendencies and possessing about 10,000 to 12,000 guns'. British officials in Kenya would not heed Sir John Kirk's call for the ending of Masai raids by 'an aggressive war which to be successful must annihilate every vestige of the present Masai system'. The British realized that 'any premature collision could scarcely breed any but evil consequences for themselves'. Administrator P. W. Forbes of North-Eastern Rhodesia subdued his desire to punish the Bemba and warned Bishop Dupont in 1897: 'I would ask you always to bear in mind that although the Company will do their best to assist you in any way, we are not at present in a position to fight the whole Awemba nation.' Even Rhodes chose in the end to enter Central Africa by outflanking the Ndebele rather than by confronting them.

Europeans sometimes refused to accept these facts. Some believed that they really could go where they liked and do what they liked; but they rarely believed it for long. The German East Africa Company, wrote a contemporary, 'did not care to take any steps to conciliate the natives; their policy, judging from their conduct, was to treat the latter as conquered people, whose feelings it would be absurd to consider'. But the Company 'was quite unable to cope with the insurrection which it had deliberately incited', and its experiences served as a warning to other East and Central African administrations. In Southern Rhodesia, too, especially after the overthrow of the Ndebele in 1893, the administration acted as if Africans did not exist as a factor in the local balance of power. But the risings of 1896-7 cost the Company more than £7,000,000 and gravely endangered their Charter. The British Colonial Secretary received the news of the rising in the spirit of the more cautious and more general tradition: 'Are you absolutely certain', he asked, 'that the precautions you are taking will furnish force amply sufficient? The history of war with South African natives contains several disasters both to Colonial and Imperial troops.' Most colonial administrators in East and Central Africa were accordingly aware of their limitations. Colonial rule, writes Professor Oliver, spread slowly, 'very conscious of its military weakness and its financial dependence, never, if it could be avoided, taking more than a single bite at a time'.

The colonizers' weakness, however, was by no means all to the advantage of African societies. In many ways it contributed towards making the impact of European intrusion more rather than less grievous. It could produce, for instance, exercises of force and injustice over and above those implicit in the whole process. 'Under-investment in a decent administration', Mrs. de Kiewit Hemphill tells us of Kenya, 'is sometimes worse than the most thoroughly arbitrary rule.' The officials of the British Imperial East Africa Company were led through their lack of support or resources into 'unsavoury expedients' and into penny pinching 'where economy was unwise or dangerous'. The Kikuyu, for example, were drawn into bitter conflicts with the whites because the British attempted to make company stations in Kikuyu country self-supporting, which led to raiding and looting by company officials. Thus British financial weakness 'established a series of patterns and precedents which, for better or worse, gave direction to the subsequent history of African and European relations'. In Southern Rhodesia the British South Africa Company at first tried to solve its financial difficulties by calling on unofficial white settlers and prospectors. Instead of establishing a regular machinery of native administration the company allowed unofficials to recruit their own labour, to collect taxes on the company's behalf and even to mete out 'justice', with disastrous results. This state of affairs continued until 1896, when W. H. Milton was called in from the Cape to reorganize the Chartered Company's administration in Rhodesia and to bring about major reforms.

Colonial weakness not only resulted in violence and injustice but was also liable to shatter whole African polities. . . . The weakness of Harry Johnston's administration in Nyasaland led directly to 'the rapid disintegration' of African political systems. Unlike Lugard in Northern Nigeria, who possessed a force formidable by colonial standards and was able swiftly to conquer and take over a functioning indigenous political system, Johnston faced 'an initial weakness in military and financial power which made it necessary to destroy rather than preserve. . . .

Yet the colonizers' weakness was often the African's opportunity. Even in Nyasaland Johnston's step-by-step extension of colonial administration allowed the African peoples of the north time to come to terms with other European influences, and to escape the disintegrating effect of Johnston's policies. . . . Recent studies of the Northern Ngoni and Tonga peoples have shown a two-way process of accommodation between black and white. The mission acted as 'a foreign institution which provided certain services and which through its mere presence came to play its role in Tonga politics—a role which was to some extent independent of the intentions of the missionaries themselves'. This pattern continued, once the administration had been set up. . . .

To establish itself and to extend its power, a colonial authority often required native allies. Hence there was wide scope for African initiative. Of course the position varied a good deal from region to region. When the British fought against the Ndebele in Southern Rhodesia, they employed only a relatively small number of African auxiliaries. But the British position in Uganda depended on the British alliance with the Ganda aristocracy. . . . The Ganda could thus assert themselves as virtually equal partners and gain a position of entrenched power and privilege established in law. None of the others achieved so much; some were abandoned by the colonial administration when the value of their alliance had gone. But in every case the alliance was a two-way process; each party made use of the other.

Many recent studies have concentrated upon the use made by Africans of these situations, and the skill with which African rulers exploited the need, weakness and ignorance of the colonialists. Perhaps Mrs. Stahl's study of the Chagga has done this most clearly. 'The chiefs showed through the centuries,' she tells us, 'a remarkable ingenuity in progressively enhancing their own powers. . . . They made use of every new thing and every new kind of human being entering the life of Kilimanjaro to enhance their own positions.' They became adept at assessing European officers, 'utilising each new officer serving a term of his career on Kilimanjaro as another element in their strategems . . . they employed a whole range of new political gambits centring on the Boma.' This is a far cry from African helplessness.

Such Afro-European alliances sometimes profoundly influenced the pattern of subsequent politics. Some chiefs managed to secure more power for themselves, as well as special access to new sources of prestige and profits. . . . In some areas in fact the advantages gained by cooperating ruling classes within their own society amounted to radical political change.

Advantages could also be gained by one African society over another. Some Africanists have spoken of Ganda 'sub-imperialism.' But there was also a Lozi sub-imperialism. The extension of Lozi control to Balovale and Mankoya partially compensated the Lozi for the loss of other privileges. There was a Toro sub-imperialism, a sub-imperialism exercised by the family of Chief Mumia in Nyanza, and others. In many cases the subjects of these sub-imperialists experienced colonial rule more through their Ganda or Lozi overlords than through British control. The struggle against these sub-imperialisms forms one of the dominant themes in the modern political history of East and Central Africa.

The effect of African initiative exercised through such alliances has been so far-reaching that some historians have limited their attention to African societies that chose to collaborate with the whites. Many scholars have argued that the collaborators, by influencing the pattern of pacification, helped to determine the shape of colonial administration, and also gained a pathway to the future by exploiting the colonial situation. Investigators have often contrasted such societies with those that chose to resist the whites by force of arms. Oliver and Fage's general history emphasizes this point. If African political leaders, they argue,

> were far-sighted and well-informed, and more particularly if they had had access to foreign advisers, such as missionaries or traders, they might well understand that nothing was to be gained by resistance, and much by negotiation. If they were less far-sighted, less fortunate, or less well-advised, they would see their traditional enemies siding with the invader and would themselves assume an attitude of resistance, which could all too often end in military defeat, the deposition of chiefs, the loss of land to the native allies of the occupying power, possibly even to the political fragmentation of the society and state.

Resisting societies or groups not only ran the risk of disintegration but of cutting themselves off from modernization, education and economic development. Resistances, write Robinson and Gallagher, were 'romantic, reactionary struggles against the facts, the passionate protest of societies which were shocked by a new age of change and would not be comforted.' They are to be contrasted with 'the defter nationalisms' which 'planned to reform their personalities and regain their powers by operating in the idiom of Westernisers.'

The distinctions between the fortunes and potentialities of co-operating and resisting societies are thus held to be great. Hence attempts have been made to explain the disposition to resist or to co-operate in terms of profound differences in the structure of pre-colonial systems. 'The more urbanised, commercial and bureaucratic the policy,' Robinson and Gallagher tell us, 'the more its rulers would be tempted to come to terms. . . . On the other hand the more its unity hung together on the luxuries of slave-raiding, plunder and migration, the less its aristocracy had to lose by struggle against the Europeans.' In this way Robinson and Gallagher account for the co-operation of the progressive Lozi and Ganda and the resistance of the plundering Ndebele and Ngoni.

The view of African resistance as a gallant anachronism, essentially negative and backward looking, has been challenged, especially by Soviet Africanists. 'It is impossible to understand the African past without the re-establishment of the truth about this resistance,' writes Professor A. B. Davidson of Moscow.

> This is the main reason why it must be re-established. And without making a study of what was the answer of one people or another to the establishment of colonial rule it is difficult to understand not only the past of that people but its present as well. It is difficult to comprehend the character of the liberation movement in the recent revolutionary years. . . . Resistance left its mark on the most important internal processes of the development of the African peoples; in the course of resistance tendencies to change developed more quickly.

Soviet historians have not provided much solid evidence to buttress these conclusions, but to my mind Russian scholars have assessed the significance of African resistance to colonial rule in a more accurate fashion than their Western colleagues. The former have a better understanding of the 'resisters'; the latter have a better grasp of the 'collaborators.' But if we are fully to understand the nature of African reactions to colonial rule, we must take account of collaboration and resistance alike. My aim in the remainder of this chapter is to show how resistance, as well as collaboration, shaped African political history.

To begin with, I disagree with many of the generalizations made by 'Western' scholars. I do not consider that resisting societies were necessarily different in structure, motive or atmosphere from co-operating ones; I do not believe that co-operating societies necessarily desired modernization more than resisting societies, or even necessarily achieved it more rapidly. The foremost among the societies engaged either in resistance or in collaboration had more in common with one another in fact than with those small-scale societies that could neither resist nor exploit colonial rule. Thus the most notable resisters had some experience of foreign contact. They were centralized, sometimes highly so, and they had some capacity for intelligent choice. Again, some communities which—according to Robinson and Gallagher—should have resisted, and were expected to do so at the time, did not, in the end, do so. In certain instances, migratory military groups or societies organized for slave-raiding and looting, successfully accommodated themselves to the whites. Such communities included the Northern Ngoni of Nyasaland, the Bemba of North-Eastern Rhodesia and the Masai of Kenya.

Some resisting societies desperately attempted to avoid the necessity of resistance. Some co-operating societies made it plain that they were ready to resist if their cherished privileges were attacked. A historian has indeed a difficult task in deciding whether a specific society should be described as 'resistant' or as 'collaborative' over any given period of time. Many societies began in one camp and ended in the other. Virtually all African states made some attempt to find a basis on which to collaborate with the Europeans; virtually all of them had some interests or values which they were prepared to defend, if necessary, by hopeless resistance or revolt.

To illustrate this point we should consider, for instance, the contrast between Matabeleland and Barotseland. The former resisted; the latter collaborated. Superficially, the distinction seems clear. . . . The Ndebele, with their raiding system, had no interest in foreign commerce. The Lozi had an elaborate bureaucracy and were strategically placed athwart the transcontinental trade routes. The Ndebele seemed fated to clash with the whites. The Lozi were likely to take from the Europeans whatever was needed to improve the Lozi bureaucracy and to further Lozi trade. But what would the Lozi have done if, like the Ndebele, they had been faced with a white invasion of their eastern raiding grounds, if their regiments had been driven back, if they had faced at long last a white column marching on their capital? They surely would also have resisted. (The white missionaries at the Lozi court certainly expected them to do so.) . . .

Resistance on the part of an African people did not necessarily imply a romantic, reactionary rejection of 'modernity,' though a lengthy war might of course occasion repudiation of European influence. Similarly, non-resistance, in the sense of abstaining from armed struggle, did not always imply a readiness to modernize. Professor Low tells us that the price exacted by the Masai for the implied alliance with the British was the preservation of the Masai way of life. 'An official report of the E.A.P. Government was later to complain,' he writes, 'that "no punitive expedition has ever been undertaken against the Masai"; an omission, it said, which subsequently enabled the Masai to eschew British pressures for change.'

On the other hand, some societies that did offer armed resistance, nevertheless desired contact with Europeans under their own control. Gungunhana of Gazaland had Protestant missionaries at his kraal, including an African minister. Gungunhana negotiated with Rhodes and desired increased trade while preparing to fight the Portuguese. Chief Makombe of Barwe, rebelling against the Portuguese in 1917, expressed his anxiety for continued intercourse with the British 'who have enriched his subjects.' Other societies developed a driving desire for modernization after the first bitter resistance was over. In terms of their eagerness for Western education, there was little to choose between the Nyasaland Tonga, who did not resist, and the Kikuyu, who did.

I must also take issue with the standard interpretation that 'nothing was to be gained by resistance' under any circumstances. Much, of course, depended on the local situation and on the military resources and psychology of the colonizers. Herero resistance against the Germans certainly turned out to be a disaster for the Herero nation. But some societies did gain benefits by demonstrating the ability to take up arms when forced to do so. The Basuto rulers wanted mission education, economic contact with the outside world and British protection. They had to fight to achieve these. It would be hard to argue that their final struggle, the so-called Gun War of 1879–81, was futile. Arising out of Basuto resistance to forced disarmament, it dragged on for seven months, cost the Cape Government £4-3/4 million, and ended in complete failure. . . . On March 18, 1884 the Basuto finally became British subjects directly under the Queen.

The Ndebele provide another, though rather different, example. After the Ndebele war of 1893, the Ndebele state was disrupted. The new rulers no longer recognized any indigenous authority. The regimental system was broken, cattle were confiscated, land was taken—all without any machinery of complaint or redress. In 1896 the Ndebele had little to lose from further armed resistance. It turned out that they had something to gain. Their rebellion threatened to smash the whole position of the British South Africa Company in Southern Rhodesia. Suppression exhausted the Company's financial resources; it also involved large numbers of British troops and a great extension of British political authority. Under these circumstances Rhodes was compelled to gamble on negotiating a peace settlement so as to prevent the war from dragging through the rainy season into another year, with back-breaking expense to the company and a probable British assumption of direct control. The High Commissioner had proscribed the Ndebele leaders; the settlers demanded unconditional surrender and condign punishment. But Rhodes dealt with the leaders and came to terms. The Ndebele did not get much—the recognition of rebel leaders as well as of loyalists as salaried indunas and spokesmen for the people; an apparatus of complaint and redress; a regular system of native administration; a new commitment to make more land available to them. But it was considerably more than they would have got without a rebellion. Resistance, far from preventing future political activity, helped the Ndebele to move into a new political era.

The Wahehe of Tanzania seem to be a perfect example of a people broken by futile resistance. They were crushed by military might. They did not even achieve a negotiated peace. Defeat left the people in a desperate state. . . . [But] Memories of their resistance dominated subsequent German and Wahehe thinking alike. Partly because of pride in these memories Wahehe institutions, or more accurately a Wahehe sense of identity, survived so well that Uhehe became the site of the most successful Tanganyikan experiment in indirect rule. Both the Germans and the British felt respect for the Wahehe, so that in later years Wahehe objections were taken especially seriously. . . . Oliver and Fage tell us that

> for the African peoples the most important factor at this stage of colonial history was . . . the intangible psychological issue of whether any given society or group was left feeling that it had turned the colonial occupation to its own advantage, or alternatively that it had been humiliated.

The Wahehe can hardly be said to have turned the early colonial situation to their profit, but they did not come out with a sense of humiliation. 'Today all Wahehe idolize Mkwawa,' wrote a British district officer in the early Mandatory period. 'This may be because he actually beat the white man in battle.'

These examples have shown that the fact of resistance could influence very greatly the later political history of a particular African Society. But resistance had a wider impact. Thus it was resistance and rebellion that provoked the most extensive theoretical debates among the colonizers and had most impact on their attitudes. In territories like Tanganyika and Southern Rhodesia, which had experienced the terrifying challenge of great rebellions, memories of war or fears concerning new outbreaks dominated the white man's mind. While indigenous policies of accommodation served, on the whole, to support white assumptions of African readiness to accept white moral leadership, the rebellions challenged all easy generalizations about African gratitude and readiness to accept colonial rule, and all assurance that whites understood the Africans. Rebellions instead provoked almost anguished professions of incomprehension and disillusion. . . . African loyalty could never again be taken for granted.

Thereafter, as Dr. Iliffe has written of Tanganyika, 'the fear of rebellion became the decisive argument in any political debate.' Freiherr Von Rechenberg always dreaded another rebellion. Von Rechenberg's successor, H. Schnee, 'never ceased to be afraid . . . he had never forgotten the files (on Maji-Maji) and always present in his mind was the thought that it could happen again.' 'The principal motivation of settler politics was fear,' writes John Iliffe. 'After Maji-Maji settler thinking was defensive.'

The same was true in the Rhodesias. Officials regularly expected renewed outbreaks. In 1903 a general inquiry from Native Commissioners as to the state of African opinion found one 'firmly convinced that we are in for such a row as we have not had up here yet . . . the whole attitude of the natives leads one to believe that they are going to have another slap at us.' . . . Similar fears were being expressed in 1915. Even in 1923, at the time of the change to Responsible Government, reports of instructions to Africans by priests and prophets were causing official concern. The settlers' memories of the rebellions remained vivid. . . .

The consequences of white preoccupation with the possibility of black rebellions are hard to assess. There was much argument over the cause of past risings and over future policy to prevent further outbreaks. Some Europeans wanted the iron hand, others the velvet glove. Fear undoubtedly had much to do with the growing expression of white prejudices against the blacks. . . . Nevertheless, particular African societies did profit by resistance, and the white man's awareness that—if pushed too far—black men could strike back also gave certain advantages to Africans as a whole. Black resistance also convinced Europeans of the importance of continued alliances with co-operative black communities. In Tanganyika, according to Dr. Iliffe, Von Rechenberg devised his economic policy to meet peasant demands, lest rebellion become the only outlet for Africans trapped in an unjust economic system.

In Southern Rhodesia the fear of rebellion led to withdrawals of over-provocative measures. . . . Fear of native risings, occasioned by excessive fiscal demands, profoundly affected British official thinking. In 1904, for instance, Colonial Secretary Lyttleton remarked that in future tax questions of this kind "the attitude of the natives will have to be taken into account." . . .

Secondly, African resistance sometimes stimulated important changes in the structure of African societies. It is already well established that such changes could be brought about by collaborating groups. Through collaboration a society, or its leaders, could gain better schools and greater economic opportunities. Historians have, in fact, distinguished a number of so-called 'Christian Revolutions' in which key collaborators tried to solve some of the weaknesses of nineteenth century African state systems, to make their bureaucracy more efficient through literacy and to render the central power independent of traditional sanctions and limitations arising out of kinship or regional groupings. 'Christian Revolutions' of this kind were effected in Barotseland, Bechuanaland and Buganda. They were not, of course, identical in character, but they all tried to apply what historians have called the Christian 'great tradition' to solve problems of scale and effectiveness.

I would not deny the importance of these 'Christian Revolutions' which did effect substantial changes. But they had serious weaknesses. They provided opportunities for minority groups only. They rested upon alien sanctions and did not achieve mass commitment. They broke with traditional restraints and often weakened the mass sense of belonging. Even internal reforms designed to improve the popular lot by abolishing serfdom, forced labor and tribute may have weakened the feeling of identity between the rulers and ruled. . . .

Like these 'Christian Revolutions' the modern nationalist movements of East and Central Africa attempt to erect effective bureaucratic and other institutions for a territorial state. But they also have to try to modernize at a more profound level by achieving mass commitment to reform. We can see the experiments of the 'Christian Revolutions' as forerunners of one part of modern nationalism. But if we seek forerunners in the attempt to commit the masses to an effective enlargement of scale we have to turn rather to the resistance movements.

We must distinguish, of course, between short wars fought against the incoming whites and later protracted rebellions. In many instances the initial war was fought with the traditional military system. Little attempt was made to modify it, or to involve in the struggle wider social strata or neighbouring African peoples. But a long-drawn-out rebellion was a different matter. The insurgents faced new problems and had to search for new solutions. The distinction made by Dr. Iliffe between initial tribal wars waged against the Germans in Tanganyika and the Maji-Maji rising is of great significance. 'Maji-Maji,' Dr. Iliffe says, was 'a post-pacification revolt, quite different from the early resistance. That had been local and professional, soldiers against soldiers, whereas Maji-Maji affected almost everyone. . . . It was a great crisis of commitment.'

The point can be well illustrated for the Southern Rhodesian rebellions. The Ndebele had fought the 1893 war using their old military system. The subject peoples and the lower castes had taken no part in the fighting; neither had there been any attempt by the Ndebele to ally themselves with the peoples of Mashonaland or farther afield. The result had been disaster. The Ndebele then faced colonial pressures of greater intensity than anywhere else in East and Central Africa, except perhaps in the plantation areas of German East Africa. They desired to rebel—and this presented problems of organization and of scale. In 1896 not only the surviving members of the regiments and the adults of the royal family but also the subject peoples of Matabeleland and the tribes of Western and Central Mashonaland all joined to fight the whites.

The problem for the Shona was different. Their political fragmentation had prevented them from putting up any co-ordinated initial resistance to the arrival of the whites. As the implications of white rule were realized, individual paramounts began to refuse demands for taxes or labour, always ineffectively. Thus to 'rebel' effectively, the Shona had to discover a principle of solidarity and to recover at least some degree of the political unity which they had once possessed. The Maji-Maji rebels faced similar difficulties. It is not certain that their rising was in any sense planned. But once it had broken out, the insurgent leaders had to effect some co-ordination between the militarized Ngoni and the original rebels. This had to be achieved without any tradition of political centralization. Risings therefore led to political experimentation. Some rebels attempted to revive older centralizing institutions. But at the same time 'new men' came to the front with new ideas. (The Shona, for instance, tried to revive the ancient Rozwi kingship. But younger men also elbowed aside aged paramounts.) Above all, such insurgents developed the notion of charismatic as distinct from bureaucratic or hereditary leadership.

In considering what this involved I have found helpful a recent article by M. A. Doutreloux on prophets in the Congo. He argues that the prophet cults which have been a feature of the history of the Congo from at least the early eighteenth century onwards have their roots in an essential weakness of Congolese society. This society could not find a solution to the problem of fragmentation and instability. . . . The prophet movements rose in order to remedy this situation. These movements were assaults not only on witchcraft but also on traditional limitations; they proclaimed a church or creed for all Africans and imposed their own regulations and codes of conduct upon believers; they endeavored to provide an indigenous Great Tradition to rival the alien Great Tradition used by the Christian revolutionaries. They pre-eminently involved the masses.

The most striking resistance movements of East and Central Africa were clearly led by prophetic figures. Among the Nandi one may trace the rise to authority of the *Orkoiyot* prophets in face of British pressure. I have pointed out the key role of the oracular priesthood of Mwari in Matabeleland, and of the spirit mediums in Mashonaland in the Southern Rhodesian rising of the 1890s. Prophets also played a major part in the Maji-Maji rebellion. In the last two instances especially, we can discern the features described by Doutreloux. The prophets imposed new regulations and new instruction on the faithful; they brought believers into the congregation by dispensing 'medicine'; they promised immunity both from witchcraft and from bullets; they promised success in this world and a return from death. They spoke to all black men. This was true in Southern Rhodesia even though the leaders involved were members of traditional religious systems with roots deep in the past. Under the stress of the rebellion situation what L. H. Gann has recently described as a 'theological revolution' took place. The officers of the old cults were able to appeal to the centralizing memories with which they were associated, but they enjoyed too an extension of power and function; they asserted a new authority over chiefs and indunas; and they imposed new obligations on their followers. For a time the charismatic leadership of the prophets brought together Ndebele aristocrats, subject peoples, deposed Rozwi, Shona paramounts. As Gann puts it, 'The proud Matabele chieftains now agreed to operate under the supreme direction of an ex-serf, a remarkable man who in "normal" times would hardly have acquired much political influence.'

There were many other upheavals on a smaller scale. A list of risings allegedly led by 'witch-doctors' in East and Central Africa amounts to some thirty-five to forty instances. These prophetic leaders appealed to notions of past unity but also attempted to reconstruct society. Religious leaders of resistances often came from outside the societies concerned and appealed for co-operation with peoples who had formerly been their rivals. Sometimes the religious leader claimed to speak in the name of a long-dead hero figure who had established a now vanished unity; sometimes he claimed to be the bearer of a new divine commandment that black men should unite. . . .

Thus Resistance movements of this sort can hardly be regarded as tribal-conservative ones, involving as they did calls to recognize new authorities, new injunctions and co-operation on a new basis. Neither were they completely reactionary and anti-modernizing. The situation gave scope for the 'new man' with specially relevant skills—like the trained Ndebele policeman in 1896. Gann has pointed out that among the followers of the chief Shona religious leader in 1896, Kagubi, were 'men who had been in touch with Europeans and picked up some of their skills.' Kagubi's daughter was a school-girl in the Catholic mission at Chishawasha. I have myself described elsewhere how in the Makombe rising of 1917 in Portuguese East Africa there was a return to the new opportunities of leadership by men who had gone to seek their fortunes in the colonial economy, producing a 'leadership of paramounts and spirit mediums and returned waiters and ex-policemen.'

Of course these attempts to create a large-scale mass movement failed. Although in a single tribal situation, as with the Nandi or the Kipsigis, the charismatic leadership of the prophets continued to provide coherence even after defeat, where attempts at unity had been made over much larger areas, involving many more disparate peoples, defeat brought the new forms of co-operation to an abrupt end. In some cases, indeed, defeat led to a sudden abandonment by many of the ex-rebels of their commitment to African religious leadership and a turning instead to mission Christianity. The new religion was felt to have proved itself the more effective. . . .

The future belonged, it seemed, to the representatives of the 'defter nationalisms' which operated 'in the idiom of the Westernizers.' Leadership passed into the hands of the educated *élite,* often drawn from co-operating groups with access to modern ideas and skills.

So runs the standard argument. But this argument needs to be probed. Students of African nationalism are coming to pay increasing attention to the current of mass political emotion and to the continuity of rural radicalism, as well as to the development of *élite* leadership. Therefore we must ask if there is any continuity between expressions of mass political emotion in the twentieth century and the risings we have discussed. . . .

It can be suggested that the resistance tradition runs into modern mass nationalism just as does the tradition of the 'Christian Revolution.' But I do not wish to suggest an essential conflict between the *élite* solutions of the co-operating societies and the mass solutions of the resisters. The 'resisters' and 'collaborators' were not fundamentally distinct. There has always been a complex interplay, also, between mass and *élite* expressions of opposition. The establishment of colonial rule took a long time. 'Primary resistance' to the whites still continued in some areas of East, Central and Southern Africa while 'secondary' oppositions had already developed elsewhere. Independent churches, trade unions and welfare associations overlapped and co-existed with tribal or pan-tribal resistance. There was a fascinating interaction between them. . . .

This sort of interplay continued into the 1920s and 30s. African trade unionists in Bulawayo in 1929 looked to the resistant Somali as an example of successful unity; on the other hand, surviving leaders of the Ndebele rebels looked with envy at the successful collaborators, Lewanika and Khama, who had retained their land. The resistant Kikuyu looked with admiration at the institutions of the accommodating Ganda and sought at first to achieve them through a Kikuyu Paramount Chief movement. The ancestry of modern African politics, in short, is a complicated one. What we *can* say with certainty is that its patterns do not derive merely from decisions conceived in the capitals of the colonial powers and put into effect in East and Central Africa. In so far as they derive from the period of the 'Pacification' and of the establishment of the colonial administrations they derive from the participation of African societies in those processes; through both accommodation and resistance; through eager demands for modernization and stubborn defenses of a way of life.

problem III

Indirect Rule in Theory and Practice

Of all the problems of European colonialism in Africa none has captivated students and scholars so much as the theory and practice of Indirect Rule. Like assimilation in French colonial policy, Indirect Rule has been many things to many people. None, however, can yet determine whether the policy was to the detriment or benefit of British tropical Africa, but no other subject of colonial Africa has evoked more argument, more condemnation, and more praise. The problem of Indirect Rule is first to understand its principles and practice as defined by Lord Lugard in his *Dual Mandate* and *Political Memoranda,* and second to contrast the policy and its execution with the condemnation of its critics. To them, a policy that began as a practical expedient characterized by flexibility and common sense soon hardened into rigidity, or in the words of Lord Hailey, Indirect Rule "passed through three stages, first of a useful administrative device, then that of a political doctrine, and finally that of a religious dogma."[1] In the 1930's Sir Donald Cameron sought to meet these criticisms. He revived Indirect Rule by liberalizing its application and redefining its principles, calling them Indirect Administration. This restatement of Indirect Rule, however, neither resolved all the problems of native administration nor stilled the critics. Consequently, when Indirect Rule, or rather Indirect Administration, was officially abandoned in 1947 in favor of an unabashed policy of local government, a great assessment of its strengths and weaknesses, the good and the bad, the relevant and the irrelevant began and continues to this day with undiminished vigor. This is the Problem of Indirect Rule in British Tropical Africa.

The principles of Indirect Rule were most clearly and eloquently presented by one of Britain's greatest colonial administrators, Lord Lugard, in his book *The Dual Mandate in Tropical Africa.* Certainly, no other book of its time had such a profound influence on the formulation of

1 Lord Hailey, "Some Problems dealt with in *An African Survey,*" *International Affairs,* March/April, 1939, p. 202.

British colonial policy. To Lugard the two most important administrative principles to employ when ruling alien peoples were "decentralization" and "continuity." If the foundations for rapid material and moral progress were to be properly established, the colonial government must combat the tendency to overcentralize by delegating the powers local district officers needed to carry out the governor's orders. At the same time, however, continuity must be maintained on all administrative levels. If this were not accomplished, each new official would have to start afresh. Progress would stop or even be set back.

If decentralization and continuity were the basic principles of Lugard's administrative system, the relationship between the British officials and the "native" rulers was the key. This relationship must be based on cooperation and directed toward facilitating evolutionary change. The "Native Administration" must be advised rather than directed by the British administrator and allowed to develop along its own lines into a system of modern local government. Only in this manner, Lugard argued, could the proper foundations be built upon which might rise the future improvement of the colonial peoples.

Turning from principles to techniques, Lugard described in his *Political Memoranda* the administrative methods necessary to carry out the principles in *The Dual Mandate.* The *Political Memoranda* were detailed instructions for British administrative officers written before World War I and revised some years before the publication of *The Dual Mandate.* Lugard intended that these detailed instructions would implant the spirit of his system while preserving the continuity it required. First of all, he stressed the importance of recognizing and ruling through the indigenous authorities. The role of the British officers, except in such critical areas as taxation, military forces, and the alienation of land, was to advise, not demand. Their task was difficult and delicate. Not only did they have to use the indigenous institutions, which were alien to British officials, but they were expected to improve them by educating the chiefs without simultaneously destroying the authority of the traditional rulers. By thus utilizing the indigenous institutions and authorities, the British officials could preserve continuity with the past while laying the foundations for the progressive improvement of the indigenous society.

Lugard regarded his *Political Memoranda* as a manual to aid British officers in establishing a pattern of rule and insuring continuity of administration. He never conceived of his instructions as an unchanging doctrine to be rigidly applied everywhere, yet the critics of Indirect Rule soon complained that what had begun as an administrative expedient in Northern Nigeria had become an inflexible doctrine imposed throughout the territories of British Africa. W. R. Crocker, a former District Officer in Nigeria and an admirer of Lugard, was one of the first to suggest that this balance was not being preserved. Rather than a flexible, practical expedient, Indirect Rule, Crocker argued, had become by the 1930's an "occult science . . . dead of creative development" which could be neither challenged nor changed. The system merely preserved the old and often corrupt oligarchies. It did not develop efficient local administration. Moreover, despite Lugard's emphasis on local initiative, British officers were frequently punished for deviating from the principles and practices as laid down by Lugard and interpreted by his successors. Those officials who were not sufficiently "indirect" failed to obtain promotions, a situation that produced cynicism and a loss of morale which often weakened the entire administration. Crocker predicted that the traditional tribal structures would not survive the influx of new ideas and new methods, and Indirect Rule would thus be reduced, as a viable administrative technique, to only the small hamlet or rural village. The rest of the vast structure was "much ado about nothing" and should consequently be ignored if not dismantled.

Crocker attacked Indirect Rule because of its failure as an administrative device. J. F. J. Fitzpatrick criticized Indirect Rule because of its deleterious effects on the people of Northern Nigeria. Instead of efficient local government and material progress, Indirect Rule sustained tyrannical and corrupt governments and promoted divisions in the population. Lugard's system fostered an inefficient and unjust bureaucracy which could neither be checked by the people nor restrained by British officers. Moreover, Indirect Rule had strengthened the feudal emirates of Northern Nigeria, increasing the possibility of revolution by the oppressed peasantry. Indirect Rule had failed, declared Fitzpatrick, and the Native Administration "ought to go over the side" and be replaced by a "clean" British administration supported by an African civil service closely controlled and supervised by British officials.

These criticisms of Indirect Rule were not without validity, and Sir Donald Cameron, who became governor of Nigeria in 1931, sought to meet them by redefining Indirect Rule in his *The Principles of Native Administration and Their Application.* Like Crocker, he recognized that Indirect Rule had become a "sacred and mysterious art," and, like Fitzpatrick, he admitted that there were "abuses." Nevertheless, neither the ossified character nor the corrupt practices of Indirect Rule vitiated the principles laid down by Lord Lugard. Rather than abandon Indirect Rule altogether, Cameron redefined it, stressing the need for flexibility, long-range goals, and a just Native Administration which served the people. Native Administration must not simply be an end in itself, however, but a means to attain the progress envisaged by Lugard. Thus, the institutions of Native Administration should be sufficiently flexible to achieve this objective. In some areas this might mean that authority would be invested in a chief; in others it would be delegated to a council. Like Lugard, Cameron firmly believed that the proper way to rule was to permit the people to develop a system of government "from their own past," a system which would utilize the best institutions of England and Africa. To Cameron the principles of Indirect Rule, restated as Indirect Administration, would best achieve this end.

Like Cameron, Dame Margery Perham was a sympathetic but not uncritical observer of Indirect Rule. In her *Restatement of Indirect Rule,* published in 1934, she defended the practice of Indirect Rule while urging the need for reform along the lines of Cameron's Indirect Administration. In ruling any African people the critical point is the nature of the contact between the ruler and the ruled. Thus, the critics of Indirect Rule must look at both cultures and their interaction. They must take into account not only the "conservatism" and the "adaptability" of African society, but also the historic balance in Britain between a conservative respect for tradition and the liberal respect for the rights of all men. These pervasive factors in the two cultures made some form of Indirect Rule an inevitable product of British administration in Africa, but this inevitability, Perham warned, must not become a justification for the status quo. The practitioners of Indirect Rule should look to the future and prepare the people for independence by encouraging progressive change through Indirect Administration as defined by Sir Donald Cameron.

By the end of the 1930's, however, many perceptive observers recognized that Indirect Administration was not sufficiently viable to meet the growing demand for services—education, health, economic development—which could simply not be managed by Native Administrations; nor could that administration provide an effective government in the burgeoning cities and municipalities. If the colonial government attempted to delegate these new tasks to the traditional African authorities, they would cease to be traditional institutions. Moreover, the colonial government must find a way to deal with the new educated elite. Excluded from the traditional institutions yet wanting power, the educated African could only be incorporated into the government through some form of direct administration. These new challenges required new procedures, for change was rapidly outstripping the ability of Indirect Rule to administer effectively in inconstant circumstances. In 1947 Indirect Rule was quietly but officially abandoned in favor of a policy of instituting local government in British Tropical Africa.

The end of British colonial rule in Africa has not terminated the debate about Indirect Rule; it has only changed its focus. Today, scholars are not so concerned about the mechanics of Indirect Rule as its origins, its effects on African society, and its success or failure as colonial policy. The attitude of the educated elite toward Indirect Rule has played a central role in this dialogue. Writing in 1956, Ntieyong Akpan observed that the African elite regarded Indirect Rule as an "imperialistic device" to maintain British control. To them the merits of Indirect Rule were nothing more than camouflage for more dubious and cynical purposes. Thus, Indirect Rule was not a system based on humanitarian motives, but an administrative structure to perpetuate imperialism. It was instituted not because it was good for the people, but because it was cheap and practical. Moreover, Indirect Rule preserved the old conservative authorities who were ill equipped by education and temperament to cope with a changing environment. Correspondingly, the educated elites, excluded from both the Native Administration and the colonial government, were transformed into an alienated class who sought power through means which challenged the very existence of empire.

The fundamental question, however, is not one of means but of motives. Were the British rulers, in fact, imperialists who devised Indirect Rule as a conscious scheme to preserve their control over their African subjects or were they well-meaning men of good faith whose failures were more human errors than conscious conspiracy? Akpan appeared to discern devious designs where D. A. Low and R. Crawford Pratt have denied Akpan's suspicion of British motives. Indirect Rule, they argued, was not the product of mere rationalization. It was founded, instead, on ethics, tradition, and theory. The British genuinely hoped that Indirect Rule would help the African people adjust to the traumatic impact of contact with the West without losing their dignity and identity. They were skeptical that their own institutions could survive when transplanted to Africa, and they deeply believed that any system of government must take into account African institutions and traditions. Thus, Indirect Rule permitted the full expression of "African genius" without creating chaos. What this meant in practice, observed Pratt and Low, was a demand for African development in the context of Victorian values. In theory, at least, Indirect Rule was a happy combination of "expediency and high purpose."

The facts, however, do not always support the theory. In practice when the British District Officer dealt with an African chief, expediency often submerged high purpose. At this level the relationship between the ruler and the ruled was a blend of dialogue and demands. On the one hand the chief's position was recognized and made more secure; on the other his control was severely compromised by the British power to depose. Likewise, the British District Officer had far-reaching powers, but these powers were in fact checked by Lugard's strictures. These checks and balances failed only when what had begun as a useful, administrative device turned first into an inflexible doctrine and finally into an immutable dogma.

Lugard: Principles of Native Administration

The British Empire, as General Smuts has well said, has only one mission—for liberty and self-development on no standardised lines, so that all may feel that their interests and religion are safe under the British flag. Such liberty and self-development can be best secured to the native population by leaving them free to manage their own affairs through their own rulers, proportionately to their degree of advancement, under the guidance of the British staff, and subject to the laws and policy of the administration.

But apart from the administration of native affairs the local Government has to preserve law and order, to develop the trade and communications of the country, and to protect the interests of the merchants and others who are engaged in the development of its commercial and mineral resources. What, then, are the functions of the British staff, and how can the machinery of Government be most efficiently constituted for the discharge of its duties in those countries in Africa which fall under British control?

The staff must necessarily be limited in numbers, for if the best class of men are to be attracted to a service which often involves separation from family and a strain on health, they must be offered adequate salaries and inducements in the way of leave, housing, medical aid—or their equivalents in money—for their maintenance in health and comfort while serving abroad, and this forms a heavy charge on the revenues. Policy and economy alike demand restriction in numbers, but the best that England can supply.

Obviously a consideration of the machinery of British administration in the tropics involves a review of its relations to the home Government on the one hand, and of its local constitution and functions on the other. I will take the latter first.

The Government is constituted on the analogy of the British Government in England. The Governor represents the King, but combines the functions of the Prime Minister as head of the Executive. The councils bear a certain resemblance to the Home Cabinet and Parliament, while the detailed work of the administration is carried out by a staff which may be roughly divided into the administrative, the judicial, and the departmental branches.

The administrative branch is concerned with the supervision of the native administration and the general direction of policy; with education, and the collection and control of direct taxes, which involve assessment and close relations with the

From Lord F. Lugard, *The Dual Mandate in Tropical Africa* (London: Frank Cass & Co. Ltd., 1965, by arrangement with William Blackwood and Sons Ltd.) pp. 94–97, 102–5, 193–218.

native population; with legislation and the administration of justice in courts other than the Supreme Court; and with the direct government and welfare of the non-native section of the population.

The departmental staff is charged with duties in connection with transport, communications, and buildings (railways, marine, and public works); with the development of natural resources (mines, collieries, forestry, agriculture, and geology); with the auxiliary services of government (medical, secretarial, accounting, posts and telegraphs, surveys, &c.); and the collection of customs duties.

The task of the administrative branch is to foster that sympathy, mutual understanding, and co-operation between the Government and the people, without which, as Sir C. Ilbert has observed, no Government is really stable and efficient. Its aim is to promote progress in civilisation and justice, and to create conditions under which individual enterprise may most advantageously develop the natural resources of the country. The task of the departments, on the other hand, is to maintain the Government machine in a state of efficiency, and to afford direct assistance in material development. Their motto is efficiency and economy. The two branches work together, and their duties overlap and are interdependent in every sphere. The efficient discharge of those duties in combination constitutes the white man's title to control.

There are in my estimation two vital principles which characterise the growth of a wise administration —they are Decentralisation and Continuity. Though, as Lord Morley said of India, "perfectly efficient administration has an inevitable tendency to over-centralisation," it is a tendency to be combated. It has indeed been said that the whole art of administration consists in judicious and progressive delegation, and there is much truth in the dictum, provided that delegation of duties be accompanied by public responsibility. This is not applicable to the head of the Government alone or in particular, but to every single officer, from the Governor to the foreman of a gang of daily labourers. The man who is charged with the accomplishment of any task, and has the ability and discrimination to select the most capable of those who are subordinate to him, and to trust them with ever-increasing responsibility, up to the limits of their capacity, will be rewarded not only with confidence and loyalty, but he will get more work done, and better done, than the man who tries to keep too much in his own hands, and is slow to recognise merit, originality, and efficiency in others. His sphere of work becomes a training school, and he is able to recommend his best men for promotion to greater responsibility than he himself can confer. The Governor who delegates to his Lieut.-Governors, Residents, and heads of departments the widest powers compatible with his own direct responsibility to the Crown, will witness the most rapid progress.

But delegation to an individual who is not equal to the responsibility obviously means disaster, and it is therefore often advisable to entrust extended powers to the individual rather than to incorporate them as a part of the duties of his office. His successor, who must obviously have less experience, and may or may not be his equal in ability, will not then automatically enjoy the same latitude, until he has proved his capacity in the higher office.

Increased latitude to the individual is not, however, inconsistent with increased delegation of duties to the office, more especially in the administrative branch of the service, where posts must of necessity grow in importance as the country as a whole develops. It is a frequent ground of criticism that the Colonial Office has been somewhat backward in appreciating the value of this principle in these young and rapidly-growing dependencies.

The Governor, by delegating work to others, would seem to lighten his own task, but in point of fact the more he delegates the more he will find to do in co-ordinating the progress of the whole. Moreover, in order to have a right appreciation of the abilities, and of the personal character of each principal administrative officer and head of department, he must be in close personal touch with them, and make absolutely clear to them the essential features of his policy. He must be the directing brain, and leave the execution to others. The task he undertakes is no light one, and if he should be called on to create an administration *ab ovo,* or to lay down new lines of policy in an old one, the work may become more than the time at his command suffices for, and the personal touch with his officers may temporarily suffer from the insistent demands of his office, until he is able gradually to delegate to those in whom he has confidence. . . .

The second of the two principles which I have described as vital in African administration is Continuity, and this, like Decentralisation, is applicable to every department and to every officer, however junior, but above all to those officers who represent the Government in its relations with the native population. The annually recurrent absence on leave, which withdraws each officer in West Africa from his post for about a third of his time, the occasional invalidings and deaths, and the constant changes rendered unavoidable of late years by a depleted and inadequate staff, have made it extremely difficult to preserve in that part of Africa any continuity whatever. The African is slow to give his confidence. He is suspicious and reticent with a newcomer, eager to resuscitate old land disputes—perhaps of half a century's standing—in the hope that the new officer in his ignorance may reverse the decision of his predecessor. The time of an officer is wasted in picking up the tangled threads and informing himself of the conditions of his new post. By the time he has acquired the necessary knowledge, and has learnt the character of the people he has to deal with, and won their confidence, his leave becomes due, and if on his return he is posted elsewhere, not only is progress arrested but retrogression may result.

It is also essential that each officer should be at pains to keep full and accurate records of all important matters, especially of any conversation with native chiefs, in which any pledge or promise, implied or explicit, has been made. It is not enough that official correspondence should be filed—a summary of each subject should be made and decisions recorded and brought up to date, so that a newcomer may be able rapidly to put himself *au courant*. The higher the post occupied by an officer, the more important does the principle become.

It is especially important that the decisions of the Governor should be fully recorded in writing, and not merely by an initial of acquiescence or a verbal order. This involves heavy office work, but it is work which cannot be neglected if misunderstandings are to be avoided and continuity preserved. The very detailed instructions regarding the duties of each newly-created department which were issued when the administration of Northern Nigeria was first inaugurated, served a very useful purpose in maintaining continuity of policy, till superseded on amalgamation by briefer general orders.

In the sphere of administration there are obviously many subjects—education, taxation, slavery and labour, native courts, land tenure, &c.—in which uniformity and continuity of policy is impossible in so large a country, unless explicit instructions are issued for guidance. By a perusal of the periodical reports of Residents, the Governor could inform himself of the difficulties which presented themselves in the varying circumstances of each province, and think out the best way in which they could be met, and could note where misunderstandings or mistakes had been made. By these means a series of Memoranda were compiled, and constantly revised as new problems came to light, and as progress rendered the earlier instructions obsolete. They formed the reference book and authority of the Resident and his staff.

In a country so vast, which included communities in all stages of development, and differing from each other profoundly in their customs and traditions, it was the declared policy of Government that each should develop on its own lines; but this in no way lessens the need for uniformity in the broad principles of policy, or in their application where the conditions are similar. It was the aim of these Memoranda to preserve this continuity and uniformity of principle and policy. . . . In Africa we are laying foundations. The superstructure may vary in its details, some of which may perhaps be ill-designed, but the stability of the edifice is unaffected. You may pull down and re-erect cupolas, but you cannot alter the design of the foundations without first destroying all that has been erected upon them. . . .

If continuity and decentralisation are, as I have said, the first and most important conditions in maintaining an effective administration, co-operation is the key-note of success in its application—continuous co-operation between every link in the chain, from the head of the administration to its most junior member,—co-operation between the Government and the commercial community, and, above all, between the provincial staff and the native rulers. Every individual adds his share not only to the accomplishment of the ideal, but to the ideal itself. Its principles are fashioned by his quota of experience, its results are achieved by his patient and loyal application of these principles, with as little interference as possible with native customs and modes of thought.

Principles do not change, but their mode of application may and should vary with the customs, the traditions, and the prejudices of each unit. The task of the administrative officer is to clothe his principles in the garb of evolution, not of revolution; to make it apparent alike to the educated native, the conservative Moslem, and the primitive pagan, each in his own degree, that the policy of the Government is not antagonistic but progressive—sympathetic to his aspirations and the guardian of his natural rights. The Governor looks to the administrative staff to keep in touch with native thought and feeling, and to report fully to himself, in order that he in turn may be able to support them and recognise their work. . . .

Lord Milner's declaration that the British policy is to rule subject races through their own chiefs is generally applauded, but the manner in which the principle should be translated into practice admits of wide differences of opinion and method. Obviously the extent to which native races are capable of controlling their own affairs must vary in proportion to their degree of development and progress in social organisation, but this is a question of adaptation and not of principle. Broadly speaking, the divergent opinions in regard to the application of the principle may be found to originate in three different conceptions.

The first is that the ideal of self-government can only be realised by the methods of evolution which have produced the democracies of Europe and America—viz., by representative institutions in which a comparatively small educated class shall be recognised as the natural spokesmen for the many. This method is naturally in favour with the educated African. Whether it is adapted to peoples accustomed by their own institutions to autocracy—albeit modified by a substantial expression of the popular will and circumscribed by custom—is naturally a matter on which opinions differ. The fundamental essential, however, in such a form of Government is that the educated few shall at least be representative of the feelings and desires of the many—well known to them, speaking their language, and versed in their customs and prejudices.

In present conditions in Africa the numerous separate tribes, speaking different languages, and in different stages of evolution, cannot produce representative men of education. Even were they available, the number of communities which could claim separate representation would make any central and really representative Council very unwieldy. The authority vested in the representatives would be antagonistic to that of the native rulers and their councils,—which are the product of the natural tendencies of tribal evolution,—and would run counter to the customs and institutions of the people.

An attempt to adapt these principles of Western representative Government to tropical races is now being made in India. . . .

Though the powers entrusted to the elected representatives of the people are at first restricted under the dyarchical system (which reserves certain subjects for the Central Authority), the principle of government by an educated minority, as opposed to government by native rulers, is fully accepted. . . .

The experiment has so far shown much promise of success, but the real test is not merely whether the native councillors show moderation and restraint as against extremists of their own class, but whether, when legislation has to be enacted which is unpopular with the illiterate masses and the martial races of India, there may be a reluctance to accept what will be called "Babu-made law," though it would have been accepted without demur as the order of "the Sirkar"—the British Raj.

It is, of course, now too late to adopt to any large extent the alternative of gradually transforming the greater part of British India into native States governed by their own hereditary dynasties, whose representatives in many cases still exist, and extending to them the principles which have so successfully guided our relations with the native States in India itself, and in Malaya in the past. It is one thing to excite an ignorant peasantry against an alien usurper, but quite another thing to challenge a native ruler.

Such a system does not exclude the educated native from participation in the government of the State to which he belongs, as a councillor to the native ruler, but it substitutes for direct British rule, not an elected oligarchy but a form of government more in accord with racial instincts and inherited traditions. . . .

The second conception is that every advanced community should be given the widest possible powers of self-government under its own ruler, and that these powers should be rapidly increased with the object of complete independence at the earliest possible date in the not distant future. Those who hold this view generally, I think, also consider that attempts to train primitive tribes in any form of self-government are futile, and the administration must be wholly conducted by British officials. This in the past has been the principle adopted in many dependencies. It recognised no alternative between a status of independence, like the Sultans of Malaya, or the native princes of India, and the direct rule of the district commissioner.

But the attempt to create such independent States in Africa has been full of anomalies. In the case of Egbaland, where the status has been formally recognised by treaty, the extent to which the Crown had jurisdiction was uncertain, yet, as we have seen, international conventions, including even that relating to the protection of wild animals, which was wholly opposed to native customary rights, were applied without the consent of the "Independent" State, and powers quite incompatible with independence were exercised by the Suzerain.

The paramount chief might receive ceremonial visits from time to time from the Governor, and even perhaps be addressed as "Your Royal Highness," and vested with titular dignity and the tinsel insignia of office. His right to impose tolls on trade, and to exact whatever oppressive taxes he chose from his peasantry, was admitted, but his authority was subject to constant interference. The last-joined District Officer, or any other official, might issue orders, if not to him, at any rate to any of his subordinate chiefs, and the native ruler had no legal and recognised means of enforcing his commands. He was necessarily forbidden to raise armed forces—on which in the last resort the authority of the law must depend—and could not therefore maintain order.

The third conception is that of rule by native chiefs, unfettered in their control of their people as regards all those matters which are to them the most important attributes of rule, with scope for initiative and responsibility, but admittedly—so far as the visible horizon is concerned—subordinate to the control of the protecting Power in certain well defined directions. It recognises, in the words of the Versailles Treaty, that the subject races of Africa are not yet able to stand alone, and that it would not conduce to the happiness of the vast bulk of the people—for whose welfare the controlling Power is trustee—that the attempt should be made.

The verdict of students of history and sociology of different nationalities, such as Dr Kidd, Dr Stoddard, M. Beaulieu, Meredith Townsend and others is, as I have shown, unanimous that the era of complete independence is not as yet visible on the horizon of time. Practical administrators (among whom I may include my successor, Sir P. Girouard, in Northern Nigeria) have arrived at the same conclusion.

The danger of going too fast with native races is even more likely to lead to disappointment, if not to disaster, than the danger of not going fast enough. The pace can best be gauged by those who have intimate acquaintance alike with the strong points and the limitations of the native peoples and rulers with whom they have to deal.

The Fulani of Northern Nigeria are, as I have said, more capable of rule than the indigenous races, but in proportion as we consider them an alien race, we are denying self-government to the people over whom they rule, and supporting an alien caste—albeit closer and more akin to the native races than a European can be. Yet capable as they are, it requires the ceaseless vigilance of the British staff to maintain a high standard of administrative integrity, and to prevent oppression of the peasantry. We are dealing with the same generation, and in many cases with the identical rulers, who were responsible for the misrule and tyranny which we found in 1902. The subject races near the capital were then serfs, and the victims of constant extortion. Those dwelling at a distance were raided for slaves, and could not count their women, their cattle, or their crops their own. Punishments were most barbarous, and included impalement, mutilation, and burying alive. Many generations have passed since British rule was established among the more intellectual people of India—the inheritors of centuries of Eastern civilisation—yet only to-day are we tentatively seeking to confer on them a measure of self-government. "Festina lente" ["make haste slowly," *ed.*] is a motto which the Colonial Office will do well to remember in its dealings with Africa. . . .

The system adopted in Nigeria is therefore only a particular method of the application of these principles—more especially as regards "advanced communities,"—and since I am familiar with it I will use it as illustrative of the methods which in my opinion should characterise the dealings of the controlling power with subject races.

The object in view is to make each "Emir" or paramount chief, assisted by his judicial Council, an effective ruler over his own people. He presides over a "Native Administration" organised throughout as a unit of local government. The area over which he exercises jurisdiction is divided into districts under the control of "Headmen," who collect the taxes in the name of the ruler, and pay them into the "Native Treasury," conducted by a native treasurer and staff under the supervision of the chief at his capital. Here, too, is the prison for native court prisoners, and probably the school, which I shall describe more fully in the chapter on education. Large cities are divided into wards for purposes of control and taxation.

The district headman, usually a territorial magnate with local connections, is the chief executive officer in the area under his charge. He controls the village headmen, and is responsible for the assessment of the tax, which he collects through their agency. He must reside in his district and not at the capital. He is not allowed to pose as a chief with a retinue of his own and duplicate officials, and is summoned from time to time to report to his chief. If, as is the case with some of the ancient Emirates, the community is a small one but independent of any other native rule, the chief may be his own district headman.

A province under a Resident may contain several separate "Native Administrations," whether they be Moslem Emirates or pagan communities. A "division" under a British District Officer may include one or more headmen's districts, or more than one small Emirate or independent pagan tribe, but as a rule no Emirate is partly in one division and partly in another. The Resident acts as sympathetic adviser and counsellor to the native chief, being careful not to interfere so as to lower his prestige, or cause him to lose interest in his work. His advice on matters of general policy must be followed, but the native ruler issues his own instructions to his subordinate chiefs and district heads—not as the orders of the Resident but as his own,—and he is encouraged to work through them, instead of centralising everything in himself—a system which in the past had produced such great abuses. The British District Officers supervise and assist the native district headmen, through whom they convey any instructions to village heads, and make any arrangements necessary for carrying on the work of the Government departments, but all important orders emanate from the Emir, whose messenger usually accompanies and acts as mouthpiece of a District Officer.

The tax—which supersedes all former "tribute," irregular imposts, and forced labour—is, in a sense, the basis of the whole system, since it supplies the means to pay the Emir and all his officials. The district and village heads are effectively supervised and assisted in its assessment by the British staff. The native treasury retains the proportion assigned to it (in advanced communities a half), and pays the remainder into Colonial Revenue.

There are fifty such treasuries in the northern provinces of Nigeria, and every independent chief, however small, is encouraged to have his own. The appropriation by the native administration of market dues, slaughter-house fees, forest licences, &c., is authorised by ordinance, and the native administration receives also the fines and fees of native courts. From these funds are paid the salaries of the Emir and his council, the native court judges, the district and village heads, police, prison warders, and other employees. The surplus is devoted to the construction and maintenance of dispensaries, leper settlements, schools, roads, courthouses, and other buildings. Such works may be carried out wholly or in part by a Government department, if the native administration requires technical assistance, the cost being borne by the native treasury.

The native treasurer keeps all accounts of receipts and expenditure, and the Emir, with the assistance of the Resident, annually prepares a budget, which is formally approved by the Lieut.-Governor.

In these advanced communities the judges of the native courts—which I shall describe in a later chapter—administer native law and custom, and exercise their jurisdiction independently of the native executive, but under the supervision of the British staff, and subject to the general control of the Emir, whose "Judicial Council" consists of his principal officers of State, and is vested with executive as well as judicial powers. No punishment may be inflicted by a native authority, except through a regular tribunal. The ordinances of government are operative everywhere, but the native authority may make by-laws in modification of native custom—*e.g.*, on matters of sanitation, &c.,—and these, when approved by the Governor, are enforced by the native courts.

The authority of the Emir over his own people is absolute, and the profession of an alien creed does not absolve a native from the obligation to obey his lawful orders; but aliens—other than natives domiciled in the Emirate and accepting the jurisdiction of the native authority and courts—are under the direct control of the British staff. Townships are excluded from the native jurisdiction.

The village is the administrative unit. It is not always easy to define, since the security to life and property which has followed the British administration has caused an exodus from the cities and large villages, and the creation of innumerable hamlets, sometimes only of one or two huts, on the agricultural lands. The peasantry of the advanced communities, though ignorant, yet differs from that of the backward tribes in that they recognise the authority of the Emir, and are more ready to listen to the village head and the Council of Elders, on which the Nigerian system is based.

Subject, therefore, to the limitations which I shall presently discuss, the native authority is thus *de facto* and *de jure* ruler over his own people. He appoints and dismisses his subordinate chiefs and officials. He exercises the power of allocation of lands, and with the aid of the native courts, of adjudication in land disputes and expropriation for offences against the community; these are the essential functions upon which, in the opinion of the West African Lands Committee, the prestige of the native authority depends. The lawful orders which he may give are carefully defined by ordinance, and in the last resort are enforced by Government.

Since native authority, especially if exercised by alien conquerors, is inevitably weakened by the first impact of civilised rule, it is made clear to the elements of disorder, who regard force as conferring the only right to demand obedience, that government, by the use of force if necessary, intends to support the native chief. To enable him to maintain order he employs a body of unarmed police, and if the occasion demands the display of superior force he looks to the Government—as, for instance, if a community combines to break the law or shield criminals from justice,—a rare event in the advanced communities.

The native ruler derives his power from the Suzerian, and is responsible that it is not misused. He is equally with British officers amenable to the law, but his authority does not depend on the caprice of an executive officer. To intrigue against him is an offence punishable, if necessary, in a Provincial Court. Thus both British and native courts are invoked to uphold his authority.

The essential feature of the system (as I wrote at the time of its inauguration) is that the native chiefs are constituted "as an integral part of the machinery of the administration. There are not two sets of rulers—British and native—working either separately or in co-operation, but a single Government in which the native chiefs have well-defined duties and an acknowledged status equally with British officials. Their duties should never conflict, and should overlap as little as possible. They should be complementary to each other, and the chief himself must understand that he has no right to place and power unless he renders his proper services to the State."

The ruling classes are no longer either demi-gods, or parasites preying on the community. They must work for the stipends and position they enjoy. They are the trusted delegates of the Governor, exercising in the Moslem States the well-understood powers of "Wakils" in conformity with their own Islamic system, and recognising the King's representative as their acknowledged Suzerain.

There is here no need of "Dyarchy," for the lines of development of the native administration run parallel to, and do not intersect, those of the Central Government. It is the consistent aim of the British staff to maintain and increase the prestige of the native ruler, to encourage his initiative, and to support his authority. That the chiefs are satisfied with the autonomy they enjoy in the matters which really interest and concern them, may be judged by their loyalty and the prosperity of their country. . . .

The limitations to independence which are frankly inherent in this conception of native rule—not as temporary restraints to be removed as soon as may be, but as powers which rightly belong to the controlling Power as trustee for the welfare of the masses, and as being responsible for the defence of the country and the cost of its central administration—are such as do not involve interference with the authority of the chiefs or the social organisation of the people. They have been accepted by the Fulani Emirs as natural and proper to the controlling power, and their reservation in the hands of the Governor has never interfered with the loyalty of the ruling chiefs, or, so far as I am aware, been resented by them. The limitations are as follows:—

(1) Native rulers are not permitted to raise and control armed

forces, or to grant permission to carry arms. To this in principle Great Britain stands pledged under the Brussels Act. The evils which result in Africa from an armed population were evident in Uganda before it fell under British control, and are very evident in Abyssinia today. No one with experience will deny the necessity of maintaining the strictest military discipline over armed forces or police in Africa if misuse of power is to be avoided, and they are not to become a menace and a terror to the native population and a danger in case of religious excitement—a discipline which an African ruler is incapable of appreciating or applying. For this reason native levies should never be employed in substitution for or in aid of troops.

On the other hand, the Government armed police are never quartered in native towns, where their presence would interfere with the authority of the chiefs. Like the regular troops, they are employed as escorts and on duty in the townships. The native administration maintain a police, who wear a uniform but do not carry firearms.

(2) The sole right to impose taxation in any form is reserved to the Suzerain power. This fulfils the bilateral understanding that the peasantry—provided they pay the authorised tax (the adjustment of which to all classes of the population is a responsibility which rests with the Central Government)—should be free of all other exactions whatsoever (including unpaid labour), while a sufficient proportion of the tax is assigned to the native treasuries to meet the expenditure of the native administration. Special sanction by ordinance—or "rule" approved by the Governor—is therefore required to enable the native authority to levy any special dues, &c.

(3) The right to legislate is reserved. That this should remain in the hands of the Central Government—itself limited by the control of the Colonial Office, as I have described—cannot be questioned. The native authority, however, exercises very considerable power in this regard. A native ruler, and the native courts, are empowered to enforce native law and custom, provided it is not repugnant to humanity, or in opposition to any ordinance. This practically meets all needs, but the native authority may also make rules on any subject, provided they are approved by the Governor.

(4) The right to appropriate land on equitable terms for public purposes and for commercial requirements is vested in the Governor. In the Northern Provinces of Nigeria (but not in the South) the right of disposing of native lands is reserved to the Governor by ordinance. In practice this does not interfere with the power of the native ruler (as the delegate of the Governor) to assign lands to the natives under his rule, in accordance with native law and custom, or restrict him or the native courts from adjudicating between natives regarding occupancy rights in land. No rents are levied on lands in occupation by indigenous natives. Leases to aliens are granted by the Central Government.

If the pressure of population in one community makes it necessary to assign to it a portion of the land belonging to a neighbour with a small and decreasing population, the Governor (to whom appeal may be made) would decide the matter. These reservations were set out in the formal letter of appointment given to each chief in Northern Nigeria.

(5) In order to maintain intact the control of the Central Government over all aliens, and to avoid friction and difficulties, it has been the recognised rule that the employees of the native administration should consist entirely of natives subject to the native authority. If aliens are required for any skilled work by the native administration, Government servants may be employed and their salaries reimbursed by the native treasury. For a like reason, whenever possible, all non-natives and natives not subject to the local native jurisdiction live in the "township," from which natives subject to the native administration are as far as possible excluded. This exclusive control of aliens by the Central Government partakes rather of the nature of "extra-territorial jurisdiction" than of dualism.

(6) Finally, in the interests of good government, the right of confirming or otherwise the choice of the people of the successor to a chiefship, and of deposing any ruler for misrule or other adequate cause, is reserved to the Governor. . . .

The habits of a people are not changed in a decade, and when powerful despots are deprived of the pastime of war and slave-raiding, and when even the weak begin to forget their former sufferings, to grow weary of a life without excitement, and to resent the petty restrictions which have replaced the cruelties of the old despotism, it must be the aim of Government to provide new interests and rivalries in civilised progress, in education, in material prosperity and trade, and even in sport.

There were indeed many who, with the picture of Fulani misrule fresh in their memory, regarded this system when it was first inaugurated with much misgiving, and believed that though the hostility of the rulers to the British might be concealed, and their vices disguised, neither could be eradicated, and they would always remain hostile at heart. They thought that the Fulani as an alien race of conquerors, who had in turn been conquered, had not the same claims for consideration as those whom they had displaced, even though they had become so identified with the people that they could no longer be called aliens.

But there can be no doubt that such races form an invaluable medium between the British staff and the native peasantry. Nor can the difficulty of finding any one capable of taking their place, or the danger they would constitute to the State if ousted from their positions, be ignored. Their traditions of rule, their monotheistic religion, and their intelligence enable them to appreciate more readily than the negro population the wider objects of British policy, while their close touch with the masses—with whom they live in daily intercourse—mark them out as destined to play an important part in the future, as they have done in the past, in the development of the tropics.

Both the Arabs in the east and the Fulani in the west are Mohamedans, and by supporting their rule we unavoidably encourage the spread of Islam, which from the purely administrative point of view has the disadvantage of being subject to waves of fanaticism, bounded by no political frontiers. In Nigeria it has been the rule that their power should not be re-established over tribes which had made good their independence, or imposed upon those who had successfully resisted domination.

On the other hand, the personal interests of the rulers must rapidly become identified with those of the controlling Power. The forces of disorder do not distinguish between them, and the rulers soon recognise that any upheaval against the British would equally make an end of them. Once this community of interest is established, the Central Government cannot be taken by surprise, for it is impossible that the native rulers should not be aware of any disaffection.

This identification of the ruling class with the Government accentuates the corresponding obligation to check malpractices on their part. The task of educating them in the duties of a ruler becomes more than ever insistent; of inculcating a sense of responsibility; of convincing their intelligence of the advantages which accrue from the material prosperity of the peasantry, from free labour and initiative; of the necessity of delegating powers to trusted subordinates; of the evils of favouritism and bribery; of the importance of education, especially for the ruling class, and for the filling of lucrative posts under Government; of the benefits of sanitation, vaccination, and isolation of infection in checking mortality; and finally, of impressing upon them how greatly they may benefit their country by personal interest in such matters, and by the application of labour-saving devices and of scientific methods in agriculture.

Unintentional misuse of the system of native administration must also be guarded against. It is not, for instance, the duty of a native administration to purchase supplies for native troops, or to enlist and pay labour for public works, though its agency within carefully defined limits may be useful in making known Government requirements, and seeing that markets are well supplied. Nor should it be directed to collect licences, fees, and rents due to Government, nor should its funds be used for any purpose not solely connected with and prompted by its own needs.

I have throughout these pages continually emphasised the necessity of recognising, as a cardinal principle of British policy in dealing with native races, that institutions and methods, in order to command success and promote the happiness and welfare of the people, must be deep-rooted in their traditions and prejudices. Obviously in no sphere of administration is this more essential than in that under discussion, and a slavish adherence to any particular type, however successful it may have proved elsewhere, may, if unadapted to the local environment, be as ill-suited and as foreign to its conceptions as direct British rule would be.

The type suited to a community which has long grown accustomed to the social organisation of the Moslem State may or may not be suitable to advance pagan communities, which have evolved a social system of their own, such as the Yorubas, the Benis, the Egbas, or the Ashantis in the West, or the Waganda, the Wanyoro, the Watoro, and others in the East. The history, the traditions, the idiosyncracies, and the prejudices of each must be studied by the Resident and his staff, in order that the form adopted shall accord with natural evolution, and shall ensure the ready co-operation of the chiefs and people. . . .

Native etiquette and ceremonial must be carefully studied and observed in order that unintentional offence may be avoided. Great importance is attached to them, and a like observance in accordance with native custom is demanded towards British officers. Chiefs are treated with respect and courtesy. Native races alike in India and Africa are quick to discriminate between natural dignity and assumed superiority. Vulgar familiarity is no more a passport to their friendship than an assumption of self-importance is to their respect. The English gentleman needs no prompting in such a matter—his instinct is never wrong. Native titles of rank are adopted, and only native dress is worn, whether by chiefs or by schoolboys. Principal chiefs accused of serious crimes are tried by a British court, and are not imprisoned before trial, unless in very exceptional circumstances. Minor chiefs and native officials appointed by an Emir may be tried by his Judicial Council. If the offence does not involve deprivation of office, the offender may be fined without public trial, if he prefers it, in order to avoid humiliation and loss of influence.

Succession is governed by native law and custom, subject in the case of important chiefs to the approval of the Governor, in order that the most capable claimant may be chosen. It is important to ascertain the customary law and to follow it when possible, for the appointment of a chief who is not the recognised heir, or who is disliked by the people, may give rise to trouble, and in any case the new chief would have much difficulty in asserting his authority, and would fear to check abuses lest he should alienate his supporters. In Moslem countries the law is fairly clearly defined, being a useful combination of the hereditary principle, tempered by selection, and in many cases in Nigeria the ingenious device is maintained of having two rival dynasties, from each of which the successor is selected alternately.

In pagan communities the method varies; but there is no rigid rule, and a margin for selection is allowed. The formal approval of the Governor after a short period of probation is a useful precaution, so that if the designated chief proves himself unsuitable, the selection may be revised without difficulty. Minor chiefs are usually selected by popular vote, subject to the approval of the paramount chief. It is a rule in Nigeria that no slave may be appointed as a chief or district headman. If one is nominated he must first be publicly freed.

Small and isolated communities, living within the jurisdiction of a chief, but owing allegiance to the chief of their place of origin—a common source of trouble in Africa—should gradually be absorbed into the territorial jurisdiction. Aliens who have settled in a district for their own purposes would be subject to the local jurisdiction.

There are some who consider that however desirable it may be to rule through the native chiefs of advanced communities, such a policy is misplaced, if not impossible, among the backward tribes. Here, they would say, the Resident and his staff must necessarily be the direct rulers, since among the most primitive peoples there are no recognised chiefs capable of exercising rule. The imposition of a tax is in their view premature, since (they say) the natives derive no corresponding benefit, and learn to regard the District Officer merely as a tax-collector. Moreover, refusal to pay necessitates coercive expeditions—scarcely distinguishable from the raids of old times. To attempt to adapt such methods—however suitable to the Moslem communities—to the conditions of primitive tribes, would be to foist upon them a system foreign to their conceptions. In the criticisms I have read no *via media* is indicated between those who are accounted to rank as advanced communities, entitled before long to independence, and direct rule by the British staff.

Let us realise that the advanced communities form a very minute proportion of the population of British Tropical Africa. The vast majority are in the primitive or early tribal stages of development. To abandon the policy of ruling them through their own chiefs, and to substitute the direct rule of the British officer, is to forgo the high ideal of leading the backward races, by their own efforts, in their own way, to raise themselves to a higher plane of social organisation, and tends to perpetuate and stereotype existing conditions.

We must realise also two other important facts. First, that the British staff, exercising direct rule, cannot be otherwise than very small in comparison to the area and population of which they are in charge. That rule cannot generally mean the benevolent autocracy of a particular District Officer, well versed in the language and customs of the people, but rule by a series of different white men, conveying their orders by police and couriers and alien native subordinates, and the quartering of police detachments in native villages. Experience has shown the difficulty in such conditions of detecting and checking cases of abuse of office, and of acquisition of land by alien and absentee native landlords. There is a marked tendency to litigation, and the entire decay of such tribal authority as may previously have existed.

The changed conditions of African life is the second important fact for consideration. The advent of Europeans cannot fail to have a disintegrating effect on tribal authority and institutions, and on the conditions of native life. This is due in part to the unavoidable restrictions imposed on the exercise of their power by the native chiefs. They may no longer inflict barbarous and inhuman punishments on the individual, or take reprisals by force of arms on aggressive neighbours or a disobedient section of the community. The concentration of force in the hands of the Suzerain Power, and the amenability of the chiefs to that Power for acts of oppression and misrule, are evidence to primitive folk that the power of the chiefs has gone. This decay of tribal authority has unfortunately too often been accentuated by the tendency of British officers to deal direct with petty chiefs, and to ignore, and allow their subordinates to ignore, the principal chief. It has been increased in many cases by the influx of alien natives, who, when it suited them, set at naught the native authority, and refused to pay the tribute which the chiefs were given no means of enforcing, or acquired lands which they held in defiance of native customary tenure. . . .

Here, then, in my view, lies our present task in Africa. It becomes impossible to maintain the old order—the urgent need is for adaptation to the new—to build up a tribal authority with a recognised and legal standing, which may avert social chaos. It cannot be accomplished by superseding—by the direct rule of the white man—such ideas of discipline and organisation as exist, nor yet by "stereotyping customs and institutions among backward races which are not consistent with progress."

The first step is to hasten the transition from the patriarchal to the tribal stage, and induce those who acknowledge no other authority than the head of the family to recognise a common chief. Where this stage has already been reached, the object is to group together small tribes, or sections of a tribe, so as to form a single administrative unit, whose chiefs severally, or in Council as a "Native Court," may be constituted a "Native Authority," with defined powers over native aliens, through whom the district officer can work instead of through alien subordinates. His task is to strengthen the authority of the chiefs, and encourage them to show initiative; to learn their difficulties at first hand, and to assist them in adapting the new conditions to the old—maintaining and developing what is best, avoiding everything that has a tendency to denationalisation and servile imitation. He can guide and control several such units, and endeavour gradually to bring them to the standard of an advanced community. In brief, tribal cohesion, and the education of the tribal heads in the duties of rulers, are the watchwords of the policy in regard to these backward races. As the unit shows itself more and more capable of conducting its own affairs, the direct rule, which at first is temporarily unavoidable among the most backward of all, will decrease, and the community will acquire a legal status, which the European and the native agent of material development must recognise. "The old easy-going days, when the probity of the individual was sufficient title to rule, are gone. . . . Intelligent interest, imagination, comprehension of alien minds—these are the demands of today. . . ."

Lugard: Methods of Native Administration: Political Officers and Native Rulers

The object in view. The British rôle here is to bring to the country all the gains of civilisation by applied science (whether in the development of material resources, or the eradication of disease, &c.), with as little interference as possible with Native customs and modes of thought. Where new ideas are to be

From Lord Lugard, *Revisions of Instructions to Political Officers on Subjects Chiefly Political and Administrative* (London: Waterlow and Sons, Ltd., 1919), pp. 296–305.

presented to the native mind, patient explanation of the objects in view will be well rewarded, and new methods may often be clothed in a familiar garb. . . .

Connotation of names of ranks. The term "Resident" implies duties rather of a Political or advisory nature, while the term "Commissioner" connotes functions of a more directly Administrative character. The former is therefore applicable to the Chief Government Officer in a Province of which large areas are under the immediate rule of a Paramount Chief, who, with Native Officials, himself administers a form of Government. The latter is more adapted to Provinces, or parts of Provinces, less advanced in civilisation, where the authority of the Native Chiefs is small, and a large measure of direct Administration must devolve upon the Protectorate Government. The term "Commissioner" is, however, already used in so many other connections, viz., a Commissioner of the Supreme or Provincial Court,—a member of a Commission of Inquiry, a Police Commissioner, &c., that for the sake both of distinction and of brevity, the term Resident has been adopted to denote the two highest grades in the Administrative or Political Department, and the term District Officer though strictly applicable only to the next two grades will be used in this Memorandum to include an Assistant District Officer.

General nature of Administrative Officer's duties. It is the duty of Residents to carry out loyally the policy of the Governor, and not to inaugurate policies of their own. The Governor, through the Lieutenant-Governor, is at all time ready and anxious to hear, and to give full and careful consideration to the views of Residents, but, when once a decision has been arrived at, he expects Residents to give effect to it in a thorough and loyal spirit, and to inculcate the same spirit in their juniors. This does not mean a rigid adherence to the letter of a ruling. Among such diverse races in widely varying degrees of advancement, it is inevitable and desirable that there should be diversity in the application of a general policy by the Resident, who knows the local conditions and feelings of his people. It does mean, however, that the principles underlying the policy are to be observed and the Resident in modifying their application will fully inform and obtain the approval of the Governor.

Festina lente ["Make haste slowly," *ed.*] is a motto very applicable to Africa, provided that the coach is not set on the wrong rail, so that a wrong course—temporarily easy—is inaugurated. By shirking initial difficulties and yielding to prejudice far greater difficulties must be encountered later. . . .

The Government relies on its Administrative Officers to keep in close touch with Native opinion and feeling, and to report for the information of the Governor. It is thus only that we can produce the best results, —that the Governor and Lieutenant-Governors can keep in touch and gain information, and the Political Officer can count on support and on recognition of his work.

Difference of method in advanced or backward Communities:— (a) *Advanced tribes.* The degree to which a Political Officer may be called upon to act in an administrative capacity, will thus depend upon the influence and ability of the Native Chiefs in each part of the Province, though in every case he will endeavour to rule through the Native Chiefs.

In those parts of Provinces which are under the immediate authority of a Chief of the first or of the second grade, the primary duty and object of a Political Officer will be to educate them in the duties of Rulers according to a civilised standard; to convince them that oppression of the people is not sound policy, or to the eventual benefit of the rulers; to bring home to their intelligence, as far as may be, the evils attendant on a system which holds the lower classes in a state of slavery or serfdom, and so destroys individual responsibility, ambition, and development amongst them; to impress upon them the advantage of delegating the control of districts to subordinate Chiefs, and of trusting and encouraging these subordinates, while keeping a strict supervision over them; to see that there is no favouritism in such appointments; and to inculcate the unspeakable benefit of justice, free from bribery and open to all.

Where taxation exists the consequent duty of assessing all the towns and villages himself will throw upon the Political Officer a considerable amount of purely Administrative work, even in such districts. In this work he should invite the co-operation of the Chief, and endeavour to enlist his cordial assistance by making it clear to him that his own interests are deeply involved.

(b) *Backward tribes.* In districts where there is no Chief of the first or second grade, a Political Officer's functions become more largely Administrative, and among uncivilised Pagan tribes he must assume the full onus of Administration, to the extent to which time and opportunity permit. In such communities he will constantly endeavour to support the authority of the Chief, and encourage him to show initiative. If there is no Chief who exercises authority beyond his own village, he will encourage any village Chief of influence and character to control a group of villages, with a view to making him Chief of a district later if he shows ability for the charge. Native Court clerks or scribes, constables or couriers will never be allowed to usurp the authority of the Native Chief or Village Head. . . .

Position and duties of Resident in charge. The Resident is the senior Government Official in the Province, and represents the Lieutenant-Governor in all Administrative matters. In the absence of a responsible officer of any Department it is his duty to report any dereliction of duty on the part of any departmental subordinate to the Head of his Department, or if of a serious nature to the Lieutenant-Governor. All such officers will be guided by the instructions and wishes of the Resident, so far as they are not incompatible with the orders they have received from the head of their department, to whom they will report the matter if the Resident's instructions conflict with departmental orders. The Head of a Department issues his instructions direct to his subordinate officer, and it is the duty of the subordinate to keep the Resident fully informed of any orders he receives which it may be useful for him to know, as, for instance, a Public Works Department Officer who had received orders to commence the repair of houses, &c. If the subordinate is a Native clerk the District

Officer will be regarded as the local representative, and communications from the Head of the Department will be addressed to him. . . .

The first and most essential duties of a Resident and his staff are those in connection with the conduct of Native Administration, including the close supervision of the Native Courts and the assessment for taxation. This work is sufficiently onerous, and it cannot be adequately performed if a Resident is charged in addition with work and correspondence of a general administrative nature. As the senior representative of Government in his province, he cannot be entirely relieved of all general administrative duties, but in the scheme of administration in Nigeria for which I am responsible, it has been my endeavour to relieve him of them as far as possible (*a*) by the creation of Lieutenant-Governors with an adequate Secretariat to undertake it, and (*b*) by the appointment of Station Magistrates charged with the Police Court work at large centres, and with the conduct of non-political questions and correspondence.

Junior Staff. Residents will spare no efforts to instruct young Officers posted to their Staff, and will see that all are familiar with the Ordinances, Regulations, General Orders, and Political Memos. These constitute the "laws and usages" of the Protectorate, which all Political Officers are bound by their oath to enforce impartially. District Officers in charge of Divisions will send full reports to the Resident, from which he will extract any information useful for his half-yearly and Annual Report to the Lieutenant-Governor, to whom he will forward all assessment reports and any particular report, or quote paragraphs from it, if of particular interest, so as to afford the Lieutenant-Governor an opportunity of gauging the abilities of Junior Officers. Assistant District Officers will submit their reports to or through their Divisional Officer, as the Resident may direct. Junior Officers will not be employed at Headquarters on clerical or accounting work which the Native Staff is capable of performing. District Officers will reside at the administrative centre of the division to which they are posted, and not at the Capital of the Province. Whenever there are any Assistant District Officers in excess of the establishment, they will be temporarily posted to the Secretariat for six months' training.

Necessity for constant travelling. Political Officers must endeavour to preserve a proper equilibrium between their Judicial and Executive duties, neither allowing the former to engross all their time and to detain them at their Headquarters, nor becoming so absorbed in assessment, and other executive work, as to neglect Judicial duties and leave cases to the Native Courts which would be more advisedly tried by the Provincial Court.

"The work done by a Political Officer," said Sir H. Lawrence, "in his district, surrounded by the people, is greatly superior to the work done in office surrounded by untrustworthy officials." A District Officer should pass from place to place and endeavour to lessen oppression and bribery, and to watch over and improve the Native tribunals. He should when possible be accompanied by the local Chief or district Head. He will of course at the same time hold his Court wherever he may be, and take opportunity to do so in a formal manner in the principal towns.

The primary object of travelling through the Province is, that the Political Officer may show himself to the people and hear their complaints at first hand, not trusting to the reports which reach him at Headquarters, where the villagers may possibly often fear to carry complaints, especially if they refer to some petty oppression or illegal exaction by the Chiefs. It is only by the advent of a British Officer that scoundrels, misrepresenting the Government action, or extorting what they will from the Natives in the name of Government, can be caught; for the villagers in their ignorance, supposing them to be genuine, dare not as a rule complain.

It has been abundantly shown by experience that "unrest," resulting in murders and outrages, and eventually necessitating the use of force, inevitably take place among primitive tribes when *districts are not regularly* and systematically *visited.* By frequent touring, abuses are redressed before they become formidable, the law-abiding people are encouraged to restrain the turbulent and lawless elements, and trust and confidence in Government is fostered.

In Provinces where there is direct taxation, officials should be constantly passing from place to place, for the purpose of carrying out the assessment of every village. . . . or verifying and revising the initial assessment. But whether there is direct taxation or not, it is equally the duty of a Political Officer to travel constantly, in order to record, or to add to the statistics required for the Provincial Records; to verify or fix the areas of jurisdiction of each District Headman and Chief, or Native Court; and to become personally acquainted with the various peoples in his district. These duties are of primary importance in the early stage of administration and organisation. . . .

Travelling, it must be remembered, costs money for transport, and is not undertaken for pleasure. Each journey, therefore, should achieve some definite and useful result. . . .

A Veterinary or Forestry Officer, or Public Works Department Officer, inspecting roads and buildings, and any other departmental officer who has occasion to travel in a Province should seize the opportunity of accompanying a Political Officer on tour. It is not, however, essential that a departmental officer should be accompanied by a Political Officer, since such a course would frequently result in mutual delay, but he would generally be accompanied by one of the native political staff to facilitate his work.

Languages. All Officers of the Political Staff are required to pass an examination in the Ordinances and Regulations of Nigeria, in the General Orders, and in one of the chief Native languages of Nigeria. Proficiency in a Native language is an important qualification for promotion. Promotion will ordinarily be provisional only unless an officer has passed, and he will be liable to revert if he does not do so within the period prescribed. Assistant District Officers must pass the Lower Standard to qualify for promotion, and a Resident should have passed the Higher Standard, especially if the language he has adopted is Hausa.

Continuity essential in Africa. I regard continuity of Administration as a matter of paramount and indeed of vital importance in African Administration. It is only after many years of personal contact that the African—naturally reserved and suspicious towards strangers—will give his confidence unreservedly. More can often be accomplished in half-an-hour by an officer well known and trusted by the people, than by another, though his superior in ability, after months of patient effort.

It has, therefore, been my general rule, that the more senior an officer becomes the less liable he is for transfer from his Province. An Assistant District Officer may be posted to two or three Provinces in succession, in order that he may gain experience, and the Lieutenant-Governor may decide whether his abilities are best adapted for work in an advanced, or a backward Province. As a Second Class District Officer he has become more of a fixture, and finally when he becomes Resident in substantive charge of a Province he is never taken away from it.

These rules are of course liable to violation owing to sudden vacancies, &c., more especially of late under war conditions, but though a Senior Officer may be removed for a time he will be restored to the Province he knows and to the people who know and trust him as soon as circumstances permit. Now that there is a single Administrative roster for all Nigeria, a Southern Provinces Officer may find himself posted on promotion to the Northern Provinces and *vice versa*. But here again the change will not as a rule be permanent, especially amongst the Senior Officers, and I should endeavour to restore an Officer to the people whose language he has learnt, and among whom he can do more efficient work, as soon as an exchange could be effected. Residents in like manner will avoid changing their Staff from one division to another if it can be helped.

Relations of Departmental Officers with Resident and Native Administration. The Political Officer is the channel of communication between all Departmental Officers and the Native Administration. It is essential that a Resident shall be fully informed of any project which a Departmental Officer proposes to inaugurate, and he will inform the Emir and enlist his assistance. If after consulting the Emir he considers that the project—or the manner in which it is proposed to carry it out—is inadvisable he will refer to the Lieutenant-Governor, and it will be held in abeyance until a reply is received. The general scope of the work having thus been discussed and approved, the Departmental Officer is at liberty to give orders as to details, but if he desires to introduce any new principle he will again consult the Resident. If the work is to be carried out at some distance from the Capital, a responsible Native official will usually be attached to the Departmental Officer, through whom he can make his requisitions for labour, &c., and issue his instructions. If the matter is urgent, and the Departmental Officer finds it necessary to issue instructions without delay, he will fully inform the Resident, in order that he in turn may inform the Native Administration.

While these instructions are of especial importance where the expenditure of Native Administration funds is involved, the general principle will also be observed in the execution of duties or works which are paid for from departmental votes. In the former case the Native Administration has the right to determine the priority in which different works shall be carried out, and the method, subject to any technical objections. Thus, if with the approval of the Governor the Native Administration provides funds for the construction of several different sections of roads, the construction of which is placed in the hands of the Public Works Department, it is admissible that the Native Administration should decide which road should take priority, and if it is itself capable of carrying out the earthworks, it may request the Public Works Department to deal with the alignment, bridges, and culverts, and only to exercise a general supervision over the remainder. Since, however, the road may eventually become a metalled motor track under the Public Works Department charge, it is clear that the construction must be in accordance with technical instructions. On the other hand a Departmental Officer carrying out Government work from Departmental votes—such as the repair of telegraphs—will look to the District Officer to assist him in procuring the necessary labour and supplies, usually, as I have said, through the medium of an official of the Native Administration. Departmental Officers must bear in mind that, in order to obtain the full benefit of Native co-operation, the orders must be given not by the Resident or any of his Staff, but by the Head Chief. . . .

Where the duties of a Departmental Officer are educational, *e.g.*, Medical and Sanitary, Forestry, Agriculture, and Veterinary—and he is engaged on a tour of instruction, it is desirable that he should inform the Resident of the nature of the advice he proposes to give, especially if it involves a specific course of action, in order that the Resident may instruct his Staff and the Native Administration to co-operate, and also in order that there may be no conflict of instructions. I recollect an instance in which two Departmental Officers, visiting the same town within a short time of each other, each with a different object in view gave diametrically opposite instructions on a specific point to the local Chief. In such a case the Resident would have been able to discuss the matter with both and to arrive at a clear course of action. Political Officers are, moreover, able to put a Departmental Officer in possession of local conditions and prejudices, and so to assist him in his objects. . . .

Judicial functions. The Resident in charge of a Province has *ex-officio* full powers as Judge of the Provincial Court of the Province, of which his European Staff are "Commissioners." The Judicial powers of a Commissioner may be increased at the discretion of the Lieutenant-Governor, irrespective of his rank, on the recommendation of the Resident and of the Legal Adviser, in accordance with the ability he shows in his judicial work. Evidence of judicial ability will necessarily count much in selection for promotion. . . .

Native Courts. A Resident will establish a Native Court in every city or district where it appears advisable to do so, and will constantly supervise its work, especially in the lower grades of Courts. He must of course carefully study the Native Courts Ordinance and Memo. 8. In

Courts of Grades A and B he will watch the integrity of the Native Judges, and note their comparative ability for promotion to more important centres, and see that their sentences are in accord with British conceptions of humanity. In the lower grades he will take care that the initiative of the Chiefs who compose the Court is not interfered with by the clerk or scribe, that they do not exceed their powers, and that their sentences and findings are free from bias.

The "Province," "Division," and "District." A Province is a single entity under the control of the Resident in charge. It is divided into "Divisions" under District Officers responsible to the Resident. The Divisions must not be confused with the "districts" under Native Headmen. The more important divisions will be under first-class, and the less important under second-class District Officers. The charge of a first or second-class division is an appointment notified in the Gazette, which forms the Treasurer's authority to disburse the duty pay which attaches to it.

The division in which the Headquarters of the Province is situated will usually be in charge of a District Officer, like any other division, so far as its routine work is concerned, but it is, I think, of great importance that in the more advanced Provinces the paramount Chief should deal direct with the Resident, and he is apt to feel slighted if referred to a subordinate Officer. He should not only have free access to the Resident at all times, but should not be debarred from consulting him in any matter, even of detail, regarding the "Emirate Division" even though the matter may eventually and properly be dealt with by the District Officer. In Provinces where there is no paramount Chief and only an embryonic Native Administration, the Resident will generally be able to take charge of the Headquarter division himself with the assistance of a District Officer who can take his place when on tour.

The number of divisions in a Province is subject to the approval of the Governor, and they will be notified in the Gazette, but their boundaries may at any time be altered by the Lieutenant-Governor subject to the stipulations in this paragraph. One or more Assistant District Officers will be attached to each division, either generally or to a particular district, as the Resident may decide. Each Divisional Officer will tour constantly in his division hearing complaints, recording statistics, inspecting Native Courts, checking native agents, surveying, and assessing, and supervising the collection of taxes where these are imposed. He will reside near the principal town of the division, and each division in turn will be visited by the Resident. The Divisional Headquarters (involving the erection of new buildings, as well as political considerations) will not be transferred to another place without the prior concurrence of the Governor. The Resident himself will reside at the Provincial capital, which will also usually be the Headquarters of the Military detachment (if any) and of the Medical and Police Officers. Wherever he wishes to go on tour the District Officer in charge of the Headquarter division will deal with any urgent correspondence addressed to him or any urgent matter as may be directed by the Resident, unless the "relief Resident" is present. . . .

A Province, or even a Division, may comprise various units of Native Administration, but in no case will such a unit be comprised partly in one Province and partly in another; and the same applies as a rule to a Division. The limits of the jurisdiction and authority of Native Chiefs may not be altered, or one Emirate or Chieftainship placed under another, without the sanction of the Lieutenant-Governor, who will in any case of importance consult the Governor. Such reference is necessary when it is proposed to subordinate a Chief hitherto independent, and more especially an independent Pagan Community to a Moslem Emirate—which should very rarely, if ever, be done.

Departmental functions of Political Officers. A Political Officer has to represent various Departments and to exercise divers functions in the Province to which he belongs. He acts as *Postal Officer,* in the absence of an European Officer of the Department, and is responsible for the despatch of mails in transit, and for the various duties laid down in the Regulations under the Postal Ordinance. The Postal and Telegraph Clerks, under his general supervision, will undertake the duties of issuing stamps, and preparing receipts for parcels and registered letters, &c.

The *Police* in his Province are under the general orders of the Resident, whose relation to them and to the Commissioner or Assistant Commissioner of Police is laid down in Police Regulations and in General Orders and elsewhere. Isolated Police Constables should never be stationed in villages since it deprives the Village Headman of responsibility and initiative; and men placed in such a position of power are apt to misuse their authority. Detachments without a European are always to be deprecated. When in charge of the Government prison, the District Officer will inspect it frequently and check the prisoners with the warrants at least once a month.

Political Officers will also assist the *Customs* on those inland frontiers where it is not possible for the Department to have an European representative, and also in the collection of Customs dues on Postal parcels; and in such capacity they exercise the powers of Customs Officers, and any preventive staff is under their orders. . . .

Crocker: Indirect Rule: An Elaborate Façade

Nigeria, more particularly Northern Nigeria, enjoys considerable fame in connection with what is called Indirect Rule, or, as the latest refinement has it, Indirect Administration. A large and somewhat intricate exegesis has grown up around what in origin and in content is quite a simple matter.

What happened was this: In 1900

From W. R. Crocker, *Nigeria: A Critique of British Colonial Administration* (London: George Allen and Unwin, Ltd., 1936), pp. 213–22.

Sir Frederick Lugard (as he then was) was appointed High Commissioner of Northern Nigeria, a country he was to pacify and bring under British control. Control was established by 1903. Sir Frederick found that he was called upon to govern a population of many millions (though, as it turned out, not as many millions as was estimated at the time) scattered over an area nearly twice the size of the United Kingdom. He had to improvise an administrative personnel and there were no hopes of getting out officers to the number required for governing the new conquest directly. Further, most of the country was already under the control of the Fulani Emirates which were there as a going concern and which impressed Sir Frederick by the quality of their administrative machinery and administrative ability. He did the obvious, indeed the inevitable, thing: he left the Emirates to continue in being, subject only to certain broad limitations. That was all there was to it. Sir Frederick was not the first Colonial Governor to resort to such an expedient. British rule in India can provide examples from as far back as the eighteenth century; the French were already doing the same thing in parts of their East Indian Empire; and the Dutch were embarked upon it in the Dutch East Indies; though Lugard showed his administrative genius in the technique and the details he worked out for running the system.

On this expedient was gradually built up an imposing superstructure of ideology. It is only fair to say that it was early observed that an ideal might be extracted from or be associated with the expedient, and, further, that the ideal itself was a good one. The ideal, briefly expressed, was that it is a good thing for primitive man to evolve along his own lines instead of being made to follow the lines of an alien culture. But it is also fair to emphasize that in actual origin, as also in actual practice, the system of utilizing chiefdoms already in existence as going concerns for governing a subject people, and the ideal of the autonomous non-alien evolution of that people, are two separate things and have no necessary connection. It was another of Lord Lugard's merits that he managed to join an ideal to the expedient.

Lugard left Nigeria on his retirement from the Colonial Service in 1919. In 1923 *The Dual Mandate in Tropical Africa* was published, a book that for its effect on the minds of those interested in colonial policy can be compared only with such a work as Durham's Report on Canada of a century earlier or Burke's speeches on the Warren Hastings trial. Any book written on his craft in the reflective evening of his life by a man of such epic experience of the Empire, of such singleness, integrity, and dignity of character, and of an outlook and a background so much wider than that of the usual Imperial functionary, was bound to contain much of very great value. To praise it would be an impertinence. There is nothing else quite like it in all the literature of British imperialism. Further experience has suggested, and no doubt will continue to suggest, modifications here and there, and as an expression of the adventurousness and gallantry of the author's life the present writer prefers Lord Lugard's *Rise of Our East African Empire* (a book in the authentic line of descent of the classics of the English explorers and pioneers); but the essential substance of the *Dual Mandate* is beyond question.

The *Dual Mandate* owed its immediate reception to the fact that it was the first reasoned case for our "dependent" Empire, and that it gave a moral basis to that case. Africa, so the argument ran, could not be left shut up merely for the benefit of the African; the outside world also had an interest in and a claim to share its great and special kind of wealth, but the outside world, in exercising its legitimate claim, must heed the legitimate interests of the African and must therefore comport itself as his trustee. Obligations, like interests, were dual. And as an example of how the outside world should exercise its trusteeship, details were set out of the system of administration that had been built up in Northern Nigeria, which was described as Indirect Rule. The book came at an opportune time. Not only was the administration of all the non-Indian part of the "dependent" Empire a closed book at that day so that authoritative information was sought for its own sake, but the British conscience was becoming more and more sensitive about the Empire. *The Dual Mandate* was a comforting as well as a highly informative book.

Lord Lugard's fame and the success of his book put Nigeria on the map, and the men who had been officers in the Service there from the early days now saw themselves as the makers of history. They were then in the saddle and were not slow to appreciate their old merits or their new opportunities. The simple and healthy linking on of an ideal to an expedient was elaborated into an occult science. Indirect Rule became a formula as hieratic and as dead of creative development as an outworn theology. In fact a theocratic oligarchy closed the canon, refusing any addition to their scriptures, "the interpretation of which was their own monopoly"; and Indirect Rule degenerated firstly into a systematic glorification of a number of able but unscrupulous careerists, secondly into the practice of preserving at all costs the status and power of the families of the hereditary Emirs and chiefs, and thirdly into an undue preoccupation with Islam and the Emirates to the neglect of the Pagan peoples. From time to time a Lieutenant-Governor (until 1931 the Lieutenant-Governors of the Northern Provinces were little interfered with by Lagos, being *de facto* Governors of Northern Nigeria) would speak *ex cathedra,* his utterance being transmitted within sealed confidential envelopes to the administrative personnel, thus giving birth to a corpus of *hadiths.* The principle of Indirect Rule, indeed, was saved from being openly discredited only because most of the simple elementary government required there, notably away from the various headquarters, went on without overdue attention to the externals of the principle and because the Land Policy (dating from Lugard's time),[1] and the impossibility of European settlement being undertaken in such climate, had preserved the economic independence of the people. It is not possible to put one's finger on a single contribution or new idea or new development in the administration of the policy of Indirect Rule in Nigeria since Lugard's time. Numerous innovations

[1] Broadly speaking, land cannot be alienated in Nigeria: it is owned by the Government in trust for the natives.

there have been; but they either were of trifles (though always loudly advertised trifles) or of sheer perversions. Lord Lugard's own sense of loyalty would probably force him to deny this strongly, but nevertheless the verdict of the future historian, no doubt, will be that Lugard was not well served by his successors (most of whom were his promoted subordinates).

It is not easy to make clear to men outside the Service to what a size and to what a pitch of absurdity this bubble had been blown. As a reference for the future student one might direct him to consult the instructions and circulars issued to officers, especially those from Kaduna, and especially those issued between 1926 and 1930. Indirect Rule and its originators (then construed to be the same as the men at the top in Northern Nigeria at that day) was praised with ecstatic fervour. It was also made clear that the mystery was so profound that it was practically beyond the understanding of junior officers, not to mention persons outside the Service, and, excepting an odd man here and there of quite unusual ability and of at least twelve years' seniority, it could never really be understood by those who had not been in the Service in the pre-war years when the principle was being worked out. It was freely admitted that this was a disturbing situation, but if only junior officers would appreciate their advantage and follow unswervingly the directions of their seniors, the worst might yet be avoided. Very awkward cases sometimes arose. For example, when Cadets and quite junior A.D.O.s asked how are you going to develop these Emirates, which you have turned into medieval monarchies, into modern states, or communities? or how can most tribal societies by developing along their own lines grow into a society equal to modern life? Such men were quickly marked down as temperamentally unsuited for life in Nigeria. No more damning remark could be made in the annual secret report on an officer than that he was "direct" or not sufficiently imbued with the spirit of Indirect Rule.

A deplorable feature of this perverted form of Indirect Rule was its pretence. Officers were continuously exhorted to be "indirect" in this highly formal sense, when not only did they see that occasions in the interests of justice often called for "direct" activity, but they saw daily the very men exacting this standard of "indirectness" from them acting (and generally rightly acting) in the most "direct" way.

Another regrettable feature was the manner in which the system worked to bolster up effete and corrupt chiefs at the expense of their people. As late as 1932, thirty years after our subjugation of the country, it was found amongst the Gwari chiefdoms that forcible seizure of girls for the harims of chiefs (Kuta and Guni), continuous and heavy exactions of both goods and money from the commoners, embezzlement of tax, arbitrary imprisonment and other persecutions, forced labour on a scale whereby in some cases half the able-bodied male population were conscripted to work in construction camps for the benefit of the chief and against the will of the conscripted, and possibly even "palace" murders, were the order in some of the Gwari chiefdoms. Some of these things, as at Kuta, had been going on, unbeknown to the D.O.s, for nine years, at a distance of only a few hundred yards from the Divisional Headquarters.

At about the same time serious scandals were brought to light in the Bida Emirate, and a year or so previously they were brought to light in the Sultanate of Sokoto. The tenacity shown by those in power in Northern Nigeria in refusing to remove higher chiefs was remarkable. It required spectacular criminality to induce Kaduna to move against them, to such a degree had Indirect Rule been perverted into a policy for conserving these petty autocracies, the argument running that a native would sooner suffer injustice from a native authority than justice from an alien.

The cardinal weakness of Indirect Rule as practised in Nigeria after Lugard's departure has been the tendency to build up autocracies and to ignore the villages. Perhaps the author may be permitted to quote here what he had occasion to write towards the end of 1931: "Indirect Rule will become a mischievous policy unless steps are taken within the next few years to build up a strong village administration. All that is good in native rule and economics and culture is from and in the villages. This bolstering up of chiefs (who now enjoy a security that was unknown before our coming) can be safe only if a 'democracy,' or some such equivalent to an effective restraining public opinion, can be built up in the villages. A concentrated drive in this direction is (as I see it) the first need in native policy here to-day." It is only fair to recognize that it was not merely natural, but also to some extent unavoidable, that the Government during the first decade or so of our occupation should concentrate on the various native *central* governments; but that excuse had long disappeared.

Perhaps the best, certainly a surprising, example of the mentality of those then in charge was the proposal to make Europeans resident in Northern Nigeria subject to Native Courts. It is hard to believe that men in their sanity and knowing in their day-to-day work the exact nature of the Native Courts, their efficiency, reliability, and so on, could have gone so far as to put such a measure down in a Bill. Yet that is what happened. We have the succeeding Governor's testimony for it, the more impressive because he was obliged to state his justifiable amazement in "Parliamentary language." Speaking in the Legislative Council in February 1933, he said, ". . . I have not proceeded with the proposal incorporated in a Bill which was discussed in this Council in February 1931 . . . to subject all persons automatically to the jurisdiction of the native authority within whose area they might happen to find themselves. . . . I confess that I have never been able to understand the provisions of the Bill. . . . It is difficult to believe that it was intended that the Administrative Officers, for instance, should in fact be subjected to the jurisdiction of the native authorities, even in the organized Emirates, and if this was the case (as almost certainly it was) then we reach again the realm of pretence in administration of which I am so, unashamedly, afraid. Moreover, some of the native authorities are of the most primitive, almost nebulous, character."

The new Governor arrived in Nigeria in the second half of 1931. As his immediate task was to deal with a deficit it was some time before his ideas on native policy were made known. A Governor controls the fountain of promotion, however, and can therefore make his ideas felt very swiftly. His Excellency indicated some animosity to the old Northern Nigerian régime, inveighing against the semi-monarchism that had been allowed to grow up in the Emirates and against the neglect of the Pagans. He circulated a thesis of his to the effect that the traditional basis of native institutions was not autocratic but conciliar, and that what was needed in Nigeria (amongst other reforms) was a search for the particular form of conciliar basis suited to this or that tribe or group, and then a reorganization of the native authority in accordance therewith. This worked like magic. The beliefs of years were jettisoned and a spate of anthropological reports flowed in from all parts of the country (the springs of which had shown no signs of drying up towards the end of 1934) proving, with an impressive unanimity, that the traditional basis of the tribal institutions investigated was, in fact, as His Excellency suggested, conciliar; and the neglect of the Pagans under previous régimes did not go unnoticed. So good were they that His Excellency himself had occasion to commend the reports, especially those from South-East Nigeria; and he sent one report, by a certain Resident, accompanied by a memorandum from another official, to the Secretary of State, as being probably the most important that had been issued officially for a long number of years in the Northern Provinces.

The two documents referred to have an interest additional to their immediate subject matter because one of them showed a conversion, following more than twenty years' experience of the country and its administration, the extent of which can be measured by a document from the same hand only five years previously, when the pro-Emirate régime was at its height and the mode of interpreting and practising Indirect Rule was just that which the later Governor was reacting against.

At that time the writer of the document referred to was Resident of a certain Province, and, as was then the fashion, produced a circular on Indirect Rule for his staff and then trasmitted a copy of it to the Lieutenant-Governor of the day. The Lieutenant-Governor, who was described in it as one of the founders of Indirect Rule and received much subtle praise, had it printed and circulated to all the Administrative staff; indeed, until the later Governor came, copies of it used to be given to Cadets on their first entry into Northern Nigeria as the official statement of Indirect Rule!

The present author, who received such a copy on entering the Service, and later, with the passage of time and its turn in the wheel of fortune, received a copy of the two documents referred to above, applied to the Colonial Office for permission to publish extracts from them in his study of Indirect Rule; permission, however, was refused. It is regretted that several amusing and instructive essays must therefore continue to blush unseen. By taking sentence by sentence and comparing them one with another, and then with the very important policy speech made by the Governor to the Legislative

Council in March 1933, it is possible not only to show the doctrine of Indirect Rule as a somewhat varying quantity, both as regards its substance and as regards the interpretation of its history, according to what happens to be the school of thought of the Governor of the day (who is also, it must be repeated, the controller of the fountain of promotion), but also to throw an essential light on the morale and tone of the upper rungs of the Service.

Hence, not unintelligibly, though regrettably (for no other system can take its place), there has grown up a reaction against Indirect Rule, both within the Service and outside it. Years of observing a practice which departs and must depart widely from the theory, which theory nevertheless is extravagantly belauded and its more or less unimportant externals insisted upon, breed a disquieting kind of cynicism which shrugs its shoulders and asks, "What else can you expect? . . . *c'est la vie* . . . and see how it brings or fails to bring promotion." Here is some of the "pretence" to which a Governor himself has made reference.

As for the outside critics, odd ones, like Mr. Murray, had ventured to demur to the claims of Indirect Rule at an earlier date, but the incident which mobilized an impressive volume of criticism was Tshekedi's case. Tshekedi, it will be recalled, was the acting Chief in Bechuanaland, who, in 1933, had a white criminal flogged, and whom Vice-Admiral Evans, temporarily officiating as High Commissioner of the South African Protectorates, then arrested, following a descent into Bechuanaland with howitzers and two hundred marines. The subsequent correspondence in the Press, which included letters from ex-Colonial officials, showed that there was a body of opinion that more than demurred to, indeed that was actively hostile to, Indirect Rule.

The Tshekedi case, nevertheless, is not really relevant to the question of Indirect Rule because the conditions it brought to light were the product not of Indirect Rule, but of no rule.

In any case the principle of Indirect Rule is not in danger. It rests not on immutable laws but on immutable poverty. No other system of administration which would conform to the standards required by England can be afforded in British Africa. The impossibility of directly ruling millions of Africans makes a temporary delegation of power to native authority inevitable; thus in Kano over two million are ruled by nine Europeans. This, in general, and if adequate supervision be forthcoming, need be no bad thing. In general, indeed, it is a good thing. But it is not the most important aspect of government. Land tenure; weight of taxation; the presence or absence of a compulsion to work for the white man; education; in short, the question of the economic independence of the African is much more important than what particular administrative machinery is used for carrying out the will of the Suzerain. For, let it not be forgotten, the Suzerain does not and cannot abdicate its will, and clashes are frequent and are bound to be frequent between that will and the desires of the native authority.

That then, in origin, as in present substance, is what Indirect Rule is. Whether a series of quasi-autonomous and quasi-autocratic states of paramount Chiefs, as in Nigeria, can evolve into a single Central Government or into non-autocratic or non-oligarchic communities is for the future; for the present the question is not of any great consequence. It is enough that they now work, and work with commendable efficiency (on the whole), and that, through financial necessity, for the time being they are secure. As for the ideology that has become associated with the expedient, that is a different matter. In so far as it is practicable, and excepting certain tribes where the customs are not worth preserving or are incapable of development (the responsibility for the decision is our own), it is, to my judgment, of the utmost importance to enable the African to develop along his own lines and to develop naturally as an African instead of artificially as a pseudo-European. It is of importance, but for much, perhaps for most, of Africa, unfortunately, it is impossible. The game even now is nearly lost. Education—even the bare literacy, and its results, given by the elementary schools—and the effect of the missionaries' evangelization and of the adoption of English law and of modern commerce are new wine which the old bottles of African culture cannot always hold. The most, probably, that can be made of Indirect Rule will be to develop African self-government in local areas (which, of course, is no small thing), and to do that means concentrating more and more on the villages. The great merit of Sir Donald Cameron is that he has sought this widening of the policy. It is still not too late in Africa to avoid some errors of our Indian venture. As for the rest of the elaborate façade of Indirect Rule, it is much ado about nothing—cardboard and plaster packed up by the careerists.

Fitzpatrick: Nigeria's Curse—Indirect Rule

On October 1st the Emir of Katsina, accompanied by two of his wives and one of his sons, and attended by a suite of four or five persons, sailed from Liverpool on his return to the Northern Provinces of Nigeria, wherein his Emirate lies. The party had come to England on a joy ride, to see the Wembley Exhibition, and had spent eighteen days in this country. According to the Press, the Emir returned with a good deal in the way of purchases. His journey from Liverpool to Lagos per mail steamer will take sixteen days, then there is a rail journey of, say, eight hundred miles to Kano, and then one hundred miles by motor before he gets back to Katsina. The cost of the double journey for nine or ten people cannot have been much less than £1,000.

That is one thing to note.

The second thing to note is this, that in the autumn of last year, at

From J. F. J. Fitzpatrick, "Nigeria's Curse—The Native Administration," *The National Review,* LXXXIV, No. 502 (1924), 617–24.

Maidugari, in the Northern Provinces of Nigeria, the native troops so far forgot their duty that the European officer commanding them had to inform the Political Officer in charge of the area that he could not guarantee the safety of the Europeans (possibly a score, including at least one lady) in it.

The disaffection of the troops was due to anti-British propaganda conducted from Egypt.

There is no reason to believe that the propaganda has been abandoned, nor that it is likely to do aught else than increase in volume and in intensity: but there is every reason to believe that what it has achieved to date is merely a beginning.

The Northern Provinces of Nigeria cover a quarter of a million square miles, and contain ten millions of people. The area is administered by the Government of Nigeria, with headquarters at Lagos, on the Coast. The system of rule is called "Indirect." This means that there are two administrations working side by side—the British and the Native. The former consists as to personnel of European Political Officers and the latter of local "big men," such as the Emir of Katsina. (The title "Emir," by the way, was introduced by the British. Nigerians themselves call such people "Sarki" or "Lamido.")

There are Government Courts side by side with Native Administration Courts, Government Police and Native Administration Police, Government Treasury and Native Administration Treasuries, and so on: practically all the departments are duplicated. But whereas the personnel of the Government staff is available for duty anywhere in the area, and is, in practice, pretty constantly on the move, the Native Administration people stick in their own bit of it. There are forty or more of these Native Administrations, all organized on the same plan, each with its own Treasury, Police, Gaols, Courts, and so forth. A European Political Officer is supposed to supervise and advise and generally direct each one of them.

Funds for their maintenance are provided out of the local revenue. Of the total land tax collected they take 50 per cent. Of the cattle tax they also take half. And they take the whole of the Native Court earnings, fines, and fees, and the market dues.

In each Native Administration the local principal chief, be he called Emir or by some other title, is the head. There is a large and growing personnel, and the Emir has of course an immense amount of patronage. The whole of the staff, from judge to assistant bricklayer, depend upon him. He appoints them, fixes their emolument, dismisses or promotes them.

All that by way of introduction. Now let us see how the system works in practice.

Polygamy is universal throughout the Northern Provinces, and an Emir's job is not an hereditary one. Before the British took over the country an Emir was an Emir just so long as his hands could guard his head. The system was one of autocracy, tempered by assassination. A strong, capable, intriguing man who could get a following and keep it could become an Emir, whatever his birth. The British, on their arrival, retained and supported in power those Emirs who went over to them, and the others they disposed of.

Vacancies occurring since have been filled by men appointed by the Nigerian Government. The tempering by assassination has been abolished, the autocracy, tyranny, remain, reinforced. The Emirs to-day are maintained by British bayonets, so that there are men holding these positions at this time who would not last a week once the bayonets were to cease.

An Emir's job is well paid: anything up to £5,000 a year is the salary, and the salary in no case represents the measure of his gettings: there are estates and amenities and pickings that go with the job and the salary.

The first thing an Emir does on being appointed is to make secure his tenure of the post. To this end as many as possible of his relations and friends are put upon the pay roll. Such men are, of course, his sworn supporters, and their number is augmented by other men who hope to get on to the salary list. The effect is that the population falls necessarily into two classes—those who draw salaries and those who pay taxes. The interests of these classes are diametrically opposed.

The men on the pay roll number a good many. Besides the Emir himself there are: Emir's secretarial staff, treasurer and staff, judges and Court officials, police, prisons staff, district headmen, village headmen, road and bridge making staff, medical staff, messengers, markets staff. Quite a number of poor relations can be accommodated, and year by year these staffs are increasing in size, and the expenditure upon them is growing correspondingly.

In many cases the persons who draw the salaries are quite innocent of any knowledge of the duties they are supposed, and paid, to perform. I remember a Road Inspection Staff, the head of which was a son of the local Emir. Neither he nor any of his colleagues knew anything about the work, didn't even go through the form of going to look at it. Another case, in another Emirate, was that of the Chief of the Road Construction Staff, a relative of the Emir's, who did not even know how to set out a straight line with the help of three poles. There was a vaccination expert who averaged, he said, three vaccinations per month, in an area containing a quarter of a million people amongst whom small-pox was endemic. In Kano Province a couple of hundred or more men were working in a Government station. The junior European officer in charge formed the opinion that they were not getting any pay, though money was being paid to the Native Administration on this account. So one day he paid them himself, a couple of shillings apiece, and they went away. Less than a mile down the road they were intercepted by a Native Administration official who collected from them the coins they had received. And so on. Additional to being forced to go on to the works, which many of the men, most of them, are willing to pay money to be excused—they have their own affairs to attend to—the poor wretches are swindled out of the miserable pay that is provided for them and is rightly theirs.

On the one side there is the Native Administration, for ever, like the daughters of the horse leech, crying for more, more, more—money. On the other there is the proletariat, with its taxes for ever being screwed up. Increase in revenue *may* arise from increased prosperity of the people: it may also follow upon more efficient tax assessment and collection.

Extortion of every sort is rife. Common forms of it are:

(*a*) Taxes being collected twice over.

(*b*) People who have been turned out *en masse* to clean a road, or to build houses, or to do some other sort of work, being either given no pay at all, or a derisory sum, although an adequate amount has been voted and actually paid by the Treasury for distribution to the workers.

(*c*) Provision, compulsory, by the people of entertainment for the Emir and his followers and his horses, or for his representatives, without any payment being made.

(*d*) Presents—"dashes"—to the Emir's wives and his relatives and his hangers-on, on demand, and of course with no *quid pro quo.*

(*e*) "Loans" to Native Administration personnel, of horses, stock, women, grain, money, etc.

Theoretically the *plebs,* thus unjustly treated, have their remedy. They can go to the Native Court. There they are not likely to resort more than once. The Native Court depends upon the Emir, and is not going to get itself into trouble in that quarter. Failing the Native Court, the grievance-wallah can go to the Political Officer, who will do the best he can for him. That is not much.

Take the case of Awudu, for instance. Awudu is a cultivator, lives in a village a few miles off the telegraph line. In January the grass and scrub are at their highest and driest, the danger of damage by bush fires is at its greatest, the land under the line must be cleared. The Political Officer informs the Emir that the clearing ought to be done, asks him to arrange for it to be done, hands him a sum of money with which to pay for the doing of it. The Emir's messengers ride forth, and friend Awudu and all the other Awudus along the line are turned out to do the work. In due course Awudu gets say threepence, which he is dissatisfied with as recompense for a week's work. He talks about it in his village, says he will go to the Political Officer. His words are reported to the Emir. Awudu, the first time the Political Officer tours in his direction, goes and lays his complaint. The Native Administration produce a list showing that Awudu for the work he did was paid three shillings on January 24th, at Womba. The Native Administration produce the man who made the payment, his colleague who wrote it down in the list at the time, the list itself, and the rest of the people from Awudu's village who worked with him, each of whom testifies that he himself received three shillings, and saw Awudu get the like. Now where does Awudu stand?

The Political Officer has no option but to dismiss the complaint, knowing well enough all the time what the facts are. Nobody is going to get across the Native Administration by telling the truth about Awudu and what he got. The Political Officer goes on his way, and presently, at most in twelve months, away to England on leave; possibly he never again returns to Awudu's neighbourhood. But the Native Administration has not done with Awudu. Always provided that he has not bolted to another country, leaving his house and his farm, he will presently find himself in the Native Court, charged, say, with stealing a sheep. The animal is found on his premises, three witnesses, or thirteen, come forward to say they saw him dragging the thing in there after dark, and the owner arrives, identifies the sheep, and Awudu as the man he saw hanging about his place just before he missed the creature. Awudu goes to gaol for six months, or two years, or five, and that's the end of Awudu. The Native Court knows exactly what it has to do with him, and when he gets to prison the warders also know just how to treat him.

In these circumstances it is not surprising that nowadays the Political Officer on tour gets no complaints against the Native Administration. The people know better than to complain. It was not always so. But yearly the Native Administration grows more and more powerful, and in this matter of extortion, more efficient. To-day, it is a veritable Old Man of the Sea, fastened upon the shoulders of the poor man, daily growing heavier, grinding him down, crushing him. It is the apotheosis of inexpugnable tyranny.

And the Political Officer is helpless. He knows what is going on, and he can do nothing. Nor is adverse comment on the functioning of the Native Administration welcomed by his superiors. The Native Administration suppresses evidence, supplies evidence, just as suits its purpose. No native with a halfpennyworth of *nous* will put himself in peril by opposing the will of the Emir. Even the "big men" crawl to the Emir; he can hurt more grievously, reward more handsomely than they can, and he can break them.

Nor is the Political Officer himself safe. His native staff are usually in *liaison* with the Emir: Political Officers come and go, but the Political Officer's native staff, and the Emir, and the Native Administration, these three are constants, and they stand together. An Emir, a Native Administration, can complain to Government of a Political Officer, in regard to money, or women, or some other matter, and whatever the facts, the Political Officer's defence can only, at the most, begin and end with a flat denial of what is alleged against him. He will get no witnesses to support his case.

I don't suppose it is appreciated in England that certain of the Native Courts exercise full judicial powers, can, that is to say, award a death sentence. Certainly it cannot be understood in England that a struggling man, ironed, was not very long ago in Sokoto dragged in the afternoon along a mile of road from the gaol, first to the Emir's house, thence to the market place, where he arrived all bloody and panting, and there, in the presence of the marketeers, was knelt down, and his head hacked off with a sword. The *disjecta membra* remained there on the ground in a pool of blood. The man was ripe for execution, may be, but that was not the way to execute him. Wherever there is a Native Court exercising full judicial powers the same sort of thing can happen.

Seventeen years in the Political Service in Nigeria, with personal experience covering the greater part of the Native Administration areas, have satisfied me that my indictment of the system is true in substance and in fact. Additional to my own personal knowledge I have the testimony of friends, colleagues, not one, nor two, but a score or more, all supporting what I say about the Native Administration. It is notorious throughout Nigeria that it oppresses the poor man and extorts from him —everybody knows it.

Doubtless defenders of the system will come forward, more's the shame and the pity, men whose names carry much more weight than mine, but certainly not men with a more considerable and varied knowledge of its workings than I possess. The abuses that I have described exist, and they are increasing, they are inseparable from the system.

The British have done great work in Nigeria. They have stopped raiding for slaves and trading in slaves (they have *not* ended slavery as an institution; daily, men purchase their freedom with the hard money proceeds of a year's or two years' or more years' toil) : they have stopped internecine war: they have made a railway and they have put steamers on the rivers: they have opened up the country to trade. And they have fashioned and riveted upon the poor people the dreadful fetters of the Native Administration.

The African native is far from being a fool. He sees now the British standing behind the Native Administration. He identifies the British with it. He appreciates that if he fights the Native Administration there are British machine guns coming to support it. He feels the Native Administration a most intolerable, efficient, invincible oppression. It assesses and collects his taxes, administers his "justice," subjects him to the *corvée,* orders and oppresses him and is hated by him, at every turn in his life. If he is forty years old he remembers the time when there were no British bayonets to maintain a tyranny: if he is young, his elders tell him of those days. And he thinks that, with the British out of the way, he could deal soon and faithfully and satisfactorily with the Native Administration. He knows as well as I do that the Emirs' motorcars and magnificence, that the money for the Emir of Katsina's joy rides to Europe, come out of his pocket, and he does not approve.

In Egypt the British did a great work. So long as they held the respect and confidence of the poor people, so long as they were recognized as the protectors of the poor, so long as the poor stood behind them, they governed the country. In those days not one thousand Zaghluls could have turned them out. Those days passed. The *plebs* moved over and stood behind Zaghlul. The *fellah* came to look upon the British as oppressors. Necessity knows no law, and many things were suffered by the *fellaheen* during the war that were perhaps inevitable. Anyhow they made up their minds that the British were no more protectors of the poor, and out the British had to go. The conditions of the *fellah* are unlikely to improve, even so.

The relevance of this lies here: Egyptian anti-British propaganda in Nigeria is a fact, and the operations of the Native Administration give it a welcoming soil upon which to work. The poor people hate the Native Administration, and will presently rise against it. That is the danger, real, proximate. Feudalism is a bad system, and, anyway, it's out of date. Yet the British seem set upon maintaining it in Nigeria. With the support of the people the British can stay in Nigeria, and continue the useful laudable enterprises they are there engaged upon. With the people alienated, and themselves allied with the class of Tax-Eaters as opposed to the class of Tax-Payers, the British will presently have to get out of the Northern Provinces.

The Native Administration as at present constituted ought to go over the side. It is expensive, inefficient, oppressive. In place of it there should be an augmented European staff, associated with African colleagues as suitable candidates come along, and they, servants directly of the Nigerian Government, should undertake all those services which are at present supposed to be performed by the Native Administration. Thus would the services be efficiently performed, the cost of them lessened, and the whole business CLEAN.

Lastly, these. I am a very sick man, far from London, and without access to records or data of any kind. If it be asked why did I not raise this issue before, my answer is that as far as I could I did whilst I was in the service. There are in Nigeria papers that I wrote and submitted to Authority. . . . What I have written is the truth, and it had to be told.

Cameron: Indirect Administration

1. *Definition of Indirect Administration.* The system of native administration generally adopted in the Protectorate of Nigeria is known as 'Indirect Administration', and, based on several principles, is designed to adapt for the purposes of local government the tribal institutions which the native peoples have evolved for themselves, so that the latter may develop in a constitutional manner from their own past, guided and restrained by the traditions and sanctions which they have inherited, moulded or modified as they may be on the advice of British Officers, and by the general control of those officers. It is an essential feature of the system that, within the limitations and in the manner which will be discussed below, the British Government rules through these native institutions which are regarded as an integral part of the machinery of government (just as the Administrative Officers are an integral part of the machinery of government) with well-defined powers and functions recognised by Government and by law, and not dependent on the caprice of an executive officer.

2. *Now firmly established elsewhere.* The time is past when this system can be regarded as a sacred and mysterious art peculiar to Nigeria and understood only by a chosen few. Indirect Administration

From Donald Cameron, *The Principles of Native Administration and Their Application* (Lagos: Government Printer, 1934), pp. 1–9, 12–22, 26–27.

has become an everyday instrument of government and, after all, the conception is older than Nigeria, as Lord Lugard has himself pointed out. The novel element in Nigeria, at the beginning of the present century, was the bold manner in which the doctrine was employed, that is, in using for the purpose the Chiefs of an alien race whose forefathers had invaded and conquered the greater part of Northern Nigeria but a hundred years before; Chiefs who now, in their turn, had been overthrown by British arms. It was a wise step—if I may be bold enough to record my judgment on such a matter—and for that reason the name of Lugard will always be associated with Nigeria. Probably the outstanding feature in that wisdom was the character of the office bestowed on those Chiefs; that of "my Wakils or Governors" as Sir Percy Girouard afterwards described it. I am quite aware that it will be argued—by a few—that the conquering Fulani should not be regarded altogether as an alien race; but, even so, I do not think that I have ever heard anyone venture to assert that in the Hausa states the society is tribal. Indeed, effort has been made since my return to Nigeria in 1931 to confute my own arguments concerning the principles of Native Administration by the contention that those societies are not tribal.

3. *Reason for its adoption; existing conditions.* The primary and compelling reason for the adoption of this system of Indirect Administration is not difficult to understand. Writing of the present day [1934] I should explain the reason in this way: Nigeria is a large country and it has a large population. Its area is some 373,000 square miles, with an African population of some 19,300,000, including the Mandated Territory of the Cameroons. The Protectorate is divided into twenty-two provinces and eighty-five divisions, each of the latter with its own staff of Administrative Officers. Why must we have Administrative Officers in a country like Nigeria? They are not to be found in the Dominions or in the United Kingdom; the County of Surrey has no staff of Administrative Officers. The reason is, of course, that in the United Kingdom and in the Dominions the people are educated and have, through the course of many generations, imbibed the precepts of law and order which must regulate the conduct of a civilised people; they can readily learn, through the newspapers and otherwise, the day to day acts and regulations of the Government which affect their lives. This is not so in the Protectorate of Nigeria, save in a very minor degree. Other means must therefore be found for communicating with primitive and ignorant peoples; we must in fact administer the people, whereas in the United Kingdom it is for the reason I have given sufficient to administer the law.

"Tribal institution" defined. Now, there are over nineteen millions of Africans in the Protectorate and the Administrative staff numbers but 347 including those on leave, a proportion of from one-third to one-fourth. It must be self-evident that not every tribesman can be reached directly by an Administrative Officer and it was therefore necessary to seek some other instrument to complete the chain of communication as between the Government and the people of this vast dependency. What more natural

than that we should use for the purpose—if we can find them—the tribal institutions of the people themselves? I mean by the term "tribal institution" the tribal authority which according to tradition and usage has in the past regulated the affairs of each unit of native society and which the people of to-day are willing to recognise and obey, if—I repeat the words again—if we can find it.

4. *Reason for its adoption; early conditions.* The system was introduced in Northern Nigeria early in the century by Sir F. (now Lord) Lugard for the same reason, roughly speaking. The number of officers available to administer the country more directly through an Administrative Service was altogether inadequate and there were no funds from which the staff could be augmented, conditions which continued for many years. As the system grew there was, naturally enough at first, a tendency to endeavour to place every unit possible under some Moslem Emir, a tendency which might well have been checked in later years when a much larger Administrative staff had become available. The 'pagan' communities in the Northern Provinces would probably, we now realise, have made greater progress if they had been developed in accordance with their own tribal institutions, however primitive, under the direct guidance of an Administrative Officer, instead of as a small part of a much larger administration, under a District Head often alien to themselves interposed between themselves and the British Officer. Their own tribal institutions, moreover, based on their own decentralised and democratic system, afford them opportunity to express their own desires with great freedom, opportunity denied to them under the system described in the preceding sentence. In some cases pagan communities were placed under Moslem Emirs because, it was said, the latter had 'conquered' them before our advent: they had 'conquered' them to the extent that they had, as against other raiding chiefs, been strong enough to make a preserve of the particular pagan country for the purpose of slave-raiding. If it be correct, as it undoubtedly is, that the allegiance of a people to a tribal head, freely given and without external cause, is the essence of true indirect administration we have in fact—although we seemed to have been oblivious of this—been in many instances administering pagan communities directly and not indirectly, and even then not through our own officers but through Moslem headmen. It is for this reason, in my considered judgment, that primitive communities in the Northern Provinces have made less progress in thirty years than comparable units in the South have made in three or four years.

5. *Political Objective must be defined.* Returning to the present day, it seems to me that any system of administration of primitive peoples must be exposed to grave danger if the supreme authority has not formulated any governing policy as to the political development of the country as a whole. We must know, in short, where we are going and what are our aims. It is necessary that the Government should form some idea broadly of what the political evolution of Nigeria is likely to be and work towards that end. It is, of course, quite impossible for me to attempt to make any comprehen-

sive forecast of the political evolution of the country; that is a matter for patience and study over a number of years, and not for prophecy. But I think that it is permissible to postulate, even at this stage, that—at least for geographical and economic reasons—it is not likely that any part or parts of Nigeria will become separate, self-contained political and economic units, and that accordingly wisdom lies in the policy of treating the country as a whole, openly and without any mental reservations. That must be accepted as the settled policy of the Government and all our efforts in the direction of the development of the people from their own history and their own institutions should be governed by that central idea. It should be evident that if we did so frame our policy as to foster the development of the Northern Provinces as a separate political unit we should merely be seeking to revive a state of affairs that the amalgamation of Southern and Northern Nigeria in 1914 was specifically designed to terminate.

6. *Other advantages from the system. Preservation of native institutions and their authority.* There are other advantages to the people, of course, to be derived from the system of Indirect Administration, many of them already manifest in Nigeria. Everyone will doubtless subscribe to the proposition that it is our duty to do everything in our power to develop the native politically on lines suitable to the state of society in which he lives. Our desire is to make him a good African, and we shall not achieve this if we destroy all the institutions, all the traditions, all the habits of the people, super-imposing upon them what we consider to be better administrative methods and better principles, but destroying everything that made the administration really in touch with the thoughts and customs of the people. We must not in fact destroy the African atmosphere, the African mind, the whole foundations of his race, and we shall certainly do this if we do not bring to the political application of the policy we have adopted a full understanding of its objects and an appreciation of the steps which we must take towards their fulfilment. When I write that our desire is to make the native "a good African" I mean that he should be trained in accordance with his environment instead of being given a European veneer totally out of keeping with the conditions under which he must live in Africa, where his home and people are. We want to make him proud of being an African (just as a Canadian is proud of being a Canadian) on the basis of a true African civilisation stimulated in the first instance by our own culture and example.

7. *Danger of impairing authority of Chiefs.* It may be argued that so far as mere administration is concerned—and this is by no means the same question as the political training of the natives—we can achieve our object by adopting the practice of using the chiefs or other native institutions as our instruments, as our mouth-pieces through whom the orders of the Government are issued to the people; but with all the disintegrating influences which are at work to impair the authority of the chief over his people that authority will be undermined and completely disappear as certainly as it is disappearing in parts of tropical Africa, unless we take steps now to prevent its disappearance. As a consequence

we should have destroyed the only foundations on which it is possible to build—and train.

8. *Influence of British Officers.* As I have already written, it must be remembered that it is quite impossible for us to administer the country directly through British Officers, even if we quadrupled the number we now employ. It has been well said, moreover, that "a European officer cannot exert a personal influence on the characters of more than one or two hundred natives." If the natives so affected should be, as they are where the Native Administration is retained as a real thing, in positions to influence other natives in their turn, then a Political Officer's influence is magnified by a natural process a thousand fold. If, on the contrary, they are not so placed, then whatever influence the Political Officer may have over the few with whom he comes into contact becomes a mere drop in the bucket and is lost in the mass.

9. *Building on native institutions.* In place of the alternative of governing directly through Administrative Officers and using the Chiefs merely as our mouth-pieces through whom we give our orders to the people, there is the other method of trying, while we endeavour to purge the native system of its abuses, to graft our higher civilisation upon the soundly rooted native stock, stock that had its foundations in the hearts and minds and thoughts of the people and therefore on which we can build more easily, moulding it and establishing it into lines consonant with modern ideas and higher standards, and yet all the time enlisting the real force of the spirit of the people, instead of killing all that out and trying to start afresh. Under this system the native authorities become not only part of the machinery of Government but also a living part of it, and the political energies and ability of the people are directed to the preservation and development of their own institutions. This is a task which will provide in ever increasing measure ample scope for those progressive Africans who genuinely desire to serve their own people. The training in the art of administration, in habits of responsibility and probity which the Chiefs and their Administrative staff receive through this medium must be of incalculable benefit to the whole body of persons concerned, provided always, of course, that in this and all other respects the Native Administration is in fact what we design it to be.

10. *The real native authority according to the people's own ideas to be employed.* This leads us to the very important point of the constitution of the Native Administration, or, more correctly speaking, the Native Authority. Emphasis must first be laid on the necessity, in seeking for the authority which according to tribal tradition and usage has regulated the affairs of the tribal unit with which we may be concerned, of assuring ourselves that the authority does in fact exist and is genuinely accepted by the people affected. If the latter are not prepared to accept the orders of the so-called authority, chief or otherwise, unless we compel them to do so then, of course, the administration is not indirect and the Native Authority set up on such a basis is a sham and a snare. Pretence of any form in the administration of primitive peoples is a dangerous thing and I detest it from the bottom of my heart. It is not possible in

civilised countries; you get found out by the people themselves. Moreover, if the authority has not the true spirit of the people behind it and is no more than a foreign and artificial intrusion imposed by ourselves almost certainly in such circumstances the people will be kept in subjection and ignorance; indeed, they must be kept in subjection and ignorance if such an authority is to endure. But with the advance of education a people thus becoming enlightened cannot be expected to continue faithful to a Native Administration which is reactionary and oppressive in its tendencies, especially where, as in some instances, the Native Administration depends for its authority on fetish and superstition for the most part. The Native Authority that is not acceptable to the people and is maintained only because we impose it on them is therefore almost certainly bound to fail and it would be better to endeavour in the first instance to administer the people directly.

11. *The people must be ready to recognise the Authority.* I am always careful, therefore, to enquire when any proposition is submitted to me for the purpose of constituting a Native Authority whether the people do in fact recognise the authority proposed and are ready to render obedience to it because it is in accordance with their tradition and custom that they should do so; or because, having seen the benefits conferred on the people by a neighbouring Native Administration, they desire of their own accord to place themselves under the orders of a prominent man of their own society or under some other authority, and to obey those orders. I would add, at the risk of being thought tedious on this point, that it is ensnaring and dangerous in this connexion to proceed on the assumption that this or that must have been the tradition and custom of a people; that they must at some time have obeyed this or that authority of their own. The present generation is possibly quite ignorant of such tradition; it is they that are primarily concerned and we must be quite certain before constituting an authority on such a basis that they are going to recognise it and obey its orders.

If the native authority is not only accepted by the people but is also regarded by them as a real living force which they value owing to the reasons for its evolution and for the benefits, in the shape of justice and fairplay, which they receive under it, they themselves will supply the incentive to advancement, a point on which I shall have something further to say.

12. *The authority according to their own tradition.* As I have written, above, we seek the authority which according to tribal tradition and usage has in the past regulated the affairs of each unit of native society and which the people of to-day are willing to recognise and obey. If we are successful in our quest we use that authority as an instrument, as the instrument by means of which we can communicate—in an authoritative manner I might add—with the people of the unit. But it is a matter of paramount importance that in recognising that authority and clothing it with legal sanction by appointing it to be a Native Authority under the law enacted for the purpose, we should in the first place regard it as the instrument which it is intended to be and retain

that consideration steadfastly in our minds. Native Administration, indirect as well as direct, is a means and not an end, and our work but commences when the Native Administration is constituted as an instrument through which the people of the unit may be administered under the direction of the Administrative staff. Any tendency, therefore, to think that when after exhaustive inquiry "the tribal institution" has in fact been identified (and recognised as a Native Authority) our work is at an end and that the Native Administration so set up can be left to work out its own salvation with a minimum of interference or even guidance on the part of the Government creates a danger to the system itself and should be checked. I trust that it is not necessary for me to add that neither the Native Authority nor the Native Court is intended to be an instrument—I have used that term—for registering the wishes of an individual officer.

13. *Education of the Native Authorities; civilised standards.* It will be the primary duty and object of the Administrative officers to educate the Native Authorities in their duties as rulers of their people according to civilised standards; to convince them that oppression of the people is not sound policy or to the eventual benefit of the rulers; to bring home to their intelligence, as far as may be possible, the evils attendant on a system which holds the lower classes in suppression, so destroying individual responsibility, ambition and development amongst them; and to inculcate the unspeakable benefit of justice, free from bribery and open to all. The end to be sought is, in brief, just government according to civilised standards and the moral and material well being and the social progress of the people.

14. *Supervision by Administrative Officers.* We assume that we have the instrument, the proper instrument acceptable to the people affected; we are careful to remember that it is in the first instance an instrument—a means and not an end; and we have our programme for the general development of these institutions according to civilised standards as set out in the preceding paragraph. What is the next step? We can find the answer to this question readily if we pause to consider what the next step would be if we were administering the people directly instead of through an instrument, the Native Authority. The answer is that, as a minimum, there must be such a degree of watchfulness and supervision as will place the Government in a position to affirm at any time whether the rights of the people to justice and fair treatment under a British Administration are being fully assured and safeguarded and whether opportunity of development is also being fully assured to them. To achieve this great skill and tact and unlimited patience will be required, the degree of watchfulness and supervision varying naturally as between an organised Native Administration of standing and repute and a more recent creation of a petty order in a primitive society where those in authority are almost as ignorant as the people they are to serve. But whatever that degree of watchfulness and supervision may be we ought to be in a position to assure ourselves that the people are receiving fair and liberal treatment, not forgetting that an autocracy may need even

more vigilance than may be necessary in democratic Bantu society as I knew it in East Africa; not forgetting, further, that, using again very pregnant words, the allegiance of a people to a tribal head, freely given and without external cause, is the essence of true indirect administration, and that in the great part of Nigeria in which native society is not strictly tribal that allegiance should not be taken for granted. In these cases, as in all other cases it is almost unnecessary to add, the incentive to obedience should be just government.

15. *Failure to correct error.* Lack of adequate supervision, because in the past a sufficiently high standard of supervision may not have been defined, is bad enough but even more serious is the deliberate policy disclosed in the tendency in the past to treat the petty Native Administrations of the Southern Provinces—I do not include in this expression the important Native Administrations of the Yoruba country and Benin—some of them not Native Administrations at all, in the same way as Administrations regarded as "highly organised" and to refrain from correcting error because what has been known as the "prestige" of the Native Authority would thereby be undermined. This tendency may be observed also in the Northern Provinces. It represents the serious mistake of attaching more importance to the machine than to the people it is designed to serve, and cannot be too strongly reprobated. A Native Administration under which the people are not receiving fair play generally can have no prestige which is worth upholding; and in my view the prestige which is sought for it will be far better secured by the intervention of the Administrative Officer in a manner that will show the people that while we are anxious to correct error and injustice we are at the same time ready to punish in our own Courts those who do not obey the proper orders of the Native Authority. It is a mistake also to believe that all possible cases should be taken in the Native Courts if the "prestige" of those Courts is to be assured. There are cases which they ought not to take and some which many of them are not competent to take; and to try the Native Administrations which, after all, are but instruments in the administration of Nigeria, beyond their powers and their capacity must, surely, be unsound policy.

19. *Dangers of repressive tendencies and consequent stagnation.* A student of Native Administration has written that he is "at times disturbed by the widespread emphasis on the importance of preserving as much as possible of indigenous African life and custom." "The possibility is foreshadowed" he adds, "of a new African feudalism which is prepared to be benevolent and paternal to the native so long as he will stay put and not raise envious eyes toward a full share in all that western civilisation can give." I am particularly attracted by these words because I have so frequently said both in Tanganyika and in Nigeria that a Native Administration which exists merely because the people are at present backward and ignorant and on that account are apparently willing to "stay put" cannot and must not endure. If there is an attempt to keep the people back and the Native Administration is consequently not so framed and constituted as to progress on modern lines

alongside the Central Government of which it is but a part, but one of the instruments of that Central Government, then, naturally, the natives will, as I have previously indicated in this Memorandum, eventually refuse to "stay put" and the edifice will crumble to the ground. Moreover, it is the avowed intention of the Government that the natives should not "stay put."

20. *Publicity of our methods.* A safeguard against stagnation of this nature and other doubtful methods of applying the policy of indirect administration lies, to my mind, in publicity. I am reluctant to make conparisons but it is my considered opinion that the Native Administrations of the Tanganyika Territory are, on the whole, more securely rooted and better equipped to stand up against assaults from the outside than are most of the Native Administrations in Nigeria, and I attribute this, for the greater part, to the fact that the former have from the date of their foundation been exposed to the full glare of public opinion, which must be and does act as a stimulus and a corrective. If the system of Indirect Administration is a real living, healthy growth, a thing generally desired by the people affected, it should not fear publicity. It seems to me, moreover, to be mere folly not to endeavour to enlist educated African opinion in support of a policy which we allege to be of such paramount importance to an African country.

21. *Feudal autocracies.* I have referred in the course of this Memorandum, with more particular reference to the Southern Provinces, to Native Administrations which are reactionary and repressive in their tendencies, in some instances depending for their authority on fetish and superstition for the most part. I am not unmindful of the difficulties which are presented where the Native Administration which we have created and recognised is based on a system of medieval polity dependent on the relation of vassal and superior, but I have deferred any more specific reference to this somewhat delicate part of the question in order to say here, in what appears to be its proper sequence, that the judgment that I have been able to form is that in some measure we have departed from the intentions and principles of Lord Lugard in this respect; particularly in drifting into the habit of mind—and I use the word "drift" with intent—in drifting into the habit of mind that a feudal autocracy of this kind is the be-all and end-all of Indirect Administration. It would be a direct contradiction in terms for me to say—as I have said in the course of the Memorandum—that it is the avowed intention of the Government that the natives should not "stay put" and at the same time to say that I accept the view last stated that a feudal autocracy of this character is all that we are seeking. But we have made some progress in this respect in the last year or two. The policy accepted for some considerable time that the Moslem Administrations should be sheltered as far as possible from contact with the world was due no doubt to a feeling, however unformulated, that an unreformed feudal autocracy could not be expected to stand up against the natural forces of a western civilisation that was gradually but quite perceptibly creeping further and further north in Nigeria; a curtain being drawn between the Native

Administrations of the north and the outer world, so far as it was possible to maintain the integrity of that curtain. But we have advanced now to the stage that the curtain is being gradually withdrawn and, I hope, will be fully withdrawn within a comparatively brief period.

22. *Feudal autocracies. Doubtful whether training and supervision is sufficient.* It is doubtful, however, whether even in the Native Administrations regarded as highly organised the amount of training in administrative work, of supervision and of guidance which the Resident and his officers can impart and exercise under the system as it still exists to-day can be regarded as at all adequate if we are really desirous of building well and securing the advancement of the people. I doubt sometimes whether we have done a great deal to impress on the minds of the Native Authorities concerned that the amelioration of the social and economic conditions of a people is one of the primary duties of an Administration and that the inspiration to improvement must come from within, from the Native Administration itself. Up to a few years ago every branch of activity, every department in the affairs of a Native Administration in the Moslem areas of the Northern Provinces remained in the hands of the Emir. In a few of them, recently, there has been some delegation of powers to members of the Emir's Council, one taking this department of the public service under his charge, another taking another department, and so on. It has been thought that this was quite an extraordinary advance, affording another reason for complacency. It is a great advance in one way but from the point of view of efficiency of administration according to civilised standards too much importance can be attached to it. The situation as it was belonged to the middle ages; it is a little better now by reason of this development but the necessity for close supervision and careful training in the difficult art of administration has not been diminished.

23. *Possible very gradual reform.* We are suffering in these respects, moreover, from the embarrassing heritage of the former practice of placing every pagan unit possible under a Moslem authority, alluded to in paragraph 4 above, and from the effects of the unhallowed policy insidiously introduced during the latter half of the last decade of thinking of the Moslem Emirates in terms of the Indian States although, of course, the former have no element of sovereign power. The situation has for these reasons been rendered a difficult one and any system of reform must be a very gradual process. The question of the administration of pagans by Moslems should be examined as each vacancy occurs in the office of Native Authority in the large Emirates in which there are pagan communities. As to the rest of the problem my own view is that as opportunities offer the system of supervision by our officers should be made more evident and more effective following the principles of the Benin Minute; and that an effort should be made to devise means that will allow the people to express themselves periodically, possibly through their Village Heads and Elders in conference with an Administrative Officer, the District Head and a representative of the Native Authority. It is a striking, but not a very comforting, re-

flection that the somewhat primitive people in the Ibo and Ibibio countries of the South are in this respect in a more favourable position than the peasantry generally in the North, with the deduction that the feudal autocracy with which certain minds have been quite content and sought to consolidate, is, after all, not the best thing from the point of view of the more humble folk who form the great majority of the people.

APPLICATION OF PRINCIPLES.

24. *Types of tribal institution.* I have written above that it is the policy of the Government to administer the natives through their own tribal institutions, explaining that I mean thereby the authority which according to tribal tradition and usage regulated each unit of native society before the advent of the British Government. Those units are of different sizes. One may embrace a whole sub-tribe such as the Egbas, ruled by one Head Chief with his traditional councillors and advisers; one may embrace only a clan (or even part of a clan) administered by one chief (*i.e.* he has no superior chief above him), again with his own councillors and advisers, or by a clan or subclan council; and a third may embrace nothing more than a few grouped villages who for reasons of a common ancestry or other common heritage have agreed to work together under a council composed of their own village elders. Some of the Moslem Emirates are not true to the first of the classes enumerated above but for the purposes of this part of the Memorandum they are included in it.

25. Every unit, to be a unit, is in charge of an authority known to the people as their tribal head—a chief or a headman where the authority is not a council as described in the preceding paragraph—and every chief and headman has, as an integral part of the social scheme, his traditional councillors and advisers. He is not constitutionally an autocrat, and he and his advisers and the simple peasants know quite well the degree in which his powers are circumscribed by native tradition and custom. He knows equally well that if his people are harshly or unjustly treated they will leave him and join a more humane chief. This is a point of great importance and Administrative Officers should study it patiently and cautiously and endeavour to ascertain fully the nature and extent of the safeguards against oppression by a chief or headman, set up by native society through the ages in this manner for its own protection, safeguards which, I have no doubt, are still preserved, *e.g.*, the chief who tries cases in his open court may be said to be for the most part only the mouthpiece of the court, through whom its decision is promulgated. As I wrote in paragraph 1 we seek to use the institutions which the people have evolved for themselves so that the latter may develop from their own past guided and restrained "by the traditions and sanctions they have inherited". Where the authority is vested in a council no question of the ascendancy of an autocrat should arise.

26. *The Chief or Headman.* As I have written in the preceding paragraphs, each such native unit is, in accordance with native custom, in charge of an authority—a chief or headman or a council. It had been

alleged, it is true, that all that machinery of native government which existed before the European came to the country, or the greater part of it, had disappeared and ceased to function, indeed that in some places it had scarcely emerged; but the experience of the last few years shows clearly that such is not the case, that the machinery we are now seeking to use still in many places held a large share in the life of the people. There is a tendency sometimes to look for too much when we start to build up on autochthonous institutions in tropical Africa: I have heard it stated elsewhere, for example, that it is impossible to introduce any form of Indirect Administration unless one is able to find a potentate of the order and dignity of a king according to Western ideas.

27. *Native institutions; how given legal status.* These are the native institutions, which, in spite of neglect, had not ceased entirely to function, and we must now consider the manner in which they are brought within the ambit of our system of European directing rule. They have to be made part of our local constitution, they have to be clothed with the authority of the law, and this is effected by means of the Native Authority Ordinance whereunder such native institutions as the Government decides to recognise are given legal status by being declared "Native Authorities" with certain specified powers. This is effected by constituting the 'office' of native authority for a specified area and appointing to the office so constituted the chief or other authority representing the native institution concerned. The first, the constituting of the office, is a constitutional act of high importance (unless the native authority is a subordinate one) and should not be delegated by the Governor, although he may delegate the power to appoint to the office except in the case of First Class Chiefs.

28. *Recognition of Chiefs, etc., by the Governor.* The chief or other authority representing the native institution comes to do so in a variety of ways which will be explained later, but appointment by the Governor, in the sense in which he appoints civil servants, is not one of those ways, though he may in certain circumstances refuse to accept a particular individual. The holder of a native office is either a hereditary chief, or a chief selected by the people for themselves, or a sub-chief, hereditary or otherwise, appointed by a Head Chief, or a native official appointed by the chief. The position is the same in the case of a council which is appointed to be a Native Authority for we there declare that the holders of certain offices (*e.g.*, the senior elder of A, the senior elder of B and so on) shall in association as a council be a Native Authority, the individuals who are members of that council being those who, in accordance with the principles here discussed, are the *de facto* holders (recognised by the Governor) of the separate native offices which, in association, are the council. In the case of hereditary chiefs we recognise *de facto* holders of the position as rightly entitled to it, and in the case of the head of a Native Administration or a sub-chief who is not hereditary, we accept the person who is declared by the people to be their choice, or who is appointed by the Head Chief, if there is one, after he has consulted the people affected. Upon a chiefship becoming vacant, we recognise similarly the person

who, according to the laws of the tribe and the wishes of the people, is the rightful successor; such person is the chief, and his position does not depend on any act of appointment by the Governor, though in extreme cases the Government may exercise its undoubted right of refusing to accept an individual who, on personal grounds, is not considered fit to occupy the position: in such cases the tribe would be required to make an alternative selection if necessary, *i.e.,* if it were not decided to appoint the Senior Administrative officer to fill the office of Native Authority for the time being under Ordinance No. 5 of 1934 which was enacted for the purpose. It may be noted here that the provisions of that law should not be resorted to unless the office of Native Authority has been constituted for the purpose of Indirect Administration and is actually vacant.

What depends upon the formal act of the Governor is the legal and constitutional status of the office of Native Authority, and in performing that formal act the Governor will prescribe the powers to be exercised by virtue of that office. An analogy which will help to make the position clear may be drawn from the British Administration where by a formal act of the sovereign authority the administration is declared to consist of certain offices and institutions, *e.g.,* the Governor, the Executive Council, and so on. The manner of appointment of individuals to those offices is quite distinct from the establishment of the offices.

29. *Limitation of the powers of the Native authorities.* There are limitations to the powers of the Native Authorities constituted as in paragraph 27, the limitation lying in the fact that the Native Authorities are not independent rulers; they are merely the delegates of the Governor, whose representative is the Resident. The Government reserves to itself the right to impose taxation, to make laws, to control the exercise of such subsidiary legislative powers as may be delegated to Native Authorities, to dispose (in the Northern Provinces) of such lands as are vested in the paramount power "for the use and common benefit of the natives" and of course to raise and control armed forces. The disposal of the annual revenue of the Native Administration, the appointment and dismissal of important officers of the Native Administration and indeed all the important executive acts of a Native Authority, though emanating from itself, are subject to the guidance and advice of the Resident. It must be understood, moreover, that unless a chief (or other authority) has been "clothed with the authority of the law" in the manner indicated in paragraph 27 above his orders are not lawful orders within the Statutes of Nigeria and cannot be enforced in any of the courts including the Native Courts. The idea that any chief can lawfully enforce his orders under the cloak of native law and custom although he does not hold office as a Native Authority is therefore erroneous. The new Native Authority Ordinance makes no provision for chiefs who are not Native Authorities.

30. *Native Administrations; forms of, explained.* In the every day language of the administration the Native Authorities are generally described as "Native Administrations." There are different forms of these Native Administrations, each

constituted as was suitable to the particular native society and in accordance with its wishes. In the first place we may have the chief, the Superior Native Authority, who, with his constitutional advisers, is the fount of all authority within the unit. The Native Treasury is the Treasury of this unit alone; the higher Native Court—generally a court of appeal—is the court of this unit alone. The Native Authority may delegate some of its authority to sub-chiefs or headmen, often hereditary offices of some standing, and this is a convenient course if there are areas at a distance from the chief's headquarters. They will in such case formally be appointed to be subordinate "Native Authorities" subject to the superior authority; but it is not necessary to appoint all the servants or agents of any Native Authority to be themselves Native Authorities as they act as the officers and servants of the Native Authorities and are clothed with authority as such. Put briefly, it is not necessary to appoint any one to be a subordinate "Native Authority" within the meaning of the law unless he has in practice in the course of the duties entrusted to him to give orders occasionally on his own responsibility (his ultimate responsibility being to his chief or other superior authority).

31. *Federation of Chiefs.* In the second place, we may have Chiefs who administer clans (or other sections) of the same tribe or kindred tribes and have agreed, with the approval of their people, to form a "Federation" in order, chiefly, to pool their financial resources. Each Chief in the Federation retains executive authorty in his own unit, and is appointed the Native Authority of that unit, but occasionally the Chiefs sitting together in Council (which may itself be appointed a Native Authority) may agree to pass an order under section 8 of the Ordinance, or a rule under section 16 (subject to the approval of the Governor), applicable to the whole area embraced by the Federation. There is a danger in this practice if too lightly applied inasmuch as in native society such orders or rules if of general application should be made by the executive authority of the unit (*i.e.* its own Native Authority) with the advice and consent of his councillors; and this wholesome safeguard in a democratic society may be neglected if a Chief is allowed to assent to a measure when sitting as a member of the Council, without consulting his constitutional advisers. Administrative Officers should be careful to see that constitutional usage in this connexion is not neglected.

32. *Place of native court in a Federation.* In this class of Native Administration (which, so far, has not developed to any great extent in Nigeria) each Chief (Native Authority) has his own Native Court, sometimes with inferior Courts under it where the area of the unit is large, and the chiefs agree to form a higher Court at the Federal headquarters which is generally a court of appeal. In principle, in forming this higher Court each Chief agrees that in his capacity as the chief executive of his own unit he will within that unit engage to see that the orders and decisions of the higher Court are duly carried out. It is therefore necessary that where a higher Court is being formed in this manner the Administrative Officer should be careful to see that this

principle is clearly understood by each of the Chiefs in the Federation, that is, that in consenting to the formation of such a Court each Chief thereby undertakes to give effect to its judgments within his own unit of which he is the executive head. Where the authority is a Council and not a chief, for example, among the Jekris and Sobos, a federation can be formed on the same principles.

33. *Federal Council not a superior Native Authority in the Full Sense.* It should clearly be understood that the Federal Council is not a superior Native Authority in the sense that the Chief of a tribe may be a superior Native Authority; that it does not appoint the servants of each of the Native Authorities constituting the Federation, nor does it dismiss them. Far less does it appoint the successor to a Chief if a vacancy occurs in any of the units of Native Administration constituting the Federation; in such case the vacancy is filled according to the traditions and custom of the unit, in the same way as if no Federation existed.

34. *President of Federal Council.* In Native Administrations of this class the President of the Federal Council is generally chosen in rotation (quarterly or even monthly) from the Chiefs forming the Federation, but in some a permanent President has been appointed by the chiefs themselves. In one or two instances attempts have been made to regard the permanent President of the Council as a "Paramount" Chief but the artificial nature of this pretension is as a rule soon disclosed. It has sometimes been thought, I understand, that a unit may withdraw from a Federation at its will and pleasure. I do not take that view. Once a unit has entered a Federation interests have been created of a general nature which should not be sacrificed at the whim of a Chief. A unit should, in my judgment, not be allowed to secede save for the gravest reasons and then only in the most exceptional cases. It will have a steadying influence on the Chiefs of a Federation to remind them, if necessary, that it will be difficult, if not impossible, gradually to develop native institutions by means of larger Native Councils if even the Federal Council cannot endure.

35. *Tribal Councils.* In a third class of Native Administration a Tribal Council may be formed of a number of petty chiefs, better described as Headmen of the same tribe or kindred tribes, each with executive authority in his own unit (subject to the advice of his own Council of Elders), clothed with authority as a Native Authority. They sit as Chairman of the Council in rotation and pool the common resources in a common budget. If they cannot agree in regard to a Chairman the District Officer should himself act as Chairman. They have on occasion framed a general order or rule for the whole area served by the Council if appointed as a Council to be a Native Authority, but I consider that in administrations of this kind it is for the present, for the reasons given in paragraph 31 above, preferable that each Headman (Native Authority) should frame the order or rule in his own unit, with the consent of his constitutional advisers. In some cases a court of appeal has been appointed at the Council's headquarters. Such a Council should as a rule not be appointed to be a Native Authority

unless it is to have executive functions. Further, such a Council acting as an advisory and financial body, and possibly forming from its members a Court of Justice, may properly be designated a "Native Administration" although it may not itself, for the present, have been appointed to be a Native Authority.

36. *Clan and village Councils.* In a fourth class of Native Administration we have the Councils of the Clans, Sub-Clans and Village Groups which are being constituted after careful research by the Administrative staff in the Eastern Provinces of the South. These Councils are not all of a type but, speaking generally, it may be said that each village, through its "headman" (however nominal, generally the senior elder) and elders, or a selected number of them according to their own customs, is represented on the Council which is appointed to be the Native Authority. It seems unwieldy and topheavy, especially where the people are illiterate and all the elders of all the villages in the Group have a right to a seat on the Council (Native Authority) but it is strictly in accord with native tradition in the early years of their society, and each Council is fashioning itself and the corporate spirit is clearly functioning in many instances. In some cases an executive committee answerable to the Council is appointed and it will be interesting to see how this system will function. The members of such a committee should be appointed for a definite, brief, period. There is no doubt, and perhaps this is the most important consideration of all, that the Native Courts constituted on a parallel basis command the respect of the people and are already highly prized by them as a welcome substitute for the Court of the "Warrant Chiefs". Moreover, in some of the most unlikely areas (judged by their former history) the Councils have had the will to suppress disorder and crime and have met with some success in doing so. The Councils described in this and the preceding paragraph afford the people opportunity to express their own desires with great freedom, and in several native communities there is a marked disposition to appoint men of some education to the Councils. This tendency is an extension of native custom in a praiseworthy direction and is naturally being encouraged. In some cases there is a strongly expressed desire to get "men of sense", as they describe them, on to the Courts.

37. *Form of Native Administration not to be stereotyped.* No attempt has been made, nor should it be made, to stereotype the various Administrations and force them into one pattern or another. It suffices if, in each case, the Native Administration is in accordance with the wishes and traditions of the Chiefs and people, and adequately fulfils the object of its existence, that is, the discharge by the local native authorities of the functions of local government in native affairs to such extent as circumstances may permit in each case and with due regard to expansion in the future.

38. *Effective administration not possible without delegation of authority.* Particular care should be taken to consult the Head Chief of a unit where there is one, and to explain to him the need for delegation of authority, and the manner in which such delegation is effected by the Ordinance, while retaining un-

impaired the power of the superior authority. It should be explained that though delegation must be exercised with care in proportion to the standing and ability of the sub-Chiefs and Headmen, without it effective administration is not possible, and it should be made clear that by consenting to the establishment under the law of the offices of subordinate Native Authorities the Chief is not surrendering in the smallest degree whatever control he may now enjoy over the appointment of individuals to those offices, or the manner in which they exercise their functions.

45. *Native Authorities and their employees distinguished.* The Governor establishes, as has been explained, the office of Native Authority: that office, as also explained, normally consists of a hereditary tribal chief, invariably in association with certain elders and other persons who occupy positions of dignity and responsibility, or of some other authority. Subordinate to that office there may, it has been seen, be others of importance, whose offices may if necessary similarly be established as (subordinate) Native Authorities, and in such cases the holders of those offices must be dealt with through the principal authority, but subject to the same limitations as to recognition, dismissal, prosecution, etc., as in the case of the Head Chief, though the Governor may delegate his powers in this respect. The holders of offices not so declared to be "Native Authorities" are merely employees of the Native Administration.

46. *The Native Authorities an integral part of the machinery of government.* The prestige and influence of the Native Authorities can best be upheld by letting the peasantry see that the *Government itself* treats them "as an integral part of the machinery of the Administration." That there are not two sets of rulers, British and Native, working either separately or in co-operation, but a single Government in which the Native Chiefs have well defined duties and an acknowledged status side by side with the British officials. Their duties should never conflict and should overlap as little as possible; they should be complementary to each other, and the Authority itself must understand that it has no right to its place and powers unless it renders proper service to the State. It is obviously desirable that Government should be called upon as rarely as possible to intervene between the Native Authority and the people, for if a Native Authority has lost prestige and influence to such a degree that it has to appeal to Government to enforce its orders it becomes not merely useless but a source of weakness to the Administration. This does not of course mean that any community may be appealing to Government throw off its allegiance to a Chief, or that mere unpopularity, which may be due to the exercise of very necessary discipline, forms any grounds for the deposition of a Chief.

47. *Education of Native Authorities in art of administration.* In order that the Native Authorities may find adequate scope for their energies, take keen interest in their duties, and command the respect and obedience of their people, it is essential, provided that the general supervision by the Administrative staff is adequate and the latter is aware generally of what is going on,

that they should in the exercise of their legitimate powers be given the greatest possible latitude and support compatible with their capacity and the position they occupy in relation to the Central Government. We should endeavour to give them an interest and an object beyond the routine performance of their duties, to interest them in the scheme of Government, to show them common interests, to engage their sympathies and active co-operation in our efforts to promote the welfare and progress of their people; for their primary duty is to their people and by the manner in which they fulfil it they will be judged. At the same time it will be the primary duty and object of the Administrative Officers to educate the Native Authorities in their duties as administrators according to a civilised standard; to impress upon them the advantage of delegating the control of districts to subordinate chiefs and headmen and of trusting and encouraging those subordinates, while keeping a strict supervision over them, to see that there is no favouritism in such appointments; and, as I have written already in paragraph 13 above, to inculcate the unspeakable benefit of justice, free from bribery and open to all. So long as they prove themselves loyal and capable it is through them that the people will be governed, and as has been written above, it is the desire of the Government to uphold their authority and prestige in every legitimate way, and to encourage initiative and a sense of responsibility. Suggestions for reform or progress should always be encouraged and all orders to subordinates should be given by British officers through the responsible chief.

Perham: A Re-Statement of Indirect Rule

The outstanding point about British Africa to-day is the extension of the indirect system of administration. This is the more remarkable because, in the decentralized position of our territories, such extension is the result of free adoption on the part of the different governments. It is the endorsement of the system, after long experience, by practical administrators. Yet in England it has lately been subjected to a considerable amount of criticism. The object of this article is to restate indirect rule in the light of these criticisms, in the hope of rebutting what is misinformed and incorporating what is constructive.

From Margery Perham, "A Re-Statement of Indirect Rule," *Africa,* VII (1934), 321–23, 328–34.

I must begin by defining indirect rule in order to concentrate the argument and avoid certain diversions which have engaged far too much critical energy. The term indirect rule has generally been used to describe, not a general principle of government, but a particular and local form of its application. The expedient by which a conquering people makes use of the institutions of the conquered is as old as history. There are circumstances which, if only for a time, make it unavoidable. Direct government in the fullest sense may be practicable where neighbouring and culturally intelligible people are annexed, but it is out of the question when the agents of a distant nation are first confronted by a numerous and primitive people. An effective administrative grasp is checked by lack of power, and even more of knowledge, and the situation imposes on the rulers at least a tacit recognition of existing laws and customs.

It is not often in history that a virtue has been consciously made of this necessity, and a system dictated by the convenience of the ruler prolonged in the interests of the ruled. It has happened more than once in the history of the British Empire because the expedient is particularly congenial to the national temperament. Nowhere, however, was the expedient so consciously and systematically developed as by Lord Lugard in Northern Nigeria. It does not, as some critics seem to maintain, detract from his achievement that it was begun in response to circumstances, or that examples of similar, though less considered, response can be found elsewhere. By trial and error over the series of years he and his staff built up a practical administration adapted to the immediate needs of the country as they saw them. It was a definite and yet a highly adaptable system which incorporated native societies as subordinate units of government. It gave statutory authority, in accordance with the varying capacity of the tribes, to native courts, native authorities, and later, to native treasuries. It appeared as the years went on that Lord Lugard and his officers had built even better than they knew. A series of *ad hoc* enactments and instructions developed into a 'corpus' in which principles applicable far beyond the Western Sudan could be distinguished from their local application. But it was not until later that, in characteristic British fashion, the chief architect and others began to find a philosophical explanation for what they had done, and to realize how readily their system could be informed with the new scientific spirit. The system, like others of our constitutional inventions, is not weaker but stronger for this sequence of development, and it is strange that some critics should have turned this also into a reproach.

More than one critic has contrasted indirect rule unfavourably with the equalitarian and assimilative policy of Victorian humanitarians and the administrators they influenced. An examination of this view will throw useful light upon our subject. The Victorians, it is said, looked upon native society and saw that it was bad. They set to work with a will to civilize it. The new theory of administration has weakened this will and has even induced officials and teachers to aim at preserving rather than superseding native culture; it has therefore come to act as a drag upon natural and desirable progress. The reply is that a growing knowledge of African society has taught us a new respect for it. We begin to understand how African cultures were integrated and so to recognize the functions of certain customs which seemed to our grandfathers the perverse aberrations of the heathen. We identify in miniature and under primitive disguise the elements common to all human societies, and we begin to question whether those elements, instead of being wholly destroyed, might not be re-expressed in forms more serviceable to the needs of today. We can see by example that what one of our African governors has called the 'killing-out' of a culture, or even of selected items in it, may be an injurious process. A tribe which is made to feel that its customs are ignored or despised by its white rulers loses its self-respect and sinks into apathy or bitterness. The loss of social energy is the more complete because our society is unable or unwilling to absorb the individuals into which an African community may be disintegrated by our contact. . . .

What is the situation before us? The contact of two cultures. Each of the two groups of critics seems to be concentrating too much upon one or other of the cultures and too little upon their actual point of contact. It is upon the realities of this contact that indirect rule must be, and to a great extent has been, based. It should not be diverted from them by theories, scientific or political, as to the desirability of preserving or replacing African culture, and it should recognize that culture not in isolation, not as it was, nor as it might be, but as at a given moment of contact, it is. Indirect administration must, perhaps, especially guard itself against the temptation to try to revive or preserve what was. It should be as ready to accept the realities of assimilation as it is ready to accept those of conservatism; to invest an advanced urban population with suitable municipal institutions, as to confirm the unquestioned authority of a secluded rainmaking clan-head. It is possible that the prolonged anthropological investigations carried out by the administrations of Tanganyika and Nigeria have given a wrong impression: their object was to allow the people, in so far as they themselves desired it, to make a fresh start from familiar ground. Few tribal councils, after years of bewildering disintegration, are able to rationalize about the exact administrative forms with which they will compromise between the past and the present, nor can the political officer make an arbitrary decision for them. Once the familiar forms have been restored, the people are free, and, in the two territories to which I have just referred, are encouraged, to develop and adjust them. In this dynamic relationship the practical administrator is made aware of two apparently contradictory tendencies operating in African society, the one adaptable and the other conservative. When he endeavours, often unconsciously, no doubt, to combine these tendencies into harmonious motion, he must contrive some form of indirect administration.

If, as I have suggested, we have not yet enough experience or expert observation of the process of adaptation to European contact under indirect systems to be certain how and how quickly and successfully it will take place, there is at least encouraging evidence of the racial capacity of most African peoples for adaptation. We can reconstruct something of such adaptation to pre-European contacts. Disparate clans were bound swiftly into strong federations by some dominant personality. Tribes conquered by strangers from the Hamitic north submitted to an effective compromise between the new political centralization and the old clan-system. Pastoral people moved into tsetse-ridden country and made what must have been a deep and painful social adjustment. Groups fringing a dominant fighting tribe made a rapid and deliberate adoption of their customs: others, incorporated by conquest, were quickly indistinguishable from their masters. Although we should not generalize too soon about the Africans' reaction to the intrusion of Europe, their vigorous receptivity does at least promise an ethnologically healthier relationship than has been possible with the Amerindian, the Australian, and Polynesian peoples.

If the preservationist should be asked to take comfort from the adaptability of the African, the assimilator should be invited to consider his conservatism. The places most readily accessible to travellers, among whom these critics are sometimes numbered, are naturally those most open to European influence. Much has rightly been made of the revolution in African transport and its significance, yet there are still vast areas untraversed by any main road or railway where the old Africa remains more evident than the new, and where a single political officer with a couple of missionaries, a few native teachers, and perhaps an Indian or Syrian trader represents civilization to fifty or a hundred thousand Africans. What alternative to indirect administration is there here except a barrier between rulers and ruled crossed only by those anonymous native agents, police, interpreters, and the rest, who almost inevitably abuse the irresistible foreign authority upon which they draw?

But African social organization can also show its tenacity when exposed to prolonged European influences. This might be expected of a Kano or a Buganda, where the imposing political structures commanded our respect and recognition from the first. It is far more surprising to find that the multitudinous kinship-groups of South-Eastern Nigeria have retained their vitality for thirty or forty years in spite of the strongest social and economic influences, and of all our attempts to group them into manageable units under more convenient administrative forms. I should have found it hard to credit if I had not myself observed the enthusiasm with which they responded to the invitation to revive their old councils and groupings. Another sign of conservatism is surely the fidelity with which Africans seem to cling to their chiefs, even where the position of these has undoubtedly been changed by their association with the foreign power. Many examples could be given from tropical Africa of this fidelity and its very practical results under indirect rule. Even in Southern Africa where chieftainship has been deliberately allowed to crumble into disuse and poverty, the people continue to proffer their barren allegiance. Zulus still fight over a question of succession. The Transkei Bunga (Council) and the South African Native Conference both contain a large proportion of educated Africans, yet both have recently passed unanimous resolutions in favour of preserving the chieftainship. An African clergyman said that 'some of the natives were of opinion that the continued existence of a tribe depended on the existence of a chief'. In the Bunga requests were made for higher fees for chiefs in order that they might keep up the state and fulfil the obligations still expected of them by their people. Criminal jurisdiction was asked for them and comparisons made in favour of the policy of the Imperial Government in this respect. 'Amongst us natives', said one member, 'the word chief is far-reaching. How we pick our chiefs cannot be understood by other nations. They cannot understand the respect we give the chief. It can only be understood by us.' In Lagos, in spite of all the influences that have been brought to bear upon this large port for fifty years, the townspeople appear to take a far greater interest in the position of the titular head of the submerged kingdom, and the dynastic feuds of his house, than in the affairs of the Municipal and Legislative Councils for all their local African membership. The first impulses of African nationalism roused by the pressure of the dominant civilization seem likely in some parts to take the form of intenser loyalty towards chiefs: the Kikuyu have even asked for the innovation of a paramount chief. Yet it might have been anticipated that chieftainship, deprived of what seem to have been its most essential functions and privileges, would be one of the first institutions to atrophy. We might venture to expect that under indirect rule chiefs—and the majority of Africans under our tutelage recognize chiefs—will remain as centres round which the councils and administrations of their people will develop, themselves becoming increasingly 'constitutional'.

Yet, perhaps, it is dangerous to venture upon even so much anticipation. The great task of indirect rule is to hold the ring, to preserve a fair field within which Africans can strike their own balance between conservatism and adaptation. There is no formula for finding the mean between the two equally mistaken policies of too much and too little intervention: it remains a test of our political judgment.

These, then, are some of the characteristics of African society with which the administrator has to reckon. But in this contact there are two cultures, not one, to be considered. The point is well illustrated by the Indian story in which the Brahmans protested against the prohibition of suttee because it was a sacred custom of the Hindus which should be respected. 'Be it so', replied Sir Charles Napier. 'The burning of widows is your custom. Prepare the funeral pile. But my nation has also a custom. When men burn women alive, we hang them and confiscate all their property. My carpenters shall therefore erect gibbets on which to hang all concerned when the widow is consumed. Let us all act according to national customs.'

There are obvious African parallels. Thus, although we have moved a long way from the righteous indignation with which Sir Harry Smith forbade 'the sin of buying wives' among the defeated Xosa, there are limits beyond which, even in the face of the most convincing scientific plea for a policy of gradualness, we should be unable to extend our tolerance. But the story symbolizes far more than this. It reminds us that the general form taken by the contact is at least as much determined by the nature of our culture as of theirs. Although we may discuss these questions academically as if there were a complete freedom of choice in the selection of a policy we must recognize, without being too fatalistic, that actually certain limits are set by our national character and political traditions. Our view of the contact tends to lose perspective when we excuse ourselves from the necessity of studying our own side of it.

Indirect rule is the characteristically British reaction to the political problem of Africa. It derives partly from our conservatism, with its sense of historical continuity and its aristocratic tradition. Our experience has not taught us to believe in fresh constitutional starts, or in the existence of political principles of universal applicability, though, as the Victorian humanitarians showed, we wavered a little under the influence of the French Revolution. This conservatism may degenerate into an exclusiveness that would deny all possibility of Africans ever being able to reach civilization by way of our natural expression of it. But indirect rule derives equally from our liberalism with its respect for the freedom of others and its conscious reaction from the old selfish type of imperialism. It is another expression of the tradition which allowed, and even encouraged, colonies to develop into dominions and which guaranteed the cultural freedom of French Canadians or South African Boers. Its danger is to decline into a merely negative attitude, a refusal to undertake distasteful responsibilities. It is because of these qualities that even where British officials have not been working under a definite system of indirect rule like that initiated by Lord Lugard, they have shown a persistent preference for indirect methods and a distaste for forcing their own ideas upon Africans. The great strength of local government in England, and our increasing belief in the principle of voluntaryism made us ready to find graded constitutional settings for small African societies. The 'D' court of the small chief with his elders is no anomaly to those accustomed to the amateur justice of petty sessions. The native treasuries express our principle that executive responsibility should always be associated with financial. The critics of indirect rule have not, as far as I know, constructed an alternative system, but when they do, they should remember that, unless it is congenial to our national temperament, however authoritatively it might be promulgated from above, it would assuredly become something different in the hands of the district officer.

This raises an important and final consideration. Administration in Africa must be related to the probable destiny of the territory concerned. Since the loss of America the tradition of the Empire has fostered the development of its dependent communities, and not only those of our own race and colour, towards that form of association in independence which is called dominion status. There is no reason to think that Britain would, or could, prevent her African territories from developing in the same direction. Sir Donald Cameron, who extended indirect rule to Tanganyika and has revitalized it in Nigeria, has stated that he regards it as the best way to fulfil our task, the training of the people in the art of administration so that they may ultimately stand by themselves. It may be that indirect rule is not suited to such conditions as those of South Africa where the hope of the Africans must be to take their place one day in the colonial state, or to those of French Africa which is expected to remain an integral part of a centralized empire. It may be less essential here to preserve continuity and to maintain the pride and unity of tribal societies. Where the future is uncertain as with those native territories which contain small white communities and where British policy is perplexed by two divergent calls upon its liberalism, it is more difficult to prescribe the best form of native administration. I believe, myself, that in all circumstances indirect rule is more effective than direct as a political training for tribal Africans. The political achievements of Africans under indirect rule already stand comparison with those of their fellows who, as in South Africa, Liberia, and the colony of Sierra Leone, have been obliged to construct institutions from the foundations upwards upon foreign models. Yet indirect rule is only a transitional method. The immediate test of its success will be the frequency with which it receives and requires revision in response to progress: the ultimate test will be the ability with which the African territories take their place in the world as self-governing nations.

Akpan: Epitaph to Indirect Rule

The educated nationalists saw in the system nothing but an imperialistic device on the part of the governing power by which the subject races might be kept down for ever, or at least indefinitely. (There were some, of course, of the more discerning among these nationalists who were prepared to admit that there was some good in the system, although they strongly disapproved of its machinery.) The unfortunate thing about it all was the very strong tendency on the part of very powerful sections of the educated communities not to appreciate the real merits of the system. As has been said this tendency could at the same time be easily understood for a number of reasons, the most fundamental of which may be said to include the following:

(i) The original motives behind the European scramble for Africa, clearly borne out by the Berlin Conference of 1885, were well-known and could not be said to be honourable to African races. The parties to the Berlin Partition of Africa hardly had—or pretended to have—as their principal aim the development of the African continent *for the benefit of the African races*. Rather, their professed motive appeared to be the

From Ntieyong U. Akpan, *Epitaph to Indirect Rule: A Discourse on Local Government in Africa* (London: Cassell & Company, Ltd., 1956), pp. 26–30.

acquisition of African territories as a means of national prestige, wealth and power for the acquiring nations. Against Britain this fact appeared particularly underlined by her immediate step of handing over the administration of these territories, in the first place, to commercial companies, chartered, or formed and chartered, soon after the Berlin Conference for the purpose. Unlike, for instance, the Charter granted to the East India Company in 1600 the new charters did not require the Companies concerned to leave the natives and their territories alone and concentrate on trade, but rather the companies were required to make the administration and control of these territories one—perhaps an overriding one—of their principal concerns. Captain Lugard, later Lord Lugard, the first Governor-General of Nigeria and the generally accepted author of the Indirect Rule System, was originally a soldier in the private employ of the Royal Niger Company. The fact that Britain, where opinion on the desirability of colonial expansion was divided (sharply divided until about 1860) at the time, was clearly encouraged by humanitarian and religious influences did not quite materially affect the position from the point of view of Africans, some of whom, while gratefully appreciating the really good and lasting work of these humanitarian and religious bodies in Africa, tended to be somewhat sceptical as to whether these bodies might not after all have been a sort of camouflaging complement to the imperial plan.

(ii) It could be argued in some quarters that the system of Indirect Rule was not, in its origin, specifically designed for the benefit, or even in the interest, of the natives but was rather a child of necessity. The writings of Lord Lugard himself, and of his most outstanding disciple, Sir Donald Cameron, tend, unconsciously no doubt, to lend colour to this belief. For both agree that limited resources, in manpower and finance, made any attempt at direct rule, in Nigeria for instance, quite impracticable and so a system whereby the territory could be administered and controlled with any passable effectiveness had to be adopted. A writer—incidentally an 'interested' party in favour of the system—has suggested that Lugard in fact borrowed a leaf from, or merely developed, the practice already tried in the southern part of Nigeria where Sir George Goldie, as chairman of the Niger Company, had in 1879 (i.e. many years before the Company was chartered or Lugard came into prominence) instructed his officials that 'if *the welfare of the native races is to be considered,* if dangerous revolts are to be obviated, the general principle of ruling on African principles, through native rulers, must be followed *for the present*'. (The sections italicized leave one in doubt about supporting the argument one way or the other without proper study of the documents themselves. 'Welfare' is a very vague word and what exactly did Goldie mean by it? His own conception of 'welfare for the native races' might easily have meant quite a different thing from what modern Africa could accept. England herself in 1879 had, in fact, conceptions of welfare for her own people quite different from present-day conceptions. Again, what did the words 'for the present' really signify? Resort to direct rule as soon as conditions became favourable? This might appear to be supported by the expressed need to 'obviate dangerous revolts'. 'Indirect Rule', however, for all its faults, and in spite of whatever might have been the original motive behind it, was much more to be preferred, as better for the natives, than any form of 'Direct Rule' would have been. Another useful—though purely academic—point brought out by the above quotation, is the apparent suggestion that the birthplace of Indirect Rule was after all the south and not the north of Nigeria, and that Goldie and not Lugard was its real author.)

(iii) Another argument has been that, even granting that the preceding argument is rejected, the system in practice could not possibly be for the progress of the territories concerned, since it merely favoured, sheltered and strengthened illiterate, conservative, unprogressive and sometimes autocratic chiefs at the expense of younger educated elements who, admitted into the Native Administration Councils, would be better able to understand and follow what was going on in the Councils as well as be able to take bold initiative in matters with which the councils might be concerned.

(iv) One other point of disgust about the system was the apparent policy to keep the Administrative Service, to which the system was intricately tied, exclusively for expatriates under the belief, rightly or wrongly, that no indigenous African was suitable for admission into it. An eloquent expression of national feelings in this respect was given by Dr. Namdi Azikiwe in his *Political Blueprint of Nigeria* published in 1943, in which the following statements appear (pp. 16–17):

> It is true that I have already discussed the Civil Service of Nigeria, but I wish to make it clear that, at present, the Administrative Service is almost a separate department from the rest of Government departments in Nigeria. From time immemorial it was regarded as a sacrosanct institution from whose ranks indigenous Nigerians were barred. It is true that there have been isolated instances when Nigeria nationals were appointed Administrative Officers, but if one should say that these people were tolerated, that is not stretching the point. . . . Nigerians have often viewed with alarm the tendency of the Colonial Office to impose on them alien political officers in the Administrative Service, with the result that in certain instances alien ideologies have replaced indigenous political philosophy of government and administration, despite the worship of the political cult of the so-called 'Indirect Rule.'

Later, on page 21 of the same booklet, Dr. 'Zik' states:

> Admittedly, there is some good in the 'Indirect Rule' system but, in practice, some of the problems raised, and the attempted solutions to them—legal, political and social, etc.—have given ground for justified apprehensions.

(v) Mention of 'political cult' brings to mind one strong psychological factor. The Indirect Rule system was based on the somewhat doubtful principle of 'letting the natives alone to develop in their own ways'. Such a policy *prima facie* clearly discouraged any definite attempt to *develop* the natives into advanced cultural, political, economic and social standards anywhere near what the Europeans were enjoying. It led in real practice to a sort of quasi-apartheid policy in the colonial territories, where Europeans hardly associated with the natives; lived apart from the natives, had separate clubs, separate hospitals, in some places even separate churches, to which no African, no matter what his social standing, could be admitted; where Europeans always looked upon the natives as inferior races fit for hewing wood and drawing water; where all senior posts in the civil or other services were clearly designated *European posts.* In some places like Kenya the natives were actually put on reserves. It is true that these practices of discrimination are now matters of recent history in most territories; but they could not be expected to be of good omen for any system of government qualified by the word *Native*—and so *Native* Administration could not be trusted. . . .

Such facts—and others which may have to be mentioned in the succeeding chapters—formed the background for the violent distrust of the Indirect Rule System among nationalists. It is to be admitted that some of the points mentioned above may in themselves be controversial; but this does not remove the fact that they did exist, even though no one might have expressed them in such crystallized forms as has just been done.

Low and Pratt: British Colonial Policy and Tribal Rulers

INDIRECT RULE

Until recently British thinking on the administration of African peoples has been marked by a near unanimous adherence to a policy known as indirect rule. It has never been a precise concept. The form in which it was applied in any area depended on many variables, amongst the most important of which was the degree of centralized authority that existed in the tribal political system. Thus, in some areas indirect rule involved the appointment of councils of traditional elders whose rule hardly extended beyond the boundaries of a single village and who had laboriously to be induced to federate with neighbouring authorities. In other areas, indirect rule meant the recognition of a powerful native ruler with an acknowledged authority over hundreds of thousands of subjects. A measure of the vagueness of the concept was the disagreement between successive governors of Uganda over whether the term applied to the type of administration in practice in Buganda. Sir Philip Mitchell, Governor from 1935 to 1940, denied that Buganda was under indirect rule. His successor, Sir Charles Dundas, in contrast, re-

From D. A. Low and R. C. Pratt, *Buganda and British Overrule: 1900–1955* (Kampala, Uganda: copyright 1969, Makerere Institute of Social Research; first published by Oxford University Press, 1960), pp. 163–76.

garded Buganda as the prototype of the whole idea.

However, in all the various types of local rule to which the term was applied, the local administration was entrusted to those native chiefs and headmen whose position was rooted in custom and who thus commanded the loyalty of the people. In contrast to any system of 'direct rule', either through British officers or through Africans appointed without reference to local traditional claims to authority, 'indirect rule' meant the appointment of traditional tribal chiefs as agents of local rule, the use in local government of those men whom the people were accustomed to obey. This principle of native administration was exceedingly influential throughout British Africa in the inter-war period. A careful study of the arguments used to defend it and of its implications and limitations is essential to an understanding of British colonial policy in almost any African territory during that period. In the case of Buganda there is additional interest in noting and explaining not only the influence of the concept but the significant variations in Buganda from the normal indirect rule pattern.

Initially its attractions were mainly administrative. 'It was necessary to seek some other instrument to complete the chain of communication as between the government and the people . . . what more natural than that we should use for this purpose if we can find them the tribal institutions of the people themselves.' What more natural indeed. With insufficient troops and a limited number of administrative officers the use of local personnel as agents of British rule was essential. The decision to enlist the tribal chiefs where possible was a natural one. They were the accepted leaders. Their presence on the British side would greatly lessen the danger of serious opposition to British rule. In a very real sense, too, there could be no substitute for them. As long as the tribal chief received the unquestioned loyalty of his people, not only would no alternative strike roots, but the chiefs themselves, unrecognized and ignored, would be a threat and a danger to the occupying power. In contrast, under indirect rule, with its instructions reaching the people through the authorities they had traditionally accepted, government would be more likely to be both accepted and effective. Lugard illustrated this point when he argued: 'Though the Suzerain power imposes the taxes and the general rate is fixed by the Governor the actual assessment is in the hands of the native ruler and his representatives. . . . It therefore appears to the tax payer as a tax imposed by his own native ruler.'

Rule through traditional institutions was seen to have a further advantage. It permitted the continued enforcement along traditional lines of the customary laws of the tribe. Though purged of elements that gave offence to Christian morality and 'natural justice', these laws, especially when enforced by those who traditionally dispensed justice, would still provide a framework of ordered social life far more effective than any externally imposed system. With special reference to Tanganyika, Sir Donald Cameron in 1931 argued these matters as follows:

'Except in the detribalized areas and areas which were broken up by the

Arabs and Germans, a native is subject to a system of law and custom which he understands . . . and I claim . . . that it is because we have determined to uphold that system of law and discipline which he knows that the native in Tanganyika as a whole is so amenable. . . . If you set up native councils which are not tribal, strictly speaking, you may call them tribal institutions because they are within a tribe but if they have not got the sanctions which I have mentioned, the sanctions of custom and usage, they are not regarded by the people with the same degree of veneration as if they were indigenous institutions of the people. . . . If you set up an artificial system of native councils which are not based on tribal authority you have got that tribal authority working underneath the whole time and then you express surprise that you do not make any progress in attaching the natives to the artificial system which you have set up.'

Indirect rule soon came to rest on more than convenience and utility. In its defence were developed arguments of principle and social philosophy. The first of these expressed the fear that any other policy might destroy an established social order before alternative institutions, social controls, and values had become firmly rooted. This was seen as undesirable for both the welfare of the Africans and the security of the British rule. This combination of expediency and high purpose, often regarded by their detractors as a specifically British characteristic, clearly influenced the thinking of many British administrators. As early as 1898 it was clearly expressed by Sir George Goldie when he wrote: 'If the welfare of the native is to be considered, if dangerous revolts are to be avoided, the general policy of ruling on African principles through native rulers must be followed.' Sir Percy Girouard wrote that 'There are not lacking those who favour direct rule, but if we allow the tribal authority to be ignored or broken it will mean that we who numerically form a small minority of the country shall be obliged to deal with a rabble with thousands of persons in a savage or semi-savage state all acting on their own impulses and making themselves a danger to society generally.' Sir Philip Mitchell later argued that if the traditional communities were broken up, if the old loyalties were destroyed, other organizations, less responsible, less loyal, and more dangerous, might take their place.

It would be wrong to dismiss this as a thinly disguised self-interest. Certainly, the influence of indirect rule ideas was greatly increased because it offered practical as well as ethical advantages. The ethical considerations, however, were not mere shallow rationalizations. At the time the alternative to indirect rule was not the rapid absorption of Africans into western type democratic institutions. Rather it was their direct rule by European officers and African subordinates. This, the supporters of indirect rule argued, would rapidly shatter the whole social fabric of African communities and reduce Africans to a disorganized mass of helots. Indirect rule was offered as a means of aiding these communities to stand with dignity and autonomy against the impact of western ways and ideas, adjusting to them but not being overwhelmed by them. This argument was well and strongly put in a memorandum submitted to the Joint Select Committee on Closer Union by the Tanganyika Government:

'We believe that for the present and for many years to come the only way in which we can prevent the natives from "going under" and becoming a servile people (a condition desired for them by a large number of white folk in East Africa); the only way of keeping his society together; the only way in which he can be trained in public affairs—however simply in the early years—is by the system of indirect or tribal administration.'

This quotation also suggests a further important observation. In the inter-war years there was strong hostility between the proponents of two main approaches to African development. One of these groups stressed the need for widespread European participation in the economic and agricultural development of the territories and for European political leadership and, eventually, control by the local European population. The second group was wary of too much European settlement and suspicious of local European political leadership. Instead it stressed that the primary responsibility of Britain was to her subject peoples, and that she held power as a trustee for these people until they developed to a position where they could rule themselves. There is no doubt that in the inter-war period almost all British supporters of this second 'trusteeship' attitude towards Britain's colonial responsibilities believed that indirect rule represented the application of this trusteeship principle to the rule of African peoples. In Tanganyika, for example, Sir Donald Cameron's vigorous application of indirect rule principles was not felt to be in any way hostile to Britain's responsibilities under the mandate. Rather, quite the reverse. Cameron argued, and the Permanent Mandates Commission concurred, that Tanganyika's native administration system was compatible with both the letter and the spirit of this mandate.

Further support for indirect rule came from a conviction, widely and deeply held in the inter-war years, that European political institutions were unsuitable for Africans. This was not out of a sentiment that these institutions were too good for the African. Rather, as the Victorian confidence in the unquestioned value of Christianity, education, and commerce declined, a type of liberal racialism developed which felt that European institutions might be inappropriate in Africa. It was not argued that tribalism could be preserved indefinitely. The fact of change was recognized. Even Lugard recognized the inevitability of rapid and disintegrating change in Africa. Indirect rule was offered as a technique of social change, a means of bringing African communities into closer contact and harmony with the modern world and of raising their standards of life without any resulting social chaos. If sheltered against a too rapid disintegration, it was hoped that the indigenous institutions would adapt themselves successfully while yet remaining in basic harmony with the African temperament and environment.

In all this there was a fundamental Burkean conservatism—a scepticism of constitution-mongering, a fear of imposed changes, a belief that each people has its character and traditions and must itself evolve political institutions suitable thereto. Expressions of these sentiments were many. In 1929 the Hilton Young Commission, for example, regarded as an open question whether representative institutions would ever be suitable for African peoples. Sir Donald Cameron, with reference to the place of elections in native political development, said: 'As far as I am concerned I would leave that to their genius. I would not force it upon them.' And again: 'Whether the native . . . will turn to a western system of government with the vote and the ballot I do not know. Again I saw that that must be left to his own genius.'

It might now be expected that the use which was made of traditional chiefs in the administration of the African territories would have been regarded in the United Kingdom as a technical administrative matter, of interest to very, very few. It is true that its main protagonists have always been colonial administrators. However, interest in and support for indirect rule was in fact strong and influential amongst a much wider circle. Two sources of this support can be noted briefly.

Firstly, after 1918, not only did interest in the colonies increase greatly in the United Kingdom but also large sections of important opinion came to hold a greatly enhanced sense of responsibility towards their inhabitants. Those who felt concern for the welfare and rights of the colonial peoples almost invariably supported the indirect rule approach to local administration in Africa. The backwardness of the continent precluded any consideration of independence, but it was widely felt that some autonomy and recognition should nevertheless be given to the social and political institutions which the people knew and felt to be their own. Indirect rule was thus the native administration side of a major body of British thought about Britain's responsibilities as a colonial power.

Secondly, indirect rule benefited greatly by the support which it received from British anthropologists in the inter-war years. Their judgement, with its obvious claim to being impartial and 'scientific', further influenced important opinion in Britain. At any time, anthropologists are sensitive to the social costs of rapid change. They are more likely to see worth and utility in institutions and habits of life about which others might be impatient and critical. In addition, under the particular stimulus of Malinowski and Radcliffe-Brown, many British anthropologists in the 1920s and 1930s had become interested in 'culture contact'. Here, inevitably, interest tended to focus on the disintegrating and negative effect of the western impact. A. I. Richards made the point in 1944 in these words:

> 'To view colonial administration as a force attacking a native society has perhaps caused too great a concentration on the disruptive processes and too little on the forces of integration which are also at work.'

Thus, though approaching colonial administration from a different standpoint, the anthropologists ended with much the same opinion as most of the officials. 'My own opinion', wrote Malinowski in 1929, 'is that indirect rule or dependent rule is infinitely preferable. . . . The real difference . . . consists in the fact that direct rule assumes that you can create at one go an entirely new order, that you can transform Africans into semi-civilized pseudo-European citizens within a few years. Indirect rule on the other hand recognizes that no such magical rapid transformation can take place, that in reality all social development is very slow and that it is infinitely preferable to achieve it by a slow and gradual change coming from within.'

Contributing to this general reluctance to impose European institutions upon Africans was the traditional preference of the British for the unsophisticated. It is an attitude that is found frequently in British writings on African themes. It appears as a preference for the Masai over the Kikuyu, the northern peoples over the coastal tribes, the uneducated pagan over the mission-trained clerk, the chief over the London graduate. Cameron exhibited this general attitude when he wrote:

'Our desire is to make him a good African, and we shall not achieve this if we destroy all the institutions, all the traditions, all the habits of the people. . . . When I write that our desire is to make the native "a good African" I mean that he should be trained in accordance with his environment instead of being given a European veneer out of keeping with conditions under which he must live in Africa.'

A consequence of this attitude was that indirect rule supporters were highly critical of any system under which the British officers in fact dominated the local scene. Lugard, for example, was convinced that the native states of India had a more secure political future than the areas under direct rule. In Africa, he wrote: 'It must be in fact remembered that the policy is to support native rule . . . and not to impose a form of British rule with the support of native chiefs.' By example, by encouragement, by advice, the chiefs must be led to an enthusiasm for justice and the progress of their peoples. A Resident too enthusiastic for specific reforms and projects might make more rapid progress initially, but if he fails to convince the chief of their value, if the native authority supports him only reluctantly and hesitatingly, then the reforms will be unlikely to have lasting value. Always the primary stress, therefore, should be on the education of the rulers. Lugard from the beginning recognized that this would not be an easy task. In 1906 he wrote:

'Residents must bear in mind that . . . the irksomeness of the new régime may weigh very heavily upon the native chiefs. The powerful are deprived of the pastime of wars and raids and even the weak may feel . . . that "There can be too much even of security." Lack of any form of excitement and rivalry between neighbouring Emirates may induce a spirit of ennui caused by the Pax Britannica. Our object should be to give them an interest and an object beyond the routine performance of their duties, to interest them in the scheme of government, to teach them to recognize the new order of things, to show them common interests, to engage their sympathy for our efforts in secular education, and to promote a legitimate rivalry in civilized progress and even in sports.'

This whole section suggests that while the supporters of indirect rule were anxious to encourage the African to adapt and develop his institutions along lines of his own choosing, there were certain manly, Christian, and Victorian virtues to which he must be led. Native authorities might choose, if they wished, to be autocratic, to ignore such western institutions as elections and to scorn the idea that they should be in any direct sense responsible to their people, but they could not choose to be disinterested in progress, they could not choose blatant nepotism or a too corrupt rule. They were, in other words, to be encouraged to promote, along traditional lines, the values and objectives of Victorian England. An interesting minor reflection of this odd combination of values appears in Lugard's references to the education of the chiefs' sons: 'I hope that they would thus be taught not merely to read and write but to acquire an English Public Schoolboy's ideas of honour, loyalty and above all responsibility. It is by such means that I hope the next generation of Fulani rulers may become really efficient, reliable and honest co-operators with the British in the administration of the Protectorate.'

THE NATIVE AUTHORITIES AND THE CENTRAL GOVERNMENT

Indirect rule in British Africa was not only a set of values and attitudes. It is most usefully discussed in terms of the definite legal form which it first received in Northern Nigeria, and which later was copied in the Native Authority Ordinances of many other British territories in Africa.

Under these ordinances, chiefs were recognized and appointed by the Governor as native authorities. As such, their primary responsibility became the maintenance of law and order in their area. To this end their authority, derived from customary law, was sanctioned in so far as it conflicted neither with any ordinance of the territory nor with 'natural justice' or Christian morality. In addition, the authorities were normally empowered to issue rules and orders on a long list of matters in which, clearly, the Administration was especially interested. This list would normally include such matters as the possession of firearms, gambling, the migration of labour, the cultivation of food crops, porterage and food for administrative officers on tour, and the manufacture and consumption of intoxicating liquor.

These powers which the chiefs enjoyed as native authorities had their severe limits. There was, of course, a ban on all exercises of chiefly power which were a danger to law and order or which were offensive to Christian morality and western standards of justice. In addition, Lugard insisted on four further limitations. He withheld for the colonial power the raising of taxes, the promulgating of legislation, the disposal of land, and the levying of native troops.

In addition to such general prohibitions as these, there was placed over the chiefs a senior administrative officer, a 'Resident' as Lugard termed him, or a 'District Commissioner' as, frequently, he was called in other territories. Although Lugard referred to these officers as the sympathetic advisers and counsellors of the chiefs, it is clear that their authority far exceeded that of mere advisers. The various Native Authority Ordinances left no doubt about this. On matters of general policy his advice had to be taken, while such matters as the disposal of revenue, the issuing of rules and orders, and the appointment and dismissal of subordinate officials were not only subject to his guidance and advice but were open to his direct intervention if he judged it necessary. Finally the Governor was always able to replace an uncooperative chief. There was no doubt on either side about the officers' superior authority. Sir Percy Girouard wrote: 'I have impressed Emirs with the idea that they are my Wakila in their emirates but they must be guided by the word of the Resident who speaks for me.' These close controls suggest a further aspect of indirect rule. It had been no part of the original intention of the early indirect rule supporters to preserve a series of semi-independent native states. On this point Lord Lugard could hardly have been more categorical:

'The essential feature of the system is that the native chiefs are constituted as an integral part of the machinery of the administration. There are not two sets of rulers, British and native, working either separately or in co-operation but a single government in which the native chiefs have well-defined duties and an acknowledged status equally with the British official, their duties should never conflict and should overlap as little as possible. They should be complementary to each other and the chief must understand that he has no right to place or power unless he reaches his proper services to the State.'

The legal position of chiefs substantiated this. Once the framework of administration had been established, colonial governments usually introduced legislation defining the responsibilities and powers of native chiefs. To be sure, their powers were not derived from an ordinance of the central government. They might have strong local authority in their own right and much deference might be paid to them. Indeed, indirect rule was based on the premise that this would be the case. Legally, however, they were the agents of the central government, enjoying only those powers which it chose to delegate or recognize and subject to control and direction.

The limitations placed on the power of the native authorities were thus very great. It was, nevertheless, the hope of indirect rule supporters that the chiefs would accept these limitations and work under them without a deep sense of grievance. Indeed, it was more than a hope. Lugard judged in 1921 that the limitations had been accepted by the chiefs 'as natural and proper to the controlling power and their reservation in the hands of the Governor has never interfered with the loyalty of the ruling chiefs'. It was a judgement which several decades of experience had substantiated.

A major part of any explanation of this is the inter-war adherence of colonial administrators to the indirect rule approach to native administration. The various articles in the Native Authorities Ordinances which sanctioned direct interference and control by government officers were regarded as emergency provisions. The whole bent, however, of official thinking deprecated any blunt assertion of the administrative officers' superior powers. 'The ideal of the highest efficiency and rapidity of execution', to quote Sir Donald Cameron, 'must be subordinate to the main policy of encouraging and training the administration.' The chiefs thus enjoyed a wider autonomy than any mere reading of the relevant ordinances would suggest, a fact which surely contributed to making these ordinances more acceptable to them.

To assure that this acceptance continued, Lugard advanced two main recommendations. The first was that governments could and must leave to the chief those functions which were most important to the maintenance of his position of authority with his people. The chief should appoint and dismiss his subordinates; he and his courts should enforce the customary law. In those territories without a settled European minority, the Crown need rarely assert its rights over land alienation. The traditional system therefore should continue, with the chief retaining any powers in matters of land allocation and adjudication which were traditionally his own. Over the appointment of native authorities, there was a similar contrast between the legal powers held by the government and the powers which its officers normally asserted. Despite the reservation to the Governor of the right of appointment, the traditional rules of succession were followed in almost all cases. The Residents' influence over appointments was thus almost always confined either to a rare final veto or to the indirect influence which they might exercise within the framework of the customary process of selection on behalf of one of the contenders to a chieftainship. It would obviously be a basic contradiction of the whole indirect rule philosophy for the administration to do more than this, except in rare occasions of crisis.

Secondly, Lugard laid great stress on the behaviour of the administrative officers. At all times they must be careful to preserve and to enhance the dignity of the chief. Chiefs were not to be rebuked in public, instructions to their subordinates were to be given through them, and a most detailed protocol was to be followed by officers in their dealings with chiefs. Always the pomp and ceremony of office were to be preserved. Finally and most important, the Resident must have in himself a 'natural dignity' that would command respect. 'Vulgar familiarity' and 'assumed self-importance' were to be avoided. Happily for his peace of mind, Lugard was able to assume that 'The English gentleman needs no prompting in such a matter—his instinct is never wrong.'

Perhaps, however, we may suggest further reasons for the early success of indirect rule in addition to the limited autonomy retained by the chief in some tribal matters and the gentlemanly behaviour of the British officers. The first must be the superior power of the British. The alternatives before a chief were co-operation or deposition. In Uganda, for example, there was an obvious moral in the contrast between Apollo Kaggwa who co-operated, continued as the leading official in Buganda, and later received the K.C.M.G.; and Kaberega, the king of neighbouring Bunyoro, who did not co-operate and who spent his last years in exile on the Seychelles. However, indirect rule received more than a sullen and reluctant acquiescence. Many chiefs, overawed by the skills and knowledge of the European, were anxious to cooperate to secure the prestige which was gained by such association and to gain for themselves and their people the advantages which they hoped such association would bring. Moreover, indirect rule was not always detrimental to the chief's position. It was normally the chief alone who was recognized as the native authority. Such customary limitations to his power as councils of elders and lower chiefs received no legal recognition and inevitably, therefore, tended to be less effective. Also, the maintenance of law and order by the colonial power removed the threat of rebellion, frequently a very real check on the exercise of power in the indigenous system. Where any of these factors were at work, the chief was inclined to be sympathetically disposed to indirect rule.

Finally, in time, the interests of the chiefs and the government became more closely interwoven. They collected government taxes, heard cases that involved statute law as well as customary law, received fixed salaries and promoted centrally initiated policies. More and more were they associated in the public's mind with the Administration and more and more did they also associate their own interests with those of the ruling power. Lugard's hope that the chiefs should become an integral part of the machinery of government was becoming a reality.

Such then have been the general values and attitudes that marked British thinking on native administration throughout most of this century. They appealed to the liberal by the paramountcy they gave to African interests. They appealed to the conservative by the organic view of society which they implied, and by their stress on gradual adaptation rather than rapid change. The ideas of indirect rule acquired enormous influence in British Africa. In territory after territory in the interwar period native administrations were reorganized to fit this indirect rule model. Again and again the Northern and Western Nigerian and the Tanganyika Native Authority Ordinances were transposed to other territories, with a minimum of accommodation to local peculiarities and differences. Even the extremely atomistic indigenous political systems of Eastern Nigeria were searched for indigenous authorities who could be the basis of an indirect rule system. 'Indirect rule,' to quote Lord Hailey, 'passed through three stages, first of a useful administrative device, then that of a political doctrine, and finally that of a religious dogma.'

problem IV

Assimilation and Association and French Colonial Rule in Africa

The problem of French colonial rule in Africa is threefold: first, the difference between the colonial policies of *Assimilation* and *Association;* second, the divergence between French colonial policy and French colonial administration in Africa; third, the contrast and similarities between the French policies of assimilation and association, both in theory and practice, and the British colonial policy of Indirect Rule.

Throughout the nineteenth century, French colonial theory was dominated by the doctrine of assimilation. Although the idea of assimilation is as old as the Roman Empire, the philosophical origins of French assimilation are to be found in the Enlightenment with its deep belief in the power of reason and the concept of the universal equality of all men. Men were, of course, different, but these differences were the result of varying environments which reason, principally education and rational change, could eliminate. The French Revolution provided the opportunity to translate these ideas into action, and the *Declaration of the Rights of Man and of the Citizen* triumphantly applied to all men, not just Frenchmen, who are "born and live free and equal in rights." These egalitarian principles obviously applied to the French colonies which were promptly incorporated as constitutional and administratively equal parts of continental France. Despite the setback to the idea of assimilation during the First and Second Empires, assimilation as the theoretical framework for French colonial policy continued to reemerge with greater vigor during the more egalitarian periods of republican government.

But what precisely did assimilation mean? Martin Lewis has observed that Frenchmen held widely divergent interpretations of assimilation. It was certainly never a monolithic theory rigorously applied in Africa, and its meaning was vigorously debated, particularly in the late nineteenth century. Moreover, when France began to acquire large and populous colonies in West Africa at the end of the century, the dispute over assimilation intensified. Most French colonial thinkers agreed upon the necessity of developing a general formula by which the colonies might be rationally administered, and assimilation appeared to many to be the most logical doctrine. In the two colonial congresses which met in 1889 and 1890 the assimilationists resolved that French policy should "propagate among the natives the language, the methods of work, and, progressively, the spirit and civilization of France." The assimilationists, however, did not envisage their policy as an inflexible dogma to be universally applied throughout the colonies. Even in 1890 assimilationists were too aware of the enormity of their undertaking to expect the creation of instant Frenchmen from African peasants. Nevertheless, the resolutions of these congresses provided general definitions of policy which remained unchallenged until the turn of the century.

During the first decade of the twentieth century the assault on assimilation was in full swing. To those who believed the pseudoscientific racial theories which were popularized and widely promulgated throughout the latter half of the nineteenth century, the races were distinguished not only by color but by hereditary mental differences which made assimilation quite impossible. No amount of education or alteration of the environment, therefore, could be expected to raise the African to the level of an ordinary European. Others argued more positively that the manners, customs, and religion of the Africans should be respected, and the Africans allowed to develop "along their own lines." Such a proposition was, of course, quite incompatible with assimilation which, it was argued, should be abandoned in favor of a policy of "mutual assistance" or "association."

Although association, like assimilation, was never precisely defined, there was wide agreement on what it meant, particularly when contrasted with assimilation. Association emphasized a cooperation between ruler and ruled. Assimilation stressed the imposition of direct, centralized French control without regard for the indigenous inhabitants. Association respected the social and political institutions of the Africans. Assimilation either ignored or degraded those institutions in favor of French customs, culture, and civilization. Association envisaged economic development for the benefit of the Africans as well as France. Assimilation implied exploitation if not expropriation.

Under a policy of association the Africans were to develop within the context of their own environment and society. The French would maintain their control by ruling indirectly through the traditional authorities. The advantages were "simplicity, flexibility, and practicality." Moreover, the economic objectives of colonization could best be achieved by such a fraternal cooperation between conqueror and conquered. But this co-operation could only be realized if the rulers recognized their responsibilities for the well-being of the ruled and the integrity of indigenous society.

Raymond Betts has traced the evolution of the association policy, demonstrating that it, like assimilation, had its origins in the Enlightenment but remained indistinct until the work of Faidherbe, Gallieni, and Lyautey made association a practical reality and a pronounced policy. In West Africa, Indo-China, Madagascar, and Morocco these three remarkable administrators established French control by first utilizing the indigenous inhabitants in the conquest itself and then permitting them to regulate their own affairs through their own institutions. French authority was thus superimposed in a manner not entirely dissimilar to the Indirect Rule which English administrators employed in British African territories. Like Indirect Rule association was practical, economical, and effective, and to French colonial theorists and practitioners, a "systematic repudiation of assimilation." By 1910, assimilation appeared dead. But was it?

Although assimilation was no longer regarded as the official ideology of French colonial policy, it remained as a constitutional fiction while its attitudes and assumptions lingered pervasively to blur the distinction between assimilation and association. Martin Lewis, again, has observed that this confusion made it possible to take those aspects of each doctrine which most effectively contributed to the continuation of French rule. Such cynicism was later obscured by pious appeals for partnership and cooperation between rulers and ruled. Indeed, assimilation even assumed a respectable revival in the 1930's as an ideological counterweight to self-determination. Few can deny the appeal or the grandeur which the ideal of assimilation represented, but assimilation, like many ideologies, foundered on the contradictions inherent in its implementation. To Frenchmen, assimilation meant the imposition and acceptance of French culture. When in the late nineteenth century the French were faced with the possibility that an overwhelming majority of voters would be non-French, assimilation was cheerfully abandoned as official policy. "What was wrong with assimilation," Martin Lewis has concluded, "was not that it was illogical, unrealistic, or impossible, but rather that no serious effort was ever made to carry it out."

Raymond Betts has concurred with this conclusion, observing that assimilation lingered on because it provided a moral justification for conquest and colonialism. The decline of assimilation was, nevertheless, inevitable. On the one hand it was too idealistic and too humanitarian an abstraction to serve as a basis for the implementation of an imperialism which, in its practical application, was neither very idealistic nor very humane. On the other hand, the diversity of peoples and cultures which the French encountered in constructing their empire required a flexible policy to meet and adapt to local conditions, rather than a monolithic, rigid doctrine to be uniformly and universally applied. The gap between the ideal of assimilation and the reality of its application became too great, and its influence in French colonial policy diminished but never died. To the end of the empire its appeal remained irresistible to the French mind. Meanwhile, in facing the practical problems of ruling an empire, the French became "as expedient as any other colonizing power." Like other imperial powers they followed different practices in different colonies. These very divergent procedures, which were collectively called "association," did provide for more local autonomy, more flexible administration from Paris, and a more balanced use of the traditional authorities and the modern elite. Association was the French recognition of the realities of imperial rule, yet it too failed in the end, not so much because of its inherent weaknesses but because colonialism always brings about its own demise.

The flexible, economical, and practical characteristics of association immediately invited comparison with Indirect Rule, and Hubert Deschamps, himself a distinguished French colonial administrator, argued that the similarities far outweighed the differences. Deschamps regarded Lord Lugard as an intensely practical man, a man of common sense, decency, and good faith who sought sensible solutions to the complex problem of imperial rule. Lugard was concerned foremost with efficiency, peace, and order—not with abstractions about the universal application of reason or the fundamental equality of all men. Indirect Rule accomplished the former while ignoring the more lofty ideals of the latter. Like Lugard, the French faced similar problems of colonial rule for which the theory of assimilation offered no ready solutions. And like Lugard, Deschamps observed, the French recognized traditional authorities and maintained indigenous institutions. Although the French frequently let some such institutions fall into disuse, they supported so many that leading French colonial thinkers, like Maurice Delafosse, came to regard the policy of association as the French counterpart to Indirect Rule.

The British system of Indirect Rule rested on the recognition that peoples and their institutions were different and that these differences should be respected. Africa could thus evolve within traditional forms and with traditional leaders. Since no attempt was made to integrate the alien overrulers with traditional rulers and ruled, this policy, argued Deschamps, could only lead to separation and independence. Despite the acceptance and practice of association, the French still clung to the ideals of assimilation. Thus, old institutions must by the nature of man give way to new and modern forms which are more universal than national in character. Deschamps concluded that in the end the Lugardians and the assimilationists both won and lost. The traditional institutions vanished before modern ones, but African nationalism triumphed over political assimilation. French and British policies, so dramatically different in theory, cancelled one another out to become, in practice, virtually identical. Or were they? Michael Crowder cannot agree.

Crowder argues that Deschamps does not fully appreciate the fundamental differences between the French and British systems of colonial rule. These differences clearly emerge when comparing, for instance, the way in which the British and the French employed the native authorities. On the one hand, the British emphasized the advisory role of British officials while respecting, if not enhancing, the powers of the traditional authorities and the institutions by which they ruled. On the other, the French regarded the chiefs as petty officials in the colonial administration retained for convenience and efficiency rather than from any regard for their traditional authority and institutions of governing. Despite the official policy of association, the deep belief in assimilation on the part of French officials in the field encouraged indifference if not contempt for African customs and institutions which were largely ignored in favor of French language, customs, and administration. To Frenchmen assimilation was synonymous with the civilizing mission which reduced traditional chiefs to "mouthpieces and scapegoats" and elevated Africans who learned French and accepted French culture to an elite status which practiced power in the colonies and influence in France. Conversely, in British territories the chiefs remained powerful figures dispensing decisions and justice while the educated Africans were relegated by British officials to petty positions in the bureaucracy or excluded from government and traditional society to drift with little influence over either. Although the similarities between French and British colonial rule appear superficially self-evident, below the surface the differences between the two systems were not only differences in degree but also in kind.

Lewis: One Hundred Million Frenchmen: The Assimilation Theory in French Colonial Policy

During World War II, Jacques Stern, a former French Minister of Colonies, wrote almost lyrically of the "patient labor of assimilation" by which France had been "consolidating the moral and material ties which bind together forty million continental Frenchmen and sixty million overseas Frenchmen, white and colored" in the French Empire. . . . [And yet between 1946 and

From Martin D. Lewis, "One Hundred Million Frenchmen: The 'Assimilation' Theory in French Colonial Policy," *Comparative Studies in Society and History*, IV (1962), 129–49.

1960 the French Empire had virtually disappeared.] What went wrong? Assuredly, in the collapse of colonialism a variety of factors have been at work, many of which were quite independent of the particular policies which happened to be followed by the imperial powers. But some light may be thrown on the failure of assimilation by an examination of its place in the development of French colonial theory.

To begin with the obvious question, what does the term "assimilation" mean? While virtually all writings on modern French colonial policy use the word, confusion abounds as to its meaning. Some writers present it as the dominant and continuing characteristic of French colonial policy throughout the entire era of imperialism, as the distinctive manifestation of the French genius. Others hold that it was abandoned early in the 20th century, and replaced by a quite different policy of "association." It is easy to show that this latter term first appeared in the literature of French colonialism as a proposed alternative to "assimilation," but it is equally true that the two words did not long remain differentiated.

Some counterpose "assimilation" to "autonomy," these two terms suggesting goals supposedly characteristic of French and British colonial policy respectively—incorporation within the body politic of the mother country, on the one hand, and colonial self-government, on the other. Yet French critics of "assimilation" based their attack on the folly of extending European democratic institutions to the "inferior races" comprising the populations of the colonies and argued that the British did not engage in such irresponsible foolishness.

Some advocates of "assimilation" have given the term a purely legalistic constitutional meaning, with colonial representation in the metropolitan parliament as its most important manifestation. Others have used it in the much broader sense of making over non-European peoples in the "civilized" image of Europeans. Some have suggested that its true significance lies in the French acceptance of racial equality, as contrasted with the "colour bar" drawn by the British. Others have employed it in a narrowly administrative sense to refer to a highly-centralized direct rule in the colonies; yet the supposedly assimilation-minded French employed the protectorate technique in many of their colonies. Also in an administrative context, assimilation has been considered to mean applying a uniform set of rules in *all* colonies without taking into account differences in size, distance from France, social organization, religious patterns, economic development, etc.

Culturally, assimilation might mean the propagation of the French language among non-European peoples; but have not the English done the same with their own tongue? Finally, to complete the confusion, one finds the odd phrase "tariff assimilation" used to describe French customs policy towards the Empire.

This mélange cannot be blamed solely on the failure of scholars to define their terms, however much one might feel that it should be a part of their responsibility. At the height of the debate over assimilation as a colonial policy, a delegate to the *Congrès Colonial National* of 1889–90 complained that "among the partisans of assimilation there are not two who agree on the meaning of that expression." A decade later, virtually the same thought was expressed by a participant in the *Congrès International de Sociologie Coloniale* of 1900 who observed that "there are so many meanings given to 'assimilation' that it has become one of the most dangerous words of our colonial vocabulary."

In 1895 Arthur Girault published his *Principes de Colonisation et de Législation Coloniale* in which, with a true Gallic passion for order, he gave a systematic presentation to the ideas of assimilation as he understood them. His definition, while no more "correct" than any other, provides a useful point of departure for our discussion. Furthermore, his work, written as a text for law students, was reissued in edition after edition, revised and expanded but always retaining the same organization in its discussion of general theoretical principles. Its influence in the training of French officialdom must have been substantial indeed.

His presentation rests on an abstract schematization involving three possible alternative colonial policies: subjection, autonomy, and assimilation. Each, he cautions, is an "abstract type" and none "have ever been realized in their entirety anywhere." Nevertheless, he leaves the reader in no doubt as to his own preference for assimilation, so long as its application is both "moderate" and "eclectic." Its ideal he considers "the constantly more intimate union between the colonial territory and the metropolitan territory." Colonies "are considered as a simple prolongation of the soil of the mother country," merely as *"départements* more distant than the rest." The goal is "the progressive subjection to the same rules of the different parts of the territory" and "the progressive creation of veritable French *départements."*

To Girault, "the principal result and visible sign of assimilation" is the representation of the colony in the legislature of the mother country. Other practical measures include the following: "A single body of legislation governs all parts of the territory without distinction," and all new laws in the mother country apply automatically in all the colonies unless specific exception is made. The administrative procedures and sub-divisions that exist in the metropolis are duplicated exactly in the colonies. The very existence of a colonial ministry may be opposed, since all the various aspects of colonial administration would properly fall under one or another of the home ministries: interior, justice, education, etc. No distinct colonial military forces exist, and colonists are subject to military obligations identical with those of citizens at home. Similarly, taxes, tariffs, and financial administration will be identical, as will the extent of civil liberties, reflecting the regime in power in the mother country.

Significantly, he comments that "the assimilation of the natives is a possible consequence, but not at all the only possible one, of the principle of assimilation of colonies":

> If it is hoped to be able to inculcate them with our ideas and our customs, then one works zealously to make them into Frenchmen: they are educated, they are granted the right of suffrage, they are dressed in the European mode, our laws are substituted for their customs, and in a word, native assimilation is pursued. But if one despairs of arriving at this result, if they show themselves refractory toward our civilization, then, to prevent them from injecting a discordant note

in the midst of the general uniformity, they are exterminated or pushed back.

As a participant in the discussions at the colonial congress of 1900, he insisted that "assimilation of the natives" and "political and administrative assimilation" must be recognized as "two distinct ideas." In the third edition of this text, he commented that assimilation "has often been asked for opposite reasons, and with a view to entirely different results."

There are those who, when speaking of assimilation, are thinking primarily of the natives, and who imagine that it is the policy to be followed towards them which is in question, when in reality it is an entirely different matter. The assimilation of the colonies is so little that of the natives that in Algeria, the pushing back of the latter is precisely what is asked by the colonists who would assimilate that country completely with France.

Obviously, Girault's interpretation was not shared by all partisans of assimilation, but it is important to be aware of it as we seek to trace the development of the concept.

Late in the 19th century a great debate developed in France over assimilation as the nation, having won and then lost its first great colonial empire in the 17th and 18th centuries, entered vigorously on a new imperial career under the aegis of the Third Republic. The foundations of the theory, however, lay in the past, and in particular in the treatment accorded the surviving fragments of the first French empire during the Revolution of 1789. . . . "The policy of assimilation," wrote Girault a century later, "was in the logic of the revolution."

The Revolution had established the equality of all Frenchmen, and the rights which it proclaimed were in its thought the same for all men without distinction of latitude. What could have been more natural . . . ?

Of course, the "natural" implication of the Revolution might equally have been to extend to the colonies the right to choose their own form of government, as France itself was doing, even if that entailed their independence and separation from France. Unreal though the alternative might seem, in 1793 Jeremy Bentham had called on the Convention to do just that, in a pamphlet entitled "Emancipate Your Colonies!"

The foundations of assimilationist theory can be traced to the arguments of the *philosophes*. In Condorcet's famous phrase, "a good law is good for all men, just as a sound logical proposition is sound everywhere." Whatever their philosophical background, however, assimilationist practices were discarded with the rise of Bonaparte's star, and there began a process that would continue throughout the 19th century—assimilative measures became associated with republican governments, their abolition with the overthrow of these governments. . . .

On Napoleon's [III] downfall in 1870, the Government of National Defense, acting almost by republican reflex, restored colonial representation. It was some years, however, before the Third Republic was sufficiently stabilized to permit much attention to colonial problems. . . . Before a new republican theory on the colonial question could be fully worked out, men of action had transformed the very nature of the question by the rapid extension of the empire in the 1880s.

The forward push in Algeria and the new acquisitions in Indo-China, Madagascar, West Africa, and Tunisia provoked controversy. Twice, in 1881 and 1885, Jules Ferry was forced from office by storms of public and parliamentary protest. But alongside those who thought imperialist ventures ill became a republican government were others who saw in the new territories a field for spreading the glories of the French tradition (as well, of course, as those who sought more mundane advantages for French capitalism).

The publication in 1874 by Paul Leroy-Beaulieu of his volume, *De la Colonisation chez les Peuples Modernes,* had attracted little attention, but by the time of its reissue in 1882, colonial policy had become a burning question. While his book was primarily historical, in dealing with Algeria he ventured to discuss the merits of current policy:

> The indigenous population is at least 2,500,000. What should be done with these 2,500,000 individuals? Three possibilities exist: to push the natives back beyond the Atlas Mountains, even into the Sahara; to fuse them with the European population by imposing on them, forcibly or by propaganda, our customs, our laws, and perhaps even our religion; or to respect all their customs, make their property inviolable, and remove the Europeans from frequent contact with them. These three systems may be defined in three words: *refoulement,* fusion [i.e., assimilation, ed.], abstention.

He found elements of each approach in past policy, but complained that after fifty years of French power no clear choice had yet been made. Such a decision, he felt, was urgently required, but what should it be? The first path he considered "unjust" and therefore unthinkable. The third, "complete respect for the customs, traditions, and manners" of the Arab population, "would, if it were applied with logic, require that our army and our colonists should quit Algeria." Obviously, this too was not to be considered. "Thus, there remains only the second path, the fusion of the indigenous element with the European element." Such fusion need not mean a complete absorption of the natives, to the point that there would remain no difference in manners or customs. All that would be needed would be to create

> a state of affairs in which the two populations of different origin would be placed under the same economic and social regime, obeying the same general laws, and following the same impulse in the productive order. For a long time, perhaps forever, there would of course remain distinctions of habits and beliefs; but there would be an identity of interests from the economic, political, and social point of view; and properly considered, that is the only harmony that is indispensable from the viewpoint of peace, prosperity, and civilization.

IV

The debate on assimilation that developed in the late 1880's found its focus in the sessions of the *Congrès Colonial Internationale de Paris* of July and August, 1889, and the *Congrès Colonial National* which met in December, 1889, and again in February and March, 1890. Both meetings were attended by many high officials from various branches of the French government at home and abroad, as well as by scholars, explorers, and other private individuals interested in colonial questions. The first of the sessions, the international congress of 1889, was attended also by delegates from Spain, Portugal, Belgium and the Netherlands. Its most prominent feature was the clash of opinions which took place between Gustave Le Bon, the explorer, and Alexandre Isaac, senator from the Caribbean island *département* of Guadeloupe and one of the two vice-presidents of the Congress.[1]

At the opening general session, Le Bon presented a report "On the Influence of Education and European Institutions on the Indigenous Populations of the Colonies." It was a slashing attack on "the fatal results of the system known as assimilation."

> Daily, people speak of "Frenchifying" the Arabs of Algeria, the yellow peoples of Indo-China, the Negroes of Martinique, of giving to all these colonies the institutions, the laws, and an organization identical to that of our French *départements*.

For such ideas he had nothing but scorn. His discourse was studded with such phrases as "inferior races," "savages," "half-civilized peoples," "barbarians." He satirized the French "taste for uniformity": "Our institutions of the moment seem to us always as the best, and our temperament, which tomorrow will lead us to overturn them entirely, today impels us to impose them on everybody."

> These theoretical views have led us and are leading us more and more to organize our colonies as French *départements*. It matters little what their population may be: Negroes, savages, Arabs, yellow peoples, should benefit from the Declaration of the Rights of Man and that which we are pleased to call our great principles. All have universal suffrage, municipal councils, *arrondissement* councils, general councils, tribunals of all degrees, deputies and senators to represent them in our assemblies. Negroes, scarcely emancipated, whose cerebral development corresponds hardly to that of our Stone Age ancestors, have jumped into all the complexities of our formidable modern administrative machines.

In passing, we should note that this was a considerable exaggeration with respect to the existing state of affairs on universal suffrage and parliamentary representation; yet undeniably it was true for parts of the empire. He was particularly exercised by attempts to extend French education to the colonial territories. He denied any enmity for education as such, but argued that "the kind of instruction applicable to civilized men is not at all applicable to half-civilized man." . . .

The British experience with European-style education in India provided him with a dramatic example of the pitfalls awaiting France. It had done no more, he claimed, "than unbalance the Hindus and take away from them their aptitude for reasoning, not to speak of a frightful lowering of morality." . . . The discussion of the report was heated. As a native of the Antilles, Senator Isaac expressed his embar-

[1] Isaac's background is interesting in view of his prominence as an advocate of assimilation. He was born in Guadeloupe in 1845, but was educated in France and then entered the educational administration. On his election in 1885 as Guadeloupe's senator, he returned to France, where he played an active role in the discussion of colonial issues.

rassment at attempting a reply: "Perhaps I myself am included among those natives who should not be given a European education."

I cannot understand how, a hundred years after the Revolution, when if I am not mistaken it is a question of restoring to light the truths affirmed in that great epoch, it can be held that education is a bad thing; that between a colonizing people and the inhabitants of the colonial country there should be only a relationship of domination; that the customs, the language, the knowledge of the European nations are a reserved patrimony which the natives should not be permitted to touch; that, finally, in the external territories of which these nations have taken possession, there should be only subjects, never citizens.

It reminded him, he said, of the days of the monarchy when the kings instructed colonial governors not to develop the spirit of the colonists too much, "because in giving the colonists a certain degree of culture they would be diverted from labors profitable to the metropolis." At that time, he continued, "there were also men in Europe who were crushed under the weight of a society based on restrictions of precisely the same nature. Were the Rights of Man proclaimed for them alone?"

How better could one make friends of a colonial people "than by establishing between them and the colonizers a community of language and interests?" Otherwise, if the native population "possesses a civilization to which you wish to confine them, that civilization will become more and more hostile to your own." And if, on the contrary, they have no civilization, "you may be blamed for having wanted to perpetuate their inferiority."

To say that it is necessary to keep people ignorant in countries under European domination, because instruction brought by the dominant people will make the natives wicked, or enemies, is to make that charge against European civilization itself.

If that doctrine should prevail, it would be necessary to suppress all that has been done up to the present, and to turn boldly toward the past. It would be necessary to declare that slavery was a beneficial institution, and that there is but one means of maintaining the metropolitan authority . . . force.

Frank Puaux, a member of the Superior Colonial Council, found himself "overcome by a profound melancholy" while listening to Le Bon.

Suppose that if on the conquest of Gaul, some savant of that time had maintained that the Gauls should be left in barbarism; that singular philanthropist might have been heeded. Would we be here today, if the Romans had followed his counsel?

Do not forget, Messieurs, that we have become what we are because a people of superior civilization communicated their light, their arts, and their laws to our ancestors. Have we the right to keep this rich heritage for ourselves? Can we refuse to do today for others what the Romans did for us nearly two thousand years ago?

Others conceded some points to Le Bon's argument, but the general tenor of the discussion was critical of his viewpoint. Dr. Poitou-Duplessy, retired chief physician of the navy, recognized that "just as the stomach requires food appropriate to its age and kind, so the brain requires nourishment suitable to the degree of development which it has attained." The brain of orientals, he agreed, was not yet capable "of partaking of our intellectual nourishment without cerebral indigestion." Nevertheless, he would not accept the view that assimilation was impossible, if approached slowly and carefully, as a parent teaches a child. Furthermore, even in an inferior race, "some men's brains are equal to the average among ourselves," and are thus capable of European education. "To refuse it to them would seem to me difficult and unjust."

When Le Bon cited a recent anthropological study as proof that the impossibility of civilizing Negroes was "well settled," that to attempt it was "pure aberration," Admiral Vallon, former governor of Sénégal, replied that "the blacks lacked neither intelligence nor natural gifts, and in that respect they sometimes put us in the shade." He considered that educating the natives was not only France's moral obligation but was in the interest of France as well. "We are in the same situation with respect to these colored peoples as we are with respect to our peasants. We owe education to the former as to the latter." "It is true," he added sarcastically, "that some persons think that in sending our peasants to school, we are making them enemies of society."[2]

Several speakers criticized Le Bon's assumption that assimilation meant an attempt to transform natives into Frenchmen overnight. The remarks of Senator Barbey, former Minister of Marine and Colonies and the president of the congress, seemed to sum up the predominant view:

> I believe I am able to say that no one here is the enemy of the natives, or the adversary of those who wish to civilize them. The whole problem is to find the best methods for doing that . . . From this point of view, there remains much to be done: we have to free ourselves of a great number of prejudices, to better recognize the proper aptitudes of the various races, to determine the degree of development to which each of them is susceptible. . . . It is necessary above all to recognize that such a work will require much time. We will achieve nothing without patience, and, I may add, without generosity. Only by treating the natives benevolently and by giving them a good example can we win them to our ideas.

Senator Isaac's own role in the congress was the presentation of a report "On Methods of Government in the Colonies." His main theme was the necessity of bringing the colonial regime "into harmony with the present institutions of the metropolis." He was sharply critical of the continued existence of rule by decree [u. senatus consultus] as established under the Second Empire, and asked that the colonies already represented in Parliament be brought more completely under the rule of laws. Where colonial representation had not yet been established, and where that fact justified a maintenance of decree rule, he felt "it would nevertheless be bad and sometimes dangerous if the exercise of that regime were not tempered by the organization of

[2] Not all French officials in Africa agreed with Admiral Vallon, as was apparent from the remarks of M. Ballay, lieutenant governor of Gabon, during the discussion of a report on education in Indo-China. "Experience demonstrates that the black who has received too developed an education acquires a distaste for labor. To multiply the number of so-called educated subjects would be to create in Gabon a hotbed of idlers and *déclassés.*"

some mode of consultation with the interested populations."

He based his argument on an extensive examination of the history of French colonial administration, designed to show that assimilation was the policy truly characteristic of republican France, and even, to some degree, of France before the Revolution. . . .

"What is a colony?" he asked. "Is it a simple field of exploitation? an instrument of work composed of the territory and of those who inhabit it? Is it an establishment which has completely answered the purpose of its creation when it brings to the metropolis a benefit, when there has been procured the means of draining off its products?" . . . He insisted that "we do not intend to formulate an absolute rule equally applicable to all the colonies." "Common sense" would indicate that that was impossible. "Their institutions will be more or less similar or different according to their age, their geographical situation, the composition of their population." It was, he implied, only the tendency and direction of development that was essential.

In the discussion which followed his report, Paul Dislère, councillor of state and another vice-president of the congress, sought to pin down his meaning. Total assimilation, it seemed to Dislère, could be achieved only "at the cost of veritable political or economic revolutions." In the "old colonies," those revolutions had taken place; "the evil is past; now there is only good to be drawn from it." He saw no impediment to their complete assimilation, giving them "all our rights," and also the same burden of taxes as in the metropolis. But he boggled at the implication that "assimilation" implied the right of all colonies, everywhere, to be represented in the national parliament, and asked what this would mean in those colonies "where a very small number of French citizens found themselves in the midst of a considerable native population." Senator Isaac hastened to reply that he had never asked that all colonies should be assimilated:

> I have, on the contrary, constantly made a distinction between assimilable colonies and those which are not suited to assimilation. . . . By assimilation I mean a situation in which the French citizens of a colony enjoy all the legal guarantees accorded to the French of the metropolis, on condition that they bear equivalent charges proportionately to their ability. . . .

The *Congrès Colonial National* was organized in seven sections, the first to consider general questions of colonial organization, the others to discuss problems of specific areas: Algeria and Tunis, the American colonies, the colonies on the west coast of Africa, in the Indian Ocean, in Oceania, and finally of Indo-China. . . .

The national congress was notable for the absence of critics of assimilation among its leadership, although participants in discussion frequently challenged the proposals made and forced modifications. Senator Isaac, in charge of the discussion on general organization, sought the commitment of the congress to the general principle of assimilation, which he defended (as in the earlier congress) by an appeal to history and the French tradition. When a critic objected that discussion of "pure theory" would lead the congress into sterile debates and obscure the real task of finding "practical means" to improve colonial organization, he insisted that nothing worthwhile could be accomplished without an adequate theory. "Unless we are to abandon everything in the colonial domain to chance and empiricism, it is indispensable to declare ourselves for a system and to set forth its principles." To do so, he reiterated, would not mean either attempting an overnight transformation of the colonies or the imposition of a uniform approach everywhere. "One does not transform a society with the wave of a wand." One must find "a general formula which can be given diverse applications." The resolution which finally emerged with the approval of the congress declared that "in all the overseas lands under French authority, the efforts of colonization should propagate among the natives the language, the methods of work, and, progressively, the spirit and the civilization of France."

There was no dissent on the question of language, but before the provision on "methods of work" was accepted it was necessary to quiet the fears of some delegates. Commander Périssé pointed out that there was "no intention of introducing into our colonies the complicated industries which can only exist in the home country."

> The only goal that it is possible to attain is to lead the natives progressively to cultivate certain useful trades, or to make use of more perfected implements than the rudimentary tools which they now employ.

Senator Isaac agreed: "No one would think, for example, of transporting to the Sudan this or that one of our metropolitan industries which would not find nourishment in that country. Manifestly, everywhere one should be inspired by the resources, the possibilities, the local needs." Even greater concern was expressed at the provision for spreading "the spirit and the civilization of France." In Isaac's original draft resolution he had used the word "customs" (*mœurs*), and many delegates voiced their doubt that this could ever be achieved. After the substitution of phrasing, however, and Isaac's assurances that "assimilation does not consist of substituting from one day to the next the customs and institutions of a European people for the customs and institutions of a native people," the clause was adopted.

The second general resolution adopted by the congress adovcated a special regime for each colony, taking account of "different geographical, political, and economic conditions." This regime, however, should be defined by an organic law. "French laws should as much as possible be applied to Frenchmen residing in the colony," while "the native laws and customs should be respected insofar as they are compatible with the *mission civilisatrice* of France." This last provision, though modified somewhat in language from the original proposal to "guarantee in principle" the respect of native laws and customs, of course still glossed over the key dilemma in the idea of assimilation as a benevolent colonial policy.

The third general resolution called for parliamentary representation of all colonies "where the French establishment is sufficiently developed, both in the number of nationals [i.e., Frenchmen from France] . . . and the importance of their interests," and declared that voting for such representatives should be by "all French citizens" of the colony. "The native populations should be led gradually to the exercise of political rights, taking account of their state of civilization." The fourth resolution attacked the *sénatus-consultes* of 1854 and 1866 as "not in accord with the principles of the present Constitution" and declared that "rule by decree is not reconcilable with parliamentary representation of the colonies." The fifth called for the establishment, for the benefit of those colonies as yet unrepresented in parliament, of "a special system of consultation" in the form of a reorganized Superior Colonial Council.

The assimilationists have been misrepresented by their critics, both political and scholarly, as insisting "on a rigid universality" of their theory, making no allowances for variations between one colony and another. The inaccuracy of this is shown by the general resolutions, but it is even more clear from the special resolutions dealing with specific areas. . . . In the West African territories as yet unannexed, the congress felt a protectorate regime would be "more favorable than annexation to the development of our influence and more appropriate to the customs and interests of the natives."

Algeria was recognized as a special case. The congress declared that it was *une terre française,* not a colony, and that France should "strive to inspire French sentiments among the natives, to favor French colonization by all possible means, to assimilate the European foreigners." It opposed naturalization of the natives *en bloc* but felt "it would be useful" to offer "a special naturalization compatible with the maintenance of their personal status" (under Moslem law) "to those who fulfill certain conditions and offer certain guarantees." If this were done, these newly-created Moslem citizens of France should be allowed to vote in the elections for Algerian senators and deputies, and "to become entitled after a delay of ten years to occupy a place in the metropolitan chambers."

In the light of the general program of the assimilationists, what seems significant is not the sweeping character of the measures, but their timidity. In no instance was a further extension of parliamentary representation called for, although the maintenance of existing colonial representation was defended even where the native population was excluded from the franchise. For Algeria the congress recommended that "sufficient financial resources should be created" to make French education "accessible to the entire school-age population," but for Indo-China the congress suggested only that the government "should study ways of encouraging the learning of French and making them accessible at small cost to the native population." . . .

The resolution on the West African establishments also favored the encouragement of missionaries to teach French, and urged "that the sons of influential native chiefs should be brought to France, where they could be familiarized with our civilization and prepared to become valuable auxiliaries for French policy in Africa." Finally, with regard to Madagascar, where French control was not yet complete, the congress seemed most concerned that the government "should maintain energetically the political supremacy of France . . . *vis-à-vis* foreign powers." Assimilation came into the picture only in the request that France should "give as much support as possible to the French missionaries and their *mission civilisatrice*" in the island.

The resolutions of the 1889–90 congress appear to have had little practical effect on the actual conduct of colonial affairs. Specifically, despite Senator Isaac's concern with ending decree rule, the *sénatus-consultes* of 1854 and 1866 continued in force without change. The importance of the congress lay rather in providing a generally-accepted definition of goals for colonial policy, a definition which stood unchallenged for some time. Around the turn of the century, however, a concerted attack on the ideas of assimilation began to develop.

In 1899, Léopold de Saussure attempted, in his *Psychologie de la Colonisation Française, dans ses Rapports avec les Sociétés Indigènes,* to demonstrate that assimilation was an impossibility. The core of his argument was a pseudo-scientific theory of "the heredity of mental characteristics." (He was, of course, far from alone at the time in considering this to be profound scientific truth.)

The Frenchman [complained Saussure] is persuaded that the several human species differ only as a result of education. The profound mental differences which separate the races seem superficial to him; . . . he persists in a futile struggle against the laws of heredity.

Approvingly, he quoted Gustave Le Bon's statement that "a Negro or a Japanese can accumulate all the diplomas possible without ever arriving at the level of an ordinary European." He reviewed the experience of the freed Negro in the West Indies and the United States to demonstrate the "organic incapacity" of that race. Successful examples of assimilation never involved whole races but were limited to individuals, usually of mixed ancestry. The fact that the 1889–90 congress was moderate in its demands for assimilation made it "all the more dangerous," as it would "create illusions and reassure some minds."

Saussure's negative attack on assimilation was matched a few years later by a more positive statement of what colonial policy should be. Joseph Chailley-Bert, in *Dix Années de Politique Coloniale* (1902), argued that the real need of the day was a "native policy" adapted to the existing situation in the newly-acquired territories which, properly speaking, were not colonies but possessions. Such a policy should recognize "the differences of race, of genius, of aspirations and of needs between the native inhabitants of a possession and their European masters" and should see in these differences the need for different institutions. The European could not work in the tropics; he could "accomplish nothing without a cheap and abundant labor supply" provided by the native population. What was needed was a policy which would "limit the introduction of European ideas to those which can serve the progress of commerce and civilization." The proper role for the European colonist was to supply capital, "not to work with his hands . . . but to direct the labor of the natives."

The new ideas were most fully elaborated by Jules Harmand in his *Domination et Colonisation* (1910). Harmand, a man of much colonial experience, had been developing his views over a quarter of a century before their final publication in book form. In 1887 he had first put forward the notion of "association" between conqueror and conquered as the proper basis for colonial policy, and by the first decade of the 20th century this new term had virtually replaced "assimilation" as the catchword to describe French policy. In Harmand's view, "association" meant "scrupulous respect for the manners, customs, and religion of the natives," replacing simple exploitation and expropriation of the native by a policy of "mutual assistance." The purpose of the policy would be to make European domination work more smoothly and productively, reducing the need for force to a minimum. It would seek to ameliorate the condition of the native "by allowing him to evolve along his own lines," leaving his habits and traditions untouched as much as possible, and employing his own forms of social organization.

Such a policy Harmand considered to be a "systematic repudiation of assimilation," substituting "indirect administration" which would conserve native institutions for the "necessarily rigid and oppressive regime of direct administration." At the same time, he was careful to note, it would "preserve with unshakeable firmness all the rights of domination. . . . It does not aim to prepare for the realization of an equality which cannot be possible, but to establish a certain equivalence or compensation of reciprocal services." . . . He admitted that it was "bad" to deprive a people of their independence, but he considered it "one of the manifestations of that universal law of the struggle for life." Civilized nations could not permit "vast and fertile regions of the globe" to remain undeveloped by virtue of "the incapacity of those who hold them." He recognized that "expansion by conquest . . . seems particularly unjust and disquieting to the conscience of democracies" because it leads to "a regime *ipso facto* aristocratic."

> France has tried to resolve this paradox by assimilation, which is based on a preconceived faith in the equality of all men and their rapid perfectability. . . . The time has come to substitute for this utopian idea conceptions which may be less generous but which are surely more useful and more productive of results, since they will be in conformity with the nature of things.

The first duty of the conqueror "is to maintain his domination and to assure that it will last; everything is good which has the effect of consolidating and guaranteeing it, everything is bad that may weaken or compromise it."

It was time, he said, to put aside illusions about the "natural rights of man." He mocked what he called "the revolutionary syllogism": "All Frenchmen are equal. The inhabitants of the colonies are all Frenchmen. All Frenchmen have the right to send deputies to the Assembly. Therefore the colonies cannot be deprived of this right." The colonial representation which resulted from this reasoning "has caused the greatest evils." . . . Limiting voting rights to the small group of white settlers only aids "the spoliation of the native majority by the European minority" and fosters dissension and hatred. But in the old plantation colonies of the Caribbean, where suffrage had been extended to the liberated slaves, "the inferior majority oppresses the superior minority." "An Annamite, a Negro, an Arab" could not become a Frenchman by "the adoption of certain European habits, the knowledge of the language and literature of the conqueror." This culture would only make him "an enemy better armed against us." "Wisdom tells us not to forget the lessons of Santo Domingo."

In the light of what would follow, it is interesting to note Harmand's warning that his policy of "association" should not be construed with "excessive liberalism" so as to put the native "on the same footing as ourselves" and lead him to believe that he had "the same rights in the association" as the French. Some, he feared, had already tried to use the new term "association" to give "a new virginity" to "that old passion" of assimilation.

Betts: Association in French Colonial Theory

Although denunciations of traditional French colonial policy and doctrine often appeared to be more ardent than attempts to substitute a new policy for the old, several new, if not original, plans for native administration did emerge at the beginning of the twentieth century. Essentially all resembled one another and were more often than not grouped together under the name of association. Because of the almost generic sense in which it was used, the term, never sharply defined, was often fused with the idea of the colonial protectorate and was at times simply seized upon as a convenient catchword. Despite these shortcomings there was wide agreement on the general ideas which the term was to embrace.

From Raymond F. Betts, *Assimilation and Association in French Colonial Theory, 1890–1914* (New York: Columbia University Press, 1961) pp. 106–28.

The great virtue of this policy was proclaimed to lie in its simplicity, flexibility, and practicality. Opposed to the rigidity and universalism of the condemned doctrine of assimilation, the policy of association emphasized the need for variation in colonial practice. One of its essential tenets was the idea that the determining factors in all colonial policy should be the geographic and ethnic characteristics and the state of social development of the particular region submitted to foreign control. Evolution of native groups along their own lines was the key.

Underlying these thoughts was the realization that a strong type of cooperation between colonial and native was imperative. This would be best achieved, ran the accepted argument, through the retention of native institutions. All French efforts were to be directed toward developing the region; in this task

French and natives would be "associated," each doing what best suited its abilities and stage of development.

Such a program necessitated a degree of autonomy in colonial administration unknown in France prior to the Third Republic. The doctrine of assimilation naturally implied centralization, and throughout her modern colonial history France had attempted to control colonial administration from Paris. Now, however, the demand for flexibility in actual practice made the former policy seem untenable. The block theory of colonialism was condemned. Not an empire, unified and homogeneous, but a series of unrelated possessions existed, and these demanded separate administration. As a consequence the administrator-on-the-spot and the officials in his charge were to assume far more responsibility for the direction of the possession's affairs than heretofore, and the task of the minister of colonies, it was said, was to be limited solely to coordination of general colonial policy. In short, the tradition of colonial assimilation was being discarded.

The idea of association was, of course, not entirely new, and even the use of the term, often credited first to Jules Harmand, had an old history. René Maunier, in his work, *The Sociology of Colonies* . . . traced the origin and growth of the idea. The type of association which he called "hierarchic partnership" dovetailed with that discussed by the theorists at the beginning of the twentieth century. Maunier explained that colonial partnership went through three phases, phases which he considered in an ascendant order and in which first the idea and spirit of humanitarianism were expressed, then those of equality, and finally those of fraternity. It is in the first phase that association develops; here "there is no equality, but there is humanity and moderation. . . . There is collaboration and cooperation, but of superior and inferior."

While inklings of this idea existed before the eighteenth century, it is at the end of that century that the idea became evident. In 1789 Robinet, in the *Dictionnaire universel des sciences morales,* expressed his desire for association between colonizer and native, and in 1821 the Comte de Laborde published his *L'Esprit d'association dans tous les intérêts de la communauté,* a work which discussed the colonial situation in Santo Domingo. Then Saint-Simon's chief disciple, Enfantin, described his own idealistic concept of association in the word *affamiliation,* which connoted intimate ties established between ruler and ruled.

Germinated in the fertile soil of the Enlightenment, as were so many humanitarian ideas, and fed by the stream of thought emanating from the Quakers, association then implied mutual trust and friendly cooperation, but of two differently developed peoples whose relationship was described as one of teacher—or of "governor" in the sense of preceptor—and pupil. The idea was, perhaps, a variation on the theme of the noble savage. And it is interesting to note that the ideas of colonial association and of assimilation were largely inspired by common ideas. But whereas a conscious lineal development in the instance of the doctrine of assimilation can be easily traced, this cannot be done for association. None of the colonial theorists were aware—at least they made no indication that they were—of an earlier use of the term "association" or of the idea as such. One among them did state that the "formula is not new," but the others who interested themselves in the issue saw the origin and growth of the term and idea as being commensurate with the growth of an interest in native policy and the concept of the colonial protectorate.

The native policy which France so sorely lacked, according to contemporary observers, was evolved in the last few decades of the nineteenth century by several colonial administrators, but most forcefully by two men in particular: Gallieni and Lyautey. To understand more fully the discussion of colonial theory in France, it is necessary to analyze briefly the methods of these two colonial officers. To appreciate their methods, it is advisable to begin the story with a few words about their predecessor, Faidherbe.

Far from the effects of volatile public opinion and from the interference of a Chamber of Deputies often hostile to colonial undertakings, the new empire builders, best exemplified by Faidherbe, Gallieni, and Lyautey, were able to act as they saw fit. They were their own masters. Thus they were able to analyze the colonial situation with a detachment unknown in France and were able to pursue a personal policy relatively unhindered by changing national political pressures. On the scene, free from tradition and historic polemics, they realized what many Frenchmen did not: the essential difference between modern imperialism and the earlier forms of French colonial activity.

France was not building another "New France." No *colonies de peuplement* were necessary or desirable. With her static population and her citizens' traditional love of their native soil, France was spared the problem of searching for outlets for emigration. Moreover, her newly acquired possessions were largely unsuited to white populations. Located in the tropics for the most part, these regions, with their profuse vegetation and hostile climate, were not the sort to induce colonization. As many colonial administrators clearly perceived, the true problem for France was of an entirely different sort: the relationship between a native mass and a white ruling minority. In the second colonial empire this problem was relatively new.

The beginnings of a sound native policy can be traced back to Dupleix in India or Montcalm in Canada. Nevertheless, it was not until a century later that the French colonial administrators as a group became cognizant of the virtues or even of the need of a native policy based on mutual respect between themselves and the populations they sought to rule. It could be said that they had no other choice, and indeed their policy was expedient. But it was also humane: the outstanding French colonial figures of this period were men who loved the life they followed, approached the native populations in their charge with sympathy—of a condescending sort, perhaps—and devoted themselves to the welfare of these peoples almost as much as to the welfare of the state they served. There were scoundrels, it it true, but there were also people like Auguste Pavie. That remarkable Frenchman, who sought to be as much a part of the native life in Indochina as was possible, casts his shadow across the annals of French colonial history in the late nineteenth century. Pavie spoke of the *conquête des coeurs,* and his was really such a policy. It was not limited to him, however.

The French Third Republic in the second and third decades of its existence produced a type of military officer who found in the pacification and administration of France's overseas possessions the opportunity to practice an art not suited to the European battlefield. Organization and administration were the activities in which he showed his skill, not in military strategy. In such endeavors Gallieni and Lyautey were the outstanding figures. Although they were two of the greatest administrators of colonial policy during the Third Republic, their methods followed in the tradition of native policy which had been encouraged by Léon Faidherbe.

A professional soldier trained in colonial warfare and activities during his service with General Bugeaud in Algeria, Faidherbe developed his own methods in the Senegal where he first took up his duties in 1852 as officer in the corps of engineers. From this date, he devoted his life to the population of the Senegal and to the problems besetting it. So successful were his initial efforts that, upon the retirement of Governor Protet, the merchants of Saint Louis suggested Faidherbe as the likely candidate for the position. In 1854 he was appointed governor-general. Under his effective leadership the internecine wars between the various local native elements were soon checked, thus enabling the French to turn their full attention to matters of political ogranization and administration.

Imbued with traditional French principles of justice which led him to respect peoples of other races, Faidherbe struggled to improve the native's state while he subdued the region for France. It was his policy to use force only at the moment when peaceful methods did not bring the desired results. He assumed a position in opposition to many of the colonial administrators of his day, for he rejected the French love of abstract principles and taste for complicated bureaucracy; instead he followed a practical and simple program which was based on the needs of the local population and its environment. Wherever and to whatever extent possible he avoided any interference with the customs and habits of the local population. To his aides he solemnly declared: "The first requisite is to administer the conquered populations well. . . . Because of differences of race and religion, it is necessary to let them regulate their own affairs as much as possible."

What Faidherbe was implementing in the Senegal was a policy of penetration with the aid of the native populations. Thus he sought to maintain whatever effective native institutions he found to be of advantage. When Gallieni arrived in the Senegal, he saw before him the excellent results of Faidherbe's native policy.

Ardent republican, a man of thought and of action, endowed with acute intelligence, Gallieni left France in 1877 for the Senegal where his vocation of colonizer opened before him. "I love this life," he said, and he applied himself to colonial problems with the same enthusiasm that characterized Faidherbe. Although ten years after his arrival there he was named commandant of the French Sudan, his real talents became manifested more clearly in Tonkin.

When Gallieni arrived in Tonkin in 1892, the French colonial government there was shaken by the struggles and piracy carried on by Chinese bands in spite of the fact that France had earlier made peace with China. Under the initiative of Governor-General Lanessan, an able administrator who also contributed to French colonial theory, the Upper Tonkin, where these struggles were most evident, was divided into four military districts. One of these territories was confided to Gallieni. His lightning-like achievements led Lanessan to give him the most troubled region, that which centered around Langson. Gallieni ended the pirate problem by a careful application of his own colonial policy:

> To occupy the country firmly, to win over the natives and to make them participate in the effort we are undertaking, such were essentially the principles to be applied in order to save the Upper Tonkin from the anarchy from which it suffered.

Gallieni's method was simple, a combination of good sense and basic psychology. To protect the country against further pirate attacks, he had a chain of military posts constructed. These were made of concrete to convince the local natives of the French intention to stay and thus to rally them to the French side. He took the "inhabitants of the country as chief collaborators" against his enemies, and he employed them as often as possible in the local administration of the region.

This policy, first undertaken in Tonkin, reached its final form at Madagascar, where Gallieni gained his greatest reputation. In no region were the French more confused or insecure than on this island, the occupation of which had begun during the second ministry of Jules Ferry. Anarchy still reigned, stimulated by continual insurrection and assisted by the lack of experience among the French in charge of the occupation. These were the reasons for which Gallieni was called to Madagascar in 1896. Immediately charged with the task of pacifying the island, he destroyed the Hova Kingdom, which occupied the central plateau of the island. Then he liberated the other native peoples formerly under Hova control, confiding the region of the extreme south to Lyautey. With speed that amazed the French government Gallieni subdued all of Madagascar and, in 1905, when he left and retired from colonial life, the island was peaceful and on the way to prosperity.

It was during his mission to Madagascar that Gallieni perfected his colonial policy. The best explanations of this policy are to be found in the proclamations that he wrote at the time.

Gallieni's method was founded on the immediate, the necessary, and the opinion that: "the administrative organization of a new country must be in perfect rapport with its resources, its geographic configurations, the mentality of its inhabitants, and the goal that one proposes to attain." In his instructions of May 22, 1898, on the pacification of Madagascar he declared that the best means of attaining this goal was to employ the combined action of force and politics. This he explained in two expressions which soon became famous: *la tache d'huile* and the *politique des races.*

According to Gallieni it was best to use force in a limited way only. Immediately after the pacification of some territory, permanent posts, political centers, and means of communication were to be established. Then the advance would continue slowly; the region would be cleared of the enemy with the help of the local inhabitants now won over to the French cause and duly armed for their new task. Provisional posts would be established in the newly acquired regions, and the process would thus continue until the whole region had been conquered and pacified. "This is the method of the *tache d'huile.* New territory is not acquired until all that in the rear had been completely organized."

If force was needed as a means of assuring colonial control, political action was still more important. A knowledge of the country and of its inhabitants was imperative, for upon these elements depended the type of government which would be instituted and, consequently, the very success of this government. Gallieni believed that not only were there customs which had to be respected but also there were hates and rivalries among the peoples which could be exploited. Like every clever and able leader, he knew the value of the old adage, *divide et impera.*

Following this empirical program Gallieni pacified Madagascar. In the process he developed the second of his famous principles, the *politique des races.* As a general rule he assumed that "all administrative organization must follow the country in its natural development." The native bureaucracy was to be left intact wherever possible; administration was to be flexible and based on the needs of each region; and, finally, all reforms were to be carefully studied in terms of native needs so as to avoid the disastrous results obtained in colonies where European institutions had been introduced *en bloc.* This *politique des races* was progressive in nature and based upon means as well as ends. As Gallieni himself wrote:

> Nothing is more damaging . . . in colonial affairs than preconceived formulas, imported principles, which, based most often on European ideas, do not apply to the environments, situations, or occasions for which one has wanted to adapt them. Common sense, knowledge of the country and of its inhabitants, prudent initiative directed toward the general goal desired, these must be the principal guides of our civilian and military administrators.

Nothing could be farther from the traditional doctrine of assimilation. No method seemed more attractive to the colonial officers who were then winning new regions for the French empire. Among these officers, one incorporated Gallieni's ideas with his own, proved their worth, and won himself a name as a genius in colonial affairs. This was Lyautey.

Gallieni had no disciple more devoted than Hubert Lyautey, even though their personal backgrounds contrasted markedly. A member of a well-known monarchist family which had produced good soldiers for monarchy and empire alike, Lyautey served the Third Republic well. If Gallieni had simple tastes and prided himself on his republican sentiments, Lyautey remained a traditionalist and a lover of the refined way of life. Yet both men possessed a humanitarian spirit. In the service of Gallieni in Tonkin, Lyautey found his reason for being: he was seduced by colonial life. He admired Gallieni as man and administrator, and he hastened to adopt Gallieni's methods.

The close friendship between the two men developed in Tonkin, where Gallieni asked for and received Lyautey as his chief of staff. From this period, Lyautey's devotion for his chief continued to grow. The novice soon acquired experience and won the admiration of his senior, who took him with him when he was given the task of pacifying Madagascar.

At Madagascar Lyautey's abilities were soon recognized and, in 1900, Gallieni entrusted the high command of the south, a heavy responsibility at the time, to Lyautey. Lyautey's own development of a native policy can be dated from this period. It is the policy of Gallieni with greater emphasis placed on the idea of the protectorate. After vanquishing the rebel chief, Rabezavena, and then winning him over to the French side, Lyautey exclaimed, "*Vive la méthode Gallieni!* Here again it has proved itself; it certainly is the true colonial method." During the entire campaign in the south Lyautey applied Gallieni's techniques with success, and, when the region was completely pacified, he defined his version of the policy in the following words:

> To adopt the policy and administration of the protectorate signifies: to maintain as much as possible in their entirely native governmental machinery, institutions, and customs; to use the traditional leaders, to let them control the police, the administration—even justice—and the collection of taxes, under the simple control of a single agent residing close to the chief.

What was here suggested was to be the basis of the administrative policy which was applied with success in Morocco. In fact, Lyautey's elaboration of the protectorate regime, his respect for Moslem customs, and his retention of the old Cherifian government—if only as a façade—proved so efficacious that, at the beginning of the First World War, he could proudly send the better part of his French troops to Europe.

In 1924, at the termination of his remarkable career in Morocco, Lyautey lauded the method developed by Gallieni and perfected by himself, when, in a speech at Casablanca, he declared:

> This agreeable and candid association of the two races is the best and surest guarantee of the future in Morocco. Nothing durable is based on force. The intelligent and hard-working people we have found here have quickly realized all the material benefits we have brought them as well as the assurance of peace and order, business security, and economic equipment we have brought. But that which has brought us still more good will is the fact that we have shown our esteem for this people by having respected all they respect, by assuring them the retention of their traditional institutions. In a word we have placed our hand in theirs.

Although the colonial officers here briefly mentioned were among the best known of those who asserted a new colonial policy, they were not alone. For instance, General Pennequin, who had originally served under Pavie in Indochina, acquired two admirers in Gallieni and Lyautey by his practice of a sound native policy and the use of indigenous troops in the conquest of the area around the Red River in 1892. Pennequin's superior, governor-general Jean-L. de Lanessan (1891–94), was one of the first to see the need for a well-followed policy of association. Seeking to avoid the heavy administrative machinery with which the French often weighted their colonies, he envisaged a form of indirect rule which would utilize existing native elites by associating them with the French effort. He suggested that the French leave local administration in the hands of the Annamite officials, "whom we will guide by our counsels and surround with our control."

While Indochina remained the experimental grounds for a new and vigorous colonial policy pushed by a small group of resolved men, even in the depths of Africa, where the native problem might seem to be of a different order, the need for cooperation was asserted. Savorgnan de Brazza wrote in his *Correspondances:* "To make use of the natives, to identify their interest and ours, to make them our natural allies, this was one of the most important aims of my mission in my opinion."

If the ideas and practices of these men had been adumbrated by others before them, the growing range of agreement is of considerable importance. At home the theorists and popularizers were engaged in giving verbal expression to the body of knowledge which the colonial administrators were using. This was a time when the methods already followed in the overseas regions profoundly influenced the theories in France. Practice seemed to be preceding theory.

The ideas generally included in the policy of association for the most part mirrored the methods practiced by Gallieni and Lyautey. The true significance of "association" is found in the belief that thc cconomic betterment of the region was to be undertaken by native and Frenchman within the general framework of native institutions. It was a policy based on the acceptance of mutual interests and on a sort of fraternity, but not of equality.

No more interesting an explanation of the policy of association is to be found than that given by Jules Harmand in his *Domination et colonisation.* For Harmand, association was synonymous with cooperation, a policy by which the conqueror would be most able to develop the conquered region economically, but also one in which the conqueror realized his responsibility to the native and concerned himself with that person's mental and physical well-being. While he believed association could be applied almost anywhere as an economic principle or moral guide, Harmand insisted that as a political instrument association would be most satisfactory where a homogeneous and relatively civilized population was to be found, and where, as he frankly admitted, submission to foreign control would be most difficult to achieve.

As with all advocates of association, Harmand listed among the policy's salient features tolerance, respect for native customs and laws, cooperation and assistance in place of exploitation. The base upon which Harmand's idea of association was to be established was order. According to him the chief factor lacking in the more advanced native societies was stable, orderly government. Afflicted by a shortage of capital, a lack of scientific know-how, by external threats and internal corruption, the native governments found it impossible to emerge from their sad state. A foreign government both strong and efficient could do what the native government could not in assuring peace and prosperity. And it seems that in offering this argument Harmand sought to justify the act of force which he insisted imperialism was.

The most novel idea that Harmand had to offer was one which seemed to be inferred in the policy of association but which was first clearly stated by him: association involved a sort of contractual agreement. It was a contract which "envisages the coexistence and cooperation of two profoundly different societies placed in contact in a manner as brusque as it is artificial." In practice the arrangement would give the European responsibility to produce material benefits valuable to native civilization. For his part, the native, gradually reflecting on the values derived from his forced subordination, would begin to cooperate more fully with the European. In short, the policy was, in Harmand's opinion, the "systematic repudiation of assimilation," for it encouraged the retention of native institutions and implied a large degree of administrative autonomy.

Although Harmand praised the policy of association as the best of all available colonial policies for control of native populations, he did caution about a possible danger in its application. The acknowledged French tendency in colonial administration might easily lead to "excessive liberalism." While the idea of a contract did exist, this contract implied no equality among the participants, Harmand affirmed. The occupying power had to retain its primacy.

> The policy of association, realistic and intelligent, reserves with unshakable firmness all rights of domination and takes into account all its exigencies. It does not at all attempt to prepare and achieve an equality forever impossible, but rather it attempts to establish a certain equivalence or compensation of reciprocal services. Far from letting the domination weaken, this policy wants to reinforce it by making it less offensive and repugnant.

In no way, however, did the newly proposed policy of association as explained by Harmand and others completely repudiate France's traditional *mission civilisatrice;* it merely modified it. In the first place the occupation of a colonial region still implied a moral obligation which was to be fulfilled by the improvement of the native's material and cultural status. However, rather than repeat the errors of assimilation by attempting to utilize methods little in accord with local customs, the French were gradually to introduce institutions and benefits which would be advantageous to the natives and appreciated by them. In the second place, so that their economic goals would be reached, the French would be compelled to impose certain French institutions on the inhabitants of the subdued region. Nevertheless, these too were to be introduced, wherever necessary, within the framework of native society. Thus, in theory the policy of association differed from that of assimilation in that the former sought the improvement of the native's condition without severely altering his way of life, while the latter sought the reorganization of native society in the light of French civilization.

To the ardent adherents of the new theory practical application appeared easy, provided certain necessary conditions existed. First, respect between Frenchman and native had to be assured so that rapid cooperation between the two would ensue. Second, realization of the responsibility of the one group to the other for the betterment of the region was necessary. Third, a sufficiently developed native administration was indispensable if the natives were to govern themselves adequately so that economic cooperation and development could take place under peaceful, even harmonious, conditions. For this last reason association was usually considered most feasible for Indochina.

Although Jules Harmand was the theorist credited with first advancing the policy of association as such, it was the Minister of Colonies, Clémentel, who may be considered the first to give this policy official sanction and to forward it. In 1905, speaking on several occasions to the ardent supporters of French imperialism, he signaled the need of a native policy which made the native an associate of the Frenchman in his task of improving the colonial region. "This policy of collaboration, of association is, moreover, a necessary policy. It constitutes not only a policy of justice but also a policy of foresight and of security."

Clémentel did not limit himself to words but sought to put such a policy into effect. In December, 1905, he inaugurated his colonial program with two letters of instruction to the governors of Indochina and Madagascar. Of Indochina he wrote that its betterment had to be achieved through "the protection, education, and association of the native." These were also the means by which he hoped to gain the confidence and support of the native populations: "Participating directly in all the efforts of this nature, reassured by employment of men of their own race, they [the populations] will soon realize that the goal sought is neither contrary to their customs nor beyond their capacities." As for Madagascar, Clémentel wished to continue Gallieni's policies there. The native bureaucrats were to be increased in number and associated in the work carried on by the French in the various provinces. In addition, greater local administrative autonomy was to be granted.

Clémentel tried to introduce this new colonial policy at the same time that the colonial congresses were urging the policy themselves. These congresses, of importance because they brought together the "colonial party," were the scenes of many discussions of colonial theory. Although this particular problem received no more treatment than any other, the various publications of proceedings indicate that warm approval was given to the policy of association. At the French Colonial Congress of 1905 Joseph Caillaux insisted that "our policy must gradually be a policy of association." Again in 1906, at the large Colonial Congress of Marseilles, the policy of association was acclaimed. Finally, in 1907, at the annual French Colonial Congress, it was said with confidence: "The entire colonial group is in agreement on the necessity of following this policy of association." Paul Deschanel added that the doctrine of assimilation had seen its day, and "we are today about to apply this formula of association which the colonial congresses have already determined and illuminated."

This brief indication of the ideas expressed during the colonial congresses—in large measure the barometer of the imperialist faction in France—shows that the policy of association was now being accepted. Nevertheless, extensive studies or explanations of this policy were not to be found. By its very nature association had to be vague; it was a general policy, not a detailed program. And it was as much a solution to France's colonial problems as would be any colonial policy short of withdrawal.

Like the doctrine of assimilation before it, association was willingly accepted; it appeared to be a practical and simple idea which sold itself without the need of extensive advertising. . . .

Lewis: An Assessment of Assimilation

Discussions of colonial policy written prior to World War II, and a surprising number of those written since, have generally accepted (implicitly or explicitly) the view that the expansion of European control over non-European peoples was in the best interests of all concerned. Once this notion is accepted, it becomes easy to judge any given policy by its utility for maintaining that control. In these terms, assimilation proved wanting. It disrupted native society unduly. It taught Asians and Africans the revolutionary heresy of "the Rights of Man." As Gustave Le Bon said in 1889, European-style education only showed the natives "the distance which we put between them and ourselves." Assimilation, wrote Roberts in 1929 in his *History of French Colonial Policy,* was "fundamentally illogical." It was discarded, "association" enthroned. Yet the distinction between "assimilation" and "association" soon became blurred. By confusing the two doctrines, it was possible to combine those features of each which contributed to the perpetuation of French rule. Assimilation was preserved as a constitutional fiction, but no serious attempt was ever made to undertake the massive work of social transformation which could alone make it a reality. The new synthesis was expressed in a resolution of the Chamber of Deputies in 1917, by which France pledged

From Martin D. Lewis, "One Hundred Million Frenchmen: The 'Assimilation' Theory in French Colonial Policy," *Comparative Studies in Society and History,* IV (1962), 149–52.

> its determination to pursue ever more effectively towards the colonial peoples the generous policy of association [*sic*] which will continue to assure their progressive incorporation in the national unity and will strengthen the ever closer union of all the territories over which flies the flag of France.

Gallicization was permitted to stand as the ultimate goal, but in practice it was not to be pressed too hastily, nor too many natives permitted to attain it.

This interpretation offered the advantage that a gallicized native élite could be separated from the native mass, and used as instruments of French policy. Girault in 1903 had suggested that assimilation was a "safety-valve" by which "the man whom we keep from being first in his own country, because it is a colony," could be offered in exchange "the possibility of being the first among ourselves." The same lure was offered under "association." A select group of natives could still vote for members of the French parliament, and even aspire to sit in that body themselves.[1]

It is true, of course, that the new theory of "association," frankly put forward by Harmand as a device to insure French domination, was in later years dressed in more benevolent guise by men who did not share Harmand's scruples against "civilized lies." It was presented as a kind of partnership of the colonial peoples with the metropolitan power, for mutual benefit. The most appropriate comment would seem to be that of President Sékou Touré of the Republic of Guinea who observed recently that Africans had no objections to partnership as such, but that they did not care for the partnership of the rider and the horse.

There is a good deal of truth to Doucet's observation (in 1926) that "this 'policy of association' was new only in the writings and speeches of theorists." Assimilation in practice was never as extreme as the critics of the theory suggested. As we have seen, even the *assimilateurs* of 1889 were quite cautious when it came to proposing specific measures to accomplish their aim. One may wonder if the true spirit of assimilation was not perhaps as well expressed by General Gallieni's address to the Betsileo people of Madagascar:

> You will always be Betsileos, but you will at the same time be Frenchmen. You should learn the French language; you should dress yourselves in French fabrics, renowned the whole world over for their good quality; you should above all become the devoted helpers of our French colonists, who have come among you to bring you wealth and civilization.

On another occasion he commented again on the adoption of European clothing and added that at Tananarive "the sale of bicycles has, in a very short time, taken on great importance among the Malagasy population." "These facts," he concluded, "demonstrate once again the spirit of assimilation of the race."

After the switch to "association" had served to reassure Frenchmen that they were not about to be inundated by the votes of millions of natives in the French colonies, the

[1] The degree to which natives could participate in elections varied considerably from colony to colony. Only in the "old colonies" and the "four communes" of Sénégal was there a blanket naturalization of non-Europeans, but varying provisions existed elsewhere by which a limited number of natives could attain French citizenship through special procedures.

distinction between it and "assimilation" began to seem less necessary. By the 1930s, "assimilation" had again become a respectable term in the lexicon of French imperialism. Its motivation, however, now seemed to be less a generous urge to extend to benighted peoples the blessings of (French) civilization, than the need to provide doctrinal justification for the maintenance of French rule in the face of developing demands for colonial self-determination.

Still, this is not the entire story. Assimilationists like Alexandre Isaac have been unjustly attacked for the absurdity of their idea that "the Rights of Man" should apply to all men. There is an undeniable moral grandeur in the ideal of assimilation as it was linked by them to the democratic traditions of republican France. The critics of assimilation, on the other hand, can derive little credit from their obsession with notions of "superior" and "inferior" races. A more justifiable charge against the assimilationists might be that they failed to realize the inherent contradiction between the assimilation they favored and the kind of imperial expansion to which they freely lent their support. Democrats at home, they were unable to see (as did Harmand, for example) that in the nature of things imperialism could not be democratic.

One source of their difficulty lay in the fact that in the sugar islands of the West Indies, assimilation had been intimately linked with the abolition of slavery. So long as colonial policy was conceived primarily in terms of these remnants of the first French empire, there was no need to distinguish between "native assimilation" and "legal and political assimilation." There, the non-white population was made up of former slaves who long since had been torn from their original roots, who spoke French, who had in fact no other cultural tradition available to them. Thus, when Isaac thought of his own land, he asked only for the complete fulfillment of assimilation in constitutional terms.

But when he and his supporters came to the problem of *new* conquests in lands with far larger populations, and with their own established civilizations, they failed to recognize the basic difference in the situation. They might call for harmonizing the French colonial system with the democratic principles of the French constitution, but they had no answer when a critic demanded —as one did at the 1889–90 congress —"What would become of France if the majority of voters were of a race different from that of the French nation proper?"

> The representatives of the colonies would one day form the majority in our assemblies. Arabs, Annamites, the tribes of the African coast would dictate to us our laws; our colonial enterprises would only lead to our voluntary servitude.

They could only say that assimilation should proceed cautiously, gradually.

The new nations emerging from colonial status in the middle of the 20th century have not been motivated by a desire to return to "the good old days" before their conquest by an imperial power. They are not striving today to root out "Western" technology, but complaining instead that under colonial rule they were prevented from developing their fair share of the techniques of modern industrial society. They do not complain that "Western" education has been forced on them, but that they have not had enough of it. They do not complain that French rule was too democratic, but that it never was democratic at all. While the colonies which were represented in the metropolitan parliament at the outset of the Third Republic continued to enjoy that distinction, no further extension of colonial representation took place despite the steady development of the non-represented colonies. The result in the 20th century was a "completely incoherent" mixed system whereby one part of the empire had electoral rights (with no rhyme or reason in the apportionment) while the remainder, in the aggregate no less qualified, had none. In 1936, there were only 432,122 qualified voters in all the overseas territories, and a large part of these were Europeans.

As independent states, the former colonies are all seeking more effective ways to achieve, on their own, the benefits of civilization which their colonial masters talked about but did little to provide.

What was wrong with "assimilation" was not that it was illogical, unrealistic, or impossible, but rather that no serious effort was ever made to carry it out.

Betts: The Ideal and the Reality of Assimilation and Association

After all was said and done, what effect did the changes in doctrine and theory evidenced during the period under study have on French colonial policy? The question is both interesting and provocative, for French colonial history following the First World War indicates that a simple answer is impossible. Even though association became the official colonial policy immediately after the war, the ghost of assimilation lingered on and could still be seen flitting in and out of French colonial affairs. Yet observation of this activity does not permit one to conclude that the French always uphold the old maxim, *Plus ça change, plus c'est la même chose.*

It is clear that most of the French colonial theorists and popularizers in metropolitan France did consciously set aside the doctrine of assimilation and did uphold association in some form or other. The support they obtained for their stand was ample, as has been seen. But ever present in French colonial theory was the moral element, the responsibility which the conqueror assumed toward the conquered and without which many felt the conquest could not be justified. Around this issue association and indeed as-

From Raymond F. Betts, *Assimilation and Association in French Colonial Theory, 1890–1914* (New York: Columbia University Press, 1961), pp. 165–76.

similation were often centered and hence at times tended to overlap.

Quite frankly, some of the imperialists of the period actually believed that association was but a thin guise for assimilation. One writer stated: "Thanks to the ambiguous sentimentality upon which the policy of association is based, one has seen the policy of assimilation, thus disguised, recommence its destructive work on native institutions." Charles Régismanset, who condemned all colonial doctrine in the years before the First World War, wrote that association "which, on the whole, leans toward the same objective as its predecessor [assimilation] but which is a little more tainted with sentimental and humanitarian preoccupations, isn't worth any more than its predecessor. It is even inferior because of the cloak of hypocrisy with which it is clothed."

But even the avowed advocates of association were willing to admit that their policy contained inherent dangers. Jules Harmand had carefully stated that association "can be used as a perfected weapon in favor of assimilation, an attempt to remake for this old passion a new virginity." Although Harmand had emphasized the need for improvement of the native's intellectual and social status as part of the task of imperialism, he did fear the possible effects of France's tendency toward assimilation.

The fear was justified, for this moral obligation attributed by so many imperialists to the act of overseas expansion paved the way for a reappearance of assimilation in the context of colonial theory.

This fact is noticeable in the thoughts of Leopold de Saussure. Saussure, author of *La Psychologie de la colonisation française,* was one of the first to attack assimilation strongly, to "prove" its invalidity according to Spencerian ideas. Yet within five years of the publication of his sensational book, he was explaining how the assimilation of the natives could be accomplished by the French. Saussure, however, did differentiate between assimilation based on "realities and experience" and assimilation "from the point of view of unitary traditions which encourage proselytism by language, morals and institutions." The former type was the one he favored. He characterized it by the improvement of the *condition morale* of the native, by his intellectual betterment and transformation.

For Saussure the sole method by which the native ought to be assimilated was one which stemmed from the belief that no universally applicable rules existed in such matters. Each instance was different and necessitated study of the natives' environment and past before any attempt at transformation of institutions could be chanced. Hence the difficulties previously encountered by the French were a result more of their false ideas about human nature than of actual social conditions. What Saussure was arguing for was modified assimilation rather than *assimilation à outrance.* Still one can ask where the line was to be drawn.

Saussure was not alone in holding these beliefs. Numerous imperialists talked of the need for "tutelage" in colonial matters. The very idea of one nation imposing her will on another carried with it a picture of some sort of superior-inferior relationship, and the one of teacher-pupil was very appealing to the French mind. Again, the concern about moral obligations made itself felt and obviously influenced the interpretation of association being fostered. The possible correlation of association with assimilation was at one point made in this fashion: "The colonies request to be assimilated to the mother country, but this assimilation must bc made in the sense that it carries with it the association of the natives with our activities."

Now return to 1889 and the ideas expressed by Senator Issac at the National Colonial Congress of that year. Issac wanted assimilation and strongly demanded that it remain France's official colonial policy. But he never suggested that total assimilation should be attempted immediately. He stated that no society could be suddenly changed by a *coup de baguette*. Change was to be wrought with "prudence, with slowness, especially with benevolence." It would immediately seem, therefore, that the colonial theories held by Issac were not so far removed from those of Saussure or, for that matter, from those expressed by most of the supporters of association.

Movement away from assimilation was difficult at times. And here was a problem not restricted to the French alone. All colonial powers practiced assimilation in some form or other. The French, however, were the ones who did it most consciously. Yet how could such a policy be totally avoided? It almost seems a concomitant feature of the act of overseas expansion and for reasons other than the moral one suggested above.

Of considerable importance in the formation of such an attitude and the tendency toward such a practice is the nature of the relationship of conqueror and conquered. The success of the conquest itself suggested the superiority of the conqueror, the weakness of the conquered. And thanks to the egoism of man, to this force that sociologists call ethnocentrism, the processes and institutions deemed necessary for the development of the possession and the betterment of its inhabitants were those of the "mother country." In spite of the best intentions of many imperialists it was difficult to think otherwise. Even a people like the English, lauded for their practical nature and condemned for their supposed coldness toward their colonial peoples, had succumbed to a form of assimilation in India.

The state of European civilization at the end of the nineteenth century enhanced the ethnocentric spirit of the European colonial. Blessed with material advantages scarcely known to most regions of the world, the European judged other peoples by his own measures. Not a cephalic index but a standard-of-living index was most commonly employed, for, all too often, civilization and material progress were used as interchangeable terms. As Pierre Mille had sarcastically written in condemnation of this attitude: "The Chinese, having no railroads, no mechanical textile industry, no Napoleon, and no Moltke are extremely inferior to us."

If the French were assimilators at heart, they were, nevertheless, not alone. Yet the adoption of any new colonial theory or policy in France was definitely hindered by this dominant attitude.

Nor should it be overlooked that assimilation was not strictly unilateral. Native populations, initially awed and fascinated by the imposing appearance of the European and the material proof of the high degree of his own cultural attainment, often sought to emulate him. The imitation of European dress is but one obvious example, as was the practice of wealthy natives of sending their children, whenever possible, to good European schools. And it is as ironic as it is true that the most successful aspect of assimilation, realized in our own times, was not sought by the imperialistic powers—the nationalism drawn along Western lines now evident in most of the former colonial regions of the world.

The attitude and problem of the native populations might be summed up in the words of Leopold Senghor: "Assimilate, without being assimilated."

Finally, it should be emphasized that association, whenever seen to embrace the idea of the protectorate, had its own difficulties. Too easily the protectorate devolved from an international arrangement providing for the coexistence of two different peoples into a type of direct rule scarcely hidden behind the pretension of continued native administration. At the top echelons the French substituted their own rule for that of the existing government so that association only really worked on a limited local level.

Assimilation, consciously or unconsciously pursued, haunted those French theorists who turned toward some form of association as an answer to the native problem. Even as recently as the debates over the constitution of the Fourth Republic, evidence of this can be found. And two contemporary colonial theorists demonstrate that the opponents and admirers of assimilation have not all receded into the depths of history. Speaking about assimilation in 1954, Paul Mus, former director of the Ecole Nationale de la France d'Outre-Mer, declared: "When our policy of gallicanization and cultural uprooting leads to the disintegration of African society, it violates sacred values which, for every people, are an unalienable right. In destroying them French policy defies God as well as man." A more generous attitude toward assimilation is that of Hubert Deschamps, himself a former governor-general and now a professor at the Institut d'Etudes Politiques of the University of Paris. Considering assimilation a part of the French intellectual tradition, he saw this policy as an ennobling one, reflecting the belief in the unity of mankind.

The discussion carried on between 1890 and 1914, like the opinions expressed above, was more than academic. The interest in policy which led to changes in theory did have a salubrious effect. As one author put it, changes were felt on the periphery. More autonomy in regional affairs became evident, and the acceptance of a more flexible colonial policy by the officials in Paris did result. Not least of all, a keener interest in the overseas empire and its multitudinous problems was aroused.

A concept of the role to be played by the native elite in this system of indirect rule, which association largely was, also emerged and has a thread of history leading down to the present, with an interesting knot appearing in the Brazzaville Conference of 1944 when the ideas of Félix Eboué, governor of French Equatorial Africa, threw additional light on the advantages to be derived from the use of the native elite. Of course the importance of the native elite in the policy of association is self-evident. As one French writer said in a discussion of association: "It requires that the upper classes—that is, the elite—participate in public affairs and retain the social rank they have acquired." They were to be the go-betweens for the French and the native populations. Quite an ambitious native role, imagined along these lines, appeared in the thoughts of the deputy A. Messimy, who in a report to the Chamber of Deputies in July, 1912, spoke of the French need to draw more closely the more assimilated elements within the growing Algerian population.

> It is by this slow fusion of the elite and by the association of the rest of the population with our interests that the Algeria of tomorrow will grow, drawing in its wake all of this North Africa where the France of the future will tap a new source of vigor.

Of course attendant problems to which Messimy did not allude were bound to arise. The problem of the *déraciné* [uprooted] is the most important, and it is one which still hounds the French in their remaining overseas territories.

> Placed between a native society living in a static condition for centuries and failing to see the need for changing whatever its manner of living, working and acting, and between the colonizing elements who find it very convenient to live and act under a regime of pure domination which brings exclusive advantages, the men of the native elite are subject to rejection by the one group and are repulsed by the other. And it requires a very great civic courage to bear the anathema of the former and the repeated outrages and injuries of the other.

Even with these evident problems clearly in view, the theorists in France still found association appealing. It could be made to work more readily than assimilation, no doubt. Adaptable it was. That one finds references to the *doctrine de l'assimilation* but references only to the *politique d'association* may be an indication of this. For one of the fundamental aims of the French imperialists engaged in discussion of colonial policy was to remove rigid doctrine from colonial matters. Even though association was not considered by all French colonial theorists to be a blanket solution for all French colonial relationships, it was suggested for those areas most likely to be immediately productive and valuable: Indochina and North Africa. Indochina in particular was singled out.

The truth of the matter is that a considerable gap always existed between whatever theories and practices were formulated in metropolitan France and the practices which were followed in the overseas regions. It would be grossly unfair to accuse the French of completely succumbing to an *idée fixe* and being guided by it as if it were a North Star of the first magnitude. The French were probably as expedient as any other colonizing power, and almost any period of French colonial history reveals a variety of practices in the then existing possessions.

Even so, the appeal of assimilation to the French mind cannot be denied. That the elevation of French subjects to French citizens with all the rights thereby to be enjoyed most often did not happen —note the dreadful inconsistencies in the history of Algeria—does not tarnish any of the glitter of the doctrine. The same noble conception of mankind which gave to Stoic thought its appeal is to be found in the French idea of colonial assimilation. But perhaps the French were tempted to forget that Man is really men, and that the integrity of the individual must be respected.

In any event imperialism did not occur by invitation but by force, and in the long run, all noble doctrines considered, was only successful so long as this *ultima ratio* was apparent. The humanitarianism underlying the theory of assimilation seldom thrived in such an atmosphere. Not that French civilization meant to the native the rattle of the *mitrailleuse,* as some unfriendly critics would have it, but it seldom meant equality and fraternity. The native was more often exploited or ignored than he was educated. And without this latter quality assimilation was but a hollow sham. Does this then mean that assimilation was only a rationalization for outright exploitation? It may well have served such a purpose, but to insist that it served no other is to deny the French one of their more engaging qualities. No doubt cultural imperialism is part of the French tradition, and assimilation can be considered one aspect of it, even though sporadically practiced. The appeal of assimilation was genuine and was genuinely French.

To suggest that the policy of association was solely the result of a business psychology which emphasized economy of operation in order to assure increased profits is to ignore many of the purposes and sentiments of the French colonial theorists. They were not businessmen. As experienced administrators, as patriots, and as reasonable individuals, they wished to arrive at a native policy which would make the overseas empire a viable institution, one which would be of value to France. Association had great appeal because it answered many needs.

Whatever else, the discussion of doctrine and theory at the end of the nineteenth century and the beginning of the twentieth did awaken the French to the problems of modern imperialism and particularly to those concerning native policy. The importance of a method, a "science" of colonialism, as it were, designed to fuse the interests of the two peoples placed in contact by the act of imperialism itself, was henceforth recognized. And if the natives were still not treated as peers, their institutions and ways were generally more respected. The history of imperialism is too often written as a study in black and white; much of the French activity was in the grey zone where black and white are not distinguishable.

The French imperialists knew that the overseas regions would eventually break their political ties with metropolitan France, and many thought this would occur sooner than need be if assimilation were to be the accepted colonial theory. Yet this future problem, whatever its imagined immediate causes, was of little concern to contemporary imperialists. The theorists hoped to forge a sound economic link which would not give way during eventual political storms. In this matter association appeared to be promising. Whether the theorists and writers of the day were correct or not in so thinking, they were right about the political evolution of the overseas empire, albeit their timing was bad.

At present the French overseas empire is in the last stages of total disintegration. Colonialism, even if it is the most generous in the world, sows the seeds of its own destruction. The generation of colonial nationalism, though an anachronism in this age of political monoliths, is noticeable everywhere in the French overseas possessions, present and former. From Indochina to North Africa and even to the regions of Central Africa, the reaction against imperialism has had an almost catalytic effect. The day of colonial empires is certainly past.

The French colonial theorists who expressed their views on colonial developments in the years between 1890 and 1914 would no doubt be sorely disappointed if they were still alive today, but they probably would not be greatly astonished. Their own discussion of colonial theory was only an initial effort to study and solve those problems which have been present in all their acuity until our own day.

Deschamps: Association and Indirect Rule

Ladies and Gentlemen,

When the Executive Council of the International African Institute conferred upon me the honor of giving the 'Lugard Memorial Lecture', I was so awe-stricken by the mere name of Lugard that the possibility of any other subject matter was immediately chased from my mind. I do not know if our President, when he gave his remarkable address to the memory of the great Lord, his predecessor, in the same city in 1952, was the victim of a similar obsession. As for me, I quickly discovered that I had had something to say to Lord Lugard for a long time and that I would never have a better opportunity to do so. Please allow me then to speak to him in your presence.

Undoubtedly, being a Frenchman raised on Descartes and Voltaire, and moreover a product of this wondrous and yet abominable twentieth century, I do not especially believe in ghosts. However, my Celtic origins and my profession of historian have accustomed me to their frequentation. Therefore, in your midst and in the full light of day, and with no recourse to the subterfuges of spiritualism, I am now going to conjure up my former and highly esteemed colleague, Lord Lugard of Abinger, and address myself with respect and honesty to this venerable spirit who is so dear to us.

Lord Lugard, please be so kind to forgive me if I dare to have you come back for a moment to this

Lecture given in Brussels on June 20, 1963 under the auspices of the eighth Lugard Memorial Lecture. "Et Maintenant, Lord Lugard?", *Africa,* October 1963, vol. XXXIII, No. 4, 293–305. Translated by Mary Paquette.

abusive planet. But, knowing you quite well now, thanks to the grandiose and detailed monument of 1948 pages with which Miss Margery Perham honored you, I cannot believe that you have lost all interest in what was once the passion of your life. I rather imagine that beneath the myrtle and laurel bushes of the Elysian Fields, you are pursuing doctrinal controversies with our countless departed colleagues used to govern colonies from the time of Julius Caesar and Pontius Pilate. It is true that today the colonies themselves belong to the realm of ghosts. Therefore, I invite you to take part in a fictional dispute on an outdated topic of an eminently academic sort but serious nonetheless.

Here you are in front of me, not the Lugard of his younger days, with his unforgettable thin wolf-like face, with his nose as thin and as straight as a sword, with his awesome Turkish saber-like mustache, and with his shining dark eyes exuding a savage energy from within their deep sockets. I would no more address that Lugard than I would a black panther.

No, the Lugard who has condescended to come back among us is the founder of our Institute, its president for twenty years, a solid old gentleman, bald, calm, pale, enlightened by his lengthy experience among men. I evoke your indulgent smile for I am going to need it.

Lord Lugard, I was once your enemy. Oh, a very small enemy, so microscopic that you never chanced to see him, and one who never did you any harm. Moreover, my grudge was not against you but rather against your doctrine. You were the great victorious champion and almost the Sovereign Pontiff of the 'Indirect Administration' in the 1930's when I was trying unsuccessfully to bring back 'Assimilation'.

Most of your compatriots, with a refreshing naiveté, still believe that assimilation has always been the unequivocal goal of French colonization. For example, in a recent short work, quite good, by the way, on Senegal, an English author wrote: 'The French had for their goal the political and cultural integration of the colonial peoples, whereas the British have always had as their final goal the preparation of their colonies for self-government and independence.' Does this evident Manichaeism really take reality into account?

Has the English colonial doctrine really ever had this monolithic continuity? Our British colleagues would answer this question much better than I would. We Frenchmen who see it from the outside have a tendency to take it in as a whole and therefore to exaggerate its apparent simplicity. We find in it the spirit of Great Britain's institutions made up at the same time of respect of old institutions, of an optimistic liberalism and of a realistic empiricism. The Englishman seems to us to frown on great Platonic constructions, he does not trust abstraction but rather puts his faith in nature. He sees the various peoples, the societies, and the institutions as living beings that he allows to grow, ready to tend to their needs, to orient them, and to use them for the best. His outlook is that of the naturalist or of the gardener. It is also the businessman's view: watch over the profits and limit the general expenses. This point of view requires that the various branches and the main office never merge. 'The triumph of the British policy', writes Seeley, 'consists of having separated the destiny of the colonies from that of the parent state and of having reduced to a minimum their mutual interference.'

That such tendencies have had as their outcome self-government and independence is apparent to us Frenchmen, impenitent reasoners. I doubt that the good English gardener, in the golden age of colonization, concerned himself much with these outcomes. Life does not follow logic. It was enough to watch over the general development of the plants, to provide for their particular needs at the various stages of their growth, taking care to avoid any absurd and oppressive generalization. God would see to the rest for He is the only master of all ultimate ends.

I may be wrong, but that is how the promising leaf-mould in which your doctrine quite naturally grew and flourished appears to me. Lord Lugard, you were acquainted with the models in India where you not only hunted the tiger with rifle but the wild boar with spear. When, after your impassioned but fruitless struggle with the slavers of Lake Nyassa, you were sent to Uganda, you displayed your skill with weapons and your persuasive authority, not to abolish the native kingdoms, but to consolidate them. You enlarged the limits of Buganda, you reconstituted the Toro and reestablished its sovereign. You refused to take the place of their rulers and you acknowledged their tribal justice. Upon your return in 1893, you formulated in *The Rise of Our East African Empire,* your inflexible principle: 'The object to be aimed at in the administration of this country is to rule through its own executive government.'

This was the time when the French did not like you. The intervention of your Maxim machine-guns in the religious wars of Uganda, then your audacious trek to Borgu, and the treaty made with the king of Nikki fifteen days before the arrival of the French officer in charge of this very same thing made you the scapegoat of our chauvinistic journalistic attacks. Thus did France have some share in your reputation, for at the same time, your compatriots discovered what you were: a hero of the Empire. Chamberlain charged you with the creation of the 'West Africa Frontier Force' which was to play a decisive role in the establishment of the Nigerian frontier; Bussa, where Mungo Park met his death, was to remain English. At the turn of the century, you were at the height of your glory. Kirk and Goldie were your friends, Flora Shaw sang your praise. Your eyes had lost their disquieting flame. At the age of 42, calmer but still tireless, you gained access to the government of Northern Nigeria. You had to conquer her, to organize her. Your methods were to be applied unfailingly, they were to be clarified and defined. There they were to find their perfect testing ground, a little too perfect perhaps, because later you were to try and apply this model in different situations.

It is quite useless, except perhaps for the French public, quite ignorant about British colonization (the reverse is also true), to recall your Kano, Sokoto, and Katsina expeditions. What is important here is that you maintained the Fulani emirs in spite of how recent and questionable their power in Hausa territory might have seemed. You felt a certain repulsion for disorder, a need for efficacy and at the same time, a certain weakness in your means that caused you to be preoccupied primarily with 'stopping disintegration.' In 1906, you defined your principles in the *Political Memoranda:* recognize the Native Administration as an integral part of the governmental machine, while directing it in the direction of the abolition of slavery and of oppression, and also towards economic development. The British Governor and the District Commissioner were really to be advisors and overseers. Thanks to your methods, when a revolt broke out, the emirs remained faithful. The virtue of Indirect Rule, at least where pacification is concerned, is thereby demonstrated.

After an instructive stay in far-off Hongkong, you came back, from 1912 to 1918, as Governor General to bind together the North and the South, and to create Nigeria, a world, an African India. You discovered certain new elements, the anarchical structures of the South-East and evolutionists of Lagos who did not fit into your plan and who irritated you. You tried painfully to make the former enter into your system and you struck up contact with the latter. You had ideals, but you were first of all a great man of action, and difficulties scared you no more than bullets. You knew how to use them to enrich your outlook.

The latter, in a partial retirement very much occupied with the League of Nations, was revealed to us in your great work: *The Dual Mandate in British Tropical Africa.* It is a classic and I will limit myself to mentioning only certain formulas from it:

'Principles do not change, but their mode of application may and should vary with the customs, the traditions and the prejudices of each unit.' You evoke independence without condemning it but while showing the dangers of proceeding too quickly. One must rely upon the traditional chieftains while changing their role. 'The ruling classes are no longer either demi-gods, or parasites preying on the community. They must work for the stipends and position they enjoy. They are the trusted delegates of the Governor. . . .' You evoke 'the high ideal of leading the backward races, by their own efforts, in their own way, to raise themselves to a higher plane of social organization.' 'The endeavour is to prevent denationalization, or to develop along indigenous lines. . . .'

You were not purely an intellectual, Lord Lugard; you did not attend any university. You invented no disquieting geopolitical generalizations, such as the 'Cape to Cairo' (route) of Cecil Rhodes. You did not, just as your subordinate Temple did, push the consequences of your doctrine to the point of the conviction that the natives must follow (I quote Temple) 'the natural evolution of their races, clearly different from those of the white man.' You did not believe that it was necessary to place a moral barbed wire fence around the black world in order to prevent entry into it by politicians and missionaries. You, a practical man, are in search of methods of action for a humane advancement within the measure of man. You are not a doctrinarian. As I shall say later on, I attacked 'lugardism'. But, Lord Lugard, you were no more a 'lugardist' than Marx was a marxist, and even less so. You were simply a man of good faith searching for sensible solutions to safeguard the present and prepare the future. Lord Lugard, I am sorry, but through you, I was attacking certain French positions.

Assimilation, as I shall demonstrate later, was only rarely the official colonial doctrine of France. But it is quite true that it satisfies certain deeply rooted and constant tendencies of the French people, tendencies with origins going back thousands of years, but which the classicism of the seventeenth and eighteenth centuries expressed perfectly.

Our ancestors, the Gauls, according to all the explorers of their time, were avidly interested in novelty and were openly receptive to strangers; the Greeks referred to them as 'philhellenics' or lovers of Greeks. After resisting conquest, they became subjects and then avid Roman citizens, to the point of abandoning their own language for Latin. The taste for Roman architecture and law became second nature to them. They passed this heritage on to us. We like the logical reasoning, the monuments with their sober but not cold lines, the institutions based on simple and clear principles. The Roman Empire, in uniting the various countries, left us a model and a certain regret. Moreover, all this Romanism is built on a base of Celtic anarchy with a certain flair for change and the exotic. We are quite familiar with strangers no matter to what race they belong. Add to that a dose of equalitarian and universal Christianity capping a rather pagan vivaciousness, and you will have an approximate portrait of the typical Frenchman—such, at least, as I see him in myself and in many others, either living or dead.

The first colonial efforts by France were imbued with this spirit. The expansion of the kingdom, the conversion of the savages, the absence of racism, these were the signs. But, with Colbert, merchantile success took precedence. Slavery was about to change the small insular societies, racism was introduced, the colonists were going to seek an autonomy which would safeguard their authority. In India, Dupleix developed a system of influence and suzerainty over the Hindu princes. Autonomy and protectorate, we were soon to find these formulas in English policies. Similar local situations led the two peoples to identical positions.

But the metropolitan tendencies were those of classicism. Descartes declared Reason to be universal. The 'interior man', the same in all latitudes, became the corner stone of all philosophers' reasoning. From then on, institutions recognized as good and reasonable were applicable to all of humanity. Spiritual and sentimental assimilation attacked slavery and tyranny. These ideas triumphed with the revolutionary Republic. The Convention abolished slavery. The Directory decreed 'the human person is not a tranferable property . . . The French Republic is one and indivisible . . . The Colonies are an integral part and therefore subject to the same laws.'

We were never to know the merits of that system because the colonies were quickly lost. This loss was to be attributed to the excesses of assimilation, and from then on, the French governments, for more than a century, were looking for a colonial policy. The first original effort was that of Napoleon in Egypt. An advocate of empire without ideology, and taking inspiration only from the necessity of the moment, he ordered that the Egyptian notables be kept with 'the greatest possible latitude in their internal affairs'; he attended Moslem ceremonies and thanked the Prophet for his victories. But the Prophet did not protect him from Nelson.

In 1830, the French again met up with Islam in Algeria, and their first act was to ensure its protection. The local institutions were preserved on the whole. The Second Republic had only a vague recourse to assimilation. Slavery was once again and this time definitively abolished, the colonies elected deputies to the French Parliament. But no attempt was made to assimilate the Algerians. Napoleon III declared that Algeria was an Arab kingdom. The particularity of colonial legislation was recognized and it was put into the hands of the Executive and taken away from the Parliament; this rule lasted a century, almost the entire duration of the colonial Empire.

A change took place at the same time in French thought. The classical and abstract concept of the 'interior man' who is invariable, a product of the mathematician Descartes, started to lose ground before the discoveries of the nineteenth century. Geography, history, and sociology were on the rise. The diversity of countries, of men, and of societies was recognized. Assimilation was then as much condemned in its intellectual roots as it had already been in practice. To the universal application of principles was easily to be substituted the method based on facts. It was the colonials, the governors, the officers, and the administrators who were going to elaborate their own terms and conditions of action according to local needs.

In Senegal, Faidherbe had already based his policy on the local chieftains. He had created a 'school for chieftains' to instruct the successors. Cambon, in 1881, inaugurated the policy of the protectorate in Tunisia; he maintained the Tunisian government and administration while controlling them. Lyautey, quite a bit later, used the same system in Morocco with a modernistic trend allied with an esthetic taste for the old institutions. 'I am the Sultan's head servant,' he liked to say, and it was true. His royalist feelings, which were of no more use in France, had found their use overseas.

In Black Africa, wherever we find kings, and except in the extreme cases of open struggle or a lack of traditional attachments, we maintained them, set them up on thrones, and made them our chief agents, just as did the English, and for the same reasons: the facilitation of conquest and of economic administration. The only difference was that we were not tempted as you were, Lord Lugard, to modernize these antiquated states, nor to create embryos of states where none existed. We did not conscientiously seek to create the future out of the past. We preserved the latter because it was convenient, and we often let it deteriorate to the advantage of direct administration. In the same way, education, wherever it existed, was carried on in French, but that was due more to the multiplicity of languages, and to the desire to form useful clerks than to a pronounced desire for assimilation.

For assimilation was then dead as far as French doctrine was concerned. Arthur Girault, the greatest of our experts on colonial law, rather grimly established that as early as 1903. The hypocritical expression of the 'policy of association' born in Indo-China was substituted for it. The word 'association' seemed to affirm the existence of a contract between the dominating power and the subjects, whereas it really conjured up the idea of the association that exists between a man and his horse. Your expression of the 'dual mandate' was at least more honest: it indicated a mutual benefit. Your work, between the two wars, began to be recognized and praised in France. A man as authoritative as Maurice Delafosse taught us at the Colonial School as late as 1926, the year of his death, a doctrine similar to yours: To protect the native institutions and to have them evolve slowly within their natural limits, and not to create mere caricatures of Europe.

There, once more I apologize because I must enter onto the scene, and that might seem especially presumptuous since I was at that time in 1930, a young assistant administrator, lost in the Malagasy underbrush, a not too-typical figure, rather insignificant and ineffective. But among the concert of praises for your doctrine, mine was the only dissenting voice. I led a solitary attack, quite unnoticed, but firmly convinced that I incarnated the future.

I had deeply loved Delafosse, both the man and his work, but I was the unruly disciple, the one who reacted the most violently to the teachings of the master by setting myself in opposition to him. Raised in the leftist, republican tradition, and a militant socialist, I was hardly favorable to chieftains and kings. (However, I must admit that ten years later when I myself had authority over kings, I got along splendidly with them.) Assimilation and universalism had since taken refuge with that part of the Left that, since it was not in power, could criticize the methods and the doctrines of those who were. Colonization did not seem justified to me except in the words of Juarès, in so far as a 'duty to proceed by degrees towards the unification of the whole human race.' Add to that the fact that I was in Madagascar, a country where the traditional chieftains had been eliminated through a century of colonization, Merina and then French, and then replaced by a direct administration. That was where with all the fiery spirit of uncompromising youth, I was slowly preparing an article entitled 'Education and Colonization' that the *Grande Revue,* highly praised in university circles, agreed to publish in October 1932. Since then I have written a little more than twenty works, some very long, but these few pages which remained relatively obscure were my greatest struggle.

I maintained that the native society differed from ours not by their nature but rather by their degree of evolution. Now, because of contact with us, they are in the process of evolving at an accelerated rate. Trade, the monetary economy, the plantations, mines, and the migration of workers, the creation of cities, all these have upset the traditional societies more than did the teachers and the missionaries. The breakdown of political structures is flagrant, and it is a good thing, because they were not adapted to the new age. Education must create new social classes, already apparent, and which will serve as the instruments of the future. 'Colonization equals education,' I wrote; even etymologically speaking, since culture naturally follows colonization . . . We still seem to control the new native societies according to principles created for primitive societies that have disappeared today.' (I want to make it clear that I was not yet an ethnologist!) The idea of making them evolve 'in their own milieu', without any exterior influence, is false, reactionary and racist. 'Any archeological shoring-up of tottering ruins cannot be a living and lasting work.' The 'imported' dogma of 'indirect rule' is ill-fated. Let us turn away from the English example to meditate on that of the Roman Empire which caused *us* to rise from barbarism. Let us welcome the natives to us, since they are coming towards us anyway, and let us build the French nation extending to Africa.' In my thesis, that I was beginning to write, I enlarged my universalism to a degree most acceptable today by concluding: 'Let us be good educators and prepare good Europeans.'

I did not quote you, Lord Lugard, but I attacked you in each sentence. Actually, I did not hurt you very much. As far as I know, my article was read by only one person, my colleague Geismar, who was an avid fan of yours. Between Senegal and Madagascar, we exchanged a few long impassioned letters. Indirect Rule was none the worse for it. I was beaten by silence, and Assimilation remained buried. It arose again much later in 1945, but really, I had nothing to do with it. My glory was purely personal, that of an unknown predecessor. And at the same time, I had a vague feeling that it was too late, and that on a planet in the process of rapid change, our great doctrinal battles over colonization would soon be relegated to ancient history with not much diffusion. You never knew this stage. In the same year, 1945, which marked the end of your era, you set out for another world leaving behind in this one an unforgettable memory.

And now, Lord Lugard? Let us try and find the moral of this story. Time has judged the merits of our opposite views. We have to confront these views with the events that followed. Who was wrong? What remains of these monuments today? And what is their share in present-day Africa?

Here we are then in the court of History. The two parties appear: On one side standing proudly is Indirect Rule of long and glorious memory, accompanied by his two daughters, the conservation of African institutions and the controlled evolution of the role of chieftains who owe so much to you. On the opposing side, the group is less distinct: one can scarcely detect the French administrative policy previous to 1945; it differed from yours (at least, in Black Africa) only in its more familiar style and less clearly defined goals. Your opposition is rather the assimilative tendency of the French people, however vague and intermittent its application to the colonies may have been, its juridical structure, its leaning towards vast rational constructs which led to the French Union and then to the Community of French Nations; add to it education in French, the steadfast belief in humanity, the distrust of the feudal, the nostalgia for the Roman Empire, the Romantic vision of France the Liberator, all in all, a simplistic temperament plus naive convictions, all of this combination of obscure virtualities that I had tried to express with rigorous energy. To sum them up in a symbolic figure, I would say that it is Assimilation, that is, the Revolution of 1789 sneaking into Africa rather late on tiptoe.

To judge fairly, we must examine not only the intrinsic virtues of both systems, but also their contact with the facts, that is, the evolution of Africa since 1945, and the present outcome.

Indirect Rule was a convenient formula for submission. It caused the least possible disturbance. it tried to keep Africa on the African ancestral path. Therefore, the need to know the country, to take inventory of its peoples, its political resources, its legal customs. It was the golden age of ethnologists and administrators quite taken with the exotic and the picturesque. These traditional societies, perfectly preserved, with their ancient structures, their colorful ceremonies, their noble demeanor, their palanquins, their crowns, their sacred thrones, their perfect adaptation to nature, their order, their serenity, all these presented to Romantic minds an idealized image of long ago, the African version of Walter Scott. The lure of the past, the charm of an escape from a Europe invaded by industrial slavery and demographic inflation, were irresistible to the intellectuals captivated by esthetics. Even I, as revolutionary as I was in thought, was sentimentally seduced by this perfume of mankind of the early ages to the point, on my return to France, of giving a scandalous lecture whose theme was: 'To save humanity, let us return to the neolithic age!' I suppose that my British colleagues, faithful to the crown and the venerable institutions surrounding it, must have succumbed even more so in this anachronistic universe miraculously preserved, and over which they watched with as much love as over the natural reserves. Thus they preserved the chieftains and increased the number of rhinoceri.

Unfortunately, the chieftains, as opposed to the rhinoceri, were not merely colorful. They were scarcely inclined to modify a state of affairs that was favorable to them. The careful control, where you had seen the panacea of progress, undoubtedly suppressed the most blatant abuses, the horror of the Sultans' prisons, the razzias, the slave trade; it had regularized administration and justice; it had allowed material changes while maintaining social conservatism. The native societies, too well protected, continued to live apart, without any active participation in the modern world.

Evolution came from elsewhere, as I had predicted it would, and contrary to your system. The 'gentlemen of the bush' that you respected as squires and the House of Lords were outdated, outclassed, and finally looked down upon as completely antiquated by the rising new class of people who were not at all titled and hereditary gentlemen, the businessmen, the store clerks, the civil servants, the wealthy planters, the influential church members, the trade unionists, the townspeople, and I should not hesitate to include in this enumeration those at the head, the intellectuals, the reasoners who will not content themselves with passive obedience. I must say that it was the honor of England to have facilitated in its universities, and sooner than us, the formation of this unruly intelligentsia. For happily, your country also had sincere liberalism in its traditions.

And Great Britain set out resolutely on this liberal path as soon as she realized, with her magnificent empiricism, on which side the forces of the future lay. She did this by taking her parliamentary traditions to Africa, with all their historic decorum: the gavel, the wig, the speaker and the opposition of his Majesty. That was the English form of assimilation. As was to be expected, the original function did not last long. 'Laws,' said Montesquieu, 'must be so suited to the people for whom they were made that it is mere chance if those of one nation are suitable for another.' Which did not prevent the above-mentioned Montesquieu from having us adopt the English system which, in France, as you know, all too often has caused great difficulties. In England, the new institutions, the house and popular vote, had grown up little by little from a system inherited from the Middle Ages. To transfer them abruptly to Africa was bound to bring about conflicts, all the more serious because they clashed with the power of the chieftains developed by Indirect Rule. Your system was based on tribalism, on the ancient nations, conformable to the limits of traditional ethnic divisions. It constituted a resistance to nationalism, to the will of the new African politicians to create states, new and enlarged nations whose limits would be left by the colonizer. The two English traditions of liberalism and conservatism, so perfectly balanced in your country through a constant and harmonious exchange of power were bound to clash in Africa and complicate the birth of the new nations.

Undoubtedly, a certain regionalism corresponds in general to the nature of affairs and feelings. It binds people together in a more intimate and a more maternal way than the State, this 'cold monster' does, as Nietzsche said. As a good provincial from the South-West, I have always regretted that in our great Revolution, federalism was guillotined with the Girondins, and that Paris, that hypertrophied heart, had, for the most part, sapped the provinces of a great deal of their strength. But in Africa, the nation had to be built from one day to the next, and the young chief of state could no more respect the fortresses of the past, reinforced through your efforts, than Richelieu and the Jacobins in our country could tolerate the feudal insolences and the Vendée insurrections. The choice lay between the new State and institutional disorder.

Indeed, the conflicts were lively but rarely bloody. The State triumphed over the tribes and the chieftains, sometimes by force, sometimes by settlement, often with the aid of an English diplomatic intermediary. Some great aggregates, of artificial origin, are maintained, such as Nigeria whose unity you cemented, and where the Northern chieftains exist along side of the more equalitarian systems of the South. In spite of the differences in the political regimes and the cultural evolution that Indirect Rule had consolidated, the nations were born, and they have taken their first steps forward. British liberalism helped them and also a typically British insular attitude; a certain detachment, a certain modest reserve with regard to other peoples; an attitude where some suffered from an adolescent timidity and others from an invincible pride; and all were undoubtedly right. It does not matter, really. The result of this reserve, of this insularity, of this reluctance to be on the look out, was that autonomy and secession were relatively easy for you. Thus the centrifugal forces were quicker to start up in your territories than in ours, at least in West Africa. The emancipation of Ghana caused a furor, and from then on, all the neighboring countries, whether they were under the British or the French, sought to line themselves up behind independence.

On the other hand, the French system, before it died, made a last attempt at assimilation. Platonic, legalistic, and steeped in geometry, the French Constituent Assembly tried in 1945, to raise a noble architectural structure built to last for centuries, where both blacks and whites could find shelter. One dreamed rather vaguely of a new Roman Empire after Caracalla, of a French world transcending continents and races. This noble illusion, made up of a mixture of traditional French chauvinism and of a very sincere anti-racist ecumenism, had been born at the Liberation. It was a question for France of assuming, after her temporary loss of stature, at the same time, a lasting greatness in the eyes of the world (for ever since Louis XIV and Napoleon, these ideas of greatness have kept coming back to us from time to time), and of liberating her black children while making citizens out of them. The word 'liberation' under the sign of which the debates of the two Constituent Assemblies took place, could have a double meaning, and lead to one of two divergent paths: the first one was the emancipation of individuals into a vast whole which would make them equal citizens, this was republican assimilation, the principle of the First Republic and the leftist parties; the second path would be the birth of new autonomous nations, a path recommended by the charter of San Francisco and the two great victorious federations; the United States and the U.S.S.R. One of the notable consequences of the French cultural assimilation was (except for the people of Malagasy forever conscious of their individualism) that the African deputies themselves attached more importance to the first tendency than to the second. The Constitution of 1946, which created the French Union, gave freedom of the city to all blacks, with deputies in the three Parisian assemblies, where government and the laws were created. Incorporated or attached to French parties, the African parliamentary members blossomed forth in the friendly atmosphere behind the scenes; they passed their political apprenticeship in a French atmosphere, interdependent with their colleagues like the black and white keys of the famous piano of Doctor Aggrey.

Nothing there that recalled the differences and limits among peoples so dear to your disciples, Lord Lugard, and to the ethnologists. In the National Assembly, in the senate, in the National Assembly of the French Union, there were only men dressed in suits or costumes, speaking French, and who were divided not along ethnic lines, nor according to territories, but according to their political parties. Had assimilation then won? Descartes and the 'interior man', were they to triumph after a century and a half of unobtrusiveness?

No, we know that today. Assimilation came too late, at a time and in a world where the Asiatic and then the African were going to start a chain reaction. The African parliamentary members could not overlook the emancipation of India, of Indonesia, and later, the Bandung Conference and the autonomy of Ghana. They slowly broke away from the metropolitan parties which were dragging them into internal quarrels of little interest to them. They regrouped into autonomous parties that knew how to obtain, by bargaining their support, not only places in the government, but political concessions and economic advantages in Africa itself. The Constitution had added, moreover, to its assimilative sauce a few nationalistic ingredients such as the recognition of 'peoples' and of 'civilizations' in the plural, such as the creation of the Territorial Assemblies given much wider powers than our departmental councils. Thus, little by little, the tendency grew stronger, not towards independence which no one was seeking then, but towards federalism; what Mr. Senghor called with a slightly comical touch, 'the Republic one and divisible.' The Community of Nations of 1958 went further to the point of establishing a kind of Commonwealth rather than a very liberal and somewhat vague Club like the British Commonwealth, but a carefully juridical edifice according to French idiosyncracy. It was only a brief stop on the long slippery slide down. From 1960, in the image of Ghana, all the French speaking republics had become independent.

Thus, of the two aspects of assimilation that I had advocated in 1932 and that had been applied too late in 1945, one, the constitution of a political entity transcending the nations, finally failed; the other, modernism opposed to tradition had won. Those who honestly believed in Assimilation, (they were especially on the left) held the notion in the simplicity of their hearts that the age of nationalisms had passed, and that as in the U.S.S.R., we were going towards the formation of great entities which were the prelude to world unity. In fact, not only did nothing like that happen, but paradoxically, assimilation was the prelude to independence. It prepared limits for it. We learned thus that nationalism was the stage of the developing of an awareness in the peoples, this adolescent crisis that none can avoid on their way to maturity. The planetary government that many young people, myself included, had thought to be realized in 1919 thanks to President Wilson, will be realized one day, I am sure, in spite of everything. But it does seem that it will come about from the union of nations and not of denationalized individuals. And this especially in Africa where the individual is barely emerging from the communal society. The English, in treating the peoples as biological entities and not as legal abstractions, have shown their usual realism.

On the other hand, our nonchalant French practice with regard to the chiefdoms had in the long run a more positive effect on the construction of new nations than did your ingenious doctrine of the evolution of the old structures and your maternal solicitude over a good education. In our territories, the kingdoms and the chiefdoms abandoned to their old age by our indifference, fell apart painlessly or were easily neutralized; sometimes the old institutions were suppressed, only to be retrieved into the administrations of the most modernistic chieftains; often they were simply neutralized and left to die their own death. The religious attachment to the chieftains did not evoke the favor that certain ethnological studies might have led one to believe; it even happened that in order to hasten an evolution judged to be progressing too slowly, the subjects themselves as in the Bamileke country, had the chieftains' headquarters burned after having massacred the chieftains. Except for this and other rare examples, the 1789 of French speaking Africa took place quite painlessly. A sign that your colorful Middle Ages had had their day.

To your account must be tallied, on the contrary, the desire to create local basic constitutions, the 'Native Authorities' and 'Native Councils' that you often had so much difficulty in establishing in countries where anarchies abounded. The French system facilitated change but did not promote initiative. The administration, our country, was a paternal king (in the best and most common cases) but almost an absolute one. The last of the absolute kings and one who gave no thought to abdicating. One became concerned —and much too late—after 1945, and in too few territories, with creating rural communes to give to the people of Malagasy and to the Africans the basic sense of responsibilities. So that the new nations in our sector inherited rudimentary or worthless substructures. It is still the administrative system inherited from us and made African which governs the whole, often with the help of sections of the governmental party. There is a serious deficiency there; the habit of responsibility is not taken on in a day; its absence allows tyranny, or at least, it causes the leaders to increase their power since they have to face everything.

Finally, since we are counting the points, here is another in favor of assimilation; it is the diffusion of the French language and culture. I do not mean to make an allusion here to the great intellectuals. Without a doubt, men like Senghor or Alioune Diop, to mention only two, do great honor at the same time to the French University and to Africa. But the English speaking universities also knew how to form men of the best caliber. The originality of our system is probably the diffusion of teaching in French to the primary level. 'The knowledge of French,' states my friend Charton, 'becomes common and popular among the youngest and most active elements. It is upon a popular base of French cultural implantation that the formation of the classes and the ascension of the elite has been able to develop.' Thus we have often avoided the divorce between the masses that remain traditional and the elite that have received a foreign education. The French language has become the means of intellectual emancipation and the path that leads to unity. During a recent stay in Gabon, I found, in the smallest villages in the virgin forest, people both young and old, who would speak with me in French, and a Gabonese minister declared: 'The United States chose English, we have chosen French.' This without French speaking Africa having the feeling of giving up something of themselves. It goes without saying that the English speaking peoples could say the same thing. A comparative study would be interesting, but difficult. In any case, the diffusion of our languages causes the linguists, after the ethnologists, to pass from applied science to pure science and history. The latter has absorbed your world and ours with all our methods and colonial doctrines. It is History who will now act as judge and decide the points.

Let us sum up the results of the match between Indirect Rule and Assimilation; to simplify things, let us say between you and me, which magnifies my importance greatly.

Your system rested on the conviction of the differences between peoples and a respect for their ways. You believed in the possibility of making Africa evolve within the forms of the past and with the men of the past. This life apart would only lead in the future to separation. Even if you were not consciously aware of it, this centrifugal movement was the normal outcome of your premises.

The belief of the eighteenth century and of the French Revolution that I took up in my article and that the French Union tried later on to realize, postulated, on the contrary, the basic similarity of the human species and its possibility of evolving on a single plane. Africa could only find its place in the modern world by an accelerated revolution replacing the old structures with modern forms. From then on, there could be no obstacle to Assimilation in a same political entity.

And now let us count up the points:

You lost on the evolution in the traditional forms, but you won on African autonomy.

I won for the victory of men and of modern institutions; I lost on political assimilation.

One to one, Lord Lugard. Match void.

Actually, we were both deceived by having too absolute of viewpoints. Men are at the same time different and similar. The Africans reacted in a normal way; they sought the same political forms as the Europeans while defending the originality of their cultures. According to Senghor, they wanted to 'assimilate, not to be assimilated.' The advantage that Africa had in this double point of view was that the European domination was at the same time long enough to cause a shock and an awakening, and short enough for Africa not to have enough time to be abolished and yet to assimilate the new points brought in from the exterior without succumbing.

Some could well ask if this colonial period were not too short? If the grafting of European institutions onto the African plants will have enough strength to withstand and to make progress possible? The importance of time cannot be denied and the past cannot be wiped out in a single stroke. One can only guess that the preparation of the Africans for their new tasks, for the exercising of power and for the creation of nations has often been insufficient. It is not the time we were lacking but the application to the tasks of the future. What I was calling for against you in 1932 was not to waste our forces by maintaining an outmoded past, but rather to set ourselves through education to laying the foundation for a modern future. We all realized this only in 1945, and a mere fifteen years of formation were not sufficient. It is not the fault of the Africans, but our own for *we developed too late an ultimate goal policy.* We were fairly skilled operators and not those rare geniuses, such as Alexander the Great, who cut the Gordian knot and who consciously create new worlds by seeing problems in a new light. We were honest organizers and not gods. Thus evolution, although born of our contact and our action, for the most part, escaped us and caught us by surprise.

The evolution that put an end to our empires is only beginning today. Economically and politically, socially and culturally, Africa is just starting to develop and transform. We cannot predict the future. Besides, that is not part of the role of the historian, and this speech (which I am going to bring to an end, please be assured!) was an historical sketch, a conjuring up of the past in the light of the present. May Lord Lugard pardon me for having drawn him away from the realm of the departed for a few moments. That is the lot of great men. May his ghost not come to haunt your dreams, and thank you all for having followed me so kindly this evening in this very serious fantasmagoria.

Crowder: Indirect Rule—French and British Style

In his witty and thought-provoking Lugard Memorial Lecture, 'Et maintenant, Lord Lugard?' Gouverneur Deschamps has provided us with an excellent general appraisal of the relative achievements and failures of French and British 'native' administration in Africa. But he does not do full justice to the fundamental differences between the two systems. Though he hints at these differences on several occasions in his lecture, he contends that, far from what is generally supposed, the two were in practice very similar, since they both reposed on indigenous chiefs.[1] He insists that "the only difference was that we were not tempted as you were, Lord Lugard, to modernize these antiquated states, nor to create embryos of states where none existed; or . . . [our administrative practice] differed from yours (at least, in Black Africa) only in its more familiar style and less clearly defined goals." This seems seriously to underestimate the nature of the

From Michael Crowder, "Indirect Rule—French and British Style," *Africa,* XXIV, No. 3 (1964), 197–205.

1 In the summary of the lecture in English it is put more explicitly: 'Indirect rule has been practised by local governors at least since the second empire; from the end of the nineteenth century the official policy was that of "Association"—very close to Lugard's ideas.'

differences between the two systems, which were rather those of kind than of degree. M. Deschamps rightly insists that there has been a tendency on both sides of the Channel to over-simplify the basic characteristics of systems of colonial administration in Africa. Nevertheless there were such fundamental differences between the French and British systems that, even if both did make use of 'chiefs', it is not possible to place the French system of native administration in the same category as British Indirect Rule. It is true that both powers had little alternative to the use of existing political authorities as a means of governing their vast African empires, and in most cases these authorities were headed by chiefs. What *is* important is the very different way in which these authorities were used. The nature of the position and power of the chief in the two systems was totally different and, as a corollary, so were the relations between the chief and the political officer, who was inspired in each case by very different ideals.

The British in Northern Nigeria, which became the model for indirect rule, believed that it was their task to conserve what was good in indigenous institutions and assist them to develop on their own lines. The relation between the British political officer and the chief was in general that of an adviser who only in extreme circumstances interfered with the chief and the native authority under him. However, where chiefs governed small political units, and in particular where their traditional executive authority was questionable, the political officer found himself interfering in native authority affairs more frequently than ideally he should. This was true in many parts of East Africa and in parts of Yorubaland, where the borderline between 'advisory' and 'supervisory' in the activities of the political officer was not always clear. Though indirect rule reposed primarily on a chief as executive, its aim was not to preserve the institution of chieftaincy as such, but to encourage local self-government through indigenous political institutions, whether these were headed by a single executive authority, or by a council of elders. In Northern Nigeria a policy of minimal interference with the chiefs and their traditional forms of government was pursued. But Lugard himself had insisted on a reform of the indigenous taxation system and of the administration of native justice when he was Governor of Northern Nigeria and believed that, while the colonial government should repose on the chiefs, their administration should be progressively modernized. And, though his successors left them largely to themselves, Sir Donald Cameron, Governor of Nigeria from 1931 to 1935, who had introduced indirect rule to Tanganyika and held similar beliefs to those of Lugard, was shocked by the situation in Northern Nigeria, where he felt the emirates were fast developing into Indian-style native states.

Indeed, in the earliest inter-war period many emirs and chiefs ruled as 'sole native authorities', a position which gave them for practical purposes more power than they had in pre-colonial days, where they were either subject to control by a council or liable to deposition if they became too unpopular. They were permitted to administer traditional justice, which, in the case of certain emirs, included trying cases of murder for which the death sentence, subject to confirmation by the Governor, could be passed. They administered political units that corresponded to those they would have administered before the arrival of the colonial power. They were elected to office by traditional methods of selection, and only in the case of the election of a patently unsuitable candidate to office, would the colonial power refuse recognition. There was thus a minimal undermining of the traditional sources of authority. The main change for the Fulani Emirs of Northern Nigeria, for instance, was that they now owed allegiance to the British Government rather than to the Sultan of Sokoto, and collected taxes on its behalf, though they retained, in most cases, 70 per cent. of the amount collected for the administration of their native authority.

This system of indirect rule was, with modifications, practised wherever possible in Britain's colonies in West Africa and in most of her other African territories. There were notable exceptions, especially in Eastern Nigeria, where the absence of identifiable executive authority in most communities made indirect rule as practised in Northern Nigeria almost impossible to apply. In such societies, British assiduity in trying to discover chiefs, or invent them, might lend colour to M. Deschamps's argument; but, in practice, the goal of ruling through traditional political units on whom local self-government could be devolved was maintained, and after much trial and error a system of democratically elected councils was formulated as most closely corresponding to the traditional methods of delegating authority.

If, taking into account such variations, we use indirect rule in Northern Nigeria as a model we shall see just how greatly the French system of administration in Black Africa differed from that of the British.

The British system depended on the advisory relationship between the political officer and the native authority, usually a chief, heading a local government unit that corresponded to a pre-colonial political unit. The French system placed the chief in an entirely subordinate role to the political officer. M. Deschamps alludes only briefly to the role of the French political officer towards the end of his article, where he hints at the nature of his status as a *roi paternel* or *roi absolu*. But it is important to stress that the chief in relation to the French political officer was a mere agent of the central colonial government with clearly defined duties and powers. He did not head a local government unit, nor did the area which he administered on behalf of the government necessarily correspond to a pre-colonial political unit. In the interests of conformity the French divided the country up administratively into *cantons* which frequently cut across pre-colonial political boundaries. Chiefs did not remain chiefs of their old political units but of the new cantons, though sometimes the two coincided. In certain cases the French deliberately broke up the old political units, as in the case of the Futa Jallon where their policy was 'the progressive suppression of the chiefs and the parcelling out of their authority'. Most important of all, chiefs were not necessarily those who would have been selected according to customary procedures; more often than not they were those who had shown loyalty to the French or had obtained some education. While the British were scrupulous in their respect for traditional methods of selection of chiefs, the French, conceiving of them as agents of the administration, were more concerned with their potential efficiency than their legitimacy. We need not wonder then that as a young French administrator, after serving in Senegal and Dahomey, M. Robert Delavignette should have been astonished, on his way to duty in Niger, to find that the British political officer in Kano actually called on the Emir when he had business with him and paid him the compliment of learning Hausa so that he could speak to him direct. "For the young French administrator, such a way of administration had the charm of a tale from *A Thousand and One Nights.*" Contrast the position of the Emir of Kano with that of the Alaketu of Ketu in Dahomey. By tradition he was one of the seven most important rulers in Yorubaland, on an equal footing with the Oni of Ife and the Alafin of Oyo. A friend who visited him while Dahomey was still under French rule found him waiting outside the French Chef de Subdivision's office. He mentioned the fact that the King was waiting to the French administrator, who replied, "Is it going to kill him to wait out there?", and kept him waiting a little longer.

It is clear then that the French explicitly changed the very nature of the powers of the chief and that 'his functions were reduced to that of a mouthpiece for orders emanating from outside'. This is brought out clearly, for example, in the *Arrêté of 28th December 1936 on the organisation and regulation of the local indigenous administration in French Equatorial Africa* in the section dealing with *Chefs de Canton* (or *de Terre* or *de Tribu*).

The Chefs de Canton (&c.) are recruited:

(i) for preference from among the descendants of old families traditionally or customarily destined to command,
(ii) from among notable natives, literate if possible, who have rendered services to the French cause and who are fitted to fill these functions by their authority or influence in the country,
(iii) from among the *Chefs de Canton* (&c.) who have satisfactorily carried out their functions for at least four years,
(iv) from among old soldiers who have completed more than the normal terms of service and who qualify for special treatment,
(v) from among local civil servants (clerks, interpreters, &c.) who have worked satisfactorily for at least four years in the public service.

The following are the disciplinary measures applicable to *Chefs de Canton* (&c.):

(i) Reprimand by the *Chef de Department.*
(ii) Temporary withholding of salary.
(iii) Temporary interdiction.
(iv) Reduction of salary.
(v) Dismissal.

Since the chiefs did not, except in rare cases, represent traditional authority and, since they were the agents of the colonial power for carrying out its more unpopular measures, such as collecting taxes and recruiting for labour, they were resented in most parts of French West Africa. While they retained no traditional judicial authority such as that of their counterparts in British West Africa in their Native Courts, they were agents of the law, in this case the unpopular system of summary administrative justice known as the *indigénat*.[2] In many areas in the post-war period they became identified with pro-French administrative parties, particularly in Soudan (Mali). Hence it was not surprising that when, in 1957, just before the independence of Guinea, Sekou Touré (then Vice-Président du Conseil) decided to do away with chiefs, the operation was effected with remarkably little protest from either the indigenous population or from the French administration that had made use of them. Of the twenty-two Commandants de Cercle, still mostly French, called to Conakry to discuss the proposed removal of the chiefs (from 25 to 27 July) only four felt that the *chefs de canton* had a useful role to fulfil in the territory, and nearly all confirmed that the chiefs no longer possessed political traditional authority and had become mere agents of the administration. As far as the Commandant de Cercle for Labé was concerned: "As for me, whether they are there or not, it is the same thing." This is a far cry from Nigeria of the day, where in the North the opposition party (N.E.P.U.) were trying unsuccessfully to rouse the people against the chiefs and where the Government of Eastern Nigeria, an area in which traditionally most societies did not have chiefs, commissioned a former expatriate administrative officer to 'investigate the position, status and influence of Chiefs and Natural Rulers in the Eastern Region, and make recommendations as to the necessity or otherwise of legislation regulating their appointment, recognition and deposition'. In African countries where the British had imposed chiefs, as in Eastern Nigeria and parts of Uganda, their prestige had in fact gone up, but this has certainly not been true in the former French territories.

In formulating these general models it is once again essential to recognize exceptions to the general rule. For example, the kings of the Mossi in Upper Volta, the Fulani Emirs of the northern provinces of Cameroun, and a number of chiefs in Niger retained some power. [But in general the French system of administration deliberately sapped the traditional powers of the chiefs in the interest of uniformity of administrative system, not only within individual territories but throughout the two great federations of West and Equatorial Africa.] Thus it seems somewhat of an understatement to describe the French attitude, as Gouverneur Deschamps does, as "our practical unconcern with respect to the chiefs." Robert Delavignette in *Freedom and Authority in West Africa* (London,

[2] Concessions were made to customary law prior to 1946, when native penal law was abolished and all inhabitants of French Tropical Africa became subject to the French code. Before that time only those Africans who were French citizens could claim justice under the Code. The vast majority of *sujets* were subject to the *indigénat* already referred to and to customary law. Customary law, however, was not administered by the chief but by the French administrator, who was assisted by two notables of the area who were versed in tradition. These courts could try both penal and civil cases. Now customary law survives in questions of inheritance, marriage, and land.

1950) bears this out in his chapter on the Commandant. 'The man who really personified the *Cercle* was the Commandant. . . . He was the Chief of a clearly defined country called Damaragam (Zinder in Niger), and chief in everything that concerned that country.' Yet this was the Damaragam once ruled over by the powerful Sultans of Zinder, who are now reduced to little more than exotic showpieces of traditional Africa. So too does Geoffrey Gorer in *Africa Dances* (London, 1935), when he writes of the 'chefs de canton': 'In theory these local chiefs rule under the guidance of the local administrator: in practice they are the scapegoats who are made responsible for the collection of money and men. While they enjoy the administrator's favour they have certain privileges, usually good houses and land and in a few cases subsidies; but unless they are completely subservient they risk dismissal, prison and exile.' Gorer draws attention to a phenomenon that bears out just how much the French had changed the nature of chiefs in West Africa. In Ivory Coast, if a 'chef de canton' with no traditional rights to 'rule' were imposed by the administration, the people often elected in secret a 'real' chief. Delavignette also notes this in *Freedom and Authority in French West Africa.*[3]

[3] A somewhat extreme point of view with regard to the French attitude to chiefs is held by J. Suret-Canale in 'Guinea under the Colonial System,' *Presence Africaine,* no. 29, p. 53 (English edition): In reality, these chiefs in their role and in the powers devolved upon them had absolutely nothing traditional or customary; designed to ensure the cheapest execution (under their own responsibility) of the multiple tasks of administration, taxation, forced labour, recruitment etc., they were the exact counterpart of the caids of Algeria, subordinate administrators.

Why this great difference in approach by the two powers to the question of native administration, given that both for reasons of economy had to administer their vast African possessions with the aid of 'chiefs'? The difference has much to do with difference in national character and political traditions. While few would disagree that the British were inspired by the concept of separate development for their African territories, there is still much debate as to how far the French were inspired by the concept of assimilation even after its formal abandonment as official policy in favour of a *politique d'association.* Only by an examination of the extent of the survival of assimilationist goals in French colonial policy can we understand the reasons for the difference in the two approaches to native administration. This survival showed itself at two levels: as a dominant feature of the *politique d'association* and in the personal ethos of the French political officer.

One of the problems here is to define assimilation. M. D. Lewis has drawn attention to the many definitions of assimilation in use: (1) Assimilation as the dominant colonial policy of France, i.e. its dominant and continuing characteristics; (2) Assimilation as the policy abandoned in favour of association; (3) Assimilation as opposed to autonomy, i.e. integration versus devolution; (4) Assimilation as a legalistic definition, i.e. representation in the mother of parliaments; (5) Assimilation as civilization; (6) Assimilation as representing racial equality as against British tendency to the colour bar; (7) Assimilation as a highly centralized form of direct rule of colonies. It is of course difficult to choose any one definition as the satisfactory one. Assimilation as practised in the four communes of Senegal, the only instance of its full-scale application in French Tropical Africa, had the following distinctive features: political assimilation to the metropolitan country through the representation of Senegal in the Chambre des Députés; administrative assimilation by creating a Conseil-Général for Senegal modelled on the Conseils du Département of France, and by the establishment of municipal councils on the French model; the personal assimilation of Senegalese in the communes by according them the status of French citizens, though they were allowed to retain their *statut personnel;* the extension of French educational facilities as part of the French *mission civilisatrice.* This policy was abandoned not so much because men like Lyautey and Jules Harmand advocated Lugardian ideas about the relationship between the colonial power and African peoples, but because, to use Lewis's phrase, the French were 'not prepared to undertake the massive work of social transformation which alone could make it a reality'. But the *politique d'association* that succeeded it was certainly not that advocated by Jules Harmand, whereby the colonial power would respect the manners, customs, and religion of the natives and follow a policy of mutual assistance rather than exploitation. Rather it was one in which, while recognition was given to the impracticability of applying a full-scale policy of assimilation to African societies, a number of assimilationist characteristics were retained. First, the goal of creating French citizens out of Africans was not abandoned; it was just made more distant and much more difficult of achievement. Second, there was a high degree of administrative centralization on the mother country, which was not compatible with a true *politique d'association.* We have already seen that the French made little concession to indigenous political units in dividing up their African territories for administrative purposes. Third, the French civilizing mission was not abandoned, and though education might be sparse, it was modelled on the French system. Children spoke French from the day they entered school. No concession was made to teaching in the vernacular as in the British territories. Fourth, individual territories were not considered as having special characters, so that the same administrative organization was imposed on them all. Political officers would be posted from one territory to the other sometimes every other year, which gave them little time to learn the local language or ethnography. On the other hand the British political officer remained in the same territory for a long period of time, and in the case of Nigeria, in the same region; and promotion depended in part on the ability of the political officers to learn indigenous languages. Thus under the French system the one constant for the political officer could only be French culture, while for the British officer every encouragement was given to him to understand the local culture. As a corollary the French did give some encouragement to the formation of a native *élite,* which was absorbed into the territorial and federal administrative services, albeit not on a very large scale. The British, on the other hand, in the twenties and thirties actively discouraged the formation of a class of Europeanized Africans, particularly at the level of the central colonial administration. Miss Perham in the late thirties was advocating that no African should be appointed to the administrative service, which she regarded as an alien superstructure. Rather they should be encouraged to work with the native administration. Nigeria was, in the words of Sir Hugh Clifford, Governor from 1919 to 1925, a 'collection of self-contained and mutually independent Native States' which the educated Nigerian had no more business co-ordinating than the British administration. Thus Nigerians were by and large excluded from the senior service of government, while a number of French colonials reached high posts in the administration. Professor Lucy Mair writing in 1936 about the status of the educated African in the French colonies remarked that: 'The assumption which governs the whole attitude of France towards native development is that French civilisation is necessarily the best and need only be presented to the intelligent African for him to adopt it. Once he has done so, no avenue is to be closed to him. If he proves himself capable of assimilating French education, he may enter any profession, may rise to the dignity of Under-Secretary for the Colonies, and will be received as an equal by French society. This attitude towards the educated native arouses the bitter envy of his counterpart in neighbouring British colonies.' Jean Daniel Meyer in *Desert Doctor* (London, 1960) writes of his experiences in French Soudan in the Army Colonial Medical Service before the Second World War: 'My colleague was a full-blooded Senegalese. He had studied medicine in France, attending the Bordeaux Naval School, and had the rank of lieutenant.' Fifth, the African colonies were considered economic extensions of the metropolitan country, and as Albert Sarraut insisted in his *La Mise en valeur de nos colonies* (Paris, 1923) the colonies should provide assistance to France in the form of raw materials for her industry, and, in addition to this, troops in time of war, in return for which the African would benefit from French civilization. Colonial policy in the inter-war period was to be 'a doctrine of colonisation starting from a conception of power or profit for the metropolis, but instinctively impregnated with altruism.'

Finally it was at the level of the political officer himself that the tendency to assimilation so often manifested itself. Whatever official colonial policy may have been concerning the status of chiefs and the necessity to respect indigenous institutions, it is clear that the majority of French political officers believed sincerely in the French civilizing mission and that it was their role to bring 'enlightenment' to the African. They certainly did not believe that indigenous culture or institutions had anything of value to offer except as a stop-gap. L. Gray Cowan writing in 1958 observed: 'The young *chef de subdivision* in bush is still a proponent of assimilation through the very fact of his education as a Frenchman although it is no longer a part of official policy'. The administrator from republican France, particularly in the inter-war period, had little time for the notion of chiefs holding power other than that derived from the administration itself. This provides a marked contrast with the average British administrator, who believed sincerely that for Africans their own traditional methods of government were the most suitable, provided they were shorn of certain features that did not correspond to his sense of justice. Coming from a country which still maintained a monarchy that had done little to democratize itself on the lines of the Scandinavian monarchies, he had a basic respect for the institution of kingship and the panoply of ritual that surrounded it. The British officer respected his chief as separate but equal, though certainly not somebody with whom he could establish personal social relations. It was the educated African before whom he felt uneasy. Indeed many political officers openly expressed their contempt for the 'savvy boy' or 'trousered African'. In Nigeria, even as late as 1954, one could hear such epithets used by Northern political officers about Southern politicians. The African's place was in the Emir's court, not at Lincoln's Inn or Oxford.

The French political officer, on the other hand, was able to establish relationships with the educated African. M. Delavignette has published in *L'Afrique noire et son destin* (1962) a revealing letter which he received from Ouezzin-Coulibaly, late Prime Minister of Upper Volta, in 1939, concerning his application for French citizenship. Ouezzin-Coulibaly, then a young teacher in Upper Volta, had been friendly with Delavignette at that time for some ten years and expresses his devotion to France and her cause in the war in the warmest terms:

"I was at Sindou and there the news of mobilization reached me on August 29, 1939. I was able to observe in a corner of the bush the affection which the natives had for France. The mobilization was carried out quietly and with a rapidity which assumed a certain understanding of duty. I was amazed and that was your work, the work of all those who had passed by there and who had inculcated the native peasant, who we wrongly consider unsophisticated, the idea of France and of the Fatherland."

It would be difficult to find such an intimate relationship between a British political officer and a Nigerian teacher at that period. Even as late as 1954, such contact would have been rare. It would be interesting to make a comparison of the philosophy of the colonial service training courses of France, which were much longer established, with that of the British Devonshire courses.

In conclusion, the differences between the French and British systems of administration in Africa were not only differences in degree but in kind. Both may have used chiefs, but the position of the chief in each system was radically different. The basis for these differences may be sought in the fact that though assimilation as an official policy was abandoned after the early experiment in Senegal, it continued to be a most important inspiration both for the *politique d'association* and for the political officer charged with carrying it out. An understanding of the nature of these differences is not only essential to an understanding of colonial history in Africa, but also to an appreciation of the differences between the two main language blocks in independent Africa today.

problem V

White Settlers in Tropical Africa

The problem of European settlers in Africa began with their appearance. Thereafter opinions about their purpose, position, and prospects in Africa soon polarized around the opposing standards of their detractors on the one hand, and their defenders on the other. To their critics, the settlers were the "bad guys" who stole the land from the inhabitants and afterwards consistently controlled or manipulated the colonial government to exploit the land, the labor, and the income of the Africans for their personal profit. Far from providing an example of civilization for the African to emulate, the settlers, according to these critics, were an aggressive and unscrupulous group who were determined to keep the African in an inferior position through injustice, bigotry, and racial discrimination. The settlers, whose technical superiority was matched only by their hypocrisy, used their "moral superiority" to justify every sort of crime against Africans who only wished to live in freedom and equality in their homeland.

To their supporters, the settlers were the "good guys" who had faced incredible hardships to develop the land and provide the material progress associated with civilization. True, the development of the territory could not have been accomplished without cheap African labor, but the initiative, enterprise, and capital came from the European settler. They were invited to come by the Imperial Government and found the land unproductive. They cleared the bush, introduced new crops and methods of cultivation, and developed new markets. They fought disease, drought, and insects. They frequently failed, but by hard work and experiment, usually with their own capital, they produced a modern economy which thereby entitled them to a dominant voice in the colony's future.

They [the settlers] feel that they have built up this country [Kenya], they have turned it from wilderness to productivity, they made their homes there, and they have helped to fight off the invader twice in thirty years; and they don't see why others who live in another continent and criticize from a distance without having themselves to face or solve any of the actual problems of Africa, should, however sincere their motives, have a greater say in the shaping of the future than those who have made the future possible.[1]

Indeed, far from being rapacious villains, the settlers appeared as intrepid pioneers who had produced wealth where there was none and created civilization where there was only barbarism.

Although these contrasting views of the White settler were the response to the activities and attitudes of the settlers themselves, the arguments for and against were invariably conditioned by the political philosophy of the individual critics and supporters. Thus, the deep belief in the fundamental equality of man, arising from Christian principles and the political ideals of the Age of Reason, collided with the convictions of those who, although accepting the proposition that all men are created equal, recognized that men, having different abilities and qualifications, make disparate contributions to society. Consequently, they expect disparate rewards and privileges. It is within this larger philosophical framework that the search for the reality between these two opposing views must take place, and it is that search which is the problem of the White settler in tropical Africa.

During and after the partition of Africa, most Victorians assumed that civilization in Africa could be carried out only by White men whose Anglo-Saxon superiority not only gave them the right but the duty to rule the Black, develop his land, and civilize him. An outspoken advocate of this view was Sir Harry Johnston, one of Britain's great proconsuls in Africa, whose experience and prolific writings made his racist opinions widely influential in Victorian Britain. Johnston believed that the progressive development of Africa could only be carried out by European colonists, and that in those territories unsuitable to White settlers, the advancement of civilization could only be accomplished under the beneficent rule of European administrators. Johnston scorned the idea of Blacks ruling themselves without White support and argued that only in time when the "rills of Caucasian blood" will circulate through Black Africa will that essential element be provided "which alone has evolved beauty of facial features and originality of invention in thought and deed." White rule and settlement was thus not only justified by the racial superiority of the Anglo-Saxons; it was a necessary prerequisite to civilize those whose color marked them as distinctly inferior.

The blatant and emotional racism of Sir Harry Johnston can no longer be accepted as sufficient reason to justify White settlement and supremacy in Africa or elsewhere. Today the justification for privilege has shifted from one of color to one of qualification. Recently, Lewis Gann

[1] Elspeth Huxley and Margery Perham, *Race and Politics in Kenya* (London, 1956), p. 132.

and Peter Duignan have argued that, although all men may be created equal, a hierarchical structure of society is a lamentable but inevitable fact of life which cannot be ignored. Accepting this disparity between social theory and social fact, they realistically accept discrimination but only so long as there is a balance between privileges and functions. Thus, a man's status in society is determined not by his color but by the part he plays in that society. In Africa the case of the White settler must therefore rest on the functions and the services he performs. In other words, what the White settler contributed to the development of the territory justified the special privileges and favored position which were acknowledged and secured by discriminatory legislation.

African nationalists, like Ndabaningi Sithole, have not accepted this argument. Rather, they contend that man was created equal and that equality is absolute and even the imperfections of society cannot make it less so. Thus, not even the economic contributions of the White settler, which incidentally increased the range of alternatives and opportunities for the Africans, can reverse the fundamental equality of all men or justify economic, social, or political privileges. Unhappily, the assertion that all men are inherently equal does not explain *why* or *how* the inequality between Black and White was perpetuated in Africa. Sithole replied that color was the reason for inequality and that discriminatory legislation was the means employed to continue it. He argued that economic rewards were thus determined more by color than by the qualifications, functions, or services a man performed.

Thus, Sir Harry Johnston's belief in the superiority of the White man has become entrenched in custom and law and continues to condition not only the relations between Whites and Blacks but the delimitation of the Africans' economic, social, and political status. The key to the preservation of the privileged position of the White settler is his economic power over the Africans, which was maintained by forcing large African populations into small areas and less fertile land. Overpopulation thus resulted, creating a floating African population which provided, in turn, a source of cheap labor for the settler. The White settler then used his economic power to acquire political control and, through legislation, maintained White supremacy. The result for the African was not only the continuation of his inferior position, but the imposition of psychological hardship and educational disadvantages which perpetuate that status.

Humanitarian concern rather than political theory stirred the indignation of Leonard Woolf to denounce the hardships inflicted upon the Africans by White settlement in East Africa. Ever since the Europeans had acquired political control during the partition of Africa, the best land was alienated to the White settlers, who were encouraged to come to East Africa by the Imperial Government. The least fertile land was subsequently cordoned off as Reserves for the Africans. The results for the Africans, argued Woolf, were nothing short of disastrous, for the Africans are agriculturalists or pastoralists and are consequently dependent upon the land for their subsistence and future well-being. The loss of their land to the settlers reduced their capacity to provide this subsistence. Adding insult to injury the settlers, having ousted the African from the land, then required his labor to work it, and when Africans expressed reluctance to provide their services, the settlers insisted that the government employ some form of compulsion to make Africans work. Although some apologists attempted to cloak these means by appeals to "the dignity of labor," the methods used by the government and settlers were tantamount to forced labor. Whether by taxation or threat, the inhumanity of the system was as humiliating for the Africans as it was profitable for the settler.

Thus, the arguments for and against White settlement ranged back and forth, with African nationalists and humanitarians on one side and White settlers and their supporters on the other. Nowhere, however, did this debate reach such a level of brilliance and sophistication as in the dialogue between Elspeth Huxley and Margery Perham. In the summer of 1941 a Colonial Conference was held at Oxford during which Margery Perham invited Elspeth Huxley to discuss the problems of Kenya and its future. Although the war prevented a face-to-face encounter, Elspeth Huxley suggested that their views be put forward in a series of letters. Margery Perham accepted the invitation with enthusiasm. The dialogue commenced and ranged far and wide but always returned to the central problem of the White settlers. The humanitarians undoubtedly proclaim Margery Perham the winner, while the settlers clearly rally to their champion. The reader can keep his own score card.

Johnston: White Man's Country

We have now seen the result of these race movements during three or four thousand years, which have caused nations superior in physical or mental development to the Negro, the Negroid, and the Hamite to move down on Africa as a field for their colonization, cultivation, and commerce. The great rush, however, has only been made since 1881, and may be said to have begun with the French invasion of Tunis. Now there remain but two small portions of the map of Africa which are un-

From Sir Harry Johnston, *A History of the Colonization of Africa by Alien Races* (Cambridge: Cambridge University Press, 1913), pp. 442–51.

coloured, that is, attributed to the independent possession of a native state. These tracts, theoretically independent, or the overlordship of which is international, are the Negro Republic of Liberia on the West coast and the Ethiopian Empire in North-east Africa. The whole remainder of the continent is now allotted to the dominion, overlordship or exclusive political direction of some one European, Christian power: Britain, France, Germany, Portugal, Belgium, Italy, or Spain. Morocco, on the extreme north-west of the continent, the bulk of whose trade was formerly with England, and whose principal seaport was once in English hands, has now France for a protector, educator and disciplinarian, and Spain for recolonizer. There is Egypt, in the occupation and under the control of Britain, though still nominally a tributary state of the Turkish Empire. Since this book was first published in 1898, the truculent Muhammadan state of Wadai has been annexed and conquered by France, together with Baghirmi and Kanem, Aïr and the Saharan oases. Darfur is under Anglo-Egyptian suzerainty; Tripoli, Cyrenaica, and Fezzan are annexed to Italy as the future "Colony" of Libya; and British rule has been made very real over the eastern Fula States of Nigeria and Bornu. The South African Republic and Orange Free State are part of the Union of South Africa. Even Liberia has recently entrusted its finances to the indirect control of its original parent, the United States. Only Abyssinia—now the Empire of Ethiopia in very fact, since 1900—remains theoretically independent; and even Abyssinia is aware that three European powers—Britain, France, and Italy—while guaranteeing her independence, have in a sense agreed to take joint action if she should abuse that independence to the commercial or political injury of their interests. Abyssinia, for many reasons connected with her history, her religion, and her sturdy assertion of independence deserves more than any other state of Africa to preserve her national self-respect and her sovereign status, provided she will abstain from offence, and recognize her geographical and racial limitations. But if through ambition she should attempt to arm and to lead the peoples of the Sudan against the new order of things which is being patiently introduced by Great Britain, she will find herself restricted once more to the African Switzerland which has been the nucleus and the last refuge of this Semitico-Hamitic people. Liberia by studiously following American advice and educating herself on the right lines to be an African Negro State and not an African parody on a tiny scale of the vast United States of North America, may play an important part some day in the political development of West Africa.

What is Europe going to do with Africa? It seems as though there were three courses to be pursued, corresponding with the three classes of territory into which Africa falls when considered geographically. There is, to begin with, that much restricted healthy area lying outside the tropics (or in rare instances, at great altitudes inside the tropics), where the climate is salubrious and Europeans can support existence under much the same conditions as in their native lands. Here they can freely rear children to form in time a native European race; and in these regions (except in parts of South Africa) there is no dense native population to dispute by force or by an appeal to common fairness the possession of the soil. These lands of the first category are of relatively small extent compared to the mass of Africa. They are confined to the districts south of the Zambezi and the Kunene (with the exception of the neighbourhood of the Zambezi and the eastern coast-belt); to the fifty thousand square miles on the mountain plateaus of Northern Rhodesia, and about a hundred and thirty thousand on the highlands of Nyasaland, Katanga, South and Central Angola, Uganda and British East Africa; to the northern half of Tunisia, a few districts of north-east and north-west Algeria and the Cyrenaica (northern projection of Barka); and to parts of the northern projection of Morocco. The second category consists of countries like much of Morocco, Algeria, southern Tunis, and Tripoli; Barka, Egypt, Abyssinia and parts of Somaliland; where climatic conditions and soil are not wholly opposed to the healthful settlement of Europeans, but where the competition or numerical strength or martial spirit of the natives already in possession are factors opposed to the substitution of a large European population for the present owners of the soil. The third category consists of the remainder of Africa, mainly tropical, where the climatic conditions make it impossible for Europeans to cultivate the soil with their own hands, to settle for many years, or to bring up healthy families. Countries lying under the first category I should characterize as being suitable for European colonies, a conclusion somewhat belated, since they have nearly all become such. The second description of territory I should qualify as "tributary states," countries where good and settled government cannot be maintained by the natives without the control of a European power, the European power retaining in return for the expense and trouble of such control the gratification of performing a good and interesting work, and a field of employment and profitable enterprise for a few of her choicer sons and daughters. The third category consists of "plantation colonies"—vast territories to be governed as India is governed, autocratically but wisely and as far as possible through native chiefs and councils, with the first aim of securing good government and a reasonable degree of civilization to a large population of races at present inferior in culture and mentality to the European. Here, however, the European may come, in small numbers, with his capital, his energy, and his knowledge to develop a most lucrative commerce, and obtain products necessary to the use of his advanced civilization.

It is possible that these distinctions may be rudely set aside by the pressure of natural laws one hundred, two hundred years hence, if the other healthy quarters of the globe become over-populated, and science is able to annul the unhealthy effects of a tropical climate. A rush may then be made by Europeans for settlement on the lands of tropical Africa, which in its violence may sweep away contemptuously the pre-existing rights of inferior races. But until such a contingency comes about, and whilst there is so much healthy land still unoccupied in America and temperate Africa, it is safer to direct our efforts along the lines laid down in these three categories I have quoted. Until Frenchmen have peopled the north of Tunis and the Aures Mountains of Algeria, it would be foolish for their Government to lure French emigrants to make their homes in Senegambia or on the Congo; until Cape Colony, Natal, the Orange Free State, the Transvaal, and Rhodesia south and north of the Zambezi are as thickly populated with whites as the resources of the country permit, it would be most unwise to force on the peopling by Europeans of Sokoto or the coast lands of British East Africa. On the other hand, however healthy the climate of Egypt may be, it is a country for the Egyptians, and not for Englishmen, except as administrators, instructors, capitalists, or winter tourists. Since we have begun to control the political affairs of parts of West Africa and the Niger basin our annual trade with those countries, rendered secure, has risen from a few hundred thousand pounds a year to about £10,000,000. This is sufficient justification for our continued government of these regions and their occasional cost to us in men and money.

In the north of Africa the white Berber race will tend in course of time to weaken in its Muhammadan fanaticism, and to mingle with the European immigrants as it mingled with them in ancient times and in the middle ages, when it invaded Spain and southern Europe. The Arab will gradually draw aloof, and side with those darker Berbers, who will long range the Sahara wastes unenvied; or else he will betake himself to the Sudan, and lead a life there freer from European restrictions, even though it be under a loose form of European rule. The Egyptians will probably continue to remain the Egyptians they have been for untold centuries, no matter what waves of Syrian, Libyan, Hittite, Persian, Greek, Roman, Arab, Turkish, French or English invaders swept over the land; but they will probably come within that circle of confederated nations which will form the future British Empire—nations of every origin, colour, race, religion, united only by one supreme ruler, and the one supreme bond of peace, mutual defence, and unfettered interchanging commerce. The Negro or Negroid races of all Africa between the Sahara Desert, the Red Sea, and the Zambezi will remain negro or negroid, even though here and there they are slightly lightened with European blood, and on the east are raised to a finer human type by the immigration of the Hamites, the interbreeding of Arabs, and the settlement of Indians. It is possible that there may be a considerable overflow of India into those insufficiently inhabited, uncultivated parts of East Africa now ruled by Britain and Germany. Indians will make their way as traders into British Central Africa, but these territories north of the Zambezi will be governed also in the interests of an abundant and powerful negro population, which before many years have elapsed will be as civilized and educated as are at least a million of the negro inhabitants south of the Zambezi at the present day. South of the Zambezi great changes will take place. The black man may continue to increase and multiply and live at peace with the white man, content to perform for the latter many services which his bodily strength and indifference to health permit him to render advantageously. But as the white population increases from one to twenty millions it will tend to reserve to itself all the healthy country in the south of Africa, and inland on that great central plateau which stretches up to and beyond the Zambezi; and the black man will be pushed by degrees into the low-lying, tropical coast regions of the south-east and of the Zambezi valley—regions which with much of Bechuanaland and Nyasaland must for an indefinite period be regarded as a Black Man's Reserve.

The European nations or national types which will predominate in the New Africa are the British (with whom perhaps Dutch will fuse), the French and the French-speaking Belgian, the German, the Italian, the Greek, and the Portuguese. The Spaniard may be met with on the North-west coast and in Morocco and Western Algeria; the Portuguese may have in Angola a second Brazil, but this dream will dissolve disenchantingly unless this nation can soon recover national energy and divert her thousands of emigrants annually to Portuguese Africa rather than to Portuguese- or English-speaking America. Portugal itself requires colonists and ought to be able to support not a discontented six but a prosperous fifteen millions of people. Italy's share of colonizable territory may be comparatively small under her own flag, and Greece may have none at all, but the north, the north-east, and north-central parts of Africa will teem with busy, thrifty, enterprising Italian and Greek settlers, colonists, merchants and employés.

The great languages of New Africa will be English, French, Italian, Portuguese, Arabic, Hausa, Swahili, and Zulu. It is doubtful whether German will ever become implanted as an African language any more than Dutch has taken root in the Malay Archipelago. It is true that Dutch in a corrupted jargon has become a second language to the Hottentots and a few Bantu tribes. But Dutch is simpler in construction, and easier of pronunciation to a negro than German. I have observed that in the Cameroons the Germans make use of the "pigeon" English of the coast as a means of communication with the people when they do not speak in the easily acquired Duala tongue. In East Africa, on the other hand, they use Swahili universally, just as the Dutch use Malay throughout their Asiatic possessions. English may not become the dominant language in all countries under British influence in Africa. It will certainly become the universal tongue of Africa south of the Zambezi, and possibly, but not so certainly, in British Central Africa, where, however, it will have the influence of Swahili to contend with. In British East Africa, in Zanzibar, and in Uganda the prevailing speech will be the easy, simple, expressive, harmonious Swahili language, a happy compromise between Arabic and Bantu. In Somaliland, Egypt, the Sahara, and the Sudan, Arabic will be the dominating language; but Italian, French, and English will be much used in Lower Egypt. Italian, Arabic, and French will remain coequal in use in Barka, Tripoli, Tunis, and Eastern Algeria; French and Arabic (French perhaps prevailing) in Algeria; and French will make its influence felt in Morocco (though it will contend there with Arabic and Spanish), and right across the Western Sahara to Senegambia and the upper Niger. English will be, as it is now—either in jargon or correctly spoken—the language of intercommunication on the West coast of Africa from the Gambia to the Gaboon. French, Swahili and Portuguese will prevail in the Congo basin; Portuguese in Angola; and Hausa in Nigeria and around Lake Chad. In Madagascar French will predominate, mingling in the Komoro Islands with Swahili.

Paganism will disappear. The continent will soon be divided between nominal Christians and nominal Muhammadans, with a strong tendency on the part of the Muhammadans towards an easy-going rationalism, such as is fast making way in Algeria, where the townspeople and the cultivators in the more settled districts, constantly coming into contact with Europeans, are becoming indifferent to the more inconvenient among their Muhammadan observances, and are content to live with little more religion than an observance of the laws, and a desire to get on well with their neighbours. Yet before Muhammadanism loses its savour, there will probably be many uprisings against Christian rule among Muhammadan peoples who have been newly subjected to control. The Arab and the Hamite for religious reasons may strive again and again to shake off the Christian yoke, but I strongly doubt whether there will be any universal mutiny of the black man against the white. The negro has no idea of racial affinity. He will equally ally himself to the white or to the yellow races in order to subdue his fellow black, or to regain his freedom from the domination of another negro tribe. There may be, here and there, a revolt against the white rule in such and such a state; but the diverse civilizations under which the African will be trained, and the different languages he will be taught to talk, will be sufficient to make him as dissimilar in each national development as the white man has become in Europe. And just as it would need some amazing and stupendous event to cause all Asia to rise as one man against the invasion of Europe, so it is difficult to conceive that the black man will eventually form one united negro people demanding autonomy, and putting an end to the control of the white man, and to the immigration, settlement, and intercourse of superior races from Europe and Asia. Difficult, this conception may be, in the light of past history, and because language counts for so much, but not impossible. Any repetition of Leopoldian tactics on a large scale, any gross oppression of the negro in South, East, West or Central Africa might fuse all culture differences, blend black and yellow men of diverse religious beliefs and superstitions in one blazing rebellion against the white race which might avail to wreck the new and the growing European civilization now spreading so fast over Africa. But otherwise the indigenous races of Africa will grow up into being black or brown British subjects (unless we deny them all suffrage), Frenchmen, Portuguese or Germans. Great white nations will populate in course of time South Africa, North Africa, and Egypt; and rills of Caucasian blood will continue, as in the recent and the remote past, to circulate through Negro Africa, leavening the many millions of black men with that element of the white-skinned sub-species which alone has evolved beauty of facial features and originality of invention in thought and deed. But the black—or, as it will be in the future, the brown—race will, through bowing to many an influence and submerged by many an invasion in the long run hold its own within limits, and secure for itself a large proportion of the soil of Africa. All predictions as to the future of the Dark Continent seem futile in face of the unexpected, the strange, the unlooked-for which arises in Africa itself. A new disease may break out which destroys the negro and leaves the white man standing; or unconquerable maladies may be evolved which sweep the white man away or make it too dangerous and unprofitable for him to settle on the soil of tropical Africa. On the other hand, remedies for all African diseases may be found, and it may be no more dangerous to the white man's health to reside at Sierra Leone or on the Upper Congo than it is for the indigenous black man. No doubt, as in Asia and South America, the eventual outcome of the colonization of Africa by alien peoples will be a compromise—a dark-skinned race with a white man's features and a white man's brain.

Gann and Duignan: The White Man's Case

The case for African nationalism has made a great impression overseas, and nowhere has the impact been stronger than amongst white intellectuals, who have played a major share in forming our contemporary image of Africa. Less attention has been paid to the point of view of the white settlers, who have, after all, been more concerned with making their living than with arguing their right to do so. No one, however, can think about society without making value judgements, and the settler's case, like that of his opponents, rests in the last instance on certain fundamental assumptions.

Equality, the white man might argue, is an ideal; it is a criterion of justice whereby society periodically judges itself while recognizing that no democratic state has ever managed to attain this ideal in full. Throughout history social groups have organized themselves into hierarchies, for—except on the most primitive level—there has always been a need to provide for a ruling group and a corps of specialists who were given certain privileges in order to hold the people together and raise production. The hierarchical structure of society represented the price which any large group had to pay for its cohesion. . . .

There is nothing wrong with this kind of discrimination, provided some sort of balance is maintained

From Lewis H. Gann and Peter Duignan, *White Settlers in Tropical Africa* (London: Penguin Books, Ltd., 1962), pp. 110–21.

between privileges and functions, and provided society does its best to look after its weaker members. The social pyramid will only topple over when this balance is no longer maintained: when, for instance, the tough-fisted but hard-working French nobleman becomes the titled parasite at Versailles spending his time reading philosophy, coining *bons mots,* and making love. Society, in other words, needs to determine at what point group privileges become too expensive a luxury to maintain, and also how big should be the share that can be made available to the masses. As far as this share-out is concerned, modern industrial society is in a better position than any that have gone before it—the cake is larger than it ever has been and so everyone can have a bigger slice.

The settler's case thus must ultimately rest on his functions, and the colonist asserts that the contribution which he has made and is still making to the future of Africa justifies special privileges for his group. He asserts that 'his role is a progressive one'. Equality, he argues, should therefore be regarded as a 'regulative principle of justice', not as an absolute ideal that can be enforced here and now.

African nationalists deny this point of view. They commonly regard equality as an absolute, something that can be enacted by political means or by a code of law. Their doctrine is grounded ultimately in the doctrines of seventeenth-century Christian radicals and those of eighteenth-century thinkers. The *philosophes,* the intellectuals of their age, taught the French revolutionary leaders, some of whom then seized on the principle of equality to attract the poor. The revolutionary leaders acted as if the principle of equality could be immediately attained. But to get equality, Robespierre argued, liberty must be suppressed if necessary.

This view bitterly clashed with the principle of liberty (without social equality) which was taken up by many English merchants and factory-owners during the age of the Industrial Revolution, when they wanted a mobile society, free from outmoded state regulations. But, as the American philosopher Niebuhr points out, the belief in equality was much more dangerous than the faith in liberty. Many social groups benefit from the latter, and a balance of power came into being among the various pressure groups. Some of the advocates of equality, on the other hand, represented an intellectual *élite* possessed of a Utopian creed, and when they gained power they were apt to set up a totalitarian democracy, under which greater crimes were committed than was possible under the slogan of liberty.

Africa today is undergoing a reassessment of the privileges and functions held by colonial Powers and settlers alike. This is a necessary process and can be a healthy one. In the past Europeans have largely monopolized political, social, and economic power, but in return for these, they have made and are still making certain essential contributions; these bear re-examination since they are all too easily forgotten in the light of the new anti-colonial orthodoxy.

To recapitulate, the scramble for Africa was not just a story of a gang of white robbers hurling themselves upon a peaceful continent, where the aborigines lived in a kind of undisturbed anthropological museum. The romantic talk of tribal freedom and leisure in pre-conquest Africa has as little basis in fact as the comparable romanticization of clan life in the Scottish highlands. Pre-conquest Africans were of course not a mass of undifferentiated savages, neither were their communities devoid of history. Pre-conquest Africa in fact produced some noteworthy cultural achievements, the importance of which has become obscured, partly because indigenous civilizations, such as those which once centred on Zimbabwe, had completely decayed by the time the Europeans got to Central Africa.

Yet, when all is said and done, tribal society even at its most advanced level implied poverty. The ordinary tribesman accordingly had few choices open to him. The sons of a junior wife in Thonga society in Portuguese East Africa, to take just one example, were not free to prosper and gain status or wealth, until the mines and farms of the Rand and Rhodesia gave them an opportunity to work and acquire goods. Previously, by custom all but the children of senior wives had been committed to an inferior status. The European was not the serpent in a black garden of Eden. African leisure was usually enforced leisure; when there was a drought or when stronger enemies attacked the village and murdered or abducted the able-bodied, stole the cattle or burned the crops, the survivors had little choice but to sit and starve. It is the modern money economy that for the first time has given to the African the choice of real economic alternatives—the foundation for liberty.

The old tribal ways, moreover, were doomed, if only for purely military reasons. Once the 'gunpowder frontier' started moving inland, the existing tribal structures would have undergone far-reaching changes, even if the Europeans had never intervened. There was no real alternative to conquest. . . . The long-term alternative to imperialism was not some tribal dreamland, but a kind of rudimentary gunpowder feudalism that could only have kept Africa back. The white Powers won; they did so not only because they were militarily stronger, but also because of their superiority in the fields of economics and ideas. They had something to contribute that straightforward military conquerors like the Amhara had not, and thus they deserved to win.

Imperial conquest was in turn widely accompanied by white settlement and it was precisely in those areas where Europeans found permanent homes for themselves that economic development was most thoroughgoing. The mines, the railways, the factories, the tobacco barns, and the hydro-electric schemes that have now come into being in Central and Southern Africa are not things which the white man stole away from the Africans. They were the fruits of an enterprise in which white and black participated, but in which the lead was always taken by the Europeans, who supplied all the plans, the skill, and the capital.[1] Africa herself had unskilled labour and natural resources. But these alone would have been of no avail. To take a single

[1] In Nyasaland, to mention just one example out of many, European planters occupy no more than 2½ per cent of the total land, but account for more than half of the country's exports.

example, Ethiopia, which possessed both these assets and remained free from alien rule except for the short period of Italian occupation, is still far more backward than Southern Rhodesia with its comparatively numerous settler population.

The reason for this state of affairs is evident. Economic advancement depends on two kinds of capital: social and physical. The former consists of the skill and capacities of a vast number of technicians, administrators, skilled workers, and industrial entrepreneurs. These people are essential, but they are expensive to train on the spot. It is of course still possible to secure quite a number of such persons on short-term contracts without relying on permanent settlement. But in a world where skills are scarce there is not in existence—as some reformers imagine—a vast reserve army of highly-qualified labour, infinitely mobile, ready to go anywhere at any time, at moderate salaries and on short engagements, until they can be replaced by Africans. To put the matter more simply, it is not nearly as easy to get good hydrologists, agricultural engineers, motor mechanics—and also efficient and honest storekeepers—to settle down in some underdeveloped country, as some people are apt to make out. The immigrant wants not just higher wages, but also a congenial environment and political security; he will not go out, unless he can secure a higher standard of living than he would get at home.

There are only two alternatives to economically motivated emigration. One is emigration for ideological reasons. The other is compulsion. As far as the former is concerned, few will go abroad for purely altruistic reasons; the 'missionary-artisan' has found few successors, and idealistic clergymen dabbling in agriculture or crafts are rarely a substitute for full-time workers. Compulsion of course is another possibility, and this has been employed to some extent by the Communists for the purpose of opening up the underdeveloped areas of the Soviet Union. Nevertheless, even compulsion is not enough and now that the standard of living is rising in Russia, the Soviet rulers too find that more and more economic incentives have to be used to get Dr Ivanovitch, the able engineering specialist, to settle down in Novosibirsk rather than to remain in Moscow, with its fine libraries, theatres, and laboratories.

A democratic society cannot use the big stick at all; it must rely on the carrot alone, and the carrot necessarily consists of higher living standards and improved status for emigrants. As long as African productivity remains low, the existing sharp differences in living standards are therefore unavoidable, even though the gap must eventually narrow. There is another economic rationale for a vigorous white immigration policy in certain African countries. The new Rhodesian, as mentioned earlier, does not merely bring his physical possessions into the country of his adoption. Equally important is the fact that he imports his skill and training as permanent assets for which his homeland has paid, a major social saving.

The settler, in other words, acts as a social yeast in regions in which development has been held back by disease, malnutrition, poverty, and tribalism. The 'web of kinship', however admirable in its original setting, discourages individual ambition and prevents the accumulation of savings. Communal tenure usually inhibits improved techniques of agriculture, for it may be difficult or impossible to experiment, to improve stock, or to add to the fertility of the soil. There is thus little point in arguing, as some critics do, that the Europeans have taken all the best land. This argument is taken to its extreme by African Congress speakers who complain that when the whites first came into Rhodesia in 1890 they stole all the finest farms by the side of the railway lines! For not only do they take little account of pre-conquest land usage, when much of the land now in European possession—for example, the White Highlands in Kenya—was worked little or not at all. They also make no mention of the way in which subsequent land values depended on improvements, on dips and dams and fences, on roads and railways, on markets and trading facilities, all of which have come into existence as the result of white settlement.

Pioneering, moreover, was no picnic. The belief in Africa's wealth has been vastly exaggerated; few El Dorados have been found. Few Kenya farmers, for instance, have been out of debt until recently. The attack on white exploitation of the land only echoes the beliefs of well-meaning but often ignorant idealists about 'poverty in the midst of plenty', for which the realities of Africa afford few grounds. African poverty is real, and the pioneers soon found it out. In the past the truth has often been obscured by scores of publicity pamphlets and novels about life in the colonies, which helped to create the stereotype of the clean-limbed young Englishman of good family who took his upper-middle-class standard of living to the wild veld, 'the land of Goshen'. In more recent times this kind of dream-settler has acquired a twin brother, the 'pass-the-gin-God-damn-you-I-need-a-woman' planter of anti-colonialist mythology, who supposedly lives in wicked luxury.

The reality is very different. The early farmer in Rhodesia, for example, whether a demobilized British officer, an Afrikaner *trekker,* or a Jewish cattle dealer, had a hard life. He experimented under unknown conditions, he suffered from lack of markets, his stock died of cattle diseases, he faced all kinds of other unforeseen difficulties. These initial setbacks were inevitable, for the whole complex machinery of civilization had to be built up laboriously from rock-bottom, and it was only gradually that living standards and technical proficiency began to rise.

The opponents of white settlement certainly have a case when they speak about the potentialities of African peasant farming, but there are many tasks which the peasant farmer cannot perform; Rhodesian flue-cured tobacco, for instance, requires a skill in organization and an amount of capital that the ordinary peasant does not possess. Peasant farming, moreover is not something that just happens when there are no whites about. Portuguese East Africa and the Zambezi Valley, for instance, have enormous acres of empty land where no Europeans have settled, but no intensive kind of farming has come into being. For the peasant farmer is like any other; he does not merely need land, he also requires social traditions, skills, physical capital, communications, marketing facilities, a social setting conducive to individual effort, the right crop and the right climate—none of which simply develop by keeping out the whites. It is quite possible to argue that—despite some 'feather-bedding' for white producers during the world slump—it is precisely in a country of European settlement such as Southern Rhodesia that the African peasant has been given his best chance; for white settlement has created marketing and training facilities that have benefited white and black alike. The Southern Rhodesian master-farmer scheme for Africans stands out as the kind of thing that can be achieved in a white man's country, and compares very favourably with the state of unimproved indigenous farming that prevails in many other parts of Africa.

Similar considerations apply to the industrial economies which are now coming into existence on the so-called 'Dark Continent', and which have progressed fastest in areas of white colonization. They also had their origin in European enterprise; until recently Europeans have provided all the know-how and most of the capital for the whole of Africa. Even after intensive Africanization programmes over the past decade, Ghana and Nigeria are still desperately short of trained personnel. In a country such as Rhodesia, with its relatively numerous white population, the position is much more favourable, even though European settlement has also brought sharp social tensions, centring on the economic colour bar. Nevertheless, in areas where Europeans have settled in the largest numbers, Africans have acquired the most industrial skills. The most outstanding example is the Union of South Africa, which counts more skilled African workers in its labour force, and is able to afford a higher average wage for black men, than any other African country.

The question of African skills is not merely affected by the colour bar but also by questions of status. In Ghana or Nigeria there are no white settlers, but all the same those countries have to cope with the problem of prestige-hungry Standard 7 boys who do not wish to do manual or technical work. Too many Africans aim to be clerks, and this is true in Accra, Lusaka, or Nairobi. To sum up, the fact that Africans have not fully shared in the profits of African development is not merely the result of discrimination; the major reason is the African's lack of social capital, not white wealth.

The question of social capital closely affects in turn the question of physical capital. Capital unfortunately is scarce all the world over—it is not merely a matter of greedy investors needlessly withholding money from poor African states. When Dr Rita Hinden of the Fabian Society argues that 'the intense poverty of colonial areas is directly due to lack of capital', she is talking good sense, but she is unrealistic when she writes that the African states 'must be given their railways and roads and harbours and water and power supplies, they must be equipped with schools and hospitals; they must, in short, be endowed altruistically with a complete foundation of public services'. Altruism can do quite a lot, but it cannot supply the whole of Africa with all the capital required.

As far as private investment is

concerned, however, not all the newly created Afro-Asian states have proved themselves to be good risks. The temptation to confiscate alien property is always great for young and shaky régimes; areas of white settlement on the other hand often provide a more stable framework, and this does much to explain their economic success.

European settlement admittedly brings with it social tensions; by Western standards living conditions for the African masses are still often appalling. But by the standards of a country like Ethiopia, Nigeria, or Liberia, the conditions of the African people in Southern Rhodesia are certainly not bad. Slums, malnutrition, and disease are the results of inadequate economic development and not of colour oppression. Neither are the ill effects of black labour migrancy necessarily due to the impact of white settlement or of colour-bar legislation, as is sometimes asserted by progressively-minded critics. Kampala in Uganda, for instance, has no white settlers, no residential segregation, and no *apartheid* laws. But after two generations of town life, the black workers still leave their wives behind in the rural areas; concubinage is rife in the city and family life hardly exists.

Whenever whites have entered a country in large numbers, African standards have in fact greatly risen. The future problems of development remain vast, but they require above all two things, industrialization and greater agricultural productivity; vast progress is being made in countries of European settlement in both respects. Africans in fact, to use Lenin's phrase, are 'voting with their legs' to enter Southern Rhodesia—and also South Africa—from territories as far afield as Nyasaland and Moçambique where white settlement is sparse.

To argue, as Tom Mboya does, that Africans would be better off without white settlers, and that colonialism only benefits the mother country or her emigrants, simply ignores the facts of life. In Southern Rhodesia, for instance, Africans are beginning to rise in the civil service and business; they enjoy a comparatively efficient system of hospitals and outstanding agricultural improvement programmes; the figure of African savings is going up, and so is the Africans' general standard of living.

The belief in exploitation rests on a tacit acceptance of the Marxist labour theory of value, which idealizes the unskilled at the expense of the entrepreneur. Admittedly, it was African unskilled labour which alone has made possible all subsequent development; this factor has all too often been overlooked by Europeans in Africa. But progress has been fast; a country like Rhodesia has managed to compress a century and a half of English social history into two generations as far as attitudes towards unskilled labour are concerned. . . .

In passing through this development, the Rhodesians managed to avoid some of the worst evils of labour management that characterized the early stages of industrialization elsewhere. Early instances in the 1890s apart, there was no conscription of labour, an expedient which overseas opinion fortunately would not tolerate. The indirect pressure of taxation was certainly employed to add to the tribesmen's need of ready cash, but there was no direct force. The system of early labour migration moreover meant that Rhodesia was spared the evils of women's and children's labour in mines and factories that formed such a characteristic feature of early industrialization in Europe. The tribesmen were thus to some extent cushioned against the effects of early industrialization, though they did not for the time being reap the full benefits of it either.

It seems likely that in areas where Europeans have settled in Africa the territories concerned got their original accumulation of capital at bargain rates, at the price of certain economic, social, and political privileges for the European minority. . . .

Sithole: White Supremacy in Action

In this chapter white supremacy is to be looked at in action, and not so much as an ideology. How did this doctrine affect Africans in their daily life?

The white man had not come to Africa for the sake of ruling it. He did not rule Africa for ruling's sake. He ruled Africa so that he was in a better position to exploit the natural resources of the continent. He came to Africa purely for his own good. The benefits that the white man sought in Africa were fundamentally economic. He only established white supremacy as a means to an end, and not as an end in itself. White supremacy was merely a mechanism to enable him to have the lion's share of the economic wealth of Africa.

Since white supremacy was the watchdog of white economic interests European rulers made laws that were weighted against the African peoples. The African, legally, had to be made to hold the thin end of the economic wedge, and the white man the fat end. That the African received less of everything because his standard of living was low, was just a lie in the soul.

Land is the basis of all wealth, and the white man made sure that he controlled most of the land. At one time 13.1 per cent. of the land in the Republic of South Africa belonged to Africans who formed 64 per cent. of the total population; in Rhodesia Africans occupy, but do not own, 38 per cent. of the land although they constitute 95 per cent. of the population; in Kenya the Mau Mau revolt of 1951 was the result of the land hunger created by the process of declaring European those parts of the country the white man wanted, and then removing Africans from such lands. The Europeans often gave themselves the choicest parts of the land, and the worst parts were designated as 'Native Reserves.' But this was not all: they owned most of the land in spite of their low numerical strength.

From Ndabaningi Sithole, *African Nationalism* (London: Oxford University Press, 2nd ed., 1968), pp. 131–37.

What was the effect of this unequal and inequitable distribution of land? Although the country was sparsely populated, it created population explosions in the 'Native Reserves.' This surplus population was forced out of the 'Native Reserves' on to European farms where they had no other alternative than to be employed by European farmers at the low wages which allowed the farmers super-profits. Land-hungry Africans were allowed to build their homes and till some land in return for agricultural services rendered to European farmers during the ploughing and harvesting seasons. Thus the feudal system characteristic of the Middle Ages, but which was destroyed during the fifteenth and sixteenth centuries, was resurrected in Africa during the latter half of the nineteenth century and practised during most of the twentieth century. The Africans had to pander to the whims of the European farmer or else he lost his home on the European farm. If the African forced out of the 'Native Reserve' did not find a job or a home on European farms, he was forced to seek employment in the cities, towns, and mines. Hence African nationalists viewed these deliberately created population explosions, in scantily populated African countries, as an ingenious device of meeting European labour problems on the numerous European farms and in the expanding industries.

An African population was thus created which had no roots in the 'Native Reserves' or in the European farms, cities, towns, or mines. The African was placed entirely at the mercy of European employers who were only prepared to pay him the lowest possible wages. The African was deprived of any bargaining power for his services. The African was dispossessed not only of his land, but of his culture, his personality and integrity. A man whose home is built on a European property is not the same as the man whose home is built on his own property. Insecurity, anxiety, and uncertainty constantly gnaw at his very soul, disturb his tranquillity, and undermine the very basis of his manhood. Disturb the people's land, and you disturb their lives.

Another important result of crowding the African in the 'Reserves' like sardines in a tin was that this gave rise to overstocking or cattle population explosion. Overstocking became a real problem, and what did the European governments do about this? They passed laws limiting the number of cattle an African might own, and if the African refused to act in accordance with the destocking law, the law dealt with him accordingly. Of course, the European governments did all this in the name of preventing soil erosion, conserving soil and water and flora! And these measures, in actual practice, turned out to be effective instruments in preventing white supremacy from being ordered and in conserving white supremacy! The sore point among many Africans, however, was that the African people were, in effect, not allowed to keep the natural increase of their stock since it was in excess of the legally permissible number that each African was enjoined to keep. The European governments organized regular cattle sales throughout the 'Native Reserves' so as to facilitate the disposal of these cattle in excess of the required number. The regular buyers were, of course, Europeans who lived off the fat of the land.

The surplus population of the 'Native Reserves' was thus to the great disadvantage of the African peoples but to the great advantage of Europeans. Phyllis Ntantala has this to say about South Africa:

> If we compare the rural land area with the rural population, we find that 124,186,000 morgen of land are owned and occupied by only 700,000 whites, while 6,025,547 Africans are crowded into 17,518,977 morgen of crown land called the 'Native Reserves'. The problem of the African, the cause behind this story of a people's agony, is LANDLESSNESS: LANDLESSNESS, so that the people will be forced out into the labour market, to the mines and the farms where they will be herded together in camps, compounds and locations, where each white industrialist, farmer and housewife will be allotted his or her fair share of hands. In the towns only their labour is wanted—themselves not.

The African's problem was twofold. Human population explosion, created by the unfair distribution of land, deprived him of his land, and the cattle population explosion, again created by unfair distribution of land, robbed him of his cattle. These exploded the very basis of his livelihood and human personality, while they were the answer to the white man's labour problems and his super-profit motive. Europeans therefore took every care to see that African economic disadvantages were legalized so that they could be effectively enforced by the police and by the courts. The courts had no alternative other than to administer the law as it was, even though it was stinking with economic injustice, and this was why African nationalists usually characterized the courts as 'rubber-stamps of injustice.' If a European farmer or industrialist ran short of labour, he just applied a little pressure on the European Member of Parliament who represented his constituency, and in turn the M. P. pressed the button in the white legislative assembly and out came cheap native labour in abundance through the other end! A government which could not provide by legislation cheap native labour was considered inefficient and ran the risk of being thrown out of power prematurely or at the next general election. 'Give me plenty of cheap native labour, and I will give you my vote,' was the bargaining strength of the European elector faced by vote-seeking parliamentary candidates. There was no African vote to counteract this 'cheap-native-labour' trend of the European voter.

So much for land and cattle. The structure of wages and salaries in European-ruled Africa should now be considered. Not only did the white man apportion to himself the choicest and most of the land, but he also saw to it that the lion's share of wages and salaries went to him. It was maintained that since the white man had the skill, the experience, and the necessary qualifications it was only fair that he receive higher wages than the African who, it was argued, had less skill, little experience, and lacked the necessary qualifications. Experience in all European-ruled Africa, however, soon proved that this was yet another lie in the soul, because when the African became as skilled, as experienced, and as qualified as the European himself the wage structure was still weighted against him: the true reason was to be found only in the unwillingness of the European to share equal wages with the African. The logic of the whole foundation and structure of white supremacy was firmly set against the sound principle of 'equal pay for equal work.' It was left to African nationalism to destroy first white supremacy in order to pave the way for those congenial conditions that would help 'equal pay for equal work' to materialize. In the distribution of salaries and wages, the spirit of that exercise may be better depicted in the following story:

A lion, a hyena, and a jackal agreed to go hunting together but only on one condition, that whatever they killed they would share equally among themselves. A big fat antelope they soon sighted, and after him they went with a swiftness that seemed to bear them on the air. The big fat antelope they soon killed, and the lion quickly presided over the distribution, while the other two looked on with enthusiasm.

Giving the hyena a portion the lion said, 'You take this,' and giving himself a similar portion he said, 'and I will take this.' Giving the jackal a similar portion he continued, 'You take this,' and giving himself another portion he said, 'and I will take this.' And so he continued the supposed equal distribution of the booty, 'You take this and I will take this. You take this and I will take this.' He repeated this round six times until the distribution was finished.

The net result of this sharing showed that the lion had received most meat, and therefore the principle of 'equal sharing' had been violated, but had been scrupulously observed between the shares that fell to the jackal and the hyena who both complained that the lion had received more than had been agreed upon.

The lion, with his mane standing up, his eyes flashing with resentment, and baring his dangerous teeth, said, 'I gave you, then myself. I gave you, then myself. I gave you, then myself. I gave you, then myself,' and he repeated the round six times. He explained himself further, 'You see I started with you first, and myself last. Then you, and myself last.' He went over this explanatory round six times in the most pious attitude of 'Others first, yourself last.'

'But you have four more pieces than both of us,' pointed out the jackal.

'These extra four pieces must be divided equally among the three of us,' insisted the hyena brightening up at the prospect of having at least one more to his share.

'Touch them if you dare,' declared the lion ready to crush any move towards his four additional shares.

The answer to the problem was not to be sought in the contract of the three gentlemen, but in the appetite or greed of the lion, and there ended the matter.

How did white supremacy work socially? In the Republic of South Africa one can still see signs in large letters such as EUROPEANS ONLY, in public parks, entrances, buses, railway stations, and other public places. During the life of the Federation of Rhodesia and Nyasaland which came into being in 1958 against the monolithic opposition of the African people, but which the African nationalists helped to destroy under the leadership of Dr. H. K. Banda, such signs were the order of the day. These signs were also to be seen in Kenya. This was only open public racial discrimination; we cannot go into other subtle and sly ways in which the African was often discriminated against.

John Gunther is impartial and an authority with an unusually keen insight into the problems confronting twentieth-century Africa. He writes:

> In some respects segregation is more pronounced in the Rhodesias than anywhere else in Africa, even Kenya and the Union (South Africa) . . . racial discriminations in Rhodesia are among the most barbarous, shameful, and disgusting in the world.
>
> In Lusaka (Northern Rhodesia) when we were there Africans were not allowed in most European shops, but had to use hatchways. They stood in line out in the dust or rain in dark passageways on the side of or behind the shop, where a kind of peephole with a small ledge was built into the wall. Through this hatch they called out their wants, and merchandise was (if the white man inside chose to pay attention) pushed out to them through the slot. Africans were not allowed to touch or handle articles; they could not feel the texture of a bit of cloth or try on things, and they had no opportunity for looking around or making any choice.

This social discrimination did not end only in hotels and restaurants which closed their doors to African people. Cohabitation of black and white was made a criminal offence. In Rhodesia the Immorality Act (which became defunct in 1962) had been designed to this end. As a result of this social bar many a European female who was found cohabiting with her black lover had to cry 'rape' to satisfy the uncompromising demands of white supremacy, and in so doing sent her black lover, who sat so high in her heart, to the gallows! She had to murder her own lover to appease white supremacy.

In perusing the annals of courts in European-ruled Africa, I have failed to discover a single instance where a European was convicted of the murder of an African and sentenced to death, although many cases have been found of Europeans convicted of murder of Europeans and sentenced to death. Many cases of Africans convicted of murder of Europeans and Africans and sentenced to death have also been found. In other words, no white man in the whole colonial history of Africa was ever sentenced to death for the murder of an African! White supremacy viewed natives as things, and therefore in the eyes of white supremacy it was preposterous and unthinkable to take away a man's life for having killed a thing! Perhaps a diversion at this juncture is excusable, and by quoting from Arnold Toynbee as to how white people generally viewed the African people whom they called 'natives' these assertions may be clarified:

> When we Westerners call people 'Natives' we implicitly take the cultural colour out of our perceptions of them. We see them as trees walking, or as wild animals infesting the country in which we happen to come across them. In fact, we see them as part of the local flora and fauna, and not as men of like passions with ourselves; and, seeing them thus as something infra-human, we feel entitled to treat them as though they did not possess ordinary human rights. They are merely natives of the lands which they occupy; and no term of occupancy can be long enough to confer any prescriptive right. Their tenure is as provisional and precarious as that of the forest trees which the Western pioneer fells or that of the big game which he

shoots down. And how shall the 'civilized' Lords of Creation treat the human game, when in their own good time they come to take possession of the land which, by right of eminent domain, is indefeasibly their own? Shall they treat these 'Natives' as vermin to be exterminated, or as domesticable animals to be turned into hewers of wood and drawers of water? No other alternative need be considered, if 'niggers have no souls'. All this is implicit in the word 'Natives', as we have come to use it in the English language in our time.

Perhaps in fairness to the white people, it should be pointed out that it is not only they who tend to look at other people in this fashion. It is a universal trait among all conquerors regardless of the colour of their skins, their creeds and nationalities. The conqueror attitude always tends to downgrade the humanity of the conquered, and this was why European conquest of Africa had to be liquidated altogether, and why African nationalism—that God-sent force which gathered momentum after World War II—discharged its headwaters in the 1950s and 1960s and swept away most white supremacy into the Atlantic Ocean, the Indian Ocean, and the Mediterranean Sea. No other force in Africa could have done it so effectively. It is clear from what has been said so far that white supremacy was the European rejection of the African as a full man in his own country, and African nationalism was the rejection of that doctrine. One or the other had to give way. There was to be no compromise.

Woolf: Land, Labor, and Profits

We have now examined the results of economic imperialism in so far as they affect Europeans in Europe: we still have to attempt to obtain some idea of the conditions of life which this policy has created for the Africans in Africa. I propose to state the facts from this point of view with regard only to British East Africa. I have chosen British East Africa from among all the territories whose history I have examined in these pages for the following reasons. I wish to obtain and to give the most favourable view possible of modern imperialism as a civilizing agent. Experience and temperament have made the rule of the British over non-adult races an example of everything that is best in modern imperialism. If we examined the administration of German, Portuguese, or Belgian possessions, we might discover defects in the treatment of and attitude towards the natives which are perhaps due to the defects in the temperament or character of the European rulers. Even the French and the Italians are notori-

From Leonard Woolf, *Empire and Commerce in Africa* (New York: Howard Fertig, Inc., 1968, by arrangement with George Allen and Unwin, Ltd., first published in 1920), pp. 337–38, 343–51.

ously lacking in some of the qualities which have made the Briton born to empire. Therefore, if in any part of Africa we are to find economic imperialism justifying itself as a governmental system for Africans, it must be in a British possession like British East Africa; and if there are any defects in the administration of the natives of British East Africa by Europeans, we may be certain that those defects are ten and a hundred times greater in the African Empires of Germany, Portugal, Belgium, France, and Italy.

The population of British East Africa consists of about four million natives and a few hundred Europeans. The Europeans are either Government servants or planters and farmers. These planters or farmers again either own or lease land themselves or are the employees of joint-stock companies. Land exploited by Europeans is either devoted to cattle or sheep farming, or to the production of grain, pulse, rubber, coffee, sisal, etc. The government of the country is entirely in the hands of the Europeans. The Governor and the Civil Service are appointed by the Crown from England and are under the Colonial Office; the Legislative and Executive Council are composed entirely of Europeans. The question which we have to consider is how the Government, and the few hundred Europeans, regard their relationship, their rights and obligations, to the four million natives.

East Africa is an agricultural country, and therefore the question of the land is of the most vital importance to the condition of its inhabitants. As we have seen in a former chapter, it is only some thirty years ago that Sir William Mackinnon and the British East Africa Company "acquired" the country. At that time the land was undoubtedly in the occupation and possession of the natives. The British Government has succeeded to the inheritance of Sir William Mackinnon's Company, and it now claims possession and ownership of all the land of British East Africa. How does the Government treat the Africans with regard to the land of Africa? The Government alienates from 300,000 to 600,000 acres of land annually, but it is a remarkable fact that not one single acre of this land is either leased or sold to the native inhabitants of the country. Government either sells the freehold of these hundreds of thousands of acres, or leases them on leaseholds of, usually, ninety-nine years. The sales or leases are confined to Europeans and to British Indian subjects. The result is that no native of Africa has a legal title to a single acre of the soil of British East Africa. The exploitation of the soil of this "possession" is reserved for the British inhabitants.

But we must examine the position of the natives a little more closely. The majority of them live in tribes, and to these tribes the Government has allocated Reserves. The land within a Reserve is reserved for the use of the tribe, and is not alienated by the Government. No native, however, has any legal title to land within the Reserve, and there is no security of tenure of such land even for the tribe. Only one tribe, the Masai, has had a Reserve assigned to it by a treaty, and that case will have to be referred to again. A Reserve can at any moment be cut down or abolished by the Government, and neither the tribe nor the individual native would have any legal claim or title to the land from which they were ousted. . . .

The Masai, in their occupation of the Reserve, were "protected" by a written agreement or treaty. No other tribe in East Africa holds a Reserve on a written document. The security of their tenure is therefore, if possible, less than was the Masai's [who had been forced out of their best reserve land, ed.]. The situation is therefore that in East Africa the natives are relegated to Reserves, consisting of the least fertile and least valuable land, that they are not allowed to buy or lease land outside the Reserves, and that they have no legal title at all to the land within the Reserves. Meanwhile the best land is sold at extremely low prices or leased for very low rents to white settlers.

The effect of this system upon the social condition of the native is disastrous. East Africa is an agricultural country. The only methods by which the native can support himself are by cultivating land himself, or by cattle and sheep farming, or by working on the Europeans' land for a wage. I shall have to consider the last alternative at some length later. If the European State in East Africa had as its object the promotion of the interests of the natives, it would obviously make it its first business to encourage agriculture or cattle and sheep farming on right lines by the natives. It is only necessary to look at the budget of this colony to see that the British Government does not attempt to do this. . . .

It is no exaggeration to say that the revenue of British East Africa is spent almost entirely upon the interests of the few hundred European settlers and upon "law and order." This is all the more remarkable when it is remembered that the only property tax, the hut tax, is levied on the natives. The white settlers, who are the property owners of the country, are extraordinarily lightly taxed, for they only pay a poll tax of £1 and their share of import duties.

But the white settlers and the European Government are not content with having ousted the natives from the best land of the country and with having relegated them to Reserves where no attempt is made to introduce them to the "blessings of civilization." The land is useless to the European unless he can get the expropriated native to work for him. But the native shows a marked disinclination to work for the European and the wages offered to him; and, if anything shows the system of economic exploitation which results from economic imperialism, it is the attitude of the white settlers and the Government towards this "labour problem." I propose to end this section by giving some facts with regard to this attitude, drawn from an official document.

In 1912 the complaints of the European landowners and farmers with regard to the shortage of labour induced the Government of British East Africa to appoint a "Native Labour Commission" to enquire and report on the subject. . . .

A large number of European planters and farmers gave evidence. They all complained of the difficulty of obtaining native labour. Their evidence was confirmed by the Secretary for Native Affairs. The native would not work voluntarily for a wage, but only if he was forced out of the Reserves to work. "It was, generally speaking, not the really able-bodied, but the old and young who were forced out to work." The method of forcing the native out to work was described by this Government official. The white settlers go to an Agent who undertakes to supply native labour from the Reserves. A native who leaves the Reserve to labour has to be registered with the District Commissioner. "There was no doubt at the present time," said Mr. Hollis, "that whenever an Agent wanted labour, he went to the chiefs and bribed them, with the result that a number of men were brought to the Commissioner to be registered. If these men were asked if they wanted to go, they often said: 'No.' . . . One could not call this voluntary labour. . . ."

Such native labour as is obtained by the white settler is, therefore, on the evidence of the Secretary for Native Affairs, forced labour. Let us examine the conditions of employment which are offered and refused by voluntary, and imposed upon forced labour. The evidence of the planters and farmers shows that the wages paid by them vary from Rs.3 per month (4s. a month, or a little over a penny a day) to Rs.7 per month (9s. 4d. a month, or a little over threepence a day). One planter said that methods of indenturing young native labour appeared to him to be excellent. "He himself had had splendid results from utilizing child labour on his farm, both boys and girls of about fourteen years of age. . . . Children were paid at the rate of R.1 (1s. 4d.) for fourteen days' actual work, without food."

It is perhaps natural that an employer should consider that results are excellent when he can obtain children of fourteen years of age to work for him for one penny a day, and able-bodied men for threepence a day, the hours of labour varying from eleven to nine (with one to two hours' break at mid-day). It is perhaps also natural that even East African natives will not work for these employers unless they are forced to do so. The disinclination of the native to work on the white man's farm becomes even more intelligible when one enquires into the way in which he is treated. When the labour recruiting agent has bribed the chief and the chief has made his forced levy on the tribe and registered his victims before the District Commissioner, the labourers have to be removed from the Reserve to the white man's farm. The Commissioners reported that the disinclination of the natives to go and work on these farms was in part due to the method in which this removal was conducted on the railway. The conditions are thus described by the Commissioners:

> It is an acknowledged fact that native labourers are packed tight into the ordinary third-class coaches and even iron-covered goods vans during their journeys, which may extend to three consecutive days and nights, if they are travelling the whole length of the line, as they are not conveyed by the ordinary passenger train, and are liable to be side-tracked to allow other trains to take precedence of them. The heat during the day, owing to the want of ventilation, and the cramping for several hours at a stretch must be well-nigh intolerable. Combined with this is the custom of locking the doors for long periods during the journey, with the natural result that the coaches become fouled, adding to the already inhuman crowding an unspeakable insanitary condition. In addition, water can only be obtained now at such places where the doors are unlocked, in accordance with existing railway regulations.

Under such conditions the British Government and the English settlers have found it impossible to inculcate in the native mind the dignity of human labour. . . .

At any rate, even with these inducements in the rate of wages and the amenities of railway travel, and with the system of unofficial compulsion described above, the English settlers cannot induce the natives to work for them. The planters and farmers who gave evidence before the Government Commission were practically unanimous in their demands for a solution of this labour problem. Their solution was a simple one. They asked the Government to cut down the native Reserves so that they would be unable to maintain the native population, and to increase the hut tax to Rs.10 for those natives who did not work on a European farm, while reducing it for those who did work. At the same time many of them asked Government to fix by law a standard wage of Rs.4 (5s. 4d.) a month.

It will be seen that this is a demand for slavery pure and simple. The reader who is not familiar with the psychology of economic imperialism may, perhaps, be disposed to think that I have misunderstood or exaggerated the demands of these Englishmen. I have not. Nearly every white settler who gave evidence before the Commission was in favour of these proposals. . . .

In their opinion the native has no right to land and no right to live his life for himself; he should be compelled to work on the white man's land for a wage fixed at twopence per day by law by the white man. They propose to use the power of the State to cut down the land, in occupation by the natives, until it is unable to support the native population. The native will thus be faced by the alternatives of starvation or of working for the settler on the settler's terms. And in order to make the result still more certain, the cost of the natives' living is to be increased by taxation, so that they will be compelled to work for the white man in order to earn sufficient money to pay the taxes. It may be added that in British Nyasaland this system had already been adopted, and there the native who cannot prove that he has worked has to pay double taxes. . . .

The views of the English settlers which we have given above are merely a reflection of the beliefs and desires of economic imperialism. The Government, they hold, should see that the land and peoples of British East Africa perform the function destined for them, namely, to promote the economic interests of the white settlers. The attitude of the Commission in its Report and recommendations towards these demands is very curious. . . . The Commission in its recommendations, in effect, adopted the white settlers' demand and proposal, though it did not state them quite so baldly. It recommended that all natives living outside the Reserves be removed within them, and that the Reserve should then be re-demarcated and cut down "with a view to reserving sufficient land for the present population only." The effect would therefore be that any increase of native population would immediately make the Reserves insufficient to maintain the population, and natives would be forced out of the Reserves to work on the white man's land.

But the recommendation of the

Commission with regard to taxation is still more significant. It started by stating that "it is recognized that . . . taxation does bring natives into the labour market, but that to increase taxation . . . with a view to increasing the supply of labour is unjustifiable." In the very next sentence, however, the Commission expresses its opinion "that increased taxation should be imposed upon natives to meet the expenses of its recommendations, and that owing to their wealth they are well able to pay higher taxes upon property." The casuistry of the Jesuit is famous, but, surely, it was never equalled by this casuistry of imperialism. For the recommendations of the Commission are not intended to promote the interests of the natives; the re-demarcation of the Reserves, etc., are recommended as means of increasing the labour supply, of promoting the economic interests of the white settler. The Commission admits that increased taxation will "bring natives into the labour market"; it holds that increased taxation in order to bring natives into the labour market is unjustifiable; and then it finally recommends increased taxation (which will bring natives into the labour market) not in order to bring them into the market, but in order to pay for other recommendations the whole object of which is to bring natives into the labour market!

The white settlers of British East Africa and the Government Commission have, of course, good authority for their views. On August 6, 1901, Mr. Joseph Chamberlain in the House of Commons dealt with this question of native labour and taxation which had cropped up in another part of Africa. He thus explained the philosophy of economic imperialism:

> In the interests of the natives themselves all over Africa we have to teach them to work. . . . Suggestions have been made in the debate that it would be wrong to tax the natives. I do not agree at all. It would not for a moment be considered wrong to tax them on the ground that they were receivng benefits for which they pay their share of the cost. It is only suggested that it is wrong when there is the ulterior result that the native will have to work to obtain the money to pay the tax. Why should that which is right in itself be wrong because incidentally it will have a result which I venture to say is also right? For if by these indirect means we can get the native to undertake industry, we shall have done the best for them as well as for ourselves. . . .

Those who share the beliefs and desires of Mr. Chamberlain and the gentlemen who gave evidence before or sat upon the British East African Commission will continue to desire what they desire and to believe what they believe. And the lives of millions of Africans will be moulded by those beliefs and desires. The white settler has taken the best land from the native. The Reserves are to be cut down until they are unable to support the native population: thus the native will be forced out of the Reserve, and in order to escape starvation will be compelled to work upon the white man's land for the wage offered to him. And in order to make the process quicker and more sure, the native is to be taxed, so that he will be compelled to adopt the only means of obtaining the money with which to pay the tax, the wages of the white man. And when the white man has got his cheap labour on a legal maximum or standard wage, tied to his land or his mine by the power of the European State and by the law—not forced labour because the labourer is not forced by the lash or iron, but only by taxation, law, and starvation—when we have obtained all this, and the happy African, expropriated from all the best land of Africa, is working nine hours a day for twopence a day upon his master's land, and his children of fourteen years are producing "excellent results" at one penny a day (without food), then we Europeans are to congratulate ourselves because, as Mr. Chamberlain explained, we are not only doing good to ourselves by getting cheap labour, but also doing good to the natives by convincing them "of the necessity and dignity of labour" at twopence a day.

We may end this chapter by noticing two curious facts. If any one had suggested to Mr. Chamberlain that all persons in Great Britain who lived on "unearned increment" should be taxed 30s. in the £ in order to compel them to work and convince them of the necessity and dignity of labour, Mr. Chamberlain would have probably replied that what applies to the natives of East Africa does not apply to the natives of Park Lane. Moreover, many of the imperialists who agree to-day with Mr. Chamberlain are horrified and enraged by what is happening under Bolshevik rule in Russia. The Bolshevik Government is presenting all its subjects with the alternative of labour or starvation. The only difference between Mr. Chamberlain and Lenin is that Mr. Chamberlain said to the natives of Africa, "You must work for the white mine-owner or white land-owner (for twopence a day if that is what the white man offers) or we shall see that you starve"; while Lenin says, "You must all work for the community for an equal wage paid by the community, or the community will see that you starve." It is curious that what is barbarism in Russia should be civilization in Africa.

Huxley and Perham: Dialogue

THE SETTLERS: SHOULD THEY BE EXPROPRIATED?

22nd March 1942

Dear Miss Perham,

Thank you for answering my letter, and for explaining your point of view so clearly. To begin with, you suggest that a healthy state can't be built on a basis of rigid racial discrimination. I agree with that. But I don't agree that Kenya's feet are necessarily set on this path. For one thing, I don't see how such a state—a little South Africa, you might say, in a political sense—could possibly arise within the framework of the British colonial empire. The general principles and

From Elspeth Huxley and Margery Perham, *Race and Politics in Kenya* (London: Faber and Faber Ltd., 1956), pp. 27–39, 42–49, 228–43.

laws on which that empire is based simply wouldn't allow it. For another, I think Kenya has already passed far beyond the stage where such a rigidly repressive state *could* be organized, even if the most reactionary elements were given a chance to try.

You imply that settlers in Kenya wish to deny to Africans the 'gradual advance in economic and political status to which they are successfully rising in those other parts of Africa where they have not a white colony sitting on their heads'. The facts don't seem to me to support this. Does native education in Kenya, for instance, lag behind that in other African dependencies? Surely not. Africans are being taught skills and trades of all kinds, and as a matter of fact the settlers have frequently prodded the Government in this respect. In politics Africans have their Local Native Councils which raise and spend their own taxes, they have a record of slow but steady advance. So far as I know the settlers have opposed none of this. On the contrary, they have often supported it. Therefore to suggest, as you seem to, that the Europeans want to sit on the Africans' heads and prevent advances seems to me to give an entirely false impression.

You say that you sympathize with those who distrust and fear the settlers' influence, and you explain why. I certainly can't agree with you that these critics are always on the defensive; on the contrary, they are always attacking the settlers' position, and the Kenya Government. One has only got to read the Parliamentary questions, for instance, to see that. But that's a minor detail. The main question, granting your fears and misgivings, is—what do you want to do about it?

It seems to me that there are only two alternatives. One is that the white population of Kenya, settlers and traders and everyone but Government officials and perhaps missionaries, should go, leaving the country in the undisputed possession of the native and immigrant Indian peoples. The other is that the whites should stay where they are. And if they stay, they must somehow or other be fitted into the economic and political structure of a future East African state.

They go, or they stay. Look at the first possibility. They won't go voluntarily. But we live in an age of vast upheavals, of the tearing up of roots, of revolution and change. The settlers could be forced to go. They were, as you know, invited to Kenya in the first place by the Imperial Government, which spent time, thought and even money, from 1903 to 1923, in attracting Europeans to the Kenya highlands and persuading them to take up land. The Imperial Government is responsible for the presence of these settlers. It wouldn't be impossible for the Imperial Government to announce that it had changed its mind, to withdraw its invitation, and to turn them out again. There would be difficulties, of course. There would be breaches of faith. But it would not be beyond the bounds of the feasible to compensate the owners of land and to arrange, perhaps, for them to take up new farms, if they so wished, in one of the Dominions.

I don't suggest that this would be a popular or an easy move. The Imperial Government would have to provide the money, and would probably have to use force to carry through the eviction. I only suggest that it isn't physically impossible, given the resolve. And it is, surely, the logical goal at which those who condemn the experiment of white settlement in Kenya should aim. If white settlement is wrong, let it be liquidated: that is the honest viewpoint, or so it seems to me.

But if, on the other hand, such a liquidation is found to be impossible, then only the second alternative remains. If the settlers are not to be turned out, they must stay; and if they stay, a place must be found for them in the design of an East African future. The question at issue then becomes: what sort of place can, and should, be found for them, and what sort of attitude towards East Africa's future development would you wish them to adopt?

Now we've come to the fundamental point on which it seems to me that we disagree. If the settlers are there to stay, is it wise, is it even moderately sensible, to regard them always with this mixture of hostility and distrust? And to offer them no hopeful goal for their own future? You reject the goal that they worked towards in the past—self-government. But you don't suggest any other. Is this negative approach likely to make them more amenable to reason, to encourage them to show moderation and liberality, to persuade them (if necessary) to mend their ways?

No, I can't help but feel that this attitude is both defeatist and sterile. It takes as self-evident things which are not necessarily true: that the interests of the settlers are at all points antagonistic to those of the Africans; that, broadly speaking, all settlers have the same interests and ideas; that they can survive only by clinging to an island of privilege protected by a reef of racial discrimination; and that there's nothing to be done about it except to offer this blank wall of resistance and opposition to any move on the settlers' part.

I venture to doubt whether this attitude will lead to a fair or lasting solution to any of Kenya's problems. An entirely new approach is, I think, needed.

Now I've aired my opinion, and perhaps you'll tell me where I'm wrong. The burden of my complaint is this: that the critics of Kenya affairs are often both defeatist and unrealistic. They believe that the evils of Kenya are due to the presence there of European settlers, but they don't propose any honest and practical steps to get rid of the element they deplore. And if they believe it can't be got rid of, then I think they are more defeatist still: for by their unremitting attacks on the white population, by their constant opposition to any and all of the Europeans' aspirations, they drive the settlers more and more into a corner, they trample underfoot the shoots of co-operation, they scorch the chances of peaceful persuasion—in short, they do every thing to antagonize and embitter the settlers, to force them on the defensive, but nothing to understand, guide or persuade.

For myself, I believe that the ills of Kenya (and Heaven knows they exist) are due, in the main, to other causes altogether, causes which this attitude of blaming everything on the settlers tends to obscure.

But before we go into that, will you let me know what you think? Would you like to get rid of the settlers and start again? Do you believe this could be done? And if you don't, what do you hope may be gained by this constant opposition and active hostility towards the settlers and all their works which, as I am sure you'll agree, is so often displayed by those who are planning from London and Oxford the design of a new African world?

Yours sincerely,
Elspeth Huxley

EXPROPRIATION IMPRACTICABLE, BUT EXPANSION UNDESIRABLE

30th March 1942

Dear Mrs. Huxley,

You ask me if I think it would be better to buy out and repatriate the settlers. I think in view of the policy followed by the small number of settlers of trying to obtain domination over the three million Africans, and the repercussions this policy, if pursued, is likely to have upon the even larger surrounding African populations, that it might have been better. But if it were possible at any time, that time has gone. It may sound very practicable in a study but it is the sort of thing no Government—or, since 1939, I should say, no British Government—is ever likely to attempt against the settlers' will. Especially as the Europeans in South Africa would almost certainly oppose it on general principles and as a weakening of their continental strength.

Also I fully agree with you that the settlers came upon the invitation of the British Government. Moreover, only a few years ago, a government, and that a labour government, made a promise to the colonists upon this point. In their White Paper of 1930 they repeated the words of the White Paper issued in 1923 by then the Conservative Secretary of State for the Colonies, the Duke of Devonshire, on behalf of the Imperial Government.

'Primarily Kenya is an African territory, and His Majesty's Government think it necessary definitely to record their considered opinion that the interests of the African natives must be paramount and that if, and when those interests and the interests of the immigrant races should conflict, the former should prevail.' That is clear enough and surely unquestionable. But the statement goes on to say that the interests of the other communities must be safeguarded. 'Whatever the circumstances in which members of these communities have entered Kenya, there will be no drastic action or reversal of measures already introduced . . . the result of which might be to destroy or impair the existing interests of those already settled in Kenya.' With this, which of course, covers Indians as well as Europeans, the Labour Government concurs and it seems to me to rule out completely the compulsory, wholesale repatriation of the Colonists.

But is the alternative, as you seem to suggest, for the government to give way to the settlers' demands? This is where we must face our quite different view of the settlers. You write of the settlers as if they were unfortunate victims, who had been badly treated and were likely to be victimized further. As I see it, the settlers have suffered nothing but occasional criticism—for the criticism is by no means a ceaseless chorus—which has had little effect except to encourage the government to maintain certain fundamental defences in the interests of the African majority. The settlers have, indeed, carried most of the outworks and are now the dominant party in the country. It is not the British government or people who have been the aggressors. They have been rather sluggish defenders. The settlers whom you see as a rather pathetic group under attack, I see as a highly organized, ceaselessly alert group of shock troops, ready at any moment, when the defences are weak, by assault or by stratagem to seize the last inner stronghold of the constitutional citadel. The government therefore is right in its policy I would say, of no *more* surrenders, no *more* constitutional privileges, and, I would add, no more land or immigration for the settlers until a proper survey has been made of the native economy and the native labour which must serve them.

It is for the settlers to call off the assault; for them to say if they will accept the system as defined by the Imperial Government. In recent years the government has in some ways consolidated and improved the positions it has put up in defence of the other races. But I am not sure whether these defences are yet strong enough.

So when you ask me what the government should do about the settlers, I would say they should continue in their policy of 'thus far and no farther' to their advance, and go on righting the balance in favour of the other races, and especially, of course, of the three million Africans. Any settlers who cannot accept this check to their attempt to dominate, which will do no injury at all to their personal security and prosperity, should move to a country where the conditions allow them the full citizenship to which their traditions have accustomed them, but which Kenya conditions make impossible. No pledge was ever made—it could not constitutionally have been made—to them that they should have domination over the other races. They have already won, by their abilities, great influence. The onus, it seems to me, is now upon them, to show how their special position can be adjusted to the right of the other less privileged, less vocal groups, to advance in their turn.

To sum up, then, I can't accept the drastic 'either—or' that runs through your letter. These uncompromising alternatives are effective in argument but man's political life is not like that. There is a middle road for the settlers between domination and ruin. When you say 'a place must be found for them in the design of an East African future', I reply that a place *has* been found for them, a very privileged, favourable and influential place, even if it falls short of their large and determined political ambitions. I do not understand you when you suggest in forcible terms that there is something oppressive or unnatural about the settlers continuing to occupy this place and it appears that in this I am sharing the view of the Government and people of this country.

Yours sincerely,
Margery Perham

THE STATESMAN'S TASK: RACIAL RECONCILIATION NOT DIVISION

15th April 1942

Dear Miss Perham,

This time I think you have misunderstood me. I never said that the alternative to turning the settlers out was 'for the government to give way to the settlers' demands'. All I said was that a place must be found for the Europeans in the general design of an East African future. To which you reply that they already have a place, and they must stick to it; 'thus far and no farther' for them, but onwards and upwards as fast as possible for the Africans.

I think this statement of yours confirms my original complaint that the policy you support is, as regards the Europeans, static and sterile. It's all right for the moment, perhaps, but surely it was never suggested that the present political and economic set-up in Kenya was to endure forever; you yourself want to see it changed as soon as possible on the African side. Why should it then remain unchanged for an indefinite time to come for the Europeans? And surely this policy which you outline, and which you say is that of the Imperial Government, is lacking in the elements of statesmanship, which must be to reconcile races, not to divide them, and to try to make the most of all the human resources of a country, not to check and perhaps sterilize the group which you say is the most powerful one in the land.

Basically, I think, your solution is wrong (if I may say so) because you see everything, the whole future, in political terms of racial conflict, instead of in economic terms of racial interdependence. I don't think it's possible to separate things out in terms of black and white, as if you were dealing with chemical compounds. You can't say that these are the interests of the whites, these of the blacks, and that the dividing line is here. You can't indefinitely hold back one racial group and force on another—or if you do, you're building on sand. In any country the interests of the different groups are so interdependent, overlap at so many points, that the races must go forward together, or else run the risk of getting lost in a morass of conflict, argument and recrimination. Surely we should have learnt by now that the human community is a living organism, and that a poison generated in one part will sooner or later affect the health of every part.

Here I can't do better than to quote another letter to *The Times.* 'We who come from the colonies,' the writer says, 'utterly fail to understand that peculiarly British outlook, which must forever look for the things that divide, and completely fail to see the things which are common to us all and should therefore form a basis for reconciliation. There must not of necessity be clash and conflict because two or more ethnic groups are to be found in any one area. . . .' So writes Harold A. Moody, president of the League of Coloured Peoples. I too come from the colonies, and I share both Mr. Moody's bewilderment and his belief. This habit of looking for what divides instead of for what unifies has (it seems to me) injured British imperial policy in recent times. To build a future on the foundation of this gulf, this racial conflict, is I feel sure, to look for trouble. Surely it can have only one result: to keep open, to deepen and broaden the crack in the very foundation of the edifice. Surely one must look for the things that unite on which to build a future state and, try to bridge the gulf, not to widen it.

You say that the policy you support is to hold back the settlers to their present level: to allow them no future growth, political or economic; to stop immigration, restrict land, to offer no goal for them to work towards. You say that this would do no injury at all to their security and prosperity. Here I can't agree. It is just because they have considered their security threatened and their chances of making a living injured that they have tried to get a bigger say in political matters. Besides, such a course can be written down on paper; it can be translated into terms of flesh and blood, of human beings and their destinies. Don't you agree that no human society can stand still while those about it are swiftly changing? That it must go forward or else backward, grow or decay, change or perish? I feel sure that you would agree with this; and that you would not therefore admit, in honesty, that your suggestion would result not in the preservation of the *status quo,* so far as the settlers were concerned, but in the gradual decline of their position, their security and their strength.

Have you paused to consider what the probable results of such a policy would be? First of all you would not, I know, expect the Europeans to acquiesce. No community, however small, would agree that an alien government had a right to erect barriers across its path on every side. You may say that the white community is too weak to be able to resist effectively. But no doubt they would attempt to enlist allies on their side. I think it should always be remembered that if the leadership for which the Europeans in East Africa look to the Imperial Government continues to be withheld (and I don't mean political leadership only, or even mainly), then the Union of South Africa may provide it. There is, in fact, an alternative to British leadership in Africa, however unpalatable you may feel that alternative may be. Some years ago a Kenya friend of mine, speaking of a failure by the government to take decisive action on some question of production, remarked angrily, and rather theatrically: 'They will drive us into the arms of South Africa!' I can't imagine anything more likely to do this than a declared imperial policy of barring European development, economic as well as political, and excluding the whites from any considerable future share in directing the policies of the country that is their home.

But let's suppose that your strangulation policy, if I may call it that, is pursued. If we agree that life can't stand still, and that things which don't advance must go back, this restrictive course would probably lead to economic difficulties among the Europeans. You've got to remember that we've entered an age when very little economic development can take place without active government support, which would presumably be withheld under your policy. Do you consider it wise to create conditions likely to impoverish a group of farmers who have contended against great difficulties to win a certain measure of success, in so doing (as they hoped) benefiting the country as well as themselves; who have enjoyed for some forty years at least the government's nominal support; while at the same time leaving them there to nurse their feelings of injustice and betrayal? In fact—for this is what it might amount to—intentionally to produce a class of embittered poor whites?

Those counties which have poor whites to cope with would give a good deal to get rid of them; I've never heard of a country wishing to create them where they don't already exist. And there's no need to remind you that the more insecure a man's position, the more ruthless and unreasonable he is apt to become in defending it. Here again, I think that by your policy you would be promoting the very qualities you most deplore—race prejudice and bigotry. You aren't going to persuade a frustrated man, smarting under a sense of grievance, to display sympathy and tolerance towards African advancement which he feels is being gained at his expense. On the contrary, by your policy you may condemn the country—or so it seems to me—to a bleak future of unending racial strife, bitterness and contention: a state of affairs which could hardly fail to stultify progress, and to create an atmosphere of futility and discontent as harmful to the happiness and balance of the African as to that of the whites.

To sum up, on this question of future aims: I believe that lasting progress can only be made on a basis of racial co-operation. The right hand cannot beckon forward one race, while the left hand holds the other back. Of course, I don't pretend that the problem of securing this co-operation is easy. On the contrary, I think it's exceedingly difficult, but I also think that unless we can solve it, we shall have failed in one of our primary duties as a colonial power, and surely it's important enough to deserve deep attention from all who, like yourself, are authorities on colonial affairs.

Yours sincerely,
Elspeth Huxley

THE SETTLERS' PRIVILEGED POSITION

23rd April 1942

Dear Mrs. Huxley,

I'll begin with a comment upon the political philosophy upon which you base one of your points.

You say that human societies are like organisms, they must grow and go forward or else go backward and perish. Your suggestion is that to call a halt to the settlers' advance is to interfere with a natural and necessary movement and to be responsible for their decay, which will poison the whole society. I can't agree with this. To begin with, I think the idea of human society as an organism may land one in a number of false deductions. Modern human societies are the creation of political art, not of nature. And secondly, I think that to apply the expression 'human society' to one very small part of it and to claim for this something like a right to advance would lead to some very surprising arguments if applied to other privileged minority groups in other countries and periods. Would we now agree that this right was inherent in the Brahmins in India, or in the old French nobility or the British landowning ruling class in 1832, or in the planter aristocracy in the West Indies? I agree that élites have performed great services but the constant process of adjustment going on in human societies has mostly been in the direction of depriving ruling minorities of their powers and privileges and sharing them among widening circles of the people. The human society that must be helped to go forward is that of the people of Kenya as a whole, not of a small ruling minority. But an even deeper divergence seems to separate us.

I felt as I read your last letter that we approach Kenya from such different directions that we get wholly different views of the country. To you the conflicts of racial interest seem to be like passing shadows on an otherwise fair and open landscape. But the conflict of racial interests, actual or potential, has dominated all Kenya's history. I did not invent it. It is the reason for the present form of constitution; it is the key to the whole of the government's policy. It is the reason why we are writing to each other. No group of humanitarians could have persuaded a succession of British Governments, which were only too anxious to avoid colonial embarrassments, to oppose the settlers' wishes except for real and compelling reasons.

Here I begin to see where we diverge so far that your thrusts at me don't seem to reach home. Let me put the position in the simplest possible terms, so that we cannot again get at cross-purposes.

(1) Kenya is a country in which there are, as you say, possibilities of racial co-operation, but in which there have been, in fact a number of conflicts of racial interests.

(2) The settlers for many years made no secret of their intention to gain the dominant position in the constitution.

(3) This constitutional control was, and still is, refused them by the Imperial Government but even without it they have become the dominant party in the country.

(4) The Imperial Government—not Margery Perham—having decided that they must not advance further constitutionally, every effort should be made to develop quickly the more backward and neglected majority groups.

I am sorry to repeat myself, but I must in order to show that this policy is not one, in your surprising words (which seem to caricature what I said), of strangulation, of 'deliberately impoverishing', of 'betrayal' and the 'production of poor whites', of 'excluding the whites from all future share in the country that is their home'. On the contrary, this policy is the one now being followed. Except as regards the restriction of immigration until the effect of the labour-drain on the tribes can be fully investigated, under this policy, I repeat, the settlers have a privileged, happy and influential position, wide lands, great economic development, and no threat at all exists to their position, except in so far as the advance of the other races must, in time, gradually bridge the large gap that at present leaves them in such splendid isolation.

To deny this, to use your strong expressions suggests that you agree that the settlers must have full political domination and further privileges and still more land, at the expense of the other races, in order to save themselves from some unspecified danger of disaster or decay. Yet, as I think you are much too reasonable to maintain this, I am left somewhat at a loss. Is not the explanation, perhaps, that you are thinking of the settlers always as a group, with group rights and interests and not as individuals.

Look again more closely at the present position of the settlers and tell me how, as individuals, they are suffering under the present policy which is one not of strangulation but of 'constitutional halt'.

They have one of the most glorious regions in Africa reserved for their exclusive use. The government has helped them to get native labour, to provide facilities for research, to cater for their educational needs. They have had the help of loans for distressed farmers and a Land Bank, though no credit system has been worked out to help African farmers. The British taxpayer has just made a present to the country of the original railway. Until quite lately they were let off very lightly in taxation, and even their present peace-time income-tax is very light and generous in allowances.

I know that many have had a hard time and done valuable experimental work. But all farmers who struggle with the elements to grow food have had a hard time in recent years.

Your farmers, after all, have the great compensations that attracted them to Kenya, the adventure and freedom of a new country, with cheap farm labour, cheap domestic service, cheap sport, and that sense of importance and prestige that comes from belonging to a small white aristocracy in a black country.

No, reading Kenya's political history I can't see that the settlers have suffered much under what you call an alien government (but which is alien only to the other three races), except in the disappointment, as a group, of political hopes they pitched too high.

Yours sincerely,
Margery Perham

A DIFFERENT VIEW OF THE SETTLERS' STATUS

1st May 1942

Dear Miss Perham,

I'm sorry you can't agree with my suggestion that the human community is a living organism, and that if one important bit of it is poisoned (say by rancour or avoidable economic distress—for instance the unemployed in this country before the war), then the whole society suffers. Although I'm no historian, I still think that this is probably true, and I can't accept your comparison between the colonists of Kenya and the Brahmins, the French nobility, the English landowners before the Reform Bill, or the West Indian plantocracy. These groups were, as you say, ruling minorities; the settlers of Kenya, as you've admitted, most definitely don't rule.

Nor did I suggest, I must repeat, that these settlers *should* be given absolute freedom to rule, and so to range themselves beside the groups you mention. I merely suggested that statesmanship should be able to offer them some goal to work towards, something rather more constructive and inspiring than the policy expressed in your phrase: 'thus far and no farther'. But I never suggested that this goal should be full political domination and minority despotism. On the contrary, I suggested that co-operation between the races, not domination by one of them, should be the aim. It was because I believe that the negative policy you support would, if carried on indefinitely, seriously injure the prospects of co-operation that I questioned its wisdom.

Perhaps we do misunderstand one another here. You deny that your policy of 'freezing' the Europeans at their present stage for an indefinite time to come, while doing everything to stimulate African advance, would lead either to hardship or to a weakening of the European position. Whether it would or not—I won't argue that now, except to say that I emphatically disagree with your conclusions—my point is really one of psychology. I feel sure that the Europeans would see in such a standstill order, indefinitely prolonged, an attempt to injure their interests and to thrust them on one side. They might even regard it, rightly or wrongly, as a breach of the pledge which you quoted from the White Paper of 1930, that nothing would be done which might 'destroy or impair the existing interests of those who have already settled in Kenya'. For these reasons they might tend to oppose the policy of African advancement as a threat to themselves, instead of welcoming and helping it as a means of strengthening the position of the whole colony. That is really my point.

Inviting me to look again at the settlers' position, you paint such a glowing picture of their advantages that I feel sure you'll be offered strong inducements, after the war, to write brochures advertising the glories of the settlers' life in the highlands. I agree with you that it's an attractive life with many advantages, though I think perhaps you have allowed the subject to run away with you a little. You write as if a kindly government had showered gifts on them; but after all, the things you mention, facilities for research and education, have been paid for by the Europeans, not given away with a pound of tea. You don't mention the hard struggle they have often had to get these things. For instance, credit. You write as if the settlers had been treated with special generosity, and the African, as usual, neglected. As a matter of fact, the lack of any proper system of agricultural credit, such as exists in almost every other farming country in the world, was for a long time one of the most yawning gaps in Kenya's economy. The work of development had to be financed mainly by means of bank overdrafts at the very high rate of 8 per cent. As early as 1919 the need for a Land Bank was pointed out strongly by the Governor of the day, but it was not until 1931 that one was finally established, on a very small scale. And it's certainly not, as you seem to imply, a form of government charity to settlers. The farmers who borrow from it pay 6½ per cent on their loans—one of the highest rates of interest payable under a government-sponsored scheme in the world. Loans are exceedingly well secured; the Land Bank is entirely self-supporting, and is in no way subsidized by the government, or by anyone else.

There is, as you rightly say, no parallel bank for Africans. It's hard to see how such a scheme could be applied, at present, to peasant cultivators. The essentials are sound, realizable security—land, properly secured title deeds, immovable property. This presupposes, to begin with, the individual ownership of land. As you know, individual tenure is not the prevailing indigenous system of land ownership anywhere in Kenya. There is as yet no system of registration, no holding of title deeds. On what can you base a credit structure when the borrowers have no negotiable security to pledge for their loans? And when, moreover, they have little or no tradition or personal responsibility and private property, such as we have acquired through centuries of individualism? I agree entirely that a credit system for advanced African farmers is badly needed and ought to be devised; but the failure to introduce one up to date isn't due (as I think you feel) to racial discrimination, but the practical difficulty of devising a workable system in the present state of African development.

But I won't try to follow you point by point. Most certainly I agree that the people of Kenya as a whole must go forward, not just the white minority; but I stick to my point that the progress of the whole will be warped and embittered if that minority is frustrated, alienated, and driven finally and fruitlessly into a hostile camp. The question, as I see it, is really whether you are going to make the attempt to achieve all-round progress by agreement and co-operation, or whether you are going to force the progress of the African race down the throats of the white race whether they like it or not, by methods that must in that case be dictatorial, and that may need the backing of force.

Yours sincerely,
Elspeth Huxley

THE LAND: VIEW FROM AN AEROPLANE

10th June 1942

Dear Mrs. Huxley,

The first subject I should like to raise with you is land. It governs the whole situation, past, present, and future. You may say that you might have hoped after all the controversies in the past, culminating in the two recent Orders in Council confirming the position of the 'European Highlands' and that of the native reserves, that the land of Kenya might have been allowed to rest.

I wish it could as I really know hardly how to begin on such a large subject. I feel rather like the walrus and the carpenter, who 'wept like anything to see such quantities of land', or, at least, of land questions. It certainly would be grand if we could clear them away.

You obviously don't want to follow me into the details of past history. Well, one must sometimes appeal to details to illustrate generalities. And you must turn to history to show the meaning of any current situation. The suspicions of the Africans about land which cloud our relations with them would seem to be mere perversity apart from Kenya history. So would all the doubts that have led the British Government to refuse to allow the white minority to rule the country.

But I would agree that it is difficult to discuss history adequately in a letter. Let's deal with this land question, then, in the broadest terms of the present and the future. Kenya looks big enough on the map to hold a very large population. But you know well, as an agricultural expert, that considerably less than half can carry an agricultural population. Cut out the Northern Frontier, and Turkana Province, most of the Coast, the Masai grazing steppes and some of the marginal pastoral land now tacked on to the Native Reserves, and only about a quarter remains. This being so, it puzzles me that the present distribution of land between the races can be defended.

After long use people come to take injustice so much for granted, so much part of the normal scenery of life, that it is only by stepping on to new ground and seeing the whole situation afresh that they realize that it does not square with the political or religious principles they profess.

Imagine then that you are in an aeroplane over Kenya accompanied by a stranger of common sense and a feeling for justice who is completely ignorant of the Kenya situation. We will confine your flight to the highlands area on which, beside the European farmers, are the two great blocks of the Native Reserves which carry three-fifths of the African population, and those the most advanced peasant farmers.

Your stranger, leaning over, observes the crowded little farmsteads of the Kikuyu and remarks the dense population.

'Yes,' you say, being very well informed. 'In this district these people are 283 to the square mile, and as certain areas of the land are unfertile there are parts where they rise to 500 the square mile, and in parts of the Kavirondo Reserve, to as much as 1,000.'

Your stranger, impressed, wonders why this should be, and you reply that they are backward people who were not able to cultivate much land.

'But,' he says leaning out over the Fort Hall and Kiambu area, 'unless I mistake at this height, I seem to see some very nice-looking crops and plantations of trees, and neat little farmsteads.'

'Oh yes,' you admit, being honest, 'they are rapidly improving and learning to make better use of their land.'

'And increasing in numbers?'

'Almost certainly.'

At this moment your plane sails over the boundary of the European highlands. The stranger makes an exclamation of astonishment, and then sits silent. At last he says:

'Who lives in these large farmhouses and wide estates?'

'These are Europeans.'

'Why do they have such huge farms compared with the other people?'

'I've told you. They are Europeans, different sort of people, and —but if you don't understand, it's rather difficult to explain.'

'How much land have they and how many are there?'

'There are just under 2,000 landholders in 16,000 square miles, but only just over 10,000 square miles is reckoned as available as good farming land.'

'I see, about five and a half square miles to each European landowner.'

'Oh, no, not quite that, because some of the land is unoccupied, and much of the nominally occupied land, as you can see, isn't being used.'

The stranger brightens.

'I'm glad to see that. That's very fortunate. Then as they learn better farming, those poor overcrowded people back there can gradually fill up all these unused lands.'

'Oh, no, they can't!'

'Why not? Don't they want more land?'

'Yes, they want it badly enough. But you see it is all being kept for Europeans.'

'Then there are a lot of Europeans who are as overcrowded as the Africans and need the land. I suppose we shall fly over their part soon.'

'No, we shan't. They aren't in Africa at all.'

'Do you mean they are overcrowded somewhere in Europe?'

'No.'

'Do they want to come very badly? Will they pay a lot of money to come?'

'No, on the contrary. The government has to spend a lot of money looking for them, and persuading them to come. Then it has to find more money to help to settle them on the land and to give them training and loans and so on, as they haven't enough themselves.'

'But I can't understand. Who wants them to come? The British Government and people?'

'No, they aren't much interested, I'm afraid.'

'Then, *who?*'

'Well, the other Europeans down there.'

'But why?'

'Well, that would take rather a lot of explanation.'

The plane is passing again over the crowded, overworked plains of central Kavirondo.

'Why does the government allow such a thing?' bursts out the stranger.

'It gave a promise to the European settlers.'

'Was that not a promise', the stranger asks, 'which no government ought to have given? And,' looking more closely at the close intricate pattern of native huts and cultivation and stock, 'is it not a promise that no government will be able to keep?'

But now the plane has roared on over Uganda and the pattern below seems to give the stranger more pleasure.

Yours sincerely,
Margery Perham

THE LAND: VIEW FROM ANOTHER

2nd July 1942

Dear Miss Perham,

You put the question of land squarely if not, I feel, quite fairly. I'll try to suggest another point of view to your airborne passenger and his somewhat inarticulate guide.

Let's suppose that, anticipating the Wright brothers, you had made the same flight some forty years ago, before white settlement began. You would have seen below the same little clusters of round, thatched huts, with their small stockades; the pocket-handkerchief patches of maize (only most of it would have been millet then), sweet potatoes, and beans. But, of course, you'd have seen far less cultivation, and fewer huts, and noticed a protective wall of forest surrounding every homestead.

'How sparsely inhabited this country is!' your passenger might have observed. 'And yet, from the appearance of the forest and vegetation, I should say it was well watered and the soil good.'

'None better,' you would have answered.

'Then I wonder why it isn't more thickly settled? I should think it would hold two or three times its present population.'

At this point the aeroplane, following the route that you chose, would leave behind the forested foothills of Mt. Kenya (now Kikuyu reserve) and soar over the great Laikipia plain (now part of the European highlands).

'How abruptly the country changes!' your passenger would remark. 'How parched and dry these plains appear, after the well-watered, forested region we've just left behind. And not a sign of human life anywhere.'

'Yes,' you would say. 'It's totally different country. Pastoral land. As you see, there are practically no rivers, and the rainfall's less than half what it is in the Kikuyu country.'

'Does no one live on all this empty land?'

'No one. Occasionally the Masai drive their cattle up this way, and until we stopped it a few years ago, they used to come over the mountains to raid the Kikuyu back there.'

'These Masai must be rather a problem,' your stranger would remark.

'Yes they are. Until a few years ago they roamed about raiding the agricultural tribes everywhere from Marsabit and Mombasa.'

'Yes I daresay a lot of the land they roam over could be put to a much better use.'

'Yes, indeed. And I hope it will be, when the railway is built.'

'The railway? But how can you have a railway in country like this? No towns or even villages, no farming or industry, hardly any people—how can it possibly pay its way?'

'It can't, I'm afraid.'

'Then who *is* paying?'

'The British Government has built it, but of course that's just the trouble—the taxpayers aren't willing to go on paying huge losses every year for ever.'

'I should think not.'

By now, the plane has left behind the Laikipia flats and is flying across the great crack of the Rift Valley.

'What a view!' the stranger exclaims. 'Is all this lovely country uninhabited too?'

'Yes, it is—the marauding Masai again. They don't occupy the land, they only roam over it occasionally, sometimes after an interval of several years; but they keep everyone else out. And of course most of it's like Laikipia—not agricultural land. There's the railway down there, do you see?'

'It looks absurd—not so much as a village or a patch of maize in sight.'

'The Government wants to open up all this land to white settlement. They believe that if they can get a British Colony going, the settlers will start new industries—cattle-breeding, sheep, perhaps wheat and so on—which will give the railway something to carry, and some hope of paying its way.'

'Yes, that sounds a good idea,' the stranger would observe. 'I suppose they don't mean to turn the peaceful natives out?'

'Oh, no. The commissioners who are marking out the land for settlement have got instructions to draw a line between inhabited and uninhabited parts, and not to give out land on the inhabited side. That's to be native reserves. Besides, you can see for yourself that there *aren't* any natives in occupation in all this pastoral land.'

'It sounds fair enough. But suppose the natives increase?'

'There's plenty of room for them. You could see, back there, what a lot of land was quite uncultivated.'

'Yes, it seemed to be mostly forest and bush.'

'Besides, it's hard to see how you can even begin to civilize the Africans until you can get an export trade going, so that the country can import a few bare necessities. There are no exportable products at present—only a little ivory.'

'That's true. So I suppose the quickest way *is* to get a white colony started?

'And to open up some of this unused land.'

I think that's roughly how the situation appeared to impartial and fair-minded men when the decision was taken to encourage a British colony in the Kenya highlands. I think it is wrong to impute to the authorities motives of injustice or greed, or to assume that the intention was present to dispossess African cultivators of their land. On the contrary, the whole policy of establishing reserves, which you now seem to condemn, was intended to safeguard the lands of the different peasant tribes against encroachment. Mistakes were made, of course, and we are paying for them in Kenya today. But the point is that they were mistakes, and not part of a deliberate plan to oust African cultivators to make way for whites.

Lord Lugard, after all, was one of the first advocates of white settlement in Kenya, and you can hardly call him a man indifferent to African interests. He wrote of the Mau Escarpment: 'This area is uninhabited and of great extent; it consequently offers unlimited room for the location of agricultural settlements or stock-rearing farms. . . . I think it not impossible that a fruit export, such as has been so successfully developed in New Zealand and California, might prove one of the industries of future settlers. . . . The speciality of this district would, I think, be the establishment of ranches and cattle-runs on the rolling savannahs. . . .' And the first Governor, Sir Charles Eliot, wrote: 'At times one may make a journey from Naivasha to Fort Ternan [i.e. up the Rift Valley and over its western wall] without seeing a single human being or a hut.' These quotations do, I think, illustrate the fact that the great bulk of the land set aside for settlement in the early days was empty of native inhabitants, and not being put to any good use.

Also, I think it's important to remember that white settlement was in those days considered desirable as an end in itself, not only for economic reasons, but as the quickest way of bringing civilization to the Africans. If this belief seems to some a little quaint to-day, it was nevertheless held sincerely and even ardently by men of the highest principles who were thinking of the interests of the African first and foremost. David Livingstone, after all, said that in his opinion white settlers and traders would do more good than missionaries, and offered the profits of one of his books towards the cost of establishing a settlement in Nyasaland.

Your pilot and his passenger failed to make any distinction between agricultural and grazing land. But one of the basic facts about the European highlands is that most of the land isn't agricultural land at all, it's pastoral. I know there's often no hard and fast dividing line between the two. But it's certain that you couldn't conduct peasant cultivation on the ranching lands of, say, central Queensland, Arizona, or over most of the Kenya highlands: Laikipia, the Rift Valley, the Molo downs. (Any more than you could mark out allotments or small holdings on the sheep-walks of the Welsh mountains or even on top of the Sussex downs.)

What people often fail to realize is that by far the greater part of the land owned by the Europeans is grazing, or at best wheat, land, not suitable for peasant agriculture, which requires not only a good soil but an abundance of water. I think it has been roughly estimated that only about one-fifth of it is good agricultural land, comparable with that in the Kikuyu or Kavirondo reserves. It's significant that of the four and a half million acres in European occupation, over three million acres is classified as 'natural grazing'. If it were really good agricultural land like the Kikuyus', but lying idle, it would be classified as 'natural forest'. For that matter, there are well over half a million cattle and sheep in European ownership—an average of about 130 head per holding. As an average this is just about as useless a figure as the average acreage per holding, but it does show that a great deal of land must be used for grazing and is unsuitable for cultivation.

And when you come to those parts of the European highlands that *do* embrace first-class soil, what do you find? One of two things. Either, as in the coffee districts near Nairobi, the land is very intensively cultivated; or else much of it is occupied by squatters, whose density to the square mile isn't far short of that in the reserves. I could fly you over districts where your inquiring passenger would certainly exclaim:

'I see we have come to another reserve: the ground below is thickly encrusted with huts and covered with patches of maize and other crops'; and you would reply: 'No, this isn't reserve, but part of the European highlands; those are squatters' huts below.'

And if your plane flew on a bit further you would find yourself over a vast, empty, rolling savannah which would inspire your passenger to remark:

'This, I suppose, is another stretch of the European highlands, since it looks so empty and undeveloped'; and you would have to answer: 'Not at all, this is part of the Masai reserve, which is actually bigger than the whole of the European highlands (less forest reserve) and contains some of the best agricultural land in the country, although it's never cultivated.'

So much has been written about 'the settlers owning all the best land' that a lot of people think Kenya consists mainly of European farms. How many people know that less than 7 per cent of the total land area has been alienated to Europeans? Of course, I know that a great deal of the country is unsuited to settlement by either black or white.

You suggest that three-quarters of Kenya's area can be dismissed as infertile. This is a higher estimate than usual; I think three-fifths would be a better guess. Shall we put it at two-thirds, a more pessimistic estimate than most? That leaves us with about 74,000 square miles of potentially usable land, of which the Europeans have about 10,000 square miles—a little over 13 per cent. The native reserves occupy 50,000 square miles, five times as much as the Europeans. And they contain most of the richest and best watered land in the colony. If you want proof of this, look at a rainfall chart—not a bad guide to soil fertility in tropical Africa. You'll find two belts of high rainfall: one round Lake Victoria, the other round Mt. Kenya. The Africans have practically the whole of these two high rainfall belts. The

Europeans have a fringe at the edges, and here and there a patch. But by far the greater part of their land in area has a relatively low rainfall, say forty inches or under. This means that on the whole their land is less fertile, less reliable for crops and more suited to stock farming.

Your remarks about the size of Kenya farms made me wonder if you had been dipping into some of the romantic novels that have been written about the colony. 'Large farmhouses and wide estates' sounds glamorous enough, but is it a true picture? Certainly there are large farms or ranches—20,000 or 30,000 acres is nothing out of the way for a sheep farm, where fifteen or twenty miles may separate one watering place from the next. (In Australia there are sheep and cattle stations far larger than this.) But in the agricultural districts, two or three hundred acres is a more normal size. There are large houses, too; but the farmsteads I remember are roughly built, small, mud-and-wattle or wooden bungalows with tin or shingle roofs: The big average holding of land is reached partly because of the size of the ranches, occupying marginal land; partly because a few companies and individuals own large acreages, some of which are divided into medium-sized farms and run as independent units by various managers; and partly because a certain amount of land given out as farms is actually nearly worthless, and unused.

I don't want to suggest that I believe everything to be perfect as regards the allocation of land. I do suggest, however, that little constructive good will be done by spreading a false impression that the Europeans have most of the good land in Kenya, and that they got it by unfair means, when in fact most of the good soil is still in African possession, and most of what the Europeans have was not previously in native occupation, and was sold to them in good faith by the government.

Yours sincerely,
Elspeth Huxley

RECAPITULATION: DANGERS OF DIVIDING THE RACES, AND NEED FOR ECONOMIC EXPANSION

10th August 1943

Dear Miss Perham,

It was no part of my contention—or at least it wasn't meant to be—that our contact with Africans has brought them nothing but good. I quite agree that life before the white man came had many advantages and charms. It was a life that at any moment might turn bad on you, but on the other hand it was a life in which everything was properly ordered and explained; in which you believed that someone, the chiefs or the witchdoctors, knew all the answers, and in which you had your own established and useful place. I could feel, dimly and imperfectly, some of its attractions when I was writing *Red Strangers,* which attempted to sketch an African society before European contact, and to trace the disruptive effect of that contact on the society.

Life nowadays has far more scope—tribal society was essentially static—but it is also far more confusing. The old ways are seen to be foolish, the old answers are lost, but the new ways, and the new answers, are still unformed and contradictory. If I were an African (a man, though, not a woman), I'm sure I should often sigh for the good old days. But, funnily enough, they don't. I've asked many Africans, young and old, male and female, if they would like the old days back again, and I've never yet met one who said yes. I think that must be our answer, Africans themselves, and I'm talking of Kenya Africans, think that on balance they have gained more, far more, than they have lost from contact with us, settlers and all. And that was all I ventured to suggest.

Of course the bad side exists and we must try to improve it—urban squalor, monotonous diet for labourers, and so on. Incidentally the third evil you mention, Africans imprisoned for offences unknown to their own code, is not, perhaps, quite such a hardship as we assume. As you know, the stigma and disgrace that goes with imprisonment in this country is entirely lacking among Africans. On the other hand the food is often better, and the work lighter, than that met with elsewhere (cutting the grass in the District Commissioner's garden, for instance), and certain trades are taught. Only the other day I came across rather an illuminating paragraph in a report about the aftercare of prisoners. It said that difficulty was met with in finding work for released prisoners, as they considered that nothing less than a foreman's job was good enough for them. Of course, the fact that imprisonment isn't very onerous doesn't alter the necessity to tackle this problem. It agree it's wrong that people should suffer detention for offences that merely puzzle them, and the whole question of applying our justice in Africa is a very difficult one. But to be fair, you must compare conditions then and now. Which is worse, to be liable to suffer a few weeks' detention in these not uncomfortable conditions for reasons which appear insufficient to Africans, or to be liable to be burnt alive or speared to death on suspicion of sorcery, a reason which certainly seems insufficient to us?

However, this discussion on the good versus bad we have brought to Africa is academic; the revolution, as you say, has taken place, and it must go forward, not back. You accuse me of accepting this fatalistically, while impatiently urging that the Europeans' grievances should be met. I could retort that the one is a fact of history which neither I nor anyone else can alter, whereas the settlers' difficulties are immediate political and economic problems which could be dealt with at once. But—if you can stand some more generalizations—I would rather answer this accusation in a different way. The fact that you make it at all seems to show that, in spite of all the ink and paper we have used up, I still haven't made clear to you the main point that I have been trying to get across.

This point was not to urge that all the settlers' grievances should be met. The urgent political problem in Kenya is not just to appease the settlers, as you seem to suggest I believe, but to take bold and constructive action to bring the races together before they drift far apart, to break down the barriers dividing them, and to get them working together for the good of all. It's because I don't believe this can be done unless more sympathy and imagination is shown to the Europeans than you seem to display, and because of the need for economic advance, that I've suggested treating Europeans as well as Africans, with more understanding, and also injecting a greater sense of urgency into the affairs of government. I suggested that this treatment should be part of a much larger plan to advance the development and prosperity of the Colony as a whole, and all races in it—the Africans above all—and not an isolated piece of special treatment for Europeans only.

In spite of all you've written to me—and it adds up to a lot of words—I've seen no sign that you admit the danger of trying to push on with the advance of the African race only, leaving the Europeans with the impression that it's to be at their expense; the danger of trying to change only part of the pattern and not the pattern as a whole. It's surprising to me that you don't admit this danger, and see how it is likely to deepen the gulf between black and white, to strengthen the colour bar, and even to lead, eventually, to a situation where extreme action might be taken by either side; and how it might retard the progress of the African himself, and perhaps warp his outlook. It seems to me a great pity that people in England should so often do the right thing—and of course it it the right thing to push ahead vigorously with African development—in so clumsy a way that they wound and embitter those who might become their strongest allies.

A phrase in your last letter seems to me to epitomize very well your attitude to the Kenya situation. You speak of the 'disturbing and distracting addition of a white colony.' So long as white settlement is regarded—and I know a lot of people do so regard it—as a sort of unnecessary and tiresome growth on what might otherwise be a healthy organism, so long, I believe, shall we fail to make any real progress in solving Kenya's problems.

White settlement isn't a disturbing and distracting addition. It's a part and parcel of the whole Kenya set-up. It's built into the very foundations of the Colony. That may not be a palatable fact to some, but it's nevertheless a fact, and one which it is useless, and dangerous, to ignore.

The question then becomes not, as I think you regard it, how to minimize the disturbance and distraction, but how to use the fact of white settlement to the best advantage of the people of Kenya as a whole. My real complaint against many of Kenya's critics, for whom you've been acting as spokesman, is that they have scarcely begun to consider this question at all, since they are so busy attacking the settlers and trying to get white settlement discredited and weakened. (Or, as you might prefer to say, controlled and restricted.) Therefore the larger question escapes them.

As you say, and I agree with you, tribalism will gradually go—perhaps much faster than once seemed likely—and the Africans will move forward towards their own version of our civilization. As you say again, they will need all the help they can get from the Europeans, who have set the pattern. From Europeans of all types: not only officials and missionaries, but settlers and traders too.

The white settlement which you so much distrust has one solid quality. It provides for our civilization permanent roots which are lacking in all other colonies where Europeans go only for a few years to work, leaving their families, their homes and at least half their hearts behind in their own country. Their work in Africa is often self-sacrificing and devoted. But it is transient, and their thoughts must often travel forward and back to the land where they were born, where their children live, and where they hope to retire. Their life is in a sense artificial, for their roots are elsewhere.

There are advantages in this situation, of course. But it doesn't weld our European way of life into the very frame of Africa. Settlement does, for better or for worse. You may think for worse, because you look forward to the day when we shall withdraw, leaving the Africans in sole charge. But that day is still distant, and a lot may happen before then. It might even be that a country with a permanent white population, stimulating and stiffening as well as distracting and disturbing, would prove better able to face and solve the problems of the future than a country without. That is, provided the two races learn to co-operate and not to quarrel. Everything comes back to that in the end.

Finally, the question of political versus economic progress. Of course you can't separate the two. Both must advance together. But I don't agree with you that we can't expect far-reaching economic and social changes until Africans have achieved political independence from us. If we waited for that we should have to wait a long time, and I'm afraid that political independence, when it came, would be ill-managed and short-lived. I think you are putting the cart before the horse. Until Kenya, to be specific, is far more developed economically, and until its people are far, far more educated (the two go together, because the economic development must pay for the education), political independence would be little better than a dangerous farce.

I don't think your analogy with Russia goes very deep. The people of Russia were held back, in the main, by an outmoded and short-sighted régime operated by a ruling class who tried to keep the mass of the people in an ignorant, non-industrialized and partially feudal state. Russia threw off this ruling class and substituted another, drawn from the people, whose aim was to spread literacy and industrialization as quickly and widely as possible. We all know how tremendous has been their success. But Africans are not being held back by a ruling class. They are being held back, and have been for centuries, by ill health and disease, by ignorance of good farming methods, by lack of tools, by superstition and mental lassitude, and by other similar things. The ruling class, if you like to call it that, the British officials, missionaries and (though you may not admit it) settlers, are striving constantly and striving hard to slay these dragons in the African's path, and to arm the Africans so that they can slay the dragons too. If the Africans are going to give only half-hearted support to these endeavours until they get political independence, as you seem to suggest, I'm afraid they will only delay grievously their own deliverance. For what sort of independence will they be able to maintain until the mass of the people (not just a small *élite*) are educated, knowledgeable and sensible, and how long would they be able to keep it unless they were strong enough and sound enough to undertake its defence?

I do agree with you, however, to this extent, that it's very hard to create the sense of urgency that's needed if things are to be tackled with real vigour, under the present form of remote-control colonial government. That was why I ventured to put forward some suggestions for transferring the focus of government from Whitehall to Africa, where the sense of urgency is certainly greater—suggestions which you severely sat on. It seems to me that your arguments lead you to a rather defeatist and depressing goal. We can't, you say, hope for the really great effort in social and economic remoulding, which we agree is needed, until Africans attain political independence. But they won't be fit for this independence until that great effort has been made, until education is universal and good and the standard of living greatly improved. And I don't see how *that* can be achieved until enormous economic strides have been taken. So it seems to me we're left with a sort of chicken-or-the-egg situation.

I still believe that the place to break through this is on the economic front, that the most pressing problems to-day are not so much political as economic and social. In fact I would venture to define the central problem thus: how to create the wealth needed to raise the standard of living, moral and material, of the African people. In that, to my mind—that, and not primarily the question of the best sort of constitution—lies the real challenge of Africa to-day. The African of the future will thank us little for a trade union ticket and a vote if he lacks a job because trade languishes, a farm because the soil is worn out, water because erosion has dried up the springs, good food because he can't afford to buy it and doesn't know how to grow it, and good health because he is full of parasites and germs.

How can this challenge be met, except by a great development of natural resources, brought about by intensification of the technical services: the services rendered by doctors and vets, by teachers and preachers, by farmers, stockbreeders, by planters and engineers, by anthropologists, plant pathologists and entomologists, by surveyors, foresters, economists, plant breeders, aviators, geneticists, roadbuilders, and all the rest?

Surely, looked at from this point of view, your policy—or, as you say, the Imperial Government's—of going slow and clinging to the *status quo,* for fear of European political gains, becomes one of mere negation. (Leaving aside the question of whether preservation of the *status quo* in a rapidly changing world *is* a policy at all.) In the case of Kenya don't you need, not fewer Europeans, and weaker ones, but more, with greater economic security and wider opportunities?

You, I believe, would like to see the white population as weak and small as possible, so that it could never hope to gain constitutional power. I've already given one reason why I disagree with this: because a weak, frightened community, on the defensive, is bound to be more obstinate, unreasonable and reactionary than a community moderately secure and hopeful about its future.

There are other reasons, too. For instance, the larger the community, the better the chance that it will throw up good leaders of common sense and breadth of mind—even, occasionally, a man of outstanding qualities. (We could do with a few more like General Smuts.) The more prosperous the community, the better the education it can afford to give its children, and therefore the more fair-minded and adaptable its citizens are likely to be. The more secure the community, the greater the progress it is likely to make in the arts and sciences, in everything that men do when they have leisure over from the struggle to exist; and it's in this direction that European influence may be of greatest value to future generations of Africans.

But these are negative reasons. I believe that a permanent population of Europeans, settlers as distinct from civil servants, may be a positive asset to East Africa, if only the political question can be settled. Europeans who live in Africa and become white Africans themselves can provide the leadership which Africans will need for many years to come. They, the Europeans, are heirs to an inheritance of ingenuity, ambition, restless energy and technical skill which is desperately badly needed in the raw, undeveloped, poverty-ridden territories of Africa. By raising the standard of living, by introducing new crops, improving the blood of stock, making discoveries about disease and nutrition and cultivation, building roads and railways, opening up markets, finding metals and starting industries, Europeans are adding greatly to the stock of Africa's still meagre resources.

For here in Africa we have, not great riches to be shared, but great poverty to be overcome; not a crowded, saturated land, but on the whole a sparsely inhabited region, with fields yet to be tilled, forests to be planted, industries to be devised, cities to be planned. We stand at the very beginning of things, with all yet to make and to build: nature still to be mastered, culture to be born, the shape of the future to be moulded. Isn't it a sign of decadent vision that we squabble so much about who should do the work, instead of planning the work that needs to be done?

Surely there's room for everyone who will make a contribution. There's room for more settlers to intensify cultivation, to improve yields and crops and water supplies, to import bloodstock, experiment with new crops, to mend and enrich the land, and therefore the country. There's room for their children to be trained as scientists and engineers, teachers and architects, doctors and nurses, chemists and carpenters, missionaries and pilots, typists and policemen and vets. There's room too for older folk, for men with experience of administration and leadership in other countries, to enter politics, and supply the oil of wisdom and good sense without which any constitutional machine will creak and seize.

There's not only room for them, there's a real need. There's a need not only for their technical services but for their counsel, not only for their skill but for their visions and dreams. Africa hasn't a surplus of brains and skill and enterprise. It wants more, not less, leadership and capital, energy and ideas. One day it may need again the military strength which an established white population can bring to the defence of Africa. It's my belief that Kenya would be a sounder and better country, for the Africans and everyone else, if the number of settlers were doubled or trebled. The obvious proviso is that they must be good settlers, and that if they work hard and intelligently they must have a fair chance to maintain decent standards for themselves and their children and to earn a reasonable living.

I know that your chief objection to an expansionist policy of this kind is the fear that a larger white population would have a better chance of gaining more political power. I've already agreed that a small white population—and even if it trebled its present size it would still be very small in relation to the African population—shouldn't have political control over millions of Africans. I've already explained how I think this could be prevented, so I won't go into it again.

Perhaps it would help if a new declaration of policy were to be made for Kenya. The Imperial Government could make its policy crystal clear: that the Europeans as a group couldn't hope for political control, and that self-government, when it came, would be self-government by all races, and not only by one. It could reaffirm its creed that no barriers of colour or race should be allowed to bar the way of those of its citizens who were fitted for higher responsibilities. But it could add that white settlement had its own contribution to make, and a big one, and that, within its well-defined political and territorial limits, it would be encouraged and fostered. (I don't mean by subsidies, but by things like the stabilization of markets, cheap credit, water schemes and so on.) It could add that fresh settlers would be invited to come to land already in white ownership, that local self-government would be developed as rapidly as possible in both European and African areas, and that both Europeans and, as they qualified for responsibility, Africans, would be associated as closely as possible with the government in its work. In short, the Imperial Government could extend a hand to the Europeans, welcome their co-operation, and guarantee their security, so far as it could, for the future; and it could seek their aid in carrying out the great work, the major work, of African advancement.

Of course, I'm not suggesting that all these problems of Kenya we've been discussing can be solved by a government declaration. It would have to be followed by action of a genuinely bold and imaginative kind.

I do venture to suggest, however, that in dealing with the tangled situation of Kenya you should, while remaining true to your principles, consider the tactics of sympathy rather than suspicion, co-operation rather than hostility, appeals to reason rather than recrimination; and behind that, consider the strategy of winning support for the cause of African advancement from the settlers, instead of drifting into the position where it might have to be carried through in the teeth of their opposition.

Yours sincerely,
Elspeth Huxley

THE CONTROVERSY SURVEYED. KENYA IN THE COMING WORLD

20th August 1943

Dear Mrs. Huxley,

I seem to detect in your last letter a note of finality; a sense, which I share, that we have emptied our quivers. Let this, then, be the end of a controversy which I have found strenuous indeed but fully worth the waging. Therefore, I will, like you, try to sum up our difference and then endeavour to wrest from what you all too rightly call 'a lot of words' some elements of agreement and of construction for the future of Kenya.

As I look back over our correspondence it seems to me that, taken line by line and page by page, the divergencies in our views are small—matters of emphasis, or wording, often of misunderstanding. And yet, their sum total is not small. It is a wide difference of perspective, arising from one of approach. I know that you have said that you want all races to go forward equally and yet I feel that as you close your eyes and look at the future your attention is drawn always to that little band—to which you yourself belong—of highly civilized whites, whom you see leading and leavening the vast backward masses of the other races. The whites are the important people, the *élite, they* must be given more understanding, sympathy, and security. *They* can make or mar Kenya. When, on the other hand, I close my eyes, I see the same scenes but the high lights fall differently. My gaze is riveted upon a huge African population, some twelve millions if we visualize federation. I admit all their backwardness and disunity now, but I believe that the powerful modern administrative and educational techniques could be used—and we have learnt much about their use in this war—to bring them forward with a speed of development hitherto unknown in human history. Then, after this, I see the settlers, a minute fraction in numbers, but relatively to the Africans, strong in their high cultural quality, their land and their economic and political advantages. I see that all through their history, and even in very recent years, this group has with a strong and united voice claimed the right to rule the other races. And yet, committed as our country is to the development of self-government for the colonial people, how can we imagine that this handful of our own countrymen will be able, in the midst of this great indigenous electorate of the future, to maintain its present superior position?

There are other signs of this difference of perspective. Remember, for instance, that when I suggested that a tropical altitude might explain the sometimes unreasonable politics of the settlers—have I not felt its effect upon my own nervous system?—you asked at what altitude, among other people, the framers of the Declaration of Independence lived? I get your point and yet—is not the comparison a little out of scale?

In Kenya itself, there is this same tendency to lack a sense of proportion. There, year by year, in the European newspapers and in settlers' speeches, you will read that 'public opinion in Kenya' will not stand for some government measure or that 'the people of this country' resent Imperial control. But there can be no doubt that over 90 per cent of the 'people of this country,' that is the Africans and Indians, desire with all their strength to retain this same Imperial control. If this is so, the admitted inconveniences and even, if you are right, occasional injuries to their interests which the settlers endure from Whitehall can weigh little in the balance. For, as Canon Broomfield suggests in his recent wise book, founded upon his long experience of East Africa (and with much of which you will agree) all the Empire and indeed the world is open to the European minority if East Africa does not meet their needs, but the East African people have nowhere else to go, 'African civilization will remain unrealized if its development is frustrated in the African's own country.'

Thus to me, it is all part of our difference in approach that in your last letter you see leadership and civilization in terms of the European group and write with real enthusiasm of the great part they will play in Kenya, being rooted in the country. Whereas I think of civilization more in terms of ideas and influences planted in the minds and hearts of men: I do not think that the presence of your restless, inventive white colony will act necessarily and automatically as a stimulus. It might indeed, if things go wrong, stimulate the Africans into unity as against the Europeans, cemented by that deep, anti-white feeling so widespread in the Union of which traces can already be seen in Kenya. In that case they might find their leadership under the Indians, whose position we have for sheer lack of time, neglected in our letters. Or, a third alternative, the presence of a dominant group might cut African self-confidence at the very roots and keep them leaderless and numbed with a sense of inferiority.

It is for reasons such as these that almost everyone in this country who has made an impartial study of the Kenya problem fears lest the Imperial Government, by lending itself to an attempt to entrench the privileged group-position of the settlers, should warp the infancy of a great African nation. 'Primarily' says one formal statement of the Imperial Government 'Kenya is an African territory' and to this another, signed by members of both houses and all parties, may be added . . . 'the interests of the overwhelming majority of the indigenous population must not be subordinated to those of a minority belonging to another race, however important in itself.' While, a good many years ago, Mr. Churchill said: 'It will be an ill day for these native races when their fortunes are removed from the impartial and august administration of the Crown, and abandoned to the fierce self-interest of a small white population.'

I cannot agree that, in reiterating these facts of Kenya's racial proportions and the Imperial Government's declared policy, and in facing their combined implications, I and the other so-called critics deserve the hard things you have said about us and the much harder things that have been said in Kenya. Even your relatively moderate words charging to our account 'suspicion,' 'hostility,' and 'recrimination,' are unjustified. They ascribe a personal antagonism.

But why should we feel that towards our own people in just this one part of the world? Why should the settlers and their apologists always direct their attack against a negligible fringe of unreasonable opinion and leave unanswered the great body of reasonable opinion upon which the Imperial Government's policy is founded? Is not this the natural, almost unconscious, device of those who feel that their case is weak? The settlers could well afford to ignore a few unreasonable critics, if, indeed, such exist. What they cannot ignore or evade is the extremely difficult situation in which they find themselves and for which neither they nor their critics are responsible but rather the inescapable facts of population and of the great flow of ideas in the Empire and the world.

Hostility towards the settlers would indeed be a poor contribution to their problem. Sympathy, though some of them might now proudly and angrily resent that word, would be more appropriate. For surely, not as individuals but as a group, the settlers are now at an apex of importance and influence from which, relatively to other groups, they can only decline. The Indians, backed vigorously by a great new Dominion Government, are likely to improve their position while every year the Africans will almost surely advance in education, in economic importance and in political activity.

You assent to this, I think. You say in your last letter that not even treble the present European population should have political control over the Africans. Here you and I are at one but I have given evidence to show that this represents a complete abandonment of the hopes upon which up to the latest date we have evidence of their group claim, the settlers built their conception of the future. Their hopes of a great white Dominion in East and Central Africa are now deserting them. Their plans for further settlement depend, as the latest news from Kenya shows, upon their success in persuading the big landholders who already hold more than they can possibly develop, not (to quote a very recent speech by their own leader) 'to stick to the land and buy more whenever they see an opportunity' but to make a sacrifice in the interests of further immediate settlement. The new settlers, though nine-tenths of the value of the land will be advanced to them, are advised to bring between £1,500 and £2,000 of capital. In addition to these difficulties Kenya must compete for emigrants from a Britain with a declining population which can ill spare the best of its youth and at a time when South Africa, Canada and above all, Australia, are making urgent and more justifiable demands to increase their British populations. Moreover, the whole trend of population movements seems to be in the opposite direction from that which peopled our Dominions by spreading men over the surface of new agricultural lands, and is towards their concentration in industrial activity.

It is hard, in these circumstances, to see that Kenya's settlement is likely to increase very greatly, or that Britain has any interest to-day in sending her people to East Africa. Sentiment alone will make little headway against economics and demography. Meanwhile, the leading British settler in Northern Rhodesia has just declared that medical opinion has pronounced against Northern Rhodesia being a white man's country except to 'a limited degree' and for whites living at a high standard. Northern Rhodesia has not, of course, the altitude nor the attractiveness of Kenya but it was to be a link in 'the White Dominion from the Limpopo to the Nile.' Even in South Africa the outlook is not untroubled. And this in spite of a temperate climate, and the immensely less alarming racial proportion for the whites of 1 in 6 as against 1 in 300 in Kenya. In spite also, of having that freedom to work out their own salvation, to generate an African policy in Africa free from remote control, which you have asked from Kenya. When I discussed the future outlook with leading men there, with General Hertzog, with the Minister for Native Affairs and others, I found they could not bear to look ahead for more than one or two generations. *Après nous*—Only the other day General Smuts—and who more than he has been in command of the situation?—said of the native problem, 'If we fail in this, we fail in everything,' and again, when speaking of the future position of the natives, 'The political road in this country is strewn with so much prejudice and difficulty that when you look to the future it appals you. . . .'

I cannot, then, but feel that the Kenya settlers face a difficult future whatever policy is followed. As you rightly pointed out, they went there at the invitation of the government and at a time when none but the most prescient could have visualized the position that we can now see ahead. Others of our nation have attempted the same adventure in other tropical countries, in the West Indies, in India, in Ceylon. How greatly has the position and, still more, the prospects of these communities changed since those early, easy days? The British in Fiji, arriving a little earlier than the Kenya settlers, like them demanded democratic rights and self-government and railed against the Crown Colony system and its native policy. Now, when they have taken full stock of the racial and political future, they have changed their minds, and have even by their own wish, shifted in part from a basis of election to one of nomination. I believe that it would be wisdom and foresight on the part of the Kenya settlers, instead of attacking, to preserve by all possible means the control of Britain because they may one day find in it their life-line.

It was necessary for me to restate my case in the light of our correspondence as you have restated yours. But that would be a barren end to the last letter. I want to make a final effort to get closer to your mind and to understand more nearly what divides us. Let me try then, to put what I know must be in your mind as you read this, the point you made in your first letter, and make again in your last, and at many places between, and one which I think you feel is your most important charge against me. It is that my attitude is utterly negative, that I emphasize past division and not possible unity, and that, in face of a given racial situation, I am empty of any constructive proposal. In trying to answer you here I have been all the time under three difficulties.

One is that before the great, inescapable facts of the situation in Africa I feel a sense of intellectual humility. I do not think I can produce some plan that will change what seems to me, in view of the racial numbers and our imperial promises to our subjects, the inevitable trend of events. There is, perhaps, a margin within which, for good or ill, we can direct their course, and about that margin I was ready to debate. For your dynamic personality, your desire for large and immediate action, this could not be enough.

My second difficulty was that I was never able to understand quite what you asked for the settlers. You have said so many things with which I have been able to agree, not grudgingly but with all my mind, about racial equality, about the impossibility of the minority controlling the majority and so on. And yet all the time you seem to have been asking for an undefined *something* that would satisfy the settlers—more influence, a more constructive future, more delegation in a situation where only they are yet politically influential. Thus I could not meet you with an outright 'yes' or 'no.' Is there perhaps some division between your mind, which clearly recognizes the limits which justice sets upon colonial ambitions, and your heart, which is with the colonists in their struggles and their hopes?

My third difficulty, which really arises from this, is that I felt myself to be carrying on a dual debate. There were you, so moderate in most ways, with so much knowledge of your world and such liberal conceptions of race relationships. You have said more than once that you do not claim to speak for the settlers, that you have not discussed these matters with them for some ten years. I think you are right and that you do not speak for them, for I have discussed these things with them much later than ten years ago, and have tried to learn more of their views by studying all the records I could find. I have already given you quotations to show what their policy has been. I will only point out now that because, in spite of your disclaimer about not speaking for them, you were, in general, standing with them, and defending them, I have all the time been carrying on a dual argument trying to meet at once your moderation and their intransigence. (And—since I would try to the end to avoid any unnecessary misunderstanding or bitterness—let me repeat, the intransigence of their group-attitude, as represented by their political leaders.)

There is another reason which seems to explain our difficulty in coming to grips, still more to terms. You have, I see, been genuinely impatient with me because I seemed unable to accept your reiterated assertion that you did not aim at future political domination but at equality and co-operation. I think I *have* been slow to believe that you really meant this, but the impressive words you have used since we embarked upon race-relations have at last convinced me. Convinced me, that is, that *you,* with your generosity and imagination, believe this. But are you not asking—indeed you have explicitly asked—for a great act of faith upon my part with regard to the settlers? In personal life it is a virtue to make upon one's own behalf an act of faith. In public life to make such an act on behalf of others may be a vice. Let there, at least, be good grounds for the faith.

What ground have I? You have throughout kept your eyes fixed almost entirely upon Kenya. But I am thinking all the time of what we can learn from elsewhere and from other times about race relationships and where can I learn except perhaps in Jamaica—and Kenya Europeans might not relish that analogy—that Anglo-Saxons are willing to accept negroes as full fellow-citizens. You yourself, I know, are making this act of faith in your own people. Do you realize how much and how new a thing you are asking from them? That they should serve the Africans, bring them on to equality and perhaps to predominance, adjust themselves decade by decade to a relationship always changing in the Africans' favour? The strain may not be great for this generation or even for the next. But I must honestly say that I would not care to leave my grandchildren to take over such a difficult inheritance. You have more courage and more faith than I and I do, in all seriousness, honour you for it. And if you are right, then all my arguments, all the criticisms from England, and much of Imperial policy would at once become superfluous.

Then you beg me to trust the man on the spot and ask derisively whether I think there is some special virtue in being a long way off and therefore making judgments at second-hand. I must answer that this is just what I do think. That is, be it understood, in the framing of general policy for backward peoples. This, too, can be learned from history, that of the Spanish, the Dutch, or the British Empires and, I believe I might add, the Roman. The reason is clear. The people who are up against backward tribes, who have, perhaps, some fear of them, and also claims upon their land and labour, are not in a position to make and carry out a policy based on general principles of justice and equality. There is always a gap between ideas in the metropolis and those on the frontier. It was in Spain, not in Central America, that the wrongs of the American-Indian was recognized. It was in Britain, not in the West Indies, that it was believed that slavery both should and could be ended. And Norman Leys, in his more humble way, is in the tradition of Las Casas, Wilberforce and Buxton. And there is not so long a time-lag to-day between the ideas of the metropolis and the frontier. Ideas fly fast and now will, very literally, fly faster yet. We who in England judge the potentiality of Africans by the first negro students in our universities, may make a more valid decision for the future of Africa than those who—unavoidably—judge by their raw 'labour' or the half-naked goatherds who trespass on their lands.

Here, then, are some areas in our field of controversy where, I think, for all the honesty of our attempts, we have failed to meet each other. Are we to conclude then, that nothing has been distilled from all this ink that has flowed except a little mutual understanding and a big agreement to differ? I do not think so. We have at least agreed upon the main lines of a federal constitution and have differed only about the date when it might safely be enacted. We have agreed fully, mind and heart, about the future of race relations, and as these are the foundations upon which all future policy must be built I may cherish the hope —which you cannot now exorcize—

that your political ideas will come nearer to mine than you now believe possible.

But is there not even more than this? It would be unworthy, I hope, of both of us to force a note of optimism in order to make a good peroration to the last letter. Our differences remain and they are great. But it is surely not unworthy to end with what Italian equestrians call 'the forward impulse.' I am not such burnt-out wood to your constructive fire as you think. I stand by all I have said, and do not regret my insistence in judging the present and the immediate future, by the past. Yet I recognize that we stand on the edge of a world in revolution and that there can be no harm in straining to look ahead at its profound turnings and heavings, and to wonder daringly whether the final shape of things to come might not be more favourable to a solution of our problem than reason and experience seem to promise. We might even face the possibility that our argument has been the last round of an old controversy and that a new era is about to begin in our problem colony because it is to be part of a new world.

Let us then search for favourable symptoms. Here is one. In the last few months there are voices—you have quoted that of our friend, Mr. S. V. Cooke—which can just be heard from East and Central and even from South Africa, which suggest a new realization of the claims and rights of the African masses; a new sense of the need for a community, not cut into racial segments, but welded into a more solid and sound whole. Leading Kenya settlers have agreed to African representation in Legislative Council. Large plans for African betterment have been gladly accepted. Is this something more than a temporary response to this war's moment of peril and weakness? Does it promise a change in the deep Anglo-Saxon sense of colour superiority? It may, and though there is little that we in England can presume to do in a matter so vital and intimate for our countrymen in Africa, we will be with you and any others who try to break through the present hard stratification of race-relationships.

Again, you have set over against the rooted colonist, the more ephemeral type of the temporary official. But, perhaps, this antithesis, this conflict of two types, will be swallowed up in a relationship so much fuller and richer that nearly all facets of British community life will come into contact with those of the colony, and the current of civilization will no longer be carried along single lines, whether official or colonial. We can surely see the first beginnings of this wider contact now.

And this leads on to another thought. As the present chaos subsides we shall, let us hope, find the world settling into a new framework which, if not universal in extent, will at least be widely regional. Is it possible that as the desire for nineteenth-century independence fades, and countries find themselves contained with the setting of wider securities and interests, the old fears of minorities and the head-on local collisions between racial groups may begin to appear superfluous? Fear on both sides, we have agreed, has been the chief creator of the two conflicting policies we have presented. But opinion in England would, I hope and believe, be as sensitive about injustice to settlers as it is to injustice to Africans. And if the settlers were certain that their legitimate individual or even minority rights would be protected within the embrace of an enduring and active Commonwealth, itself set in an inter-national framework, they might have less motive for clinging to their claim for local domination. And we in Britain, equally sure of the strength of imperial and international controls, might lose our constant fear lest some irreparable injustice should be done in distant colonies that bear our name. Things have not indeed been standing still even while we have been writing these letters. Imperial promises of growing liberalism and clearness about the determination to develop self-government among colonial peoples have been followed by several important measures in fulfilment, and have culminated in the speech last month in the Commons by the Colonial Secretary, Colonel Stanley, which seems to breathe a new practical and virile spirit. Meanwhile, the idea of regional councils within which this strong Imperial policy would find radiating centres, is being developed further month by month.

Thus I own that at the end of this correspondence I feel somewhat less anxiety about the political prospects of the Kenya Africans than I did at the beginning. I have lost some, at least, of my fear that the Imperial Government could, in a moment of weakness or distraction, block the political future of the people either in East or Central Africa. The more so as the tide of British opinion is flowing in the direction of greater justice and generosity to the under-privileged, whether they live in Stepney or Kiambu. And behind British opinion, Allied opinion, interested or inconsistent though some of it may be, seems to be turning in this same direction.

Kenya, then, seen from the broadest angle, presents something more than an isolated problem, a localized, irritating conflict between Whitehall and Nairobi, or between interfering pro-natives and wicked settlers. It is simply the problem of making adjustments on the equator to deep changes in ideas and purposes at the centre. Under the stress of a war that demands of the British people hitherto unimagined standards of individual quality and social unity, we have been forced to remould our society and our ways of living. New machinery for achieving the common good—and for achieving it quickly—have opened up wholly new visions of the meaning of those two words, of the spreading to the masses of those good things for the mind and the body which have been the privilege of the few. Private interests, through no fault of their own, have become crystallized round the old restrictive structure. They must bend or break, whether here or in Kenya. You believe that in Kenya they will bend, will adapt themselves willingly to the new demand to serve and to share, a demand much harder to meet in Kenya than in Britain. We, with our new, daring hopes for our own country and our awakened sense of colonial responsibility, will watch. Past history, as shown in these letters, may make us a little wary, but I am sure there will be no lack of help and appreciation if the settlers are able to play the fine and immensely difficult part you have imagined for them. It would, I think, be the first time in history that a ruling minority had actively helped a subject people to undermine their own supremacy. If this should, indeed, come to pass, let me say with all sincerity, as the last words of this long correspondence, that no one would rejoice more than I that my reading of history should be proved wrong and your political intuition should be proved right.

Yours sincerely,
Margery Perham

problem VI

Exploitation and Development in Colonial Africa

Did European colonialism exploit or develop Africa? The controversy aroused by this question has, perhaps more than any other problem in African history, been influenced by European ideologies and perpetuated by the dearth and inaccuracy of statistics about the African economy. Too often rational debate about the colonial economic system has degenerated into polemical diatribe based more on an individual's political ideology than African realities. Development to one individual is exploitation to another, as each cavalierly gerrymanders the meager statistics to support fact and fancy. The Problem of Exploitation or Development in Tropical Africa is consequently to steer between the Scylla of irrelevancy and the Charybdis of irresolution. Thus, the widely divergent assertions about European economic policies and practices in Africa, which range from almost total condemnation to positive approval, must first be examined. Then, the effects of these policies and practices on the African masses must be assessed. Clearly, the authorities are as divided on the economic impact on the Africans as they are in opposition on the nature and benefits of the European colonial economic system. Not only do the authors differ in kind but in degree, their differences frequently the product of their own political ideologies. In fact, the personal political ideologies and subjective assumptions of the reader himself will undoubtedly condition his attitude toward Exploitation or Development in Colonial Africa, frustrating those who seek objective solutions while stimulating others who enjoy the vagaries of endless dialogue, if not impassioned debate.

Writing immediately after World War I, a prominent British Socialist, Leonard Woolf, argued that European colonialism was both produced and perpetuated by the need for capitalists "to buy cheap and sell dear." The principal folly of colonialism was demonstrated when economic imperialism, which caused the quest for empire, proved neither profitable nor productive. The colonial powers were never able to create monopolies out of their markets, and the markets which did exist failed to expand, as many imperialists had predicted, and remained an insignificant factor in the total foreign trade of any of the European colonial powers. Of even greater significance was the failure of the colonies to provide employment for European workers as many advocates of empire had predicted during the days of the scramble for Africa. Rather than provide profits and produce for imperial powers, markets for manufactured goods, and employment for European workers, colonies had been merely the cause of rivalry and war in Europe. Those who benefited were a handful of wealthy financiers who profited from inflated interest rates, cheap African labor, and exploitable products. The failure of economic imperialism did not mean, however, that colonialism had no effect on Africa. Unfortunately, it had too much. Capitalism had brutally exploited the peoples of Africa in order to assure the wealth of a few financiers. Thus, a handful of capitalists, with the support of the colonial regime, were, in fact, deciding the destiny of Africa, not on the basis of the needs of the African people, but on the needs of European capital. Such exploitation, Woolf concluded, could end only when the European peoples replaced capitalism with socialism.

D. K. Fieldhouse has disagreed. He argued that the idea of colonial exploitation was a "dangerous myth." The modern colonial empires were not founded by looting, revenue transfers, and unfair trade terms as were the older mercantile empires. They were "political" empires in which economics was never a critical factor. Thus, the economic exploitation often associated with colonialism was not, in fact, a product of that colonialism. Exploitation was instead determined by the general "imbalance of power" between Europe and the rest of the world and by economic factors unconnected with colonialism. The features commonly associated with economic exploitation—low wages, low taxes, and extraction of minerals and produce at low prices—were in fact prevalent in other states independent of European colonial rule. There was, to be sure, economic exploitation, but such exploitation was the result of Europe's economic power and would have occurred whether or not the imperial powers established formal political control in Africa.

Lewis Gann and Peter Duignan have replied to the Marxist critics of colonialism, arguing in rebuttal that the principal economic result of colonialism was the development, not the exploitation, of Africa. Colonialism provided that necessary condition to attract capital to Africa—peace. Once peace had been established by the colonial powers, the capital investment needed to develop the untapped wealth of the continent entered Africa in increasing amounts and, at last, began to transform the economy of the continent. Thus, instead of causing economic stagnation, colonialism produced economic growth. Large mining combines used capital, which Africa could never have provided herself, to unlock previously unobtainable natural resources while creating new "non-metallic sectors" in the economy which were beneficial to all the people. Certainly, the imperialists employed cheap African labor, but to regard such practices as profitable exploitation is to ignore the taxes they paid and the great risks they assumed. In fact, the African people paid far less for "incipient industrialization" than did the English in the eighteenth century and the Russians in the twentieth. To disregard these advantages and assert, as do the Marxists, that colonialism was detrimental to Africa's economy since it did not establish sufficient industry and the Africans did not receive a just price for their labor and natural resources is, Gann and Duignan have argued, to damn European capitalism unfairly for not meeting a subjective goal unconnected to objective criteria.

Gann and Duignan have stressed the economic benefits which Africa received from colonialism. For example, African agriculture was not stagnant during the colonial period. They have asserted that in fact the opposite was true. Many African peasants were able with the help of European capital and scientific knowledge to make "astonishing progress." The cocoa farmers of Ghana and the peanut growers of Senegal were two examples of the ability of Africans to take advantage of the opportunities offered by colonial rule. To be sure, this progress was accompanied by the disintegration of the small family farm, the appearance of the migrant worker, and the creation of a landless peasantry, but by and large these problems were overshadowed by the advances. African agriculture was further improved by the White settlers and the large plantation companies. On the one hand, European farmers did, of course, alienate land, aggravating the problems of land hunger and migrant labor among the Africans. On the other, the European farmers introduced more advanced and intensive farming methods which helped to improve African agriculture. Gann and Duignan have concluded that European colonialism developed rather than exploited the continent and, on balance, was beneficial for Africa and its peoples.

Michael Crowder has disagreed. Discussing the economic impact of colonialism on West Africa, he has argued that colonialism had little impact on the socio-economic patterns of African life before 1940, and those effects that it did have were invariably bad. For example, the transportation systems, which are usually regarded as the first step in African economic development, were designed solely for the interests of the mother country. Crowder has made the same charge for almost all other European development schemes in West Africa. Thus, "any benefits" accruing to the Africans from European economic development in West Africa were "from accident not design." True, the European rulers did build railroads, introduce regulated currency, and prevent large-scale land alienation in West Africa, but they did not regulate the expatriate firms, carry out sufficient agricultural research, or provide the education and social services required to fulfill their civilizing mission. Thus, the economy of West Africa was not characterized, particularly during the interwar years, so much by development or exploitation as by "immobilisme" or stagnation.

The West African masses, Crowder has contended, were affected very little by colonial rule. In most areas cash crop production was merely a means to pay taxes and buy luxuries. It had, therefore, no profound effect on the social and economic way of life of the African peasant. Furthermore, the agricultural techniques which the Europeans introduced into Africa were largely irrelevant to African farming which continued to depend on traditional methods. As a result there was little improvement in the "basic standard of living" even in the areas where coffee and cocoa were grown as cash crops. The same was true for migrant workers on plantations and in mines. Their wages were so low and their contact usually so brief that their way of life remained largely unchanged. In fact, Crowder has concluded, the social and economic effect of colonialism "was much less than has been assumed."

Jack Woddis has refused to accept either the view of Gann and Duignan that colonialism produced economic development in Africa or the position of Michael Crowder that it had little impact at all. On the contrary he has forcefully argued that the effects of colonialism in Africa were many and all bad. Colonialism was, for Woddis, synonymous with robbery. The Europeans stole African land, labor, and natural resources by "every means open to them." In some colonies large amounts of land and in all colonies the "best" lands were alienated for European use. The loss of land produced migrant workers and rural poverty, aggravated by European agricultural methods which were "incorrect" for the African situation. The results of colonialism were thus almost entirely harmful. Woddis has concluded that the Europeans had done "nothing" to help the Africans; they had merely "made a wilderness and called it peace."

Woolf: Economic Imperialism, Exploitation, and the Future of Africa

The question which we have to answer is this: What has been the general effect of these beliefs and desires of economic imperialism which we have traced in Mediterranean Africa, in Abyssinia, in East Africa, and on the Congo? . . . There can in fact be no doubt that the protectionist policy of France in Algeria and Tunis succeeded to some extent in reserving those countries as partially closed markets for French goods. The fact that nearly nine-tenths of Algerian imports and over half of the Tunisian come from France might lead to a hasty conclusion that the policy of economic imperialism had entirely justified itself from the point of view of French economic interests, and was mainly responsible for providing Frenchmen with two large reserved markets for their goods. But there are certain facts which throw doubt on the validity of this conclusion. In the first place, it overlooks the fact that France is the nearest large industrial country to Algeria and Tunis, and that therefore under any circumstances the French would naturally have a great share of their import trade. Thus in 1885, when the existence of the Capitulations still prevented France from establishing a system of colonial preference with Tunis, she nevertheless supplied 50 per cent of the Tunisian imports. Similarly with Algeria. M. Girault points out that the tariff assimilation, which has been "a delusion" and "provokes bitter recriminations" in other French colonies, "raises no protests in Algeria." The reason is that in this case tariff assimilation "does not interfere with the natural course of commerce; on the contrary, it favours it." In other words, Algeria would, in any circumstances, be among the largest of France's customers, and *vice versa;* and economic imperialism, while it has increased the flow of trade between the two countries, has not, as it most certainly has in many French colonies, forced that trade into unnatural channels for the economic benefit of Frenchmen and to the economic detriment of the colonies.

These conclusions are, for our purpose, not very satisfactory. What we want to know is the extent to which this policy of economic imperialism in the acquisition and subsequent handling of Tunis and Algeria has affected the economic interests of the inhabitants of France. Our figures and our facts give us a certain amount of information on the subject, but they do not enable us to give a very precise

From Leonard Woolf, *Empire and Commerce in Africa: A Study in Economic Imperialism,* (New York: Howard Fertig, Inc., 1968), pp. 316, 328–31, 333–36, 352–58. First published by George Allen and Unwin, Ltd., 1920.

answer to the question. The evidence points to the conclusion that the policy has not succeeded in reserving for French industry any stores of African raw materials. The idea that any French workers would be out of employment if Britain or Italy had acquired Tunis instead of France—because iron and phosphate would thereby have been diverted to English or Italian and away from French industry—has proved a delusion. The raw materials of Algeria and Tunis have not benefited French manufacturers or workers but only a very small number of French capitalists—and that accounts for the fact that economic imperialism always receives greater support from finance than it does from either industry or labour. On the other hand, there is some reason for believing that the policy has increased the sales of French commodities in this African territory. To some extent economic imperialism has created here a market for French goods, and has therefore increased the profits of French industry and the employment of French workers. But to what extent? That after all is the real question; for the economic justification of economic imperialism—apart from its moral and political justification—must depend upon the number of manufacturers and workers whose economic interests have been actually affected by the French acquisition of Tunis and Algeria.

It is possible to furnish some answer to this question by considering the exports of France to Tunis and Algeria in relation to the total quantity of her exports to all countries. In 1912 France exported to Algeria and Tunis goods to the value of about 648 million francs; her total exports to all countries from 1906 to 1910 averaged in value 5527 million francs annually. If therefore economic imperialism could claim the credit for the whole of the French exports to these two possessions, it would have created a market for French goods which takes only 11 per cent of all the commodities exported by France. But such a claim on the part of economic imperialism would be, of course, absurd. Compare these figures with those for the early years of the decade 1880–1890, when economic imperialism had not yet been adopted as a policy. In 1885 French commodities exported to Algeria and Tunis were valued at 172 million francs, while the value of all exports of French product and manufacture in 1885 was 3088 million. Therefore the very highest which economic imperialists can claim is that their policy has in twenty years succeeded in creating a market in Algeria and Tunis for French goods which takes about 5½ per cent of all the commodities exported by France. When it is remembered that the value of French exports to Algeria and Tunis is about 2½ times greater than the value of all French exports to the other French colonial possessions, it will be seen how extremely small the effect of economic imperialism must have been upon the volume of the foreign commerce of France, and therefore upon the economic interests of producers.

An examination of French commerce with French possessions on the continent of Africa points to the same conclusion. The following table shows for the year 1910 the total French exports to and imports from all French colonies and possessions in Africa:

French Exports to:	Francs.
Algeria	483,000,000
Tunis	58,000,000
Other French possessions in Africa	118,000,000
	659,000,000

French Imports from:	Francs.
Algeria	401,000,000
Tunis	58,000,000
Other French possessions in Africa	135,000,000
	594,000,000

Now compare these figures with the total commerce of France in the same year: the total of all French exports was 8,100,000,000 francs, and of all French imports 9,100,000,000 francs. Therefore in 1910 her African empire was responsible for less than 8 per cent of her export trade, and less than 7 per cent of her import trade. In the philosophy of economic imperialism the United Kingdom and Germany are economic enemies and rivals of France, while her African empire is a weapon to be used against those enemies and rivals. Truly a strange philosophy when we find that the United Kingdom and Germany are infinitely more important in the trade and commerce of France than the whole of this African empire. In 1910 France exported goods to the United Kingdom valued at 1230 million francs or about 100 per cent more than to her African empire, and to Germany goods valued at 764 million francs or 15 per cent more than to her African Empire, while her imports from these two countries together were nearly three times in value the imports from her African empire. Nothing could show more clearly that the economic beliefs behind economic imperialism are dreams and delusions.

BRITAIN AND EAST AFRICA

Sir William Mackinnon, Mr. Chamberlain, *The Times,* Captain Lugard, and Mr. McDermott all held the opinion that the acquisition and retention of British East Africa and Uganda were vital to British industry and commerce. They even went so far as to warn the British working-classes that, if a Liberal Government gave up Uganda, they would find themselves without employment, for the cotton goods and other commodities which they made for sale to the inhabitants of these territories would be made by Germans or Frenchmen, and the raw materials upon which British industry depended and which came from East Africa and Uganda would go to French or German factories. These prophecies were made in the 'eighties and early 'nineties: a quarter of a century has passed, and it is now possible to form some opinion upon the extent to which the prophecies have been fulfilled. . . .

The figures show quite clearly the importance which these territories have, in about a quarter of a century, attained in supplying raw materials to British industry. The exports from the whole of the East Coast of Africa to the United Kingdom consist almost entirely of food or raw materials. These exports have increased enormously between 1884 and 1913. From the whole coast (*i.e.* including Portuguese and German as well as British territory) the annual average between 1884 and 1888 was £115,000, while between 1909 and 1913 it was £1,427,000, an increase of 1140 per cent. Clearly the importance of the East Coast of Africa as a source of raw materials for British industries has materially increased since 1884. But its importance does not depend only upon the absolute increase in the exports between the two dates; it also depends upon the relation between the raw materials supplied to British industries from this part of Africa and the raw materials supplied from the rest of the world. I have added statistics in the tabular statement which allow us to make this comparison. The annual average value of food and raw materials imported into the United Kingdom from all countries and British possessions between 1909 and 1913 was £526,743,000; the annual average of all imports (which are mainly food and raw materials) from the whole East Coast of Africa in the same period was £1,427,000. That means that to-day this part of Africa supplies 2 per cent of the food and raw materials required by British industry—in other words, a completely negligible quantity.

But so far we have been considering this coast of Africa as a whole and including in it Portuguese and German possessions. The whole case of the economic imperialist rests on the assertion that the possession of African territory by the European State is essential for the supply of raw materials for its industry. We must therefore exclude the German and Portuguese territory and examine the importance of the British territory alone. Of the total imports of £526,743,000 all the British possessions in East Africa together supplied £785,000, or 1 per cent; Uganda, which *The Times* and Captain Lugard said in 1891 was essential to the continued existence of British industries, supplied £218,000, or .04 per cent.

Imperialists often assume that the mere fact of a piece of African territory not being under the British flag implies that no raw materials produced by it are available for British industries. The absurdity of this hypothesis is shown by the statistics in the tabular statement. The increase of imports of raw material from East Africa into the United Kingdom between 1898 and 1913 rose by 422 per cent; those from British possessions in East Africa rose by only 306 per cent. The increase in the value of raw materials which British industries derived from German East Africa was immeasurably greater in this period than the increase in the value of raw materials which they derived from our own East African possessions, and greater even than the value of the materials derived from British East Africa and Uganda. The evidence of these figures is conclusive that German East Africa in German hands was no less valuable as a source of supply of raw materials for British industries than were British East Africa and Uganda in British hands.

If we turn to the second part of the table, we get a very good idea of the value of East Africa as a market for the products of British industry. Between 1884 and 1913 the rate of increase in the value of the produce and manufactures of the United Kingdom exported to the East Coast of Africa was almost the same as the rate of increase in the value of the raw materials from that part of the world imported into the United Kingdom, *i.e.* about 1200 per cent. Yet by 1913 this part of the world still took a minute and negligible quantity of the products of British industries. For the years 1909–1913 it took on an average goods to the value of just over 2¾ million pounds, while the total annual value of all produce and manufactures of the United Kingdom exported to foreign countries and British possessions was 455 million. Thus the whole coast, including German and Portuguese possessions, furnished a market for about .6 per cent of the total exports of British industries. But the figures are even more startling if we examine only those which relate to the British possessions on this coast. In the first place the rate of increase in the exports to the British possessions has actually been less than that in the exports to German East Africa. The significance of this fact is obvious when it is remembered that Mr. Chamberlain and the economic imperialists of the British East Africa Company argued that the main reason why Britain should seize and retain Uganda and British East Africa was in order to keep the Germans out and prevent them from closing these territories to the products of British industry. Twenty-five years have revealed the falseness of this argument and of the terrible picture drawn by them of the unemployment which would fall upon the British worker if Sir William Mackinnon and his fellow-capitalists were not allowed and encouraged to acquire Uganda. According to these figures, the number of workers in Britain to which German East Africa has afforded employment by taking the products of British industry has increased at a higher rate between 1890 and 1913 than has the number to which Uganda and British East Africa has afforded employment.

Secondly, it is necessary to consider the relative importance of the British possessions on the East Coast of Africa as a market for British products. The annual average value of British produce and manufactures exported to these countries during the period 1909–1913 was £884,000; that of British produce and manufactures exported to all foreign countries and British possessions was £455,000,000. Therefore all these British possessions on the East Coast only take .1 per cent of the exports of British industry. Uganda, that country which was to save the British workman from unemployment, actually takes no more than .006 per cent of the total exports of British industries. It is clear that the incorporation of Uganda in the British Empire has had no more and no less effect upon British trade, industry, and employment, than if it had been sunk in the Indian Ocean and blotted off the map of the world. . . .

And what is true of British colonial policy in this respect, is true of the policy of the other European States. Neither Germany nor France has succeeded in effectually reserving the raw materials in their African possessions for their own industries and industrialists. The reason is that the raw materials are mainly exploited by European capital, and European capital is always strong enough to protect its own interests. Its own interests are not to provide patriotically raw materials for the national industries, but to sell them to the highest bidder. Hence in practice the English manufacturer finds no difficulty in obtaining raw materials from the French capitalist in Tunis or the German capitalist in German East Africa; and the French or German manufacturer finds no difficulty in getting his supplies from the English capitalist in the British possessions. Once more we see that it is national financiers, not traders or industrialists, who benefit from the acquisition of territory by Britain, France, or Germany.

The other delusion of the economic imperialist has to do with the importance of these African territories as a market for European manufactures. "We must acquire Uganda and British East Africa for the British Empire," said *The Times* and Captain Lugard, "in order to reserve these rich and populous districts as a market for British exports, and so keep the wolf of unemployment from the door of the simple, British working-man." But these imperial economists forgot the law of economics that supply must depend upon demand. The rich and populous markets upon which they turned covetous eyes consist of a few hundred white men and several million Africans. The importance of these territories as a market for British industries depends therefore upon the demand of the Africans. Now the African is, according to European standards, wretchedly poor, and he is accustomed to invest such wealth as he has, not in the products of British industries, but in cattle. If a free man, he lives upon what he himself produces in a Native Reserve; if he works, he works for a white man who pays him at the rate of about 4s. a month. It is obvious that a population where wages work out at between £2 and £3 a year will never provide a very rich market for the products of European industry. Is it very surprising, in these circumstances, that Captain Lugard's hopes have not been fulfilled, and that British manufacturers are only able to sell goods to the people of Uganda of the annual value of £39,000? . . .

The facts examined in this book at any rate warrant the conclusion that Africa and the lives of its inhabitants, as we know them to-day, have been moulded very largely by the communal beliefs and desires to which we have given the name economic imperialism. One peculiar thing in this situation is that the political good and evil fortune of this continent and of its millions of inhabitants has been determined, during the last thirty years, mainly from outside, by the social and economic ideals and philosophy of alien white men. It is true of course that the communal beliefs and desires of the Africans are part cause of their present political and economic condition; if they had had the psychology of European civilization instead of African savages, they would never have fallen under the dominion of Europeans. But the psychology of the African has been only the passive agent in the making of his life and history; the active agent has been the beliefs and desires of Europeans.

In the last chapter I have attempted to trace the general effects of European policy in Africa. In my judgment those effects have been almost wholly evil. The European went into Africa about forty years ago desiring to exploit it and its inhabitants for his own economic advantage, and he rapidly acquired the belief that the power of his State should be used in Africa to promote his own economic interests. Once this belief was accepted, it destroyed the idea of individual moral responsibility. The State, enthroned in its impersonality and a glamour of patriotism, can always make a wilderness and call it peace, or make a conquest and call it civilization. The right of Europe to civilize became synonymous with the right of Europe to rob or to exploit the uncivilized. The power of each European State was applied ruthlessly in Africa. In bitter competition with one another, they partitioned territory which belonged to none of them. By fraud or by force the native chiefs and rulers were swindled or robbed of their dominions. Any resistance by the inhabitants to the encroachments either of individual Europeans or of European States was treated as "rebellion," and followed by massacres known as wars or punitive expeditions. In this process tribe was used against tribe and race against race, and wherever any native administration existed it was destroyed.

This work was accomplished by men who were not more rapacious or evil than the ordinary man; it was accomplished by men often of ideals and great devotion, but who accepted a political dogma, namely, that their actions were justified by the right and duty of the European State to use its power in Africa for the economic interests of its European subjects. Just in the same way those who burnt and tortured heretics were probably no more cruel or evil than the majority of their fellows; they were men of ideals and great devotion who accepted the religious dogma that it was the right and duty of the Church to torture men's bodies for the sake of their souls.

The dogma of economic imperialism prevailed with the aid of modern rifle and gun. The slaughter of the most warlike Africans encouraged the survivors to submit, and peace descended upon the greater part of Africa. The first stage of economic imperialism was accomplished, and the European looked round and openly proclaimed that the work he had done was good. The reason which he gave and gives for this opinion is interesting and deserves a little examination. The policy of conquest and partition which we have described is usually defended on two grounds: first, that it was inevitable; and secondly, that it eventually substituted a system of law and order for one of lawless barbarism.

It is true that if men believe and desire certain things, and then translate their beliefs and desires into actions, effects inevitably follow. But it is difficult to see why the inevitability of these effects justifies either the beliefs, the desires, or the actions. If the ruling classes believe that it is their duty to burn heretics and desire to burn heretics, heretics will inevitably be burnt; and if irresponsible traders armed with European rifles conceive that it is their right and duty to exploit Africans armed with assegais, Africans will inevitably either be shot or exploited. This no doubt raises a difficult problem for the European State. If it does not interfere to regularize the exploitation and regulate it under the name of conquest, the ferocity and cupidity of the European are themselves unregulated, and the native is either exterminated or enslaved. There is no doubt that non-adult races like the Africans suffer worse things when they are left under "independent" rulers to deal with white traders and financiers, than when the white man's State intervenes and conquers the African's country. Such intervention has, in fact, always proved to be inevitable. But the final situation is created by the beliefs and desires of the European traders and financiers, and neither those beliefs nor desires, nor the conquest and the methods by which the conquest is made, are justified because the last stage in this process follows inevitably from the first.

The second argument is that this last stage in the process is actually better than the first, that the inhabitants of East Africa under British rule, and of Algeria and Tunis under French rule, are better off and happier than they were before the European State entered Africa. Put in this way, the statement is not easy to prove or disprove. It is, however, quite certain that those who have been disgusted by the effects of the rapacious and bloodthirsty European exploitation of Africa, and who by a natural reaction have looked back to a Golden Age of peace and innocence before the European came there, are wrong. There have been no Golden Ages of uncivilized peace and innocence in the world's history, least of all in the continent which was scourged by the slave trade. The African was a savage with all the vices of savagery. Like all human beings, the natives of Africa, not satisfied with the perpetual and unavoidable sufferings which Providence inflicts upon their species, contrived to make their own and their neighbours' lives as miserable as possible. Their methods, when compared with those of our own, were crude; they consisted in war, religion, cannibalism, and cruelty. But the savage has not that organized and intelligent persistence in making his neighbour's life unbearable which is so characteristic of Western civilization. His efforts are spasmodic, often ill-contrived and inconsistent. . . .

Life in Africa during the first fifty years of the nineteenth century was undoubtedly ugly and cruel and bloody. But its misery was not, like that of civilization, organized or continual. This fact accounts for the contradictory descriptions and estimates of it which we find in the works of travellers and missionaries. The villages and country of the Congo, which the civilization introduced by King Leopold subsequently converted into a desert, seemed to Coquilhat when he visited them in 1883 to be idyllic, the inhabitants prosperous, peaceful and happy. On the other hand, men like Grenfell, who knew and denounced the atrocities perpetrated by European economic imperialism in the Belgian Congo, furnish evidence of the horrors of barbarism which preceded them.

It is, however, for our purpose unnecessary to attempt any accurate comparison between the misery of African savagery and the misery of European exploitation. Even if we admit that the atrocities of the first far outweigh the atrocities of the second, and that Europe has given to Africa the inestimable gift of law and order, this is no justification of the system of conquest, partition, and economic exploitation which we have examined. When Europeans are forced to defend the evil that they have done in Africa by pleading that the evil has been less than that done by the savage rulers and the Arab slave traders whom they have destroyed, their case must be a singularly weak one. Economic imperialism stands self-condemned if the only thing which it can say for itself is that the present conditions in British East Africa, for instance, are rather better than they were when Captain Lugard led his expedition into Uganda.

The past and the present of Africa are dark pages in the world's record. What of its future? The European is here faced by a problem with which his own future, and that of his civilization, are inevitably bound up. He can, if he will, continue to follow the path of those beliefs and desires which we have examined, and the public policy of European States will be the policy of economic imperialism. But in that case we must not delude ourselves with the belief that we can escape from the consequences of our actions, or that the political sins of one generation are not visited upon the next. The African question has not been settled either for white man or black man by the partition of Africa among four or five European States. If the same economic beliefs and desires continue to govern our policy and shape our actions as they have done in the past, the social results within Africa, and the international results outside it, can be predicted with considerable certainty. The States which possess territory there will attempt to reserve it for economic exploitation by their own subjects. The tariff, the differential export duty, the subsidy, the manipulation of railway rates, and the concession, will continue to be used as economic weapons. The concessionaires and small groups of prominent capitalists in the possessory States will make fortunes, and Labour will be induced to believe that it is guaranteed against unemployment by making goods of the annual value of £30,000 for a few million natives under the national flag, although it makes goods of the annual value of hundreds of millions of pounds for purchase by those peoples who are represented to be its enemies and rivals. Meanwhile the citizens of non-possessing States who see themselves apparently shut out of rich markets and denied access to the stores of raw materials will, as in the past, refuse to believe that God has chosen only four or five peoples to bear the white man's burden of lucrative imperialism, and will determine to take the first opportunity of upsetting the *status quo*. International relations will again, unconsciously perhaps, be firmly established on a foundation of rivalry, cupidity, aggression, fear of aggression, and force. The land-owning nation, knowing that it won and holds what it owns solely by the right of force, will also know that the landless nation will, when the opportunity presents itself, challenge that ownership by appealing once more to force. The peace of the world will depend upon a shifting balance of power, or rather upon the calculations of a few statesmen and soldiers as to whether the balance has at last shifted to their side. For if anything is certain in international politics, it is that you cannot base international relations in one quarter of the world upon right and law and co-operation, and in another quarter upon economic hostility and force. You cannot combine the ideal of a League of Nations in Europe and America with the ideals of economic imperialism and *Machtpolitik* in Africa and Asia. If the power of the European State is to be used to promote the economic interests of its citizens and to damage the economic interests of those who are not its citizens, the final test of power or force will not be made in Africa and Asia, but upon the old graves in the battlefields of Europe.

Such must be the inevitable international effects outside Africa of economic imperialism. Within the continent the policy must proceed to its logical conclusion. The millions of Africans, who belong to the black non-adult races, will remain subject to the autocratic government of alien white men. The belief that the economic development of the country should be the first duty of the administration in order that it may fit into and serve the economic—the industrial and financial—system of Europe will be the main principle of government. The acceptance of the principle that the power of the European State should be used in Africa to promote the economic interests of European citizens will subject the Colonial Offices and Colonial Governments to the irresistible pressure of the handful of white men who have economic interests in Africa. If those interests require that the native shall not be educated, he will not be educated; if they require that he shall be demoralized and poisoned by gin, gin will be sold to him; if they require that the native shall be forced to work on the white man's land for a penny a day, taxation or starvation will furnish the necessary inducement; if they require that land occupied by natives shall be sold to Europeans, the natives will be removed into Reserves, and the Reserves will then be cut down until the native is forced to return to work for a penny a day on the land from which the European expropriated him. In this process of what Mr. Chamberlain called "convincing the native of the necessity and dignity of labour," the whole tribal organization, and the bonds which bound together the fabric of native social life, will necessarily be destroyed. The Government will be powerless to substitute, whether by education or otherwise, anything in their place; for any real education will unfit the native to take his place as a docile labourer on a penny a day in the scheme of economic imperialism. Thus the natives will receive an ever larger measure of the blessings of law and order, and the European an ever increasing measure of cheap labour. The exploitation of Africa by Europe internally as well as externally will be based upon force, the primitive right of the stronger to enslave the weaker. At the worst this right will be enforced with the cruelties and atrocities which Europe associates with the Belgian Congo and the German and Portuguese Colonies; at the best the right will be enforced by the milder, more respectable, and no less efficacious British method of legislative enactment.

Such must inevitably be the future of Africa if it be shaped, like the past and the present, by the desires, beliefs, and policy of economic imperialism. The conditions necessary, if the evils are to be turned into blessings and the professions of our civilization made good, are not really so obscure or complicated as the economic imperialist would have us believe. Africa is a continent inhabited by a population which belongs almost entirely to non-adult races. It is true that for Europe to withdraw to-day from Africa and to leave these non-adult races to manage their own affairs is impossible. For generations Europe has exploited Africa for economic ends, at first by the slave trade, and later by commerce, agriculture, mining, and finance. No change for the better would be brought about by the European State withdrawing its control. Economic imperialism has itself created conditions in which that control must inevitably continue. We are thus faced with a curious position in Africa. Primitive peoples are suddenly confronted with a highly complex alien civilization in which social policy is mainly directed towards safeguarding its most cherished principles, the sacred rights of property and the even more sacred right (and duty) of selling in the dearest and buying in the cheapest market. In all the relations of organized political, economic, and social life the primitive peoples are unable to hold their own with the civilized. Only the sun, malaria, and sleeping sickness have saved and will continue to save the African from extermination at the hands of the white man. The white man is inferior to the native only in this inability to exist and propagate in the greater part of Africa. Thus millions of Africans must continue to co-exist with European civilization. But the ideals of Europe, the economic principles upon which our society is based, inevitably result in the political subjection and the economic exploitation of Africans by Europeans. The European State, if it remains in Africa, is necessarily an instrument of that exploitation; if it withdraws, it merely hands over the native to the more cruel exploitation of irresponsible white men.

Fieldhouse: The Myth of Economic Exploitation

The most commonly held and dangerous myth connected with the modern empires is that they were great machines deliberately constructed by Europe to exploit dependent peoples by extracting economic and fiscal profit from them. Its corollary is that the new states had a moral claim to be compensated for losses suffered in the past by being helped to become advanced industrial economics. None denied that it was desirable for wealthy industrial states to help those with primitive economies: but to base their claim to assistance on the premise that they were exploited in the past was wrong. The myth of imperial profit-making is false.

To start with, the modern empires were not artificially constructed economic machines. The second expansion of Europe was a complex historical process in which political, social and emotional forces in Europe and on the periphery were more influential than calculated imperialism. Individual colonies might serve an economic purpose; collectively no empire had any definable function,

From D. K. Fieldhouse, *The Colonial Empires: A Comparative Survey from the Eighteenth Century* (New York: Delacorte Press, 1966), pp. 380–87, 391–92.

economic or otherwise. Empires represented only a particular phase in the ever-changing relationship of Europe with the rest of the world: analogies with industrial systems or investment in real estate were simply misleading.

Yet, though the colonial empires were undoubtedly functionless in origin, this is not to say that they did not later provide an economic return, a 'profit,' to their owners. Certainly many colonial enthusiasts in Europe alleged that they could and did. Were they right?

To answer this question requires a careful analysis of its meaning. It is, in fact, highly theoretical. An industrial company exists to produce profits: colonies were human societies belonging to a different order of things. It is really as meaningless to ask whether a colony such as Nigeria was 'profitable' to Britain as to ask whether Wales or England was. In each case some form of 'advantage' was obvious. But this was not necessarily economic; and if it was it cannot necessarily be called 'profit' and need not result from 'exploitation.' In short, such concepts reflect a perverted form of thinking about colonies which derived from the 'mercantile' theories of the first empires. The fact that they were commonly held does not make them true. The task of the historian is to analyse the various forms of 'profit' Europe may have gained from her colonies; to compare these with countervailing disadvantages; and to decide whether on balance empire gave economic advantages which Europe would not otherwise have obtained.

The crux of the matter is to define what empire meant in economic terms. A colony differed from an independent state only in that it was governed by an alien power: colonial status was primarily a political phenomenon. This immediately limits the field of inquiry, for it excludes all those influences exerted by Europe which fell short of full political control: 'economic imperialism' and 'informal empire,' for example. If empire generated 'profit' this must be directly attributable to alien rule. The question can therefore be redefined: what economic advantages did Europe extract from her colonies which she could not have gained from other countries, however similar in other ways?

There were at least six obvious ways in which this might be done. The first was simply to loot an occupied country of its treasures. This was very rare in the modern empires. Few new colonies possessed hoarded wealth on the scale of Mexico, Peru or India in the past: there was little that could profitably be seized from African or Polynesian chiefs. Moreover, although 'pacifying' armies were often barbarous in their methods, they were normally under direct metropolitan control and conquest was quickly followed by civilized methods of government. The rape of Bengal in the 1760s was not repeated after 1815.

A more sophisticated way of extracting profit before 1815 was to transfer colonial revenues to the metropolitan treasury. This also became very rare. From 1831 to 1877 the Dutch transferred Indonesian surpluses through the 'Culture System'; the British East India Company and other chartered companies sometimes paid dividends out of colonial taxation; but no normal colonial government ever did so. Some demanded contributions to defence costs; the French confused things by integrating the accounts of some colonies with their own. But most colonies were left to use their own revenues and were more likely to receive subsidies than to be robbed of surpluses.

A third possible source of imperial advantage was to transfer money or goods from colony to metropolis as interest on loans, payment for services rendered, the pensions and savings of colonial officials and the profits made by business firms. Much has been made of this 'drain,' particularly by Indian historians; but the Indian case is misleading. The greater part—interest charges, profits of alien enterprises, etc.—would have been equally due from independent states which borrowed in the British capital market or in which British firms operated. The net 'drain' was therefore the cost of services, such as the Indian army, which Britain controlled and which India might not otherwise have chosen to pay for, and the transferred salaries of alien officials. The damage to India was not the absolute cost but the loss of currency and international exchange by a country short of both.

A fourth possible form of exploitation was the imposition of 'unfair' terms of trade on a colony. This had been the basic device of the 'mercantile' empires, and, in its pre-nineteenth-century form, may well have provided artificially high profit levels for metropolitan merchants and producers. But no modern empire operated a comparable system of monopoly. By the 1860s the old controls had been dismantled. Although tariff preferences, shipping subsidies, navigation acts and import quotas were soon disinterred, no country ever entirely closed colonial ports to foreign competition. Even the proportion of colonial trade which fell to the parent states was unimpressive. Britain's share of her empire's trade fell from an average of 49 per cent in the decade after 1854 to 36 per cent in 1929–33: thereafter, even revived protection only increased it slightly. France kept a larger share, always more than half, of the trade of her colonies; even so, the proportion declined with time. Most other empires had a similar experience: only the United States and Russia, which entirely enclosed their colonies within domestic tariff systems, really had a commercial monopoly; and this probably benefited the dependencies as much as the metropolis. Although modern protectionism harmed the interests of colonial subjects as much as it did metropolitan consumers, it was at least reasonably impartial and the losses of colonial consumers were compensated by guaranteed and preferential markets in Europe. It is therefore unlikely that 'neo-mercantilism' produced substantial net 'profits' for metropolitan countries.

By a curious paradox, however, it has been argued that during their era of free trade the British 'exploited' colonies by making it impossible for them to protect their own industries against her exports, so holding back their industrial progress. This did not apply to the settlement colonies, which were allowed their own protectionist policies from 1859, but may have been true of others. India was again the test case, since she was the only British dependency in the nineteenth century with the evident capacity to develop large-scale mechanized industry. There is no doubt that free trade had serious consequences for her. In the early nineteenth century free import of British cottons destroyed Indian hand-loom weaving on a commercial scale: thereafter the British ban on protective tariffs held back mechanized cotton production and kept the market open for Lancashire. Indian cottons were not protected until about 1926, and textile imports from Britain then dropped significantly. . . .

Yet it is impossible to be certain that these disadvantages were specifically the result of British imperial authority, for other and totally independent states were also forced, during the nineteenth century, to reduce or abolish import duties in the interests of British exports. China, for example, was restricted by treaty after 1842 to a maximum tariff of 5 per cent on all imports. An 'open door' might, in fact, have been imposed on any weak state by European powers: an independent India might have been as unable as China was to protect her own industries against foreign demands for freedom of access. Thus the 'open door' was a typical product of Europe's general preponderance. Formal empire was one way of imposing it, but by no means the only way; and the benefits resulting from free commercial access to non-European states cannot be regarded as an exclusively imperial 'profit.'

The most commonly alleged form of imperial profiteering was to 'exploit' the natural endowments of dependencies—oil, minerals, natural rubber, ivory, etc. If these were extracted without giving compensating advantages, an ex-colony might hypothetically find itself robbed of assets which might otherwise have financed the creation of a modern industrial economy. A simple model would be the use of petroleum deposits by a company wholly owned and run by citizens of an imperial state. If no colonial labour was employed, no taxes were levied for local use, and the oil was exhausted before independence, the new state might be said to have been looted.

Examples of 'exploitation' on this scale are, however, difficult to find. Extractive industries were never entirely insulated from their environment. All had to use local labour. They paid wages lower than they paid to Europeans but vastly higher than those normal in subsistence economies. All had to build modern communications and other amenities which benefited the colony as a whole. Some part of company profits were always spent locally, lubricating the colonial economy. Most overseas companies had to pay taxes to the colonial government. Thus no extractive industry failed to provide some advantages to the dependency in which it operated. The question is whether these were enough: whether an independent state could have gained more.

The question was pragmatic rather than moral. The value of natural endowments was for the most part created by demand elsewhere: in most cases only alien capital and skills could give them commercial value. What tax was due to the indigenous owners of the soil? The only useful yardstick was what happened in comparable independent countries; and evidence provided by states such as Persia and the Latin American republics suggests that this would have been small simply because their bargaining power also was small. Independence enabled ex-colonies to impose stricter terms on foreign companies, but these were matched by the higher demands also made by previously independent states after 1945. If neither was able to undertake such complex economic operations on its own account, its demands were limited by the fact that Europeans might cease to operate altogether. In short the same principle applied as had always operated in the deserts of the Middle East and the Sudan: caravans passing through could be mulcted only to a certain point, beyond which they would use alternative routes.

It is impossible, therefore, to measure the 'profit' Europe gained from 'exploiting' the natural resources of her dependencies because they were formal colonies. By mid-twentieth-century standards Europeans showed a cavalier disregard for the interests of other societies, taking what was profitable and putting back only what was necessary. Yet this had little to do with political empire and was not limited to it. One-sided use of natural resources reflected an imbalance of power between the west and the non-industrialized areas of the world; and while this lasted no non-European society had sufficient bargaining power to impose fully equitable terms.

The last and most sophisticated way in which empires have been alleged to give economic profit was through the higher return Europeans could obtain by investing capital in colonies than they could get at home. This theory dated back at least to Adam Smith and the classical economists, who were concerned mainly with the advantages of applying capital to fertile land in settlement colonies rather than to marginal land in Europe. In its most influential form, however, the theory was based on the Marxist principle of 'surplus value,' and turned on the greater profitability of using capital in tropical lands where labour was cheaper than in industrialized Europe. Lenin, for example, argued in 1916 that the growth of industrial monopoly and 'finance-capitalism' in western states created 'an enormous "superabundance of capital" '. This could not profitably be invested at home without raising wage levels, and therefore reducing profits, simply because the labour supply could not be expanded. The rest of the world lacked capital but had ample labour and raw materials. European capital could generate a higher surplus value there than at home, and this enabled metropolitan capital to go on accumulating. If it could not go abroad, capital would stagnate and capitalism would crack. Lenin predicted that in course of time the non-industrial world would be entirely absorbed by European 'imperialists' (finance-capitalists), and that this would lead to wars for imperial redivision which would destroy capitalist society and usher in the socialist revolution.

Shorn of its ideological trimmings, Lenin's theory simply asserted that the combination of cheap labour, political power to make it work at subsistence wages, and commercial monopoly to exclude foreign rivals, generated excess profits for European empires. The desire for these advantages led to tropical colonization. Was he right?

He was wrong on one point at least, for, as has already been seen, it is impossible to explain the expansion of European empires after 1815 in terms of economic need: there simply was no correlation between the time-scale of European 'finance-capitalism' and imperial expansion, nor between colonies and areas of greatest investment. Yet, once empires existed, the question must be faced: did they provide higher profits for European capital than could have been obtained in Europe or in independent foreign states?

This is the most difficult of all questions to answer. A straight comparison between dividend rates on European and colonial investments is impossible since European rates were necessarily raised by the very possibility of investment overseas. The only useful comparison is between rates actually obtained in Europe and those gained in colonies and in foreign states. . . .

Such figures are far too limited to prove anything; but they do suggest, in conjunction with other evidence, that the profitability of investment in primary-producing non-European economics, many of which were colonies, depended more on international economic factors than on the special advantages which Lenin thought colonies provided for their masters. By comparison the political status of non-industrialized countries was of little importance, and empire could not of itself generate super-profit for European capital.

It is, in fact, impossible to state whether or not colonies were more profitable for European investors than their own countries or foreign states: only generalizations are safe. Some colonial areas offered high profits because of their natural endowments, but they would have been equally advantageous as independent states. If Europe benefited economically from other parts of the world by 'exploiting' them, it was because of her immense military and economic preponderance. Empire in the formal sense was merely one form in which this was expressed, and had no colonial empires been created in the nineteenth century Europe would still have taken whatever economic assets she needed and dictated the terms on which she did so. By 1964 formal empire was practically over: yet still the advanced western economies were able to dictate to the 'developing' countries, and western capital was even more essential to their development. The balance of advantage may at all times have been unequal, but this was the result of more being added to those that already had the advantage.

Gann and Duignan: Exploitation or Development

African statistics are sparse and unreliable. Even modern sources on the subject are often of questionable accuracy. Official reports and yearbooks can easily produce an impression of accuracy which the facts do not warrant. Southern Rhodesia, closely administered and efficiently run from the early days of the occupation, stands out as one of the African territories best provided with statistical data, yet until compara-

From L. H. Gann and P. Duignan, *The Burden of Empire, An Appraisal of Western Colonialism South of the Sahara* (New York: Frederick A. Praeger, 1967), pp. 227–51.

tively recently even much of this material had to be taken with a grain of salt. . . .

Information concerning European trade or investment in Africa is equally hard to assemble. An economist could fill a whole book concerning just the obstacles. Statistics are often unreliable or incomplete; they are drawn from dozens of different countries and hundreds of different sources; types of classification may vary, and comparisons are often impossible. Yet these difficulties are nothing compared with those facing an investigator interested in African economic life. We know, for instance, that around 1910 some African peasant farmers in Southern Rhodesia began to invest money in plows and carts, in boreholes, and in new kinds of European breeding stock. African-grown cocoa became big business on the Gold Coast, and in 1927 cocoa accounted for nearly 83 percent of the colonies' exports. Nigerian peasants became major palm-kernel producers; Africans in Uganda cultivated cotton on a large scale.

Until very recently, however, statisticians have not accumulated much reliable information on local capital formation anywhere in Africa, especially for agriculture. . . . Africa experienced great difficulties in securing capital compared with other, more favorably placed parts of the world. Foreign capitalists, far from pouring their money into the newly founded colonies, were chary of placing funds in the Dark Continent. The rate of interest on overseas capital had been rising steadily for some years before the outbreak of World War I, and between 1914 and 1918 the supply of outside funds virtually ceased. After the war the rate of interest continued to remain high. . . .

The rate of interest varied considerably from territory to territory. From 1935 on self-governing Southern Rhodesia, with its cautious financial administration, managed to borrow money at only 3.85 percent, the lowest rate for any British territory in Africa. South Africa obtained loans on conditions not much worse than Southern Rhodesia's, but Nigeria had to pay more, while Kenya, at an interest rate of 5.06 percent in 1935, carried the highest rate of any British territory. Even so, money was hard to get. Africa was not the reputed El Dorado of the Stock Exchange, and many leaders could secure more favorable conditions elsewhere. Yet there was economic progress. Frankel calculated that the total foreign investments in Africa, up to the end of 1936, amounted to some £1,322 million. Between 1914 and 1936 probably more money flowed into Africa than during the whole period from 1870 to 1913. The 1920s and 1930s, in other words, were not a period of total economic neglect, but saw considerable development. The rate of investment, however, remained uneven; only certain countries benefited to any great extent, and most of the money loaned went into the mining industry. . . .

South and South Central Africa thus developed into major mineral exporters. Mining dominated the local economy, and minerals from the southern portion of the continent accounted for most of sub-Saharan Africa's foreign trade. In addition, other territories as well made advances. The proclamation of imperial rule over the Gold Coast encouraged an influx of European capital. Foreign entrepreneurs imagined that deep-level mining might also create a second Rand on the West Coast. British and South African investors, however, suffered many disappointments. The gold-bearing strata proved insufficiently rich, and the African people were too numerous and tenacious to give up long-established rights. Gold mining nevertheless made some advance; by 1935 about 41 percent of the country's exports consisted of minerals, mainly gold and diamonds. Gold mining, together with the need to secure a firm hold over the Ashanti, also caused the government to embark on railway building. The opening of the forest by railways and later by motor roads in turn gave great stimulus to the production of cocoa on the part of individual peasant owners. But from the standpoint of Africa's mining economy as a whole, the West Coast cities no longer played a major part. Commercially speaking, the axis of Africa had shifted to the southern portion of the continent.

Most of this mining enterprise rested on huge foreign-owned combines, able to mobilize vast amounts of capital and to pay for expensive machinery and equipment. The Northern Rhodesian companies thus carried out extensive geological research and conducted large-scale aerial surveys completely beyond the means of the old-fashioned prospectors who had pioneered the search for minerals. Big companies put up model townships; they provided health services, cleared the mining areas of malaria, and constructed mining hospitals and training establishments. Amalgamation into large units also brought major financial and political advantages. Production could be planned over longer periods of time. The companies acquired a stronger position for getting their share in the world market. Marketing became more economical. Overhead expenses diminished, and the companies as a whole could deal with the administration to greater advantage. Big concerns, moreover, could wait much longer for their money than the small entrepreneurs who had pioneered the gold industry of Southern Rhodesia and diamond production at Kimberley. . . .

Large-scale mining enterprise unlocked a tremendous amount of new wealth inaccessible by traditional methods of production in Africa. But almost from the start the big mining companies faced a barrage of criticism, sometimes from quite unexpected quarters. In Northern Rhodesia, for instance, the first attacks on the system came not from the Africans, but from the very settlers who had been drawn to the Copper Belt by the big mining concerns. Alien capitalists, the colonists claimed, were drawing superprofits from the territory and were stripping the protectorate of its natural wealth. The country's economic development was lopsided; secondary industries were being neglected. The bulk of the country's wealth went into the pockets of investors abroad; what little was left within the colony's borders benefited a small group of privileged people rather than the workers. White-settler leaders in Northern Rhodesia (and also in Kenya) therefore advocated all kinds of *étatiste* solutions —state-planned location of industries, marketing controls, and state enterprise to speed up economic growth. Soon black leaders put forward similar arguments; in many ways they shared the economic misconceptions of white mine workers, or even of European farmers, but they gave a specifically African slant to the settlers' reasoning and stressed that white miners and employees were both part of a privileged minority.

European socialists, arguing in a similar fashion, elaborated these strictures. The Communists especially saw the development of these mining territories as a deliberate conspiracy, designed to retard the colonies in question and keep their peoples enslaved to alien monopolies. They stressed the high rate of profit and implied that these profits were in some part due to the imperial connection. The colonial system, in their view, provided the metropolitan countries with terms of trade much more favorable than would have been enjoyed between countries of equal political status. The big mining men formed a specially privileged stratum even among their fellow capitalists; their superprofits played an essential part in shoring up Western capitalism as a whole. Mineral exploitation, the argument continued, was not in any way a progressive form of enterprise. Extractive industries took all of Africa's natural wealth and benefited none but the imperialist exploiters. Large-scale mining with its superprofits was a particularly objectionable form of enterprise which either failed to stimulate or, indeed, actively restricted development in all other sectors of the economy. . . .

The Communist argument has, in one form or another, become accepted in most of the emergent states of Africa. Foreign-owned mammoth mining enterprise is widely regarded as the most characteristic and also the most dangerous form of colonial or neocolonial exploitation. . . .

The gold- and copper-mining industries of southern Africa, with their high rate of investment and profits, are commonly cited as the most characteristic and also the most onerous form of colonial exploitation. All too often, however, this censure rests on certain unacknowledged assumptions which deserve further discussion in the context of African mining development.

The first of these preconceptions concerns the respective roles of primary and secondary industries. All Marxist and many non-Marxist economists believe that a country which makes a living by selling raw materials to foreigners necessarily stays poor. Prosperity supposedly cannot be gained without factories, especially steel mills and machine-tool manufactures. There is, however, no justification for this belief. The doctrine rests in the highly ethnocentric assumption that the chronological pattern of the British industrial revolution must prevail all over the world. . . . The question of priority also needs to be considered. Modern Zambia may well make money in manufactures, but this does not mean that Northern Rhodesia would have done better in the 1920s and 1930s, at an early stage in its development, by directing funds into factories. Thirty years ago the country lacked an economic infrastructure; manufacturing would have been expensive in social as well as economic terms and might merely have led to a dead end.

The next point concerns the general relationship between colonial capitalism and secondary industry. Marxist arguments notwithstanding, a capitalist economy does not necessarily preclude industrial development in colonial or ex-colonial territories. South Africa and Southern Rhodesia both started as mining and farming countries. In time they built up factories and steelworks with money made in primary industries, an economic policy which they shared with countries as diverse as Australia and the United States. . . .

The third argument concerns the method of development. Many critics, both white and black, assumed that imperial administrators should, as part of their trusteeship obligations, have accelerated progress in countries such as Northern Rhodesia by setting up state-owned or state-supported industries. The colonial government could, of course, have set up factories of that kind, but either such enterprises would have had to compete with foreign firms on a free market or else manufactured goods from abroad would have had to be excluded by high tariffs. The former course of action might well have led to the speedy collapse of such industries; the latter would in all probability have compelled local inhabitants to buy products of lower quality at higher prices than would have obtained in a free market. Neither course of action would have benefited Northern Rhodesia.

Looking at this controversy from the metropolitan point of view, it is difficult to see what type of commercial policy the imperial power should have adopted at home. Free trade, the anticolonial reasoning asserts, milks the dependent territories of their resources, but protective barriers raised by the mother country against imports deprive the colonies of markets. Both courses would therefore have incurred equal censure. The problem of foreign loans puts the colonial power into a similar quandary. Large-scale foreign investment supposedly robbed Africa of its economic wealth, but had the colonial governments kept out foreign funds, they would have incurred even harsher criticism. The imperial powers would rightly have been accused of running their dependencies in a "game-warden" spirit. . . . Such arguments, which damn the colonialists if they do and damn them if they don't, must be accepted for what they are—bastions to defend a position taken up in advance for political or ethical rather than economic reasons.

Many Marxist writers assert at present, and imperialist writers argued in the past, that Great Britain needed colonies to improve its terms of trade. Colonial domination supposedly enabled the imperialists to sell at high prices and to buy at low ones. An examination of the figures concerning the British terms of trade does not bear out this contention. The argument also ignores the fact that up to the early 1930s, that is to say during the heyday of British imperialism, the British Empire was built on free trade. Northern Rhodesian mining magnates, for instance, did not give any special preference to British purchasers. They sold where they got most for their copper. The Northern Rhodesian government, for its part, did not give special favors to lenders from the United Kingdom. Anybody who would invest was at liberty to do so. South African, American, and even some Continental investors bought Northern Rhodesian mining shares; hence the territory could borrow where money was available at the most favorable rates at the time.

The robbery-of-resources argument has a more obvious appeal. Large-scale mining, according to this case, stripped countries such as the Congo and Northern Rhodesia of irreplaceable wealth; the indigenous people lost their heritage; foreign mining enterprise should therefore be entered on the debit side of imperialism. The case cannot, however, be easily sustained. The foreign investors did not in fact take away from African tribesmen a form of wealth which they had previously enjoyed. Foreign capitalists did not, like the Soviets in Manchuria or Eastern Germany, dismantle machinery or strip the country of existing equipment. The mining companies created a new form of enterprise; they mined ores which communities such as the Lamba and Lala could not have exploited with the technological means available to tribal society. The Northern Rhodesian mining companies, moreover, showed considerable courage and capacity for long-range planning. . . . A government-directed economy would not, in the early 1920s, have gone ahead with large-scale development work even if the administration had possessed the men and the money to embark on such a program. In Marxist language, the Northern Rhodesian mining concerns therefore performed a progressive function.

Large-scale mining, moreover, was not confined to purely extractive processes, but also set off development in what might be called the "nonmetallic" sectors of the economy. Here a distinction must be made between simpler forms of enterprise, such as alluvial gold washing, and complex ventures, such as the deep-level excavation of copper, vanadium, or gold. The technology of alluvial gold production is comparatively simple and requires little capital. Many African communities in countries as widely separated as Ghana and the ancient kingdom of Zimbabwe knew the art of washing the yellow metal and worked this natural resource. . . . Large-scale mining, however, made for much greater changes. The mines created markets for more agricultural produce. The flow of investment was not confined just to sinking shafts and driving tunnels. Smelters and electrolytic plants went up in the bush. Mining gave rise to railway development, to road construction, and to the provision of port facilities. Money went into workshops, electric power plants, waterworks, and cement factories. The concentrations of population created a demand for permanent housing. The emergence of townships, large and small, required public utilities and public services. Development in turn attracted a multitude of people eager to meet the growing demand for building material, food, fuel, clothing, and all kinds of services. Banks and trading stores opened their doors. White and black farmers alike found new opportunities for selling their grain and cattle, and "the basis was thus laid for a multiplier-accelerator process of economic growth."

The African mining territories paid the price of development in the form of profits to overseas investors. These were high, and as John Strachey, a moderate British socialist, has put it, "It is impossible to become aware of them without understanding the sense of outrage which possesses a subject people as soon as it comes to know what is happening to it under imperialism." . . . He concludes that "a gross profit or surplus, call it what you will, or some £24 million, or two-thirds of the total, was transferred to the United Kingdom and America," implying that foreign investors pocketed two-thirds of the country's mining wealth. The realities are, however, not so dramatic. Strachey fails to mention the expenditures incurred by mining companies on imported raw materials, imported services, and depreciation. The investors' net gains were thus only a fraction of what he believes them to have been.

Strachey also expresses indignation over the figures devoted to African wages. He points out that only £2 million in money and rations went to Africans working on the mines, out of a gross value of output amounting to £36,742,000. The mineowners, however, also had a case. The mines, according to Miss Deane's figures, paid £3,600,000 into the public coffers. The government spent some of this on projects benefiting Africans on the Copper Belt, a contribution to African living standards ignored by the conventional Marxist argument. Wages for unskilled men were small because the supply of such labor was large and its competence was low. But African copper miners went to work because they wanted to; in Northern Rhodesia there was no compulsory labor of the type practiced under the fully collectivist system that then prevailed in the Soviet Union. The Central African mines, with their high level of technology and their paternalistic outlook, also eschewed the kind of underground labor on the part of women and children that was utilized during the early industrial revolution in Great Britain. The African proletariat in some ways, therefore, paid a lower price for incipient industrialization than did the British workers in the eighteenth century. African mine workers on the Copper Belt enjoyed a higher standard of living than they did in their native villages; they received better housing and food than at home, so much so that their average physical well-being consistently improved in employment.

African workmen also experienced some disadvantages. They kept one foot in the rural areas and retained their land rights in the African villages. Wages, however, were generally assessed in terms of the needs of single men, not in terms of family needs. African mine laborers, with their traditional obligations to an extended circle of relatives, had to carry a burden much heavier than that which a British workman would be expected to bear on behalf of his kinsfolk. In times of slump, African mine workers could always go back to their villages, which gave them some form of protection. Moreover, the African subsistence economy perforce acted as a buffer, shielding the money economy from fluctuations; this provided what in fact amounted to unemployment and old-age benefits, and, of course, saved the companies and the state large welfare costs. Cash wages remained stabilized over long periods, and the problem of raising real wages hinged on the provision of fringe benefits, such as better housing and ration scales. Nevertheless the new wage economy did allow for a certain amount of spread in wages.

Surprisingly enough, by the beginning of the present century a skilled black Rhodesian laborer may in certain cases have been better off than an unskilled English workman.

African living standards were thus by no means uniformly bad. Black wages and economic progress, on the other hand, were almost certainly retarded to some extent by the restrictive practices of white trade unionists. European labor unions throughout southern Africa successfully obstructed the entry of black people into various branches of highly skilled employment. Admittedly, these restrictions affected only a limited group of African workmen at the time; they did, however, significantly contribute to the development of apartheid. But this raises issues which, though extremely important, are different from those usually discussed under the heading of colonialism.

The problem of the artificially managed wage did not originate in the colonies and was not confined to them. Strachey's attack must thus rest on a more general basis. Like so many other critics of Western enterprise in Africa, he assumes in the manner of a medieval Schoolman that there is a "just price" for labor as for any other commodity. But he does not say what this price ought to be. Nor does he specify what he would consider a just return on capital invested, or to what extent financial risks and services should be properly remunerated, if at all. Again, there is no attempt to analyze the kind of situation which would have occurred if the mines had paid an uneconomic wage high enough to create a privileged group of African as well as European mine workers. In the absence of any such objective standards, the economist has nothing more to say, and the pamphleteer must take over.

For many decades mining dominated the cash economy of sub-Saharan Africa. From the first decade of the 1900s, however, agricultural exports began to rise sharply, and agriculture rapidly increased in relative importance. Much of this development centered on South Africa, by far the most advanced country and the most important pioneer on the African continent. Yet economic growth in many other parts of Africa also went forward at a rapid pace. There is, accordingly, no justification at all for the view, fashionable among critics of the colonial system in the 1920s and 1930s, which saw Africa as nothing but a stagnant pool, whose people, under the imperial aegis, either stood still or were retrogressing. Africa's agricultural progress was all the more surprising in view of the many natural obstacles faced by cultivators black and white alike. Many parts of Africa suffer from alternating cycles of drought, followed by heavy tropical downpours which leach the soils. Erosion forms an ever-present threat to inexpert farmers. The peoples of Africa faced all kinds of human, plant, and animal diseases peculiar to tropical areas. Development was desperately hampered until Western research found means of coping with afflictions such as malaria, sleeping sickness, and parasites attacking cattle. The lack of transportation facilities further impeded development. Most parts of Africa lacked good riverine communications; because of the great distances, inland producers in the past could rarely market their crops. The imperial impact vastly changed this situation. The period from 1880 to 1920 was the great age of railway building in Africa. By the end of the 1930s about 32,000 miles of railroad track were in operation, about two-thirds of which served South Africa, the Rhodesias, the Congo, and the Portuguese colonies. . . .

Agricultural development in twentieth-century Africa stood, so to speak, on three legs. There was cultivation by African peasants; there was farming by European settlers; there were some large-scale plantations run by big concessionary companies. Of all these, African enterprise was by far the most important, but it was also the form of enterprise that varied most extensively in methods, technical skill, and output. African peasants faced many obstacles. They had to contend not only with the difficulties of nature, but also with lack of physical and social capital. Throughout most of Africa their work continued to depend on hoes and axes and on the unaided power of the human muscle. In most parts of Africa tribesmen lacked incentives for intensive cultivation. Land was plentiful; whenever cultivators had exhausted the fertility of their gardens, they moved on, allowing nature to restore the fertility of the soil. As long as the supply of land seemed unlimited and storage facilities and markets few or nonexistent, African cultivators would only have wasted time and effort by producing more specialized crops. Where conditions became favorable, however, African farmers did make use of new opportunities and in some areas made astonishing progress.

One of the best-known success stories concerns the development of cocoa in the Gold Coast (now Ghana). The Gold Coast had an ancient tradition of overseas trade. The commerce in palm oil and other commodities had created a certain amount of capital. Longstanding links with the Western world and improved railway and port facilities created under British aegis put bush farmers in touch with metropolitan customers. Contacts with other countries also introduced new cultivable plants, including the cacao tree. *Theobroma cacao,* a native of Central and South America, was first carried to the islands of São Thomé and Fernando Po by the Portuguese. In 1879 Tete Kwashi, an enterprising Accra man, brought the plant to the mainland; government and mission agriculturists popularized the crop, and by 1891 the Gold Coast exported its first cocoa crop, amounting to just eighty pounds. The plant prospered in the hot and humid atmosphere of the West Coast, and its cultivation quickly caught on. African peasants soon understood the potential of the crop; they displayed precisely those gifts of foresight, calculation, and economic acumen that their detractors so often deny. . . . African growers therefore had to invest a good deal of capital in relation to their resources and had to wait a considerable time for their profits. This they managed to do, and within a few decades the output of the Gold Coast multiplied several thousand times. The colony's agricultural department provided valuable help, and by 1935–1936 output amounted to 285,351 tons, that is, nearly half the world's supply. Cocoa enabled the Gold Coast to pay for substantial imports of cement, machinery, flour, and so forth, commodities unknown to the country in the 1890s. Carriers and canoes gradually gave way to steam locomotives, trucks, and bicycles, and conditions of life underwent a major transformation.

The achievement of black cultivators in the Gold Coast was by no means unique. Around 1820, peanuts were introduced to Senegal from Central America. African peasants first grew the new plant as a food crop and later accumulated surpluses for export. The suppression of the slave trade, the decline in the exploitation of wild rubber, and improved communications gave a great stimulus to peanut cultivation. Marseilles soapmakers bought large quantities of peanut oil. African cultivators quickly responded to the new demand, and between 1841 and 1854 the export of Senegalese peanuts jumped from 1,000 to nearly 5 million kilos. The French administration tried to stimulate production further. Government agronomists developed superior seeds, which were distributed to farmers through Sociétés Indigènes de Prévoyance, government-controlled cooperative societies with compulsory membership. After 1932 these bodies were used to educate farmers in better methods of cultivation; they supplied modern equipment, stored produce, and in some places transported and sold crops in officially controlled markets. The world depression dealt French West Africa's exports such a severe blow that France for the first time came to the rescue of a colonial crop and, at least temporarily, sacrificed the interests of metropolitan consumers and oil millers to those of African producers. After the early 1930s the principle of guaranteed price and marketing for peanuts was generally respected, though pressure from opposing French interests sometimes succeeded in either limiting peanut imports to France or setting the guaranteed price at such a low level as to provoke bitter protests from Senegalese producers and exporters.

The effects of French policy are difficult to assess. French officials, like the British, were often convinced that private middlemen must be "parasites." They tried to control trade by various means, but official marketing control may well have hurt the peasants by reducing competition for their products and thereby reducing their incomes. French official pressure on Africans to cultivate "industrial crops" induced farmers to expand the area under cultivation and to exhaust the soil. In Senegal millet became a subsidiary crop, and its people were increasingly dependent on imported rice. Africans augmented their purchasing power, and thus were increasingly dependent on guaranteed prices and markets artificially sustained by the French government. Famines became exceptional occurrences in French West Africa, but its people continued to remain at the mercy of droughts, plant diseases, and locusts, while the rural population remained undernourished. The French, again like the British, almost certainly underestimated the black peasants' ability to adjust themselves to market fluctuations and to respond to economic motives; enforced cultivation constituted exploitation in the true sense of the word in that it did away with the producer's free choice. French West Africa nevertheless saw some real economic progress and became a substantial producer of tropical export crops. Senegal was one of the world's great production centers of peanuts and by 1937 exported more than half a million metric tons. . . .

African cash farming, like any other kind of economic development, brought many new problems in its wake. The Gold Coast, for instance, now depended largely on a single crop; traditional crops were neglected, and the country became a major importer of foreign food. As long as cocoa prices held, this did not matter; black cultivators enjoyed a higher income than they could have achieved with traditional crops. But when prices fell, cocoa farmers found themselves in grave difficulties. The cocoa growers' predicament was also made more difficult by technical deficiencies. Farmers generally turned a deaf ear—sometimes not without justification—to expert advice that plots should be weeded, manured, and kept free of insect pests. In many areas land became scarce, and what was worse, the early cocoa farms began to die out.

African society at the same time experienced a new kind of social differentiation. The old pattern of a small family farm, run entirely by the labor of the peasant's own kinsfolk, gradually disintegrated. The majority of growers came to rely on hired labor; some accumulated great wealth, but others fell into poverty. West Africa as a whole now had to face the problem of migrant labor, with the additional disadvantage that small proprietors could not afford welfare facilities remotely comparable to those provided by big European-owned mining companies. The growers also believed that foreign buyers combined to keep down cocoa prices. In 1937 most of the big European firms entered into an agreement to restrict competition and to prevent local prices from rising above the world market level. The African growers, to their good fortune, were not then tied down by any official distribution monopoly, and they retaliated by refusing to sell to the buyers' combine. Some European firms, moreover, remained aloof from the restriction scheme, and in the end the two parties to the dispute concluded a truce which once again allowed cocoa to be sold abroad. There were many other difficulties, but by and large African agricultural enterprise made considerable progress, especially on the West Coast; the black farmer became what he had never been before in the history of his continent—a factor of some importance in the world economy.

In relation to the enormous size of the African landmass, white agricultural enterprise remained restricted in extent, being confined to a few relatively limited areas. . . . European farming in sub-Saharan Africa generally remained confined to the lands south of the Zambezi, and even here progress was slow. More than two centuries elapsed after the initial Dutch settlement on the Cape before the white population of South Africa passed the 200,000 mark. Farming in South Africa attracted little foreign capital; although Europe's wealth increased, its investors preferred countries like the United States, Australia, and New Zealand, which did not offer the same climatic difficulties and which, except for the latter, did not have to worry about an extensive "native problem," with all the accompanying military and administrative complications. As with capital, so it was with labor. Unskilled white workmen could not find jobs in South Africa. The Cape used to import slaves, and the local whites developed a marked contempt for unskilled work, which became associated with tasks fit only for men of color. In the early nineteenth century the British abolished slavery and lightened the lot of the Hottentot, but the Bantu of the interior provided white South Africans with an additional source of cheap unskilled labor. The indigenous people of Australia and North America had been mainly hunters and food gatherers, whom white settlers could employ only to a limited extent as trackers, herdsmen, or suppliers of fur. The Bantu, on the other hand, were an Iron Age people, familiar with agriculture and pastoral farming of a simple kind; they could easily be trained to work on farms, especially at a time when the frontiersmen's own methods of production were fairly elementary. . . .

After about the middle of the nineteenth century, moreover, European farmers at the Cape strengthened their economic potential and found a modest kind of prosperity. Growing ports and expanding mining compounds furnished farmers with additional markets. Engineers put up roads, bridges, railways, and dockyards. The growth of shipping and banking helped to put the country in touch with new customers overseas. Some farmers began to work out more intensive methods, and various technological improvements made their appearance in the countryside. Landowners experimented with new products such as mohair and ostrich feathers, while South African Merino wool acquired a recognized place on the world markets. In the twentieth century, technological change acquired increasing momentum. Agricultural mechanization and progress in agricultural processing industries such as fruit canning, tobacco manufacture, and meat refrigeration vastly added to the country's wealth. Farmers developed better methods of plant selection, stockbreeding, and soil management. Veterinary surgeons learned how to cope with various kinds of animal diseases. Despite large remaining islands of backwardness, South Africa developed into the most skilled and most versatile of Africa's agricultural exporters.

From the end of the nineteenth century on, European farmers also penetrated beyond the confines of South Africa into what are now Rhodesia and the railway belt of Zambia. Throughout a large part of this tremendous region the European agriculturist usually followed in the miner's footsteps. The widely scattered mining townships and marketing centers required food; European farmers thus settled on the highveld, usually along the railway lines constructed to serve the miner's needs. As on every other frontier, grazing and tilling normally started as a scratch affair. There was the old story of vast distance and scanty markets. Both immigrant cultivators and stockmen could buy land and native cattle at low prices, yet at first they found great difficulties in making ends meet. Pioneering brought hardships; settlers frequently had to eke out their livelihoods by selling firewood, by transport riding, and by prospecting. In addition, they had to shoulder numerous experimental risks. A newcomer might spend a large amount of money to improve his herds, only to have his pedigreed beasts struck down by some little-known disease. The properties of the soil were often unfamiliar to strangers, and a farmer might lose all his capital by planting the wrong kind of crop. . . .

In terms of technical performance, European forms of agriculture achieved considerable success. European farmers produced vast quantities of flue-cured tobacco, a commodity which required more skill and capital than indigenous black cultivators possessed. They developed dairy farming and introduced various specialized crops unknown to traditional African farming. They put up dips and dams, tobacco barns, fences, and windbreaks, thereby improving the value and productivity of their land. European settlement even changed the very appearance of the landscape by bringing in new trees such as wattle and eucalyptus, with beneficent ecological effects on the countryside.

European farming also had profound social effects. In Southern Rhodesia something like half the available acreage gradually passed into European ownership. Black men found themselves confined to a much smaller area than in the pre-occupation days. In many parts of Rhodesia, European settlement brought about heavy pressure on the land; white landownership in many cases produced an intractable African tenant-farmer problem, as well as a system of absentee ownership popularly known as "kaffir farming." Worse still, the world slump led to government intervention. The smaller white maize farmers made up for their inadequate capital resources with their voting power; they secured featherbedding measures to shield themselves against competition both from the more efficient large-scale white producers in the country and from African peasants working at lower cost. Nevertheless, in other ways white occupation helped to stimulate African farming enterprise. In Southern Rhodesia the Europeans moved into a country nearly twice the size of Great Britain and inhabited at the beginning of the present century by considerably less than a million indigenous people. Southern Rhodesian Africans, unlike the Indians of North America, the Araucanians of Chile, or the Maori of New Zealand, in the end managed to retain something like 40 percent of the total acreage and kept a base sufficiently large to develop a more intensive kind of agriculture than that practiced before the white occupation. They learned new techniques of agriculture and benefited from government stock- and agricultural-improvement programs.

In many areas, such as the Northern Rhodesian railway belt, white farmers acquired their holdings in districts only thinly settled before the arrival of the white man. European-initiated development, in fact, sometimes attracted black newcomers from other parts of the country. The effects of white land occupation were often contradictory, and the debit and credit sides of the account are not always easy to draw up from the African cultivator's point of view. White conquest often displaced black people from their ancestral acres, yet pacification also allowed the weaker African communities to use their remaining lands more effectively. Tribesmen no longer had to construct their villages with an eye to tactical defense possibilities, hence black peasants could move out farther afield in search of tilling and grazing grounds without having to worry about raiding parties. There was an end to the interminable stock lifting and crop thefts engendered by tribal wars. The European impact for the first time created a market for indigenous as well as white farm products. Not only white townsmen, but also white dairymen, and tobacco farmers, bought African-raised beef and maize to feed their workmen. African farmers bought new implements such as plows and carts, and later on even motortrucks, from their white neighbors. The white farmers' lobby was on the whole sufficiently intelligent not to oppose government-directed improvement schemes in the reserves; the administration constructed dips and dams in the native areas; agricultural instructors gave advice on improved methods, with the result that the numbers of African-owned cattle and of acres under African cultivation vastly expanded under the new regime in Rhodesia.

Black and, to a lesser extent, white farmers carried the main burden of agricultural development in Africa. The third, and on the whole least important, instrument of progress was company enterprise. Big business preferred to put its resources into mines and railways and, in South Africa, into factories. There were, however, some notable exceptions. Unilever in the Congo and the Cameroons Development Corporation in West Africa promoted extensive agricultural enterprises. Liberia also owed much of its development to similar foreign initiative. In 1926 the Finance Corporation, a Firestone subsidiary, concluded an agreement with the Liberian government and advanced money to the small, financially unstable republic under very onerous conditions. The Liberians accepted Firestone's terms, partly because they wished for American diplomatic support against their colonial neighbors and partly because they anticipated a substantial infusion of American investments. To a certain extent, Monrovia got what it wanted. Long-standing boundary troubles with the French came to an end. The Liberians secured sufficient cash to satisfy some of their creditors and attained the unusual distinction of being one of the few nations to repay their war debts to the United States in full. Firestone received extensive land and tax concessions and in turn initiated the world's largest rubber undertaking. Furthermore, the company acquired a good reputation as an employer. It paid its workmen much more adequately than the government and other local entrepreneurs and also subsidized wages by bonuses for increased output and by selling low-priced food to its employees. Plantation laborers could work their own plots in spare-time hours; debt peonage was strictly avoided. The company put up hospitals, built roads, and established a public radio service and other undertakings. Firestone had sufficient perception to encourage independent rubber production in Liberia, proving thereby that company enterprise need not necessarily conflict with private initiative. The company provided free rubber seeds to independent growers, as well as high-yielding clones, or buds, and trained instructors to advise on methods. "The Firestone Plantations Company," wrote a standard handbook some twenty years after the start of these operations, "represents the one concrete evidence of economic progress in Liberia since 1926."

Company enterprise, on the other hand, led to a great deal of friction. The Firestone enterprise, in fact, produced all the tensions that come with the impact of a great capitalist concern on a weak and underdeveloped country. Liberians complained that leading positions in the enterprise were reserved to Americans. There was much resentment with regard to the company's exemption from corporation taxes and other public charges. The company disputed the Liberian figures and asserted that its contributions amounted to about one-third of the country's revenue. Firestone's profits came under attack; Liberians spoke of exploitation, even though the wages paid on Firestone estates were much higher than elsewhere in the country. A much more substantial criticism concerned the size of the concession. Firestone received a grant of 1 million acres, a very large area for a country no bigger than the state of Ohio. The company actually worked only a small portion of the available land, but its very presence may possibly have discouraged other foreign investors from putting money into the country. Liberians also accused Firestone of wielding undue political influence, though the country's ruling stratum displayed considerable skill in pitting the company, the American government, the League of Nations, and various foreign powers against each other. Firestone thus aroused a great deal of antagonism, some of it justified and some of it ill-founded, but all typical of the kind which a successful foreign corporation, whether a British firm like Unilever or an American concern like Firestone, so often arouses in an underdeveloped country dominated by an economically weak but self-conscious and sensitive ruling class.

In summary, the interwar period saw tremendous economic growth in Africa. There is, accordingly, no justification for the view of this period of African history as one of imperial neglect in contrast with Communist progress. True enough, development was uneven. Large areas of Africa were little affected by change; only South Africa, the oldest white-settled area on the continent, managed to build up substantial industries, while the continent as a whole remained a primary producer which devoted its resources to the export of minerals and crops. Africa did, however, see vast additions to its real resources in the shape of railway lines, roads, mines, plantations, hydroelectric plants, and other assets. These economic changes came about without large-scale liquidations and without forced labor of the Stalinist variety. Imperial rule indeed shielded sub-Saharan Africa from other foreign pressures and prevented internecine struggles; colonial Africa bore but a minor military burden; it operated with a relatively small and inexpensive state machinery, so that comparatively few resources were diverted into civil service and defense expenditure (the Gold Coast had fewer than 150 civil servants in the 1930s).

The new enterprise, by the very speed of its impact, created a host of social tensions. The clash of black peasant agriculture, white farming, and company ventures, for instance, might engender sharp competition for labor and natural resources.

Competition, on the other hand, might also imply cooperation. Firestone's activities to a certain degree assisted idigenous Liberian rubber producers; white Rhodesian tobacco farmers bought native-grown maize. The various new enterprises in some ways complemented one another. Critics of existing colonial practices often erred, therefore, when they advocated reforms in terms of a rigid either-or choice and contrasted black with white farming or primary with secondary industries as mutually exclusive categories.

Contact with the white man, whether as merchant, mineowner, farmer, or manufacturer, also brought about economic changes of a more intangible kind. Europeans taught African villagers the art of storing ideas. In the past, tradition had depended on memory and word of mouth; the old knew most and the young least. Now missionaries and others showed how words might be committed to paper and permanently preserved. Not only were labor migrants enabled to communicate with their fellow villagers back home by means of inky marks on paper, but also they were enabled to read books and newspapers. Of equal significance was the creation of a vernacular literature which began, as in Europe, with translations of the Scriptures and the compilation of hymnbooks in indigenous languages. Cashbooks and catechisms both demand literacy of their users, and these skills in turn helped to speed up economic transformation.

Crowder: Peasants, Workers, and Colonial Development in West Africa

1 THE NATURE OF COLONIAL DEVELOPMENT

In 1926 Alan McPhee wrote of what he described as *The Economic Revolution in British West Africa* in eulogistic terms: 'English capital has come in and built the railways and constructed the harbours and cleared the channels; it has also introduced new cultures and improved old ones; it has built roads and towns and established markets; it has introduced banks and a convenient currency; it has exploited minerals. More than this, English government has brought peace and security and abolished slavery. The result is an enormous expansion of trade, in which the natives performed their part and reaped their reward.' Cosnier, taking a harder look at the situation in French West Africa eight years earlier, wrote: 'We have left almost nothing for the producer in return for the considerable riches our commerce has gained. Almost nowhere are there any fixed riches.'

From Michael Crowder, *West Africa under Colonial Rule* (Evanston: Northwestern University Press, 1968), pp. 273–75, 345–53.

Looking back on the early years of colonial rule, indeed the whole period up to the Second World War, Cosnier's account is the more accurate of the two. Only the railways remain as a major legacy of the economic policies of the colonial powers of that period, and they were paid for by taxes imposed on the African himself. In both British and French West Africa economic policy on the part of the newly established governments subordinated African interests to those of the needs of the Metropolis. The railways, and later the tarmac roads, tell the tale most clearly: simple feeders linking areas that produced the crops and minerals Europe needed with the ports on the coast. There was little attempt to develop communications in such a way that the internal as distinct from the export economy of the colonies would be stimulated. So West Africa was subjected to an administrative system whose avowed purposes were to bring the material as well as the spiritual 'benefits' of Europe to the African, but saw these not in terms of the rational development of these colonies in their own interest, but in the interest of the mother country. Thus in the Gambia the peasant produced groundnuts to the exclusion of rice, so that that colony imported rice. The same was true of Senegal. In 1911, for instance, in the Fouta-Djallon, there was a shortage of rice created by the insistence of the Guinea colonial administration on the production of rubber, so that the money earned from the latter was lost in buying rice, normally domestically produced in sufficient quantities, at inflated prices.

Whereas before colonial occupation groundnuts and palm-oil had been produced by the African in a situation where he could balance the comparative advantage of concentration on subsistence crops against growing export crops to exchange for imported goods, the colonial system, primarily through taxation, forced him to concentrate on export crops to the detriment of his subsistence crops. Thus in the Gold Coast, where there was no taxation, but a shortage of labour for the cocoa plantations and gold mines, migrants from the heavily taxed regions of the Upper Volta filled the gap. Seasonal labourers from Sudan worked on the groundnut-producing lands of Senegal and Gambia in order to pay their taxes. Development took place only in those areas that were of interest to the Metropolitan economies, with the result that vast areas of West Africa remained untouched by the colonial régime until the beginning of economic planning in the 1940's, when the colonies were looked at not exclusively in terms of their usefulness to the mother country but as economic entities in themselves. Under colonial rule any economic benefits that may have accrued to the African resulted from accident not design, by-products of the primitive economic system the colonial powers instituted to carry from Africa its raw materials for processing in the factories of Europe, in exchange for a strictly limited range of European manufactures. The principal beneficiaries were the stockholders of the companies importing and processing the raw materials, and those that produced the goods exported to Africa in exchange: assorted cloths, tobacco, alcohol and rice, and of course the materials for the development of the transport system that could facilitate this economic régime.

European governments played a much more dominant role in the economics of their African colonies than they ever did at home. State ownership of the means of production which would have been rejected by an anti-socialist Britain or France if it concerned the Metropolis was never challenged as far as Africa was concerned. Commerce was unwilling to invest anything but short-term capital in West Africa. Thus government had to provide the bulk of capital for long-term investment like railways and ports. Government also made an impact as the agency for law and order in which commerce would thrive. Much too much, however, has been made of this aspect of government's role in the economy by writers of the colonial period such as McPhee. West Africa, as we have shown, was not in the state of disorder colonial apologists liked to suggest it was before the imposition of the colonial régime and was in fact, even in conditions of disorder, as in Yorubaland, supplying Europe with the products she needed without European control. Nevertheless the colonial régime did facilitate economic exchange between regions that had been previously hostile to each other, and by building railways, which it is unlikely they would have done if they did not have control of the countries through which they passed, they did increase opportunities for commercial intercourse dramatically.

The economic impact of the colonial governments in the period up to 1918 was felt most in the following fields: the development of a communications system; the introduction of a portable currency; and in a negative sense, the prevention of the alienation of the land from Africans to Europeans. They failed to take the initiative where it was needed in three important fields: first the regulation of the activities of the expatriate commercial companies and their Lebano-Syrian adjuncts so that these would not be detrimental to the peasant who, with the exception of gold from Ghana, tin from Northern Nigeria and the cocoa, coffee and bananas of the Ivory Coast and Guinea plantations, produced everything on which the economies of the West African colonies were based. Second, they devoted a minimal amount to research into and improvement of the agriculture of West Africa, even though this was the basis of these economies. Finally the 'mission civilisatrice' faded into the background and the educational and social services for the African that an enlightened man like Cosnier saw were essential to economic improvement played a very minor role in government activities. . . . The economic impact of colonial rule on African society was much less profound than colonial administrators liked to think. The period 1919–39 was one of 'immobilisme' in which what little change there was did not stand comparison with what was taking place in the outside world. The railway systems had for the most part been completed by 1918—only the introduction of the motor vehicle was a significant factor for change in this period. The African found himself the simple producer of raw materials for which Lebanese were the agents of sale and European companies the exporters. Conversely these same companies imported the goods which the African bought, mainly at the shops or through the agencies of Lebanese traders, with the money he earned from the sale of his crop. Only in rare cases did the African survive as an importer, almost never as an exporter, and in neither role was he significant after 1920. Except in the cocoa-producing areas of the Gold Coast and Nigeria, the African was squeezed out of his pre-colonial role of middleman between peasant producer and expatriate exporter by the Lebanese. This meant that the African's role in the colonial economy became almost exclusively that of petty trader and primary producer of cash crops, on his own account or as labourer on the farms of others, African or European, in the case of the few plantations that existed in French West Africa. A small number were employed in mining industries in Ashanti, Jos and Enugu, on the railways and as casual labourers in the urban centres. The income they derived from the colonial economy was for the most part so low that it brought about no significant change in their standard of living. Only cocoa and coffee fetched high enough prices to affect the traditional socio-economic structure of the peoples producing it. The other cash crops, most of which had, like palm products, groundnuts and cotton, been exported before the imposition of colonial rule fetched such low prices that the peasant produced just enough to pay taxes and satisfy his immediate needs for imported clothes, utensils and foodstuffs like sugar. The narrow range of goods in the Lebanese stores was not substantially different from those which the African middleman used as the basis of barter in pre-colonial times.

For the African peasant the growing of cash crops during the colonial period was, except in the cocoa- and coffee-producing areas, primarily geared to paying taxes and supplementing the subsistence economy with imported luxuries. If the price for cash crops was low, his marginal propensity to produce cash crops for sale over and above those necessary for the purposes of paying taxes fell also. For the peasant could provide most of his basic needs from internal sources. Even when the price for crops was high, immense effort was required in labour terms to produce larger quantities. This problem was solved, partially, by the importation of labour from other areas. This migratory labour was available, as we have seen, because of taxes imposed on peoples inhabiting areas on which no cash crops would grow. In certain areas the peasant would involve himself in commitments based on the previous year's price for a crop, and be forced to produce greater quantities of his cash crop in order to meet them if it fell. Where immigrant labour was scarce, he would have to transfer labour from the subsistence crops to the cash crops. In parts of Senegambia this situation, aggravated by the long-standing dependence on imported goods, reached the point where peasants were importing rice which they could grow themselves, and going without food for nearly two months a year, because they had neglected the subsistence economy in favour of the cash crops. Counteracting the propensity of the peasant to abandon cultivation of the cash crop in favour of subsistence crops, was his tendency to incur debts to the Lebanese traders, who were quite aware that indebtedness was one of the only ways over and above taxation which could force him to produce for a low price. The French, however, resorted to the introduction of compulsory production of crops in areas where the peasant would otherwise have refused to grow them because of the low price. Thus, anxious to be independent of cotton supplies from outside the French empire, the administration in French West Africa forced the peasant to produce it under threat of imprisonment if the quality was not good enough or the quantity insufficient. The ease with which people moved out of the cash economy into a purely subsistence economy also related to the dependence their society had built up on imported goods. In Senegal, where by the time of the Depression many families had been involved in the export of groundnuts to Europe for over seventy years, imported cloths, utensils and rice had become part of their way of life. But even they, despite predictions of famine and political upheaval, were able to revert to subsistence production in 1932. . . .

The extent of the involvement of the peasant in the cash crop economy was limited by the extent of the colonial transportation system. Vast areas, such as Bornu in Nigeria, remained largely untouched by it because no railway passed through them, and until after the Second World War long-distance road haulage of the low-priced cash crops did not pay. Even the term cash applied to these crops is inappropriate, for in many areas the exchange of 'cash' crop for imported goods was largely by barter. It was the migrant labourer rather than the peasant farmer who became the pioneer of currency as a means of exchange.

Just how little the bulk of the people were affected by the European-dominated import-export economy is brought out by Governor Clifford's report to the Nigerian Council in 1923: 'The vast majority of the indigenous population are still independent of the outside world for all their essential supplies. They can and do spin their own thread, weave their own garments, provide their own foodstuffs, and even, when the necessity arises, forge their own tools, and make their own pottery. For them imports from Europe are still, in the main, luxuries with which, if needs must, they can wholly dispense; and the sole exception to this, in pre-war days, was imported spirits of European manufacture.' And for these latter they had 'illicit' substitutes. Twenty years later, with regard to the whole of British West Africa, the Leverhulme Trust Commission reported that 'all Africans are, to a very large extent, and very many of them wholly, outside the system of money economy which dominates the economic life of Europe and the rest of the world.' The African, encouraged in times of good prices to produce cash crops, and ignorant of the fluidity of prices on the world commodity markets, was easily convinced that he was being robbed and deceived by the whites if they offered him a low price, and refused to continue production unless under pressure of taxation, indebtedness or force.

2 THE AFRICAN PEASANT AND NEW CROPS

The colonial régime did little to improve growing techniques of low-value export crops: they remained the same as in pre-colonial times. For most peasants the European agricultural officers were an irrelevance. There was of course no attempt to improve the methods of production of subsistence crops, as the Germans had done in Togo. Thus the peasant, whether farming for himself or working on the farms of others, did not gain any new knowledge of agricultural techniques under colonial rule. Even the labourer in European plantations used for the most part his traditional instruments, and stayed there as short a time as possible, learning nothing about improvement. Rather the peasant was allowed to exhaust the land. . . .

The colonial administration did nothing to prevent situations such as that in Gambia where rice that could have been grown by the peasant more cheaply was imported and to pay for it he devoted more of his energies in the cultivation of groundnuts. Indeed it favoured the colonial economic system, for French rice exporters in Indo-China could find a market in Senegal. Only when Indo-China became independent of France did France make efforts to develop Senegal's own rice potential. Similarly, Cardinall, commenting on the imports of foodstuffs in Gold Coast of 1930, noted that the country could have produced itself half 'the fresh fish, rice, maize and other meal, beans, salted and fresh meat, edible oils, spices and fresh vegetables (imported), or in other words would have saved 200,000 pounds.'

The only crops that did radically alter the standard of living of their producers were cocoa and coffee in the Gold Coast, Ivory Coast and Western Nigeria. For both these crops the price was consistently sufficiently high for the farmer safely to depend on imported goods in substitution for domestically produced goods. . . .

The cocoa industry in Ghana created a rich class of farmers who were able to undertake social innovations at their own initiative, and who showed that the African peasant, if prices were good, did not have to be forced into production. Sir Hugh Clifford was full of praise for him:

'This man, reputed to be lazy by the superficial globe-trotter or the exponent of the damned nigger school, has carved from the virgin forest an enormous clearing, which he has covered with flourishing cocoa farms. Armed with nothing better than an imported axe and machete, and a native-made hoe, he has cut down the forest giant, cleared the tropical undergrowth, and kept it cleared. With no means of animal transport, no railways and few roads, he has conveyed his produce to the sea, rolling it down in casks for miles and carrying it on his own sturdy cranium. Here is a result to make us pause in our estimate of the negro race.' . . .

Of the peasant-farmers in West Africa, only those producing cocoa and coffee were significantly involved in the money economy and experienced substantial social change as a result. . . .

Unfortunately, as Field has pointed out, the acquisition of wealth did not mean a necessary improvement in basic standards of living and nutrition, for far too much money was spent on luxuries, and at the same time concentration on cocoa farming led to neglect of subsistence farming. No other group was brought into the money economy in the way the cocoa and coffee farmers were. The migrant labourer depended on currency, but he earned very little, and most of it was taken in taxes and by his family on his return.

3 THE AFRICAN LABOURER

Those employed on the European plantations of the Ivory Coast or Guinea were little affected by their experience. Their terms of labour were seasonal for the most part, and they were not only underpaid, but not given, as we have seen in Ivory Coast, all that they earned in cash. No rural proletariat arose from among the workers on the European plantations. Before 1940 only the railways employed a large number of regular workers, among whom many were, or were trained as, skilled artisans. The only comparable industries to the railways as employers of labour were the mines. But much of the labour on the mines was irregular. In Jos, the tin mines employed for the most part daily paid unskilled and illiterate labour to dig at the faces of the open mines. In the gold mines of Ashanti the main problems were the shortage of labour and its irregularity. And most of those employed were immigrants who intended returning home eventually. In Enugu labourers were press-ganged by unscrupulous chiefs into work on the coal mines in the early years from 1915 till 1922. After that labour flowed freely into the mines so that by 1930 the management, which was a government agency, was able to be selective in the employment policy. The peoples of the area in which the mines were situated tended to be less educated than those from neighbouring divisions, and management deliberately pursued a policy of recruiting illiterate locals rather than their neighbours who were 'relatively more educated and could voice their grievances and were therefore regarded as trouble makers.'

The mines, then, employed a labour force which was either of temporary immigrant nature as in the case of the Gold Coast gold mines, or, where locally recruited as in the case of the Jos and Enugu mines, largely illiterate. Wages on all three mines were low for the ordinary labourer: in the coal mines in 1929 they were about 7d.–1S. 6d. per day; in 1930 in the gold mines they were 1S. a day for unskilled surface labourers and between 1S. 3d. and 1S. 9d. for unskilled underground labourers; on the tin mines in 1S. 6d. per day for unskilled labourers.

The wages for these labourers were too low to alter their standard of living significantly. Before 1940 none of the mine workers had organised themselves into effective trade unions, though wild-cat strikes had taken place before that time . . . . Indeed until the Second World War trade unions were of no real significance in either British or French West Africa. In the latter they were illegal until the advent of the Popular Front Government in 1937. In the former they were tolerated but not recognised until about the same time. Trade Union Ordinances were passed for Gambia in 1932, Sierra Leone in 1939, Nigeria in 1939 and Gold Coast in 1941. The attitude of the Sierra Leone Government to Trade Unions was not much different from that of the Southern Nigerian Government with respect to employment on the Enugu mines. In 1921 it refused to recognise a union on the grounds that 'a tribal ruler is elected for each tribe in Freetown by the members of the tribe themselves. These tribal rulers are recognised by law and form the intermediaries between the members of the tribe and the government, and it is not possible for the government to deal with or recognise any rival authority introduced by strangers to the colony.' Only some ten trade unions of any importance seem to have been formed and to have survived any length of time in West Africa before 1940. Significantly of these five were African Civil Servants unions, and two were railway workers unions. Civil servants and railway employees formed the only two major coherent groups of workers among whom there was an educated élite in any way capable of organising workers against government. . . .

In French West Africa the railways too were the main focus of strikes. In 1925 railway workers on the Dakar–St. Louis line went on strike, and in the same year Bambara conscripted for work on the Thiès-Kayes line provoked a general strike after three of their leaders were arrested as a result of discontent among them. The troops, many of whom were Bambara, refused to be involved in any action against the strikers and the administration had to release the Bambara leaders to bring an end to the strike.

From a social point of view, then, the impact of the colonial economy was much less than has usually been supposed. Perhaps the most important effect was the ousting and consequent frustration of the African businessman from a share in the profits from the expansion of the economy that took place under colonial rule.

Woddis: The Rape of Africa

The history of Africa's relations with the West has been a history of robbery—robbery of African manpower, its mineral and agricultural resources, and its land. Even though direct slavery no longer exists, labour, resources and land remain the three dynamic issues over which the struggle for the future of Africa is being fought out. The form of this struggle, it is true, is a political fight for national independence; but the abolition of foreign control of labour, resources and land is the substance for which this independence is being sought.

Despite important changes that have taken place in Africa in the last twenty years, the main characteristic of its economy remains its colonial character, its basis in cash crops and mineral extraction for the profit of foreign monopolies. . . .

Both during and since the great scramble for Africa by the Western imperialist powers at the end of the

From Jack Woddis, *Africa: The Roots of Revolt* (New York: The Citadel Press, 1962), pp. 1–2, 4–5, 7–13, 16–20, 31–34, 36–43, 46–47.

nineteenth century, land-grabbing has been a central aim. By direct seizure, conquest, pressure on chiefs, trickery, swindling, the repudiation of pledges and promises, by every means open to them, the representatives of the European powers took land. And, despite Hailey's allegation that "the period of alienation has for all practical purposes come to an end," the practice has steadily continued during these past twenty years—and even takes place today.

In the Union of South Africa, 89 per cent of the land was taken from Africans or reserved to Europeans. In Southern Rhodesia it was 49 per cent, and the same in Swaziland. Even though in other territories the percentage was less—9 per cent in the Belgian Congo, 7 per cent in Kenya, 5 per cent in Nyasaland, Ghana and South West Africa, and 3 per cent in Northern Rhodesia—it still meant that the acreage per head of the Europeans was far greater than per head of the Africans.

More important still, the land left to the Africans was the poorest, while that taken by the Europeans was the best. Speaking of Northern Rhodesia, Hinden has pointed out that despite the size of the country "land has become a very scarce and precious commodity for the Africans." Although the mere acreage figures might not bear out the above contention, says Hinden, she stresses that "crude statistics have little meaning," for the Africans are confined to the "poor soils," with poor irrigation facilities which compel them to crowd into the few areas which have water supplies. On top of this, there is "a wide distribution of the tsetse fly, which effectively rules out cattle-raising over five-eighths of the country, and infects human beings themselves with the deadly sleeping sickness. . . ." These enormous handicaps have proved, says Hinden, "nothing short of catastrophic" to successful agriculture.

And the same can be said of other African territories. The Africans have been not only robbed, and terribly robbed, of land, but their *best* land has been taken by Europeans, and they themselves have often been confined to the worst scrub-land, waterless, semi-desert, or malarial, and infested swamp-lands—land which, even with enormous reserves of capital and the utmost use of modern machinery and technique, would require a prodigious effort to make habitable and fertile. . . .

Completely understandable, therefore, is both the bitter hostility which Africans feel towards those who have robbed them of their land, as well as their desperate attempts to cling to whatever land they can. . . .

The [East African] Royal Commission was compelled to admit that:

> ". . . conceptions of 'Crown land' and of 'Public land' which relegate the customary right holders to the legal position of occupiers at the will of the state have often, and particularly in so far as the state's powers have been exercised for the purpose of disposing of land to non-Africans, or for what the African regards as purposes of non-African profit, *given the African a sense of insecurity in his land holding, notwithstanding the statements of policy and the complicated administrative machinery designed to reassure him.*"
>
> [Own italics—J. W.]

But why should the African be "reassured" by "statements of policy and the complicated administrative machinery"? On the contrary, his whole experience tells him that he has everything to fear from such reassurances. . . . Africans have remarked that each measure for their "protection" has always meant the further taking of their land. . . .

It is not intended here to go into any detail concerning the seizures of African land. Much has already been written on this score and even defenders of imperialism cannot deny what took place, even though they might try to justify it. It is, however, important to examine why this land-robbery occurred, why it is maintained and even extended, and what have been its consequences for the African people.

It is, of course, true that a basic reason for this act of robbery was a simple one of primitive accumulation—to take land because of the minerals it contained and the crops that could be grown on it. But this is only part of the answer, for an examination of European land utilisation in Southern Rhodesia, Northern Rhodesia and Kenya, for example, shows that *only a very small proportion of the land reserved for Europeans has, in fact, been used by them.* . . .

The reason for this, and for the wholesale taking of land in so much of Africa, was two-fold: to prevent the African peasant from becoming a competitor to the European farmer or plantation owner; and to impoverish the African peasantry to such an extent that the majority of adult males would be compelled to work for the Europeans, in the mines or on the farms. *Thus not only the enrichment of the Europeans but the deliberate impoverishment of the Africans became a cornerstone of official policy.*

The Europeans went to extraordinary lengths to prevent African competition in agriculture. The steps taken seem even more extraordinary when one bears in mind the official accounts of African "backwardness" and "inefficiency" as farmers. In fact, as many commentators have revealed, it is the European settlers who have been proved such inefficient farmers. Even with the best lands in their possession they have had to be constantly subsidised and aided by governments, and "protected" against African competition by the introduction of various restrictions or limitations on African agriculture, and by the introduction of various discriminatory measures in favour of the European farmer.

If railways were already built, the Europeans took good care to ensure that the lands they possessed included those portions adjoining the rail routes; and in the same way, new lines were built with European interests in mind. It was the same with access to main roads and markets. The European farmer was given all the advantages. . . .

Yet, despite the advantages provided for Europeans, Hinden was able to write of Northern Rhodesia in 1941: "European agriculture has, it is generally agreed, been a failure." And this although "all the legal provisions for its success were carefully secured by the Europeans for their prosperity."

The same applies to Southern Rhodesia. "No great examination is needed," says Brown, "to see that European agriculture in Southern Rhodesia must be among the most inefficient in the world."

A similar tale could be told of Kenya. S. and K. Aaronovitch have shown, in considerable detail, the failures of European farming in Kenya between the two world wars, despite considerable government assistance. Here, too, "the dominant thought of the settlers has been to avoid competition from the Africans."

Thus, as regards coffee-growing in Kenya, S. and K. Aaronovitch have explained how Africans were restricted in growing coffee, partly by the high cost of the license, partly by the limitation in acreage, and, after this was removed in 1939, by the restriction of African coffee-growing to certain areas, especially for the valuable arabica coffee. The fear of the Europeans, they point out, was that "increased production by Africans would not only threaten their markets, but would diminish the flow of labour from the Reserves."

This question of the flow of labour brings us right to the heart of a fundamental aspect of European land policies in Africa. *To put it in a nutshell, a major aim of European land policy in Africa is to ensure cheap labour for European mines and farms.*

When gold and diamonds were discovered in South Africa at the end of the nineteenth century, and railways began to open up the whole continent, European capital began to flow, in an ever-increasing stream, particularly into South Africa, and European settlement followed in its wake. Lenin has explained that the reason for the big export of capital to such areas as Africa is that "in these backward countries profits are usually high, for capital is scarce, the price of land is relatively low, wages are low, raw materials are cheap." Nowhere is this more true than in Africa, where the price of land was nominal. But to make these high profits, European companies and farmers needed the cheap African labour. . . .

But to secure African labour for European enterprises was to prove no easy task. A triple attack was launched, the three prongs consisting of land control, forced labour and taxation. . . .

These policies consisted in robbing the African peoples of their best land—and in some cases of most of their land—and preventing, by various measures of discrimination and restriction, the emergence of a flourishing African rural economy. The old subsistence agriculture was broken not only through land seizures and forced labour but by the introduction of the cash poll tax system which compelled Africans to obtain cash. Any attempt on the part of Africans to escape the net, to obtain the cash by turning from subsistence agriculture to the development of cash crops, and so avoiding wage labour for Europeans, was largely balked by the government policy of favouring European settlers and discriminating against and restricting Africans. Only in West Africa, where large-scale European settlement had not taken place, and in Uganda, were the African people able, to some extent, to escape this fate. . . .

The seizure of African land and the destruction of traditional African agriculture has been accompanied by a decline or even a large-scale elimination of village crafts and industries which find themselves unable to compete with imported foreign goods. In many parts of Africa imported textiles have resulted in "a complete disappearance of domestic weaving." Other crafts, it is said, "have suffered similar decline." In Nigeria, according to Forde and Scott, "traditional guilds of smiths have decayed, leaving their members impoverished and threatened with social degradation." Similarly, in French Africa "deterioration of African craftsmanship is very rapid . . . certain objects, such as household utensils, produced by African craftsmen have disappeared, calabashes being replaced by basins, wooden bowls by plates." Labouret states that the collapse of African handicrafts has been so sweeping in some areas that special vocational schools have had to be established in order to preserve these crafts. . . .

The seizure of African land, as has already been noted, did not occur solely at the time of the scramble for Africa at the end of the nineteenth century. Throughout the twentieth century, and continuing until the present day, the colonial governments in the various African territories have, by legal enactment or other drastic measures, carried forward their policy of slicing away the land from the African people. Even when land-hungry African peasants squat on land classified as "Crown land" but which has not yet been set aside for European settlement, they are brutally turned off. . . .

Throughout Africa one can witness the inevitable and tragic consequences of this European policy of land-robbery and the strangulation of African agriculture. In every African territory sixty years of imperialist exploitation have been sufficient to plunge the majority of African peasants into the most abysmal depths of poverty and misery.

The herding of Africans into the poorest land has meant a terrible land shortage which figures alone do not adequately convey. Overstocking and overpopulation have been the unavoidable result, coupled with the most intensive exploitation of the soil. The old, traditional African farming method of shifting cultivation, which allowed land to return to grass for considerable periods (a few years at a time) and so regain its fertility, is no longer possible. Instead, in a desperate attempt to provide sufficient food, the peasant is driven to keep his land continually under crop. This exhausts the land —and so the crop yield diminishes, and the crisis, for man and soil, deepens. . . .

And this is precisely what has happened in so much of Africa. The population has become "too dense for its area" largely because government policy has crowded it into insufficient reserves.

Brown has shown how this process has gone ahead in Southern Rhodesia. It is often argued, he says, that if Africans were given more land, they would only ruin it.

> "This is a fallacy," replies Brown. "The fact is indisputable that when, before the advent of the Europeans, Africans had abundant land, *the erosion they caused was negligible* and the *soil maintained its fertility and structure.*"
> [Own italics—J. W.]

It is, he asserts, *"the coming of the Europeans which has changed this and caused most of the soil erosion and soil exhaustion in the Reserves."* Among the reasons he gives for this deterioration are the limitation of land for Africans, and the agricultural policy pursued by the Native Agriculture Department. While many authorities tend to put the main blame for the spread of erosion and the exhaustion of the soil on to the shifting system of agriculture practised by Africans, Brown argues that, on the contrary, "from a conservation point of view, and particularly on sandveld soils, the system was almost perfect."

But the Native Agriculture Department has done its best to switch the Africans in the Reserves from shifting cultivation (which left the land fallow for several years so as to restore its fertility) over to continuous cultivation. From a conservation point of view, stresses Brown, "this system of continuous cultivation is basically wrong for the Native Areas." Such advice, he says, would never be given in the European farming areas, but in the Reserves the land development officers "can advise nothing else because of the shortage of land."

The contention that it is the agricultural methods of the Africans, and their refusal to accept "modern" Western methods, which are the prime cause of the decay of the African agrarian economy does not stand up to any serious examination. In fact, many recent studies have stressed the suitability of African methods for African conditions, *given an ample supply of land.* And these same studies have also warned of the indiscriminate use of Western methods which, though of value in European conditions, can do immense harm in the very different conditions of Africa. . . .

No one would want to claim that traditional African agriculture has said the last word on the matter. But much expert opinion is coming round to the view that what is required technically speaking—and this is quite apart from the question of land-ownership and distribution—is "a synthesis of modern technology and the empirical knowledge of the peasant." As Wilson has said, "The traditional African farmer has a profound understanding of his environment and it is essential that this should not be lost under the influence of Western education." . . .

Thus overcrowding and land shortage, combined often with incorrect advice from European officials, have resulted in the decline of soil fertility, erosion, and, for the African peasant, ruination. By 1946, Col. C. E. Ponsonby was telling the House of Commons: *"Already eighteen districts in Kenya itself are receiving famine relief."* Negley Farson noted: *"All but a minute proportion now spend some six months of every year in a state of semi-starvation."*. . .

For a number of years now Africans have been under pressure from colonial governments to abandon their traditional system of communal land tenure and to adopt instead individual title to land, either freehold or leasehold. In this way African land, like European land, would become a commodity to be bought or sold on the market, or rented out. The East Africa Royal Commission Report goes to considerable lengths to argue in favour of such a change, emphasising, in the customary fashion of official reports, that it would be in the interests of Africans to make this change. Coupled with this imperialist proposal to go over to the commercialisation of land is the renewed pressure to abandon subsistence farming in favour of the growing of certain cash crops under conditions, however, which will prevent real competition with Europeans, and at prices determined by European settlers or by European monopolies controlling the international market.

Although by the end of the nineteenth century classes were in process of formation in parts of Africa and forms of feudal land ownership were coming into being, over most of the continent the land was still held in common and was valued for its *use*. *Ownership* of the land in the commonly accepted sense of the term in Europe, carrying with it freehold rights and the power to sell land, did not exist.

"Land," says Batten, "was considered by most Africans in much the same way as Europeans think of sunshine and air—equally plentiful, equally necessary, and equally to be shared by all members of the community according to their needs. Land had no price and was not for sale."

Batten points out that although an individual, under this traditional form of tenure, "may have the *use* of a particular farm, his rights in it, and what he can do with it, are limited by other rights over the same land held by the members of his family, clan or tribe." There were, of course, many variations of custom within this generalisation.

The situation was sometimes modified, says Batten, by conquest or by the development of strong central governments ruling over large areas, as among the Chagga and the Baganda in East Africa, the Basuto in South Africa, and, in West Africa, in the emirates of Northern Nigeria, and the kingdoms of Dahomey, Ashanti and Benin. In these cases the central authority was strong enough to take over from smaller groups their traditional function of allocating land.

At the same time, in areas of dense population, where trade was developed and land less plentiful, other modifications were already taking place, even before the advent of European imperialism. Among the Kikuyu in Kenya, for instance, a man could pledge his land to his creditors—but he parted only with the *use* of it; and once his debt was paid, he could take his land back. Also, persons from other tribes were allowed to hold land after donating gifts to the clan authorities; yet even here, the gifts were not recognised as the payment of an actual price for the land, but merely as a thank-offering for being admitted into the community. "Membership of the community, not payment of price, was the condition of land-holding."

Over most of Africa customary forms of land tenure, varying in the details of their application, continue to this very day, although conquest by Western imperialism has introduced important modifications into them. A key factor in the development of traditional land tenure in Africa was the fact that there was a plentiful supply of land, and that production was for subsistence. Owing to usurpation by Europeans, land is no longer so plentiful for the African people; and the general consequence of European land policies has been the break-down of subsistence agriculture. Moreover, colonial governments have directly introduced new forms of tenure by law, as for example the institution of the *mailo* system under the Buganda Agreement, as well as the system of leasing Crown lands to Africans, as is done in Northern and Southern Rhodesia.

In Kano in Northern Nigeria, land was even being sold before the arrival of Europeans; and since then, with the introduction of money and the spread of cash crops, the tendency to sell or lease land has become more marked, though it is still on a limited scale. . . .

But will the commercialisation of African land, the introduction of rent and the buying and selling of land, bring to the African peasant any more security than he enjoys at present?

Batten rightly doubts whether the development of individual tenure "does in fact promote that security which is urged as one of its chief advantages." He points out that under customary tenure neither drought nor trade depression affect the landholder's security as a landholder. "He may go hungry, and he may have to reduce the quantity of the produce he gives to his chief, but he has no *money* rent to pay as a condition for remaining in possession." To those who might interpolate that a system of freehold tenure would give equal security, Batten points out that a system of landholding which enabled individuals to raise credit on land could lead to debt and the polarisation of classes on the land. . . .

The commercialisation of land, the creation of individual holdings, *under present-day conditions in Africa,* in which African economic development is held back by European control of land, natural resources and labour, and where the African producer, whether buying or selling, finds himself in a market dominated by powerful European monopolies, can provide no lasting solution to the lot of the African peasant. At best it can lead to the emergence of a stratified rural population, with a small comparatively rich section at the top, and a growing army of poor, landless or semi-landless proletarians at the bottom. . . .

Even in West Africa, where there already exists a pattern of individual farmers—small, middle and rich—the pressure for full commercialisation of land is being exerted.

> "West African land law frequently puts obstacles in the way of an African pledging as security his land and buildings. Such legislation, originally designed to protect the African from exploitation and to preserve local custom and tradition, has now outlived its usefulness; the safeguards have become shackles. . . . This question is one which merits the early attention of West African Governments, for the introduction of land registries and the replacement of the present multifarious, intricate and uncertain laws by something like a uniform system of land tenure would be a boon to the business community."

But what may turn out to be "a boon to the business community" and apparently of benefit, too, to the Bank of West Africa Limited, is not necessarily in the interests of the African peasant. As long as Western monopolies and European settlers monopolise the land of Africa and dominate its markets, the majority of peasants will continue to live in abject poverty, and no changes in land tenure systems will, of themselves, save the peasants from their plight.

In fact, proposals for encouraging the development of an African farming class too often turn out to be mere devices for robbing the bulk of Africans of their land. This, for instance, is what has happened in Southern Rhodesia.

"The Native Land Husbandry Act is ostensibly intended to produce a middle-class of small African farmers, holding land in freehold instead of communally. But so far, *its main result has been to force thousands of Africans off the land* —providing a useful float of labour for European enterprise."

[Own italics—J. W.]

Coupled with proposals for individual title to land is the concentration on cash crops. The cultivation of cash crops, on which government officials put so much stress as a means of strengthening the economy of the African territories, is pursued so relentlessly and with such a ruthless disregard for anything but the utmost and quickest possible profits, both for the European plantations as well as for the big European trading companies which buy up the crops from the African peasant-farmers, that the fundamental agrarian crisis is only aggravated. . . .

Monoculture, a typical symbol of colonialism, is nowhere more marked than in Africa. Whole territories are given up entirely to one or two crops—cocoa in Ghana, cotton in Uganda and Sudan, coffee in Kenya, palm oil in Nigeria, sisal in Tanganyika, and tobacco in Southern Rhodesia. No matter whether such production is conducted in the form of large European plantations as in Kenya or Tanganyika, or is based on individual African holdings as in Ghana or Uganda, the soil becomes overexploited and deterioration rapidly sets in.

Crop rotation, to maintain the fertility of the soil, was "often used by Africans before the coming of Europeans" says Batten, but "the effect of cash-cropping has been that in many areas traditional rotations have been abandoned for the continuous planting of one type of crop, and the effect on the soil has naturally been bad."

Another danger introduced by cash crops is plant disease, which Batten says is "greater now than it was in earlier times." Many of the present cash crops, such as cocoa, coffee, sugar, cotton, citrus, wheat, maize, were not indigenous to Africa. Grown under African conditions, without the necessary scientific preparation or fully taking into account the different climate, these crops have become more liable to disease. The import of diseased seeds and plants are another cause of the spread of plant disease in Africa itself. The cotton boll-worm, for example, is said to have been brought into Africa from America.

The growth of cash crops, whether by European plantations or African farmers, has resulted in the wholesale destruction of valuable forest land. Coming on top of the considerable cutting down of trees by European timber farms, by mining companies to clear land and make pit props, and to provide firewood for both domestic and industrial purposes, the result has been little short of disastrous. . . .

Moreover, with so much land, manpower and resources given over to cash crops, mainly for export, the production of food for domestic requirements becomes neglected and famine and undernourishment spreads.

Dependence on one, or a few, cash crops leaves these territories dangerously exposed to all the vicissitudes of price changes for their products on the international market, and makes for economic instability.

The slump of the 1930s, with its accompanying catastrophic drop in agricultural prices on the world market, produced a deep crisis for African farmers, even in the relatively more prosperous areas of western Africa where the growing of cash crops by African farmers was well developed. Indebtedness—the dreaded Asian symbol of peasant poverty—made its appearance. . . .

But even with favourable market prices, it is not the poor African farmer who benefits from the growth of cash crops. Batten gives the interesting illustration relevant for Uganda, of the history of a cotton shirt, passing through its various stages from raw cotton to a cotton shirt bought by Africans.

"First, there is the labour of planting, hoeing and picking, with seed and tools as the necessary equipment. To this must be added the labour of transport to a buying centre and, perhaps, some capital in the form of sacks or baskets, or possibly a bicycle. At the buying station a price is paid—*perhaps a penny in the case of enough cotton to make the shirt*. . . . Up to this stage only African labour and capital have been involved. The price is low, but little skill and hardly any capital have been used.

"The raw cotton is now ginned and baled. Here the labour is not great. It is made easy by the use of capital in the form of expensive machines and by some highly skilled labour which keeps them in good order. The reward for this service is again only a very small sum, but the great quantities of cotton the machines can quickly deal with enrich the owners of the capital and give the highly skilled men in their employ a much higher reward than the farmer enjoys. *Africans do not share much in the wealth produced at this stage:* most of the ginneries are owned by Asians or by Europeans: some Africans help to supply skilled or semi-skilled labour and are rewarded accordingly, but *the majority work as porters and at other jobs requiring little skill.*

"The cotton is now sold at a higher price to the spinners and the price is further raised to pay for the labour and capital involved in *transporting the cotton by road, rail and sea to some cotton-manufacturing country*. There the spinner and the weaver both apply further labour and capital, and the price steadily rises as the cotton takes on a more useful form. More labour and capital are employed by the wholesale and retail merchants who guide the manufactured cloth back to the African consumer. Only at the last stage, and not always then, does the African reenter the picture, if he owns capital in the form of a sewing machine, uses African labour, and takes his reward by selling imported cloth at a higher price in the form of shirts. *But most of the labour and capital applied to turning raw cotton into shirts is non-African, and hence most of the reward*—the difference in price between a few ounces of raw cotton and the manufactured shirt—*cannot add to the total wealth owned by Africans.*" [Own italics—J. W.]

While what Batten says here regarding the addition of more capital and more labour at each stage in the process is largely true, this is not the whole explanation. The reason why the African farmer is paid one penny for the raw cotton which he later purchases back, in the form of a shirt, for a number of shillings, is because the market at both ends—when he sells and when he buys—is dominated by the big European monopolies. It is big European companies which force the price of the raw materials produced by the African down to the barest minimum, just as it is big European companies which compel the farmer, now a purchaser, to pay through the nose for the goods he requires. This "scissors spread" between the low prices paid to Africans for agricultural raw materials and the high prices they have to pay for imported manufactured goods is a common phenomenon in all colonial countries. It is, in fact, the source of the super-profits which European capitalists make from colonial exploitation. Obviously the Western monopolies have no intention of "killing the goose that lays the golden eggs," and therefore all the official emphasis on cash crops is simply a further means of favouring the interests of the big companies which enrich themselves at Africa's expense.

In his competition with European farmers or plantation owners, the African farmer finds all the cards stacked against him. Batten is forced to admit that the European plantocracy in Africa "can bring to bear on colonial governments a weight of influence out of all proportion to their numbers, and that there is a possibility that this influence may be used to advance their own interests at the expense of those of Africans." The "possibility," at Batten calls it, is, in fact, usual practice.

In this way the European farmers and their families receive privileges in education, health, social services, and public utilities as compared with Africans. Further, they receive, in addition to such social benefits, economic advantages which favour them at the expense of African farmers—tax concessions, favoured prices, access to rail routes, financial credits. And, in addition, the colonial governments favour the Europeans in the matter of the workers who are employed on their plantations: plantations are the last form of enterprise in the African colonies in which Africans are allowed to form trade unions (and, even then, they function with still greater difficulty and harassment than most); and wage minima for farms and plantations are generally much below other wage minima, and in many cases do not exist at all.

In short, European farms and plantations in Africa are given every possibility by the colonial system to flourish at the expense of both African workers and peasants. Significantly Batten remarks:

> "Some people may doubt whether plantations could be successful in tropical Africa if they had to withstand free competition from peasant farmers while contributing their full share of taxation to the central government."

But as long as the European plantocracy retains the political power in its hands, and remains, with the mineowner, the virtual ruler of so much of the African continent, the African peasant will never be given the opportunity to engage in "free competition" with his European rival.

While in East and Central Africa, the home of the big European capitalist farm and plantation, the official talk is all of "aiding the individual African farmer," in West Africa, the traditional home of the "sturdy peasant," the striking new development is the growth of plantations, mainly European-owned.

There is no contradiction here. In East and Central Africa, the white settlers, who largely dominate the political and economic life of the territories, and who occupy a commanding position in agriculture, are seeking, very late in the day, to establish a small stratum of individual farmers who, they hope, will become their political allies and supporters in the face of the growing mass discontent of the mass of impoverished peasantry. Hence the gestures towards aiding African farmers, gestures which, as we have already seen, are largely illusory.

In West Africa, on the other hand, where the territories are rapidly winning their political independence, the traditional method of imperialist exploitation has been through the large European trading companies to whom, via countless middlemen, the African producers have had to sell their crops. Political independence will increase the power of these African capitalist farmers, who will certainly demand higher prices for their products. To offset this, and partly also to act as a means of pressure, the European monopolies are now passing over to plantation development in this part of Africa.

Thus in Ghana, acting on the advice of *European* advisers, the government is apparently going to develop the large-scale production of rubber. "The main hope of the government," states a correspondent in *West Africa,* "is clearly placed on attracting foreign capital to establish and manage rubber plantations: approaches have already been made to the U.S. Government."

Similarly in Nigeria, plantation development has made considerable progress in the past few years. Since 1952 nearly forty new estates covering 125,000 acres have been developed, and it is estimated that by 1962 the 1952 plantation acreage in Nigeria (excluding the Cameroons, where there have been for some time considerable plantations) will have increased some six hundred per cent! Oil palms and rubber are the two commodities being most affected, the great Dunlop plantation of 20,000 acres in Eastern Nigeria being described by *West Africa* as "one of the most exciting economic developments Nigeria has seen." There is no doubt that the Dunlop company is more excited by the prospects than the people of Nigeria. It has been estimated that in Africa to put a man to work in a plantation costs about £500, whereas to put a man to work in a modern factory needs an investment of £2,000. It is understandable, therefore, that for some Western companies the plantation is the more attractive proposition for investment.

It is in the face of such giant plantation firms, favoured in every way, as we have seen, by colonial legislation and practice, that the African farmer strives to develop. The main beneficiary of the cash-crop concentration is the big European monopoly, both in the form of planter and as trader, along with the auxiliary transport, shipping, docks, banking, insurance, and so on. . . .

In bringing about the destruction of the old order in Africa the imperialists have, just as in India, done nothing to "emancipate or materially mend the social condition of the mass of the people." On the contrary, they have plunged the African peasant down to the utmost depths of poverty and disaster, producing as a result that peculiarly African phenomenon, the *continually migrating peasant-worker,* confronted with the "loss of his old world," yet "with no gain of a new one." It was not without reason that a report on the effects of migrant labour in Nyasaland, in 1953, correctly forecast that: "the Nyasaland-born natives will have acquired a mistrust and loathing for administration by the white people which has made a wilderness and called it peace."

But a "wilderness called peace" exists not only in Nyasaland. Similar wildernesses are to be found throughout the African continent. Sixty years of imperialist exploitation have been sufficient to wreak this terrible damage. Real peace, and the transformation of these wildernesses into the flourishing fields and farms which a free people, aided by modern technique and State aid, could create, demands, as a first step, the elimination of colonial rule and the return of the land to the African people.

problem VII

The Elites, the Masses, and African Nationalism

The Problem of the African elite, the African masses, and African nationalism is the final, the most comprehensive, and the most contemporary historical problem presented in this collection. On the one hand, the decolonization of Africa is not yet complete, and this Problem merges history with the present. In the Portuguese colonies, for instance, this question is not simply academic. On the other hand, however, student and teacher alike must look back over the colonial period to consider the nature of African resistance, European settlement, and the administrative theories and practices of the imperial powers in order to perceive the beginnings and transformations of African nationalism.

The problem of African nationalism is essentially twofold. First, one must assess the relationship between the influence of European ideas and the influence of African realities. Second, one must examine the relationship between the Western-educated elite and traditional society in forming and conditioning the nationalist movement to determine whether the elite manipulated, compromised, or cooperated with the masses. Traditionally, African nationalism has been regarded as a phenomenon which emerged after World War II and was sharply distinguished from the proto-nationalist movements of the early colonial period. Thus, scholars have focused their research on the development of towns, voluntary associations, education, and a Westernized elite. Recently, however, other Africanists have suggested that the contribution of the traditional authorities and the peasant masses to African nationalism was neither reactionary nor futile but positive and necessary. This change in perspective, a shift which is characteristic of the preceding Problems in this volume, has been accelerated by historical research carried out after the independence of African territories and continues to this day as an essential part of the evolving historiography of Africa.

James Coleman has argued that such concepts of the nation-state and nationalism are Western ideas which are fundamentally alien to Africa. Thus, primary resistance, messianic movements, separatist churches, and tribal associations, although related to nationalism, were basically "reflections of the persistent desire of the masses to preserve or recreate the old by protesting against the new." Rather than being committed to a "positive and radical alteration of the power structure," these traditional forms of protest were essentially "negative." Moreover, if the Western-educated elite committed themselves to mass discontent, they would compromise their basic goals of "modernization," "political unity," and "stability." Since the divisive traditions of clan and tribe tended to undermine the unifying purpose of the nationalist movement, the traditionalists, Coleman has argued, were essentially antagonistic to African nationalism.

Therefore, European colonialism emerged as an "indispensable precondition" to African nationalism. The strength and vitality of the nationalist movements depended not so much upon any African element but upon the influence of the European economic system, urbanization, and education. Variations in the nationalist movements were caused not by the presence or absence of primary resistance or nativistic responses, but rather by the degree of acculturation of the elite, the intensity of European influence, and the accommodation of the colonial system. Since the British created an acculturated elite that, unlike the elite in Francophonic Africa, was denied an opportunity to participate in ruling the colony, these same colonies experienced the most pervasive and successful nationalism.

Georges Balandier cannot accept the exclusion of such neotraditional movements as messianic cults from modern African nationalism. Although they were ostensibly religious, the messianic movements displayed political overtones which were the "unequivocal" if "unsophisticated" progenitors of African nationalism. They were, as Coleman has pointed out, primarily protests against all aspects of European domination, but they were not simply negative retorts to colonial rule. They were rather an attempt to create leaders with "real authority" just as the later nationalist movements spawned leaders who cut across clan, age-set, or tribe. Furthermore, the messianic movements were the first real attempts to build institutions which could not only recapture the loyalty of the African masses, but could unify the people and express their discontent. In this way, Balandier has argued, religion became a "smokescreen for politics" at the time when there was no means of political dissent. The messianic movements and nativistic churches, therefore, like the later nationalist movements, were "xenophobic" and "racist" reactions to colonial rule which sought to unify the people, provide new leaders, and build new institutions to replace the pervasive influences of European colonial rule.

T. O. Ranger broadens Balandier's thesis to include the movements of primary resistance during the late nineteenth and early twentieth centuries. He has argued that African nationalism was tied to the past because its leaders could not ignore either the local political environment or the necessity of including "mass emotion." Ranger has sought to demonstrate, moreover, that there was an "important connection between resistance and later political developments." By helping to shape the pattern of colonial rule, resistance obviously helped shape the environment out of which emerged modern African nationalism. There is even a more direct correlation between primary resistance and the secondary resistance of messianic cults, nativistic movements, or elite associations which are commonly regarded as the beginnings of African nationalism. Since primary resistance and secondary opposition to colonial rule were often contemporaneous, the leadership of the two movements were frequently in communication if not the same individuals. This was the first point of contact. The second was the types of "organizations and inspirations" originating in primary resistance which "directly" or "indirectly" provided a viable link to future opposition or national movements. The prophetic, charismatic leadership, for example, which inspired many primary resistance movements, was later employed by modern nationalists to solve problems of "morale," and "trans-tribal coordination." Their efforts to unite by appealing to past unity were similar in aims, and even methods, to the earlier proto-nationalists and the contemporary nationalist movements.

Unlike James Coleman, T. O. Ranger has argued that there were direct human and indirect symbolic links between modern nationalism and the African past. Nationalist leaders, whether educated elites or traditional authorities, had to be cognizant of the memories of resistance and the methods of the prophets if they were to build a mass movement. Thus, the African past conditioned the development of the nationalist movement as much as the ideas and techniques which the African elite had borrowed from Europe. To ignore or even deny the role of the traditions of resistance was to distort the character of the nationalist movement.

Closely related to the part which the African past has played in shaping the nationalist movement is the problem of assessing the role the elite and the masses played in leading and conditioning the nationalist movement. James Coleman in his pioneer work on Nigeria has argued that the beginnings of nationalism evolved from the relationship between the European rulers and the educated elite. This elite was excluded from British society and politically ignored. They were frequently treated with contempt as inferior imitations of Englishmen. Thus, even when the Nigerian achieved Western education and wealth, he was not accepted by British officials as a social or political equal. Not unnaturally the elites "resented" this attitude of superiority and the dramatic differences in the standard of living of expatriate officials and Nigerians of equal education and ability. The practice of the British colonial administration to exclude Nigerians from senior positions in the civil service was hardly calculated to assuage this resentment. Before World War I and during the interwar years this social and political ostracism was largely accepted by the elite. In the late 1930's and particularly after World War II, however, they were no longer content to be excluded from determining the future of Nigeria. They found themselves increasingly checked by the British and opposed by the leaders of the native administrations. Frustrated at every turn, the elite became "convinced" that to acquire an appropriate influence in governing Nigeria they must "wrest control of the superstructure [of government] from the British." In origin and objectives the nationalist movement, therefore, developed out of the special grievances of the Westernized elements in Nigerian society.

Martin Kilson in his examination of political change in Sierra Leone has not found the evolution of nationalism so divorced from traditional authorities and institutions. In Sierra Leone nationalism emerged more from the interplay of modern and traditional elements than as the sole creation of the elite. To acquire mass support the elite manipulated and "exploited" traditional institutions and customs throuth ties with the indigenous leaders. The "ritualistic flattery," "charismatic" leadership, and the financial links between the elite and traditional authorities all served to demonstrate the traditional character of nationalism in Sierra Leone.

J. M. Lonsdale, in his research on nationalistic movements in East Africa, has argued that the roots of nationalism lie neither in the rich loam of grievances by a frustrated elite nor in the sandy soil where the elite of Sierra Leone adopted and exploited traditional forms, but in the red clays of East Africa where flourished the discontent of the rural masses. Thus, nationalism in East Africa could only become a coherent movement when the elite united with the peasants to challenge the colonial rulers at the center of power. Emphasizing the role of the peasants in the national movement, Lonsdale has argued that the disintegration of rural society was accompanied by a shift in loyalty from the lineage, to the tribe, and finally to the nation. The problem was thus one of developing local and then national leadership which could both unite the people and communicate their grievances to the government. There were three stages in this process. Before 1925 the traditional leaders dominated politics. The focus of politics was thus diffuse. Gradually, as the colonial impact weakened the power of the traditional authorities, new leaders began to assert themselves. The focus of politics consequently shifted from the lineage to the tribe. This second and transitional phase ended in the late 1930's when British intervention increased the pressures on African societies. Educated men began to eclipse the influence of the chiefs at the local level, but these new leaders and the peasants realized that local control could not resolve peasant discontent. Thus, as the demands for change increased after World War II, the focus of politics shifted once more to the center of power. The process was not, as Coleman has suggested, one in which the elite mobilized and manipulated the masses, but rather one in which the masses "threw up" their leaders and demanded a role in the central government in order to resolve their grievances.

Coleman: What Is African Nationalism?

I. WHAT IS AFRICAN NATIONALISM?

Not the least burdensome of our tasks is the problem of correlating or distinguishing between the generally accepted political concepts elaborated with specific reference to developments in the Western World (i.e., state, nation, nationality, nationalism) and the conceptual tools developed by the Africanists. The latter have tended to feel that the traditional concepts and methods of the political scientist are unserviceable in the study of the political structure and life of pre-literate societies. Yet notwithstanding the importance of the lineage, clan, or tribe; the role of the diviner, the chief, or the age-grade society; or the wide variations in the organization of power within such societies, the concept and the institution of the modern nation-state, towards the creation of which African nationalism tends to be directed, is distinctly Western in its form and content. It is as exotic to Africa as Professor Toynbee has suggested that it is to the rest of the non-European world. Nevertheless, just as the Indian National Congress has largely created an Indian nation, so African nationalists are endeavoring to mould new nations in Africa (e.g., "Ghana," "Nigeria," and "Kamerun").

Not only is a political scientist quite precise in his use of the concept "nation," but in poaching on the insights of the Africanists he also finds it difficult to place under the cover of "nationalism" all forms of past and present discontent and organizational development in Africa. Thus, it is believed useful at the outset to distinguish the following:

A. TRADITIONALIST MOVEMENTS

1. Spontaneous movements of resistance to the initial European occupation or post-pacification revolts against the imposition of new institutions, or new forms of coercion,

From James S. Coleman, "Nationalism in Tropical Africa," in *American Political Science Review,* XLVIII, No. 2 (1954), 404–14.

referred to herein as "primary resistance."

2. Nativistic, mahdistic, or messianic mass movements—usually of a magico-religious character—which are psychological or emotional outlets for tensions produced by the confusions, frustrations, or socioeconomic inequalities of alien rule, referred to herein as "nativism."

B. SYNCRETISTIC MOVEMENTS

1. Separatist religious groups, which have seceded and declared their independence from white European churches either because of the desire for religious independence or because the white clerics were intolerant regarding certain African customs; hereafter referred to as "religious separatism."

2. Kinship associations, organized and led by the Western-educated and urbanized "sons abroad" for the purposes of preserving a sense of identity with the kinfolk in the bush and "brothers" in the impersonal urban center, as well as of providing vehicles for pumping modernity—including the ideas and sentiment of nationalism—into the rural areas.

3. Tribal associations, organized and led by Western-educated elements—usually in collaboration with some traditionalists—who desire to resurrect, or to create for the first time, a tribal sentiment ("tribalism"), for the purpose of establishing large-scale political units, the boundaries of which will be determined by tribal affiliation (i.e., those who accept the *assumption* of common blood and kinship) and the forms of government by a syncretism of tribal and Western institutions.

C. MODERNIST MOVEMENTS

1. Economic-interest groups (labor unions, cooperative societies, professional and middle-class associations) organized and led by Western-educated elements for the purpose of advancing the material welfare and improving the socioeconomic status of the members of those groups.

2. Nationalist movements, organized and led by the Westernized elite which is activated by the Western ideas of democracy, progress, the welfare state, and national self-determination, and which aspires *either* (a) to create modern independent African nation-states possessing an internal state apparatus and external sovereignty and all of the trappings of a recognized member state of international society (e.g., Sudan, Gold Coast, Nigeria, and possibly Sierra Leone); *or* (b) to achieve absolute social and political equality and local autonomy within a broader Eur-African grouping (e.g., French and Portuguese Africa) or within what is manifestly a plural society (e.g., except for Uganda, the territories of British East and Central Africa).

3. Pan-African or trans-territorial movements, organized and led by the Westernized elite, frequently in association with or under the stimulus of American Negroes or West Indians abroad, for the purposes of creating a global *racial* consciousness and unity, or of agitating for the advancement and welfare of members of the *African* race wherever they may be, or of devising plans for future nationalist activity in specific regions.

Once these very arbitrary analytical distinctions are drawn it should be stressed that none of the categories can be treated in isolation. Each of the movements is in one way or another a response to the challenge of alien rule, or of the intrusion of the disintegrating forces—and consequently the insecurity—of modernity. The recent so-called nationalism in Central Africa has been a mixture of "primary resistance" by the chiefs and traditionalists of Northern Rhodesia and Nyasaland and the nationalist agitation of the Westernized elite. Until the project of Federation became an active issue, African movements in this area were confined principally to religious separatist groups, tribal associations, or, in the case of Northern Rhodesia, labor unions. On the West Coast, where nationalism is far more advanced, traditionalist and syncretistic movements have not been and are not absent. In some instances, kinship associations and separatist religious groups have been the antecedents of nationalist organizations; in others they have provided the principal organizational bases of the latter (e.g., the National Council of Nigeria and the Cameroons was first inaugurated as a federation mainly of kinship associations, and the African National Congress of the Rhodesias and Nyasaland was the product of fusion of several African welfare societies). In certain cases unrest or protest of a nativistic flavor has been instigated by nationalists for their modernist ends; in others nationalists have claimed such uncoordinated uprisings, as well as purely economic protest movements, to be manifestations of "nationalism," when in reality the participants were unaware of such implications.

One of the interesting differences between prewar and postwar nationalism on the West Coast of Africa is that in the former period nationalism tended to be—as Lord Lugard insisted—the esoteric pastime of the tiny educated minorities of Lagos, Accra, Freetown, and Dakar; whereas in the latter period these minorities—greatly expanded and dispersed in new urban centers throughout the interior—have made positive efforts to popularize and energize the nationalist crusade in two ways. The first has been to preach education, welfare, progress, and the ideal of self-government among the masses, largely through the nationalist press, independent African schools, and kinship and tribal associations. The aim here has been, in the words of one of their leading prophets, Dr. Nnamdi Azikiwe of Nigeria, to bring about "mental emancipation" from a servile colonial mentality. The second method has been to tap all existing nativistic and religious tensions and economic grievances among the tradition-bound masses, as well as the grievances and aspirations of the urbanized clerks and artisans, and channel the energies thus unleashed into support of the nationalist drive. The technique here has been (1) to make nationalism, and in particular its objective of self-government, an integrating symbol in which even the most disparate goals could find identification, and (2) to politicize—one would like to say nationalize—all existing thought and associations. Until recently, many observers—including colonial administrators—tended to live in the prewar climate of opinion and therefore underestimated the power which had thus been harnessed to the nationalist machine.

In the case of the Mau Mau movement in Kenya we are confronted with a complex mixture of nationalism, with a strong traditional bias on the part of the Westernized leaders, and nativism, manipulated by the leaders, on the part of the masses. Both have been generated to an especially high level of intensity as a consequence of the acute and largely unassuaged sense of frustration on the part of the Westernized elite, growing out of the very bleak outlook arising from the almost total absence, until recently, of meaningful career and prestige opportunities within either the old or the new systems, and of the masses, resulting from the land shortage and the overcrowding on the reservations. The presence of a sizable Asian "third force," which virtually monopolizes the middle-class sector, and which has been and is politically conscious, provides a new variable of no little significance in the total situation. The fact that the pattern of organization and the strategy and tactics of the Mau Mau revolt indicate a higher level of sophistication than sheer nativism would imply suggests that our analytical categories need further refinement or qualification.

A particularly striking feature of African nationalism has been the literary and cultural revival which has attended it. A renewed appreciation of and interest in "African" culture has been manifested, in most instances by the most sophisticated and acculturated Africans. . . . In some cases this cultural renaissance has had a purely tribal emphasis; in others it has taken a "neo-African" form, such as the African dress of Dr. Nnamdi Azikiwe, nationalist leader in Nigeria. It has usually been accompanied by a quest for an African history which would in general reflect glory and dignity upon the African race and in particular instill self-confidence in the Western-educated African sensitive to the prejudiced charge that he has no history or culture. In short, there has emerged a new pride in being African. In French areas, the accent until recently has been upon French culture and literature, but there are increasing signs of a shift to African themes amongst the French African literati. The important point is that African nationalism has this cultural content, which renders more difficult any effort to separate rigidly the cultural nationalism of the urban politician from the nativism of the bush peasant.

Yet the differences are important to the student of African nationalism. Primary resistance and nativism tend to be negative and spontaneous revolts or assertions of the unacculturated masses against the disruptive and disorganizing stranger-invader. They are a reflection of a persistent desire of the masses to preserve or recreate the old by protesting against the new. Syncretism is different in that it contains an element of rationality—an urge to recapture those aspects of the old which are compatible with the new, which it recognizes as inevitable and in some respects desirable. Whereas all forms of protest are politically consequential—at least to colonial administrators—only nationalism is primarily political in that it is irrevocably committed to a positive and radical alteration of the power structure. In brief, nationalism is the terminal form of colonial protest.

Another reason for distinguishing between the various categories of assertion, which are basically differences in goal orientation, is not only to provide some basis for judging the nature of the popular support of a nationalist movement during its buildup, but also to have some means of predicting the stability and viability of the political order established by the nationalists once they achieve self-government. . . . If a colonial nationalist movement comes to power atop a wave of mass protest which is primarily or even in part nativistic in character, this would have a direct bearing upon the capacity of the Westernized leaders of that movement, not only to maintain political unity and stability but also to carry out what is at the core of most of their programs —rapid modernization by a centralized bureaucratic machine. Any thorough study of the anatomy of a nationalist movement, therefore, must seek to determine the linkages and compatibilities between the goal orientations of the several forces from which that movement derives its élan and strength.

II. FACTORS CONTRIBUTING TO THE RISE OF NATIONALISM

It is far easier to define and describe nationalism than it is to generalize about the factors which have contributed to its manifestation. Put most briefly, it is the end product of the profound and complex transformation which has occurred in Africa since the European intrusion. It is a commonplace that the imposition of Western technology, socio-political institutions, and ideology upon African societies has been violently disruptive of the old familistic order in that they have created new values and symbols, new techniques for the acquisition of wealth, status, and prestige, and new groups for which the old system had no place. The crucial point here is not that nationalism as a matter of fact happened to appear at a certain point in time after the "Western impact," but rather that the transformation the latter brought about has been an indispensable precondition for the rise of nationalism. Nationalism, as distinguished from primary resistance or nativism, requires considerable gestation. A few of the constituent elements have been:

A. ECONOMIC

1. *Change from a subsistence to a money economy.* This change, consciously encouraged by colonial governments and European enterprise in order to increase the export of primary products, introduced the cash nexus and economic individualism, altered the patterns of land tenure and capital accumulation, and, in general, widened the area of both individual prosperity and insecurity.

2. *Growth of a wage-labor force.* This development has resulted in the proletarianization of substantial numbers of Africans, which has weakened communal or lineage responsibility and rendered those concerned vulnerable to economic exploitation and grievances.

3. *Rise of a new middle class.* Laissez-faire economics and African enterprise, coupled with opportunities for university and professional education, have been factors contributing to the growth of a middle class. This class is most advanced in Senegal, the Gold Coast, and Southern Nigeria, where it has developed despite successive displacement or

frustration by the intrusion of Levantines and the monopolistic practices of European firms.

B. SOCIOLOGICAL

1. *Urbanization.* The concentration of relatively large numbers of Africans in urban centers to meet the labor demands of European enterprise has loosened kinship ties, accelerated social communication between "detribalized" ethnic groups, and, in general, contributed to "national" integration.

2. *Social mobility.* The European-imposed *pax* coupled with the development of communications and transport has provided the framework for travel, the growth of an internal exchange economy, and sociopolitical reintegration.

3. *Western education.* This has provided certain of the inhabitants of a given territory with a common lingua franca; with the knowledge and tools to acquire status and prestige and to fulfill aspirations within the new social structure; and with some of the ideas and values by which alien rule and colonialism could be attacked. It has been through Western education that the African has encountered the scientific method and the idea of progress with their activistic implications, namely, an awareness of alternatives and the conviction that man can creatively master and shape his own destiny.

C. RELIGIOUS AND PSYCHOLOGICAL

1. *Christian evangelization.* The conscious Europeanization pursued by Christian missionary societies has been a frontal assault upon traditional religious systems and moral sanctions. Moreover, the Christian doctrine of equality and human brotherhood challenged the ethical assumptions of imperialism.

2. *Neglect or frustration of Western-educated elements.* Susceptibility to psychological grievance is most acute among the more acculturated Africans. Social and economic discrimination and the stigma of inferiority and backwardness have precipitated a passionate quest for equality and modernity, and latterly self-government. Rankling memories of crude, arrogant, or insulting treatment by a European have frequently been the major wellspring of racial bitterness and uncompromising nationalism.

D. POLITICAL

1. *Eclipse of traditional authorities.* Notwithstanding the British policy of indirect rule, the European superstructure and forces of modernity have tended to weaken the traditional powers of indigenous authorities and thereby to render less meaningful pre-colonial sociopolitical units as objects of loyalty and attachment. There has been what Professor Daryll Forde calls a "status reversal"; that is, as a result of the acquisition by youth of Western education and a command over Western techniques in all fields, there has been ". . . an increasing transfer of command over wealth and authority to younger and socially more independent men at the expense of traditional heads. . . ."

2. *Forging of new "national" symbols.* The "territorialization" of Africa by the European powers has been a step in the creation of new nations, not only through the erection of boundaries within which the intensity of social communication and economic interchange has be-

come greater than across territorial borders, but also as a consequence of the imposition of a common administrative superstructure, a common legal system, and in some instances common political institutions which have become symbols of territorial individuality.

These are a few of the principal factors in the European presence which have contributed to the rise of nationalism. As any casual observer of African developments is aware, however, there have been and are marked areal differences in the overt manifestation of nationalism. Such striking contrasts as the militant Convention People's party of the Gold Coast, the conservative Northern People's Congress of Nigeria, the pro-French orientation of the African editors of *Présence Africaine,* the cautious African editors of *La Voix du Congolais,* and the terroristic Mau Mau of Kenya are cases in point.

There are a number of explanations for these areal variations. One relates to the degree of acculturation in an area. This is a reflection of the duration and intensity of contact with European influences. The contrast between the advanced nationalism of the British West Coast and of Senegal and the nascent nationalism of British and French Central Africa is partly explicable on this basis.

A second explanation lies in the absence or presence of alien settlers. On this score the settler-free British West Coast is unique when contrasted to the rest of Africa. The possibility of a total fulfillment of nationalist objectives (i.e., *African* self-government) has been a powerful psychological factor which partly explains the confident and buoyant expectancy of West Coast nationalists. On the other hand, as previously noted, the tendencies toward accommodation or terrorism in the white-settler areas is a reflection of the absence of such moderating expectancy.

Certain African groups exposed to the same forces of acculturation and the same provocation have demonstrated radically different reactions. The Kikuyu versus the Masai peoples of Kenya, the Ibo versus the Hausa peoples of Nigeria, and the Creole and Mende of Sierra Leone are cases in point. It is suggested that the dynamism, militancy, and nationalist élan of the Ibo peoples of Nigeria are rooted partly in certain indigenous Ibo culture traits (general absence of chiefs, smallness in scale and the democratic character of indigenous political organization, emphasis upon achieved status, and individualism). Much of the same might be said for the Kikuyu peoples of Kenya.

Differing colonial policies constitute another cause of these areal differences. Nationalism is predominantly a phenomenon of British Africa, and to a lesser extent of French Africa. Apart from the influence of the foregoing historical, sociological, and cultural variables, this fact, in the case of British Africa, is explained by certain unique features of British colonial policy.

It was inevitable that Britain, one of the most liberal colonial powers in Africa, should have reaped the strongest nationalist reaction. A few of the principal features of British policy which have stimulated nationalism deserve mention:

1. *Self-government as the goal of policy.* Unlike the French and Portuguese who embrace their African

territories as indivisible units of the motherland, or the Belgians who until recently have been disinclined to specify the ultimate goals of policy, the British have remained indiscriminately loyal to the Durham formula. In West Africa, this has enthroned the African nationalists; in Central and East Africa, the white settlers.

2. *Emphasis upon territorial individuality.* More than any other colonial power, the British have provided the institutional and conceptual framework for the emergence of nations. Decentralization of power, budgetary autonomy, the institution of territorial legislative councils and other "national" symbols—all have facilitated the conceptualization of a "nation."

3. *Policy on missionaries and education.* The comparative freedom granted missionaries and the laissez-faire attitude toward education, and particularly post-primary education, has distinguished and continues to distinguish British policy sharply from non-British Africa.

4. *Neglect, frustration, and antagonism of educated elite.* Not only have more British Africans been exposed to higher education, but the British government until recently remained relatively indifferent to the claims and aspirations of this class, which forms the core of the nationalist movements.

5. *Freedom of nationalist activity.* The *comparative* freedom of activity (speech, association, press, and travel abroad) which British Africans have enjoyed—within clearly defined limits and varying according to the presence of white settlers—has been of decisive importance. It is doubtful whether such militant nationalists as Wallace-Johnson of Sierra Leone, Prime Minister Kwame Nkrumah of the Gold Coast, Dr. Nnamdi Azikiwe of Nigeria, Jomo Kenyatta of Kenya, and Dauti Yamba of the Central African Federation, could have found the same continuous freedom of movement and activity in Belgian, Portuguese, and French Africa as has been their lot in British Africa.

All of this suggests that African nationalism is not merely a peasant revolt. In fact, as already noted, nationalism where it is most advanced has been sparked and led by the so-called detribalized, Western-educated, middle-class intellectuals and professional Africans; by those who in terms of improved status and material standards of living have benefitted most from colonialism; in short, by those who have come closest to the Western World but have been denied entry on full terms of equality. From this comparatively affluent—but psychologically aggrieved—group have come the organizers of tribal associations, labor unions, cooperative groups, farmers' organizations, and—more recently—nationalist movements. They are the Africans whom British policy has done most to create and least to satiate.

Balandier: Messianism and Nationalism in Black Africa

One of the most characteristic phenomena of sociocultural change occurring during the colonial period in numerous societies of Christianized Black Africa is the appearance of messianistic movements which gave rise to more or less ephemeral *Negro churches*. Although they are outwardly religious, these movements rapidly develop a political aspect; they are at the origin of nationalisms which are still unsophisticated but unequivocal in their expression. . . .

The area of diffusion of these messianisms is mostly in South and Central Africa, but they appeared sporadically among the peoples of the Gulf of Guinea. The action of the prophet Wade Harris, a Liberian who introduced himself as a "messenger of God" guided by the angel Gabriel, was sufficiently active to reach a great many people as far as the Gold Coast, early in this century. His teachings have not entirely disappeared: an ethnologist has just discovered a sect in the lower Ivory Coast which maintained a large part of the doctrine and ritual. The phenomenon appears oldest and most deeply rooted in South Africa. The first manifestations go back to approximately 1890, and some 800 so-called "separatist" churches group 760,000 adherents, i.e., approximately one-fourth of the number of Africans belonging to the recognized churches. In the French and mostly in the Belgian Congo, prophetic types of reactions appear after the First World War and have never stopped since, though they have gone through alternating phases of expansion and retreat. To these movements which are African in inspiration, one must add those fostered in South and West Africa by the introduction of the Watch Tower Congregation. The latter has spread widely in the Bantu area, under special names (Kitower, Kitawer, Kitawala, etc.), but maintaining everywhere its aspect of *total* reaction against, and refusal to accept, the *status quo*, and, among other things, the presence of Europeans. Its teachings, and particularly its early diffusion by the Cape mission of pamphlets written in seventeen dialects, have certainly made an impact on some later messianisms, by stressing radical subversion and facilitating the elaboration of apocalyptic myths.

Apart from the internal and external rivalries which they provoke, and apart from the attempts they make to differentiate themselves, these *Negro churches* share common

From Georges Balandier, "Messianism and Nationalism in Black Africa," in Pierre L. Van den Berghe, *Africa, Social Problems of Change and Conflict* (San Francisco: Chandler Publishing Company, 1965), pp. 443–48, 457–58.

characteristics, and can unite, at least temporarily. In order to define them, if only in a gross way, the following aspects should be emphasized. These religious groups seceded from Christian missions (hence the expression "separatist churches") or were fashioned after the missions; their central element is a prophetic personality who developed a set of teachings announcing an end to all the disabilities suffered by Black Africans. Such groups have great drawing power; they appear essentially unstable as organized churches, but durable as to the needs they satisfy and the aims they seek. Churches rise and disappear, but the messianistic movement has remained remarkably permanent for several decades.

The phenomenon is at the same time cultural and sociological. It constitutes either an attempt to adapt the message of the Christian missions to the African context, or a revival in a Christianized framework of the still active elements of traditional religion. This syncretism is linked to another very apparent characteristic: the new religions are often violently opposed to the old particularistic cults (thereby stressing their unitary tendency), and to manifestations of sorcery and magic which have proliferated in disrupted societies. The phenomenon is also a reaction to the colonial situation, and to the domination exercised by European minorities. By insisting on the aspect of social reorganization and of rejection of a situation regarded as radically detrimental, the anthropologist R. Linton has presented messianistic movements as a relatively common consequence of relations of domination and submission. Negro messianisms, insofar as they constitute a protest and a return to certain authentically African values, seem linked to the awakening of nationalism. This aspect is all the more apparent in that the Negro church seeks to recreate a real authority; either the pontiff assumes the characteristics of the traditional chief, or the latter becomes pontiff and endeavors to reestablish a system of obligations as a substitute for old taboos that have disappeared. . . .

The first clear-cut manifestation of this autonomous Christian movement is the foundation in 1892 of the so-called "Ethiopian" Church which established relations with the American [African] Methodist Episcopal Church, founded in the United States by Negroes and for Negroes. Racial kinship between the adherents of the two churches was significantly stressed. The unity of the movement was quickly shattered along lines of ethnic particularism, but the initiative had been taken and new churches appeared, with more radical teachings of an "apocalyptic" character. These became vigorous when the first measures of racial discrimination after the creation of the Union of South Africa were applied: prophetic movements then proclaimed total subversion and the expulsion of Europeans. Incidents occurred which obliged the government to define precisely the conditions necessary for official recognition. In 1945, of some eight hundred registered churches, only eight of the oldest and numerically largest were recognized. The remarkable fact to remember is the sensitivity of these religious groups to the social climate created by the relations between the Africans and the Europeans.

Dr. Sundkler[1] distinguishes two types of churches, the "Ethiopian" and the "Zionist," and he defines their respective characteristics. The "Ethiopian" churches remain markedly influenced by the organization and the teachings of the missionary groups from which they seceded. They limit to the greatest degree contamination by traditional elements. Their aims are twofold: first, to prove that a Negro church remains alive even outside the control of Europeans; second, to create a center of political life in the only form possible, namely inside the church, since Africans are denied any opportunities for political action in lay groups. The teachings of Ethiopian churches are a school of African nationalism; the organization of the groups resorts to old notions of chieftainship or kingship, and sometimes the function of priest and that of tribal chief coincide. These churches are therefore regarded favorably by elements belonging to the traditional hierarchies. One might say that they remain more aristocratic than popular.

Churches of the "Zionist" type are more unstable, and threatened by splinters; they show more religious fervor. Their attraction resides in the very fact that they are syncretic and tolerate greater freedom for the faithful. Priests have a more prophetic character, model their role more after that of divine, healer, and witch finder than after that of chief, and remain in more direct and close touch with their flock. The cult makes a wide allowance for traditional beliefs and practices; baptism is linked with complex purification rituals; revelation through dreams, taboos, dancing, and fits of seizure play an important role. Religious practice in these churches reaffirms the efficacy of the old social therapies. This explains the refusal of all modern instruments of "cure": medicines, vaccinations, medical visits. The African finds in these sects a religious practice and an efficacy which are familiar to him. There is a reaction against the abstract, formalistic teachings of the missions. . . . At the same time, there is a return to authentically African forms of prayer and of expressing one's fervor. Missionary teachings, on the other hand, are often found to be only a series of precepts and moral exigencies, most of them radically hostile to traditional behavior, and the missionary church appears to be largely an annex of the missionary school. Finally, the Zionist churches react against a Christianity which seems to have neither the same scope nor the same meaning, according to whether Africans or Europeans are involved. Most of the *Negro churches* reject, according to their expression, the "pale Christ of the Whites," and substitute for him a Black Christ with whom the various church founders are often merged. Thus, the role of racial relations is evident even inside the churches. . . . Opposition to a policy of racial discrimination entails exaltation of African values and a return to the old culture in order to take a stand vis-à-vis the Europeans. A resort to the Bible favors utopian constructs and belief in a salvation of the black race guided by the prophets who founded the churches. To a large extent, the idea of salvation and of

[1] Lutheran missionary of Swedish origin, B. G. M. Sundkler has undertaken a detailed study of South African "Separatist Churches."

access to the Heavenly City, or that of a natural revolution which will overthrow the established order, is linked with a racism induced by the racism of the colonizers. . . .

What deeper significance must be attributed to such an undertaking? It seems, first of all, to be a reaction against "missionary" influence which has been constraining, multiple, contradictory (with rivalries between Protestants, Catholics, and members of the Salvation Army), hostile to the fundamental beliefs of the group, and incompatible with certain characteristics of social organization (notably, polygyny). It represents an attempt at adaptation (helped to a certain extent by the examples of syncretism spread by the Salvation Army), as well as at social reconstruction. This is necessary in a sociocultural whole where religious functions are still hardly distinguishable from political ones. The group reacted at the level where it was most menaced, namely that of fundamental beliefs and behavior, and at the only level where emancipation was possible; the group could otherwise only yield to the economic and political imperatives of the colonial powers. This transfer of political reactions to the level of religious activities is common in colonial or dependent situations. Religion becomes to a certain extent a smokescreen for politics.

Secondly, these movements canalize protest against a certain form of economy which upsets traditional equilibria and introduces insecurity. The three periods of grave conflicts coincide with the three periods of economic crisis: in 1921–1922 the crisis affected colonial products, thereby reducing the only important source of monetary income; in 1930–1931, the world depression had local repercussions; and after 1940 there was a period of scarcity of goods and rise in prices. Adverse economic conditions act as a tidal wave which calls into question the temporarily established order. Poverty and insecurity are then accentuated, and recourse to old systems of protection is impossible. In these altered societies where living conditions are made more precarious by dependence on an economy which became monetary but remained quite rudimentary, any disturbance has an immediate repercussion and acts with an intensity which we hardly suspect.

Finally, messianistic movements are a reaction against the continuous process of group disintegration. Opposition between pagans and Christians, and among Christians themselves; individualism growing out of ever more numerous modernist elements; multiplication of conflicts between the sexes; interest rivalries that become more acute with the progressive implantation of the money economy; disaggregation of clans, lineages, and villages—these are some of the principal aspects of the process. The movements we just studied aim, more or less consciously, to reestablish broken ties, and to recreate a community. They gather and unify people. A whole ethnic group finds again the meaning of its unity, and takes conscience of its *situation*. This reconstruction takes place only through radical opposition, which leads people to xenophobic reactions, and to a kind of racism. At the same time, the group acquires a feeling of being a *chosen people* which has a mission to accomplish vis-à-vis less conscious ethnic groups.

These are the main objectives which these religious movements seek to achieve more or less consciously, depending on the personality of their leaders. But it is important to insist on the subjective significance which they have for each of their members. They serve as a framework for a true utopian construct, for the announcement of a kind of golden age when all present difficulties will disappear and which will come after cataclysms shall have given Africa back to itself. These movements create hope, and allow one to escape, in an illusory manner, a situation hitherto passively tolerated.

Ranger: Primary Resistance and Modern Mass Nationalism in East and Central Africa

The argument for East and Central Africa has to begin, I think, by establishing what is perhaps an obvious but yet insufficiently appreciated fact; namely that the environment in which later African politics developed was shaped not only by European initiatives and policy or by African cooperation and passivity, but also by African resistance. In this sense at least there is certainly an important connexion between resistance and later political developments.

In some cases the environment of later politics was shaped by the consequences of the total defeat of attempted resistance. . . . Yet there has been a curious failure to appreciate the wide significance of such defeats as a psychological factor. Let us take the case of Kenya as an example. British rule was established in Kenya with few spectacular or large-scale displays of force. For this reason it was possible to write about the 'pacification' of Kenya in the terms employed by A. T. Matson in 1962: 'Except in abnormal cases . . . the amount of force used was minimal, with the result that the pacification of the Protectorate and the settlement of its tribes were accomplished with astonishingly little loss of life . . . Most of the operations were carried through by local forces acting more as police than conquerors.' But such a view overlooked the fact that, for each Kenyan African society that suffered what Matson would describe as a police action, the experience of rapid and total defeat could be traumatic. The point is well brought out by Professor Low. 'It was force and military prowess which in the main effected the critical submissions to British authority of the peoples' of the Kenya uplands, he tells us.

From T. O. Ranger, "Connexions Between 'Primary Resistance' Movements and Modern Mass Nationalism in East and Central Africa," Part I in *Journal of African History,* IX, No. 3 (1968), 440, 443–48, 452–53; and Part II in *Journal of African History,* IX, No. 4 (1968), 631–39, 641.

> Any map which outlined the operational theatres of the many small British military expeditions during the first fifteen years of British rule . . . would exhibit few interstices . . . And for all the exiguousness of these expeditions in European terms, they were often vastly greater, more lethal demonstrations of force than any which the defeated tribes had experienced from any quarter in the past, since they almost invariably took the form of a wholly unequal encounter between guns upon the British side and spears upon the African. . . .

Resistances also helped to shape the environment of later African politics because of their impact upon the thinking and action of the colonial authorities. Thus actual or potential resistance brought about the collapse of the commercial companies which were at first employed by the Germans and the British to open up their East African spheres of influence, and forced the two governments to assume direct responsibility. Moreover, both under company and colonial office rule, the possibility and actuality of resistance was a main factor in bringing about those alliances between the colonial administration and co-operating African societies which are generally agreed to have been so important to later political activity. Despite their technological superiority, the new colonial regimes were weak in men and finance and needed allies to deal with resistance or rebellion. Finally, African rebellions did much to shatter the early European attitude of masterful complacency. The thinking of administrators and settlers, especially in Tanganyika after Maji-Maji and in Rhodesia after the Ndebele and Shona risings of 1896–7, was dominated by the fear of the repetition of such outbreaks. This fear had many and complex effects, but among other things it led to certain concessions to anticipated African discontent as well as to military and police contingency-planning. If Africans in Tanganyika wanted at all costs to avoid another Maji-Maji rising, so also did administrative officers.

But it was not only the attitudes of defeated African societies and those of apprehensive white settlers which were affected by resistance and rebellion. There was a complex interplay between so-called 'primary' resistance and manifestations of 'secondary' opposition. We have seen . . . that many scholars have employed a rather rigid periodization in their approach to African nationalist historiography. The period of resistance is followed by hiatus; then arises the new leadership. But we must remember that the effective establishment of colonial rule throughout southern, central and eastern Africa took a very long time to achieve. 'Primary' resistance to it was still going on in some areas while 'secondary' movements were developing elsewhere. Independent churches, trade unions, welfare associations, Pan-Africanist movements all existed at the same time as expressions of tribal or pan-tribal resistance. This fact was important in forming the attitudes of the more radical 'secondary' politicians.

In another paper I have given two examples of this. One concerns the interaction of the career of the South African leader, Tengo Jabavu, and the fact and memories of the Ndebele rising. The second example is the fascinating one recorded in Shepperson and Price's account of the contacts between Nyasaland

and Zululand. In 1896 Booth, the radical missionary, travelled from Nyasaland, taking with him one Gordon Mathaka, because the Yao wished 'to send a messenger to the other tribes in the south who had known the white man a long time to find out what they thought'. Mathaka heard the opinion of the Zulu Christian *élite*. 'No matter what the Yao thought', they told him, 'no living white man, whether carrying guns or not, would in the end be the friend of the black men.' And when Booth himself gathered together some 120 African intellectuals to discuss his projected African Christian Union, 'after a twenty six and a half hour session they rejected his scheme on the simple grounds that no white man was fit to be trusted, not even Booth himself . . . No trust or reliance at all could be placed in any representative of "the blood-stained white men, who had slain scores of thousands of Zulus and their Matabele relations".' These Zulu intellectuals did not perceive as sharply as some modern historians the gulf between primary and secondary resistance.

Nor, indeed, did the men who met in London in 1900 for the first Pan-African Conference. These Afro-Americans, West Indians, West Africans, and so on, stated that they were meeting partly because of their concern over the wave of violent conflict between black and white which appeared to be sweeping Africa, instancing the Sierra Leone tax revolt and the Ndebele rising of 1896 as examples. Partly as a result of the impact made by the Ndebele rising, this first Conference appealed to Queen Victoria for reforms in Rhodesia.

This sort of interaction lasted into the 1920s. One example, again a Rhodesian one which refers back to Ndebele resistance, must suffice. In June 1929 the first militant African trade union was holding its meetings in Bulawayo; weekend after weekend it hammered away on the theme of African unity, appealing not only to the pan-tribal union movements of South Africa but also to successful examples of continuing armed resistance. . . .

In all these ways, then, resistances formed part of the complex interaction of events which produced the environment for modern nationalist politics. I now want to turn to a more complex and interesting argument. This argument runs that during the course of the resistances, or some of them, types of political organization or inspiration emerged which looked in important ways to the future, which in some cases are directly, and in others indirectly, linked with later manifestations of African opposition. . . .

The point can be well illustrated in the cases of the two greatest rebellions in East and Central Africa, the Ndebele-Shona risings of 1896–7 and the Maji-Maji rising of 1905. The main problem about these risings is not so much *why* they happened as *how* they happened. How was it possible for the Ndebele and their subject peoples to rise together in 1896, when in the 1893 war the subject peoples had abandoned their overlords? How was it possible for the Ndebele and the western and central Shona to cooperate in the risings in view of their long history of hostility? How was it possible for the Shona groups to co-operate among themselves in view of their nineteenth-century history of disunity? How was it possible for the very diverse peoples of southern Tanzania to become involved in a single resistance to the Germans? Finally, how was it that these apparently odd and patch-work alliances offered to the whites a more formidable challenge than had the disciplined professional armies of 1893 or the Hehe wars?

In the Rhodesian case part of the answer certainly lies in the appeal back to traditions of past political centralization. But both in Rhodesia and in Tanzania the main answer lies in the emergence of a leadership which was charismatic and revolutionary rather than hereditary or bureaucratic.

The African societies of East and Central Africa could draw in times of emergency upon a number of traditions of such charismatic leadership. Two emerge as particularly important in connexion with the sort of large-scale resistance we are discussing. The first of these is the prophetic tradition. Many African societies of East and Central Africa had religious systems in which specialist officers played an institutionalized prophetic role, speaking with the voice of the divine either through possession or through dream or oracular interpretation. Such prophet officers have usually been regarded by scholars, in common with 'traditional religion' as a whole, as conservative and normative forces. The prophet has been thought of as the ally of the established political order and as the guardian of its customary moral norms. But, as I have argued in a recent paper, the prophetic authority could not be so confined; the claim to speak with the voice of the divine was always potentially a revolutionary one, and if the prophet could invest the ordinary operations of a society with divine sanction he could also introduce new commandments. . . .

In the various resistances to the establishment of colonial rule, there is no question that religious leadership played an important part. The character of this leadership varied greatly, however. Sometimes the establishment religion of an existing unit committed itself to resistance alongside the established political and military system. Sometimes the established religious officers resisted the movement of the established political authorities into a 'Christian Revolution'. But sometimes, in the great movements of rebellion and resistance that we are now particularly discussing, innovating religious leadership sprang up to revitalize or to challenge the established religious structure as well as the whites and, where necessary, the African political authorities. Such innovating religious leadership sprang out of either the prophetic or the witchcraft-eradication traditions. In their different ways both called for the creation of a new order in which neither sorcery nor colonial pressures nor the tensions of small-scale society would exist; both offered protection and invulnerability to those who observed their new commandments. They thus offered solutions, on however temporary a basis, to the problem of morale, to the problem of the combination of different groups, and to the problem of co-ordination. . . .

Almost everywhere this kind of leadership was seen by the Europeans as profoundly reactionary, as endeavouring merely to preserve the tribal past and to exclude all innovation. In fact it was often revolutionary in method and in purpose and sought to transcend tribal limitations. Prophet leaders were often men able at one and the same time to appeal to past notions of unity . . . and also to attempt to restructure society. Thus they appealed to a wider unity than had been achieved in the past and they were not afraid in its service to challenge the authority of secular leaders. . . .

Resistances of this sort, then, can hardly be adequately defined as 'reactionary' or as essentially backward-looking, however passionate and romantic they may have been. In many ways they were tackling the problems which more recent proto-nationalist and nationalist movements have faced. But there still remains a key question. The great 'primary resistance' movements may have been *similar* to later expressions of opposition to colonial rule but were they *connected?* They may not have looked to the fragmented tribal past and attempted to preserve it, but did they look to the future and provide the basis for, and tradition of, the mass political movements of the twentieth century? . . .

It has most often been argued, of course, that 'primary' resistances were *not* connected, either directly or indirectly, with later forms of opposition. Resistances were followed, it was held, by 'a period of calm,' out of which emerged 'other leaders and other motives.' And it is unquestionably true that after, say, 1920 there were very few 'tribal' risings and that different sorts of political organization were developed by new men. To that extent periodization of African nationalist history is legitimate enough. But, as I suggested in the first part of this article, we need to look for continuity in mass emotion as well as for continuity in *élite* leadership, if we are to establish a satisfactory historiography of nationalism. It is obviously important to ask whether there was any continuity in terms of mass emotion between the sort of risings I have been discussing and modern nationalism.

The first part of an answer is that there is undoubtedly a link between these resistances and later mass movements of a millenarian character. Nor is this link merely a matter of *comparing* the Shona-Ndebele or Maji-Maji risings with later prophet movements or witchcraft eradication cults. There is often a quite direct connexion. . . .

The most direct connexions, of course, are provided by examples like that of Nyabingi, which provided the basis both of 'primary resistance' and of persistent twentieth-century millenarian manifestations. Next come movements like that of the Mumbo cult in Nyanza province, Kenya. The Mumbo cult has recently been examined in a very interesting paper by Audrey Wipper. It arose among the Gusii, apparently around 1913, after the defeat of various 'primary resistances.' It reached peaks of activity in 1919, in 1933, and to a lesser extent in 1938 and 1947; it was one of the movements banned in 1954. Thus in point of time it bridged the period between the suppression of the Gusii risings of 1904, 1908 and 1916 and the emergence of modern mass nationalism. In character it was strikingly similar to the sort of movement we have already discussed. Although arising among the Gusii, it was 'a pan-tribal pagan sect,' creating its own society of true believers, whom it bound by its own codes of conduct and to whom it promised eventual triumph and reward. The colonial period, in its mythology, was merely a testing period devised by the God of Africa to sort out the true believers from the faint-hearted; before long those who remained true would enter into the wealth and power of the whites. Mumbo had the most direct links with the period of primary resistance. 'The Gusii's most venerated warriors and prophets, noted for their militant anti-British stance, were claimed by the movement,' Miss Wipper tells us. 'Zakawa, the great prophet, Bogonko, the mighty chief, and Maraa, the *laibon* responsible for the 1908 rebellion, became its symbols, infusing into the living the courage and strength of past heroes . . . Leaders bolstered up their own legitimacy by claiming to be the mouth-piece of these deceased prophets.'

Indeed, if Miss Wipper is right, we are close here to the idea of an 'alternative leadership,' stemming from traditions of resistance and opposed to officially recognized authority. 'Especially successful in effecting such claims were the descendants' of the prophets and chiefs concerned. 'Thus, with the progeny of the Gusii heroes supporting the sect, a physical as well as a symbolic link with the past was established. Here was a powerful symbolic group whose prestige and authority could well be used to arouse, strengthen and weld the various disunited cults into a solid anti-British opposition.' Miss Wipper makes the important point that the cult looked back only to those figures who themselves stood out from and tried to transform traditional small-scale society; 'it looks to the past for inspiration and to the future for living.' 'Its goals,' she tells us, 'are Utopian and innovative rather than traditional and regressive,' involving attacks upon small-scale traditional values as well as upon European values. It would seem that Professor Ogot has considerable justification for applying the word 'radical' to the cult, and in claiming that 'the history of African nationalism in the district must be traced back' to its emergence. . . .

Similar examples of direct 'physical' and indirect 'symbolic' connexion with primary resistances can be given for Christian independent church movements. In the first category comes, for instance, Shembe's Nazarite Church in Zululand, so vividly described by Professor Sundkler. This impressive manifestation of Zulu, rather than South African, nationalism referred back to 'one of the most dramatic occasions in the history of Zulu nationalism,' the Bambata rising of 1906. It was physically linked to this rising through the person of Messen Qwabe, one of its leaders. Shembe himself proclaimed: 'I am going to revive the bones of Messen and of the people who were killed in Bambata's rebellion.' All five sons of Messen have joined the church, which was given posthumous spiritual approval by their dead father, and it is taken for granted that all members of the Qwabe clan will be members of it. In the second category comes Matthew Zwimba's Church of the White Bird, established in 1915 in the Zwimba Reserve in Mashonaland, which appealed to the memory of the 1896–7 rising by regarding all those who died in the fighting in the Zwimba area as the saints and martyrs of the new church. It is important to note also that Zwimba regarded himself as very much a modernizer and succeeded, at least for a time, in establishing himself as the intermediary between the chiefs and people of Zwimba and representatives of the modern world.

It can be shown, then, that some at least of the intermediary opposition movements of a millenarian character, which are usually by common consent given a place in the history of the emergence of nationalism, were closely linked, as well as essentially similar, to some movements of primary resistance. Can we go further than this? It would be possible to argue, after all, that whatever may be the interest of such millenarian movements in the history of African politics, they have not in fact run into the main-stream of modern nationalism and in some instances have clashed with it. A movement like Dini Ya Msambwa might be cultivated for short-term purposes by a political party—as KANU [Kenya African National Union] is said to have cultivated it in order to find support in an otherwise KADU [Kenya African Democratic Union] area—but it can hardly be thought to have had much future within the context of modern Kenyan nationalism.

It seems to me that there are a number of things to be said at this stage. I have argued that modern nationalism, if it is to be fully successful, has to discover how to combine mass enthusiasm with central focus and organization. This does not mean that it needs to *ally* itself with movements of the sort I have been describing which succeeded, on however limited a scale, in arousing mass enthusiasm. Indeed, it will obviously be in most ways a rival to them, seeking to arouse mass enthusiasm for its own ends and not for theirs. But it would be possible to present a triple argument at this stage. In the first place, one could argue, where nationalist movements *do* succeed in achieving mass emotional commitment, they will often do it partly by use of something of the same methods, and by appealing to something of the same memories as the movements we have been discussing. In the second place, where nationalist movements are faced with strong settler regimes, as in southern Africa, they will tend to move towards a strategy of violence which is seen by them as springing out of the traditions of 'primary resistance.' And in the third place, where nationalist movements fail, either generally or in particular areas, to capture mass enthusiasm, they may find themselves opposed by movements of this old millenarian kind, some of which will still preserve symbolic connexions at least with the primary resistances. . . .

The new mass party in East and Central Africa, as it spreads to the rural districts, comes to embody much of the attitude which has hitherto been expressed in less articulate movements of rural unrest. It often appears in a charismatic, almost millenarian role—the current phrase, 'a crisis of expectations,' which politicians from Kenya to Zambia employ to describe their relations with their mass constituents, is not a bad description of the explosive force behind all the movements we have described. Often the party locally—and nationally—appeals to the memories of primary resistance, and for the same reason as the millenarian cults did; because it is the one 'traditional' memory that can be appealed to which transcends 'tribalism' and which can quite logically be appealed to at the same time as tribal authorities are being attacked and undermined. My own experience of nationalist politics in Southern Rhodesia certainly bears out these generalizations. It was the National Democratic Party of 1960–1 which first really penetrated the rural areas and began to link the radical leadership of the towns with rural discontent. As it did so, the themes and memories of the rebellions flowed back into nationalism. 'In rural areas,' writes Mr Shamuyarira of this period, 'meetings became political gatherings and more . . . the past heritage was revived through prayers and traditional singing, ancestral spirits were evoked to guide and lead the new nation. Christianity and civilization took a back seat and new forms of worship and new attitudes were thrust forward dramatically . . . the spirit pervading the meetings was African and the desire was to put the twentieth century in an African context.' So Mr George Nyandoro, grandson of a rebel leader killed in 1897, and nephew of a chief deposed for opposition to rural regulations in the 1930s, appealed in his speeches to the memory of the great prophet Chaminuka round whom the Shona rallied in the nineteenth century; so Mr Nkomo, returning home in 1962, was met at the airport by a survivor of the rebellions of 1896–7, who presented him with a spirit axe as a symbol of the apostolic succession of resistance; so the militant songs copied from Ghana were replaced by the old tunes belonging to spirit mediums and rebel leaders. . . .

This brings us to the second point. It is natural that a nationalist movement which is still engaged in an increasingly violent struggle for independence will turn even more exclusively to the tradition of resistance. This has certainly happened in Southern Rhodesia, for example. The present phase of guerrilla activity in Rhodesia is called by the nationalists 'Chimurenga,' the name given by the Shona to the 1896 risings. 'What course of action will lead to the liberation of Zimbabwe?' asks a Zimbabwe African National Union writer. 'It is not the path of appeasement. It is not the path of reformism. It is not the path of blocking thirds. It is the path of outright fearless defiance of the settler Smith fascist regime and fighting the current war for national liberation. It is the path of direct confrontation. It is the path of Chimurenga.' Here, within the Rhodesian movement, there is not only an attempt to stress the mass, radical characteristics of the nationalist parties as with TANU, but in many ways a repudiation of the party as an organizational form in favour of a return to the older tradition. . . .

It is time to move to the third point—that these traditions of resistance can sometimes be used *against* nationalist movements as well as *by* them. Indeed the whole question of African resistance to *African* pressures is one which urgently needs investigation before we can obtain a balanced view of the significance of resistance as a whole.

A number of preliminary points, however, can already be made. In the first place, of course, the extension of the concept of resistance to include African resistance to African pressures reminds us that historical discussion of the role of resistance as a force for change cannot be restricted to the period of the Scramble and the Pacification. This is true even if we limit the idea of resistance to European-African confrontations: the Shona, for instance, had a long tradition of rebellion against the Portuguese which served as the background to their rebellion against the British. But it is even more importantly true if we consider African resistance to African pressures. During the nineteenth century, East and Central Africa were exposed to a number of powerful African intrusions which threatened the very existence of certain societies. Partly in response to these intrusions, the existing secular authorities in some African societies attempted to build up new powers; sometimes this attempt also provoked resentment and resistance within the society.

Some at least of these resistances to external African invaders or to the expansion of internal central authority took the form of the reactions to European rule which I have described above. The prophetic and witchcraft eradication traditions were as available to movements of this kind as to later movements of protest against the whites; certain features of the later movements which historians have felt to be characteristic of response to colonialism as such were almost certainly present in these earlier manifestations. . . .

Then again, during the colonial period itself, a good deal of what we can properly call African resistance, in the sense of movements similar to those categorized as 'primary resistance' movements, has taken the form of protest against dominance or sub-imperialism by other African peoples. A few examples may be given. The violent opposition of the Kiga clans to the control of the Ganda agents of British over-rule; the rebellion in 1916 of the Konjo people against Toro control, which is being followed up at the present time by a second rebellion of the Konjo for the same reasons; the disturbances in Balovale and elsewhere against the control of local government by the Lozi; these are all instances of resistance which clearly have to be fitted into any general discussion of the topic. . . .

However strange their mythologies and structures may appear to us, these movements require to be taken seriously and with sympathy as consistent expressions of aspirations which in the end have to be met in one way or another by the rulers of East and Central Africa, whether white or black. The aspiration to 'put the twentieth century in an African context'; the aspiration towards a new society 'conceived of as a gigantic village made up of thousands of small villages in which the people find their own authenticity'; the aspiration towards gaining control of their own world without surrendering its values; all these are still characteristic of the rural masses of East and Central Africa. It is, of course, true that these movements have not offered lasting or effective solutions; . . . they have been 'revolutionary in method' but also 'anarchic in effect.' It is the task of the nationalist movements of East and Central Africa, therefore, to maintain mass enthusiasm for their own solutions. It is their task to demonstrate that they can institutionalize and make permanent their answers to the problem of how to increase effective scale without destroying African communalist values more successfully than the primary resistance leaders or the millenarian cults.

Coleman: The African Elite and African Nationalism

EUROPEAN ATTITUDES TOWARD THE EDUCATED ELITE

The special grievances of the westernized elements were crucial factors in the awakening of racial and political consciousness. Much of their resentment, of course, was the inevitable outcome of the disorganization following rapid social change. Their desire to emulate Europeans tended to separate them from their traditional milieu. Had they been accepted completely and unconditionally as dark-skinned Englishmen—as, in fact, certain members of the first generation were accepted—and had they been permitted to achieve a social and economic status that was both psychologically meaningful and materially satisfying, the course and the pace of Nigerian nationalism would most likely have been quite different. This did not happen, however, mainly because of the attitudes of many of the European residents and the policies of the British administration in Nigeria. In the trenchant words of Sir John Rodger: "We are busy manufacturing black and brown Englishmen—turning them out by the score, and cursing the finished article when the operation is complete. . . . [We] create an alien and then leave him to work out his own salvation."

With many notable exceptions, the characteristic attitude of resident Europeans toward the educated African was one of contempt, amusement, condescension, or veiled hostility, depending upon the individual relationship. From the turn of the century until the late 1940's, many visitors to Nigeria, and to other parts of British West Africa, commented on the tension and animosity between Europeans and educated Africans. An observer in 1912 noted that "the relations between the Anglo-Saxon and the Anglicized African in West Africa are delicate and difficult." In 1925 another observer said: ". . . one frequently hears people of all kinds remark how superior the untutored primitive villager is to the African who has come into contact with Europeans." Charles Roden Buxton made a similar observation in 1935: "Few white people have a good word to say for the educated African. . . . [His] failings and absurdities are one of the stock subjects of conversation among White people in West Africa."

Apart from color prejudice, cer-

From James S. Coleman, *Nigeria: Background to Nationalism* (Berkeley: University of California Press, 1963), pp. 145–66.

tain aspects of the Nigerian situation helped to create the disparaging attitude of Europeans toward the educated African. In the first place, some educated Africans, particularly in the pre-World War II period, appeared comical, and perhaps ridiculous, in their awkward attempts to imitate the mannerisms in dress, speech, and behavior of the "English gentleman." Because they made the latter their prototype, rather than the common English clerk, farmer, or laborer, their endeavors were all the more ludicrous. . . .

There are, of course, obvious explanations for the exaggerated imitative tendencies of the educated Nigerian. He had been taught in school to imitate the "English gentleman"; most of the advertisements he saw in newspapers and magazines, particularly in the early days, were addressed to such a type; and, except for traders and missionaries, most Europeans in Nigeria were colonial officials who until recently were of the aristocracy or *haute bourgeoisie,* and tried to perpetuate in Africa the mode of living of the English upper classes. In a sense, therefore, European attitudes were the product of class snobbery. . . .

European resentment of the educated African stemmed in part also from the universal urge to ridicule the imitator. Of course, in the early period of colonialism, missionary effort, the educational system, and other Western forces and institutions were explicitly aimed at transforming the African into the European image. And any human relationship cast in the model-imitator mold tends toward a superior-inferior stratification of attitudes. It is psychologically difficult for a model to regard an imitator as his equal; he is hypercritical of, rather than flattered by, awkward efforts at imitation. It was no doubt the confession of inferiority implicit in extravagant imitation that led many postwar nationalists to lampoon the earlier generation of educated Africans, frequently with the epithet of "hat-in-hand Uncle Tomism."

One can in fact draw a rather sharp distinction between the first generation of educated Nigerians, who revealed a strong urge to imitate, and the generation that came of age in the late 1930's and early 1940's. This difference in perspectives and behavioral patterns is of crucial significance. Generalizations about the perspectives and predispositions of one generation are likely to be invalid for its successor. In Nigeria there is fairly strong evidence that the attitudes of the second generation were partly determined by a reaction against the attitudes of the earlier generation. Indeed, one of the main themes in Premier Nnamdi Azikiwe's *Renascent Africa* was an appeal to the upcoming generation for "mental emancipation" from the attitudes of the older generation. All this, of course, was closely linked with the development of cultural nationalism in the second generation of educated Nigerians.

Many resident Europeans also felt that the educated African was congenitally dishonest or unscrupulous, or had otherwise failed to achieve the minimum standards of character prescribed by the model of an acceptable European. This sentiment was reflected in the great emphasis placed upon moral and character training in the schools by European educators and officials. It also appeared in the disinclination of the European banks to grant credit to

Nigerians, and in the unwillingness of commercial firms to elevate Nigerians to positions of responsibility, especially those involving financial matters. . . .

European beliefs and feelings about African financial dishonesty were not, of course, without foundation. The incidence of theft, corruption, and dishonesty on the part of Africans in contact with Europeans was high, but not necessarily higher than in similarly placed groups in other societies. . . .

Other factors caused Europeans to consider the educated African deficient in character. They believed that an African who obtained a position of power over other Africans would exploit them mercilessly for his own ends. This charge was usually documented by references to the arrogance and exploitative practices of the Afro-American ruling minority in Liberia; or to the fact that employees of African firms were paid less and treated worse than employees of European firms; or to Lagos barristers who charged unconscionable legal fees and deliberately provoked costly litigation in which the illiterate bush farmer was the financial victim; or to the pomposity, venality, and nepotism, and the ruthless exaction of bribes from illiterate members of the public, on the part of African clerks, male nurses, customs employees, and police. This petty oppression by many educated Africans confirmed and strengthened European prejudice. . . .

Although prejudice might account for the condescension or contempt of Europeans toward educated Africans, it did not explain their veiled or frequently open hostility. Friction was most acute at the personal level. Many Europeans felt that educated Africans were insulting, assertive, and "uppity"; that they refused to reciprocate social overtures and created imaginary disabilities, slights, and rebuffs; and that they maintained a "chip-on-the-shoulder" attitude in their personal relationships. . . .

Tensions of this character, of course, are well-known phenomena in interracial situations. The Nigerian problem, however, has distinctive features. In the first place, until recently the vast majority of educated Nigerians were political and social outsiders in their own country. Second, the educated Nigerian suffered more than anyone else from the discriminatory behavior of the white community, not only because he aspired most intensely to the status of equality, but also because he was the thankless intermediary between European officials and the Nigerian public. Most educated Nigerians either served directly under or were only one stage removed from daily contact with the white man, and the relationship was on a master-servant basis. The Nigerian's aggressiveness was either a defense mechanism hiding a deeply ingrained inferiority complex, or a natural human retaliation to the insults, imaginary or real, which he received from his European superior. . . .

The antagonism of the white community, and especially of officialdom, toward educated Nigerians became more pronounced when it was realized not only that they were the source of political agitation, but also that they aspired to greater participation in the government with the ultimate aim of displacing the white administration. It was the educated Nigerians who organized mass meetings in Lagos, provoked disturbances in the provinces, published vituperative articles in the local press, and made life miserable and insecure for British administrators. There was nothing a district officer, a resident, or a governor dreaded more than political disturbances and unrest during his tour of duty. He would have to face the inevitable parliamentary question, or a visiting commission of inquiry, not to mention added work and an unfavorable efficiency report. In a colonial milieu political tranquillity was the norm, and an administrator's failure to achieve that norm was presumed to be a reflection upon his ability. The educated African was the bête noire of the European administrator . . . .

It was in the social sphere, however, that European attitudes and prejudices toward educated Africans were most embittering. The vast majority of Nigerians—the illiterate and unsophisticated—were little disturbed by white pretensions to superiority, but educated Africans were genuinely resentful. In the early days, when Nigeria was indeed a "white man's grave," separate European and African residential areas and hospitals might have been justified on grounds of sanitation and public health. Yet long after modern prophylaxis had rendered Nigeria suitable for white habitation, the distinction was rigidly maintained. Separateness was not only openly asserted and therefore officially supported in the civil service, residential areas, and hospitals, but it existed in most places where interracial contact occurred, including motion picture theaters, social clubs, and recreational facilities.

And yet it was not the separateness, but rather the qualitative differences in the facilities provided for the two races, which aroused the greatest hostility. The extreme contrast between the well-paved roads, the street lighting, and the palatial homes in the European quarter on Lagos Island (Ikoyi), and the chaotic squalor of the native quarter, was a constant reminder to educated Nigerians living in Lagos and other urban areas of the wide gap between their style of living and the "white" standard to which they aspired. Moreover, the refinements and comforts of European facilities were supported by taxes paid by Nigerians. . . .

Color discrimination, as it was practiced in Nigeria, was the product not only of preconceptions regarding African inferiority, reinforced by a magnification of the faults of educated Africans, but also of the firm conviction that peaceful colonial administration and the perpetuation of imperial rule were directly dependent upon the doctrine of white superiority. This attitude is most poignantly brought out in Joyce Cary's novel *The African Witch*. Even those Europeans in Nigeria who were not color-conscious—and there were many, and at high levels—were effectively prevented from reducing social tensions and establishing rapport between European groups and educated Africans. The ban against familiarity, the rigid maintenance of separate African and European standards and facilities, and the painful, albeit subtle, penalties inflicted upon Europeans or educated Africans who violated the color bar were all part of a determined effort to preserve the doctrine of white superiority, not necessarily for its own sake, but for political tranquillity. Nor was this simply an unwritten code, as evidenced by the following wartime instructions given to white troops stationed in West Africa:

> In all contact with the natives, let your first thought be the preservation of your own dignity. The natives are accustomed to dealing with very few white people and those they meet hold positions of authority. The British are looked up to, put on a very high level. Don't bring that level down by undue familiarity.

OFFICIAL POLICY TOWARD THE EDUCATED ELITE

From the beginning of formal British administration in Nigeria the government faced a serious dilemma in connection with the status and role of the educated elements. On the one hand, educated Nigerians were absolutely indispensable not only for the government of the country, but also for its development, as intermediaries between the tiny group of European officials and the vast mass base. On the other hand, under British prewar policies, particularly indirect rule, there were few roles beyond clerkdom which educated Nigerians could be permitted to perform. Of course, the size of Nigeria and the small number of British officials made indirect rule itself a requisite of imperial control. In order to govern Nigeria the British needed both the educated elite and indirect rule, yet each pointed toward a very different political formula. One of the important strands in the political history of British administration in Nigeria has been the effort to resolve this internal contradiction.

CENTRAL GOVERNMENT

Before World War II the educated elements, with few exceptions, were excluded not only from the central government but also from the native administration of local government. At the central level only four Africans were elected as members of the Legislative Council between 1923 and 1946. Three were elected from the township of Lagos and one from Calabar, by an electorate composed of the wealthier members of the communities. In addition, the governor appointed seven Africans to the council during the period 1923–1938, and ten during the period 1938–1946, to represent the interior of the Southern Provinces. Before 1946 there was no African representation from the Northern Region. All the elected and appointed African members came from the educated class (five clergymen, six lawyers, one journalist, one wealthy trader, and one district chief from the Cameroons). Yet only two of them, both elected from Lagos, would have been considered nationalist-minded at the time they served, and they were all repudiated by postwar nationalists.

Two educated Africans (Sir Adeyemo Alakija and Justice S. B. Rhodes) were appointed to the governor's Executive Council in 1943, but both were considered by the nationalists to be "safe" government men. Before 1943 no African had participated directly in policy formulation at the central executive level. Furthermore, with few exceptions, Africans were excluded from the various functional councils and boards appointed by the government to advise on specific problems.

. . . There is, however, little evidence that before World War II the government considered the Africanization of these advisory bodies politically expedient, notwithstanding African criticisms in the Nigerian press and elsewhere.

It was their exclusion from the administrative, judicial, and technical branches of the senior (European) civil service, however, which the educated elements felt most keenly. Despite the comparatively large number of Nigerian barristers, the Nigerian judiciary remained predominantly European until the 1940's. By 1939, there were only twenty-three educated Africans in the senior service. But educated Nigerians were unimpressed by these appointments. One reason was that most of the appointees were either repatriated "Brazilians" or native foreigners, and not "sons of the soil." The three most senior Africans in the senior service belonged to the alien categories, as did most of the early appointees to the judiciary. The two members of the Executive Council, Rhodes and Alakija, were Sierra Leonian and Brazilian respectively. Second, it was believed that even those few Africans who were elevated to senior-service rank did not enjoy equality with Europeans in the perquisites and conditions of service. One senior African, for example, had a European subordinate who received a higher salary than he did. Finally, educated Nigerians believed that Africans appointed to office were selected because they had ingratiated themselves with Europeans and not because they were more competent than others.

Salary scales in the African clerical service ranged from £36 to £400 a year. The highest salary accrued only to the oldest and most senior African chief clerks, about twenty-five in number. Most Africans in the civil service received an annual salary of £100 or less. By contrast, a European official fresh from his university in England started at £450 a year, and within seventeen years his salary could increase to more than £1,000. The gap between the two services was further widened by the more favorable conditions of service and the higher perquisites in the senior service.

The feeling of denial regarding elevation to the (European) senior service might have been assuaged had a more fluid situation existed within the African civil service. But even in that service only 3 per cent of the positions (185 out of 5,841) had been classified as senior (that is, with a salary above £100 a year) by 1936. This meant that the great bulk of government employees were competing for a few highly prized positions with a very slow turnover. The African's frustration was further aggravated because most of the senior posts in the African service were held by native foreigners. Since the government service provided the pattern for other employing agencies in Nigeria, this situation was general throughout the country.

It is also possible that the grievances of African civil servants would have been lessened had they been eligible for promotion from the ranks. As it was, the sharp differentiation between the European and African sectors of the civil service created or exacerbated tensions which developed along racial rather than purely economic lines. The few Africans who were appointed to the senior service had no bonds or feeling of identity with the thousands of

Africans in the junior service, either because they were native foreigners, or because the gap between the two services was so wide that the great mass of Nigerian clerks did not feel that one of their own kind had been promoted.

In a large measure, however, the rigid stratification in the civil service simply represented the transfer to Nigeria of the bureaucratic organization characteristic of the British civil service, in which there was, until recently, a marked distinction between the administrative class and the clerical services. In Great Britain, of course, the distinction largely followed class lines, whereas in Nigeria it automatically followed racial lines. In any event, although the Nigerian pattern was not necessarily devised to preserve white supremacy or to discriminate against Africans, it nevertheless had that effect which, from a political standpoint, is just as significant.

The virtual exclusion of educated Nigerians from meaningful roles in the central government was an explicit policy of the British administration. It was based upon the following oft-quoted principle, enunciated by Lord Lugard in 1920:

> It is a cardinal principle of British Colonial policy that the interests of a large native population shall not be subject to the will . . . of a small minority of educated and Europeanized natives who have nothing in common with them, and whose interests are often opposed to theirs. . . .

The same principle was stated even more forthrightly by Sir Hugh Clifford in his famous 1920 address before the Nigerian Council. His remarks were largely provoked by the demands of the National Congress of British West Africa:

> "There has during the last few months been a great deal of loose and gaseous talk . . . which has for the most part emanated from a self-selected and a self-appointed congregation of educated African gentlemen who collectively style themselves the 'West African National Conference.' . . . It can only be described as farcical to suppose that . . . continental Nigeria can be represented by a handful of gentlemen drawn from a half-dozen Coast tribes—men born and bred in British administered towns situated on the sea-shore, who in the safety of British protection have peacefully pursued their studies under British teachers. . . ."

The denial of the political claims of educated Nigerians was based not only on the smallness of their number, but also on the belief that the educated minority lacked cultural identity with the masses. During Lugard's governorship, and indeed until the early 1930's, there was evidence to support such a belief. In 1921 approximately 18 per cent of the English-speaking Africans in Nigeria were native foreigners (that is, educated Africans mainly from the Gold Coast and Sierra Leone). In the townships of the Northern Provinces, with which Lugard was more intimately acquainted, the proportion was nearly 40 per cent. As late as 1936, this alien group still tended to dominate the upper ranks of the African civil service and the clerkship hierarchy in commercial firms. It is more likely than not that most of the educated Africans whom Lord Lugard and other high-ranking European officials encountered in the early 1920's were not Nigerians at all, but native foreigners. Indeed, Sir William Geary reports that in the early period the terms "native foreigner" and "educated native" were virtually synonymous.

If Lugard was referring to this

group when he spoke about educated Africans, he was quite right—they had no identity with the indigenous Nigerian masses. Moreover, the Nigerians themselves, unlike Europeans who did not differentiate among Africans, knew that the native foreigners were not sons of the soil even though they were dark-skinned. . . . The majority of them had no intention of settling in Nigeria, but were saving their money for eventual retirement in their home territories. As late as 1936, outward remittances by native foreigners totaled £545,875 a year, which exceeded Nigeria's average prewar annual expenditure on education. In the decade 1921–1931, however, the number of native foreigners declined, and by the end of World War II native-born Nigerians constituted all but a tiny fragment of the educated elements.

It is, of course, an open question whether educated Nigerians accurately represented the views of the inarticulate masses, or whether the interests of the two groups diverged. In any event, the principal basis for the charge that they were unrepresentative was that they had become "detribalized." This was a frequently expressed, and much resented, European stereotype of the educated Nigerian. The concept of "detribalization," useful though it may be in referring to social change as a general process, frequently conveys a false picture when applied to groups or individuals. As stated elsewhere, "the concept tends to evoke the distorted image of polar extremes—of 'tribalized' witch doctors and secret societies on the one hand and of 'detribalized' barristers and their 'national congresses' on the other, with very little connection between the two." Most educated Nigerians either sought to recapture, or had never lost, a significant measure of identity with their lineage and with African culture.

There were many ways in which educated Nigerians manifested the tenacity of the lineage and tribal attachment. The wealthier professional classes made efforts to procure chieftaincy titles or councilorships in their native villages. They also coöperated with teachers, clerks, and artisans to organize and maintain lineage or tribal unions in urban communities. These unions were an organizational expression of the persistent feeling among educated groups of loyalty and obligation to the kinship group and to the town or village where the lineage was localized. Their widespread existence, their strength, and the devotion and interest of their members, including most of the educated Africans, provide positive evidence that Europeans have grossly exaggerated the detribalization of the educated class. On the other hand, some educated Nigerians, especially those who glorify African culture, have endeavored to minimize the extent of their own acculturation by denying that their European values, loyalties, behavior patterns, and aspirations were in any sense un-African or were blindly copied from Europeans. Race-conscious Africans have resented terms like "detribalization" and "Europeanization" as implying that Africans abandoned their own culture because it was inferior and embraced European culture *in toto* because it was superior.

Another official argument for limiting the participation of educated Africans in government was that they were not qualified to hold political power or responsibility. Lord Lugard claimed that "the educated native, generally speaking, [has not] shown himself to be possessed of ability to rule either his own community or backward peoples of his own race, even under favourable conditions." Apart from his personal prejudices, Lord Lugard was influenced in his views by the exploitative and oligarchical character of Negro self-government in Haiti and Liberia. . . . In any event, to the generation of educated Nigerians who came of age in the late 1930's and early 1940's, disqualification by analogy was as empty as an argument that Europeans were incapable of self-government because of the Nazi and Fascist dictatorships.

A persistent theme in official responses to the demands of educated Nigerians for the Nigerianization of the senior service was that the high standards of the service could not be compromised, and that few educated Africans could meet them. In the abstract, of course, the maintenance of high standards is laudable, but to the educated Nigerian the argument smacked of sophistry. . . . In any event, African clerks were acutely aware of the striking contrast between their own salaries and conditions of service and those of the Europeans under whom they worked, and were convinced that they could readily replace the Europeans without reducing efficiency or lowering standards. . . .

But educated Africans were not totally excluded from government at the central level. Although Lord Lugard refused to give them power over the African masses, nevertheless he permitted them a limited outlet for their energies. In his view self-government for Europeanized Africans should be "along the same path as that of Europeans—increased participation in municipal affairs until they prove themselves fitted for the larger responsibilities of Government of their *own* communities. . . ."

Yet there was another strand in official policy which resulted in a fatal dualism. This strand comprised institutional arrangements and explicit official statements pointing toward ultimate self-government for a united Nigeria. A few educated Nigerians had actually been admitted to the central administrative service. They had also been appointed to serve as unofficial members of the Legislative Council, whose purview included not only the colony, but also the Southern Provinces and, for certain financial purposes, the Northern Provinces of Nigeria. Indeed some educated Africans had been members of the Legislative Council since the beginning of the century, and new members had been appointed during the 1930's.

These actual developments were buttressed by explicit official statements which clearly gave educated Nigerians the notion that all Nigeria would ultimately be governed by a central administration controlled by Africans. When discussing the reconstitution of the Nigerian Council in 1921, Sir Hugh Clifford stated that the new body should be "a *serious* factor in the Government of the Colony *and Protectorate*" and as "truly and practically representative of *all* Nigerian interests" as possible. He also expressed the hope that it would ultimately be "the Supreme Council of State—the 'Parliament' of Nigeria. . . . In this instance, however, the ultimate goal was considered to be in the distant future, and could be realized, as Sir Hugh had in fact stated, only "when the Native Chiefs become properly and efficiently organised throughout the country." Yet this qualification did not dim the brightness of the future envisioned by educated Africans; it merely meant that they would have to mark time. This they were not content to do.

In retrospect, the tempo and course of Nigerian nationalism might have been different had the British authorities avoided the dualism of excluding educated Africans on grounds of principle, but at the same time giving them the vision of ultimate control. The policy of dualism created frustration and bitterness which a more consistent policy, pursued steadfastly from the commencement of British rule, might have prevented. . . .

Guided by the Lugardian principle of separating educated Nigerians from the masses, the British administration delayed coming to grips with the problems of where the educated classes would fit into the total picture, and of who would control the superstructure holding the native authorities together in a modern political unit. Educated Nigerians became convinced that they were destined to serve forever as clerks and subalterns, and that the superstructure was, as Lugard perhaps assumed, a perpetual British preserve. . . .

In the early 1930's, however, official thought regarding the relationship between educated groups and the native authority system, particularly in the Southern Provinces, began to change. Several factors were responsible. The most obvious was the great increase in the number of educated Nigerians. It was no longer a problem of a few thousand concentrated in Lagos and other urban centers, but of hundreds of thousands scattered all over southern Nigeria. In the decade after World War I the number of secondary schools had jumped from two to twenty-six. The second factor was the sudden burst of organizational activity among educated groups in the early 1930's, which reflected their strong desire to participate in the affairs of their home villages or districts. Organized into lineage and tribal unions, educated sons abroad asserted a claim to have their voices heard in native authority councils. In general, their demands were moderate and showed a sense of responsiblity. The British change in policy was in part a response to this challenge. In the late 1930's and early 1940's, the government gave increasing encouragement to the activities of these unions. At the same time it insisted that the educated influence must be persuasive rather than dictatorial, and that it must be channeled through and have the consent of the traditional authorities. In short, although Lugard's idea of keeping all political development in Nigeria within the framework of the traditional system was retained, his policy of educating and reforming that system from within, which had meant the exclusion of the educated elements, was abandoned.

Policy changes were further stimulated by warnings from observers and students of the African scene, who felt that meaningful roles must be provided for the previously excluded and unwanted group of educated Nigerians. In 1935 Charles

Roden Buxton warned that "we neglect the *intelligentsia* at our peril," and added:

> The educated Indian—the Babu—was regarded with precisely the same mixture of contempt and jocularity as the educated African is today. Yet, what has happened? In less than a half a century those Babus, whom we thought we could ignore, . . . had become the statesmen of India. . . . They were still a tiny minority, but they had become the people without whose consent and co-operation we could no longer carry on the government of India at all. I venture to prophesy, confidently, that it will be the same in Africa. . . .

In similar vein, Lucy P. Mair, one of Britain's leading Africanists, pointed out in 1936 that demands for change had always come from minorities with specific grounds for discontent and that the African educated class would ultimately triumph.

Perhaps the most direct examination of the problem in its Nigerian setting was undertaken by Margery Perham in 1936. Acknowledging that the emergence of the educated Nigerian was absolutely necessary for Britain's colonial mission, she urged that it be accomplished by (1) employing more Nigerians in "positions of trust" (but not in the administrative service), and (2) "doing everything possible to find or create opportunities for them within the Native Administrations." Obviously referring to Nnamdi Azikiwe, she raised this question: "But what scope . . . can the rudimentary Ibo groups offer to one of the tribe who has spent ten years at American universities accumulating academic qualifications?" The question was answered by Azikiwe himself; ten years later he was the leader of a Nigeria-wide nationalist movement, and twenty years later the premier of Eastern Nigeria.

As subsequent events proved, this late prewar effort to channel the energies of educated Nigerians into the traditional structure did not satisfy their aspirations. It is difficult to make broad generalizations because of wide tribal variations in the composition of native authorities, the uneven tribal and geographical distribution of educated Nigerians, and the division of the group into sharply defined conservative, moderate, and radical elements. The attitudes of educated Nigerians in prewar Lagos, the most sophisticated and enlightened urban center, provide a few clues. The older and more conservative progovernment members of the Lagos intelligentsia gave unquestioning support to the system of native administration in the provinces, but strongly objected to extending the system to Lagos or the colony area. Were they not "British subjects"? Lagos barristers, who comprised about half of the total African representation in the pre-1946 Legislative Council, opposed one aspect of the system of indirect rule on personal and professional grounds. They protested their exclusion as counsel from the native court system. As more barristers arrived from the London Inns of Court, the protest became louder. The thousands of educated clerks, artisans, and subalterns in Lagos expressed their dissatisfaction over the exclusion policy through their lineage and tribal unions. Whether moderates who sought partial representation, or radicals who pressed for total control, they all wanted the old and illiterate members of the native authority councils replaced by the young and educated—namely, themselves.

By the time of World War II the grievances of educated Nigerians had increased and the radical tendency had become dominant. There were two principal reasons for this development. First, the British administration was either disinclined or unable, because of the war and the strong resistance of traditionalists, fully to integrate the educated elements into the traditional structure. The scattered efforts that were made affected so limited a number of educated Nigerians that few sensed any change in policy. The second reason was increasing acceptance of the notion that the system of indirect rule was "not only a form of government specially invented for backward peoples, but one designed to perpetuate their backwardness by preserving their isolation and tribal divisions." . . .

The expression "indirect rule" had taken on imperialistic connotations because educated Nigerians believed that district officers, residents, and governors sometimes insulted chiefs and elders or emasculated their powers by vetoing their actions, dictating taxes, arbitrarily establishing local rules, appointing and deposing titled chiefs, and interfering with local customs; in short, the British administration, in their view, imposed a petty autocracy under the pretense of training Nigerians for self-government.

There was a second reason for the opposition to indirect rule. Because emirs and chiefs held office at the pleasure of the resident or the governor, they seemed to be merely puppets—"imperialist stooges" in nationalist jargon—of the colonial government, and hence could not be independent representatives of the people, least of all of the educated groups. It was the subservience of most traditional authorities to the white man, whether fancied or real, which provoked the more race-conscious educated Nigerians into uncompromising hostility to the whole system of indirect rule. The fact that British plans for constitutional reform did not deviate from the basic Lugardian purpose of channeling Nigerian energies and power through the native authority system, served only to strengthen the suspicion that the traditional authorities were agents of imperialism. This aggravated the growing antagonism between the educated elements and the chiefs, which in turn increased the latter's subservience to the British and the former's demands for control at the center. Members of the intelligentsia became convinced that the only sure way of making their influence felt was to wrest control of the superstructure from the British.

Kilson: Nationalism and Traditionalism in Sierra Leone

NATIONALISM AND TRADITIONALISM

The competing ideas, values, and methods in Sierra Leone party politics are readily classifiable under the terms nationalism and traditionalism. The former term refers to those types of political perceptions, values, and modes of action that resulted primarily from European domination of Sierra Leonean society. The latter term embraces those sociopolitical values and methods that are essentially indigenous to the society or that resulted from a qualified fusion of indigenous and expatriate modes.

In general, the militant anticolonial nationalism found elsewhere in Africa was not a prominent feature of party operations in Sierra Leone, either at the time I observed them in 1960–61 or prior to this period. This was especially the case for the SLPP [Sierra Leone People's Party], the dominant party since the commencement of bona fide party politics in 1951. Neither in the SLPP's constitution nor in its first election manifesto (1951) do the favored words in the vocabulary of militant African nationalism like "colonialism" and "imperialism" appear. They do appear twice in the SLPP's 1957 election manifesto, but in the rather obscure and diffident context of a "Message" written by Albert Margai, then party chairman, and appended to the main body of the manifesto.

The relatively small role of the nationalist outlook in the politics of the SLPP was apparent as well from its leaders' view of the process by which colonial peoples gain independence. Militant nationalist parties like the Convention People's Party (CPP) in Ghana and the *Parti Démocratique de Guinée* (PDG) conceived this process as a struggle by colonial peoples to wrest power from expatriate authorities. SLPP leaders, however, saw it largely as an operation through which power was granted by, not wrested from, the colonial authorities when the subject peoples proved their ability properly to handle power. This conception was quite evident in a political broadcast by Sir Milton Margai during the 1957 general election. "We [SLPP leaders] were the first Ministers ever in Sierra Leone," he said. "We were pioneers. The evidence of how well we have done our jobs is seen in the readiness with which Her Majesty's Government has agreed for us to take another step towards self-government." . . .

From Martin Kilson, *Political Change in a West African State: A Study of the Modernization Process in Sierre Leone* (Cambridge: Harvard University Press, 1966), pp. 252–56, 259–64.

The absence of a militant nationalist approach by the SLPP reflected both the circumstances of the party's rise to power and the conscious preference of its leadership, especially Sir Milton Margai. As we have seen . . . the SLPP did not pursue mobilization of the rural masses as a means of gaining their support at elections. Rather, it relied upon, and articulated its political structure to, the traditional institutions controlled by Chiefs, who held legitimate—though not uncontested—claim upon political allegiance of the rural populace. The Chiefs . . . were themselves transformed significantly enough under colonial institutions to lend their status and role to the modern party process.

Circumstances and preferences reinforced each other. Sir Milton Margai in particular had little understanding of or sympathy for the kind of expedient democratic outlook required of a political leadership whose claim for power rested upon an organized mass basis. Sir Milton's thought was alien to the kind of political outlook that admitted a measure of autonomous, self-interested rationality to the political needs and orientation of the masses. . . .

There were, of course, other leading figures in the SLPP during its formative period—notably Albert Margai and Siaka Stevens, respectively Minister of Local Government and Minister of Lands, Mines, and Labour 1953–1957—who personally inclined toward allowing the rural populace political expression outside traditional institutions and values. But the circumstances were so favorable to the kind of approach espoused by Sir Milton Margai, combined with his large personal influence in the SLPP, that these figures followed suit. . . .

POLITICAL USES OF SECRET SOCIETIES

Given the significance of the leader in modern African politics, we cannot overemphasize the seminal role of Sir Milton Margai in fitting the SLPP's behavior to traditional patterns. His social origins and status as the son of a chiefly family, and the fact that his father's brother was an influential Mende Chief in Bonthe District throughout his political career, certainly predisposed Sir Milton toward this method. Moreover, during two decades of service (1932–50) as a medical officer in the hinterland prior to entering party politics, he had himself experimented with the use of Mende tribal associations like the Sande Society, an initiation order for females, in disseminating modern health and household practices and in training a corps of midwives.

Indeed, in a certain sense Sir Milton inherited a predisposition toward the synthesis of traditional and modern forms from Mende society itself. The Mende, more than other Sierra Leonean tribes but not unlike tribes elsewhere in Africa, initially experimented with the use of traditional cultural associations to cope with aspects of the Western intrusion as early as the turn of the twentieth century. As Kenneth Little points out, during the Hut Tax War of 1898 (also known as the Mende War, since the Mende carried a major share of it), the

Mende Chiefs "called warriors to arms over a wide area by sending round the Poro sign of war—a burned palm-leaf." Ever since this event the Poro Society has been used variously by Chiefs and peasants for political purposes connected with the colonial situation. Throughout the twentieth century educated Mende—and also Temne, to whom Poro had spread—never hesitated to join Poro Society, and, according to Little, even when well established in modern professions or trades, they were likely to "continue to play a part in Poro activities."

It is no surprise, then, that the modern elite in the Protectorate who founded the SLPP in 1951 adopted the traditional Poro symbol, the palm leaf, as the party symbol. Incidentally, a not implausible alternative explanation of this act might run as follows: If the conservative nationalist method of SLPP leaders is viewed psychologically as a function of a Caliban-like personality trait—otherwise called an Uncle Tom personality or the Sambo syndrome—in the context of a colonial situation, then the adoption of the palm leaf as a party symbol may be a subliminal form of radical or revolutionary expression. This is especially so when it is noted that the most symbolically significant use of the Poro palm leaf in the context of the colonial situation was at the time of the Hut Tax War. Further credence is lent to this type of psychological explanation of the symbolic side of SLPP political behavior by the fact that the SLPP chose the date of April 27 as Independence Day, which was the same date on which the Mende War broke out. Whatever the limitations of this type of explanation, there are certainly many features of African political behavior under colonial rule—and equally in the post-colonial period, given the persistence of neo-colonial relations—that are illuminated by it.

Besides the palm leaf, the SLPP exploited other features of Poro for political purposes. Sir Milton Margai was most astute at manipulating Poro obligations in his relations with Chiefs and other traditional notables; and throughout Sierra Leone, individual candidates drew upon Poro obligations at every opportunity. . . .

This . . . incidentally, points up an important feature of the utilization of Poro obligations for modern political purposes: persons exploiting these obligations were invariably of high traditional status, mainly sons of Chiefs. This conformed to traditional uses of Poro authority and influence, for traditionally Chiefs virtually claimed ascriptive right to exercise this authority. . . . This pattern of Poro authority was weakened under colonial change, with the result that the peasant disturbances of the 1930's and the postwar period saw the rebellious exercise of Poro obligations by commoners. But within the structure of the SLPP's nationalist politics, such perversion of traditional authority patterns and values was *verboten,* and the few SLPP politicians of commoner origin were keen to recognize this.

RITUALISTIC FLATTERY: PERSONALISM AND LEADERSHIP

The personal style of SLPP politicians in their relations with each other, and especially with the party leader, was equally governed at many points by traditional patterns. Ritualistic flattery, widely used traditionally as a means of gaining influence with Mende and Temne Chiefs, was common in interpersonal relations among politicians. SLPP legislators and ministers were particularly keen in using ritualistic flattery when confronting Sir Milton Margai. This not infrequently entailed a minister or party official indulging in self-negation, all to the end of symbolizing one's dependence upon the leader as well as the leader's own omnipotent sagacity.

Institutionally speaking, ritualistic flattery creates a symbolic relationship of dependence between the persons concerned. Among the Mende in particular such a bond is highly valued, reinforced as it is by the transfer of benefits or prestige. This style of interpersonal relations among politicians is prevalent elsewhere in Africa and has been a factor in the rise of a highly personalistic dictatorial leadership under single-party rule, as in the case of the Nkrumah regime in Ghana and the Houphouet-Boigny regime in the Ivory Coast. Although dictatorial rule has not yet occurred in Sierra Leone, the prevalence of ritualistic flattery in interpersonal political relationship is a facilitating factor, emanating from, and reinforced by, traditional society, where the life cycle of the average man is still imbedded.

VOLUNTARY ASSOCIATIONS IN THE SLPP: A RECIPROCITY MODEL OF AFRICAN POLITICS

The SLPP's adherence to traditional norms of socio-political relations affected nearly every aspect of its behavior. This may be illustrated by an account of the party's relationship with modern and quasi-modern (or neo-traditional) voluntary associations.

The SLPP had a distinct preference for voluntary associations that were formed through a fusion of modern and traditional elements. Thus the party's initial ties with voluntary associations were with the Mende Tribal Committee and the Temne Tribal Union in Freetown. Both grew out of the system of tribal headmen administration employed by the colonial government in Freetown, beginning with the statutory establishment of a Mende tribal headman in 1905. These associations invariably touched the lives of a major segment of the urban population; throughout the postwar period, during which they grew, they performed, quasi-legally, an array of basic administrative functions under their tribal headmen, like the registration of births and deaths, settling disputes of a traditional nature, performing marriages, registering migrants from the hinterland. Community development functions were also performed, such as the collection of £20,000 by the Temne Tribal Union to build two mosques in the late 1940's and the raising of a comparable sum by the Mende Tribal Committee to build in 1960-61, an additional church of the United Brethren in Christ Mission, which was erected within a stone's throw of the Tribal Committee's headquarters.

Within the Mende Tribal Committee and the Temne Tribal Union, the political process was in some measure traditional. For example, the home of the Mende tribal headman (or rather headwoman—Madame Nancy Koroma—

when I observed the institution in 1960-61) was also the headquarters of the Tribal Committee. This kind of personalization of roles and functions is ubiquitous in traditional society, and, like the setting of the chiefly role in hinterland areas of Sierra Leone, the home office of Nancy Koroma was a beehive of activity where modern, traditional, and ritual functions intertwined and overlapped. In a sense, then, the political process within these tribal associations centered more around the charismatic position or attributes of the headman than around the functions of the office. It was not, however, a situation of either the one or the other, for the charismatic (or ritual) role gained credence in the non-traditional, urban environment through the secular role ordained by colonial government.

The combination of the ritual and secular roles within the tribal associations naturally rendered them attractive to the SLPP as bases for spreading its influence in the urban areas and towns. The associations were, among other things, capable of maintaining traditional relationships between leaders and followers even in the non-traditional urban environment—a goal central to the SLPP's political values. The SLPP always preferred linkage with associations headed by persons who had both Western education and high rank in traditional society. Nancy Koroma and Kandeh Bureh, the heads of the Mende and Temne tribal associations respectively, both claimed the latter attribute. Madame Koroma was of a chiefly Mende family in Moyamba District, and her father was the first Mende tribal headman in Freetown, appointed by the colonial government partly because he possessed high traditional rank. Kandeh Bureh was a member of a Temne ruling family in Mange Bure Chiefdom, Port Loko District. Both were also comparatively well-educated, at the upper primary level, and Kandeh Bureh was a schoolteacher for many years. Both were experienced, too, in the running of modern organizations. Madame Koroma, for example, was a leading and long-standing member of the United Brethren in Christ Church in the Mende Community of Freetown, as well as a member of other welfare bodies. Likewise, Kandeh Bureh, besides his teaching career, organized a group of recreational associations of young Temne males in Freetown called "dancing compins," established a night school for literacy training, and founded an agricultural settlement for unemployed Temne males. . . .

Traditionally in African society, a person contracts ties beyond his primary unit more as a member of the primary collectivity than as an individual, thereby continuing basic allegiance to the primary unit and its needs and obligations. In other words, the primary collectivity itself mediates one's wider social relations. Something like this principle of traditional social relations was evinced in much of the SLPP's relations with voluntary associations. Few members of voluntary associations held outright membership in the SLPP; they were linked to the party through the intermediary of the associations and their leaders. Even if the individual member of a voluntary association held outright membership in the SLPP, it was understood that the act of membership intimately embraced his relations with the voluntary association. And the voluntary associations themselves were linked to the SLPP less through outright membership (in fact, the constitution of the SLPP made no provision for such membership) than through a pattern of interlocking leadership. Invariably the leaders of the major voluntary associations—who were themselves possessed of both high traditional status and modern-leadership attributes—simultaneously held posts in the formal structure of the SLPP.

Thus, the SLPP both integrated the masses, after a fashion, into modern politics and preserved the efficacy of traditional modes of mediating socio-political relations. The party, moreover, reinforced this arrangement by dispensing finance and general patronage in a traditional manner. Wealth in traditional society as Marcel Mauss brilliantly showed in his *Essai sur le don* (1925), circulated in a manner congruent with the prerequisites of the maintenance of kinship and general social obligations. Seldom was wealth used, as in modern society where production and exchange of goods and services revolve around the cash nexus and the impersonal market system, to subdue or overcome primordial social relations. When it was so used, it became politically (and socially) redundant through conspicuous consumption by authorities or was flushed off through warfare.

This traditional principle of circulating wealth can be detected in the SLPP's use of finance to bind voluntary associations to it. A variety of voluntary associations received a major part of their operating finance from the SLPP government. The Ex-Servicemen's Association, for example, received annual grants during 1957–60 which totaled £4,433; the Sierra Leone Football Association shared in the £6,725 government grant to the Sierra Leone Sports Council, a quasi-government body, over the same period; the Sierra Leone Students' Union in London received a £500 grant in 1959–60; and, also in 1959–60, some 283 Producers' Cooperative Societies with a membership of 15,624 obtained a variety of government assistance valued at £68,605, plus a government-guaranteed loan of £120, 000, and influential members of the societies received "advances . . . to buy building materials to improve their houses."

The recipients recognized, above all, the principle of reciprocity implicit in the exchange (gift) between themselves and the SLPP. Primitive exchange binds the individual and his social unit. This lent the SLPP a convenient political lever: Lacking adequate political machinery for the manifold purposes of modern politics, it could, through reciprocity, leave to voluntary associations the matter of ensuring that their members supported the party when required. Related matters of political discipline and sanction could, within certain limits, also be left to voluntary associations. The members, cognizant of the fact that they *and* their kinship unit were bound, were not inclined to falter when the party needed support. The system, then, was, in a certain sociological sense, rather oppressive—and worked partly because of this. It worked also because it met certain needs of individuals and groups. But in the context of a developing society this type of political process also had its drawbacks, some consequences of which are noted presently.

A number of interesting political consequences emerge from the type of relationship the SLPP established with voluntary associations. When compared to the direct mode of integrating an individual *qua* individual into the party politics of developing African societies, the method adopted by the SLPP may be less conducive to the growth of politically alert citizens. Nevertheless, the political experience acquired within voluntary associations—at a sub-governmental level, so to speak—may eventually foster the organizational pluralism that seems to be a precondition of viable competitive politics. But in the short run at least, the type of political relationship established by the SLPP between the new elite and the masses is unlikely to advance the average voter much beyond the traditional authority system.

For the ruling elite this has obvious advantages when they wish to stabilize socio-political relations in the course of modernization. African voluntary associations, rooted as they are in traditional relations, reduce the tension and cleavage that stem from a change in the individual's primary social loyalties, obligations, and expectations. But from the viewpoint of the masses, the stability produced by this socio-political pattern may well hinder their advance. This is especially so when it is recognized that the new elite in Africa incline toward a pattern of resource allocation or use that is basically Western, in the sense that it is governed more by individual preference than by obligations of traditional kinship—particularly where such allocation concerns the share claimed by the elite groups themselves. Yet these same elite groups, cognizant of the persistence of traditional perceptions of social relations among the population, formally infuse the modern political process with as many traditional norms or evaluations as they can. Hence an interesting and far-reaching contradiction.

Much of post-colonial politics centers around this contradiction between the elite's self-serving approach to the allocation of scarce resources, on the one hand, and their political espousal, on the other hand, of traditional norms and obligations as guideposts for political behavior. The single-party tendency so widespread in post-colonial Africa is not, for instance, unrelated to this contradiction; through the single party the elite endeavor to curb political groups likely to question this contradiction and exploit it for political purposes. Thus many facets of politics within the elite and between the elite and the masses may be expected to revolve around the contradiction I have delineated.

Lonsdale: Nationalism and Traditionalism in East Africa

The belief that African nationalism is the political expression of social change may be summarized quite simply. In general the colonial period saw within each territory the creation of a single, if deeply divided, political and economic system out of the multitude of pre-existing societies, tribes, peoples and kingdoms. For all but the most isolated of Africans there was a vast increase in social scale. With this there came the beginnings of proletarianization, especially in Kenya, and a growth of economic individualism through the introduction of marketable cash crops and outlets for food surpluses. On a lowly and obvious level, the social preconditions for a wider political consciousness—nationalism eventually—were provided. More importantly for this paper, the developing colonial situation was accompanied by a growing depersonalization of relations within African society. This process, with exceptions and variations, seems to have been marked by three broad phases. . . .

There was the initial period in which the administrations were establishing themselves, finding or creating political communicators, points of contact with the subject peoples. In the ideal case the political communicator, king or chief, whether traditionally legitimate, traditionally recognizable as usurper, or jumped-up mercenary and buccaneer, remained also a social communicator, in close relationship with his tribesmen or peasants. His administrative duties, little more than tax collection and the maintenance of order, were not yet heavy enough to disrupt the known social pattern. Strains there were of course. But face-to-face relations were retained within the African societies, intrusion on the part of the British being confined to manipulation of the points of contact.

Then, with colonial authority firmly established, officials felt less dependent upon their African allies, being more preoccupied with administrative efficiency, development, and immigrant pressures. There was increasing economic and institutional change which tended to undercut the relationship between chief and people and between the people themselves. . . .

The structure of communication remained founded upon the officially recognized chief in his tribal location. But in order to mollify the newly articulate educated men, administrators had 'strained to the utmost the loyal support of the old chiefs, by demanding the inclusion of younger men' in tribal councils, even before the institution of Local

From J. M. Lonsdale, "Some Origins of Nationalism in East Africa," *Journal of African History,* IX, No. 1 (1968), 120–29, 135–38, 140–46.

Native Councils (L.N.C.s) in 1925. Whatever their shortcomings, these L.N.C.s were crucial in that they enlarged the circle of recognized communicators between people and government. Their membership comprised not only chiefs *ex officio,* but teachers, traders and the like. Executive orders were still transmitted downwards through the chief; communication upwards from the people did not always have to pass through the same narrow channel to secure official notice. The points of contact were multiplying, and with them the strains of chiefship. . . .

In this second phase, then, governments were in some areas assisting in the social decline of the political communicators on whom their authority rested, a decline which was in any case likely with the widening influence of the market economy. To mark the third phase, in the 1930s a crucial new factor was added in each of the three mainland territories, namely increasing government intervention in the everyday business of life. There was a proliferation of marketing controls, stricter supervision of the educational system and, most important of all, the first attempts to change African methods of land usage. All this government activity had two significant and related results. The more enterprising Africans, traders, teachers, improving farmers, came in increasing individual contact with the machinery of central government. Secondly, African authorities were either by-passed by departmental experts or, if efficient, became faceless co-ordinators of improvement schemes, much like the new breed of deskbound white officials themselves. The old communicators no longer occupied a sole focal point in local society.

The conclusion of this argument is vital. The combined effect of social change and the erosion of one form of African leadership was the emergence in some areas of groupings recognizable as peasantry. The term has been used already in this paper in contradistinction to tribesmen. There are difficulties in its application to the African situation, but if it is accepted that the distinguishing condition of a peasantry is its semi-autonomy or partial self-sufficiency in political, economic and cultural spheres, it seems clear that the introduction of the colonial authority structure, agricultural production in excess of subsistence requirements, and the spread of Christian and Islamic literary cultures together produced such a condition, certainly in those areas most exposed to change. . . .

An independent landowning peasantry was emerging. Chiefs, the old communicators, were irrelevant to many of the peasants' dealings with economic agencies or new social communities; for example, the churches. And, as members of a stable bureaucracy, their prestige and wealth was less dependent upon such involvement in local society. In Professor Low's phrase, there was an atrophy of face-to-face relations, not only between the peasantry and their political leaders but, with the new incompetence of these leaders as social communicators, between the peasants themselves. In such a situation, with its openings for new leadership, Wolf sees the classic opportunity for effective political action on the part of the peasantry. The way was clear for new communicators either to re-knit the old society in relevant terms, or to join the new interests in new associations, in order to regain effective popular contact with the colonial authority, if necessary through the medium of open conflict. The choice of unifying symbols, whether tribe or peasant class and nation, was determined by the pressures, from above and from below, which developed within the colonial situation. In the inter-war years the pressures from above, from the colonial authority, were still mediated almost exclusively through the official chiefs. The new opportunities for social mobility and status outside the chiefships were the most awkward signs of pressures from below. Together, they focused political attention on the possible alternatives for securing an effective African voice in the local councils of empire. The varied political focus employed by Africans was an index both of the changing nature of the colonial pressures and of the social confidence of their leaders. This focus was controlled by three factors: an estimate of the popular basis of support for a given action—an awareness of social change; an understanding of the enemy's most responsive and responsible point—a knowledge fostered by government action; and an appreciation of those features of the administrative and legal framework which could be turned to advantage. It defined political aims, tactics and organization. . . .

Until the end of the First World War, the African political focus in Kenya remained diffuse in the sense suggested above. The hardships of the war itself, and immediately thereafter increased taxes, reduced wages, an influx of fresh settlers, their rising demands for labour, and the renewed threat to African lands implicit in the change of status from East Africa Protectorate to Kenya Colony—all these factors presented Africans with a 'clearly defined enemy.' In the protest associated with Harry Thuku there was then a nationalist understanding of the situation; but the new social bases for a sustained nationalist organization were lacking. The centrality of Thuku's focus was blurred. He applied pressure on the governor and settlers, in association with the African population of Nairobi and the Asian community, both in their different ways concerned with politics at the centre of the colony. The impact of his demands was lessened by the nature of his organized support, recruited from groups at the same time wider and narrower than Kenya's territorial bounds. The membership of his East African Association included Baganda and some individuals from Tanganyika, but the sense of 'Africanness' which this collaboration implies is not the same thing as nationalism. More significant for the future was the response within Kenya's localities. Part of Thuku's appeal among his own tribe, the Kikuyu, seems to have been due to his demand for a paramount chief, a demand which later Kikuyu associations echoed. Luo leaders similarly called for one of their own, educated and elected. Such slender evidence as exists for Masai connexions with Thuku suggests that most interest was shown by the Kaputei clan, supporters of Seggi ole Lenana, who had recently been removed from his paramountcy. The Kamba, perhaps because they lacked such potential focus for presenting their grievances, showed little enthusiasm.

These demands for paramount chiefs were an integral part of the politics of local focus. The outburst of African protest in the early 1920s had been met, in Nairobi at least, with bloody repression. Despite the subsequent declaration of the doctrine of 'native paramountcy,' it was clear that the central government was more deferential to settler than to African opinion. Appreciation of this settler strength at the centre was coupled for many Kenyans with a knowledge of the relative independence enjoyed by the Kingdom of Buganda. If government could not be effectively challenged at the centre, perhaps it was possible to question the legitimacy of its authority in local concerns. . . .

The demand for paramounts started as a non-controversial item of policy supported by all those articulate members of society who were anxious to erect defences against the central government. It promised greater local control over land and the allocation of resources for development. By the late 1930s the demand was related more to internal social concerns, with the popular election of a paramount chief seen as a means of overthrowing the official chiefs, who were government appointees. The struggle between the old communicators and their rivals was joined. The imperatives of political defence and social change were interdependent. If the district commissioner, as was argued by the Luo, was subject to settler pressure, so too were the government chiefs. And if missions and government implemented their educational and other development programmes in alliance with the chiefs, so also the chiefs were often the first beneficiaries of change. If it was impossible for Africans to control their chiefs through a voice in the central government, the alternative could only be the introduction of popular control within the localities, both over the political communicators and over the incidence of social and economic benefits. The growth of new interest groups seeking political recognition of their educational and econonomic attainments; disappointment in the official chiefs' performance as political communicators and demands for their popular accountability; these factors were concurrent and inseparable rather than a simple chain of cause and effect. . . .

Failure on the political front accelerated the desire for internal social reform, with the aspirant new social communicators demanding political roles. The localities became cockpits of competition. On the one hand the official chiefs, by selection increasingly committed to material progress and sometimes allied to senior mission adherents, tended to support government and mission programmes. Thanks to their official status they could hope, by their protests or their enthusiasms, to influence schemes for development; and in so doing they could manipulate the opportunities for patronage within the locality. On the other hand were those numerous individuals of enterprise who were excluded from the narrow executive structure, seeing official programmes not only as generally insufficient, but also as tending to favour the official communicators who helped to implement them. In the areas most subject to change, there were then two competing *élites,* the 'established *élite,*' and that on 'the growing edge of social activity,' distinguishable in many cases only by their differential access to official goodwill. The manner in which this competition expressed itself and later influenced nationalist politics seems to have depended much on the extent to which the colonial authority structure accommodated itself to indigenous social patterns. . . .

By the end of the Second World War, the politics of local focus, entailing the reform of the colonial system, were in Kenya and Tanganyika proved to be a failure on the external front. Statutory L.N.C.s in Kenya could not even prevent the further excision of tribal land—as shown in the Kakamega Gold Rush of the 1930s. In 1951 the Meru of northern Tanganyika were powerless to prevent their own eviction to make way for white settlers. And local pressure could do little to influence the central governments' allocation of resources for development. Internally also, L.N.C. elections in Kenya too often excluded those enterprising individuals who, travelling in trade or permanently employed outside their tribal reserves, lost touch with their lineage constituency. This lack of political adjustment to social change was officially admitted to be even more pronounced in Tanganyika's localities before the Second World War. But the futility of these attempts to find local solutions to African problems does not mean that the inter-war period can be dismissed as of no account in the history of East African nationalism. The experience of failure was itself important. For in the long years before the local focus was discarded, emergent African groups became fully aware of the strength of officially entrenched privilege within their own societies. This awareness is a constituent part of the ideology of African socialism. And failure meant not only that many future nationalists would be radicals, but also that they would have a low estimate of the potential of local government as an instrument of change. The implementation of national goals would be the function of a greatly strengthened central government after independence.

These generalizations point to similarities in the pre-nationalist inheritance of Kenya and Tanganyika. The experience of their first nationalist movements brings out the contrasts within that inheritance, contrasts that have here been explained in terms of the differing indigenous societies that were subject also to differing colonial situations. In its first three or four years, T.A.N.U. [Tanganyika African National Union] achieved a much stronger organization and wider network than did K.A.U. [Kenya African Union] in the seven years of its legal existence. In other words, T.A.N.U. was much more successful in its encounter with the central paradox of any national movement. To be effective and credible, nationalist leaders must appeal for mass support; but such an appeal brings into central focus those rivalries of tribe, language and culture which have hithero been contained within their respective localities. In the inter-war years, the period of local focus, political argument had centered on the allocation of resources to the localities and the distribution of the ensuing benefits within them. The debates were conducted within fairly circumscribed groups of rival modernizers, African officials and those outside the mission or government hierarchies. These tended to present their conflicting claims to governments with but little attempt to mobilize popular followings. It is important to discuss why this was so—especially remarkable in Kenya by contrast with the mass meetings held by Harry Thuku and other leaders in the early 1920s. Fear of government repression or a tacit acquiescence in alien rule provide only a very partial answer.

A complex question has been asked. A brief and oversimplified answer will be attempted. It will be argued that the mass of Africans were in the inter-war years bereft of effective political communicators with the colonial authority. There were two main reasons for this. The first was the lack of heavy external burdens on the tribesmen or peasantry until the mid-1930s. The second was the existence of what may be conveniently called Christian Revolutions, not only in the initial colonial period, as in some of the Uganda kingdoms, but inherent in the later development of missionary education elsewhere. This lack of effective political communication was a new development. In precolonial society each colonizing unit, based generally on the lineage, possessed its communicators over against similar and neighbouring units. In resistance to European occupation the mobilizers of mass action within the colonizing unit had been these traditional communicators, whether chiefs, warriors or religious leaders. If short-lived, military resistance took traditional forms; if drawn-out, new principles of organization might evolve. In post-pacification revolts, demanding a more conscious commitment than resistance, the task of communication within the rebellion seems to have been carried out more often by religious figures. Religious appeals, whether by priests of an established order or by revolutionary prophets, and in themselves implying a reorientation of society, permitted social mobilization on a wider scale than appeals by leaders of kin groups. That African societies should commit themselves to the crisis of rebellion is striking evidence of the existence of leaders who could communicate effectively with their people. It was in the religious field that corporate action on a lowly social plane retained most vitality in the years that followed the collapse of armed African resistance and rebellion. Independent churches and indigenous sects were of many kinds, fulfilling as many social needs. Some sought relief for the oppressed poor in confused millennial dreams; some aimed at social sanity and order at a humble level on earth; others saw salvation in educational schemes as ambitious as any offered by the mission churches in which, as may tend to be forgotten, many political leaders continued to find 'a place to feel at home.' However much these churches differed in aims and recruitment (the above categories were not necessarily mutually exclusive), they all had one thing in common. They were able to enlist the continuing loyalties of many ordinary Africans, at however local a level, and however prone to further schism and segmentation. This was a quality more often lacking in explicitly political associations until the late 1930s.

The two reasons advanced for this lack—the absence of heavy governmental burdens on ordinary Africans and the effects of the introduced Christian literary culture—were closely linked. Together, they both obviated the need for a continuing, committed presentation of mass problems before the colonial authority, and seemed initially to provide the individual and society with an assured, non-political means of attaining equality with the European rulers. When external pressure was felt by the mass of Kenya Africans immediately after the First World War, the reaction had been dramatic enough, not least because the officially appointed communicators felt their local positions to be threatened by popular discontent. Thereafter burdens on both chiefs and tribesmen were relaxed, partly through government policy, partly because of the growing African acceptance of the cash economy. Tax liabilities were increasingly easy to meet from employment or agriculture. Those Africans whose conditions were perhaps the hardest, the squatters on European farms, were also those most cut off from the potential communicators, whether chiefs or politicians. Economic development in all three mainland territories before the late 1930s consisted almost entirely in providing better access, both institutional and physical, to the world market. Production methods and land tenure, even where the crops themselves were new, continued unaffected by direct external pressure, though there were, as already noted, changing attitudes to land, voluntarily and from within. In this atmosphere, there were rarely acute peasant complaints to articulate, and such as there were seemed to demand social rather than political remedy. On the other hand there was great scope for competition amongst the rival *élites* for access to the resources of modernization and to marketing outlets. This was the hallmark of the politics of local focus, political debate within the tribe. Certainly, part of that debate was over who would be the most effective communicators with the colonial power. But this was not an issue to generate a common front or mass meetings—rather the reverse. In such local concerns, lineage groups were still the rival interest groups. If the ground swell of social change had diminished the importance of the old communicators, it had not yet provided a mass constituency for the new. . . . Effective national movements could not emerge until the aspirant new communicators had realized their potential role. This was a difficult task. In the 1920s, educated men had tended to ally with the traditional communicators. The known unit, the tribe, was seen as the focal point of the desired independent society. For some the focus was the wider ethnic community of which neighbouring tribes were but components. This wider scale of social endeavour was still more evident in the later phase of local political focus. The official nationalism of sectional chiefs was opposed by more radical movements demanding paramounts. More recently young nationalist movements have used locally traditional communicators, but for national ends. The focal point of the desired society was now the nation. The new men of the 1920s had made their alliances with the chiefs out of a sense of their own relative weakness. They recognized social facts. The nationalist politicians entered their alliances from a position of relative strength. They saw them as the prelude to social reform. But the politicians' freedom of action was not limitless. It depended rather on the continued exercise of diplomatic skill. And, in the words of one East African leader, the post-Independence strategy of development has still to use tradition in order to abolish tradition, to use the clan in order to create communities which are not clannish. Above all, nationalist parties were, and are, dependent on their local communicators whose political effectiveness depends on their social support.

Many accounts of African nationalism emphasize the role of the political party in creating this support, in rousing the people from the 'inertia of loyalty' that attaches to any government in power, in this case the colonial regime. It seems possible to exaggerate this external morale-building function. For if in the inter-war period the mass of Africans were deprived of political communication by the lack of widely felt burdens and the minority attractions of western Christian culture, so from the late 1930s these conditions were reversed. As already suggested in the preliminary discussion of social change, purposive government action in economic, educational and agrarian spheres brought individual Africans, many of whom were now more peasants than tribesmen, into much closer and more irritating contact with the colonial regime. At the same time as many ordinary people were for this reason developing a more explicitly political interest, the potential new communicators, teachers, traders and clerks, were shedding their illusions. Improved education did not remove the colour bar, but it did help to remove a sense of cultural inferiority. The secondary school-leaver was better equipped than the barely literate to distinguish between the material and cultural aspects of the West. Concurrently, the new governmental pressures felt by the peasantry meant also the end of any hopes for effective local political focus. The expenditure of greater resources on economic development and social services brought with it more stringent central government control.

Such was the setting for the spontaneous contribution to nationalism. Of the many facets to this contribution, only four will be discussed here. Together they illustrate the shift in mass concerns from a political focus that was diffuse or local to one that was central. First, there is the question of agrarian change generally, which focused attention on central government as a sometimes incompetent agent of reform. Secondly, the social philosophy which inspired governments' land tenure policies, namely the creation of a stable rural middle class, provoked a clearly radical social response. Thirdly, the cavalier treatment of elected local authorities by governments in a hurry forced the new communicators, often members of these authorities, into open opposition on a popular issue. Lastly, and perhaps most importantly, the development of producers' co-operatives gave to the peasantry organizations that were both locally based and centrally concerned with governments' economic policies.

Soil erosion had been recognized as a threat by the East African governments long before the Second World War. Customary land usage was increasingly destructive of the soil with the growth of population and commercial pressure on the land. Both physical anti-erosion measures were needed and, in the long term, changed methods of African farming. Improved husbandry was required if African cash crops were to be assured of a continuing welcome on the world market. The wartime emphasis on increased production, together with a shortage of the necessary departmental staff, meant that the agrarian problem had reached crisis proportions by 1945. More widely, the post-war era promised a new deal for the colonies from which both the dependent and metropolitan economies would benefit. In both the metropolitan and local contexts, the governments were in a hurry. In Kenya, urgency was added by the hope that economic development would silence political unrest. The 1954 Swynnerton Plan for the intensified development of African agriculture was a direct response to Mau Mau. Government hoped to solve a political problem by economic means: it was this very economic solution which precipitated the wider rural revolt which hastened the end of colonial rule. . . .

Government motives were suspect. The social implications were disturbing too. One of the features of precolonial African history had been the existence of free cultivators, unencumbered by landlords or indebtedness. But, in Kenya especially, it was accepted that development must be empowered by the individual profit motive. Land must be consolidated, not only to give the secure tenure necessary for capital improvement, but to enable African farmers to mortgage their land against development loans. Hitherto, government had not interfered with customary conditions of tenure, to limit the dangers of such indebtedness. In 1954 it was proposed that 'former Government policy [should] be reversed, and able, energetic or rich Africans will be able to acquire more land, and bad or poor farmers less, creating a landed and a landless class. This is a normal step in the evolution of a country.' The proposals were accepted. They were implemented, like all other government programmes, through the official chiefs. These were in a position to reap disproportionate benefits in the land cases attendant on consolidation, and from the agricultural department's farm planning services. To the peasant, agrarian reform was not only change, but also another stage in the accretion of chiefly power and wealth, with individual land titles consolidating both. The danger was the greater where the peasantry were also migrant workers. On balance—it is a moot point—it seems that families whose heads were frequently away in European employment were less likely to change their farming methods. The rural modernizers were rather the old welfare association leadership and the chiefs—some of whom were retired agricultural instructors. These were the 'able, energetic or rich Africans,' long associated with government departments. When land consolidation was started, it seemed likely that those already dispossessed in the towns or on European farms would be permanently dispossessed in their home areas also. Urban and rural radicalism nurtured each other. In Kikuyuland this situation led to something approaching civil war. More generally, this deepening alienation of the peasantry from their chiefs provided an open opportunity for a rural counter leadership.

This alternative leadership was present already in the elected element of the District Councils that in Kenya superseded the L.N.C.s, and in Tanganyika supplanted the native authorities. In line with overall British colonial policy, these local government bodies were after the war given more democratic form, greater authority and increased financial responsibility. The irony was that these new features were being inculcated by the same governments which, in their haste to solve agrarian problems, were resorting increasingly to enforcement rather than consultation. This was a long-standing African complaint. In 1935 the 'loyalist' Kikuyu Provincial Association had asked agricultural officers to order their African subordinates, on going out 'to advise other natives, [to] give their advice in the form of advice and not as a compulsory order . . . Further they should explain the benefits of their advice.' An African farmer's association near Dar es Salaam similarly complained of agricultural inspectors in 1948, that 'instead of teaching us how to produce more crops etc., they tell us to clean our coconut shambas at once and in the case of failing to do so, . . . heavy fines and imprisonment are imposed . . .' This same sentiment was expressed in the District Councils. In 1947, Oginga Odinga, then a junior councillor, 'emphasized that if the soil was to be preserved, it was the duty of the community to do the work on their own land rather than waiting or depending on someone else to come and do the work for them.' Resentment of outside direction was combined with desire for improvement under African control, for African benefit. District Councils were quick to protest that their new powers were a sham. They had no say in the elaborate schemes of government departments. Early in 1959 the Luo African District Council of Central Nyanza, acting under strong local pressure, voted itself into dissolution rather than accept government terms for the management of an afforestation scheme. The government had to rely on nominated councils in Kikuyuland during the Mau Mau Emergency. In Sukumaland, Tanganyika, there was the same story of council opposition to government instruction, even though the council was dominated by chiefs. Two points here must be emphasized. Most of the stimulus to such council opposition came from within the localities. Peasants and councillors knew like frustrations. This first observation is reinforced by the second. Many of the elected councillors, greatly increased in number with the extension of local democracy after the war, were already closely associated with the people by virtue of their leading positions in trading companies or co-operatives.

These too had a long history. In the inter-war years independent traders had been a minority group. They were often involved in the more radical movements within local political focus, resentful of the marketing advantages enjoyed by the chiefs. The generally increased peasant participation in the cash economy during the war, and the business aspirations of demobilized servicemen thereafter provided a much broader base for such commercial activity. African business careers were dogged by lack of capital and entrepreneurial experience, by Asian dominance in retail trade and produce marketing, by government marketing regulations and credit restriction. Many failed. Bitter experience taught the need for political assistance in the attack on economic privilege. Concurrently, there was a great expansion of producers' co-operatives, with which the majority of peasants in the more advanced areas had at least some connexion. They were concerned with the whole range of central governments' economic policies. Each co-operative society was also a miniature cockpit of tension between the initiative of their African organizer and officials, and the paternalism of government co-operative officers. It is significant that co-operative or other commercial organizers were as prominent as the trade unionists in the national movements. Koinange, Odinga and Muliro in Kenya; Musazi in Uganda; Bomani, Kahama and Kasambala in Tanganyika; all these and many more were genuine communicators in their relationship between their co-operative membership and central government. The national party had need of the same type of communicator with the localities.

The passion of peasant resistance to government dictate had moved the 'inertia of loyalty' to the colonial regimes. In many cases it had forced governments to admit failure, weakening colonial morale. Rural radicalism had in many areas provoked open opposition to the old communicators, the chiefs. The opportunities for an effective opposition leadership were confirmed in government treatment of elected local authorities. Rural economic enterprise joined peasant and new communicator in the co-operative societies. A peasant revolt had thrown up its leaders—local men with central interests. As such the revolt was atypical. Peasant movements are historically anarchic. It was the function of the conscious element, the nationalist leaders, to maintain that centrality of focus. It remains their more exacting task after Independence. . . .